Hands-On Novell® NetWare® 6.0/6.5
Enhanced Edition

Ted Simpson

Hands-On
Novell Netware
6.0/6.5

6192 5453022

THOMSON
™
COURSE TECHNOLOGY

Australia • Canada • Mexico • Singapore • Spain • United Kingdom • United States

THOMSON

COURSE TECHNOLOGY

Hands-On Novell NetWare 6.0/6.5, Enhanced Edition

is published by Course Technology.

Managing Editor
William Pitkin III

Quality Assurance Testing
Marianne Snow, Chris Scriver

Editorial Assistant
Amanda Piantedosi

Product Manager
Amy M. Lyon

Product Marketing Manager
Jason Sakos

Cover Design
Abby Scholz

Developmental Editor
Lisa M. Lord

Senior Manufacturing Coordinator
Trevor Kallop

Text Design
GEX Publishing Services

Production Editor
Summer Hughes

Associate Product Manager
David Rivera

Compositor
GEX Publishing Services

Technical Editor
David Mansheffer

Disclaimer
Course Technology reserves the right to revise this publication and make changes from time to time in its content without notice.

ISBN 0-619-21545-3

BRIEF
Contents

PREFACE xi

CHAPTER ONE
Defining Network System Components 1

CHAPTER TWO
Implementing eDirectory Services 33

CHAPTER THREE
Designing the File System 77

CHAPTER FOUR
Managing User Access 141

CHAPTER FIVE
Securing the File System 185

CHAPTER SIX
Working with eDirectory Security 235

CHAPTER SEVEN
Configuring the User Workstation Environment 279

CHAPTER EIGHT
Implementing Network Printing 331

CHAPTER NINE
Accessing and Managing the Network with Novell's OneNet Utilities 389

CHAPTER TEN
Implementing Internet Services 431

CHAPTER ELEVEN
Implementing Messaging Services 473

CHAPTER TWELVE
Installing NetWare 6 511

APPENDIX A
CNA Objectives 557

APPENDIX B
Forms and Worksheets 563

APPENDIX C
Network Pathways and Protocols 585

APPENDIX D
Forms and Worksheets 611

APPENDIX E
NetWare 6.5 Security Enhancements 645

APPENDIX F
Novell Services for Linux 657

APPENDIX G
Command-Line Utilities   675

GLOSSARY   679

INDEX   687

TABLE OF

Contents

PREFACE   xi

CHAPTER ONE

Defining Network System Components   1
    Novell's OneNet Strategy   2
    Universal AeroSpace Orientation   3
        Company Tour   4
    Introduction to Network Components and Services   6
        Login Security Services   7
        Directory Services   12
        File Services   14
        Print Services   16
        Application Services   16
    Network Entities   18
        User Workstations   19
        Servers   19
        Server Accessories   21
        Shared Storage Devices   22
        Printers   22
    The Network Pathway   23
    Network Protocols or Rules   25
        NetWare IPX/SPX   25
        TCP/IP   25
        NetBEUI/NetBIOS   27
    Chapter Summary   28
    Key Terms   29
    Review Questions   30
    Universal AeroSpace Case Projects   32

CHAPTER TWO

Implementing eDirectory Services   33
    Implementing the Client   34
        Web Browser Clients   36
        Using the Microsoft Client   36
        The Microsoft Client Service for NetWare   40
        The Novell Client   42
    Novell eDirectory Services   45
        eDirectory Components   46
        Directory Context   48
    Designing an eDirectory Tree Structure   51
        Introduction to NetWare Management Utilities   53
    Implementing the eDirectory Tree   60
        Creating Alias and Volume Objects   60
        Creating Organizational Units with iManager   62
        Completing the Tree Structure with ConsoleOne   64
    eDirectory Partitioning and Replicating   66
        eDirectory Replicas   67
        eDirectory Partitions   68
    Chapter Summary   72
    Key Terms   72
    Review Questions   73
    Universal AeroSpace Case Projects   75

CHAPTER THREE
Designing the File System   77
  NetWare File System Components   78
    Disk Partitions   79
    Storage Pools   81
    Volumes   81
    Directories and Subdirectories   92
  Establishing the Universal AeroSpace Directory Structure   95
    Defining Processing Needs   95
    Designing the Structure   98
    Implementing the Directory Structure   100
    Working with Network Files   111
  Planning Drive Pointer Usage   118
    Planning Drive Mappings for Universal AeroSpace   120
    Establishing Drive Pointers   122
    The MAP Command   123
    Using Directory Map Objects   125
  Backing Up Network Data   127
    The Storage Management System   127
    Establishing a Backup System   130
  Chapter Summary   134
  Key Terms   135
  Review Questions   136
  Universal AeroSpace Case Projects   139

CHAPTER FOUR
Managing User Access   141
  Establishing Login Security   142
    Implementing User Account Restrictions   142
    Implementing Intruder Detection Limits   145
  Creating and Managing Users and Groups   149
    Increasing Admin User Security   149
    Defining and Creating Groups   150
    Creating User Templates   152
    Creating User Objects from Templates   156
    Using iManager to Create Users and Groups   161
    Updating Multiple User Accounts   165
    Using LDAP to Import Objects   168
  Establishing Organizational Role Objects   171
  Deleting, Renaming, and Moving Objects   173
    Moving a Container Object   174
  Chapter Summary   177
  Key Terms   178
  Review Questions   178
  Universal AeroSpace Case Projects   181

CHAPTER FIVE
Securing the File System   185
  Access Right Security   186
    NetWare Access Rights   186
    Trustee Assignments   188
    Inherited Rights   195
    Combining Trustee Assignments and Inherited Rights 198
    Calculating Effective Rights   200
    Working with Supervisor Rights   202
  Planning File System Security   204
    File System Security Guidelines   205
    Universal AeroSpace File System Security   207
  Attribute Security   217
    File and Directory Attributes   217
    Planning Directory Attribute Usage at Universal AeroSpace 221
    Planning File Attribute Usage at Universal AeroSpace 221
    Implementing Directory and File Attributes   222
    The FLAG Command-Line Utility   225

Chapter Summary 227
Key Terms 227
Review Questions 229
Universal AeroSpace Case Projects 231

CHAPTER SIX
Working with eDirectory Security 235
Introduction to eDirectory Security 236
    Assigning eDirectory Rights 239
    eDirectory Default Rights 253
eDirectory Security for Universal AeroSpace 255
    Defining Trustee Assignments 256
Assigning Rights Through Administrative Roles 268
Chapter Summary 273
Key Terms 273
Review Questions 274
Universal AeroSpace Case Projects 276

CHAPTER SEVEN
Configuring the User Workstation Environment 279
Login Script Processing 280
    Types of Login Scripts 281
Login Script Programming 286
    Login Script Variables 288
    Using Login Script Variables 291
    Writing Login Scripts 293
    Documenting Login Scripts 303
Implementing Login Scripts for Universal AeroSpace 304
    Identifying Login Script Requirements 304
    Writing Login Scripts 305
    Entering Login Scripts 310
    Testing and Debugging Login Scripts 313
Managing User Environments with Z.E.N.works for Desktops 314
    Z.E.N.works for Desktops 3 Overview 315
    Installing Z.E.N.works 316
Managing Workstations 317
Chapter Summary 322
Key Terms 323
Review Questions 324
Universal AeroSpace Case Projects 327

CHAPTER EIGHT
Implementing Network Printing 331
Network Printing Overview 332
    Queue-based Printing System Components 332
    Setting Up Queue-based Printing 336
    Troubleshooting Queue-based Printing 343
Implementing Novell Distributed Print Services 344
    Setting Up NDPS Components 345
    Installing NDPS Printers on User Workstations 359
    Troubleshooting NDPS Printing 361
iPrint and the Internet Printing Protocol (IPP) 365
    Enabling Printers for iPrint 365
    Installing the iPrint Client and IPP Printers 366
Defining a Printing Environment 370
    Step 1: Defining Printer Requirements 370
    Step 2: Determining Printer Location and Attachment Method 371
    Step 3: Defining Printer Names 372
    Step 4: Planning the eDirectory Context 372
Setting Up the Printing Environment 373
    Creating and Configuring Printer Agents 373
    Configuring Printers on Client Computers 378

Chapter Summary   382
Key Terms   383
Review Questions   384
Universal AeroSpace Case Projects   386

CHAPTER NINE
Accessing and Managing the Network with Novell's OneNet Utilities   **389**
Working with iFolder   390
    iFolder Components and Installation   391
    Managing iFolder   396
    Using iFolder   400
Installing and Using NetStorage   403
    Installing NetStorage   404
    Using NetStorage   405
Using NetWare 6 Remote Management Utilities   406
    The Remote Manager Utility   406
    The iMonitor Utility   414
    The RConsoleJ Utility   417
Managing Novell Licensing Services   419
    Using iManager to Install and View License Certificates   420
    Using Remote Manager to View License Information   422
Chapter Summary   423
Key Terms   424
Review Questions   424
Universal AeroSpace Case Projects   427

CHAPTER TEN
Implementing Internet Services   **431**
NetWare 6 Internet Service Components   432
    Apache Web Server for NetWare   433
    Tomcat Servlet Engine for NetWare   434
    Novell Portal Services   434
    NetWare Web Search Server   436
    NetWare Enterprise Web Server   436
    FTP Server   437
    NetWare Web Manager   437
Installing and Configuring Web Services   437
    Working with NetWare Enterprise Web Server   438
    Operating and Configuring Enterprise Web Server   439
    Working with NetWare FTP Server   445
Working with Certificate Services   450
    Novell Certificate Server   453
Securing Net Services   454
    Internal Security   455
    Firewall Security   459
    Protection Against Virus Attacks   461
    Defense Against Denial-of-Service Attacks   464
Chapter Summary   466
Key Terms   466
Review Questions   467
Universal AeroSpace Case Projects   470

CHAPTER ELEVEN
Implementing Messaging Services   **473**
Implementing an E-mail System   474
    E-mail Components   474
    E-mail Protocols   475
    Common E-mail Clients   475
    Common E-mail Back-End Servers   477
    Installing GroupWise 6   479
    Setting Up GroupWise Client Computers   486

Configuring and Managing the GroupWise System   490
   Adding GroupWise Snap-ins to ConsoleOne   490
   Creating GroupWise Post Office Users   492
   Creating Additional GroupWise Post Office Objects   496
   Deleting and Renaming Post Office Objects   497
   Establishing Mailbox Security   499
Monitoring and Troubleshooting a GroupWise System   500
   Monitoring GroupWise Agents   500
   Identifying and Troubleshooting E-mail Problems   504
Chapter Summary   505
Key Terms   506
Review Questions   507
Universal AeroSpace Case Projects   509

CHAPTER TWELVE
Installing NetWare 6   **511**
Directory Services   512
   X.500 Directory Standard   512
   eDirectory Architecture   518
Preparing for NetWare Installation   519
   The Server Planning Worksheet   519
   Server Identification   521
   System Information   522
   Disk Driver Information   523
   Partition Information   523
   Network Card Information   524
   Protocol Information   524
   Server Context   525
   Installation Component Options   525
Installing NetWare 6   527
   Phase 1: Preparation of the DOS Partition   527
   Phase 2: Initial Installation and File Copying   528
   Phase 3: GUI Installation   530
Working with the Server Console   534
   Console Commands   535
   NetWare Loadable Modules (NLMs)   541
   Using Java on the Server   546
   Modifying the Server Startup Files   547
Upgrading an Existing Network to NetWare 6   548
   Upgrading the Existing Tree to eDirectory 8.6   549
   Upgrading the Certificate Authority Object   550
   Installing a NetWare 6 Server into an Existing Tree   551
Chapter Summary   552
Key Terms   552
Review Questions   553
Universal AeroSpace Case Projects   556

APPENDIX A
CNA Objectives   **557**

APPENDIX B
Forms and Worksheets   **563**

APPENDIX C
Network Pathways and Protocols   **585**
Designing a Network Pathway   586
   Network Cables   586
   Network Topology   589
   Network Interface Cards   592
Implementing the TCP/IP Protocol   597
   IP Addressing   597
Key Terms   610

APPENDIX D

Upgrading to NetWare 6.5   **611**

NetWare 6.5 Installation and Upgrading Enhancements   612
Performing a NetWare 6.5 Server Installation   614
Managing Branch Offices   622
Server Consolidation   623
Remote Upgrades   624
Network Administration and Business Continuity   624
iManager 2.0 Enhancements   625
File System Enhancements   633
End User Enhancements   636
Virtual Office   636
Virtual Teams   637
NetWare 6.5 eGuide   640
iPrint Enhancements   640
Web Services   641
Developer Tools   641

APPENDIX E

NetWare 6.5 Security Enhancements   **645**

Introduction to Encryption Security   646
Cryptography Techniques   647
Encryption Protocols   648
NetWare 6.5 Authentication Security Enhancements   651
NDS Passwords   652
Simple Passwords   652
Universal Passwords   652
Message Digest 5 (MD5)   654
CertMutual   654
Universal Smart Card   654
X.509 Certificate   654

APPENDIX F

Novell Services for Linux   **657**

Growth of Linux   658
Linux Benefits   658
Linux Concerns   659
Novell Services for Linux   661
Support Services   661
Products and Solutions   662
Setting Up Role Based Services   664
Commitment to Open Source   667
Training and Certification   672

APPENDIX G

Command-Line Utilities   **675**

NetWare 6 Workstation Utilities   675
Legacy Workstation Utilities Compatible with NetWare 6   677

GLOSSARY   **679**

INDEX   **687**

Preface

Since the 1980s, Novell has been a leader in the development of LAN technology. The requirement for secure access to resources and services across LANs and the Internet has created a need for more powerful and complex network systems, but the variety of computer operating systems and network protocols can make it difficult to access and manage company information and services from different locations. Novell has responded to this need with the NetWare 6.0 operating system, which includes an updated directory system and a variety of network services designed to bring diverse computer environments and networks together so they can work as one network, or what Novell refers to as "OneNet." In addition, with the release of NetWare 6.5, Novell has continued its tradition of providing networking solutions by enhancing OneNet administrative utilities and strengthening its support of open-source software standards, including Linux, Apache Web Server, MySQL, and PHP/Perl. Coverage of NetWare 6.5 features, improved security, and Linux support is provided in Appendices D, E, and F.

To be competitive, companies and organizations need competent network professionals who can manage network environments. Novell instituted the Certified Novell Administrator (CNA) program to help establish credibility for network administrators who have the knowledge and skills needed to implement Novell networking services. Appendix A lists the latest CNA exam objectives and maps them to the chapter and section of the book where they are covered. You can find more information on Novell certification options and testing at *http://education.novell.com*.

Hands-On Novell NetWare 6.0/6.5 is intended to provide the concepts, skills, and hands-on experience you need to pass the Novell CNA exam and be able to use NetWare 6.0 to build network systems. These skills, along with the CNA designation, will put you in a position to take advantage of the many opportunities in the rapidly growing and changing field of networked computing.

NetWare Versions

Several versions of NetWare are still in use today, including NetWare versions 4 and 5. This textbook focuses on the latest versions, NetWare 6.0 and NetWare 6.5. Because NetWare 6.0 is the version used for the CNA exam objectives, the main body of the textbook still focuses on that version. The latest version, NetWare 6.5, includes many enhancements, such as more powerful Web-based management tools, new user productivity software, more security options, and support for open-source software. These NetWare 6.5 features are covered in the three new appendices.

Approach

I wrote this book to meet the Novell NetWare 6.0 CNA exam objectives. As a result, the textbook examples and activities are written using a NetWare 6.0 server with client workstations running Windows 2000 and Novell Client 4.83 (the most up-to-date configuration at the time). If you're working with a NetWare 6.5 server, you'll find that the NetWare 6.5 Web-based tools look slightly different from the screen shots in Chapters 2, 3, 4, 8, 9, and 10. To help you out, special captions have been added for screen shots that vary widely between NetWare 6.0 and 6.5. These captions refer you to updated screen shots shown in the appendices. If you're using a NetWare 6.0 server for the main textbook, you might want to install an evaluation copy of NetWare 6.5 to do the activities in the appendices. Appendix D includes a NetWare 6.5 installation example and activities using the new iManager utility and Novell's new Virtual Office software.

Intended Audience and Use

Hands-On Novell NetWare 6.0/6.5 is intended for people who are getting started in computer networking or want to prepare for the CNA certification exam. To understand the material in this book, you should have a background in basic computer concepts and have worked with applications in the Windows environment. Although this book is intended for use in a classroom or an instructor-led training environment that has a NetWare 6.0 server installed as described in the classroom setup guide on the Instructor Resource CD, you can also use this book with self-paced or Web courses where you work on your own server. If you're using a self-paced approach, you might to obtain a copy of VMWare, which enables you to run the NetWare 6.0/6.5 server along with a client on your desktop. For more information on VMWare, visit its Web site at *www.vmware.com*.

Chapter Descriptions

Chapter 1, "Defining Network System Components," introduces Novell's OneNet strategy, explains the basic network system components—including servers, clients, pathways, and protocols—and describes the network environment for this book's Universal AeroSpace case study.

In **Chapter 2**, "Implementing eDirectory Services," you begin building your version of the Universal AeroSpace network by installing client software, designing the eDirectory tree structure, and creating network objects.

In **Chapter 3**, "Designing the File System," you continue building the Universal AeroSpace network by learning how to design and create a network file system, based on the new Novell Storage Services system. In addition, you learn how to back up the file system and implement drive pointer mappings to ensure standardized access to data.

In **Chapter 4**, "Managing User Access," you learn how to create groups, user accounts, and Organizational Role objects to give users secure access to the network. You also learn how to improve network security by setting up password restrictions, account restrictions, and intruder detection policies.

In **Chapter 5**, "Securing the File System," you learn how to grant appropriate access rights to users, and how to make trustee assignments to directories and files for users, groups, and containers in your Universal AeroSpace network. You also learn how to effectively use inherited rights to enable users to access and manage files and folders.

In **Chapter 6**, "Working with eDirectory Security," you continue working with trustee assignments, inherited rights filters, and administrative roles to grant effective rights through user, group, and container objects. You also learn how to delegate administrative functions to users and groups by using eDirectory security.

Chapter 7, "Configuring the User Workstation Environment," explains how to implement login scripts to meet users' access needs and how to provide a standard set of drive mappings and desktop functions. In addition, you learn how to use Z.E.N.works to configure and manage desktop policies for users and workstations.

In **Chapter 8**, "Implementing Network Printing," you learn how to set up and maintain a network printing system that enables users to send output to network printers easily and reliably. You learn how to work with queue-based printing, Novell Distributed Print Services, iPrint, and the Internet Printing Protocol to plan and implement a network printing system. In addition, you learn basic troubleshooting techniques to identify and fix network printing problems.

Chapter 9, "Accessing and Managing the Network Using Novell's OneNet Utilities," delves into Novell's OneNet strategy of allowing information and services to be accessed and managed from any computer with Internet access. You learn how to set up and implement the new NetWare 6.0 utilities, such as iFolder, NetStorage, Remote Manager, and iMonitor, and how to use iManager to add user licenses and view license information.

Chapter 10, "Implementing Internet Services," covers the NetWare 6 Internet delivery services, including Net Services and Web Services components. You learn how to implement these services and secure them from unauthorized access and attacks. You also learn how to use Novell Certificate Services, firewalls, and antivirus software to protect data and services when users are accessing information across a public network.

In **Chapter 11**, "Implementing Messaging Services," you learn the components of the Novell GroupWise messaging system. You also learn how to set up and configure GroupWise servers and clients so that you can implement e-mail services, create post office objects, and troubleshoot common e-mail problems.

In **Chapter 12**, "Installing NetWare 6," you learn how to plan for and perform a NetWare 6.0 installation, how to work with common NetWare 6.0 console commands, and how to load and work with NetWare Loadable Modules. You also learn the steps to upgrade an existing NetWare 5 network to NetWare 6.0.

Appendix A, "CNA Objectives," lists each CNA certification objective along with the chapter and section where information about the objective is covered.

Appendix B, "Forms and Worksheets," contain copies of forms students can use to complete the end-of-chapter case projects.

Appendix C, "Network Pathways and Protocols," provides more in-depth coverage of network pathways and protocols, including network media, physical and logical topologies, and protocols. TCP/IP addresses, masks, and gateways are covered, in addition to TCP/IP network services, such as DHCP and DNS.

Appendix D, "Upgrading to NetWare 6.5," covers NetWare 6.5's major new features, including installation, iManager 2.0, and the new Virtual Office. In addition, this appendix gives you an overview of eGuide, Snap shot backups, new Web development services, support for the new iSCSI standard, and the Nterprise Branch Office Appliance.

Appendix E, "NetWare 6.5 Security Enhancements," covers authentication security standards and how they are implemented in NetWare 6.5.

Appendix F, "Novell Services for Linux," discusses the growth of Linux and open-source standards and explains how Novell is providing support and services to meet these growing demands. In addition to learning about Novell's exciting new Linux direction, you learn the steps for installing iManager 2.0 on Linux and using Apache Manager to manage NetWare and Linux Web sites. This appendix also lists the objectives for the new Novell Certified Linux Engineer (CLE) certification.

Appendix G, "Command-Line Utilities," offers a reference for using common commands, such as NDIR and NCOPY.

Features

Hands-On Novell NetWare 6.0/6.5 differs from other networking books in its unique hands-on approach and its orientation to real-world situations and problem solving. To help you comprehend how Novell NetWare concepts and techniques are applied in real-world organizations, this book incorporates the following features:

- **Chapter Objectives**—Each chapter begins with a detailed list of the concepts to be mastered. This list gives you a quick reference to the chapter's contents and is a useful study aid.

- **Hands-On Activities**—Concepts are explained in the context of a hypothetical company (Universal AeroSpace) that casts you in the role of a student intern working for the network administrator. The hands-on activities are incorporated throughout the textbook, giving you practice in setting up, managing, and troubleshooting a network system. The activities give you a strong foundation for carrying out network administration tasks in the real world. Because of the book's progressive nature, completing the hands-on activities in each chapter is essential before moving on to the end-of-chapter projects and subsequent chapters.

- **Chapter Summary**—Each chapter's text is followed by a summary of the concepts introduced in that chapter. These summaries are a helpful way to recap and revisit the material covered in each chapter.

- **Key Terms**—All terms introduced with boldfaced text are gathered into the Key Terms list at the end of the chapter. This list gives you an easy way to check your understanding of all the terms introduced.

- **Review Question**s—The end-of-chapter assessment begins with a set of review questions that reinforce the material introduced in each chapter. Answering these questions ensures that you have mastered the important concepts. The review questions can also be used to help prepare for the CNA exam.

- **Universal AeroSpace Case Projects**—At the end of each chapter, you have the opportunity to reinforce and apply the chapter's concepts and techniques by building the Business office for the Universal AeroSpace network on your own. Although each chapter's case projects build on previous chapter case projects, they are independent of the hands-on activities, meaning that students don't need to do the case projects to complete the hands-on activities in subsequent chapters.

Text and Graphic Conventions

Additional information and exercises have been added to this book to help you better understand what's being discussed in the chapter. Icons throughout the text alert you to these additional materials:

 Tips offer extra information on resources, how to attack problems, and time-saving shortcuts.

 Notes present additional helpful material related to the subject being discussed.

 The Caution icon identifies important information about potential mistakes or hazards.

 Each Hands-on Activity in this book is preceded by the hands-on icon.

 Case project icons mark the end-of-chapter Universal AeroSpace projects, which are scenario-base assignments that ask you to independently apply what you have learned in the chapter.

Instructor's Materials

The following supplemental materials are available when this book is used in a classroom setting. All supplements available with this book are provided to the instructor on a single CD-ROM. You can also retrieve these supplemental materials from the Course Technology Web site, *www.course.com*, by going to the page for this book, under "Download Instructor Files & Teaching Tools".

Electronic Instructor's Manual. The Instructor's Manual that accompanies this textbook includes:

- Additional instructional material to assist in class preparation, including suggestions for classroom activities, discussion topics, and additional projects.

- Solutions to all hands-on activities and end-of-chapter materials, including the review questions and Universal AeroSpace case projects.

ExamView®. This textbook is accompanied by ExamView, a powerful testing software package that instructors can use to create and administer printed, computer (LAN-based), and Internet exams. ExamView includes hundreds of questions that correspond to the topics covered in this text, enabling students to generate detailed study guides with page references for further review. The computer-based and Internet testing components allow students to take exams at their computers, and they save instructors time by grading each exam automatically.

PowerPoint presentations. This book comes with Microsoft PowerPoint slides for each chapter. These slides are included as a teaching aid for classroom presentation, to make available to students on the network for chapter review, or to be printed for classroom distribution. Instructors, please feel free to add your own slides for additional topics you introduce to the class.

Figure files. All figures and tables in the book are reproduced on the Instructor's Resource CD in bitmap format. Similar to the PowerPoint presentations, they are included as a teaching aid for classroom presentation, to make available to students for review, or to be printed for classroom distribution.

CoursePrep Test Preparation Software

The CD included with this book contains CoursePrep test preparation software for the Novell CNA 050-677 exam. This CoursePrep software provides 50 sample exam questions that mirror the look and feel of the CNA 050-677 exam. For more information about MeasureUp test prep products or to order the complete version of this software, visit the Web site at *http://www.measureup.com*.

ACKNOWLEDGEMENTS

Although I have spent many hours updating this book to NetWare 6.0 and 6.5, it would never have been completed without the help of Course Technology management and staff, especially Amy Lyon, who directed and managed the project, and Will Pitkin, for his vision for the book and his persistence in working with Novell to obtain the latest information. I want to express my many thanks to my excellent editor, Lisa Lord, whose patient help and hard work, along with her mastery of technical jargon (also known as GeekSpeak) and the English language, brought life to the words in these chapters. I also want to express my thanks to my excellent technical editors, Warren Wyrostek and David Mansheffer, who contributed so much to the technical content and applicability of the chapters and appendices. I also owe a big thanks to Jim Greene and the staff at Novell for providing ongoing information on NetWare 6.5 and the CNA objectives.

Credit for identifying technical problems with the hands-on activities goes to Marianne Snow and Chris Scriver, who did an excellent job of checking each step. No book can be completed without all the work required to get it ready for printing. I feel fortunate to have had such an excellent production editor as Summer Hughes to make sure this book was ready for publication. I take my hat off to the excellent reviewers—David Anfinson of Williston State College, John Crowley of Bucks County Community College, and Cynthia Mason-Posey of Prince Georges Community College—for their consistent hard work in ensuring that the content and activities would meet the practical demands of teaching NetWare 6 concepts in the classroom environment.

Finally, I want to thank my wife, Mary, who made many alterations in our schedule and helped me through the sometimes daunting challenges of meeting the ever-changing schedules and requirements that go with writing a book. I want to dedicate this book to the students at WITC and other colleges who are pursuing the challenging field of computer networking. In addition to students who are pursuing the challenging field of computer networking, I want to dedicate my writing efforts to my mother, Rosemarie (Ode), who although she's not a technical type, has a great depth of knowledge and wisdom about life and work.

Read This Before You Begin

To do the case projects and set up your own version of the Universal AeroSpace network, you will be assigned to a NetWare classroom server and given a student reference number (an Admin user name preceded by your student number) and a data volume identified with your student number. Your user name will have the necessary privileges to build your own network system by creating and managing network objects, such as users, groups, printers, and files, without affecting other students' use of the server. Your assigned data volume is the work area on the classroom server where you have been given all rights to create and manage files and directories so that you can complete the projects and activities. If you're doing the activities and projects on your own computer network, you need a computer to use as the NetWare server; then install an evaluation copy of the NetWare 6.0 or NetWare 6.5 on your server as described in the classroom setup instructions available in the Instructor's Resources and on the Course Technology Web site, *www.course.com*. You can also use VMWare to run the NetWare 6.0 or 6.5 server along with the client on your desktop. For more information on VMWare, visit its Web site at *www.vmware.com*.

Minimum Lab Requirements

Hardware:

- Each student workstation requires at least 128 MB of RAM, an Intel Pentium or compatible processor running at 166 MHz or higher, and a minimum of 500 MB of free space on the hard disk. A CD-ROM drive is also important for loading software and performing certain activities. If you're using VMWare, each student workstation needs 512 MB RAM, a Pentium II processor running at 700 MHz minimum, and 2 GB free space on the hard drive.

- To use NetWare 6.0, you need a classroom server with at least 512 MB of RAM, an Intel Pentium II or higher processor running at 500 MHz or higher (Intel Pentium III 700 MHz recommended), a minimum 8 GB hard drive (4 GB for the NetWare SYS volume and at least 500 MB for each student), a CD-ROM drive, a Super VGA or higher resolution display adapter and monitor, and a mouse.

- To use NetWare 6.5, you need a classroom server with at least 1 GB of RAM, an Intel Pentium III or higher processor running at 700 MHz or higher (Intel Pentium 4 1.2 GHz recommended), a minimum 8 GB hard drive (6 GB for the SYS volume and at least 500 MB for each student), a CD-ROM drive, a Super VGA or higher resolution display adapter and monitor, and a mouse.

Software:

- *Windows 2000 Professional or Windows XP (Windows 2000 Professional recommended)* for each student workstation.

- *A copy of the Novell NetWare 6.0 or 6.5 operating system for the server.*

- *Licenses for each student account*—NetWare 6.0/6.5 uses a new licensing system called User Access Licensing (UAL) that assigns a license to each user account when the user logs in. UAL requires multiple licenses for each student because he or she will be creating multiple users. So if you're using UAL, you should plan on each student needing at least four licenses. If all licenses in the UAL are used, you can use iManager to revoke user account licenses to make more connections available. Another option is contacting Novell about obtaining an educational license. Educational licenses do not assign a license unit to each user, but allow multiple users to share a single license unit by releasing the license unit each time a user logs out. When using an educational license, only one license unit is needed for each student.

- *Z.E.N.works for Desktops version 3.2 or higher*—You can download an evaluation version of Z.E.N.works for Desktops by visiting *www.novell.com/products/zenworks*.

- *Latest support pack for NetWare 6.0*—At the time of this writing, you can download the latest support pack (nw6sp3) from *http://support.novell.com*. Select the Product Updates option, and under the Product Categories section, click on the applicable NetWare product to display a list of NetWare-related products. Click NetWare 6 to see a list of products and fixes. You can then select and download the support pack. Note that support packs are quite large and should be downloaded with a high-speed Internet connection.

- *GroupWise 6*—Chapter 15 requires installing GroupWise on the classroom server. You can download a three-user GroupWise 6 evaluation version from *www.novell.com/products/groupwise*.

- (Optional) *An evaluation copy of the Novell NetWare 6.5 operating system for the appendix activities.*

- (Optional) *VMWare licenses for each student workstation (www.vmware.com).*

1

DEFINING NETWORK SYSTEM COMPONENTS

After reading this chapter and completing the exercises, you will be able to:
- Describe the Novell OneNet strategy
- Describe the operation of the fictitious Universal AeroSpace Corporation
- Identify network components and services, describe their functions, and access common network services
- List and describe the network entities
- Describe a sample network pathway
- Understand the major workstation protocols used in a NetWare network

To be competitive in today's rapidly changing information age, organizations and individuals need fast, reliable, and secure access to resources and services. Computer networks provide the information highway to connect people with information sources and services. As a result, computer networks have become one of the most vital parts of an organization's information system. Because of the key role computer networks play in providing organizations with access to information and resources, technical people who can implement and manage diverse networks are in high demand. Therefore, Novell has implemented a certification test for Certified Novell Administrators (CNAs). CNA certification demonstrates to potential employers that you have the knowledge base and aptitude to succeed as a network administrator. In this book, you will learn what a Certified Novell Administrator needs to know to work with and administer the NetWare 6 environment.

NOVELL'S ONENET STRATEGY

Computer networks come in many shapes, sizes, and configurations. Networks can generally be categorized as local area networks, metropolitan area networks, or wide area networks. **Local area networks (LANs)** are used to connect computers that are physically close to each other, such as those in the same building or office. LANs usually consist of a copper cable system that connects the computers to a central wiring hub. **Metropolitan area networks (MANs)** use fiber-optic or microwave towers to connect computers in the same geographical area, such as a city or county. **Wide area networks (WANs)** use carriers such as the phone system to connect computers over long distances, including across the country or even around the world. In the past, computer networks tended to be isolated entities owned and controlled by a specific company or organization. Many computer networks used proprietary systems that made it difficult to connect them to share information. Today, the Internet is breaking down these barriers with standards and technology that enable secure data transmission between almost every type of networked computer.

Since the beginning of microcomputer-based business systems in the early 1980s, Novell has been a leader in LAN technology. Earlier versions of the Novell NetWare product excelled at offering rapid and secure access to file and print resources to a wide variety of locally attached computers. Today, Novell is developing products that help make the Internet's many diverse network systems operate as a single network. Novell uses the term **OneNet** to describe its strategy of developing products and services to make diverse networks separated by MANs and WANs act as a single network. Novell's OneNet strategy is to simplify the complexities of managing and accessing networks and accelerate an organization's ability to implement Internet applications by providing tools and solutions that work across different network environments.

Networks can get quite complicated with different types of computers attached in different locations. As illustrated in Figure 1-1, an organization's computer network might be a combination of LANs connected by MANs or WANs. In addition, employees often need to connect to the network from home or another remote location and access files or transmit data. In Figure 1-1, each division has its own LAN to connect the computers. Universal AeroSpace headquarters in Salt Lake City, Utah, consists of Business and Manufacturing divisions in the same city connected with a fiber-optic cable to form a MAN for both divisions to communicate with each other. AeroDyn is a subsidiary company in a different city. The LAN at AeroDyn is connected to Salt Lake City over a WAN provided by leasing a line from a long-distance carrier. Using the WAN, computers attached to the LAN in the AeroDyn office can communicate with computers attached to the LANs in Salt Lake City. With Novell's OneNet products and services, an employee or network administrator with a laptop can use the Internet to connect to the Salt Lake City office. Once connected to the LAN in Salt Lake City, employees can access any information they have rights to on the entire company network. Novell's OneNet strategy is to make complex networks, such as the one shown in Figure 1-1, easier to access and manage from any type of networked computer.

Although the NetWare 6 network operating system is a key part of Novell's OneNet strategy, Novell offers other products and services—such as eDirectory, Z.E.N.works, iFolder, and iPrint—that can run on a number of network operating systems, including Windows NT, Windows 2000, and Linux. By running on a variety of operating systems, these services and products are essential in making networks of diverse systems work together as OneNet. In this chapter and throughout the book, you'll learn more about the OneNet strategy and how it can be applied to an organization by working with the hypothetical Universal AeroSpace Corporation's network.

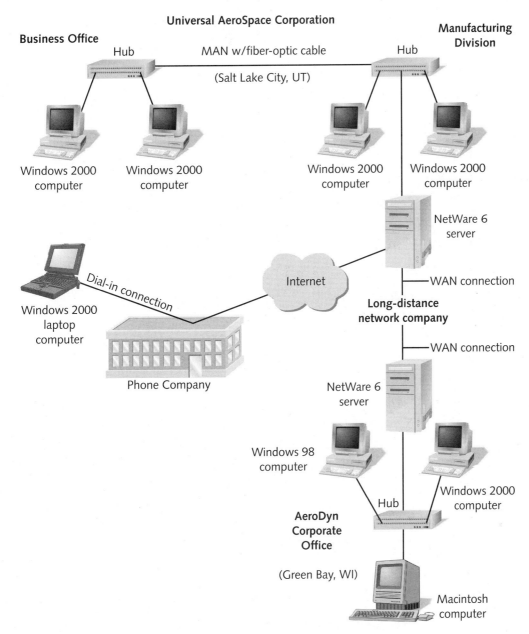

Figure 1-1   Sample computer network for Universal AeroSpace

UNIVERSAL AEROSPACE ORIENTATION

Having practical experience with networks, such as through internships while you're a student, enhances your ability to pass the CNA exam. In this book, you will gain some practical experience with NetWare 6 by playing the role of a student intern for the fictitious Universal AeroSpace (UAS) Corporation. By setting up and working with this company's network throughout the book, you'll learn how to apply network concepts and techniques and gain hands-on experience working with network services and resources. In the following chapters, you'll learn how to administer a network by creating your own version of the Universal AeroSpace network system.

UAS is a small engineering firm founded in the mid-1980s to design and manufacture specialized parts for aircraft companies. The company's strength has been designing and manufacturing aircraft components with high-strength aluminum alloy materials. Last year, UAS was reorganized under new management. The organizational chart shown in Figure 1-2 illustrates the current company structure.

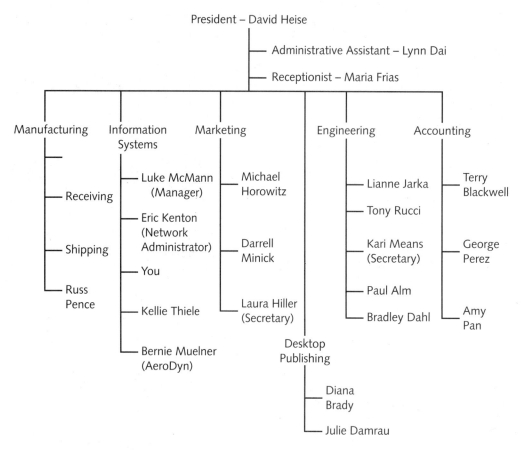

Figure 1-2 Universal AeroSpace organizational chart

In the 1990s, the president of UAS worked to expand the corporation into other high-tech markets by actively pursuing a NASA contract. As a result of a proposal drafted by the Marketing and Engineering departments, the corporation was recently awarded a NASA contract to design and build specialized components for a new international space station. As a result of the NASA contract, UAS has been expanding its operation, including hiring design engineers and office staff. One of the expansion priorities is installing a network information system that allows office staff and engineers to communicate and share computer resources. The new contract requires UAS engineers and office staff to frequently travel to NASA facilities, making it necessary to have access to resources and information while on the road.

After working with an outside consultant to help analyze existing systems, management decided to install a NetWare 6 network based on the system's reliability, proven technology, scalability, and ability to integrate resources into a OneNet solution. Your assignment as a student intern will be to work with UAS personnel to learn how the network works and then build a similar network in the classroom.

Company Tour

Figure 1-3 illustrates the layout of the Universal AeroSpace building with the current locations of computers and printers in each department. All office computers have Windows 2000 installed. Although several of the computers have inkjet printers attached, most printing is done through networked printers. The administrative computers are used to run accounting software and perform spreadsheet functions. The administrative assistant, Lynn Dai, along with each department secretary, currently has a Windows 2000 computer and laser printer used mostly for word processing. Diana Brady and Julie Damrau have powerful computers and laser printers used to run the desktop publishing software for creating and editing instructional manuals and sales material. Julie's computer has a DVD recorder she shares with Diana for creating DVDs. Each salesperson has a Windows-based laptop computer with word processing and spreadsheet software to create documents and access the customer database system and cost sheets. Because the salespeople often need access to their information while on the road, Novell's OneNet strategy will be important in providing solutions that gives them access to their files and allows them to print documents when they are away from the office.

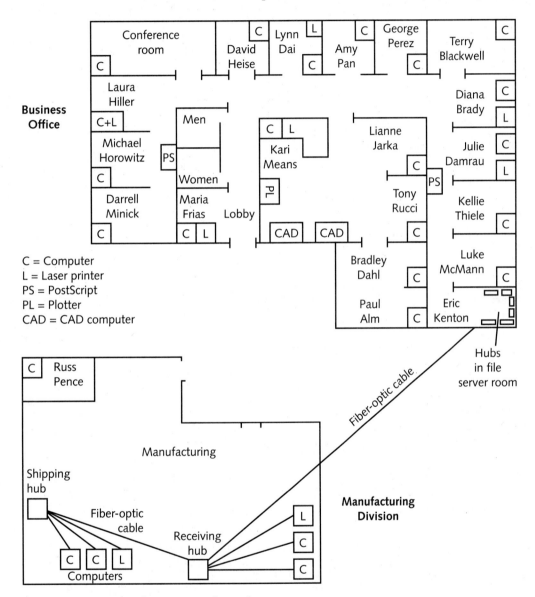

Figure 1-3 Universal AeroSpace floor plan

The Engineering department is responsible for designing components that meet the buyer's specifications. Currently, the department has two computer-aided design (CAD) computers attached to a shared plotter. Engineering files that contain information the business staff needs for writing contract agreements and other documentation are shared. Most shared files are kept on the server, but certain large files are copied directly between workstations.

As a result of the NASA contract, the company has expanded the Manufacturing facility by hiring additional machine tool specialists and adding new computer-aided manufacturing (CAM) machines to fabricate parts and components. All computers in the Manufacturing facility are attached to the network system to share resources and communicate more easily.

The Information Systems department, managed by Luke McMann, currently consists of a programmer/analyst, Kellie Thiele, and network administrators, Eric Kenton and Bernie Muelner. As a programmer/analyst, Kellie is responsible for network application services along with software development, configuration, and deployment. Eric's responsibilities as a network administrator are establishing and maintaining network users and security, implementing and securing the network file system, setting up and maintaining network printing, developing and implementing the backup and recovery system, supporting network communications, and managing the NetWare server and network performance. Bernie is responsible for administering the LANs at UAS subsidiaries.

INTRODUCTION TO NETWORK COMPONENTS AND SERVICES

As a **Certified Novell Administrator (CNA)**, you will need to be familiar with the hardware and software components that make up networks so that you can select, implement, and maintain a network system that meets your organization's communication and processing needs. This section introduces the major components and services that make up a local area network and explains how they are applied in the Universal AeroSpace Corporation network.

As illustrated in Figure 1-4, any network, including human networks, consists of four major types of components:

- Entities that need to communicate
- Services that provide access to network resources
- A common pathway for communications
- Rules (protocols) that control the communication process

 Novell identifies network components as servers, workstations, peripherals, transmission media, and network interface cards (NICs). These detailed components are included in the major types of components covered in this chapter. Workstations and peripherals are examples of network entities. Servers are entities that provide network services, and transmission media and NICs are included in the network pathway component.

In a LAN, entities typically consist of client computers, servers, and shared resources, such as printers and volumes (a logical division of disk storage space). A network service is a combination of computer hardware and software that provides network resources the client computers can access. As a CNA, you will need to know how to administer network systems that consist of several types of network services, including those for security, directories, messages, files, printers, and applications. The pathway consists of the cables and NICs used to connect the computers and transmit data, and the rules are the communication standards (protocols), such as TCP/IP, that control the format and transmission of data.

All services require client and server components. The **client** component runs on the user's computer and connects the application and the service running on the server computer. The **server** component consists of the computer hardware and software necessary to run the network services and provide access to resources. Common network services include the following:

- **Security services** authenticate users to the network by using login names and passwords and determine what rights and privileges users have to the network. NetWare security services include login security, file system security, eDirectory security, printer security, and server console security. Each of these security services will be covered in later chapters.

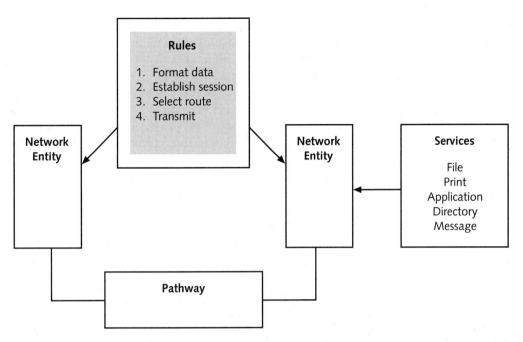

Figure 1-4   Major network components

- A **directory service** maintains information about network objects, such as users, printers, and data volumes, in a hierarchical database called the directory. Network entities use the information provided by the directory service to locate and access network resources and services.

- A **message service** is used to transfer e-mail messages and event notifications between client computers and servers.

- A **file service** enables client computers to access and save data on a shared file system.

- A **print service** allows printers to be attached to the network system and then used by client computers.

- An **application service** assists in running programs, such as spreadsheets, word processing programs, and database systems, by performing certain processing functions for client computers.

In the following sections, you will be introduced to these network services in the Universal AeroSpace system. In later chapters, you will learn how to implement and manage these network services.

Login Security Services

Before accessing resources or services on a network, users must authenticate themselves by providing a valid user name and password to the client software. The client software then uses the user name and password to authenticate the user to the network. Novell uses the term **logging in** for the process of entering an authorized user name and password before gaining access to the network. To access the local Windows 2000 workstation, Microsoft also requires the user to authenticate by using a valid user name and password, and refers to this authentication process as **logging on** to the workstation. As a result, when you access the Novell network from a Windows 2000 workstation, you need to perform two authentication processes. First, you log in to the network using the Novell Client. The Novell Client then attempts to log on to the local Windows 2000 workstation with the user name and password you supplied to the Novell Client. If the local workstation has a user account with this user name and password, the user is automatically logged on to the local workstation. However, if the local workstation doesn't have a user account that matches the Novell Client user name and password, the user sees a Windows logon window and must then enter a valid user name and password to authenticate to the local workstation before proceeding.

To allow users to access the Novell network, the network administrator needs to create a user account in Novell's eDirectory for each user. To make accessing the local workstation easier, the network administrator can also create a user account on the Windows 2000 computer with the same user name and password as the Novell user name. Because Novell's eDirectory service stores user accounts in containers stored in a tree structure, users must supply their user names and passwords when logging in, along with the container and tree where their user names are located. The location of the container in eDirectory is referred to as its "context." Figure 1-5 shows the Novell Login window after clicking the Advanced button. Notice that the window contains text boxes called Username, Password, Tree, Context, and Server. It also contains the Windows NT/2000 tab, used to specify the local user name for logging on to the Windows 2000 workstation. The user name entered in this tab must exist on the local computer and is initially set to Administrator. (Your instructor will supply a local user name.) The local user name determines the rights and desktop environment users will have on the local workstation. If multiple users share a workstation, you should create a local user account for each user.

The concept of "context" is explained in more detail in Chapter 2.

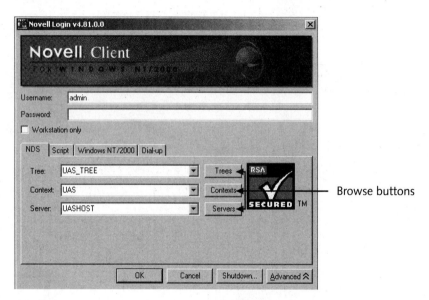

Figure 1-5   Using the expanded view of the Novell Login window to select context information

By default, the Username text box contains the name and context of the last user who logged in from your workstation. If no one has logged in since the client was installed, the Username text box is blank. The Password text box is where you enter the password associated with your user account. This field is kept blank to prevent someone else from logging in as the previous user. Your password is used like a signature, allowing the eDirectory service to verify that you are the actual user of the account. As shown in Figure 1-5, clicking the Advanced button enables you to select the tree and context information identifying the location of your user account.

The Context text box is used to specify the path leading to the container where your user name is stored. You can use the buttons to the right of each text box to browse for a tree, container, or server instead of typing in the object's exact name. The list arrows next to each text box enable you to select from previously used trees and contexts. In the following activities, you log in to both the Novell network and your local Windows 2000 computer to change passwords and send messages.

Activity 1-1: Logging in and Changing Your Password

Time Required: 10 minutes

Objective: Explain and perform the login procedure.

Description: Logging in plays a critical role in network security. The login process of entering authorized user names and passwords is how people are identified as valid users of the network. To improve security, users should keep passwords secret and change them periodically. To build your own version of the Universal AeroSpace network system, you have been assigned an Organization container named ##UAS (the ## represents your assigned student number) that stores the ##Admin user account, which has supervisor rights to your organization. Currently, your administrative user name does not have a password. In this activity, you log in with your assigned ##Admin user name, and then change your password to make your account more secure.

1. If necessary, start your computer, and press **Ctrl+Alt+Del** to open the Novell Login window.

2. Log in by specifying your assigned ##Admin user name and ##UAS context:

    a. In the Novell Login window, enter **##Admin** (replacing the **##** with your assigned student number) in the Username text box.

    b. Enter **password** in the Password text box.

    c. Click the **Advanced** button and verify that UAS_Tree is displayed in the Tree text box.

    d. To find your user name, you need to tell the computer which context to look in. To change the context to your ##UAS container, click the **Contexts** browse button to open a window showing the UAS_Tree structure (see Figure 1-6).

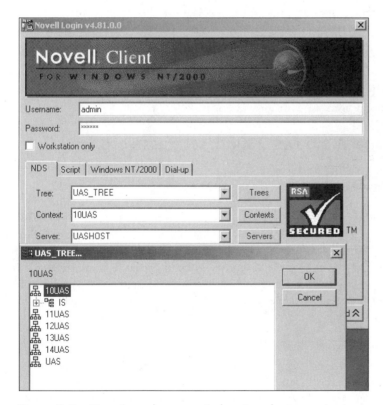

Figure 1-6   Opening a browse window to select a context

    e. If necessary, expand the Class container. Click your **##UAS Container**, then click **OK**.

3. Windows 2000 requires a user to log on to the local computer as well as the Novell network. The local Windows 2000 computer keeps its own directory of users. When logging in to the Novell network, you can click the Advanced button to select a local user name and password for logging on to the Windows 2000 computer. To change the local user name for logging on to the Windows 2000 computer, click the **Windows NT/2000** tab and, enter the local Windows 2000 user name that your instructor supplied.

4. Click **OK** to log in to the Novell network. If your login attempt fails, repeat Step 2, being careful to correctly enter the user name and password. After successfully logging in to the Novell network, enter the password for your local Windows 2000 user name and click **OK** to log on to your Windows 2000 computer.

5. To protect your ##Admin user name from unauthorized access, you need to change your password to one that only you know. A secure password should consist of at least eight characters and include both numbers and letters. Windows passwords are case sensitive (meaning that the lowercase *a* is considered different from the uppercase *A*), but Novell's passwords aren't. To change your password, follow these steps:

   a. Press **Ctrl+Alt+Del** to open the NetWare Security dialog box, and click the **Change Password** button.

   b. Highlight the **UAS_Tree** in the left pane.

   c. In the Old Password text box, enter **password**.

   d. Enter the new password for your ##Admin user in the New Password and Confirm new password text boxes.

   e. Click **OK** to change your password, and then click **OK** to close the confirmation message box and return to your desktop.

   f. Log off by clicking **Start**, **Shut Down**, **Log off** *username* (*username* is your Windows local user name).

6. Now test your password by logging back in to the network with your assigned ##Admin user name. Record the results on your student answer sheet.

Activity 1-2: Changing the Windows 2000 User Password

Time Required: 5 minutes

Objective: Describe and access common network services.

Description: When logging in to the network, Novell Client attempts to log on to the local Windows 2000 computer with the user name you entered in the Windows NT/2000 tab and the password for your Novell user name. If the passwords for the local Windows 2000 user name and the Novell user name are not the same, a dialog box opens, asking you to enter your Windows 2000 user name and password. To prevent entering two passwords, Eric changed the password on his local computer to match the password of his Novell account. In this activity, you log on to your local workstation and change your password to match the one you set in Activity 1-1.

1. If necessary, start your computer to open a Novell Login window.

2. Click the **Workstation only** check box and enter **Administrator** in the Username text box. (If you do not have access to the Administrator password, your instructor will provide a user name and password with rights to create new users.) Enter the password for your Administrator account in the Password text box, and then click **OK** to log on to your workstation.

3. Right-click the **My Computer** icon, and then click **Manage** to open the Computer Management console.

4. Expand the **Local Users and Groups** icon and then click the **Users** folder to display all users in the details pane on the right. On your student answer sheet, record the existing users.

To add a new user, you click Action, New User on the menu bar and then enter the user name and password information in the New User dialog box.

5. Right-click your local user name, and then click **Set Password** to open the Set Password dialog box.

6. Enter the password you used for your ##Admin user name in Activity 1-1 in the New password and Confirm password text boxes, and then click **OK** to change the password.

7. Close the Computer Management console, and log off.

8. You can also change the passwords of your current Novell and Windows 2000 user names by holding down the Ctrl+Alt+Del keys. Follow these steps to see how to use this method to coordinate your Novell and Windows 2000 passwords:

   a. Repeat Steps 1–4 of Activity 1-1 to log in to both the Novell network and your local Windows 2000 workstation, replacing "password" with the new password you established in Activity 1-1.

   b. Press the **Ctrl+Alt+Del** keys to open the NetWare Security dialog box, and then click the **Change Password** button to open the Change Password dialog box. Notice that both your UAS_Tree user name and your Windows 2000 workstation user name are highlighted in the pane on the left.

   c. You can change both passwords at the same time by entering your existing password in the Old Password text box and a new password in the New Password and Confirm New Password text boxes. For this activity, click **Cancel** to leave your passwords unchanged.

9. Click **Cancel** again to close the NetWare Security dialog box, and log out.

Activity 1-3: Using Message Services

Time Required: 5 minutes

Objective: Describe and access common network resources.

Description: Message services provide many functions, including delivering e-mail, notifying users when documents are printed, and sending messages. In this activity, you use message services to send a message to another student. In Chapter 8, you will learn how to use message services to receive notifications from network printers.

1. If necessary, start your computer to open the Novell Login window.

2. Enter your ##Admin user name, new password, and context. Click **OK** to log in to the Novell network and your local Windows 2000 computer. On your student answer sheet, record whether you were asked to enter a local user name and password to log on to the Windows 2000 computer.

3. Obtain the ##Admin user name of another student.

4. Right-click the red **N** on the taskbar, point to **NetWare Utilities**, point to **Send Message**, and click **To Users** to open the NetWare Send Message dialog box.

5. If necessary, click **Show Connected Servers** to display UASHOST in the Available Servers box. Click the **UASHOST** server, and then click the **Select** button.

6. Enter a message in the Enter message text box.

7. Click on the student ##Admin you want to send a message to, and then click the **Send** button.

8. Click **OK** to close the Send Message Results dialog box.

9. Respond to any messages you receive. Record the steps you use to respond to a message on your student answer sheet.

10. Click **Close** to close any Send Message dialog boxes, and then click **Close** to close the NetWare Send Message dialog box.

11. Log off.

Directory Services

Directory services are essential in networks so that users can log in and locate network objects and services. Most directory services currently in use are based on the IEEE X.500 object–naming system and include the Lightweight Directory Access Protocol, Windows 2000 Active Directory, and Novell's eDirectory. In this book, you'll be working with the Novell eDirectory service to set up and configure your version of the UAS network. In Chapter 12, you'll learn more about how X.500 and Active Directory compare to Novell's eDirectory service.

In early versions of NetWare, users were required to log in separately to each server they needed to use, so the network administrator had to maintain a separate list of valid user names and passwords on each server. In NetWare 6, Novell has made this job easier to manage by providing a global database of network resources and user information called the **eDirectory** (formerly the NDS, Novell Directory Services). The eDirectory database is called a global database because it's available to all servers. Having a global database means that users can authenticate themselves once to the entire network rather than to each individual server. After users have logged in to the network, they can access the resources they have authorization for, regardless of which server contains those resources.

In addition to user information, the eDirectory database stores information on all network resources. To improve organization and management, users and resources in the eDirectory database are stored in containers, similar to the way files and programs are organized into directories on a disk drive. Containers in the eDirectory database are arranged in a hierarchical tree structure, starting with the [Root] object, as shown in Figure 1-7. The location of an object in the tree is referred to as its context, which is specified by starting with the lowest container and working up. For example, in Figure 1-7, the user Paul is in the Engineering.UAS context, and the Bus_HP3 printer is in the Business.UAS context.

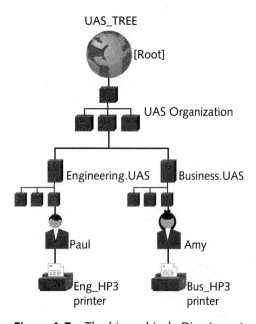

UAS_TREE
[Root]
UAS Organization
Engineering.UAS   Business.UAS
Paul   Amy
Eng_HP3 printer   Bus_HP3 printer

Figure 1-7   The hierarchical eDirectory structure

The eDirectory service is an important part of Novell's OneNet strategy because, in addition to running on NetWare 6, it can be run on other platforms, such as Windows 2000, Windows NT, and Unix. Running the Novell eDirectory service on multiple platforms allows networks consisting of diverse clients and servers to appear as OneNet to both users and administrators.

The eDirectory database tree is created and given a unique tree name when the first server is installed. Initially, the eDirectory tree consists of only a single container housing server objects and a user account named Admin. The Admin user account has Supervisor rights to the eDirectory tree and is allowed to create and manage other objects. In NetWare 6, creating and managing network objects in the eDirectory tree is often accomplished by using the ConsoleOne utility, shown in Figure 1-8.

Notice that in addition to the menu and toolbars, the ConsoleOne window is divided into two major frames. On the left is the Navigation frame, which contains a browse window used to display and navigate the eDirectory tree structure. The Navigation frame displays container objects, such as the UAS Organization, and is used to select a network context. On the right is the Object frame, which displays the individual network objects from the network context selected in the Navigation frame. In the following activity, you practice using ConsoleOne to browse the existing UAS tree and view information on network users.

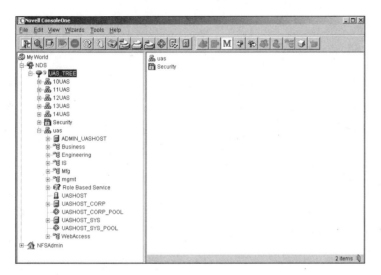

Figure 1-8   The Novell ConsoleOne utility

Activity 1-4: Viewing eDirectory Information

Time Required: 10 minutes

Objective: Describe and access common network resources.

Description: Kari Means needs to verify that the job description information for all the Engineering users is up to date. In this activity, you assume the role of Kari Means and use the ConsoleOne utility to explore the sample UAS tree structure and view information on the user objects in the Engineering container.

1. If necessary, start your computer to open the Novell Login window.

2. Log in with the user name KMeans located in the Engineering.UAS context:

   a. Enter the user name **KMeans** in the Username text box, and **password** in the Password text box.

   b. Click the **Advanced** button.

   c. If necessary, enter UAS_Tree in the Tree text box by clicking the **Trees** browse button, clicking the **UAS_Tree** item, and clicking **OK**.

   d. Click the **Contexts** browse button and, if necessary, double-click the **UAS** container to expand it.

   e. Click the **Engineering** container, and then click **OK**.

   f. If necessary, enter UASHOST in the Server text box by clicking the **Servers** browse button and then double-clicking the **UASHOST** server.

    g. Click **OK** to log in as Kari. If your login attempt fails, repeat this step, being careful to enter the user name, password, and context correctly.

3. If Kari's Novell password is different from your local Windows 2000 password, a dialog box will open, asking for the local user name and password. If necessary, enter the password for your local Windows 2000 user name, and then click **OK** to finish logging in.

4. Double-click the **User Information** application service to start the Novell ConsoleOne utility.

5. To expand the UAS_Tree, you might need to click the **+** symbol to the left of the NDS icon first. Next, click the **+** symbol to the left of the UAS_Tree icon in the Navigation frame, and then click the **+** symbol to the left of the UAS Organization.

6. Click the **Engineering** container to display user accounts in the Object frame.

7. Double-click **LJarka** in the Object frame, click the **General** tab (if necessary), and record the job description information on your student answer sheet. Notice that the information in the property fields cannot be changed. This is because the user you are logged in as, Kari Means, has been granted rights to just read the information.

8. Click **Cancel**.

9. Repeat Step 7 to record job information for each of the Engineering department users on your student answer sheet.

10. Click **Cancel**.

11. Practice using ConsoleOne to display users and objects in other contexts. Record any observations on your student answer sheet.

12. Exit the ConsoleOne utility by clicking **File** and then **Exit** on the menu bar.

13. Log out (follow the same procedure you used in Activity 1-1).

File Services

File services provide access to network data in such a way that the client computer appears to be accessing a local drive. The client software running on the user's workstation takes requests for shared data and sends these requests to the file service. It also allows drive letters to be mapped to network shared directories so that application software can easily access network files. The file service running on the server computer responds to the request by sending the data back to the client. To make file services faster, operating systems, such as NetWare, cache commonly requested data in memory. Accessing data from a memory cache is up to 100 times faster than accessing the disk system. Reliability and fault tolerance are critical parts of any network file service because they ensure continued access to network data despite hardware failures. NetWare offers improved fault tolerance by providing hot fix, disk duplexing, and server clustering capabilities for servers. If a disk block on the server fails, a hot fix enables the server to redirect that block to another area of the disk. With disk duplexing, the server records the same data on two disk drives (a process called "synchronizing") and on different controller cards so that one drive can continue to provide data access if the other drive or card fails. With server clustering technology, two or more servers can share a common disk system, making the data available in case one of the servers has a hardware failure. In Chapter 3, you will learn how hot fixes, duplexing, and clustering are implemented in the Universal AeroSpace network.

In addition to speed and reliability, another important part of any network file service is securing network data against unauthorized access. File services secure shared data by requiring users to have assigned permissions or rights. The permissions or rights control what type of activity each user can perform on the shared data. Network administrators assign permissions and access rights, which allow users to view filenames, read file contents, write to files, create or delete files and directories, and modify filenames and attributes, among other activities. With NetWare's iFolder service, users can access their data across the Internet by using a browser, such as Netscape Communicator or Internet Explorer. In Activity 1-5, you use network file servers to access documents and files on the Universal AeroSpace network.

Activity 1-5: Working with Drive Mappings

Time Required: 10 minutes

Objective: Describe and access common network services.

Description: One of the ways a client computer can access network file services is through drive mappings. Drive letters can be mapped to link directly to a specific directory in the network file system. As the UAS network administrator, Eric needs to plan which drive letters should be used to access certain standard volumes and directories. In this activity, you use My Computer to identify which drive letters are mapped by NetWare when logging in as Tony Rucci, and then use Novell Client to map a drive letter to a network directory.

1. If necessary, start your computer, and press **Ctrl+Alt+Del** to display the Novell Login window.

2. Click the **Workstation only** check box, and log on to your Windows 2000 computer with your local Windows 2000 user name and password.

3. Double-click the **My Computer** icon, and record the local drive letters available on your student answer sheet.

4. Log off your Windows 2000 workstation by clicking **Start**, **Shut Down**, **Log Off** *username*, and then clicking **Yes** in the Log Off Windows dialog box.

5. Log in as Tony Rucci by following these steps:

   a. Enter the user name **TRucci** in the Username text box and **password** in the Password text box, and then click the **Advanced** button.

   b. If necessary, enter UAS_Tree in the Tree text box by clicking the **Trees** browse button, clicking the **UAS_Tree** container, and clicking **OK**.

   c. Click the **Containers** browse button and, if necessary, double-click the **UAS** container to expand it.

   d. Click the **Engineering** container, and then click **OK**.

   e. If necessary, enter UASHOST in the Server text box by clicking the **Servers** browse button and then double-clicking the **UASHOST** server.

   f. Click **OK** to log in.

   g. If necessary, enter your local user name and password, and then click **OK** to log on to your local computer.

6. Double-click the **My Computer** icon, record the network drive letters and paths on your student answer sheet, and then close the My Computer window.

7. Map drive letter R to the Engineer\NASA\Rover directory and make the drive letter appear as the topmost or "root" level every time you start Windows by following these steps:

   a. Right-click **My Network Places**, and then click **Novell Map Network Drive** on the shortcut menu.

   b. Click the **Choose the drive letter to map** list arrow, and then click the **R** drive letter in the list of options.

   c. Click the **Browse** button to open the NetWare Resource Browser dialog box.

   d. Click the **+** symbol to the left of the UAS_Tree icon to expand the tree structure.

   e. Expand the **UAS** Organization to display all objects in UAS.

   f. Expand the **UASHOST_CORP** volume object to view the directories, expand the **Engineer** directory, and then expand the **NASA** subdirectory.

   g. Click the **Rover** subdirectory, and then click **OK**.

   h. Click the **Check to make a folder appear as the top most level** check box.

   i. Click the **Check to always map this drive letter when you start Windows** check box.

   j. Click the **Map** button to map drive letter R: and display the contents of the Rover subdirectory.

   k. Close the Rover subdirectory dialog box.

8. Double-click **My Computer**, and verify that drive letter R: is pointing to the Rover subdirectory.

9. Close the My Computer window, and log out.

10. Follow the procedure in Step 5 to log in as Tony Rucci.

11. Use My Computer to determine whether drive letter R: is mapped to the Rover subdirectory. Record your results on the student answer sheet, and then close the My Computer window.

12. Remove the drive letter R: mapping by following these steps:

   a. Right-click **My Network Places**, and then click **Novell Map Network Drive** on the shortcut menu.

   b. Click the **Choose the drive letter to map** list arrow, and then click the **R** drive letter in the list of options.

   c. Click the **Disconnect** button, and then click the **Close** button.

13. Log out.

Print Services

Print services are similar to file services in that print services include client software that makes accessing network printers the same as accessing a printer attached directly to the workstation. Network print services also provide security measures for determining which printers each user can access and which users can control and manage the network printers. In addition, network print services can download printer drivers and automatically install printers on user desktops. NetWare 6 includes the Internet Printing Protocol (IPP) service that enables users to install new printers and view their printer status in their Web browsers. IPP also enables users to send output to printers across the Internet. In later activities in this book, you will practice using network print services by accessing a printer defined in the UAS network system.

Application Services

Application services can be classified as centralized, distributed, or client-server. In a **centralized application service**, such as the Microsoft Terminal Server and Citrix, software is run on a central server computer with the clients simply acting as input/output terminals. These types of products allow applications to run from a central server with the workstation acting as a terminal using what's commonly called a **thin client**. Thin client software provides a browser window to the terminal server, allowing screens to be displayed and data to be entered. A disadvantage of centralized application services is that they require powerful and expensive servers to achieve fast performance.

A **distributed application service** allows each user's desktop computer to run its own software and process information independently. The Universal AeroSpace Corporation currently uses distributed processing to run its applications so that its employees can use a wide variety of specialized software packages that require sophisticated graphical user interfaces (GUIs). Distributed processing gives UAS more flexibility than a centralized application service would, and at a lower cost.

Client-server application services are often part of database systems in which client computers make requests for specific data records from database services running on a server computer. The database service running on the server then scans the database and returns either the requested data or a message indicating that the record could not be located. For example, UAS uses a client-server database system for its inventory application, so salespeople can efficiently use their laptop computers to access inventory data with a dial-up connection to the network. Because the dial-up connection operates at relatively slow speeds, the client-server database system makes accessing the database faster because only the requested inventory information is transmitted over the phone line. Without a client-server database, the laptop computer would need to look up the requested data record itself, causing much unnecessary data to be transmitted over the phone line. In Activity 1-6, you see how Universal AeroSpace uses Novell's Z.E.N.works application service to distribute different applications to users depending on their needs.

Activity 1-6: Using Application Services

Time Required: 15 minutes

Objective: Describe and access essential network services.

Description: A challenge for network administrators is installing and maintaining applications on many different user workstations. Novell's Z.E.N.works for Desktops is an application management tool that helps network administrators deliver applications to user workstations without having to install the application software at each workstation. For example, when a user at Universal AeroSpace logs in, Z.E.N.works displays a list of applications that the user is authorized to start. When the user selects an application, Z.E.N.works determines whether that application is installed on the user's workstation and, if necessary, automatically downloads the files needed to run the application. In this activity, you log in as two different users in the Engineering department and compare the applications they are authorized to use.

To perform this activity, verify that your instructor has installed Z.E.N.works version 3 on your network. You will work more with Z.E.N.works in Chapter 7.

1. If necessary, start your computer to open the Novell Login window.

2. Log in as Kari Means by following these steps:

   a. Enter **KMeans** in the Username text box and **password** in the Password text box, and then click the **Advanced** button.

   b. Verify that UAS_Tree is displayed in the Tree text box. If necessary, click the **Tree** list arrow, and then click **UAS_Tree** in the list of options.

   c. Click the **Contexts** browse button, and then double-click the **UAS** Organization.

   d. Click **Engineering**, and then click **OK**.

   e. Verify that UASHOST is displayed in the Server text box. If necessary, click the **Server** list arrow, and then click **UASHOST** in the list of options.

   f. Click **OK** to log in, and if necessary enter your local user name and password to log on to your Windows 2000 computer.

3. On your student answer sheet, record the applications displayed in the Novell-delivered Applications dialog box, and then log out.

4. Log in as the design engineer, Lianne Jarka, by following these steps:

   a. Enter **LJarka** in the Username text box and **password** in the Password text box, and then click the **Advanced** button.

   b. Verify that UAS_Tree is displayed in the Tree text box. If necessary, click the **Tree** list arrow, and then click **UAS_Tree** in the list of options.

   c. Verify that Engineering.UAS is displayed in the Context text box.

   d. Verify that UASHOST is displayed in the Server text box. If necessary, click the **Server** list arrow, and then click **UASHOST** in the list of options.

   e. Click **OK** to log in, and if necessary enter your local user name and password to log on to your Windows 2000 computer.

5. On your student answer sheet, record the applications displayed in the Novell-delivered Applications dialog box.

6. Record the following information on your student answer sheet:

   a. Record which application(s) are the same for both users.

   b. Record which application Kari Means has that Lianne Jarka does not have.

7. Log out.

NETWORK ENTITIES

Before you can set up a LAN to provide network services to users, you must define the required network entities and determine how they will be connected. As shown in Figure 1-9, network entities generally consist of a combination of devices that can communicate through a LAN, including user workstations, servers, shared storage devices, printers, and accessories. In the following sections, you learn about each of these network entities, along with how the UAS network implements them by using Novell NetWare 6.

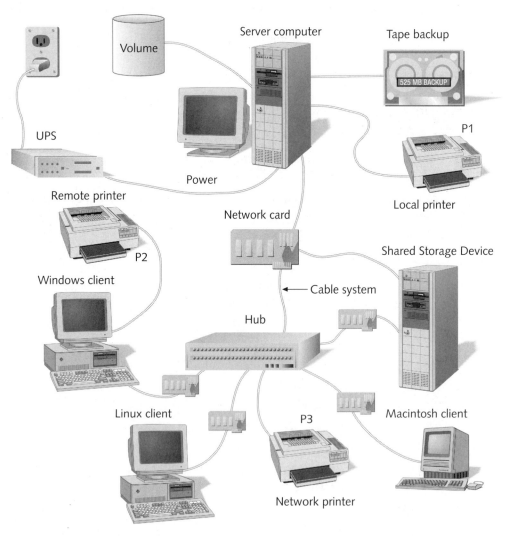

Figure 1-9   Sample network components

User Workstations

A user workstation is a computer used to run applications that access network resources and services, such as files, printers, and communication systems. A critical part of any network system is giving user workstations access to the shared data and resources they need to run user applications. Because different types of workstation operating systems are needed to run user applications and meet user preferences, a network system should be able to support a variety of desktop operating systems. For example, UAS has a combination of Windows, Linux, and Macintosh computers to meet the processing needs of the Engineering, Accounting, Marketing, and Desktop Publishing departments. One of the reasons UAS selected NetWare 6 is for its ability to support a wide variety of workstation environments, allowing them all to communicate and share data and other resources as one network.

Servers

Shared resources and information are made available to the network through network services, which are combinations of computer hardware and software that provide network resources that client computers can access. A server is a computer that runs one or more network services. Servers often use hardware and software that is optimized to respond reliably and quickly to requests for network services. However, any computer on the network with the necessary memory and processor capacity can act as a server by running software that offers one or more of the previously identified services. Operating systems that provide network services are referred to as **network operating systems (NOSs)** and can be divided into two basic categories: peer-to-peer and server-centric.

Peer-to-Peer Systems

Some network operating systems allow a computer to be both client and server, enabling users to share resources from their computers with other users on the network. Networks that have client computers performing server functions are commonly referred to as **peer-to-peer** network systems; these systems are easy to set up and offer a lot of flexibility, along with a low initial cost. Computers in peer-to-peer networks are organized into logical clusters called **workgroups**. One or more computers in each workgroup provide network resources and services to the other computers. Because Windows NT Workstation and Windows 2000 Professional have a limit of 10 incoming connections, workgroup size should be kept to 10 or fewer computers.

In a peer-to-peer network, each computer maintains its own user and password information. As networks become larger, maintaining password security on each computer makes peer-to-peer systems difficult to manage and secure. In addition, when a user's computer is not on, certain data and services might not be available to the network. Currently, the UAS network uses peer-to-peer networking in the Engineering department so that users can share large CAD files instead of copying them to the central server. Peer-to-peer networking is also used in the Desktop Publishing department so that other staff can access the DVD recorder on Diana Brady's computer. The DVD recorder is not used frequently, so there's little impact on the performance of Diana's computer. In Activity 1-7, you use peer-to-peer networking to share a folder on your computer. In Chapter 2, you will learn how NetWare servers can act as peer-to-peer servers when working with computers that have only the Microsoft client installed.

Activity 1-7: Peer-to-Peer File Sharing

Time Required: 15 minutes

Objectives: Identify network components and describe their functions.

Description: A Windows 2000 Professional workstation can also be used as a peer-to-peer server that allows other users to access its files and printers. Tony Rucci has been working on a diagram of components for the international space station. In this activity, you download a document file from the UASHOST server and share it on your workstation. You then work with another student to access his or her shared directory.

1. Log in as Tony Rucci:

   a. Enter **TRucci** in the Username text box and **password** in the Password text box, and then click the **Advanced** button.

   b. Verify that UAS_Tree is displayed in the Tree text box.

   c. Click the **Contexts** browse button. If necessary, expand the **UAS** Organization, and then click the **Engineering** container.

   d. Verify that the UASHOST server is displayed in the Server text box.

   e. Click **OK** to log in.

2. If necessary, log on to your Windows 2000 computer with the Administrator user name and password.

3. Create a directory on your workstation's C: drive named **Designs**.

4. Use the Paint program to open the vehicle.bmp file in the G:\Engineer\NASA folder. Make a few modifications to the file, and then save the file in your C:\Designs directory using the name **##Mars** (## represents your assigned student number).

5. Share your Designs directory with the default permission of Read Only by following these steps:

   a. Right-click the **Designs** directory, and then click **Sharing** on the shortcut menu to open the Share Properties dialog box.

   b. Click the **Share this folder** or **Share as** radio button. The share name is the name other users see when they access your computer. By default, the share name is the same as the folder name, truncated to 12 characters. In this activity, leave the default share name and proceed to the next step.

6. To prevent other users from changing or deleting data in your shared directory, you need to set the shared permissions to Read Only:

   a. Click the **Permissions** button to display the Permissions for Designs dialog box. Click to deselect the **Full Control** and **Change** permissions check boxes, leaving only the Read permission selected.

   b. Click **OK** to save your permission changes.

   c. On your student answer sheet, record the possible shared permissions.

   d. Click **OK** to share your Designs directory.

7. Access another student's Designs directory:

   a. Obtain the name of your partner's computer.

   b. On your computer, click **Start**, **Run**, and then enter your partner's computer name preceded by \\. For example, if your partner's computer is named pro1, enter **\\pro1**, and click **OK**.

   c. If necessary, enter a valid user name and password to log on to your partner's Windows computer.

8. Open your partner's ##Mars design file, and save it in your Designs directory:

   a. Double-click your partner's **Designs** directory to view the contents.

   b. Double-click the **##Mars** file to open it.

   c. Save the file to the Designs directory on your local hard drive.

9. Close all windows and log out.

Server-centric Systems

In the NetWare operating system, Novell separates server functions from client functions by using a specialized NOS to control the server computer. User workstations are required to communicate through client software to gain access to services running on the NetWare servers. Because user workstations must communicate through a server rather than directly with each other, as in peer-to-peer systems, NetWare networks are classified as **server-centric**. An important concept of a server-centric network is that a user needs to log in only once to access services and resources hosted by any server that is part of the network tree. As you learned earlier in this chapter, the single login is made possible by the eDirectory service, which allows network servers to share a common directory database of users and other network objects. Another advantage of server-centric networks is the performance and reliability you achieve by running the server software on specialized computers designed to perform network services. For example, Eric recommended that UAS purchase a Compaq computer for its server because it has features that enhance reliability and speed. Additionally, because NetWare 6 is designed as a dedicated NOS, its servers offer better performance, security, and reliability for network services than what's available in peer-to-peer network systems.

To provide access to information and software, NetWare requires the server's disk space to be organized into one or more volumes. A **volume** is a logical division of a server's disk system consisting of a physical amount of storage space on one or more hard disk drives. All network files are accessed through volumes, and each volume is associated with a specific NetWare server. In addition to representing disk drive space, volumes can represent other physical storage media, such as a CD-ROM or optical disks, that need to be accessed on the network. Each server is required to have at least one volume named SYS, which is created during installation to contain operating system files and programs. To store company data and software, the network administrator often creates additional volumes. For example, the UAS network currently contains two volumes housed on the UASHOST computer: the SYS volume, used only for the NetWare operating system, and the CORP volume, used to store company data. In Chapter 3, you will learn how to design a file storage system consisting of multiple volumes for your version of the UAS network.

Server Accessories

In addition to the disk volumes and network operating system, servers need to be protected from power problems and have a method of protecting and restoring network data. To provide these network capabilities, the UAS server has an uninterruptible power supply and tape backup attached.

Uninterruptible Power Supply

If a server loses power without going through the proper shutdown procedure, it's likely that some of the data stored in the file cache memory will not be completely written to the disk drives, resulting in corrupted or damaged files and directories. Therefore, the UAS network includes an **uninterruptible power supply (UPS)** for each server on the network. The UPS provides backup power from batteries in the event of a commercial power failure or brownout. In the UAS network, the UPS has a NetWare-compatible serial interface that attaches to the file server's serial port and notifies the NetWare operating system when the server is on battery power. If commercial power is not restored in a specified time period, NetWare goes through the server shutdown procedure to prevent data loss before the UPS is exhausted.

Tape Backup

Implementing and managing a daily tape backup system is a critical part of administering a network system. The tape system and software should be certified by Novell to ensure that it correctly backs up data and security information. All backup systems should be tested to make sure that data and software could be reliably restored. Backups of data that are essential to an organization's operation, such as payroll, accounts payable and receivable, and inventory, should be kept offsite in case the building is damaged or destroyed. For example, when Luke McMann designed the UAS backup system, he planned a weekly backup of all files and daily backups of any updated data. He then made arrangements with a local firm to have the weekly backup tapes rotated to an offsite storage facility.

Shared Storage Devices

Shared storage devices are disk systems that attach directly to the network cable and can be shared by multiple servers. Typically, shared storage devices use RAID (redundant array of independent disks) technology to combine several disk drives, thus offering additional capacity and reliability. Because RAID technology stores redundancy information on each drive, if any of the drives on the RAID device fails, information is still available to the network. By using NetWare 6 clustering capability, multiple servers can share volumes on the same shared storage device. In this way, if any one of the servers has a hardware failure, another server can automatically take over and continue to give clients access to the networked data. For increased reliability and speed, shared storage devices are often placed on dedicated networks called storage area networks (SANs). SANs are specialized networks that support storage devices by using a reliable high-speed fiber-optic cable to connect the storage devices to the NetWare servers. Using shared storage devices and SANs, along with NetWare 6 clustering services, can help ensure continuous access to critical network data.

Printers

Providing shared access to sophisticated, high-speed printers is an essential capability of a local area network. Among the advantages of placing printers on a network are cost savings, increased workspace for employees, flexible printer selection based on application needs, and printer fault tolerance. Printers can be connected to a NetWare network in one of three ways:

- Attached to the NetWare server
- Attached to user workstations
- Attached directly to the network cable

In most organizations, printers are not attached to the NetWare server because the server computer is usually secured in a locked room. Attaching network printers to user workstations provides easy access, but also results in slower performance when printing high-resolution graphics from desktop publishing or presentation graphics applications. Attaching a printer directly to the network gives you the best performance and reliability, but is more expensive because of the need for a dedicated network card inside the printer or an external control box for printer attachments. For example, UAS has network-attached printers in each department, and Diana Brady and Maria Frias have shared laser printers attached to their computers. In Activity 1-8, you use your classroom printer to print out a plan that identifies the Universal AeroSpace network equipment needs.

Activity 1-8: Identifying Universal AeroSpace Network Components

Time Required: 15 minutes

Objectives: Identify network components and describe their functions.

Description: When Luke McMann first started with Universal AeroSpace, he assessed the needs of all users served by the network and what equipment they currently used or needed. From this information, he created the floor plan shown previously in Figure 1-3. This floor plan identifies all current and planned workstations, printers, and servers. In this activity, you log in to the UAS network tree as Luke and access the equipment list form in the Forms directory. You then fill out the form, print it, and save it in the network's Shared directory for documents.

1. If necessary, start your computer to open the Novell Login window.

2. Log in as Luke McMann by following these steps:

   a. Enter **LMcMann** in the Username text box and **password** in the Password text box, and then click the **Advanced** button.

b. Click the **Contexts** browse button, and then click the **IS** department under the UAS Organization.

c. Click **OK** to log in. If necessary, enter the local Windows 2000 password, and then click **OK** to complete the login.

3. Open the NetList.doc file:

a. Double-click the **My Computer** icon on your desktop.

b. Double-click the **G** drive letter, double-click the **Forms** directory, and then double-click the **NetList.doc** form to open the WordPad application.

4. Refer to Figure 1-3 to record the number of computers and printers in each department in your NetList document.

5. Save your revised document in the G:\Shared directory using the name **##Equip.doc** (## represents your assigned student number).

a. Click **File** on the menu bar, and then click **Save as**. Click the **Save in** list arrow, and then click the **G** drive letter.

b. Double-click the **Shared** directory.

c. Enter **##Equip.doc** in the File name text box, and then click the **Save** button.

6. Set your workstation's printer to default to the IS department network printer by following these steps:

Depending on how your network was installed, your classroom networked printer should be installed as UASClass_P. If you do not have this printer on your workstation, see your instructor for printing instructions.

a. Click **Start**, **Settings**, **Printers** to open the Printers window.

b. Right-click **UASClass_P**, click **Set as Default** on the shortcut menu, and then close the Printers window.

7. Print your document to the default printer by clicking **File**, **Print** on the WordPad menu bar.

8. Click **File**, **Exit** on the menu bar to exit the WordPad application.

9. Log out.

THE NETWORK PATHWAY

The LAN pathway is based on the cable system and network cards used to connect the network entities. The network cable system consists of the cable media along with the cable layout, or **topology**. As described in Appendix B, a variety of cable and topology options are available for LANs. Most LAN cable systems currently use the star topology to connect each computer to a central hub with unshielded twisted-pair wire. **Hubs** are the central connecting point in a star topology and repeat signals to other computers on the network. The network pathway for UAS consists of a star topology, with unshielded twisted-pair cable connecting each computer in the business office to the hubs in the file server room. As shown in Figure 1-3, computers in the Receiving and Shipping departments are connected to hubs in the Manufacturing facility. Because the Manufacturing facility is in a different building and contains equipment that generates a lot of electrical noise or static, Luke chose to use fiber-optic cable to connect the Shipping and Receiving hubs to the main network. Although fiber-optic cable is more expensive than unshielded twisted-pair cable, it's immune to electrical noise and can transmit more data over longer distances.

After deciding on the cable system and topology, another important step in setting up the network pathway is to select and install the network interface cards (NICs). As described in Appendix B, the two most popular types of NICs are Ethernet and token ring. Because these cards use different methods to send and receive data, you cannot combine computers with token ring and Ethernet cards on the same network cable system. Token ring cards are useful in IBM mainframe systems, but Ethernet cards are more commonly used today. Ethernet cards are available for different types of cable systems. The most common are 10BaseT or 100BaseT. The 10 or 100 designates the speed of the card in megabits per second (Mbps), and the term 10BaseT or 100BaseT comes from the Ethernet network having a transmission speed of either *10* or *100* Mbps using digital *base*band signals over *t*wisted-pair cable segments. Modern Ethernet cards can automatically switch between 10 and 100 Mbps, depending on the network speed. Luke selected 100BaseT Ethernet cards from the same manufacturer to connect each computer to the network. Getting NICs from the same manufacturer makes configuring the computers easier because all NICs use a common software driver. As a CNA, you'll need to be able to install and troubleshoot NICs; common problems include incorrect drivers and misconfigured hardware settings. In Activity 1-9, you use Windows 2000 to check the NIC on your computer and document its driver settings and configuration.

Activity 1-9: Identifying Network Adapter Properties

Time Required: 5 minutes

Objectives: Identify network components and describe their functions.

Description: Bradley Dahl's computer has been displaying network error messages. Eric has decided to verify that Bradley's computer is using the same NIC settings as the other computers in the Engineering department. In this activity, you simulate Eric's task of comparing Bradley's NIC settings by using My Network Places and Control Panel to document your NIC settings. You then compare your findings to those of another student.

1. If necessary, start your computer, and log in to your local workstation as Administrator:

    a. When you see the Novell Login window, click the **Workstation only** check box.

    b. Enter the administrator user name and password you use to manage your local Windows workstation.

    c. Click **OK** to log in.

2. Document your network adapter settings:

    a. Right-click **My Network Places**, and then click **Properties**.

    b. Right-click **Local Area Connection**, and then click **Properties**.

    c. Click the **Configure** button.

    d. Click the **Driver** tab, and record the driver date on your student answer sheet.

    e. Click the **Resources** tab, and record the interrupt and memory range on your student answer sheet.

    f. Click **Cancel** twice to return to the Network and Dial-up Connections dialog box.

    g. Close the Network and Dial-up Connections dialog box.

3. Compare your network adapter settings to those of your lab partner and document any differences on your student answer sheet.

4. Log out.

NETWORK PROTOCOLS OR RULES

The network pathway provides the hardware necessary to transmit signals representing binary bits from one computer to another, but the bits must be organized into packets that the receiving computer can understand and process. A networked computer's **protocol stack** is the collection of related network protocols, or rules, responsible for formatting packets of data to be transmitted by the NICs. Although delivering data packets throughout the network system is the responsibility of the network pathway, the functions of the protocol stack include routing packets between different networks, verifying delivery, and requesting network services. Certain protocol stacks, such as IBM's Synchronous Data Link Control (SDLC), Microsoft NetBEUI, and Novell IPX/SPX, are called proprietary protocols because they are owned and controlled by a specific company. Other protocols, such as TCP/IP, are nonproprietary and are controlled by an industry organization consisting of vendors and users.

Because today's networks often need to support multiple protocol stacks for computers to communicate and access services using different operating systems, NetWare 6 is designed for multiple protocols. For example, the Universal AeroSpace UASHOST server supports both TCP/IP and IPX/SPX. TCP/IP is needed to allow access to the Internet and use Novell's OneNet services, and Novell's proprietary IPX/SPX protocol is needed to support legacy NetWare applications and older clients. In this section, you learn about these protocols and their advantages and disadvantages.

NetWare IPX/SPX

The IPX/SPX protocol is the Novell proprietary system that manages routing and formatting NetWare packets on the network. To communicate, IPX (Internetwork Packet eXchange) must be loaded on each network client as well as the file server. In addition to IPX, each client and file server must have a network card driver loaded to transmit the packets. The IPX protocol and the NIC driver are brought together during client installation with a process called binding.

Besides IPX, NetWare uses two other protocols to provide network services: SPX and NCP. Sequential Packet eXchange (SPX), used by some client software to ensure successful delivery of packets, works by using special control and acknowledgment packets from the receiver that inform the sender if any data needs to be retransmitted. **NetWare Core Protocol (NCP)** is the language that applications use to access services on NetWare servers through the client software running on the workstation computer. Currently, Novell provides the Novell Client, designed to take advantage of all the available services by using NCP. In addition to supporting the Novell Client, Novell introduced the Native File Access Protocol (NFAP) with NetWare 6. NFAP enables diverse clients to communicate directly with a NetWare server by using their native protocols. For example, Windows, Macintosh, and Linux clients can use NFAP to access shared files from a NetWare 6 server with their native protocols. Using NFAP makes setting up clients and accessing basic NetWare file and print services simpler. However, you will need the Novell Client on a workstation to perform certain server management functions or access specialized Novell services. For example, to gain access to specialized Novell services, such as Z.E.N.works, UAS has installed Novell Client on most computers in the Engineering department and Business office. In Chapter 2, you will work with both NFAP and Novell Client to access network services on the NetWare 6 server.

TCP/IP

The **Transmission Control Protocol/Internet Protocol (TCP/IP)** was first developed in the 1960s to support communication among mainframe computers in government agencies and educational institutions. Like IPX/SPX, TCP/IP is responsible for formatting packets and then routing them between networks by using Internet Protocol. IP is more sophisticated than IPX in fragmenting packets and sending them out over WAN links, such as those used when connecting to the Internet. The TCP/IP specifications were developed and are still maintained by an independent agency, the Internet Access Board (IAB). Because TCP/IP was developed to connect a large number of independent organizations, it was designed to support communications between diverse computers and operating systems. The TCP/IP model actually consists of four major layers, as shown in Figure 1-10.

Moving from the bottom to the top of Figure 1-10, the Network layer provides the communication pathway consisting of network cards and drivers. The Internet layer, or IP, is responsible for routing packets to different networks. The Transport layer, also called the host-to-host layer, consists of both the TCP and User Datagram Protocol (UDP) services. Both transport services use port numbers to identify the sending and receiving applications. For example, a Web server typically uses port 80, but the FTP server defaults to port 21. In addition to the basic services of UDP, the TCP transport service guarantees the delivery of packets by sending and receiving acknowledgments. With this acknowledgment system, the sender and receiver can establish a window for the number of packets to be acknowledged. The windowing capability offers better performance than WANs do because each packet does not need to be individually acknowledged before another packet is sent. The Application layer represents a network service, such as a Web server or an FTP server, that is processing client requests and returning information via the Transport and Network layers.

 Because of the popularity of the TCP/IP protocol stack for LANs and WANs, starting with NetWare 5, NetWare can use only TCP/IP for its network clients and services. Older versions of NetWare required NetWare administrators to support the IPX protocol for access to NetWare servers and TCP/IP for Internet access. By eliminating IPX, network administration and support can be simplified and made more efficient.

| **Application Layer** |
| This layer includes network services along with client software. |
| **Transport Layer**
TCP/UDP Services

This layer is responsible for getting data packets to and from the Application layer by using port numbers. TCP also verifies packet delivery by using acknowledgments. |
| **Internet Layer**

This layer uses IP addresses to route packets to their appropriate destination network. |
| **Network Layer**

This layer represents the physical network pathway and the network interface card. |

Figure 1-10   TCP/IP layers

In TCP/IP, each computer attached to a network is called a "host" and is assigned a unique address. Routers connect independent networks and transfer packets from one network to another by using the IP network address. The IP address allows packets to be sent over different routes and then reassembled in the correct sequence at the receiving station. IP addresses consist of 32-bit numbers that are expressed as four bytes separated by periods. Each IP address contains network and host components, as illustrated in Figure 1-11.

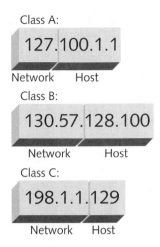

Class A:

127.100.1.1

Network   Host

Class B:

130.57.128.100

Network   Host

Class C:

198.1.1.129

Network   Host

Figure 1-11   IP address components

Setting up and working with IP addresses is an essential part of network administration. The first step in planning and setting up an IP address scheme is to select a network address for each LAN. Network addresses used to access the Internet need to be assigned by an Internet service provider. Certain IP network addresses are reserved for private internal networks, so when setting up an IP address scheme for these networks, you should use one of the private IP network addresses listed in Appendix B. For example, because all the UAS computers in Salt Lake City are attached to the same LAN, Luke decided to use a private network address of 172.20.0.0 for those computers. Each computer is then given an IP address consisting of the network address component and a unique host component. As described in Appendix B, IP addresses can be assigned manually or automatically. In Activity 1-10, you learn how to check your computer's IP address configuration.

NetBEUI/NetBIOS

NetBEUI is the Microsoft protocol stack integrated into Windows products. Of the three protocols described in these sections, NetBEUI is the smallest, fastest, and easiest to use. It also has the fewest features, so it's more limited in large networked environments because it does not support the Network layer needed to route packets between networks. As a result, NetBEUI is limited to communicating with other computers attached to the same network cable system. Because NetBEUI does not have the overhead of providing routing functions, it is extremely small and fast, making it ideal for small networks of 10 to 50 devices.

The NetBEUI protocol stack consists of NetBIOS and Service Message Blocks (SMBs), which provide a standard, well-defined way for servers and clients to communicate. Many peer-to-peer applications have been written to interface with NetBIOS to communicate with applications running on other computers, thus allowing an application to span multiple computers. As a result of the popularity of NetBIOS-based applications, both IPX/SPX and TCP/IP provide support for the NetBIOS protocol. The UAS network uses NetBIOS to allow workstations to run peer-to-peer applications while still accessing services from NetWare file servers.

Being able to set up and manage protocols on user computers is an important task for network administrators. In Activity 1-10, you use Windows 2000 to identify the network adapter properties and protocol configuration on your workstation.

Activity 1-10: Identifying Workstation Protocols

Time Required: 10 minutes

Objective: Identify common network systems and protocols.

Description: Paul Alm's computer is unable to log in to the UAS network, so Eric has asked you to check Paul's network settings because he suspects that the protocol configuration information might have been changed when Paul installed a new Internet application package. Eric would like you to compare Paul's protocol configuration to other computers in the Engineering department. In this activity, you simulate checking out Paul's computer by documenting the IP configuration of your workstation and then comparing it to your lab partner's configuration.

1. If necessary, start your computer to open the Novell Login window.

2. Simulate not being able to log in by clicking the **Workstation only** check box.

3. To view your workstation's TCP/IP settings, you need to log on to your Windows 2000 computer with the local Administrator user name and password. (If necessary, your instructor will supply a user name/password that has Administrator rights to your local workstation.)

4. Identify the protocols installed on your computer:

   a. Right-click **My Network Places**, and then click **Properties**.

   b. Right-click **Local Area Connection**, and then click **Properties**.

   c. Record the installed protocols on your student answer sheet.

5. Identify your IP address by following these steps:

   a. Click the **Internet Protocol (TCP/IP)** list arrow, and then click **Properties** in the list of options.

   b. On your student answer sheet, record the IP address settings.

6. Click **Cancel** twice to close the windows.

7. You can also find IP configuration information from the command prompt by using the IPCONFIG command. If your IP address is set to Automatic, you need to follow these steps to find your IP address information:

   a. Click **Start**, **Run**, enter **cmd** in the Open text box, and click **OK** to open a command-prompt window.

   b. Enter **IPCONFIG/ALL** at the command prompt, and then press **Enter**.

   c. If necessary, record your IP address information.

   d. Enter **Exit** at the command prompt, and then press **Enter** to close the command-prompt window.

8. Compare your protocol settings with your lab partner's and document any differences on your student answer sheet.

9. Log off your local computer.

In this chapter, you have identified the essential network services that make up the UAS network, including directory services, file services, print services, and application services. In addition, you have learned about the components that make up the UAS network infrastructure, such as user workstations, printers, servers, the network cable system, and protocols. In Chapter 2, you will begin implementing your version of the UAS network by installing client software and creating your eDirectory tree.

CHAPTER SUMMARY

- To set up and manage a network, you need to be familiar with the services and components that make up a network system, including user workstations, servers, volumes, printers, cabling, network cards, and protocols. User workstations run the application software and use client software to make requests for file services, print services, message services, and application services. Server computers provide network services to clients.

- In peer-to-peer networks, a computer can be both a client and a server, allowing it to share data and resources with other computers. Although peer-to-peer networks are flexible and easy to set up, they can be difficult to administer because of the lack of centralized control.

❏ NetWare networks are referred to as server-centric because they use dedicated server computers whose network operating systems are geared toward providing network services to other clients rather than running application software. In addition to better performance and security, NetWare servers offer improved reliability over peer-to-peer servers because the NetWare NOS is designed specifically to provide network services.

❏ The network cable system provides the infrastructure over which signals can travel between network components, using such media as twisted-pair, coaxial, and fiber-optic cable.

❏ Network interface cards allow computers to transmit signals over the cable system. The standards commonly used in today's networks are token ring and Ethernet 10/100BaseT. Although 10/100BaseT is the most popular because it delivers the best performance for the cost, token ring is useful in industry applications that require uniform throughput on heavily used networks.

❏ A network protocol consists of software that formats and routes data packets between servers and clients. Because the client computer operating systems on your network can use different protocols, network administrators often need to support multiple protocol stacks on a NetWare network. Common protocols supported by NetWare servers include TCP/IP, IPX/SPX, and NetBIOS.

KEY TERMS

application service — A service that assists client computers in running certain software functions.

centralized application service — A system in which all processing is done on a centralized server. The workstations act as terminals to send and receive data from the server computer.

Certified Novell Administrator (CNA) — An administrator who has passed the Novell Certified Administrator certification test; the objectives for this test are covered in this book.

client — A computer that accesses network services such as shared files, printers, applications, or communication systems.

directory service — A network service that stores configuration information on network objects, such as users, printers, groups, and containers, in a global database that's accessible to all network servers.

distributed application service — A system that supports each user's computer running its own software.

eDirectory — A global database in Novell containing information on all network objects, including users, groups, printers, and volumes, that is available to all servers.

file service — A service that enables client computers to access and save data on its disk storage system.

hub — A central connecting point for computers attached to a star topology network.

local area network (LAN) — A high-speed communication system consisting of cables and cards (hardware) along with software that enables different types of computers to communicate and share resources over short distances, such as within a single building or room.

logging in — The process of authenticating yourself to a Novell network by supplying a user name and password.

logging on — The process of authenticating yourself to a Windows network by supplying a user name and password.

message service — A network service responsible for sending and receiving network messages and notifications.

metropolitan area network (MAN) — A network that uses fiber-optic or microwave towers to connect computers in the same geographical area.

NetBEUI — A Microsoft nonrouting protocol stack commonly used on Windows.

NetWare Core Protocol (NCP) — A protocol used by NetWare to access services on a NetWare server.

network operating system (NOS) — The software that runs on server computers to provide services to the network.

OneNet — Novell's strategy of making multiple networks, consisting of diverse clients and services, work together as one network.

peer-to-peer — A network operating system in which a computer can be both client and server.

print service — A network service that makes printers attached to the network available to user workstations.

protocol stack — The collection of protocols responsible for formatting and routing packets of data between network devices.

security service — A network service that authenticates users to the network and determines which network rights they have.

server — A computer that provides one or more network services.

server-centric — A network operating system, such as NetWare 6, in which server functions run on a designated computer.

thin client — The workstation component of a centralized application service that acts as an input/output terminal to an application running on the server.

topology — The physical layout of the cable system.

Transmission Control Protocol/Internet Protocol (TCP/IP) — The protocol commonly used to format and route packets between Unix computers; also used on the Internet.

uninterruptible power supply (UPS) — A backup power system that uses batteries to supply continuous power to a computer during a power outage.

volume — The major division of NetWare storage. All files are stored in volumes associated with a specific NetWare server.

wide area network (WAN) — A network that uses carriers such as the phone system to connect computers over long distances.

workgroup — A group of two or more peer-to-peer networked computers.

REVIEW QUESTIONS

1. The network interface card is an example of which of the following network components?

   a. network entity

   b. network service

   c. pathway

   d. protocol

2. Which of the following is an application service in which each user's computer runs its own software?

   a. file service

   b. centralized application service

   c. distributed application service

   d. directory service

3. Novell's OneNet utilities work only with NetWare 6. True or false?

4. You log in to a Novell network and log on to a Windows 2000 workstation. True or false?

5. Which of the following network services stores user names and passwords?

   a. security

   b. eDirectory

   c. file

   d. application

6. A(n) _____ computer accesses network services such as shared files and printers.

7. Which of the following services enables multiple clients to access its disk system to retrieve and save data?

   a. file service

   b. centralized application service

   c. distributed application service

   d. directory service

8. Which of the following services assists client computers in running application software?

   a. file service

   b. centralized application service

   c. distributed application service

   d. directory service

9. Which of the following services runs applications for client computers?

   a. file service

   b. centralized application service

   c. distributed application service

   d. directory service

10. Which of the following specifies the location of your user name in the eDirectory tree structure?

   a. pathway

   b. container

   c. context

   d. protocol

11. Operating system software that provides network services is referred to as the _____.

12. _____ network systems allow client computers to perform server functions.

13. Dedicated servers are used with _____ operating systems.

14. When using NetWare 6, the _____ service provides a global database of user and other network objects.

15. The network _____ describes the physical layout of the cable system.

16. Which of the following networks consists of a fiber-optic or microwave link between buildings in the same city?

   a. WAN

   b. MAN

   c. LAN

   d. SAN

17. How would you configure a user's Windows 2000 computer to prevent him or her from having to log on to both Novell and the local workstation?

18. Which of the following is a proprietary protocol owned by Novell?

   a. NetBEUI

   b. NetBIOS

   c. IPX

   d. TCP/IP

19. Which of the following application services is often part of database systems in which client computers request records from database services running on a server?

   a. server-centric

   b. clustering

   c. peer-to-peer

   d. client-server

20. Which of the following is the term for logical clusters of computers in peer-to-peer networks?

    a. clusters

    b. domains

    c. workgroups

    d. trees

UNIVERSAL AEROSPACE CASE PROJECTS

Case Project Background

AeroDyn, a manufacturer of aircraft control systems, is relocating to a new facility. Bernie Muelner, the network administrator for AeroDyn, would like you to design a network infrastructure for the new facility. AeroDyn will implement a centralized server running NetWare 6 along with two Windows 2000 servers to provide file, print, and application services for all clients. The server will be connected to a NetWare-compatible UPS and have a tape system installed to perform daily backups. Duplexed controller cards and disk drives will ensure additional fault tolerance. A Pentium IV processor running at 1.5 GHz and 512 MB of RAM for file caching will provide high performance for all network clients. An extra disk drive, controller card, and system board should be kept in-house to reduce downtime in the event of a hardware failure.

In addition to the server, the peer-to-peer network system in the Engineering department will continue to be used so that engineers can share large design files. Providing convenient access to printers is an important objective of the AeroDyn network system. To provide access to laser printers for all users, Bernie is planning to attach each department's laser printer to the network through the secretary's client computer, as illustrated previously in Figure 1-3. The Postscript laser printers should be directly attached to the network to provide the high speed needed for desktop publishing and presentation graphics output.

Case Project 1-1: Creating a Local User Account on Your Computer

Kari Means's computer was recently upgraded to Windows 2000. Whenever she logs in to the Novell network, she gets a Windows NT/2000 Workstation dialog box asking her to log on to the Windows 2000 computer. Currently, she has to enter "Administrator" along with a password to complete the login. She would like to be able to enter her login user name and password only once in the Novell Login window. On your student answer sheet, explain how you can fix this problem, and then use the steps you followed in Activity 1-2 to automate the Windows logon process.

Case Project 1-2: Exploring the UAS Organization

The administrative assistant, Lynn Dai, has asked Kari Means to document the job descriptions for all users in the Accounting department. Follow the procedure in Activity 1-4 to log in as Kari Means and then use ConsoleOne to record the requested job description information for the following Accounting department users on your student answer sheet:

- Terry Blackwell

- George Perez

- Amy Pan

Case Project 1-3: Sharing a CD-ROM

Julie Damrau will be using peer-to-peer networking to share the DVD drive on her computer with Diana Brady. In this case project, you will work with another student to simulate Julie Damrau's shared DVD by sharing the CD-ROM drive on your computer with your lab partner. On your student answer sheet, document the steps needed to share the drive as well as the steps needed to access the drive from Diana's computer.

2

IMPLEMENTING eDIRECTORY SERVICES

After reading this chapter and completing the exercises, you will be able to:

♦ Configure a workstation to communicate with the network by using both Microsoft and Novell Client software

♦ Describe the function and purpose of eDirectory and use distinguished and relative names to access network objects

♦ Install and use NetWare management utilities to work with the eDirectory tree

♦ Install and use NetWare Administrator, ConsoleOne, and iManage to browse the eDirectory tree, view object properties, and create new objects

♦ Use ConsoleOne to view and work with partitions and replicas

---

In Chapter 1, you learned about the major components and services of a network and how they have been applied to the Universal AeroSpace network. Starting with this chapter and continuing throughout the book, you learn how to use NetWare 6 to implement your own version of the Universal AeroSpace network. The NetWare 6 operating system enables network components and services to work together as OneNet by allowing client computers to use their included client software, and have the NetWare operating system installed on the servers. In addition to allowing communication among the physical components and services, the NetWare operating system provides a secure way for users to access only the resources and services they are authorized to use. To set up a secure network system that is easy to use, Certified Novell Administrators (CNAs) must be able to install client software as well as define network users and the objects they will be authorized to access or control. In this chapter, you learn what a CNA needs to know about implementing network clients and designing and maintaining an eDirectory structure for an organization such as Universal AeroSpace.

IMPLEMENTING THE CLIENT

As a CNA, one of the tasks you will need to perform is installing and configuring user workstations on your network. To communicate and access network services, a user's computer requires a network interface card (NIC) along with client and protocol software components, as shown in Figure 2-1. Before setting up the client computers for your UAS network, you need to understand the role that each of these software components plays in the network communication process.

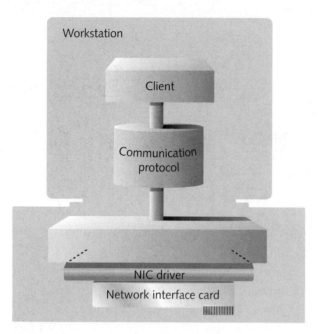

Figure 2-1 Client components

The NIC driver controls the network interface card so that it can send and receive packets over the network cable system. Information on the correct driver program for your NIC should be included in its operating manual. Most common NIC drivers are included with Windows 2000. You can refer to the Microsoft Windows Hardware Compatibility List for a list of NIC manufacturers compatible with your version of Windows. Often, Windows automatically detects the NIC and loads the drivers for you. If drivers for your NIC are not included in Windows, you can click the Have Disk button in the Driver Installation dialog box to load the drivers from the manufacturer's disk or CD-ROM.

In Chapter 1, you learned that the communication protocol is responsible for formatting the data in a network packet as well as routing packets between different networks. In the past, communication protocols were closely linked to the client software. For example, early versions of Novell Client required Novell's IPX/SPX protocol to communicate with NetWare servers, but Microsoft clients and servers required NetBEUI/NetBIOS protocols. Because TCP/IP is necessary to access Internet services, many network administrators had to install and manage several protocols on the same network cable system. Supporting multiple protocols on a single network requires more time and can cause extra traffic, thus reducing network performance. Because modern clients can use any of the major protocols to access network services, most networks today use TCP/IP to access both local services and the Internet.

As described in Chapter 1, network services need both client and server software components to operate. The client software component must work closely with the local operating system and the server to provide access to network services. The client software formats a request and then uses a network protocol to send that request to a server. A service running on the server processes the request and then sends the results back to the client. As shown in Figure 2-2, each type of NOS requires its own client to be loaded on the workstation to communicate with services running on the server. To access services on Windows servers, Microsoft clients use the Common Interface File System (CIFS) to format service requests. Before

NetWare 6, accessing file services on NetWare servers required the workstation to have Novell Client to format requests with NetWare Core Protocol (NCP). Unix clients use the Network File System (NFS) protocol to access files on other Unix systems, and Apple clients use AppleTalk Filing Protocol (AFP) to access file services on other Apple computers. Web browsers such as Internet Explorer are clients that use Hypertext Transfer Protocol (HTTP) and the Web Distributed Authoring and Versioning (WebDAV) protocol to access resources and services running on Web servers.

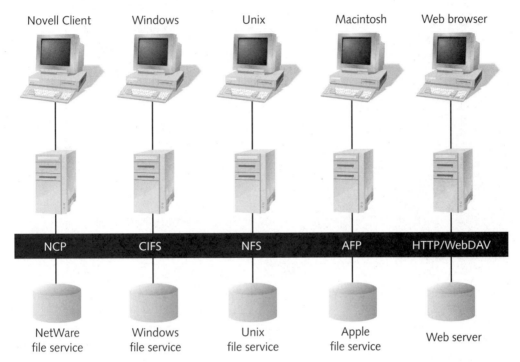

Figure 2-2   Client protocols

An important part of Novell's OneNet strategy is to provide network services that are compatible with the variety of clients shown in Figure 2-2. Previous versions of NetWare depended on the Novell Client being installed on user workstations, but NetWare 6 adds direct support for Web browser clients along with support for native file access from Windows, Apple, and Unix workstations. Another client for accessing NetWare servers is Microsoft Client Services for NetWare, included with all versions of the Windows operating system. With multiple client alternatives for accessing NetWare servers, network administrators can now select a client that best suits the needs of the user's workstation environment and applications. Table 2-1 lists the clients that can be used with Windows to access NetWare 6 servers, along with the advantages and disadvantages of each.

To make accessing NetWare file services simpler in a multiclient environment, NetWare 6 includes Novell's new Native File Access Protocol (NFAP), which enables NetWare 6 servers to process file service requests formatted by non-Novell clients, such as Microsoft, Apple, and Unix. Using Novell's NFAP helps simplify network administration by eliminating the need to install Novell Client software on computers that simply need to access files on NetWare servers. To provide access directly from Windows, Unix, and Apple clients, the NetWare 6 server needs to have NFAP installed by selecting the NFAP option during server installation or by adding it later with the server console's install feature, as described in Chapter 12. Although supporting Apple and Unix clients is important in many networks, in the following sections, you focus on how to use NFAP to work with Microsoft clients.

Table 2-1   NetWare Client Options

Client	Advantages	Disadvantages
Web Client	■ Allows access to NetWare services and administrative tasks from any computer attached to the Internet. ■ Does not require a Novell client on the workstation.	■ Does not yet provide access to all NetWare services and resources.
Microsoft Client	■ No additional clients required on the Windows computer. ■ Users view the NetWare server in the same way as other Windows servers.	■ Requires NFAP to be installed on the NetWare server. ■ Uses different passwords that are not as secure as Novell Client passwords. ■ Users might have to maintain multiple passwords. ■ Does not allow access to certain NetWare services and administrative utilities.
Microsoft NetWare Client	■ Easy to install and configure on Windows. ■ Requires less administrative overhead to maintain. ■ Uses the same Novell eDirectory user names and passwords as Novell Client.	■ Does not allow access to certain NetWare services and administrative utilities. ■ Requires IPX/SPX on the NetWare server.
Novell Client	■ Provides access to all NetWare services and administrative utilities.	■ Requires more administrative time to install and maintain. ■ Might conflict with some Windows features.

As shown in Table 2-1, accessing certain eDirectory or application services on a NetWare server still requires Novell Client to be installed on the workstation. Because eDirectory services are necessary to provide the best security and to administer certain eDirectory objects and services, Novell Client still plays an important role in a Novell network. In the following sections, you also learn how Novell Client software is installed and configured on user workstations.

Web Browser Clients

Web browsers, such as Internet Explorer and Netscape, are clients that use the HTTP and WebDAV protocols to make requests to Web servers. Many Internet applications are now written to access data and services from Web browsers. An essential part of Novell's OneNet strategy is allowing administrators and users to use their Web browsers as clients to manage the network and to access file and print services. In this book, you will learn about a number of Web-enabled applications included with NetWare 6, such as iManager, Remote Manager, iFolder, and iPrint. Later in this chapter, as well as in Chapter 4, you will learn how to use iManager to set up and manage the eDirectory tree for your version of the UAS network. In Chapter 9, you will learn how to configure iFolder so that users can access their files from any location by using browser software. In Chapter 8, you will use the iManager utility, along with the Internet Printing Protocol (IPP), to set up and maintain the network printing environment. You will use Remote Manager in Chapters 3 and 9 to manage directory structures and consoles from a Web browser.

Using the Microsoft Client

The Microsoft client is needed to access shared resources and services from other Windows-based computers. This client is optional on Windows 9x, but is automatically installed with the Windows 2000 operating system. Because the Microsoft client is so common on desktop computers, it's a natural choice for accessing NetWare file services on workstations that do not need additional Novell services. For example, in the UAS network, the computers in the Shipping and Receiving departments need only file and print services to access inventory files on the NetWare 6 server and to print shipping labels. As a result, Eric Kenton decided to simplify these computers' configuration by using only the Microsoft client.

> In peer-to-peer networks, Windows servers are organized into workgroups. For Microsoft clients to access the NetWare server, NFAP makes the NetWare 6 server appear to the Windows client as another Windows server in a workgroup. During NFAP installation (refer to Chapter 12), a Microsoft server name and a workgroup are assigned to the NetWare 6 server along with the volumes to be shared with the Microsoft clients. The default method is to share all volumes and place the NetWare server in the WORKGROUP workgroup, using a Microsoft server name composed of the NetWare server name followed by an underscore and a *W*. For example, the Microsoft server name for UASHOST would be UASHOST_W. A user can access data volumes on the NetWare server by using My Network Places from the Windows desktop to browse the network, or by entering the universal naming convention (UNC) path for the data volume. A UNC path has two backslashes preceding the server name and a backslash separating the server and shared volume name. For example, the name for the CORP volume on the UASHOST_W server would be \\UASHOST_W\CORP.

When a computer running a Microsoft client attempts to access a NetWare 6 server running NFAP, the Windows client submits its local user name and password to the NetWare server in the same way it would attempt to log on to a Microsoft server. Access is granted if the user account and password exist on the NetWare server. If the user account and password on the NetWare server do not match the user account and password used to log on to the Microsoft client, an Enter Network Password dialog box opens, requesting the user name and password for the UASHOST_W server.

In addition to the user's eDirectory password that Novell Client needs, NetWare keeps a separate password for each user account to use when logging on from Microsoft clients. Keeping separate passwords for use with NFAP is necessary because the Microsoft client uses a different password encryption system than Novell's eDirectory-based clients do. Novell refers to NFAP passwords as "simple" passwords because they do not have the same security encryption as eDirectory passwords. If users log in from two different computers, one using only the Microsoft client and another using the Novell client, they need to maintain separate passwords—one password for the Novell client and a simple password for the computer that has only the Microsoft client. For example, as supervisor of the Manufacturing department, Russ Pence needs to log in from both his office computer, which uses the Novell client, and the Receiving department's computer, which uses the Microsoft client. Therefore, Russ needs to maintain two passwords for use with these two computers.

In the following activities, you remove Novell Client from your workstation and then simulate setting up a new computer in the UAS Receiving department by using NFAP to log in to the NetWare 6 server and access network files on the CORP volume using only the Microsoft client. In Activity 2-2, you use a UNC path to map a drive to the UASHOST_W server's CORP volume.

Activity 2-1: Removing Novell Client

Time Required: 5 minutes

Objective: Uninstall Novell Client.

Description: At times, Eric has been asked to remove Novell Client to make a major configuration change, return the workstation to its initial state, or correct problems caused by an improper installation or corrupt client file. In this activity, you remove Novell Client to simulate Eric's occasional requirement to uninstall it.

To perform this activity, you must have access to a user name and password with administrative rights to the local workstation.

1. If necessary, start your computer to obtain the Log On to Windows window. Enter a user name and password with administrative rights to your local workstation, click the **Workstation only** check box, and then click **OK** to log on to your Windows 2000 computer.

2. Right-click **My Network Places**, and then click **Properties** to open the Network and Dial-up Connections dialog box.

3. Right-click **Local Area Connection**, and then click **Properties** to open the Local Area Connection Properties dialog box.

4. Record the components listed in the Components checked are used by this connection section on your student answer sheet.

5. Click **Novell Client for Windows 2000** in the Components checked are used by this connection section, and then click the **Uninstall** button.

6. Click the **Yes** button in the Uninstall Novell Client for Windows message box. Novell Client will be removed.

7. When it's finished uninstalling, click the **Yes** button in the message box to restart your computer.

8. When the computer restarts, on your student answer sheet, record the name of the dialog box that appears in place of the Novell Login window.

9. Log on using your local Windows administrator user name and password.

10. Repeat Steps 2 and 3 to record the network components on your student answer sheet.

11. Click the **Cancel** button to close the Local Area Connection Properties dialog box.

12. Close the Network and Dial-up Connections dialog box, and log out.

Activity 2-2: Using the Microsoft Client to Access NetWare Services

Time Required: 10 minutes

Objective: Use the Microsoft client to access NetWare 6 file services.

Description: The computers in the Receiving and Marketing departments are used only to access the Inventory database from the NetWare 6 server. To simplify the setup of these computers and to increase network security, Eric decided to use Novell's NFAP to eliminate the need to install Novell Client on these computers. In this activity, you simulate setting up a computer in the Receiving department by using NFAP to map a network drive to the Inventory directory on the NetWare 6 server.

1. Start your computer, and log on to your local Windows computer with your ##Admin logon name and password.

2. Verify your workstation's workgroup by following these steps:

    a. Right-click **My Computer**, and then click **Properties** to open the System Properties dialog box.

    b. Click the **Network Identification** tab, and record your computer's workgroup name on your student answer sheet.

    c. Click the **Cancel** button to return to the Windows desktop.

3. Follow these steps to browse to the NetWare 6 CORP volume in the workgroup named WORKGROUP:

   a. Double-click **My Network Places** to open the My Network Places dialog box.

   b. If your computer is in the WORKGROUP workgroup, double-click the **Computers Near Me** item to display all the computers in WORKGROUP.

   c. If your computer is not in WORKGROUP, double-click the **Entire Network** item to open the Entire Network dialog box, click the **entire contents** option, and then double-click **Microsoft Windows Network** to display all existing workgroups. Double-click **Workgroup** to display all computers in WORKGROUP.

   d. Double-click the **Uashost_w** computer to open the Enter Network Password dialog box.

   e. In the Connect As text box, type **Receiving1**, and in the Password text box, type **password**.

   f. Click **OK** to log in to the NetWare server.

   g. Record the shared volumes on your student answer sheet.

   h. Double-click the **SYS** volume.

   i. Right-click **Software.cti**, and then click **Properties** to open the SOFTWARE.CTI Properties dialog box.

   j. Record the size of the Software.cti directory on your student answer sheet, and then click the **Cancel** button.

   k. Close the SYS on Uashost_w dialog box, and log off.

4. Log on to your local Windows computer with your ##Admin logon name and password.

5. To access the Inventory data, the software running on the workstations in the Receiving and Shipping departments needs drive letter I: mapped to the CORP volume, which contains the Inventory directory. In this step, you use your Microsoft client along with NFAP to map drive letter I: to the UASHOST_W\CORP volume.

   a. Right-click **My Computer**, and then click **Map Network Drive** to open the Map Network Drive dialog box.

   b. Click the **Drive** list arrow, and click drive letter **I:** in the list of options.

   c. In the Folder text box, enter the UNC path **\\Uashost_w\Corp**.

   d. Click the **different user name** link.

   e. Enter **Receiving1** in the User name text box, and then enter **password** in the Password text box. Click **OK**.

   f. Verify that the Reconnect at logon check box is selected, and then click the **Finish** button.

   g. Close the Corp on 'Uashost_w\corp' (I:) dialog box.

6. Double-click **My Computer**, and verify that drive I: is mapped to the CORP volume. Record the drive mappings on your student answer sheet.

7. Close the My Computer window, and log off.

8. Verify that drive I: will be mapped to the Inventory directory each time the workstation is started:

   a. Log on to the local workstation by clicking the **Workstation only** check box, and then entering your ##Admin user name and password.

   b. Double-click **My Computer**, and verify that drive I: is mapped to the Inventory directory.

9. Using this technique, Eric set up all computers in the Receiving and Shipping departments to automatically map drive I: to the Inventory directory. To return your workstation to its default configuration, you should disconnect the drive mapping for drive I: as follows:

   a. Right-click **My Computer**, and then click **Disconnect Network Drive** to open the Disconnect Network Drive dialog box.

   b. Click **I: \\Uashost_w\Corp** to select it, and then click **OK** to disconnect the drive.

   c. Use My Computer to verify that the I: drive has been removed.

10. Close the My Computer window, and log off.

The Microsoft Client Service for NetWare

As you learned in the previous section, NFAP enables computers with only the Microsoft client to access files on the NetWare server by using its own simple password system. However, users who use both the Novell and Microsoft clients to log in must maintain two passwords. An alternative to installing Novell Client on Windows computers is to use Microsoft NetWare client. Windows 9x and 2000 come with an optional NetWare client—Microsoft Client Service for NetWare—to access services on NetWare 6 servers. With this client installed, users can access NetWare files and printers by using their eDirectory user names and passwords. Using the Microsoft NetWare client rather than the full Novell client helps keep computer configurations simpler, thus reducing the maintenance needed to configure the more complex Novell client. Using the Microsoft NetWare client can also lessen the chance of system failures caused by system conflicts with Novell Client. The disadvantage of the Microsoft NetWare client is that it does not support Z.E.N.works applications or administrative utilities, such as NetWare Administrator or ConsoleOne. In addition, the Microsoft NetWare client requires the NetWare 6 server to use IPX/SPX. If you are planning to use only TCP/IP on your network, the Microsoft NetWare client will not be able to access the NetWare servers. In the following activity, you install the Microsoft NetWare client on your workstation and then use it to log in and attempt to run the NetWare Administrator utility.

Activity 2-3: Installing Microsoft Client Service for NetWare

Time Required: 15 minutes

Objective: Use the Microsoft client to access NetWare 6 file services.

Description: Because the UAS network will initially use both IPX and TCP/IP, Eric decided to use the Microsoft NetWare client on the Desktop Publishing computers to keep configurations simpler. When the network is converted to TCP/IP, he will upgrade these computers to Novell Client (described in the following section). In this activity, you install the Microsoft NetWare client on your computer and then use it to log in to the Novell network. Note: In order to perform this activity you will need to have a local user named ##Admin on your Windows workstation. If necessary, log on to your local workstation as Administrator and then follow the note on page 11 of Activity 1-2 to create a local user named ##Admin.

1. If necessary, start your computer to display the Log On to Windows dialog box.

2. Log on to the workstation with the Windows administrator user name and password.

3. Right-click **My Network Places**, and then click **Properties** to open the Network and Dial-up Connections dialog box.

4. Right-click **Local Area Connection**, and then click **Properties** to open the Local Area Connection Properties dialog box.

5. Click the **Install** button to open the Select Network Component Type dialog box.

6. Record the component options on your student answer sheet.

7. Click the **Client** component, and then click the **Add** button to open the Select Network Client dialog box shown in Figure 2-3.

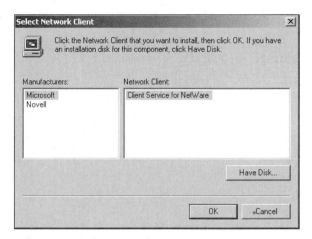

Figure 2-3   The Select Network Client dialog box

8. In the Manufacturers section, verify that Microsoft is selected.

9. In the Network Client section, verify that Client Service for NetWare is selected.

10. Click **OK** to open the Select NetWare Logon dialog box, and record the NetWare logon options on your student answer sheet.

11. Click **OK** to accept the default settings.

12. Click **Yes** to restart your computer.

13. Log on to your local Windows computer with your ##Admin user name and password. You should see the Select NetWare Logon dialog box shown in Figure 2-4.

Figure 2-4   The Select NetWare Logon dialog box

14. Click the **Default Tree and Context** radio button.

15. Enter **UAS_Tree** in the Tree text box.

16. Enter the context to your ##UAS container (**.##UAS** or **.##UAS.CLASS**) in the Context box (replace ## with your assigned student number).

17. Click the **Run Login Script** check box.

18. Click **OK** to log in to the Novell tree. When you log on to Windows with your ##Admin user name, Windows will log you in to the Novell network.

19. Log off.

20. Remove the Microsoft NetWare client by following these steps:

a. Log on to the workstation using the Windows administrator user name and password.

   b. Right-click **My Network Places**, and then click **Properties** to open the Network and
      Dial-up Connections dialog box.

   c. Right-click **Local Area Connection**, and then click **Properties** to open the Local Area
      Connection Properties dialog box.

   d. If necessary, click to select the **Client Service for NetWare** component, and then click the
      Uninstall button.

   e. Click **Yes** to confirm that you want to uninstall Client Service for NetWare.

   f. Click **Yes** to restart your computer.

The Novell Client

Although the Microsoft NetWare client can be used to log in and access basic NetWare file and print services, it does not have all the capabilities of the Novell client included with NetWare 6. Novell Client offers
the following advantages over the Microsoft NetWare client when logging in to the UASHOST server:

- Easy access to network services through the addition of the Novell menu in the taskbar and
  extra NetWare options in the My Computer, Network Neighborhood, and Explorer menus

- More secure passwords

- The ability to use NetWare utilities, such as ConsoleOne and NetWare Administrator

- Support for Z.E.N.works application services

As shown in Table 2-2, there have been several versions of the Novell client for different operating sys-
tem environments. Earlier versions required the use of IPX/SPX to communicate with NetWare servers.
As a result, some applications still need IPX/SPX to operate. The Novell Client version included with
NetWare 6 has backward-compatibility with earlier clients and applications because it supports the
IPX/SPX application interface over TCP/IP.

Table 2-2   Novell Clients

Novell Client Version	Description
NetX	The NetX client, used with DOS and Windows 3.1, provided network access using only IPX/SPX; the NetX client acted as a shell to the DOS environment, enabling it to use network services. It was loaded with the Autoexec.bat file to run the NIC driver, load the protocol, and run the client.
Client 32	Client 32, an early version of Novell Client, was used with Windows 95. Like the NetX client, Client 32 depended on IPX/SPX to access NetWare servers. Client 32 used the capabilities of a 32-bit operating system to enhance the client's features and performance. Because operating systems such as Windows 95 are more network-aware than DOS, Client 32 worked with the operating system to provide access to Netware services instead of acting as a DOS shell.
Novell Client	Novell Client is an improved version of Client 32 that provides access to NetWare services by using IPX/SPX or TCP/IP. Versions of Novell Client are available for Windows 9x and 2000 computers. The latest Novell Client version is required if you need to use NetWare 6 management tools, such as ConsoleOne, and access application services, such as Z.E.N.works.

Installing Novell Client from a CD-ROM on every workstation in a network would be a time-consuming
task for most organizations. Fortunately, Novell offers multiple installation or upgrade methods to make

implementing Novell Client easier. As a network administrator, you can select any of the following methods to install Novell Client, depending on the workstation's configuration and your personal preferences:

- *Install from CD-ROM*—This method is best used on new workstations that are not currently connected to the network. If the workstation has a CD-ROM drive, Novell Client can be installed quickly from the client CD-ROM.

- *Install from the network*—Another good use of Novell NFAP is installing Novell Client on a new Windows computer. With NFAP, a new computer can log in to the network using only the default Microsoft client. Novell Client can then be installed from a shared copy of the client installation software on the NetWare server. This method is faster and more convenient than installing from a CD-ROM. In Activity 2-4, you learn how to use this method to install Novell Client on your workstation.

- *Automatic Client Upgrade (ACU)*—You can use the ACU method to automate upgrading older Novell Client versions to the latest Novell Client when a user logs in from the workstation. The ACU method involves placing special commands in the container login script file, as described in Chapter 7, that starts the upgrade. This method can be a little tricky to set up, but it's valuable when you're upgrading multiple computers to the latest version of Novell Client.

In the following activities, you install Novell Client using the network method and then learn how to customize Novell Client installation options.

Activity 2-4: Installing Novell Client

Time Required: 10 minutes

Objective: Install, uninstall, and configure Novell Client.

Description: When setting up a new computer, Eric often installs Novell Client from a directory on the NetWare server rather than from the client CD-ROM so that he can install several clients at once without needing multiple copies of the client CD-ROM. To install Novell Client from a network directory, Eric uses the Microsoft client on the new computer to access Novell Client directory on the NetWare 6 server. In this activity, you learn how to install Novell Client from a network directory. To change your Windows 2000 network configuration in this activity, you need to log on with a user name and password that has administrative privileges on your workstation.

1. Start your computer, and log on to your local Windows computer with your assigned Windows administrator user name and password.

2. Map drive letter F: to the \\Uashost _W\SYS\Public folder:

   a. Right-click **My Computer**, and then click **Map Network Drive** to open the Map Network Drive dialog box.

   b. Click the **Drive** list arrow, and then click the **F** drive in the list of options. (If drive F: is in use, select the first available drive letter.)

   c. In the Folder text box, enter **\\Uashost_W\SYS\Public**.

   d. Click to deselect the **Reconnect at logon** check box.

   e. Click the **different user name** link.

   f. In the User name text box, enter **EKenton**, and in the Password text box, enter **password**.

   g. Click **OK** to return to the Map Network Drive dialog box, and then click the **Finish** button to map the drive and open the Public on 'Uashost_w\sys' (F:) dialog box.

3. Start the Novell Client installation:

   a. Double-click the **Clients** directory to open it.

   b. Double-click the **Winsetup** program to start the Novell Client Installation Wizard.

    c. Click the client installation option for Windows NT/2000.

    d. Read the license information, and then click the **Yes** button to accept the license agreement.

    e. Click the **Custom Installation** radio button and then click **Next** to display the Select the components you wish to install window. Click to place a check mark in the **Novell Distributed Print Services** component and then click **Next** to display the protocol selection window. Click **Next** to accept the default **IP and IPX protocol** option and display the Login Authentication window. Click **Next** to accept the default **NDS (NetWare 4.x or later**) option, and then click **Finish** to complete the installation.

    f. After the installation is finished, click the **Reboot** button to restart your computer.

4. When the computer restarts, the Novell Login window should be displayed. Do not log in at this time. Proceed to the next activity to log in and test your Novell Client installation.

Activity 2-5: Customizing Novell Client

Time Required: 10 minutes

Objectives: Describe client options for logging in to a Novell server. Install, uninstall, and configure Novell Client.

Description: To make it easier for users in each department to log in, Eric has customized the Novell Client software in each department to default to the department's container. In this activity, you explore some of the options available when customizing Novell Client.

1. If necessary, start your computer to obtain the Novell Login window.

2. Click the **Workstation only** check box, and log on to your local Windows computer with your Windows local administrator user name and password.

3. Right-click **My Network Places**, and then click **Properties** to open the Network and Dial-up Connections dialog box.

4. Right-click **Local Area Connection**, and then click **Properties** to open the Local Area Connection Properties dialog box.

5. Record the items listed in the Components checked are used by this connection section on your student answer sheet.

6. Click to select **Novell Client for Windows 2000**, and then click the **Properties** button to open the Novell Client for Windows 2000 Properties dialog box.

7. If necessary, click the **Client** tab to select it, as shown in Figure 2-5. Notice the text boxes called First network drive, Preferred server, and Preferred tree. These text boxes can be used to change the initial settings when a user first logs in. In addition to the drive, server, and tree settings, the Client tab contains the client's version number and latest service pack. This information is important to ensure that the client is current. The bottom section of the Client tab contains the default context where eDirectory looks to find the user name.

8. Verify that the First network drive is set to F, and then enter the following defaults: **UAS_TREE** in the Preferred tree text box and **UASHOST** in the Preferred server text box.

9. Change the default context to point to the Engineering container in the UAS Organization:

    a. In the Tree text box, enter **UAS_TREE**.

    b. In the Name context text box, enter **.Engineering.UAS**.

    c. Click the **Add** button to insert the context information.

10. Click the **Advanced Login** tab, where you set which options are displayed when you click the Advanced button during login. Record the current settings on your student answer sheet.

11. Click the **Advanced Menu Settings** tab, where you can set the options available on various menus. Click the **Change Password** option, and then record the description on your student answer sheet.

2

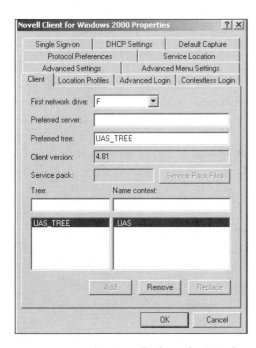

Figure 2-5   The Novell Client for Windows 2000 Properties dialog box

12. Click the **Advanced Settings** tab, where you control parameters used to communicate on the network. Click the **File Caching** option, and then record the description on your student answer sheet.

13. Click the **Contextless Login** tab, which is used to specify a global catalog of objects. The global catalog makes it possible to log in or access a resource without specifying which container the user account or resource is located in. On your student answer sheet, record whether contextless login is enabled on your computer.

14. Click **OK** to close the Novell Client for Windows 2000 Properties dialog box.

15. Click **OK** to close the Local Area Connection Properties dialog box.

16. Click **Yes** to restart your computer.

NOVELL EDIRECTORY SERVICES

As described in Chapter 1, eDirectory services play a critical role in managing, securing, and accessing network services and resources. In NetWare 6, directory services have improved from being simply a login authentication method to becoming the central database of all network objects and configuration information. Starting with NetWare 4, Novell pioneered a directory service, using a global database of network objects, called **Novell Directory Services (NDS)**. NDS was based on an industry-standard naming system called X.500. By using X.500 standards, Novell made NDS compatible with naming services used by many other systems, including the Internet. NDS pioneered a global database of network objects that all servers on the network have access to, thus eliminating the need for network administrators to manage user accounts on multiple servers. NDS also enabled a network administrator to separate network users and objects so that it was easier to manage large numbers of users or to delegate control of certain objects to other administrators. Today, eDirectory, based on the original NDS used in NetWare 4 and NetWare 5, extends the global directory database to multiple server platforms, such as Windows 2000 and Linux. In addition, eDirectory provides enhanced security and support for more advanced network applications and services. In the following sections, you learn how to use eDirectory to organize the network objects for your version of the UAS network and make them available only to authorized users.

eDirectory Components

To work with Novell eDirectory Services, you need to know the components that make up its database and how they work together. The eDirectory system uses a tree structure to organize network components, called **objects**, in a way that is very similar to how files and directories are organized on a hard disk. The eDirectory database consists of three major types of objects:

- The [Root] object
- Container objects
- Leaf objects

The **[Root] object** is important because it represents the beginning of the network directory service tree, in much the same way the root of a disk volume represents the beginning of the disk storage space on a drive. Each eDirectory tree can have only one [Root] object, which is used to identify the name of the eDirectory tree and represent all objects within the tree. For example, if you give the root of the tree the rights to access a specific data file, all users defined in your eDirectory database will inherit those rights. In this way, the [Root] object can be used to assign rights to all valid users on your network system.

Container objects are used to group and store other objects. eDirectory supports three major types of container objects:

- Country
- Organization
- Organizational Unit

Country container objects must be assigned a valid two-digit country code and can exist only within the root of a directory service tree. Because they create an extra level in the directory tree, most network administrators do not use Country container objects unless they work in a multinational organization. **Organization container objects** must exist within a Country container or directly under the root of the directory service tree. Every tree must have at least one Organization container object. **Organizational Unit (OU) container objects**, which must exist within an Organization container or within another OU container, divide users and other leaf objects into appropriate workgroups, such as company divisions or departments.

Figure 2-6 illustrates the sample eDirectory tree for UAS. Notice that the UAS Organization has three OU containers: IS, Engineering, and Manufacturing. The Manufacturing OU is further divided into the AeroDyn and UAS OUs.

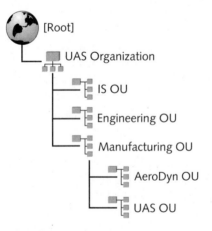

Figure 2-6   Sample UAS tree structure

Leaf objects represent network entities, such as users, groups, printers, and servers. Leaf objects can exist only within Organization or Organizational Unit containers. Table 2-3 describes the network objects in the UAS network, along with the object types and graphical icons. Each type of object has certain properties associated with it. A **property** is a field that can contain information about an object. Not all object types have the same properties associated with them; a leaf object, such as a printer, would have different properties than a user object.

Table 2-3 eDirectory Object Types

Object Name	Abbreviation	Type	Icon	Description
[Root]		Root of tree		The beginning of the eDirectory tree. The root of the tree is given a name when eDirectory is installed on the first server.
Country	C=	Container		Optionally used to designate the country where your network resides and is used to organize Organization container objects. Must be a valid two-character country abbreviation.
Organization	O=	Container		Represents a company or an organization and is the first level that can contain leaf objects. An eDirectory structure must have at least one Organization container object.
Organizational Unit	OU=	Container		An optional container object frequently used to represent a department or division within a company. An Organizational Unit object can exist within an Organization or another Organizational Unit container.
Alias	CN=	Leaf		A pointer to an object in another container. Alias objects are used to make it easier to access objects that are not in your current context.
Computer	CN=	Leaf		An object used to represent a client computer (user workstation).
Group	CN=	Leaf		A group object can be used to represent one or more users. Group objects are often used to grant access rights to several users.
NetWare Server	CN=	Leaf		An object representing a NetWare 6.0 server and its location in the eDirectory structure.
Print Server	CN=	Leaf		A print server object represents a process that takes jobs from print queues and sends them to the assigned network printer.

Table 2-3   eDirectory Object Types (continued)

Object Name	Abbreviation	Type	Icon	Description
Printer	CN=	Leaf		An object representing a network printer and its configuration.
Print Queue	CN=	Leaf		An object representing a print queue on the network containing print jobs and configuration information.
User	CN=	Leaf		A user object represents a person who uses the network. This object is used to manage and maintain information about the user, including login restrictions and his or her access rights.
Volume	CN=	Leaf		A volume object is used to represent a physical file storage area on a NetWare server. Volume objects are created when a server is installed on the network.

You can assign values to each property of an object. Some object properties, such as a user's telephone number or the print queue of a printer object, are multivalued (contain more than one entry). Each object has certain property values that are required when the object is created. For example, each user object must be assigned a login and last name value when the user is created. Other property values are optional and can be added later.

The Admin user object is created when the first server is installed in the eDirectory tree. **Admin** is an important user object because it has the Supervisor right to the entire eDirectory tree, allowing the Admin user to create and manage all other objects in the tree structure. A password is given to the Admin user during the initial server installation. If you're the Admin user, you should remember this password because without it, you must reinstall the eDirectory tree to regain the Supervisor right.

Directory Context

The location of an object within the eDirectory tree is referred to as its **context**. Just as a path is used to specify the location of a file on a disk drive, the context is used to specify the location of an object within an eDirectory tree. One difference between a disk path to a filename and an eDirectory context is that the context is specified with X.500 notation, which starts with the object and works up the tree. In contrast, a disk path is specified from the root of the drive down to the filename. For example, to identify the disk path to the Memo file located in the Document directory of the C: drive, you would use C:\Document\Memo, but to identify the context of the user EKenton in the IS container shown in Figure 2-6, you would use .EKenton.IS.UAS. Another difference between the eDirectory context and the disk path is that the eDirectory context is formatted with periods to separate each level instead of the slashes or backslashes used in disk paths. The period at the beginning of the context is used to specify starting at the [Root] object of the eDirectory tree in much the same way a slash is used at the beginning of a disk path.

Each object in the eDirectory database can be uniquely identified by its **distinguished name**, which consists of the object's name along with its complete context, leading to the root of the eDirectory tree. A context specification that includes the object abbreviations is referred to as a **typeful name**. For example, the user LJarka could be identified by using the following as her typeful distinguished name:

```
.CN=LJarka.OU=Engineering.O=UAS
```

The two-letter abbreviation preceding the name of an object identifies the object's type: CN= identifies LJarka as the common name for a leaf object, OU= identifies Engineering as an Organizational Unit container object, and O= identifies UAS as an Organization container object. (To see the abbreviation for each eDirectory object type along with its eDirectory definition, refer back to Table 2-3.) Using typeful distinguished names that include the object type abbreviation along with the context requires extra time and opens up the possibility of errors, however. As a result, eDirectory can assume object types as long as the rightmost object is an Organization or Organizational Unit. A distinguished name that does not contain the object type abbreviations is referred to as a **typeless name**. For example, the typeless distinguished name for the user LJarka would be specified as follows:

```
LJarka.Engineering.UAS
```

The location of your client computer within the eDirectory tree is referred to as its **current context**. In the previous section, you learned how to customize Novell Client to set the current context of your computer to the Engineering container. By setting the client's current context, you make it easier for users to log in by simply typing the common name for their user account. If users need to log in outside their current contexts, they can do so by specifying the distinguished name for their user accounts. For example, Eric wants to log in from Kari Means's computer, which has its current context set to the Engineering OU. To log in, he could type his distinguished name—.EKenton.IS.UAS—in the Username text box, or click the Advanced button to set the current context to the IS container, as you did in Chapter 1.

If your client computer's current context is set to one of the containers specified in the distinguished name, you can save keystrokes by using a relative name. A relative distinguished name, often referred to as just a **relative name**, starts with the current context and is specified by omitting the leading period. For example, if the current context is set to the UAS container, Eric could log in by using a relative name or distinguished name in the Username text box:

- EKenton.IS (relative name—note that the name does *not* start with a period)

- .EKenton.IS.UAS (distinguished name—note that the name starts with a period)

Another way to specify a relative name is by ending the name with a period, which causes the eDirectory system to move the current context up one level before searching for the object. For example, if the default context of the Novell client is .Engineering.UAS, Eric Kenton could log in to the IS container by entering "EKenton.IS." in the Username text box. In the following activities, you practice logging in by using relative and distinguished names.

Activity 2-6: Using Distinguished Names

Time Required: 10 minutes

Objective: Use distinguished and relative names to access network objects.

Description: Eric typically has to log in from computers in other departments to test and maintain network services. In this activity, you practice logging in as Eric Kenton from a workstation in the Engineering department by using a distinguished user name instead of clicking the Advanced button to change your current context.

1. If necessary, start your computer to obtain the Novell Login window.

2. Log in using a typeful distinguished user name for EKenton in the IS Organizational Unit of the UAS Organization:

    a. In the Username text box, enter Eric's typeful distinguished user name as shown:

    ```
    .CN=EKenton.OU=IS.O=UAS
    ```

    b. In the Password text box, enter **password**.

    c. Click the **Advanced** button to display the NDS Information tab. Click the **Tree** list arrow, and click **UAS_Tree** in the list of options.

d. Click the **Server** list arrow, and then click **UASHOST** in the list of options.

e. Click **OK** to log in as EKenton. If necessary, enter the password for logging on to the Windows 2000 computer, using your local ##Admin user name.

3. CX is a command-line utility (see Appendix C for more information) that you can use to view your current context. Follow these steps to use the CX command to record your current context:

a. Click **Start**, **Programs**, **Accessories**, **Command Prompt**.

b. At the command prompt, enter **CX**, and then press **Enter**.

c. Record the current context on your student answer sheet.

d. Enter **Exit**, and then press **Enter** to close the command-prompt window.

4. Log out by clicking **Start**, **Shutdown**, **Log off**.

5. Use the procedure in Step 2 to log in as Eric Kenton, using a typeless distinguished name. On your student answer sheet, record the name you enter.

6. Log out.

7. Use the procedure in Step 2 and attempt to log in as Eric Kenton by entering the typeless name **EKenton.IS.UAS**, which does not contain a leading or ending period. Record your results, along with the reason this method does or does not work, on your student answer sheet.

8. Use the procedure in Step 2 to log in as **KMeans** in the Engineering.UAS container by using a typeful distinguished name and a password of **password**. On your student answer sheet, record the name you enter.

9. Log out.

10. Use the procedure in Step 2 to log in as **RPence** in the Mfg Organizational Unit of the UAS Organization, using a typeless distinguished name and a password of **password**. On your student answer sheet, record the typeless distinguished name you use.

11. Log out.

Activity 2-7: Using Relative Names

Time Required: 5 minutes

Objective: Use distinguished and relative names to access network objects.

Description: When he knows the current context settings of a workstation, Eric often uses a relative name when logging in to the network to save time and reduce the chance of typos. In this activity, you learn how to use relative names to log in from workstations configured for different default contexts.

1. If necessary, start your computer to obtain a Novell Login window.

2. Click the **Advanced** button, and change your default context by entering .**UAS** in the Context text box.

3. Follow these steps to log in using the relative name EKenton.IS:

a. In the Username text box, enter the relative name **EKenton.IS**, and enter **password** in the Password text box.

b. Click **OK** to log in to the Novell network.

c. If necessary, enter the password for logging on to the Windows 2000 computer using your local ##Admin user name.

4. Log out to display a new Novell Login window.

5. Click the **Advanced** button, and verify that the default context is set to UAS.

6. Follow the procedure in Step 3 to use a typeful relative name to log in to the Engineering container as KMeans, and enter **password** in the Password text box. On your student answer sheet, record the typeful relative name you use.

7. Log out to display a new Novell Login window.

8. Click the **Advanced** button, and enter **.Engineering.UAS** in the Context text box to change your current context to the Engineering container.

9. Follow the procedure in Step 3 to log in as Eric Kenton by entering the typeless relative name **EKenton.IS.** (note the period following the relative name) in the Username text box and **password** in the Password text box.

10. Log out to display a new Novell Login window.

11. Click the **Advanced** button, and change your current context by entering **.IS.UAS** in the Context text box.

12. Use a typeless relative name that contains a trailing period to log in as the user KMeans in the Engineering context. Record the typeless relative name you use on your student answer sheet.

13. Log out.

DESIGNING AN eDIRECTORY TREE STRUCTURE

One of Eric's first jobs when setting up the UAS network was to design the eDirectory tree structure for the organization. The first step was to define and document all users and other objects in the network. After identifying all the network objects, his next step was to determine what containers would be needed. Eric did this by grouping the objects into containers based on resource sharing. When grouping objects, you should keep the design as simple as possible to reduce the number of containers that will be needed. A general rule is to avoid containers with fewer than 10 users unless the objects are in separate geographical areas with their own server and independent resources. Although this task can be involved and complex for large corporate networks, it can be quite simple for small single-server networks. The final step was to design the UAS eDirectory tree structure by placing the containers in a hierarchical structure. Novell recommends that each tree have only one Organization container for objects shared by the entire organization. In a simple tree design, the Organization container might be the only container object needed. Figure 2-7 illustrates applying the simplest eDirectory tree design to the UAS network, with a single Organization container holding all user and network objects.

Although this design would work for a smaller company, because of UAS's projected growth, Eric decided to divide the network objects into OU containers for the Business office, Engineering, Management, and IS, as shown in Figure 2-8. Because the Engineering department monitors many of the manufacturing processes, Eric initially decided to place the container for Manufacturing (the Mfg OU) in the Engineering OU. Universal AeroSpace and AeroDyn have manufacturing facilities in different cities, so Eric identified separate containers for AeroDyn and UAS within the Mfg OU. The Business OU will include all leaf objects for the Desktop Publishing, Accounting, and Marketing departments.

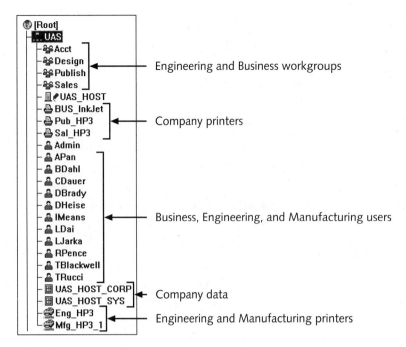

Figure 2-7 A simple eDirectory tree design

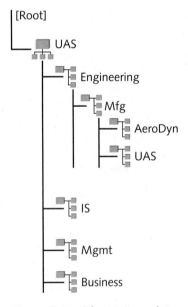

Figure 2-8 The Universal AeroSpace tree design

Because the users in each department have different needs in terms of resources and access rights, separating them will make it easier to assign user access rights, partition the database, and manage the network in the future. Although the Marketing and Desktop Publishing departments could also be separated from the Business OU, the complexity of the additional network directory design would not justify its use for the relatively few objects in the Marketing or Desktop Publishing workgroups. In addition, because of their physical proximity, users in these departments often share access to network printers and other resources, compared to the Manufacturing department, which has network objects spread between the AeroDyn and UAS facilities in two different cities. Using this model, Eric installed the NetWare 6 operating system, which placed the server, volumes, and other system objects in the UAS container, as shown in Figure 2-9. As network administrator, Eric then used the NetWare management utilities to create the OUs he identified in Figure 2-8.

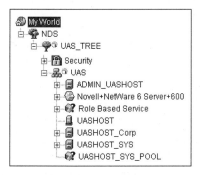

Figure 2-9   The UAS tree structure after installing NetWare 6

Introduction to NetWare Management Utilities

To work with the eDirectory tree, you need to become familiar with Novell's management utilities. In previous releases of NetWare, implementing and managing the eDirectory tree have required running the NetWare Administrator utility on a computer with the Novell client installed. In NetWare 5, Novell introduced the ConsoleOne utility, which was written using the Java language so that it could run on multiple platforms, including the NetWare server's console. With NetWare 6, in addition to NetWare Administrator and ConsoleOne, Novell has introduced a new network management tool called iManager. With this utility, network administrators can manage their eDirectory trees from a Web browser, such as Internet Explorer, instead of requiring a workstation with the Novell client. Because it does not require the Novell client running on a Windows-based computer, the iManager utility is an integral part of Novell's OneNet vision, allowing network management from any client on a connected network.

The version of iManager that ships with NetWare 6 is referred to as a "pre-release" utility because it allows for only limited eDirectory object management. Until Novell is able to incorporate all management tasks into the iManager utility, network administrators need to be able to use the legacy Novell Client utilities—ConsoleOne and NetWare Administrator—to perform certain management tasks.

Each utility has its advantages and disadvantages. For example, currently ConsoleOne has the most capability to manage NetWare 6 features, NetWare Administrator has the advantage of providing high performance on older computers, and iManager has the advantage of being able to be used from any network through a standard Web browser. Because of their different capabilities, a CNA should be familiar with all three utilities. Although ConsoleOne will be the primary utility used in this book, you will also learn how to use NetWare Administrator and iManager to perform network tasks, and the activities in this book introduce you to using all three utilities. In the following sections, you learn how to install ConsoleOne and NetWare Administrator and then use these utilities to view the UAS tree structure that Eric designed.

Using NetWare Administrator

To run NetWare Administrator, you need a Windows 9x or 2000 workstation with at least 64 MB of RAM and the Novell Client software. Although the Microsoft client allows users to access NetWare file and print services, it does not have the necessary components to run ConsoleOne or NetWare Administrator. During server installation, the NetWare Administrator software is loaded into the Public directory of the server's SYS volume. There are multiple versions of NetWare Administrator for different operating system environments. In this book, you will be using the Nwadmn32.exe program in the Public\Win32 folder. In the following activities, you learn how to create a shortcut to run NetWare Administrator, and then use this utility to browse the tree structure and view information on network objects.

Activity 2-8: Creating a NetWare Administrator Shortcut

Time Required: 5 minutes

Objective: Install and configure NetWare Administrator.

Description: As the network administrator, Eric Kenton often uses NetWare Administrator to implement and maintain the UAS network system. To make it easier to start NetWare Administrator, Eric created a Windows desktop shortcut, but also added NetWare Administrator to the Start menu of his workstation so that he had another way to start the utility if the desktop icon was deleted. In this activity, you add a NetWare Administrator shortcut to your desktop as well as to your Start menu.

1. If necessary, start your client computer, and log in to the network with your assigned ##Admin user name:

   a. Enter **##Admin** (## represents your assigned student number) in the Username text box, and enter the password you assigned to your ##Admin user in Activity 1-1.

   b. Click the **Advanced** button.

   c. Enter the context to your ##UAS container (**.##UAS** or **.##UAS.CLASS**) in the Context text box (replace ## with your assigned student number), and click **OK** to log in.

2. Open the F:\Public\Win32 folder by following these steps:

   a. Double-click **My Computer**.

   b. Double-click the **Z:** drive.

   c. Double-click the **Win32** folder.

3. Right-click the **Nwadmin32** program, and then click **Send to**, **Desktop (Create shortcut)** to create a shortcut on your desktop.

4. Close the Win32 dialog box. A shortcut to Nwadmin32 should now appear on your desktop.

5. To add Nwadmin32 to your Start menu, right-click the **Start** button, and then click **Open** to open the Start Menu dialog box.

6. Right-click the **Nwadmin32** shortcut, and drag it from the desktop to the Start Menu dialog box.

7. Release your right mouse button, and then click **Copy Here** on the shortcut menu to place a copy of the shortcut in your Start menu.

8. Close the Start Menu dialog box.

9. If you're continuing to the next activity, stay logged in. If not, click the **Start** button (the Shortcut to Nwadmin32 option should appear in the upper half of the Start menu), click **Shut Down**, and log out.

Activity 2-9: Browsing with NetWare Administrator

Time Required: 10 minutes

Objective: Use NetWare Administrator to browse the eDirectory tree, view object properties, and create new objects.

Description: Because of its good performance and ability to open multiple browse windows, Eric periodically uses NetWare Administrator to manage his tree structures. In this activity, you learn how to start NetWare Administrator, open multiple browse windows, change the context, and view objects in the eDirectory tree.

1. If necessary, start your client computer, and log in with your ##Admin user name:

   a. Enter **.##Admin.##UAS** in the Username text box (replace ## with your assigned student number).

   b. Enter your password in the Password text box, and click **OK** to log in.

2. Start NetWare Administrator by clicking **Start**, **Shortcut to Nwadmin32**. The NetWare Administrator utility contains a number of buttons on its toolbar for performing various activities, as illustrated in Figure 2-10. If necessary, read the tip in the Welcome to NetWare Administrator window, and then click **Close**.

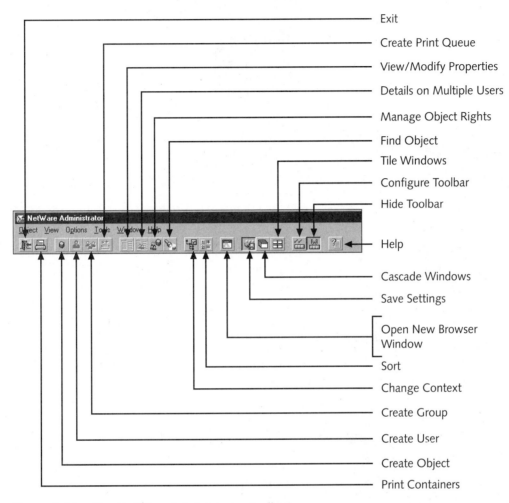

Figure 2-10   The NetWare Administrator toolbar

3. After NetWare Administrator is started, you see a browse window similar to the one in Figure 2-11.

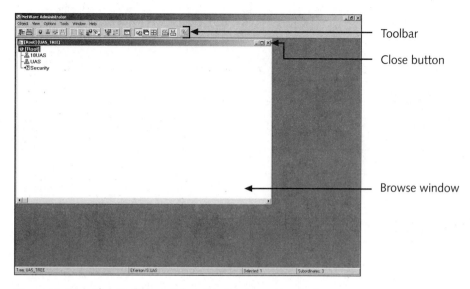

Toolbar

Close button

Browse window

Figure 2-11 The NetWare Administrator browse window

4. Close the existing browse window by clicking the **Close** button.

5. Open a browse window to the root of the tree by following these steps:

a. To open a new browse window, click **Tools** on the menu bar, and then click **NDS Browser** to open the Set Context dialog box. Notice that the Context text box displays your workstation's current context in the UAS_Tree.

b. Click the **Browse** button to the right of the Context text box to open the Select Object dialog box shown in Figure 2-12. The Browse context section on the right is used to change your current context. The Available objects section on the left contains a list of objects in the selected context.

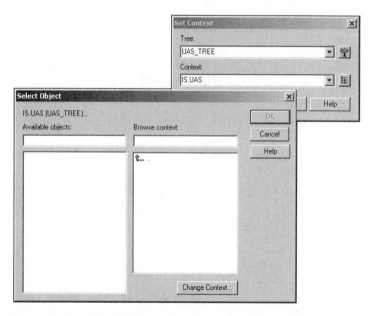

Figure 2-12 The NetWare Administrator Select Object dialog box

c. To move your current context up one level, double-click the **up arrow** in the Browse context section. All objects in the [Root] container of the tree are then displayed in the Available objects section.

    d. To set the context of the Browse context section to the [Root] of the tree, double-click the **[Root]** object in the Available objects section.

    e. Click **OK** to save the new context setting. The browse window should now display all the Organization containers.

6. On your student answer sheet, record the names and types of all objects displayed in the browse window.

7. To view all objects in the UAS container, double-click **UAS** in the browse window.

8. On your student answer sheet, record the names of all Organizational Unit objects in the UAS Organization.

9. On your student answer sheet, record the names of all group objects in the UAS Organization.

10. To view objects in the IS container, double-click the **IS** container in your UAS window to expand it.

11. Record the members of the ISMgrs group on your student answer sheet:

    a. Click the **ISMgrs** group name, and press **Enter** to open the Identification dialog box for the group.

    b. To view group members, click the **Members** button to open the Members dialog box, and record all members on your student answer sheet.

    c. Click the **Cancel** button to return to the browse window.

12. Double-click the **UAS** Organization entry in the browse window to collapse it.

13. It is often useful to open multiple browse windows to see objects in two or more containers simultaneously. In this step, you'll open an additional browse window to your ##UAS Organization and then tile the two browse windows.

    a. Follow the procedure in Step 5 to open a new browse window to your ##UAS Organization (replace the ## with your assigned student number).

    b. Tile your browse windows by clicking **Window** on the NetWare Administrator menu and then clicking **Tile**.

14. On your student answer sheet, record any objects currently in your ##UAS Organization. Later in this chapter, you will begin building your version of the Universal AeroSpace tree in your ##UAS Organization.

15. Close NetWare Administrator by clicking **Object** and then **Exit** on the menu bar.

Installing and Using ConsoleOne

ConsoleOne remains the primary utility for managing most aspects of the NetWare 6 eDirectory tree. In addition to having Novell Client installed, ConsoleOne requires a workstation to have at least 128 MB of RAM and a 300 MHz processor to run effectively. Although the ConsoleOne software can be run directly from the SYS volume of the NetWare 6 server, loading the ConsoleOne files across the network is slower and uses up network bandwidth. As a result, it's much faster to start ConsoleOne if you install it on your local computer. In the following activities, you install ConsoleOne on your desktop and then practice using it to browse the existing Universal AeroSpace tree.

Activity 2-10: Installing ConsoleOne

Time Required: 15 minutes

Objective: Use ConsoleOne to browse the eDirectory tree, view object properties, and create new objects.

Description: After installing Novell Client on his workstation, Eric wanted to install ConsoleOne on his local workstation to enable him to perform the management tasks necessary to implement and maintain the UAS network for multiple locations. To make it easy to install ConsoleOne on additional stations, Eric copied the ConsoleOne installation files to the Client directory of the SYS volume. In this activity, you use the ConsoleOne installation files in the Client directory to install ConsoleOne on your workstation so that you can use it to implement and manage your version of the UAS directory tree.

1. If necessary, log in with your assigned ##Admin user name:

2. Start the ConsoleOne installation program in the Public\Client\ConsoleOne directory of the server's SYS volume:

   a. Double-click **My Computer**, and then double-click the **Public on 'UAShost\Sys' (Z:)** drive to open the Public folder.

   b. Double-click the **Clients** folder to open it.

   c. Double-click the **ConsoleOne133** directory to open it.

   d. Double-click the **c1_nw_win.exe** program to display the WinZip Self-Extractor dialog box.

3. Click the **Setup** button to start unzipping the ConsoleOne files and display the Welcome window of the ConsoleOne Installation Wizard.

4. Read the information in the Welcome window, and then click the **Next** button to continue.

5. View the License Agreement window, and then click the **Accept** button to continue.

6. Record the default installation path on your student answer sheet, and then click the **Next** button to accept the path and continue.

7. Record the default ConsoleOne components on your student answer sheet, and then click the **Next** button to accept the defaults.

8. In the License Agreement window, click the **I DO accept the terms of this license agreement** radio button, and then click the **Next** button to continue.

9. On your student answer sheet, record the components listed in the Products to be installed window, and then click the **Finish** button to complete the installation. Wait for the files to be copied to your local hard drive. This could take several minutes, so it's a good time to take a short break. The Installation Complete window is displayed after all files are copied to your local computer and a shortcut to start ConsoleOne is added to your desktop.

10. Click the **Close** button, and wait for the WinZip window to close and return you to the Client Installation ConsoleOne options.

11. ConsoleOne uses snap-ins to extend its ability to manage network objects. To enable the full features of ConsoleOne on your workstation, follow the steps below to copy the updated ConsoleOne files to your system.

    a. Use My Computer to open the Public on Cbe_admin (Z:) folder.

    b. Navigate to the Mgmt\ConsoleOne folder.

    c. Right-click the **1.2** folder and click **Copy**.

    d. Close ConsoleOne window.

    e. Use My Computer to navigate to your C:\novell\consoleone folder.

    f. Click **Edit | Paste** and then click the **Yes to All** button as many times as necessary to replace existing files.

    h. Close the consoleone window.

Activity 2-11: Introduction to Using ConsoleOne

Time Required: 10 minutes

Objective: Use ConsoleOne to browse the eDirectory tree, view object properties, and create new objects.

Description: One of Eric's first tasks after installing the NetWare 6 server was to create his own user account for testing or accessing network services. In this activity, you use ConsoleOne to browse the UAS directory tree and then create a user account for yourself in your ##UAS organization.

1. If necessary, log in with your assigned ##Admin user name:

2. Start ConsoleOne by double-clicking your newly created desktop shortcut.

3. In the Novell ConsoleOne window, expand the UAS_Tree and ##UAS Organization to display a window similar to the one shown in Figure 2-13:

   a. If necessary, click the **+** to the left of the NDS icon to expand this object. Next, expand **UAS_Tree**.

   b. Expand the **UAS** Organization.

4. On the left is the Navigation frame, which displays structure objects, such as containers, servers, and volumes. On the right is the Object frame, which displays leaf objects, such as users, groups, and printers. To display leaf objects in the UAS Organization, click the **UAS** Organization container. On your student answer sheet, record all user names listed in the Object frame.

5. Click the **Engineering** Organizational Unit to display all objects in the Engineering department.

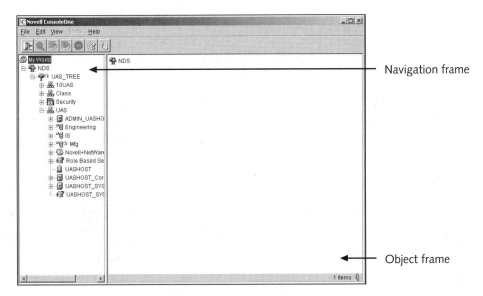

Figure 2-13   The ConsoleOne window

6. Display the members of the Design group:

   a. Double-click the **Design** group object to open the Properties of Design dialog box, and record the available tabs on your student answer sheet.

   b. Click the **Members** tab, and record the group members on your student answer sheet.

7. Click the **Cancel** button to close the Properties of Design dialog box.

8. Close the ConsoleOne window by clicking **File** on the menu bar and then clicking **Exit**.

9. Log out.

IMPLEMENTING THE eDIRECTORY TREE

Now that you have been introduced to the management utilities, you'll begin learning how to use them to set up your version of the UAS eDirectory tree, as shown previously in Figure 2-8. Your classroom eDirectory tree has been set up to allow you to create your own version of the Universal AeroSpace structure in your assigned ##UAS Organization (the ## represents your assigned student number). Initially, your ##UAS Organization contains only your ##Admin administrator name that was created during the classroom server's setup. The actual NetWare server and SYS volume objects are located in the UAS Organization. In the following sections, you learn how to use NetWare Administrator to create objects in your ##UAS Organization that represent the server and volume objects contained in the UAS Organization after server installation. After creating these initial objects, you use the iManager and ConsoleOne utilities to establish your UAS tree structure by creating OUs for the IS, Engineering, and Management departments.

Creating Alias and Volume Objects

You have been assigned to your own UAS Organization, but there is only one server object, which all student organizations need to share. Alias objects are a solution to accessing a single object from multiple containers. An **alias object** is a pointer to the real object located in another container. Alias objects are useful when you need to access physical resources, such as files and printers, from different contexts (several departments in a company, for instance). Using alias objects enables you to create a single object containing information about a resource and then access this object from other containers. To simulate having a server object in your ##UAS Organization, you will need to create an alias object that points to the actual server.

Volumes are the basic logical components of the network file system. A server's disk space is divided into one or more volumes, much as a file cabinet is divided into one or more drawers. In Chapter 3, you will learn about the components that make up the NetWare file system and how volumes are created on a server. Every NetWare server is required to have one volume named SYS that contains operating system files and utilities. The network administrator then creates additional volumes to store user data and applications. **Volume objects** point to the physical data volumes on the server and are used to access data and store volume configuration and status information. When a new volume is created on the server, a corresponding volume object is created in the server's eDirectory container. Additional volume objects can then be created in other containers to make it easier to access volume data and statistics without browsing the tree or changing your current context. In the following activity, you simulate the UAS network environment after Eric installed NetWare 6 on the UASHOST server by using NetWare Administrator to create an alias object and a SYS volume object in your ##UAS Organization.

Activity 2-12: Creating Alias and Volume Objects with NetWare Administrator

Time Required: 10 minutes

Objective: Use NetWare Administrator to browse the eDirectory tree, view object properties, and create new objects.

2

Description: In this activity, you use NetWare Administrator to create alias and volume objects in your ##UAS container that point to the UASHOST server. You will then be able to access information about the server and volumes without having to change context to the UAS container.

1. If necessary, start your computer, and log in to the network with your assigned ##Admin user name.

2. Start NetWare Administrator by clicking **Start**, **Shortcut to nwadmin32**. If necessary, click **Close** to exit the Welcome to NetWare Administrator window.

3. If necessary, open a browse window in NetWare Administrator to show the contents of your ##UAS container.

4. Click your **##UAS** container, and then press the **Insert** key to open the New Object dialog box, similar to the one in Figure 2-14.

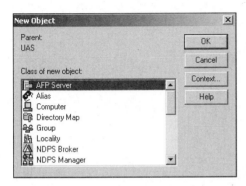

Figure 2-14   Selecting an object type in the New Object dialog box

5. Double-click **Alias** in the Class of new object list box to open the Create Alias dialog box.

6. Type **UASHOST** in the Alias Name text box.

7. Click the **Browse** button next to the Aliased Object text box to open the Select Object dialog box. Use the Browse context section to navigate to the **UAS** container.

8. Double-click the **UASHOST** server object in the Available objects section to insert the UASHOST server into the Aliased Object text box.

9. In the Create Alias dialog box, click the **Create** button to create the server alias object.

10. Double-click your new alias object to display the NetWare Server: UASHOST dialog box. Record the status and version information shown in this dialog box on your student answer sheet.

11. Click the **Cancel** button to return to NetWare Administrator.

12. Follow these steps to create a volume object named UASHOST_SYS that points to the SYS volume of the UASHOST server:

    a. Click your **##UAS** container to highlight it.

    b. Click the **Create Object** button on the toolbar or press the **Insert** key to open the New Object dialog box.

    c. Scroll down the Class of new object list box, and double-click **Volume** to open the Create Volume dialog box.

    d. Enter **UASHOST_SYS** in the Volume Name text box.

    e. Click the **Browse** button next to the Host Server text box to open the Select Object dialog box.

f. Double-click your **UASHOST** alias in the Available objects section.

g. Click the **Physical volume** list arrow to display a list of all volumes on the UASHOST server.

h. Click the **SYS** volume, and then click the **Create** button. A UASHOST_SYS volume should now be displayed in your ##UAS container.

13. When you're finished, your NetWare Administrator window should look like the one shown in Figure 2-15.

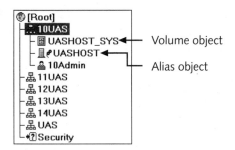

Figure 2-15   The results of adding an alias and a volume object in NetWare Administrator

14. Close NetWare Administrator by clicking **Object**, **Exit** on the menu bar.

15. Log out.

Creating Organizational Units with iManager

In keeping with Novell's OneNet vision, NetWare 6 introduces a number of new utilities and features that enable you to access and manage network resources by using standard Web browsers. With the new iManager utility, network administrators can create and manage eDirectory objects from any network or client by using a Web browser such as Internet Explorer or Netscape. Although the functions of iManager are limited in its initial release, in the future Novell plans to use this utility to replace both ConsoleOne and NetWare Administrator. By default, the Admin user of the tree has the necessary rights to use iManager to perform all tasks, but by creating administrative roles, the administrator can grant rights to other users to perform certain management tasks in iManager. In Chapter 6, you will learn more about how to assign these administrative roles to delegate tasks to other users. A special administrative role has been created for your ##Admin user name so that you can use iManager to create and maintain objects only in your ##UAS container. You could easily create your remaining OUs with NetWare Administrator, but in the following activity, you practice using iManager to create container objects in your ##UAS Organization.

Activity 2-13: Creating Objects with iManager

Time Required: 10 minutes

Objective: Use NetWare management utilities to browse the eDirectory tree, view object properties, and create new objects.

Description: Eric began implementing the UAS directory tree by creating OUs for the IS, Engineering, and Management departments. Although you could create OUs with NetWare Administrator or ConsoleOne, in this activity, you should pretend you're working from home and accessing your server through the Internet with iManager.

1. Bypass the Novell Client login to simulate operating from your home computer. Click the **Workstation only** check box, enter your local Windows 2000 user name and password, and click **OK**.

2. Start your Internet Explorer or Netscape program, and open the iManager utility by following these steps:

 a. Enter the following URL: **https://*server_ip_address*:2200**, replacing *server_ip_address* with the IP address or DNS name assigned to your UASHOST computer.

 b. If you receive any security alert message boxes, record the messages on your student answer sheet, and then click **Yes** or **OK** to continue. The Novell Web Manager window opens (see Figure 2-16).

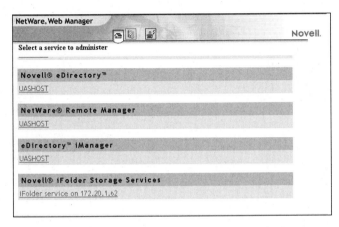

Figure 2-16   The Novell Web Manager window
When using NetWare 6.5, you will see the NetWare 6.5 Welcome as shown in Figure D-17.

 c. Click the **UASHOST** link beneath the eDirectory iManager option to open a Novell Login window.

 d. Enter your assigned Admin username in the Username text box, enter your password in the Password text box, and enter the context to your assigned UAS container (for example, on the classroom server use either **.##UAS** or **.##UAS.CLASS** depending on the tree structure in use) in the Context text box.

 e. If necessary, enter **UAS_Tree** in the Tree text box.

 f. Click the **Login** button to open the iManager window, showing your ##UAS Organization name in the navigation pane on the left (see Figure 2-17).

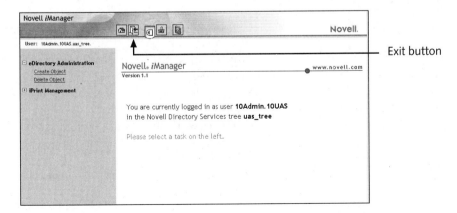

Figure 2-17   The iManager window listing your task options

3. Click the **+** symbol to the left of eDirectory Administration to display a list of tasks you are authorized to perform.

4. Create the IS Organizational Unit by following these steps:

    a. Click the **Create Object** link to open the Available Classes window. On your student answer sheet, record the possible objects you can create with iManager.

    b. Click the **Organizational Unit** item, and then click the **Next** button to open the Create Organizational Unit window, similar to the one in Figure 2-18.

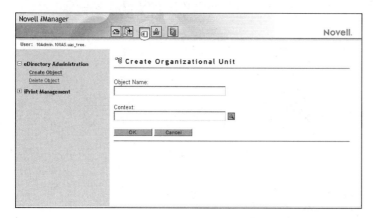

Figure 2-18   The Create Organizational Unit window

    c. Enter **IS** in the Object Name text box.

    d. Click the Browse button next to the Context text box. In the browse window that opens, navigate to your ##UAS container.

    e. Click **OK** to create the object and display the Create Object request succeeded message box.

    f. Click **OK** to acknowledge the message and return to the iManager task list.

5. Repeat Step 4 to create the Engineering Organizational Unit.

6. Repeat Step 4 to create the Mgmt Organizational Unit.

7. Click the **Exit** button on the iManager toolbar to return to the Novell Login window.

8. Close your Web browser by clicking **File**, **Close** on the menu bar.

9. Log off Windows.

Completing the Tree Structure with ConsoleOne

As a network administrator, you are also a network user when you perform such tasks as word processing or sending e-mail messages. When you log in with the Admin user name, you risk accidentally changing the system configuration or erasing or corrupting server files. In addition, if the workstation from which you're logging in has a computer virus in memory, the virus could infect program files on the server, causing the virus to quickly spread throughout the network. To reduce the chance of these problems occurring, you should create a separate user name for everyday tasks, such as e-mailing or word processing, and log in as Admin only when you need to maintain or configure the network. In the following activity, you use ConsoleOne to complete the setup of your eDirectory tree and create a standard user account that you can use to log in to the network.

Activity 2-14: Creating Objects with ConsoleOne

Time Required: 10 minutes

Objective: Use NetWare management utilities to browse the eDirectory tree, view object properties, and create new objects.

Description: In this activity, you use ConsoleOne to finish your UAS tree by creating the Manufacturing department within your Engineering OU, as shown previously in Figure 2-8. You also create a standard user account for yourself and then test the account by logging in.

1. If necessary, start your computer, and log in to the network with your assigned ##Admin user name.

2. Use your desktop shortcut to start ConsoleOne.

3. In the Navigation frame, expand the UAS_Tree and your ##UAS Organization by clicking the + symbol to the left of each object. Notice that the IS and Engineering Organizational Units you created with iManager are displayed.

4. Create an OU named Mfg in your Engineering container:

   a. Right-click your **Engineering** OU, point to **New**, and record the available options on your student answer sheet.

   b. Click **Organizational Unit** on the shortcut menu to open the New Organizational Unit dialog box.

   c. Enter **Mfg** in the Name text box, and then click **OK**. The Mfg OU should now appear under the Engineering container in the ConsoleOne window.

5. Create two OUs named AeroDyn and UAS in your Mfg container:

   a. Expand your **Engineering** container.

   b. Right-click your newly created **Mfg** OU, point to **New**, and then click **Organizational Unit**.

   c. Enter **AeroDyn** in the Name text box, and then click **OK** to create the container.

   d. Right-click your newly created **Mfg** OU, point to **New**, and then click **Organizational Unit**.

   e. Enter **UAS** in the Name text box, and then click **OK** to create the container.

6. Create a user name for yourself in your IS OU:

   a. Click the **IS** OU.

   b. Click **File** on the ConsoleOne menu bar, point to **New**, and then click **User** to open the New User dialog box (see Figure 2-19).

   c. In the Name text box, enter a user name consisting of the first letter of your first name followed by your last name, and then enter your last name in the Surname text box.

   d. Click the **Create Home Directory** check box.

   e. Click the **Browse** button to the right of the Path text box.

   f. Click the **up arrow** to view all Organizations.

   g. Double-click the **UASHOST_SYS** volume.

   h. Click the **Students** folder, and then click **OK** to enter the path to your home directory.

   i. Click **OK** to create your user account and home directory.

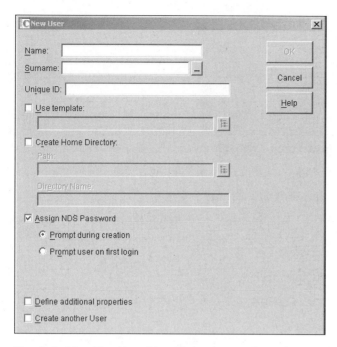

Figure 2-19   The New User dialog box in ConsoleOne

  j. When you see the Set Password dialog box, enter and confirm a password for your user account, and then click the **Set Password** button. You should now see your user object in the ###UAS Organization in the ConsoleOne window.

7. Close ConsoleOne by clicking the **Exit ConsoleOne** button.

8. Log out to display a new Novell Login window.

9. Click the **Workstation only** check box.

10. Log on to your Windows computer with the Administrator user name and password.

11. Follow the procedure in Activity 1-2, "Creating a Windows 2000 User Account," to create a new local user account with the same user name and password as the NetWare user you created in this activity.

12. Log out.

13. Log in to both Novell Client and the local Windows 2000 Professional computer, using your new user name and password. Record the results on your student answer sheet.

14. Log out.

Congratulations on completing the eDirectory tree structure for your version of the UAS network! To make your tree structure more fault tolerant and scalable for future growth, in the next section, you'll learn how to partition the tree and place replicas of network objects on multiple servers. By partitioning and replicating the eDirectory tree on multiple servers, for example, Eric was able to increase performance and provide continuous network access to the UAS network, even if one of the servers has a hardware failure.

eDirectory Partitioning and Replicating

As described earlier, the eDirectory tree is a global database containing information on network objects that's shared among all servers in the eDirectory tree. Each record in the database represents a single network object. The database itself is a hidden file stored on the NetWare server when the first server is installed on the network.

eDirectory Replicas

Universal AeroSpace Corporation has only one NetWare 6 server, so the global eDirectory database currently resides on the UASHOST NetWare server; that means this server must be up and running for users to be able to access the network. Future expansion plans for Universal AeroSpace include adding a dedicated NetWare 6 server for the Engineering and Manufacturing departments. When the new server is added, NetWare 6 will automatically place a copy of the entire eDirectory database on the new server, as shown in Figure 2-20.

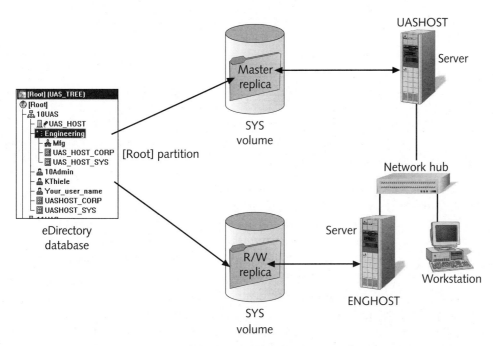

Figure 2-20   Adding a copy of the eDirectory database to the new server

The copy of the eDirectory database placed on the new server is called a **replica**. There are five types of replicas: Master, Read/Write, Filtered, Read-Only, and Subordinate. Eric learned in his eDirectory design and implementation class that the eDirectory service creates Read-Only and Subordinate replicas, so these two types are not a concern for small or medium-sized networks. A Master replica is the original main copy of the eDirectory data. As network administrator, you might want to create additional Read/Write (R/W) replicas for two major reasons: They improve performance by reducing the time required to authenticate or access a network object, and they ensure additional reliability and fault tolerance. Placing an R/W replica on the Engineering department's server, ENGHOST, would improve performance for those users because the ENGHOST server could authenticate access to network objects immediately, without having to communicate with the primary UASHOST server. Reliability and fault tolerance would also be improved by maintaining separate replicas of the eDirectory database on the Engineering server. For example, if the Business server, UASHOST, is down, users in the Engineering department could still log in and access the resources on the ENGHOST server. In addition, the eDirectory replica stored on the ENGHOST server would enable Business department users to log in and access resources, such as network printers and e-mail, and use information stored on the ENGHOST server. The data files stored on the primary UASHOST server's file system would, of course, not be accessible until that server is brought back online.

Filtered replicas are similar to R/W replicas, except that you can use a filter to specify what types of objects are included in the replica. These replicas are useful when remote users in an organization must use a slow WAN connection. For example, placing a Filtered replica that contains only user accounts on the remote server enables users to log in without the overhead of keeping the organization's entire eDirectory database synchronized with the remote server. When users at the remote location log in, the server at their location can check its copy of the eDirectory database to authenticate the logins without needing to use the slow WAN connection to access the main server. Without a replica at the remote server, each user's login request would need to be sent across the WAN connection for authentication.

eDirectory Partitions

Although keeping a complete copy of the eDirectory database on each server offers more reliability and improved performance when authenticating objects, it can also create extra communication overhead time, especially when servers are connected over WANs. The extra communication time is caused by the need to synchronize any changes to eDirectory objects across all servers containing replicas of the eDirectory database. Creating Filtered replicas of the database on servers located on other LANs can help reduce synchronization time by synchronizing only certain object types, such as user accounts. Although using Filtered replicas helps reduce synchronization traffic, it can still require a lot of data to be sent between the server with the Filtered replica and a server with a full replica when users access object types that aren't included in the Filtered replica. To reduce this overhead, Novell has added the ability to partition the eDirectory database. A **directory partition** is a division of the eDirectory database that enables a network administrator to replicate only a part of the entire eDirectory tree. Initially, the eDirectory tree contains only one partition that starts at the root of the tree: the **[Root] partition**. Additional partitions must start with a container and include all objects and subcontainers from that point down the tree. The start of an eDirectory partition is referred to as the "partition root."

In addition to the new server in Engineering, the IS manager, Luke McMann, is planning to install another server in the Desktop Publishing department. Eric is concerned that creating replicas of the entire eDirectory tree on all three servers would create extra communication overhead to maintain partition synchronization. As a result, Eric is planning to make the Engineering container a separate partition from the [Root] partition, which would allow the objects in the Engineering partition to be replicated only on the ENGHOST and UASHOST servers. The Desktop Publishing server, PUBHOST, could then contain only an R/W replica of the [Root] partition. Figure 2-21 illustrates this partitioning scheme.

Notice that the [Root] partition contains all objects in the UAS Organization except for the Engineering objects, which are stored in the Engineering partition. The PUBHOST server contains only an R/W replica of the [Root] partition objects. UASHOST contains Master replicas of both the [Root] partition and the Engineering partition. The ENGHOST server contains only an R/W replica of the Engineering partition. When changes such as adding new users to the IS department are made to the [Root] partition, these changes have to be synchronized only between the UASHOST and PUBHOST servers. Additions or changes made to objects in the Engineering department are synchronized only between the UASHOST and ENGHOST servers. In addition, notice that Eric arranged the replicas so that if any of the servers goes down, at least one replica of each partition is available to the network. For example, if the UASHOST server goes down, all objects in the [Root] and Engineering partitions are still available from both the PUBHOST and ENGHOST servers.

2

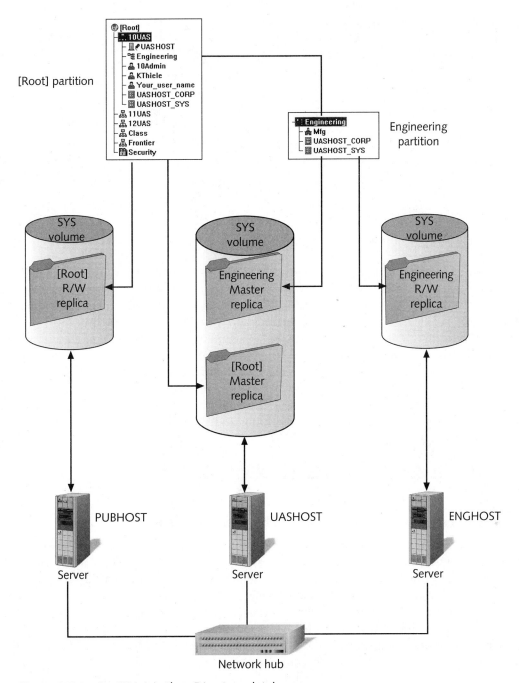

Figure 2-21   Partitioning the eDirectory database

With NetWare 6, the ConsoleOne utility is used to view, create, move, or merge partitions. As shown in Figure 2-22, the ConsoleOne utility enables you to identify which partitions exist in the eDirectory tree and determine on which servers the partition replicas are stored.

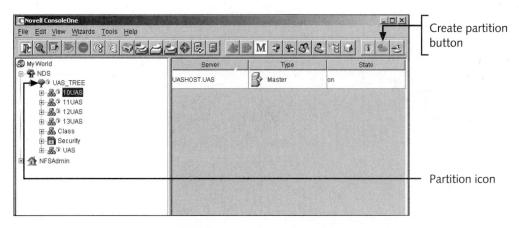

Figure 2-22 The Partition and Replica view in ConsoleOne

Notice that partition icons indicate the containers that are separate partitions of the UAS_TREE. The first partition icon is next to the UAS_TREE; this partition is the eDirectory tree [Root] partition, the first and only required partition in the tree. It contains the Class and Security containers. Additional partitions have been created for the UAS Organization container and for each ##UAS Organization container. On the right is the Replica frame, which displays the servers that contain replicas of the selected partition and indicates the replica type and state. In Figure 2-22, the UASHOST server contains a Master replica of the highlighted UAS partition. If your classroom network contains multiple servers, you might find that the UAS partition is also stored on other servers. The State column indicates the status of the replica on that server. You should not create or merge partitions if the state is not "on." In the following activities, you learn how to use ConsoleOne to view current partitions and create a new partition for the Engineering container.

Activity 2-15: Viewing Partitions and Replicas

Time Required: 10 minutes

Objective: Use ConsoleOne to view and work with partitions and replicas.

Description: At a UAS meeting, David Heise expressed concern about scaling the network to meet the company's rapid growth expectations. Luke assured David that NetWare 6 is very scalable and will be able to handle the expected growth. His plan includes adding more servers and then partitioning the eDirectory database to ensure better performance and fault tolerance. Although Universal AeroSpace's eDirectory tree isn't currently large enough to require partitions, Novell recommends creating partitions before installing multiple servers into different containers of the eDirectory tree. Eric plans to follow Novell's recommendation by creating a separate partition for the Engineering container so that he will be prepared to add servers in the Engineering and Desktop Publishing departments in the near future. Before creating partitions, Eric used ConsoleOne to view and document the existing partitions and replicas in the UAS_Tree. In this activity, you use ConsoleOne to identify partitions and find the servers that contain replicas of the partitions.

1. If necessary, start your computer, and log in to the network with your assigned ##Admin user name.

2. Double-click your **ConsoleOne** desktop shortcut.

3. Change the ConsoleOne window to the Partition and Replica view by clicking the **UAS_Tree** object, and then clicking **View**, **Partition and Replica View** on the menu bar.

4. If necessary, expand the CLASS Organization to view your ##UAS container. Notice that each container that is a partition has a special icon (shown previously in Figure 2-22). On your student answer sheet, record whether or not your ##UAS container is a separate partition.

5. Click your **##UAS** Organization to view all replicas of your partition in the Replica frame. Record the replica information on your student answer sheet.

6. View all replicas stored on the UASHOST server by following these steps:

    a. Expand the **UAS** container.

    b. Click the **UASHOST** server to view all replicas in the Replica frame.

    c. Record the replicas and their types on your student answer sheet.

7. Leave the ConsoleOne Partition and Replica view open for the next activity.

Activity 2-16: Creating a Partition

Time Required: 10 minutes

Objective: Use ConsoleOne to view and work with partitions and replicas.

Description: Universal AeroSpace is expecting rapid expansion in the Engineering department and is planning to add servers dedicated to engineering and desktop publishing applications. To prepare the eDirectory tree for this expansion, Eric made a separate partition for the Engineering OU to prepare for installing additional servers in the tree. In this activity, you use ConsoleOne to create a new partition for the Engineering department.

1. If necessary, log in to the network with your ##Admin user name, and start ConsoleOne.

2. In the ConsoleOne Partition and Replica view, expand your **##UAS** Organization, if necessary. (If you aren't continuing from the previous activity and need to open this view, click **View**, **Partition and Replica View** on the menu bar.)

3. Click your **Engineering** OU to select it.

4. Click the **Create Partition** button on the ConsoleOne toolbar, or click **Edit**, **Create Partition** on the ConsoleOne menu bar.

5. Click **OK** to create a partition from your Engineering container. The system will then check system availability and rights to perform the operation.

6. After the system has performed the checks, the Creating Partition message box is displayed with Close and Cancel buttons. Do not click either button; wait for the partition creation operation to finish.

7. After a short time, the partition will be created and a partition icon will appear to the left of the Engineering container. The Replica frame will display the location of your Engineering partition replicas. Notice that the Master replica of the new Engineering partition has been placed on the UASHOST server.

8. Right-click the replica of your partition in the Replica frame to display the replica options. Record the available options on your student answer sheet.

9. Click the **Add Replica** option to open the Add Replica dialog box. Record the replica types on your student answer sheet.

10. Click the **Browse** button next to the Server Name text box to select a server to place the replica on. Click the **Up one Context Level** button twice to display all Organizations. Double-click the **UAS** Organization to display the UASHOST server object. Double-click the **UASHOST** server to open the Add Replica dialog box.

11. Select the **Read-only** replica type, and then click **OK**.

12. On your student answer sheet, record the error message you see. Click **Close** to close the message box.

13. Click the **Cancel** button to return to the ConsoleOne window.

14. Close ConsoleOne by clicking the **Exit** button on the ConsoleOne toolbar.

Good job! Your tasks for this chapter are finished, and you can now log off the network and proceed to the end-of-chapter projects to apply your skills to creating the eDirectory tree structure for the Business department.

Chapter Summary

- Using Native File Access Protocol, NetWare 6 can process requests for file services for Microsoft, Apple, and Unix clients. You must have Novell NetWare Client installed to take advantage of certain eDirectory features, such as enhanced security and Z.E.N.works application services.

- One of NetWare's major features is the global eDirectory database, which allows NetWare servers to share access to a common set of network objects that can be organized into a hierarchical tree structure. In addition to the [Root] object, which represents the beginning of the eDirectory tree, eDirectory objects can be classified as container objects or leaf objects. Container objects are used to store other objects and include the Country, Organization, and Organizational Unit objects. Leaf objects represent actual network entities, such as users, printers, groups, servers, and volumes. Small networks can have a simple tree structure consisting of leaf objects within a single Organization container. Larger organizations require more complex trees with multiple Organizational Units.

- The location of an object within the eDirectory tree is called its context. Specifying its name along with its complete context path (its distinguished name) uniquely identifies an object. A distinguished name can be typeful or typeless. A typeful distinguished name includes the object type along with the name of the object. A typeless name does not include the object type specification; although it's not as specific, it's much easier to enter.

- The location of the client computer within the eDirectory tree is called the current context, which can be used to make access to objects easier by simply entering the object's common name.

- NetWare 6 has two graphical Windows-based utilities for managing eDirectory objects: ConsoleOne and NetWare Administrator. ConsoleOne is the primary utility, but NetWare Administrator can offer better performance on older computers. These utilities are used to browse an eDirectory tree structure, view information about specific objects, and create leaf and Organizational Unit objects.

- Replicas are copies of the eDirectory database placed on NetWare servers; they provide fault tolerance if a server is down and enable faster access to network resources. When an eDirectory database becomes large or is spread over several servers, a network administrator can increase performance by breaking the database into smaller segments, called partitions. Replicas of partitions can be kept only on servers that need that data, thereby decreasing the network traffic required to keep all servers synchronized.

Key Terms

Admin — An important user object with supervisor rights to the entire eDirectory tree.

alias object — An object used as a pointer to another object located in a different container of the eDirectory tree.

container object — An eDirectory object used to contain other objects.

context — The location of an object in the eDirectory tree.

Country container object — A special type of container object used to group Organization container objects by country. Country containers must be assigned a valid two-digit country code and can exist only at the root of an eDirectory tree.

current context — The default location of the client computer in the eDirectory tree.

directory partition — A division of the eDirectory structure that starts with a single container and includes any subcontainers.

distinguished name — A name that uniquely identifies an object in the eDirectory database.

2

leaf object — An eDirectory object used to represent network entities, such as users, groups, printers, and servers. Leaf objects must exist within Organization or Organizational Unit containers.

Novell Directory Services (NDS) — Used in versions before NetWare 6, a global database containing information on all network objects, including users, groups, printers, and volumes, that are available to all servers.

object — A network component of the eDirectory database.

Organization container object — An eDirectory object used to group objects that belong to an organization. Organization objects can exist at the root of an eDirectory tree or within a Country container.

Organizational Unit (OU) container object — An eDirectory object used to group leaf objects that belong to a subdivision of an Organization container. Organizational Unit containers can exist within an Organization container or within another Organizational Unit.

property — A field containing information about an object. Not all object types have the same properties.

relative name — Starts with the current context of the client, but omits the leading period.

replica — A copy of the eDirectory database stored on a NetWare server.

[Root] object — An eDirectory object representing the beginning of the network directory service tree.

[Root] partition — The initial division of the eDirectory tree that starts at the root of the tree.

typeful name — A distinguished name that includes object type abbreviations (O, OU, and CN).

typeless name — A distinguished name that assumes object type based on position instead of including the object type abbreviations.

volume object — A pointer to physical data volumes on the server, used to access data and store volume configuration and status information.

REVIEW QUESTIONS

1. Which of the following protocols is used to access network servers from a Web browser?

   a. NCP

   b. IPX

   c. HTTP

   d. NSF

2. Which of the following clients requires NFAP to be installed on the NetWare 6 server?

   a. Microsoft client

   b. Web browser client

   c. Microsoft NetWare client

   d. Novell Client

3. Novell's Z.E.N.works application service will run on which of the following? Select all that apply.

   a. Microsoft client

   b. Microsoft NetWare client

   c. Novell Client

   d. Web browser client

4. List two advantages of using Novell Client.

   _____

   _____

5. Which of the following is an advantage of Client Services for NetWare compared to the Microsoft NetWare client? (Choose all that apply.)

a. uses the Novell eDirectory password and context system for logging in to NetWare

b. allows access to Novell's Z.E.N.works application service

c. allows use of the Novell management utilities, such as ConsoleOne

d. does not require the user to have a separate user name on the local Windows workstation

6. Which of the following industry naming standards is the basis for the object-naming system used in Novell's eDirectory?

a. DNS

b. X.500

c. SDLC

d. NetBIOS

7. List three types of container objects.

_____

_____

_____

8. Identify each of the following objects as Country, Organization, Organizational Unit, or leaf. For all leaf objects, include the type of leaf object (user, group, printer, server, and so forth).

a. Accounting   _____   _____

b. NASA   _____   _____

c. Neil Armstrong   _____   _____

d. Spain   _____   _____

e. CTSHOST   _____   _____

9. Which of the following is a field that can contain information about an object?

a. leaf

b. property

c. value

d. container

10. Which object types can be placed in the [Root] of an eDirectory tree? (Choose all that apply.)

a. user objects

b. Organization objects

c. volume objects

d. Country objects

11. In which of the following containers can user objects be placed? (Choose all that apply.)

a. Country

b. [Root]

c. Organization

d. Organizational Unit

12. List two advantages of placing replicas on multiple servers.

_____

_____

2

13. Which of the following is a division of the eDirectory database that starts at a container?

    a. replica

    b. partition

    c. [Root]

    d. Organization

14. Which of the following refers to the location of an object in the eDirectory tree?

    a. context

    b. path

    c. partition

    d. environment

15. Write a typeful distinguished name for the user JMeek, who is located in the Marketing department of the AstorFurs company.

    _____

16. Write a typeless distinguished name for the SAL_HP3 laser printer located in the Marketing department of the AstorFurs company.

    _____

17. Write a typeless relative name for the SAL_HP3 laser printer described in Question 16, assuming that your current context is the AstorFurs Organization.

    _____

18. List four types of replicas.

    _____

    _____

    _____

    _____

19. Which of the following utilities enables a network administrator to create and manage eDirectory objects from any network or client by using a Web browser, such as Internet Explorer or Netscape?

    a. ConsoleOne

    b. NetWare Administrator

    c. iManager

    d. WebDAV

20. Which of the following starts with the client computer's current context and is specified by omitting the leading period?

    a. typeless name

    b. relative distinguished name

    c. distinguished name

    d. typeless distinguished name

CASE PROJECTS: UNIVERSAL AEROSPACE NETWORK SYSTEM

Case Project 2-1: Creating the Business Organizational Unit

Now that you have finished the structure for the Engineering department, your next task is to set up the Business OU. In this project, follow the steps in Activity 2-13 to use iManager to create a Business container in your assigned ##UAS Organization.

Case Project 2-2: Creating Initial Objects in the Business Organizational Unit

Following the steps in Activity 2-12, use NetWare Administrator to create an alias object to the UASHOST server and a SYS volume object in your newly created Business OU. Make sure you modify Step 4 to click your .Business.##UAS Organizational Unit to create the alias and volume objects in the new container.

Case Project 2-3: Modifying the eDirectory Tree Design

AeroDyn Corporation, a manufacturer of aircraft control systems, is a subsidiary of Universal AeroSpace, but its office and manufacturing facilities are in a different city. The office staff includes seven salespeople, three design engineers, four programmers, two accountants, and an IS department. Management consists of a general manager and two administrative assistants. The accountants and management share network resources, such as printers, files, and applications. The design engineers and programmers often work together on projects and need to share resources. Luke McMann, manager of UAS's IS department, would like you to modify the eDirectory structure for Universal AeroSpace. Your design should identify any additional OUs and their locations in the eDirectory tree. You should also identify any additional partitions that should be created to add a NetWare 6 server in the AeroDyn location. Have your design approved by your instructor before proceeding to the next project.

Case Project 2-4: Creating the AeroDyn Structure

After you have your design approved, use ConsoleOne to implement the design by creating the necessary containers and partitions. After finishing the project, have your instructor check your work.

3

DESIGNING THE FILE SYSTEM

> **After reading this chapter and completing the exercises, you will be able to:**
>
> ♦ Describe the components of Novell Storage Services and use ConsoleOne to create and access volumes
>
> ♦ Identify important NetWare-created directories and describe their purpose
>
> ♦ Apply directory design concepts to developing and documenting a directory structure for Universal AeroSpace Corporation
>
> ♦ Use ConsoleOne and Remote Manager to work with files and directories in the NetWare file system and perform such tasks as salvaging and purging network files
>
> ♦ Plan and implement network drive pointers

In Chapter 2, you built the base for your network by setting up the clients and establishing the eDirectory tree structure necessary to support network objects and services. Before creating user accounts and providing access to network services for Universal AeroSpace, Eric Kenton needed to establish the initial network file system to designate areas for user home directories, applications, and shared data. Designing and implementing a network file system that meets an organization's needs is an essential step that a CNA must take when setting up a network system. Another part of setting up the file system is planning for user access from the local network and through the Internet. Because local access to the file system is usually handled through drive mappings, an important part of a CNA's job is planning and implementing drive pointers. As part of Novell's OneNet strategy, NetWare 6 has new Internet file access technologies called iFolder and NetStorage that enable users to have access to their data whether in the office, at home, or on the road. In this chapter, you learn the components of the NetWare file system as well as how to design and implement a network file system for your version of the Universal AeroSpace network that will improve users' workflow. In addition, you learn how to plan a drive mapping strategy that will provide a consistent set of drive letters so that users can easily access the network data and applications they need. In Chapter 7, you will learn how to configure servers and clients so that users have convenient access to data by using login scripts, iFolder, and NetStorage.

NetWare File System Components

The NetWare file system offers many benefits for making information available on a network. These benefits can be classified into the following five categories:

- *Centralized management of data and backups*—When data is stored on a server, users can access centralized database files that contain current and accurate information. Centralizing data enables critical files to be backed up regularly and makes it easier to restore lost data or recover from a file server failure.

- *Improved security*—Netware prevents users from modifying or accessing data that they are not responsible for maintaining or authorized to use.

- *Improved reliability and fault tolerance*—NetWare's disk-mirroring and duplexing features can be used to ensure that duplicate copies of data are automatically available for users in the event of hardware failures. NetWare 6 includes disk-clustering technology that enables multiple servers to share access to the same networked disk system, thus increasing reliability and fault tolerance.

- *Shared and private storage areas*—Shared storage areas allow users to share files or transfer files to other users without having to carry disks between machines. With private storage areas, users can save their own work in a secure area of the file server.

- *Access to data*—An essential part of Novell's OneNet vision is using common clients and operating systems to give users access to the data and documents they need from computers attached to any interconnected network. As you learned in Chapter 2, through Novell's Native File Access Protocol (NFAP), NetWare can support Apple, Unix, and Windows clients, which reduces hardware costs because there's no need for separate servers to support each operating system. When more users and applications are added to the network, it's essential that a CNA know how to give users access to data they need, both inside and outside the corporate network.

Because a file system is used to organize and secure the information stored on a network, a good design is necessary to facilitate a network's setup, use, and growth. With NetWare 6, Novell has improved the network file system by implementing **Novell Storage Services (NSS)** version 3. Earlier versions of NSS included with NetWare 5 are more difficult to implement and don't support the SYS volume. As a result, NSS is an option on NetWare 5 servers, typically used only with very large data volumes. Because of the advanced features of NSS, Novell has made NSS version 3 (NSS3) the primary file system used on all NetWare 6 volumes, including the SYS volume. An NSS SYS volume of at least 2 GB is required during NetWare 6 installation. Other minimum and recommended system requirements for installing NetWare 6 are listed in Table 3-1.

Table 3-1   NetWare 6 Minimum and Recommended Requirements

Component	Minimum	Recommended
Processor	Pentium II or higher	700 MHz Pentium III
Memory	256 MB of RAM	512 MB of RAM
Video	Super VGA or higher	Super VGA or higher
DOS partition	200 MB	1 GB
SYS volume	2 GB	4 GB
Network board	10 Mbps Ethernet	100 Mbps Ethernet
CD-ROM	Bootable CD-ROM drive	50-speed CD-ROM drive
Mouse		Serial, USB, or PS/2

As illustrated in Figure 3-1, the main components of the NSS3 file system are disk partitions, storage pools, and volumes. The disk drive is first divided into one or more partitions. The partition space from one or more drives is then combined to form storage pools; a single storage pool can contain space from one or more disk partitions. After a storage pool is created, volumes can be defined within that storage pool. Later in this chapter, you will follow Eric as he creates disk partitions, storage pools, and volumes for the Universal AeroSpace network.

3

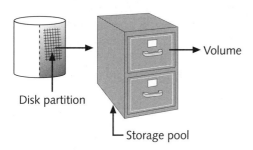

Figure 3-1 NSS3 file system components

Disk Partitions

To format and manage storage on a physical disk drive, the drive needs to be divided into one or more **disk partitions**. Originally, a disk drive could have a maximum of four disk partitions defined, but with Novell Storage Services, you can have an almost unlimited number of NSS disk partitions. As described in Chapter 12, when installing NetWare 6 on a new server, the installation program requires a DOS partition of at least 200 MB, with a recommended size of 1 GB. In addition to the DOS partition, during installation a SYS volume is created by default for operating system files. When planning how to allocate the remaining drive space, it's a good idea to leave some unpartitioned space for future expansion of storage pools. For example, when establishing the storage space for the UAS disk drive, Eric divided his 60 GB drive into three partitions, as shown in Figure 3-2. By leaving approximately 14 GB unpartitioned, Eric has the option of extending the SYS or CORP partition in the future.

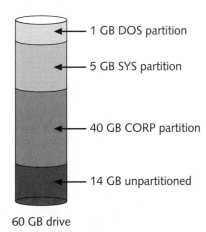

60 GB drive

Figure 3-2 UAS disk partitions

To create and manage partitions, you use ConsoleOne or NetWare Remote Manager. Because NSS partitions are considered part of the NetWare server's disk storage, they do not appear as separate objects in the eDirectory tree, but are accessed by selecting the NetWare server object. Later in this chapter, you'll use ConsoleOne to view partition information through the NetWare server object.

Partition Fault Tolerance

Having all operating system files and data on one drive creates a potential single point of failure for the file service if the drive or its controller card fails. As described in Chapter 1, fault tolerance is the system's ability to continue to function despite the failure of a major component. With NetWare, you can ensure increased reliability when you create an NSS partition by enabling the Hot Fix or Mirror options, as shown in Figure 3-3. Hot fixes increase partition reliability by detecting bad disk blocks and then automatically redirecting the data being written to the bad disk block to another area of the disk, called the eDirectory or reserved area. As shown in Figure 3-3, the size of the reserved area is specified when you enable the Hot Fix option for a new partition. The only disadvantage of hot fixes is the relatively small amount of space reserved for bad blocks along with a very small amount of server processing time. Unless you're severely low on disk space, you should always enable the Hot Fix option when creating volumes.

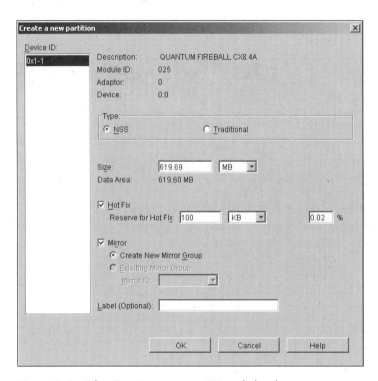

Figure 3-3   The Create a new partition dialog box

To further increase your data's reliability, you can enable the Mirror option to have NetWare automatically keep the data on two partitions (and on different drives) synchronized by writing data to both partitions. If one of the drives fails, data will still be available from the mirrored drive. The Mirror option allows you to create a new mirror group or add the new partition to an existing mirror group. When adding a partition to an existing mirror group, the data area of the new partition must be the same size as the existing partition in the group. If the partitions are different sizes, NetWare automatically increases the larger partition's hot fix area to make the data areas the same size. The term **duplexing** describes the process of mirroring disk partitions that exist on separate physical disks on separate controller cards, whereas **mirroring** means that the separate drives are attached to the same controller. Using two controller cards enables duplexing to provide faster speeds and continuous operation if you have a controller card failure. To ensure maximum speed and reliability, Eric attached the two 60 GB drives to separate controller cards on the UASHOST server to duplex the SYS and CORP partitions (see Figure 3-4). If one of the drives or controllers fails, the system continues reading and writing to the other drive. When the problem is fixed, NetWare automatically rebuilds the new drive so that the two drives are the same.

The process of enabling duplexing is the same as mirroring; the only difference is that with duplexing, the two partitions are located on disks attached to different controller cards.

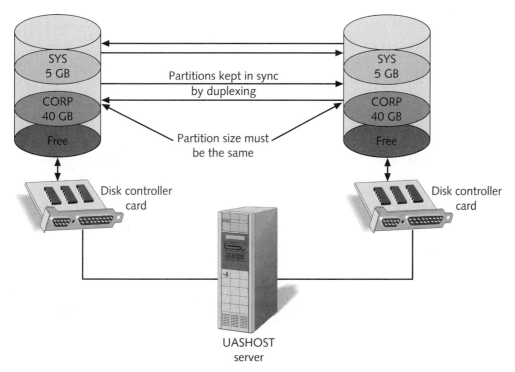

Figure 3-4   Duplexing UAS partitions

Storage Pools

After a disk has been partitioned, the next job in setting up an NSS file system is creating one or more storage pools. **Storage pools** are created from disk partitions and can be extended by adding disk partitions, as shown in Figure 3-5. When a disk partition is added to a storage pool, the amount of free space in the pool is increased by the size of the disk partition. Later in this chapter, you'll learn how to use ConsoleOne to add disk partitions to storage pools. If you're adding a disk partition from a second drive to an existing storage pool, you should consider mirroring or duplexing the new partition on another disk to prevent one drive's failure from bringing down the entire storage pool. Leaving some unpartitioned space on a new drive gives you the option of extending a storage pool without adding another drive. During installation, a storage pool named SYS is created for the SYS volume. The SYS volume is then used to hold operating system files and programs. To separate the operating system files from the organization's data, the network administrator must create one or more additional storage pools.

Volumes

As described in Chapter 1, volumes are the basic storage unit used by network file services to give users access to network directories and files. NetWare 6 supports both traditional volumes and the new NSS volumes. NSS volumes are usually preferred over traditional volumes because they offer additional capacity and high-speed mounting. Table 3-2 compares NSS and traditional volumes.

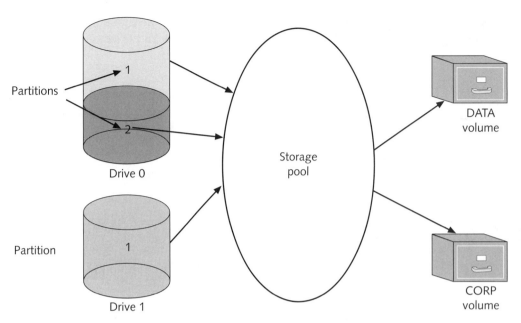

Figure 3-5   Storage pools

Table 3-2   NSS Versus Traditional Volumes

Feature	Traditional Volume	NSS Volume
Maximum number of volumes	64	255
Maximum number of files	16 million	Unlimited
Memory required to mount 20 GB volume	320 MB of RAM	32 MB of RAM
Mounting speed	Several minutes for large volumes	Less than one minute, even for very large volumes
Support for file compression	Yes	Yes
Support for block suballocation	Yes	No
Support for large block sizes (more than 4 KB)	Yes	No
Support for clustering	No	Yes
Support for data shredding	No	Yes
Support for user space restrictions	Yes	Yes
Support for directory space restrictions	Yes	Yes
Support for hot fixes	Yes	Yes
Support for automatic error correction and data recovery	No	Yes
Support for Modified File List feature	No	Yes
Software RAID support	No	Yes

As listed in Table 3-2, before NSS, the traditional file system supported up to 64 volumes per server and 16 million files per volume. By contrast, NSS3 now supports up to 255 mounted volumes per server and a virtually unlimited number of files per volume.

The increased speed of mounting NSS volumes on a server is a benefit that network administrators will appreciate. In the past, mounting a volume involved loading the file allocation table (FAT) into the server's memory. On large volumes, this process could take several minutes and require several megabytes of RAM; for example, a 10 GB volume could take 160 MB of RAM to mount. Instead of a large FAT, NSS uses a more memory-efficient file allocation system called **balanced trees (B-trees)**. Using B-trees, volumes of more than 400 million files can be mounted in just seconds and require a maximum of only 32 MB of RAM. In addition, with the B-tree system, NetWare can retrieve any file blocks not in memory in just four processor cycles, making NSS much faster than previous file systems.

NSS Volumes

NSS volumes are logical divisions of an NSS storage pool and are contained in one or more disk partitions. NSS volumes can be given a specific size, up to the storage pool's maximum size, or they can be allotted an initial size and then allowed to grow to the size of the storage pool. Configuring a volume for this growth has the advantage of allowing you to later extend the volume size by simply adding another partition to the storage pool. For example, assume that your SYS volume is the only volume in a storage pool consisting of one 10 GB disk partition. If the SYS volume is allowed to grow to the size of the storage pool, its maximum size will be 10 GB. If you add another 5 GB partition to the storage pool, the SYS volume can grow to a maximum of 15 GB.

In addition to faster mounting and lower server memory requirements, NSS volumes incorporate several new features and attributes that make them beneficial for network storage. Most of these features and attributes can be set when you create the NSS volume (see Figure 3-6) or configured later in the Properties dialog box for the volume. As a CNA, you should understand how the NSS volume features described in the following sections benefit the network file system. Later in this chapter, you'll learn how to use ConsoleOne to configure NSS volume features and attributes.

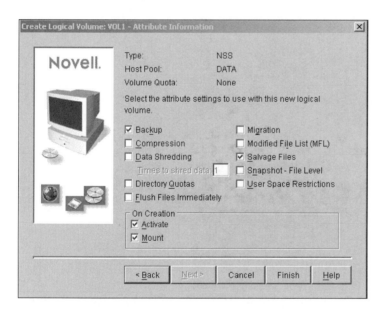

Figure 3-6   Setting options when creating a volume

Clustering   Although mirroring and duplexing can provide fault tolerance if a drive or controller fails, the server's hardware itself could still cause loss of network services. To provide fault tolerance in the event of a server failure, NSS supports **server clustering**, in which volumes are shared among two or more servers, as shown in Figure 3-7. As described in Chapter 1, shared volumes are usually placed on a networked storage device that's attached to a high-speed storage area network (SAN). If one of the clustered servers has a hardware failure, another server automatically takes on the role of making the data on the shared volume available to network users. The process of switching from a failed server to an operational server is called **failover** and occurs in just a matter of seconds.

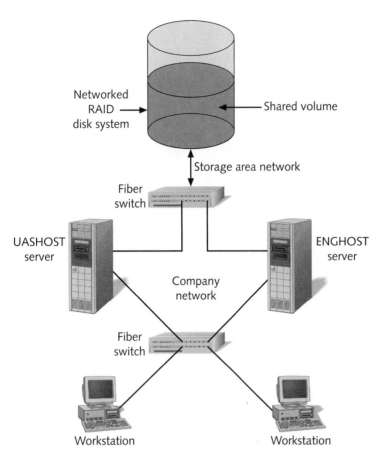

Figure 3-7   Server clustering

Another possible source of downtime is the failure of a disk drive in the network storage device. Networked storage devices usually use hardware-based RAID 5 technology to provide fault tolerance in case there's a hardware failure on one of the network storage device's disk drives. When using RAID 5, a network storage device writes data and control information to multiple drives so that if one drive fails, its information can be recovered by using the control information stored on the other drives.

Overbooking   Assume that you have a 40 GB storage pool to be divided into two volumes: one for accounting data and another for marketing data. After analyzing the storage needs for each department, you conclude that the Marketing department will eventually need 35 GB, but the Accounting department could get by with 15 GB. Although no one volume can exceed the storage pool size, overbooking allows the sum of all volumes in the storage pool to be larger than the pool size; therefore, with this feature, you could create a Marketing volume of 35 GB and an Accounting volume of 15 GB. If both volumes grow to their capacity, you could expand the storage pool size by adding more disk partitions. For example, you want to create a 1.5 GB volume named VOL3 within a storage pool named DATA, which has 1.6 GB available. When you create the new volume, you can specify its size in the selected storage pool, as shown in Figure 3-8. Notice that the Total Quotas column for the DATA pool has 2.2 GB already allocated to other volumes. With overbooking, you can specify a size for the new volume up to the capacity shown in the Available column, despite the fact that the total quotas exceed the pool size. Of course, the storage pool will be filled before all volumes can reach their allocated sizes. If this happens, you can increase the pool size by adding more partitions.

Flush Files Immediately   The Flush Files Immediately attribute can be selected during or after creating a volume and causes a file to be saved to disk immediately after it's closed, instead of waiting for the next server disk write cycle. Writing closed files to disk immediately decreases the chance of data loss if the server has a hardware or power failure.

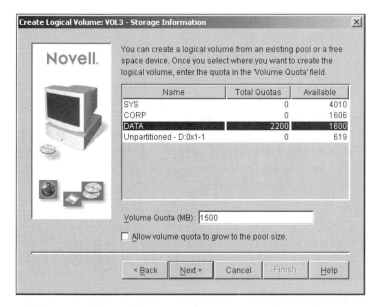

Figure 3-8 Overbooking volumes when specifiying the storage pool size

File Snapshot   In the past, backing up file servers that were accessed 24-7 created problems with backing up open files. For example, if a backup program is running while a file is being changed, the backup will contain an incomplete copy of the new data. NSS offers a solution to this problem through the use of its file snapshot capability. To enable this option, select the Snapshot - File Level attribute (refer back to Figure 3-6) when creating a volume (or later in the volume's Properties dialog box). This option saves the most recent copy of a closed file for backup purposes and ensures that if your data is lost between backup copies, you can restore a valid copy of the previously closed file.

Modified File List   Previous versions of the NetWare file system determined which files needed to be backed up by setting an attribute flag (described in Chapter 5) whenever a file's data changed. This system required the backup utility to scan all filenames for attribute flags to determine which files to back up. When you create NSS3 volumes, you can optionally select the Modified File List attribute so that the volume tracks the names of any files that have changed since the last backup. Using this feature can speed up the process of making a differential file system backup of large volumes, as described in Appendix C.

File Compression   A feature common to both traditional and NSS volumes is **file compression**. Like other volume attributes, you can enable the Compression attribute during or after volume creation with the ConsoleOne utility. When file compression is enabled on a volume, the server automatically compresses all files that have not been used for a specified time period. By default, the server compresses files that have not been used for seven days if the compression will result in at least a 5% savings in disk space. In Chapter 5, you will learn how to selectively enable or disable compression on individual files and directories.

Data Shredding   With the NetWare file system, you can easily recover deleted data files by using the NetWare salvage capability. If you need to destroy sensitive data for security purposes, however, enabling the Data Shredding attribute can add an extra level of security to your network file system by overwriting any purged files with random data patterns. By writing up to seven random patterns over the data, data shredding makes it impossible for information from deleted files to be accessed with disk editor software, such as Norton Disk Doctor.

Disk Space Restriction Options   By default, administrators could restrict space used by traditional volumes on the basis of individual users or an entire directory structure. Because managing user restrictions and directory quotas on very large volumes requires extra processing time, however, disk space restrictions are optional on NSS volumes. When creating NSS volumes, administrators can decide whether they want to be able to restrict volume space by selecting the User Space Restrictions option or the Directory Quotas option when the volume is created or modified.

Salvage Files Option   As with disk space restrictions, you can enable the Salvage Files option for deleted files in NSS volumes. When a file is deleted from a volume that supports salvaging files, the filename and data are kept until the space is needed for new files. When new space is needed, the space from the oldest deleted files is used first. On a large volume, it could be months before the operating system reuses space from a deleted file. Deleted files can be salvaged, or undeleted, until the operating system reuses the space or the file is purged. With NSS volumes, network administrators have the option of salvaging files on a volume-by-volume basis when a volume is created or modified.

Although being able to salvage deleted files can be important on volumes that contain shared user data, the extra processing time required to maintain deleted files might not be worthwhile for volumes containing application software or highly secure documents. For example, the SYS volume contains NetWare applications and system files that sometimes need to be updated. Updating the NetWare operating system with a new service pack deletes and replaces older program files with newer ones. It's highly unlikely you would want to salvage old system programs after installing a newer version because mixing the older software with the new software can cause system errors. In addition, many applications create and delete temporary files that you would not want to salvage. As a result, to save processing time on volumes such as SYS, you might want to turn off the Salvage Files option to improve system performance. Security can also be a reason to turn off this option. Some volumes might contain sensitive information that users don't want to be accessed when a file is deleted. Turning off the Salvage Files option on these volumes can help increase security on deleted files.

Traditional Volumes

Although NSS volumes offer many advantages over traditional volumes, when you upgrade a NetWare server to NetWare 6, any existing volumes remain traditional. Traditional volumes can be converted to NSS volumes by creating an NSS volume and then transferring the data from the traditional volume to the new NSS volume. Because traditional volumes are created directly from disk partitions, they do not offer the flexibility and scalability of NSS volumes, which are created from storage pools. When creating traditional volumes, you have certain options, such as block size and suballocation, that are not available on NSS volumes. Data is written to the disk in units called blocks. A **block** is the amount of data that's written to or read from the disk at one time. Block size is set when a storage pool or traditional volume is created and can range from 4 KB to 64 KB. Although the block size on storage pools is automatically set to 4 KB when the storage pool is created, you can set the block size on traditional volumes when you create the volume. Larger block sizes can speed up disk access because it takes fewer disk requests to read or write large files. As a result, network administrators often prefer to use large block sizes for traditional volumes containing large files, such as those used in desktop publishing or other graphical presentation applications.

In addition to customizing the block size, traditional volumes offer a suballocation feature not currently available with NSS volumes. Without suballocation, each block in a volume can be assigned to only one file, meaning that small files on volumes with large block sizes waste disk space; for example, if you stored a 1 KB file on a volume with 16 KB blocks, 15 KB of disk space would be wasted. This problem is solved in traditional volumes by **suballocation**, which allows data from multiple files to be stored in the same block by dividing the block into 512-byte suballocation units. When using suballocation, a file must always start at the beginning of a block; other files can then use the space remaining in the block as necessary. Figure 3-9 illustrates using suballocation to store three files on the CORP volume. File1 requires 2.5 KB and occupies the first five suballocation units in Block 1. File2 is 1.5 KB and occupies the first three suballocation units in Block 2. File3 requires 7 KB and uses all of Block 3, along with three suballocation units in Block 1 and three suballocation units in Block 2.

3

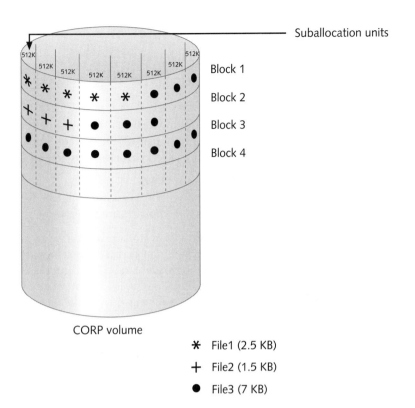

Suballocation units

Block 1
Block 2
Block 3
Block 4

CORP volume

✳ File1 (2.5 KB)
+ File2 (1.5 KB)
● File3 (7 KB)

Figure 3-9 Suballocation in traditional volumes

Viewing NSS Information

Before NetWare 6, viewing and managing file system information often required the administrator to work from the server console with the NWCONFIG utility. In NetWare 6, administrators can create, manage, and view disk partitions, storage pools, and volumes from a workstation using ConsoleOne or a Web browser running Remote Manager. In Chapter 10, you'll learn to use Remote Manager to monitor and maintain the server environment. In this section, you learn how to use ConsoleOne to view information on partition, storage pool, and volume objects.

Volume objects, which represent NetWare volumes in the eDirectory system, play an important role in eDirectory by linking the eDirectory tree objects and the network file system. As a result, before you can use ConsoleOne to access the network file system, you need to have an eDirectory object for each physical network volume. These eDirectory volume objects are created during the NetWare installation and, by default, are placed in the same container as their NetWare server. For example, the default volume object name for the SYS volume on the UASHOST server is UASHOST_SYS. As you learned in Chapter 2, you might want to create additional volume objects in other contexts to improve access to data and applications. After creating an eDirectory volume object, you can access its directories and files by selecting the volume object in the eDirectory database.

As a network administrator, you need to know how much space has been used on a volume so that you can make decisions about the location of new network directories and plan for system expansion. You can view information about NetWare volumes by using the NetWare Remote Manager utility or the Windows-based ConsoleOne and NetWare Administrator utilities. In the following activities, you learn how to view information about your NSS volumes and file system components by using ConsoleOne.

Activity 3-1: Using ConsoleOne to View NSS Information

Time Required: 10 minutes

Objective: Describe the components of Novell Storage Services (NSS).

Description: Viewing information on NSS components is useful when documenting your network file system. In this activity, you use ConsoleOne to view information about the partitions and storage pools on your server. To perform Steps 3–7, you need to log in with a user name that has administrator rights to the server. If you do not have access to an administrative user name, perform Steps 1 and 2 and then use the screenshots to fill in your student answer sheet.

1. If necessary, start your computer. When you see the Novell Client window, click the **Workstation only** check box, and log on to your local workstation using the administrative user name.

2. To use ConsoleOne to manage the server's physical disk system from a workstation, you need to turn off the File Caching option on the client so that you can update the server information in real time without caching previous information. Although file caching can increase the speed of operation when the same file is being accessed by multiple users, it can cause problems when doing a real-time update. Follow these steps to turn off file caching on your workstation:

   a. Right-click **My Network Places**, and then click **Properties**.

   b. Right-click the **Local Area Connection** icon, and then click **Properties**.

   c. Click **Novell Client for Windows 2000**, and then click **Properties** to open the Novell Client for Windows Properties dialog box.

   d. Click the **Advanced Settings** tab (see Figure 3-10).

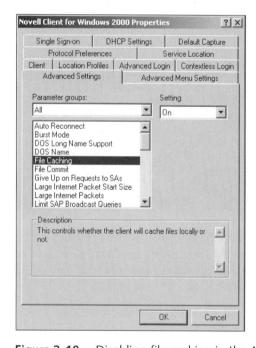

Figure 3-10 Disabling file caching in the Advanced Settings tab

   e. In the Parameter groups list, click the **File Caching** parameter, click the **Setting** list arrow, and then click **Off** in the list of options.

   f. Click **OK** twice to save the configuration settings and close the Local Area Connection Properties dialog box.

   g. Click **Yes** to restart your computer for the settings to take effect.

3. After the computer restarts, log in to the Novell network with a user name that has administrator rights to the UASHOST server.

4. Start ConsoleOne, and expand the **UAS_Tree** object.

5. Expand the **UAS** Organization.

6. To view information on the existing NSS partitions, follow these steps:

    a. Right-click the **UASHOST** server object, and then click **Properties** to open the Properties of UASHOST dialog box shown in Figure 3-11.

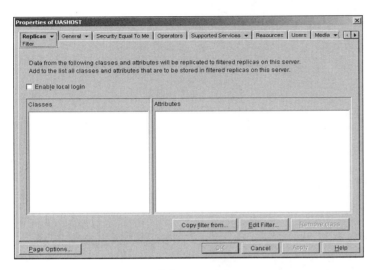

Figure 3-11   Properties of the UASHOST server

    b. Scroll to the right, and click the **down arrow** on the Media tab to display the media options shown in Figure 3-12.

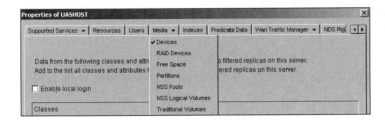

Figure 3-12   Selecting options in the Media tab

    c. Click the **Partitions** option to display the Partitions tab (see Figure 3-13).

    d. Click the first NSS partition and record the partition values requested on your student answer sheet. If you are not able to log in with administrator rights, use Figure 3-13 to fill out your student answer sheet.

    e. Click the **Mirror** button to open the Partition Mirror Group dialog box (see Figure 3-14), which displays information on mirrored partitions. If two partitions are mirrored or duplexed, their partition IDs are listed in this dialog box. In addition to the information in the Group Status section, you can click one of the mirrored partitions to view its status information to determine whether it's in sync with the other partition in the Mirror Group section.

    f. Click the **Close** button to return to the Partitions tab.

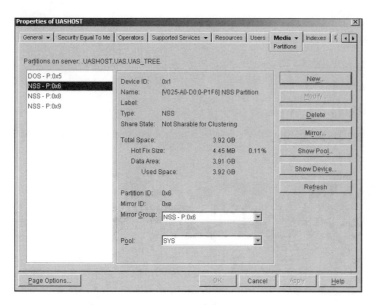

Figure 3-13   Viewing partition information

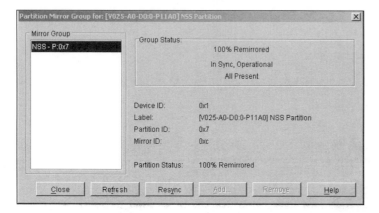

Figure 3-14   The Partition Mirror Group dialog box

    g. To view device information, click a partition, and then click the **Show Device** button to display a tab similar to the one shown in Figure 3-15 (note that the name on the Media tab has changed to Devices). On your student answer sheet, record the requested device information.

    h. Click **Cancel** to return to the ConsoleOne window.

   7. To view information on the existing NSS storage pools, follow these steps:

    a. Right-click the **UASHOST** server object, and then click **Properties** to open the Properties of UASHOST dialog box.

    b. Click the **down arrow** on the Media tab to display the media options.

    c. Click the **NSS Pools** option to display a tab showing all storage pools on the selected server (see Figure 3-16).

    d. Click the first storage pool and record the information requested on your student answer sheet. If you are not able to log in with administrator rights, use Figure 3-16 to fill out your student answer sheet.

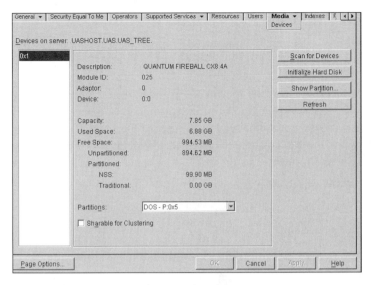

Figure 3-15   Viewing device information

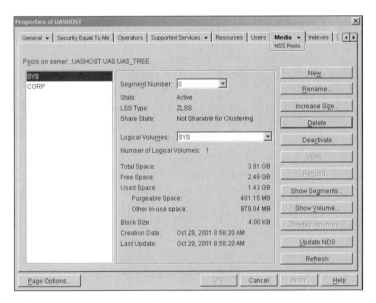

Figure 3-16   Viewing information on the NSS storage pools

   e. Click the **Increase Size** button (used when you want to add partitions to the storage pool); after recording the description on your student answer sheet, click the **Cancel** button.

   f. Click the **Deactivate** button and record the warning message on your student answer sheet. After recording the message, click **No** to cancel the operation.

 You might need to deactivate offline troubleshooting or repair, which will be described in Chapter 10.

   g. Click **Cancel** to return to the ConsoleOne window.

8. Exit ConsoleOne, and log out.

Activity 3-2: Using ConsoleOne to View Volume Information

Time Required: 5 minutes

Objective: Describe the components of Novell Storage Services (NSS).

Description: You use the volume object in ConsoleOne or NetWare Administrator to manage the network file system. Remember that to keep the server functioning, you need to make sure the SYS volume does not run out of space. Therefore, Eric periodically uses ConsoleOne, NetWare Administrator, or Remote Manager to check the status of the SYS volume. In this activity, you use ConsoleOne to display information about the SYS volume on your classroom server.

1. Log in with your assigned ##Admin user name.

2. Start ConsoleOne, expand **UAS_Tree**, and then expand your **##UAS** Organization.

3. To view volume information, follow these steps:

   a. Right-click the **UASHOST_SYS** volume object, and then click **Properties**.

   b. Click the **Dates and Times** tab, and record the volume creation and modified dates on your student answer sheet.

   c. To display the space usage along with the volume's block size and compression or suballocation status, click the **Statistics** tab. Record the information requested on your student answer sheet.

   d. Click the **Users with Space Restrictions** tab, and record user space restrictions for the volume on your student answer sheet.

4. Exit ConsoleOne, and log out.

Directories and Subdirectories

Just as file cabinet drawers are organized by using hanging folders, NetWare volumes are divided into multiple directories and subdirectories. Directories and subdirectories allow you to keep files separated in a volume, just as folders enable you to separate and find information in a file cabinet. You can also place space restrictions on directories and subdirectories to prevent certain applications or users from occupying too much of a volume's disk space. As a CNA, you will need to know which directories NetWare 6 needs as well as how to create directories for organizing data. In the following sections, you learn about the NetWare required directories along with suggested directory structures that you can use to meet your organization's data and software storage needs.

System-Created Directories

As shown in Table 3-3, the NetWare operating system stores its required system files and utilities on the SYS volume under several directories. Table 3-3 lists all the system-created directories; the most common directories that administrators use are Login, Public, and System. The following sections explain how NetWare uses these three directories and where certain types of files are stored.

Login   The **Login directory** contains files and programs that can be accessed before logging in. In the past, DOS clients used the Login directory to access commands needed to log in to the network. NetWare 6 uses the Login directory to find commands needed to access or start network services from a Web browser. Three important DOS programs in the Login directory are Cx.exe, Nlist.exe, and Login.exe; these utilities are mostly used when logging in from or working on DOS-based computers. In addition to storing the DOS commands, many network administrators like to use the Login directory to store files and programs that users often need during the startup process. When these programs release a new version, you can easily update them by copying the new software into the Login directory, instead of having to copy them to each workstation's hard disk drive.

Table 3-3   System-Created Directories

Directory Name	Purpose
Apache	Contains the Apache Web server files
Audit	Contains files for auditing system activity and Web server access
Etc	Contains configuration files for TCP/IP and the certificate server
iFolder	Contains configuration files for the iFolder service (covered in Chapter 7)
Java	Java language files
Login	Contains files and software available to clients before logging in to the network
Mail	Contains no files; used for backward-compatibility with earlier versions of NetWare
Ndps	Contains files used with the Novell distributed printing system (covered in Chapter 8)
NetBasic	Contains files needed to run the NetBasic language used with certain Web applications
NetStorage	Contains configuration files and software for the NetStorage service (covered in Chapter 7)
Ni	Contains configuration files and software used by the certificate service security
Novonyx	Contains Web server files for the Novonyx Web server
Nsn	Contains files used by the Web services
Odbc	Contains database and configuration files for the Web services
Perl	Contains programming language software used by the Web services
Public	Contains files and software available to all users after logging in
Pvsw	Contains license file information
Queues	Provides backward-compatibility with legacy NetWare print queues (covered in Chapter 8)
System	Contains files and software used by the NetWare operating system
Tmp	Stores temporary files
Ucs	Contains NetWare modules used by the operating system
Webapps	Contains Web application software for NetStorage, Web Manager, and Web Access
XTier	Contains NetWare Loadable Modules used by the operating system
Zenworks	Contains applications and configuration files for the Z.E.N.works application management system (covered in Chapter 9)

Public   The **Public directory** contains utility programs and files that are available to all users after they have logged in. ConsoleOne and NetWare Administrator, for example, are stored in the Public directory. Appendix C lists several useful command-line utilities that are also in the Public directory.

System   The **System directory** contains NetWare operating system files and utilities that are accessible only to the network administrator. Many of these system files are flagged as Hidden or System to protect them from accidental access. Only the Admin user should be given rights to the System directory to avoid the possibility of users erasing or modifying system files and using commands that affect the file server's functioning. Some network administrators move program files that they do not want users to run, such as NetWare Administrator, from the Public directory to the System directory. This improves security by preventing users from using the utility to browse the eDirectory database.

Other System Directories   In addition to the three major system-created directories, you will also find Etc and Deleted.sav directories on the SYS volume. NetWare 6 creates the Etc directory to store sample files that help configure the server for the TCP/IP network protocol. To help users recover lost files, the Deleted.sav directory is created automatically on each volume; it's the part of NetWare's file recovery system that enables you to recover a file even after the directory containing the file has been deleted. In the section "Working with Network Files," later in this chapter, you get a chance to work with salvaging and purging deleted files.

Suggested Directories

The required directories are created during installation to give the NetWare operating system the areas it needs to perform its functions. In addition to these required directories, however, your organization will need additional directories to organize data and software on the file server. As a CNA, you should be aware of the three basic types of directories that Novell suggests should be part of an organization's file system:

- Application directories
- Shared directories
- User home directories

Application Directories Application directories hold installation files that are needed to install or run software on user workstations. For example, in Chapter 1 you observed how Eric used Novell's Z.E.N.works application service to selectively install and run software on user workstations based on those users' rights. Z.E.N.works requires that certain installation application files be copied to the network file system. As a result, Eric had to create an application directory structure to store the installation files needed to deliver applications using Z.E.N.works. In Chapter 9, you will learn how to use Z.E.N.works to implement applications in your version of the UAS network.

Shared Directories One of the benefits of using a network is access to network files. As a CNA, you will need to establish shared directories so that users can work with common files and documents. Files stored in shared directories are generally available to only one user at a time, so the ability to have a file accessed by multiple users at the same time requires database software that's written to prevent one user's changes from overwriting another user's changes. At first, you might think that storing data on a server makes it less secure. Actually, by implementing proper security, data stored on a server is more secure than on a user's local computer, where someone else could gain access to his or her computer. In Chapter 5, you will learn how to use file system security to ensure that only authorized users have access to network data.

User Home Directories Each user will need his or her own home directory for storing files and documents. When planning your disk storage needs, you should allow space for all users to store personal projects and files. Generally, users are not given access to files in other users' home directories; instead, files needed by multiple users should be stored in separate, shared directory areas. In the following activity, you use ConsoleOne to view directory information, and then move on to design and create the file system structure for your version of the UAS network.

Activity 3-3: Using ConsoleOne to View Directory Information

Time Required: 10 minutes

Objective: Identify important NetWare-created directories and describe their purpose.

Description: In this activity, you use ConsoleOne to display information about the SYS volume directories on your classroom server.

1. Log in with your assigned ##Admin user name.

2. Start ConsoleOne, and expand the **UAS_Tree** object.

3. Expand your **##UAS** Organization.

4. Click your **UASHOST_SYS** volume to display directories in the Object frame.

5. Record information on your student answer sheet about the Public directory:

    a. Right-click the **Public** directory, and then click **Properties** to open the Properties of PUBLIC dialog box.

    b. Click the **Facts** tab and record the information requested on your student answer sheet.

    c. Click the **Trustees** tab and record the users who have rights to this directory.

6. Follow the procedure in Step 5 to record information about the System directory on your student answer sheet.

7. Follow the procedure in Step 5 to record information about the Login directory on your student answer sheet.

8. Exit ConsoleOne, and log out.

ESTABLISHING THE UNIVERSAL AEROSPACE DIRECTORY STRUCTURE

Now that you know the components used in a network file system, the next step is to design and implement a directory structure that meets the file-processing needs of the Universal AeroSpace Corporation. Designing the directory structure involves identifying the directories and subdirectories you will need and deciding where these directories will be placed in the structure. To implement the directory structure, you use utilities such as ConsoleOne and NetWare Administrator to create and manage the directories and files. Before you can begin, you need to analyze the processing needs of users in the organization to determine what directories will be needed. After you have defined the directories that are needed, you can then design a directory structure in a logical, organized fashion.

When designing a directory structure, you should be aware that not all network administrators agree on a best method; instead, network administrators develop their own styles and preferences for how they like to define and arrange directories. In the following sections, you learn how Eric applied the concepts of file system design to UAS and see how to implement the design by using ConsoleOne.

Defining Processing Needs

In many ways, designing a file system is similar to creating a blueprint for a building. Just as the blueprint helps the builder determine the construction details and materials needed, the design of the file system structure helps the network administrator allocate storage space and implement the file system on a network. The first step in designing a file system structure is to determine the storage requirements for the file services that the network will be providing to your users. To do this, Eric spent time meeting with users and administrative assistants in each department. After analyzing this information, he was able to summarize the processing needs for Universal AeroSpace, described in Figure 3-17.

All Users

All Universal AeroSpace users will require a home directory to store temporary files, files related to a project with which they are working, and document or spreadsheet files for which only they are responsible. All users will also need access to shared directories that they can use to exchange files with other users in the corporation. The organization has established a standard set of word processing forms for a variety of uses, including purchase orders, outside correspondence, and internal memos. These standard forms and templates need to be easily accessible by all users.

All Universal AeroSpace users will need access to Microsoft Office software. As a result, the installation and program files for Microsoft Office and Windows need to be placed in directories available to all workstations. In addition, a temporary directory should also be reserved for storage of temporary files created by certain applications.

Currently, Universal AeroSpace is hiring an Internet service provider to publish the corporation's Web site information. Kellie Thiele is responsible for the Web site and currently has all files on her computer. The Web site files should be moved from Kellie's computer and placed on the CORP volume. In the future, this will facilitate Eric's plans to move the Web site to Universal AeroSpace's own Web server.

Universal AeroSpace is replacing its old inventory system with a Windows-based package that allows shared access by users throughout the company. Terry Blackwell is currently responsible for auditing the inventory database, adding new parts, and making weekly inventory reports for the Marketing and Manufacturing departments. The new inventory package will enable the users in the Shipping and Receiving areas to enter data as well as allow the Marketing department to enter new orders and track production.

Engineering and Manufacturing

The CAD application software used by the Engineering department is installed on each workstation, but the CAD drawing files for the two NASA projects and the current aircraft design projects for Boeing need to be shared by multiple users and should be stored in separate directories on the network. The Engineering department also plans to use the network to pass CAD files between workstations as well as provide shared access to document and spreadsheet files. In addition, some drawing files need to be made available for the Desktop Publishing department to use when creating instruction manuals. At this time, the file system for Engineering will be stored on the CORP volume. However, in the near future, Eric wants to install a separate Engineering server and move all Engineering and Manufacturing data from the CORP volume to the Engineering server.

The Manufacturing department plans to install a network-based requirements planning system (RPS) to plan raw material purchases based on projected shipments. Russ Pence will be responsible for maintaining the system, but Kari Means in Engineering, as well as the users in the Marketing department, will need to be able to update the RPS database with sales projections and new requirements based on product design.

As the network administrator, you will need a work area to store software and other files with which you are working. In addition, you have several software utilities that you would like to place on the network so that you can access them from any client computer.

Figure 3-17   Universal AeroSpace processing needs

Generally, storage areas or directories can be divided into five different types: system, software package, application, shared data, and private data. Table 3-4 contains the Storage Requirements Form that Eric used to document the storage areas needed to support processing for the departments at Universal AeroSpace.

Eric identified shared work directories for each department in addition to a shared directory for the entire company. Although it would be possible to get along with only one shared directory for the entire company, multiple directories help keep the files separate, making it easier for users to find the files they need. Having separate directories also provides additional security; users in the Engineering department, for example, will not have access to budget files or other information that does not affect them.

3

Table 3-4   Universal AeroSpace Storage Requirements Form

Storage Requirements Form				
Created by: Eric Kenton				
Date:				
Organization: Universal AeroSpace				

Workgroups:

Workgroup Name	Members
Admin	David Heise, Lynn Dai, Maria Frias
Accounting	Terry Blackwell, George Perez, Amy Pan
Marketing	Laura Hiller, Michael Horowitz, Darrell Minick
Desktop Publishing	Diana Brady, Julie Damrau
Engineering	Kari Means, Lianne Jarka, Tony Rucci, Paul Alm, Bradley Dahl
Manufacturing (Mfg)	Russ Pence, Receiving station, Shipping station
Information Systems (IS)	Kellie Thiele, You, Luke McMann, Eric Kenton

Directories:

Directory Description	Type	Users	Capacity	Directory Name
Home directory for each user	Private data	All staff	.5 GB each = 10 GB	(User login name)
General word-processing (WP) forms and templates	Shared WP data	All users	500 MB	Forms
Shared documents	Shared data	All users	1 GB	Shared
Windows applications	Master software for installation	All users	3 GB	Apps
Inventory system	Vertical application package	Business, Marketing, and Engineering	1 GB	Inventry
Engineering	Software and files	Engineering	18 GB	Engineer
Engineering shared data	Shared documents and drawings	Engineering and Mfg	5 GB	Shared
Information Systems	Software and files	IS	2 GB	IS
Utilities	Software utilities	IS	500 MB	Utility
NASA ISS project	Shared CAD drawings	Engineering	5 GB	ISS
NASA Rover project	Shared CAD drawings	Engineering	5 GB	Rover
Aircraft	Shared CAD drawings	Engineering	5 GB	Aircraft
Web	Web site files	Kellie Thiele and Julie Damrau	1 GB	Web
CAD software	Installation files	Engineering	1 GB	CAD
RPS	Requirements planning software	Russ Pence and Kari Means	1 GB	RPS
Temporary	Temporary files needed by certain applications	All users	1 GB	Temp
Desktop themes	Shared Windows data	All users	1 GB	Desktop
Department shared directories	Shared files for each department	All department users	5 GB each	Shared
Management data	User home directories and data for Mgmt department	Mgmt department users	10 GB	Mgmt
Manufacturing data	Directory structure for Mfg shared data	Mfg and Engineering departments	10 GB	Mfg Data

Designing the Structure

After Eric determined what directories would be needed, his next step was to identify disk volumes and then design the layout of the directories within the network volumes. To avoid filling up the SYS volume and causing system problems, you should generally plan to place user data and applications on separate volumes. The SYS volume should be used only for NetWare operating system files. Many network administrators prefer to use at least two volumes in their network's file structure. When using multiple volumes, a network administrator usually reserves the SYS volume on each server for operating system files and possibly third-party software, such as virus detection and recovery utilities. In addition to the SYS volume, one or more volumes are defined to store the organization's data files, print queues, and applications. By placing the organization's data files and applications on separate volumes, the administrator can ensure that free space is always available on the SYS volume for NetWare's use. As a network administrator, you should use the following guidelines suggested by Novell for planning NetWare volume usage:

- Reserve the SYS volume for NetWare operating system files.

- Create one or more additional volumes for application and data files.

- Consider placing files from workstations that support special name formats, such as Macintosh or Unix, on separate volumes.

Like many other network administrators, Eric decided to separate the SYS volume from the organization's data storage by creating separate volumes for company data. Having separate volumes for company data ensures adequate free space on the SYS volume for system functions. Separate volumes also make it possible to perform maintenance and backup activities on the company data without taking the SYS volume offline, which is important because taking this volume offline prevents access to necessary system software and makes the server unavailable for network use.

Because Kellie works with many fairly short program files and subroutines, Eric has decided to create a traditional volume named SOURCE for her software so that he can use small block sizes and take advantage of block suballocation (described previously in the section "Traditional Volumes"). To help him define the company data volumes, Eric created the Volume Design Form, shown in Figure 3-18, which identifies the type of volume to be created and the volume's name, size, and attributes. For example, NSS volumes require the storage pool name as well as volume attributes, such as Backup, Compression, and Data Shredding.

When documenting the directory structure for a data volume, it is often difficult to draw all directories and subdirectories on one sheet of paper. To help document the Universal AeroSpace directory structure for the CORP volume, Eric used two different design forms. As shown in Figure 3-18, a Volume Design Form is used to document all directories under the root of the volume as well as directories containing only a few subdirectories. In addition to showing the volume's first level of directories, this form contains fields for NSS features and maximum capacity; this information will be important when you create the volumes during the installation process. You might also want to show subdirectories for directories that contain a simple structure. Eric placed all directories that contain files shared by multiple departments, such as Forms and Apps, under the root of the CORP volume. The Engineer, IS, and Mgmt departmental directories will be used to store user home directories as well as files and applications unique to each department.

For more complex directory structures, such as those for the Business, Marketing, Desktop Publishing, and Engineering departments, Eric used a Directory Design Form to show all subdirectories within that directory structure. Figure 3-19 shows the Directory Design Form that Eric developed for the Engineer directory structure.

Volume Design Form

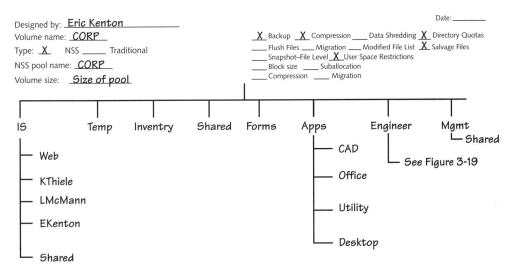

Figure 3-18 The Volume Design Form

Directory Design Form

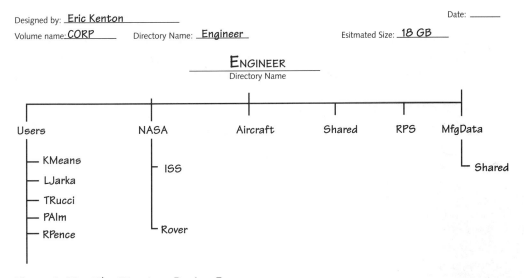

Figure 3-19 The Directory Design Form

The directory structure Eric used is referred to as a departmental structure because the user home directories, shared work directories, and applications are located within the workgroups of the departments that control them. Directories that contain files available to all users, such as Forms and Inventry, are located at the root of the volume. Shared directories are located within each department's directory to provide separate shared file access for all users in the department. The Shared directory off the root of the CORP volume is available so that users in all departments can exchange files or work on common projects. For example, the Engineering department can use the CORP:Shared directory to save drawing files that the Desktop Publishing and Marketing people will need to prepare documentation and presentations.

Another way to organize directories on a volume is by application rather than department. Figure 3-20 shows an example of how the directories for Universal AeroSpace might be organized in an application-oriented structure.

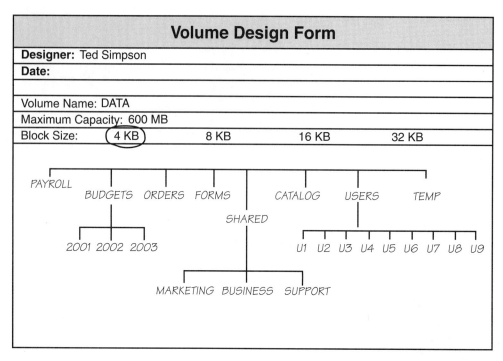

Figure 3-20   An application-oriented directory structure

Notice that in an application-oriented structure, all user home directories are placed under a common directory called Users. The shared directories can then be grouped according to their use, and applications can be placed in separate directories located under the [Root] of the volume. The advantage of an application-oriented structure is that it's fairly shallow, making it easier to locate files without going through multiple layers of directories. In larger directory structures, the shallow nature of the application-oriented structure can actually be a disadvantage, however, making it difficult to know which departments use which directories.

The organizational method you select for a directory structure depends on personal preference as well as the organization's size and type of processing. Generally, small network file systems are easier to organize with an application-oriented structure, as it keeps the design simple and easy to use. With large file systems that have several workgroups and many data directories, it's often easier to maintain security and locate data when you use a departmental structure. In some cases, you might find that a combination of both methods works best for your situation. No matter what design method you use, a good rule of thumb is not to exceed three subdirectory layers, with no more than 20 subdirectories in any one directory (this makes it easier for you to view all directories on the screen at the same time).

Implementing the Directory Structure

After the storage needs for the network file system were defined, the next step Eric took to establish the network file system was to create the NSS CORP volume. Because NSS volumes exist within storage pools, creating the NSS CORP volume involved three steps: creating a new disk partition, assigning the partition to a new storage pool, and creating the NSS volume. In the next sections, you'll see how Eric created the necessary NSS file system objects.

To create a traditional volume named SOURCE for Kellie's software, Eric used the following procedure:

1. Because creating a volume requires the Supervisor right to the server where the volume is being created, Eric logged into the network with the Admin user name and password.

2. Next, he started ConsoleOne and expanded the UAS_Tree and UAS Organization.

3. He right-clicked the UASHOST server and clicked Properties to open the Properties of UASHOST dialog box.

4. Eric clicked the down arrow on the Media tab and clicked the Traditional Volumes option to open the Traditional Volumes dialog box (see Figure 3-21).

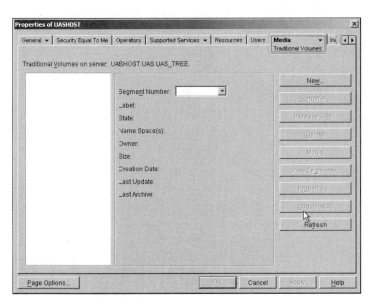

Figure 3-21   The Create a New Pool Wizard
In NetWare 6.5, storage management services are performed using either iManager or NSSMU as described in Appendix D.

5. To create a new volume, he clicked the New button to start the Create a New Traditional Volume Wizard.

6. He entered the name SOURCE in the Name text box and clicked Next to display the available unpartitioned space.

7. He clicked on an available partition and entered the maximum size in the Used column, as shown in Figure 3-22.

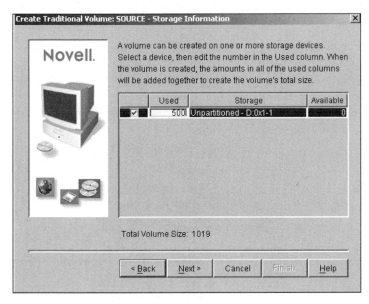

Figure 3-22   Viewing existing storage partitions in the Storage Information window
In NetWare 6.5, storage management services are performed using either iManager or NSSMU as described in Appendix D.

8. After verifying the size and partition information, Eric clicked Next to display the Traditional Volume Attribute dialog box.

9. He clicked the Block Size list arrow to select a block size of 32 KB, and then clicked Finish to create and mount the SOURCE volume.

10. He responded by clicking Yes to the message box asking if he wanted to create the partition for the volume with Hot Fix and Mirroring options enabled.

11. After creating the traditional partition and SOURCE volume, Eric returned to the Properties of UASHOST dialog box.

12. He clicked Cancel to close the Properties of UASHOST dialog box and return to ConsoleOne, exited ConsoleOne, and logged out.

Creating the CORP Partition

In previous versions of NetWare, partitions were created and maintained from the server console with the NWCONFIG utility. In NetWare 6, file system components are managed by using ConsoleOne or NetWare Remote Manager. Along with iManager, NetWare Remote Manager is one of Novell's new Web browser utilities that complies with Novell's OneNet vision of making network management possible from any networked computer. Although iManager enables you to manage the eDirectory tree and other services, NetWare Remote Manager is used to manage the server computer and file system. The following steps illustrate how Eric created the CORP partition in ConsoleOne. If you like, you can follow along on your computer, but keep in mind that certain screens or options will not be available if you aren't logged in as the eDirectory tree administrator.

1. Eric logged in to the network using the Admin user name and started ConsoleOne.

2. In the ConsoleOne Navigation frame, Eric expanded the UAS Organization.

3. Because partitions are part of the NetWare server, not separate objects in the eDirectory tree, Eric right-clicked the UASHOST server object, and then clicked Properties to open the Properties of UASHOST dialog box.

4. He then clicked the down arrow on the Media tab and clicked the Partitions option.

5. To create a new partition, Eric clicked the New button to open the Create a new NSS partition dialog box (shown previously in Figure 3-3).

6. Eric entered the size of the partition and accepted the default options of Hot Fix and Create New Mirror Group. When creating a mirrored partition on the second drive, Eric will change the default option by clicking the Existing Mirror Group radio button and then identifying the partition created in this dialog box. Entering a name in the Label text box is optional but can be helpful in locating a particular partition. You need to remember the name assigned to the partition to select it when creating or adding to a storage pool.

7. After entering the necessary data, Eric clicked OK to create the new partition and return to the Media Partitions tab.

8. After clicking the new partition and verifying that it was successfully entered in the Partitions text box, Eric clicked Cancel to return to the ConsoleOne window.

Creating a Storage Pool

Like partitions, in NetWare 6 you can create and manage storage pools by using ConsoleOne from a local computer or NetWare Remote Manager from a browser. The following list shows the steps Eric used in ConsoleOne to create the CORP storage pool on the UASHOST server. If you like, you can follow along on your computer, but keep in mind that certain screens or options will not be available if you are not logged in as the eDirectory tree administrator.

1. To create a storage pool for the CORP data, Eric first logged in to the UAS_Tree as the Admin user, and then started the ConsoleOne utility.

2. He then used the Navigation frame to expand the UAS container, right-clicked the UASHOST server object, and clicked Properties.

3. In the Properties of UASHOST dialog box, he clicked the down arrow on the Media tab and then clicked the NSS Pools option.

4. To create a new storage pool for the CORP volume, Eric clicked the New button to start the Create a New Pool Wizard, shown in Figure 3-23.

5. Eric entered the name CORP and then clicked the Next button to display the Storage Information window (see Figure 3-24), which shows the existing storage partitions along with their available space and identification.

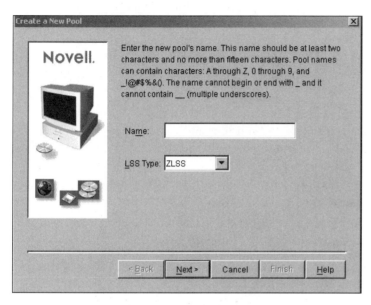

Figure 3-23   The Create a New Pool Wizard
In NetWare 6.5, storage management services are performed using either iManager or NSSMU as described in Appendix D.

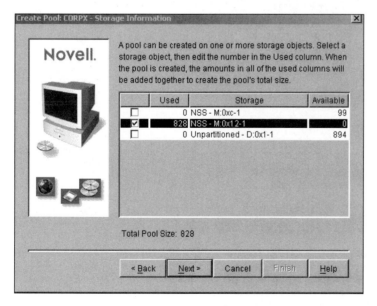

Figure 3-24   Viewing existing storage partitions in the Storage Information window
In NetWare 6.5, storage management services are performed using either iManager or NSSMU as described in Appendix D.

6. Eric clicked to place a check mark in the NSS - M:0x12-1 partition, and then clicked Next to display a summary window.

7. Eric clicked Finish to create the CORP storage pool, using the default option to Activate on Creation.

8. After Eric verified that the new CORP storage pool appeared along with the SYS pool in the Media NSS Pools tab, he clicked Cancel to return to the ConsoleOne window.

Creating an NSS Volume

Before establishing the UAS directory structure, Eric needed to create a volume in the CORP storage pool. By default, when you create a volume, a corresponding volume object is created in the same container as the server. To make accessing and managing volumes more convenient, Eric also created volume objects in other OUs. The following list shows the steps Eric took in ConsoleOne to create a logical NSS volume (the CORP volume) on the UASHOST server. If you like, you can follow along on your computer, but keep in mind that certain screens or options will not be available if you are not logged in as the eDirectory tree administrator. In Activity 3-4, you use ConsoleOne to create volume objects in your ##UAS Organization that point to the logical volumes created on the server.

1. After logging in to the UAS_Tree as the Admin user and starting ConsoleOne, Eric expanded the UAS container in the Navigation frame, right-clicked the UASHOST server, and then clicked Properties.

2. He then clicked the down arrow on the Media tab and clicked the NSS Logical Volumes option.

3. To create a new volume, he clicked the New button to start the Create a New Logical Volume Wizard.

4. He entered CORP in the Name text box and clicked Next to open a Storage Information window (see Figure 3-25) that lists the existing storage pools.

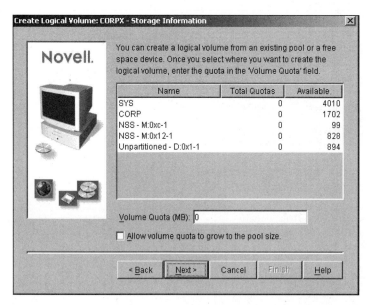

Figure 3-25 Viewing existing storage pools in the Storage Information window
In NetWare 6.5, storage management services are performed using either iManager or NSSMU as described in Appendix D.

5. After selecting the CORP storage pool, Eric clicked the Allow volume quota to grow to the pool size check box. To create multiple volumes in the pool, he could use the Volume Quota (MB) text box to set a limit for the volume.

As described earlier in this chapter, although a single volume's quota cannot exceed the size of the storage pool, when creating multiple volumes in a pool, overbooking allows the sum of all volume quotas to be larger than the pool size.

6. After entering the volume storage information, Eric clicked Next to display the Attribute Information window, similar to the one shown in Figure 3-26.

7. In addition to the default Backup and Salvage Files options, Eric clicked the Directory Quotas and User Space Restrictions check boxes to allow him to restrict directory sizes to the capacities he allotted in Table 3-4.

8. After selecting the options he needed, Eric clicked Finish to create the volume.

9. After verifying that the volume was created, Eric clicked Cancel to return to the ConsoleOne window.

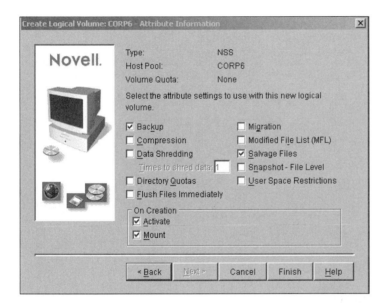

Figure 3-26 Restricting directory size in the Attribute Information window
In NetWare 6.5, storage management services are performed using either iManager or NSSMU as described in Appendix D.

 ## Activity 3-4: Creating Volume Objects

Time Required: 15 minutes

Objective: Use ConsoleOne to create volume objects in the NetWare file system.

Description: Although a volume object is automatically added to the same container as the server when the data volume is initially created, to make accessing and managing data more convenient from other OUs, Eric has adopted the policy of creating volume objects in each container. In this activity, you use ConsoleOne to create SYS and CORP volume objects in the Engineering, IS, and Mgmt OUs.

1. Log in with your assigned ##Admin user name.

2. Start ConsoleOne, expand **UAS_Tree**, and then expand your **##UAS** Organization.

3. To create a CORP volume in your ##UAS Organization, follow these steps:

   a. Right-click your **##UAS** Organization, point to **New**, and click **Object** to open the New Object dialog box.

   b. In the Class of new object list box, scroll down the **Volume** object, and then click **OK** to open the New Volume dialog box.

   c. In the Name text box, enter **UASHOST_CORP**.

    d. Click the **Browse** button to the right of the Host server text box, and then click the **up arrow** to display the Organizations.

    e. Double-click the **UAS** Organization, click the **UASHOST** server object, and then click **OK** to return to the New Volume dialog box with UASHOST.UAS in the Host server text box.

    f. Click the **Physical Volume** list arrow, and then click your **##CORP** volume object in the list of options.

    g. Click **OK** to create the new volume and return to the ConsoleOne window.

4. Follow the procedure in Step 3 to create a CORP volume object in your IS container.

5. Follow the procedure in Step 3 to create a CORP volume object in your Engineering container.

6. Follow the procedure in Step 3 to create a CORP volume object in your Mgmt container.

7. To create a CORP volume object in your Mfg container, follow these steps:

    a. Expand your **Engineering** container.

    b. Right-click your **Mfg** container, point to **New**, and click **Object**.

    c. In the Class of new object list box, scroll down and double-click the **Volume** object to open the New Volume dialog box.

    d. In the Name text box, enter **UASHOST_CORP**.

    e. Click the **Browse** button to the right of the Host server text box, and then click the **up arrow** three times to display the Organizations.

    f. Double-click the **UAS** Organization, click the **UASHOST** server object, and then click **OK** to return to the New Volume dialog box with UASHOST.UAS in the Host server text box.

    g. Click the **Physical Volume** list arrow, and then click your **##CORP** volume object in the list of options.

    h. Click **OK** to create the new volume and return to the ConsoleOne window.

8. Exit ConsoleOne and log out.

Creating the Directory Structure

You can create the network directory structure from Windows by using My Computer or Windows Explorer, just as on a local hard drive. You can also use Novell's ConsoleOne or Remote Manager utility to create and work with the network directory structure. When working from a local network with ConsoleOne, it's often more convenient to use it to perform network file system activities instead of flipping to another screen or utility. If you are working from a remote location, Novell's NetWare Remote Manager utility conforms to the OneNet vision by allowing you to manage the file system from a Web browser. As a result, to become a CNA, Novell requires you to know how to perform file system functions from ConsoleOne or Remote Manager. In Activities 3-5 and 3-6, you learn how to use ConsoleOne and Remote Manager to create the UAS directory structure shown previously in Figures 3-18 and 3-19. In Activity 3-7, you learn how to limit the amount of disk space a directory should occupy, as specified in Table 3-1.

Activity 3-5: Creating Directories with ConsoleOne

Time Required: 15 minutes

Objective: Use ConsoleOne to work with files and directories in the NetWare file system.

Description: Now that the volume objects have been created, you can use them to set up the file system structure. Although you can create directories and files from the DOS prompt or from Windows Explorer, it's often more convenient to work with the file system structure from the eDirectory tree by using ConsoleOne, NetWare Administrator, or Remote Manager. In this activity, you use ConsoleOne to build and work with the file system structure shown previously in Figures 3-18 and 3-19.

3

1. If necessary, start your computer, and log in with your assigned ##Admin user name.

2. Start ConsoleOne by double-clicking your desktop shortcut.

3. Expand **UAS_Tree**, and then expand your **##UAS** Organization container.

4. Open your UASHOST_CORP volume objects by clicking the **UASHOST_CORP** object name.

5. To create the main directories shown in Figure 3-18, follow these steps:

    a. Press **Insert** or right-click the volume object, point to **New**, and then click **Object** to open the New Object dialog box.

    b. If necessary, click the **Directory** object to select it, and then click **OK** to open the New Directory dialog box.

    c. Enter **IS** in the Name text box.

    d. To speed up creating the remaining directories, click the **Create another Directory** check box, and then click **OK** to create the IS directory. The IS directory should now appear in the browse window, and the New Directory dialog box will reopen.

    e. Enter **Temp** in the Name text box, and then click **OK** to create the Temp directory.

    f. Enter **Inventry** in the Name text box, and then click **OK** to create the Inventry directory.

    g. Enter **Shared** in the Name text box, and then click **OK** to create the Shared directory.

    h. Enter **Forms** in the Name text box, and then click **OK** to create the Forms directory.

    i. Enter **Apps** in the Name text box, and then click **OK** to create the Apps directory.

    j. Enter **Engineer** in the Name text box, and then click **OK** to create the Engineer directory.

    k. Enter **Mgmt** in the Name text box, and then click **OK** to create the Mgmt directory.

    l. Click **Cancel** to close the New Directory dialog box.

6. To create the subdirectories of Apps, follow these steps:

    a. Click the Apps directory, click the **New Object** button on the ConsoleOne toolbar, and then double-click the **Directory** object in the New Object dialog box to open the New Directory dialog box.

    b. In the New Directory dialog box, enter **CAD** in the Name text box, click the **Create another Directory** check box, and then click **OK** to create the CAD directory and reopen the New Directory dialog box.

    c. Enter **Office** in the Name text box, and then click **OK** to create the Office directory and reopen the New Directory dialog box.

    d. Enter **Utility** in the Name text box, and then click **OK** to create the Utility directory and reopen the New Directory dialog box.

    e. Enter **Desktop** in the Name text box, and then click **OK** to create the Desktop directory and reopen the New Directory dialog box.

    f. Click **Cancel** to return to the ConsoleOne window.

7. To create the subdirectories of IS, follow these steps:

    a. Click the **IS** directory, click the **New Object** button, and then double-click the **Directory** object in the New Object dialog box.

    b. Enter **Web** in the Name text box, click the **Create another Directory** check box, and then click **OK** to create the Web subdirectory.

    c. Enter **Shared** in the Name text box, and then click **OK** to create the Shared subdirectory.

    d. Click **Cancel** to return to the ConsoleOne window.

8. To create the Mgmt\Shared subdirectory, follow these steps:

   a. Click the **Mgmt** subdirectory, and then click the **New Object** button on the ConsoleOne toolbar to open the New Object dialog box.

   b. Verify that Directory is selected in the list of objects, and then click **OK** to open the New Directory dialog box.

   c. Enter **Shared** in the Name text box.

   d. Click **OK** to create the Shared subdirectory and return to ConsoleOne.

9. To create the subdirectory structure for the Engineer directory, as shown in Figure 3-19, follow these steps:

   a. Click the **Engineer** directory, click the **New Object** button, and then double-click the **Directory** object to open the New Directory dialog box.

   b. In the New Directory dialog box, enter the directory name **Users** in the Name text box, click the **Create another Directory** check box, and then click **OK** to create the Users directory and reopen the New Directory dialog box.

   c. Enter **NASA** in the Name text box, and then click **OK** to create the NASA directory and reopen the New Directory dialog box.

   d. Enter **Aircraft** in the Name text box, and then click **OK** to create the Aircraft directory and reopen the New Directory dialog box.

   e. Enter **Shared** in the Name text box, and then click **OK** to create the Shared directory and reopen the New Directory dialog box.

   f. Enter **RPS** in the Name text box, and then click **OK** to create the RPS directory and reopen the New Directory dialog box.

   g. Enter **MfgData** in the Name text box, and then click **OK** to create the MfgData directory and reopen the New Directory dialog box.

   h. Click **Cancel** to return to the ConsoleOne window.

10. To create a subdirectory named Shared in the MfgData subdirectory, follow these steps:

   a. If necessary, expand the **Engineer** directory.

   b. Click **MfgData** subdirectory, and then click the **New Object** button to open the New Object dialog box.

   c. Verify that Directory is selected in the list of objects, and then click **OK** to open the New Directory dialog box.

   d. Enter **Shared** in the Name text box, and then click **OK** to create the Shared subdirectory and return to ConsoleOne.

11. Expand all your directories. As shown in Figure 3-27, your ConsoleOne window should contain the directory structure shown in Figures 3-18 and 3-19 except for the NASA subdirectories. In the next activity, you learn how to use the Remote Manager utility to create the ISS and Rover subdirectories.

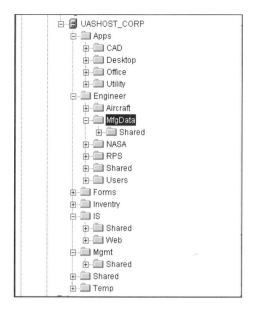

Figure 3-27   Viewing your directory structure in ConsoleOne

12. Exit ConsoleOne, and log out.

Activity 3-6: Creating Directories with Remote Manager

Time Required: 10 minutes

Objective: Use Remote Manager to work with directories in the NetWare file system.

Description: In this activity, you use Remote Manager to create the ISS and Rover subdirectories from your network browser. In Chapter 10, you will learn how to use Remote Manager to manage other server processes.

1. If necessary, start your computer to obtain the Novell Login window. To simulate being at home without Novell Client, when you see the Novell Login window, click the **Workstation only** check box, and then log on to your local computer using your Windows user name and password.

2. Start your Web browser software.

3. Enter the following URL for your server, replacing *ip_address* with the IP address of your assigned server: **https://ip_address:2200**.

4. If you see a security alert message box, click **OK** to proceed.

5. To maintain secure encrypted communications, Remote Manager uses the Novell Certificate Service to obtain a security certificate. If your browser does not have the Novell certificate server in its list of trusted certificates, you will see another security alert message box informing you that the certificate is from an untrusted company.

    a. Click the **View Certificate** button, and then click the **Details** tab to view the certificate information and verify that it is from the UAS_Tree.

    b. Record the requested certificate details on your student answer sheet.

    c. Click **OK** to return to the security alert message box.

6. Click **Yes** to open the NetWare Web Manager dialog box.

7. To start Remote Manager, click your **UASHOST** server name beneath the NetWare Remote Manager title.

8. If you see another security alert message box informing you that you are about to view pages over a secure connection, click **Yes** and then **OK**. The Enter Network Password dialog box then opens.

9. In the Enter Network Password dialog box, enter the typeless distinguished name of your ##Admin user (for example, on the classroom server use either .##Admin.##UAS, or .##Admin.##UAS.CLASS depending on the tree structure in use) replacing the ## with your assigned student number. Enter your password, and then click **OK** to log in and open the Remote Manager window, similar to the one shown in Figure 3-28.

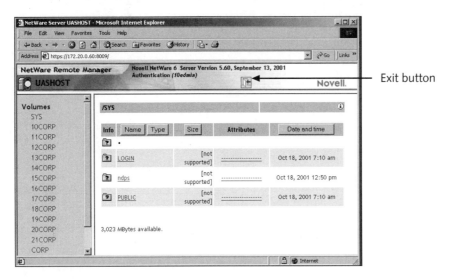

Figure 3-28   The NetWare Remote Manager dialog box

10. Click your **##CORP** volume (## represents your assigned student number) in the Volumes list to display your existing file system structure.

11. Click your **Engineer** directory to display its subdirectory structure.

12. If necessary, scroll down and click your **NASA** subdirectory.

13. Follow these steps to create the ISS subdirectory:

a. Click the folder icon to the left of the . name to display a /##CORP/Engineer/NASA window in the right-hand pane showing information about your NASA directory, as shown in Figure 3-29.

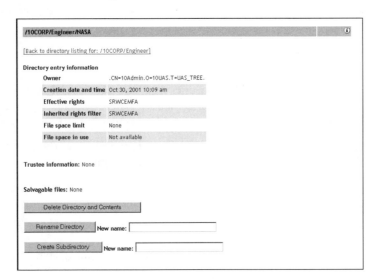

Figure 3-29   Creating a subdirectory in Remote Manager

b. At the bottom of the window, enter **ISS** in the New name text box to the right of the Create Subdirectory button.

c. Click the **Create Subdirectory** button to create the ISS subdirectory within your NASA directory and return to the /##CORP/Engineer/NASA directory pane.

14. Repeat Step 13 to create the Rover subdirectory.

15. Exit Remote Manger by clicking the **Exit** button located on the toolbar.

16. Click **Yes** to close your Web browser window.

17. Log off Windows.

Activity 3-7: Setting Directory Space Limitations

Time Required: 15 minutes

Objective: Use ConsoleOne to work with files and directories in the NetWare file system.

Description: During his analysis, Eric determined a starting directory size for each of the directories (refer back to the Storage Requirements Form in Table 3-4). To be sure that no one directory structure grows at the expense of other directory needs, you need to use NetWare's capability of limiting directory sizes. With NetWare, you can place limitations on the amount of volume space a directory and its files can occupy by using ConsoleOne, NetWare Administrator, or Remote Manager. In this activity, you learn how to use ConsoleOne to place the recommended size limits on each of the main directories you have created.

To save changes to directory size restrictions, you need to log in with a user name that has the Supervisor right to the UASHOST server.

1. If necessary, start your computer, and log in with a user name that has the Supervisor right to the UASHOST server.

2. Start ConsoleOne, and expand both **UAS_Tree** and your **##UAS** Organization.

3. Click your **UASHOST_CORP** volume to display your directories in the Object frame.

4. Right-click the **Forms** directory, and then click **Properties** to open the Properties of Forms dialog box.

5. Click the **Facts** tab.

6. Click the **Restrict size** check box, and then enter **5000** in the KB text box.

7. Click **OK** to save your directory space restriction.

8. Repeat Steps 4–7 to set the following directory size restrictions shown previously in Table 3-4:
   - 1 GB for the UASHOST_CORP: Shared directory
   - 3 GB for the UASHOST_CORP: Apps directory structure
   - 18 GB for the UASHOST_CORP: Engineer directory structure

9. If you're continuing to the next activity, you can stay logged in and leave ConsoleOne open; if not, exit ConsoleOne, and log out.

Working with Network Files

Files are used to store data in the network file system in much the same way they are used to store data and software on your local disk drives. Planning the location of files on network volumes is an essential part of organizing the file system. Although files can exist on the root of a volume, placing them in directories and subdirectories results in a more organized file system; this placement also increases file system security, as described in Chapter 5.

NetWare stores information about each file in the **directory entry table (DET)** located at the beginning of each volume. In addition to the file's name and storage location, NetWare includes such information as owner, size, creation dates, access dates, trustee assignments, and attributes. By default, the file owner is the user who creates the file. By keeping track of file owner and size information, NetWare enables the network administrator to limit disk space usage on a user-by-user basis. Network administrators also need creation and access dates to perform functions such as listing files that have not been accessed for a specified time period.

As described earlier in the chapter, one of the strengths of NetWare's file system is its ability to reliably recover files even after they have been deleted for a long time. When a file is deleted, NetWare does not overwrite its space until the space from all previously deleted files has been reused. Deleted files remain in the parent directory they were deleted from and can be salvaged from their parent directory. As a result, a user can often recover deleted files from the parent directory many months after the file has been deleted. Even if the entire directory structure that contained the file is deleted, the network administrator can still recover the deleted files from Deleted.sav.

 Standard users do not have rights to salvage files from the Deleted.sav directory. Only the network administrator has this right by default.

For security reasons or for operating system efficiency, however, sometimes you want to give deleted file space back to the operating system immediately for reuse—a process called purging files. When files are purged, NetWare reclaims their space and they can no longer be recovered. As a result, purging deleted files can be important for security purposes because it prevents the deleted files from being salvaged. If purged files exist on an NSS volume and the Data Shredding attribute is enabled, purged files will be overwritten with random patterns of characters to help ensure that the deleted data cannot be accessed or viewed. Another advantage of purging files is to make space immediately available to the NetWare server to reuse. This not only increases NetWare's efficiency, but also prevents other possibly valuable files from being reused as quickly. For example, Kellie recently installed a software package in the Apps directory of the UAS network and then decided to delete the software directory and place it on her local computer. Purging files in the Apps directory will make any disk space used by the application files immediately available for other purposes.

Although you can use NetWare Administrator to purge and salvage files, the easiest way to perform these functions is directly from Windows. For example, users can purge or salvage files in their directories by using My Computer or My Network Places to browse the network file system, right-click the directory, and then use the Salvage or Purge file option on the selected directory. When working with the network file system in Windows, it is often convenient to map a drive letter to the NetWare volume you will be accessing. Mapping a drive letter to each volume you use makes accessing network data faster than having to browse to the volume using My Network Places. By default, drive letter F: is usually mapped to the SYS volume when you log in to the network. Drive mappings to other volumes need to be mapped manually or through a login script. In the following activities, you use Windows to map a drive letter to your ##CORP volume. Later in this chapter, you'll learn how to plan drive mappings that meet the needs of your network users. In Chapter 7, you will learn how to use login scripts to automatically map drive letters to the necessary volumes when users log in. The following activities give you practice with moving directories, copying files, uploading files, and salvaging and purging deleted files.

 ## Activity 3-8: Moving a Directory Structure

Time Required: 10 minutes

Objective: Use ConsoleOne to work with files and directories in the NetWare file system.

Description: When implementing a directory structure, it's often useful to be able to move a directory along with all its files and subdirectories to another location in the volume. For example, when you created a user account for yourself in Chapter 2, the user home directory was placed in the SYS volume. To correspond to the directory structure design, you will need to move your user account's home directory to the IS directory so that it will be with the other IS department user home directories. The data, any subdirectories, and users' rights assignments are also moved to the new location. In this activity, you use ConsoleOne to move your home directory to the IS directory. In Chapter 5, you'll learn how to verify that the user trustee assignments have been moved along with the data.

1. If necessary, start your computer, and log in with your assigned ##Admin user name.

2. If necessary, start ConsoleOne, and expand **UAS_Tree** and your **##UAS** Organization.

3. Open the SYS volume by clicking the **UASHOST_SYS** volume object to display all directories in the Object frame.

4. Double-click the **Students** directory in the Object frame to open it.

5. To move your user home directory to the IS directory, follow these steps:

   a. Right-click your user home directory, and then click **Cut**.

   b. In the Navigation frame, expand your **UASHOST_CORP** volume.

   c. Right-click your **IS** directory, and then click **Paste**. Your user home directory should now appear in the Object frame.

6. If you are continuing to the next activity, leave ConsoleOne open and stay logged in. If not, exit ConsoleOne, and log out.

Activity 3-9: Copying Files with ConsoleOne

Time Required: 10 minutes

Objective: Use ConsoleOne to work with files and directories in the NetWare file system.

Description: After Eric established the directory structure for the Universal AeroSpace CORP volume, he placed some data in the structure so that users could begin to use the system. Lynn requested that standard company forms be available on the new network as soon as possible. In this activity, you use ConsoleOne to copy the company forms from the SYS volume to the Forms directory you created for your version of the UAS network.

1. If necessary, start your computer, and log in with your assigned ##Admin user name.

2. Start ConsoleOne, and expand your **UAS_Tree** and **##UAS** Organization.

3. Expand the **UASHOST_SYS** volume object.

4. Open the WP subdirectory of the Software.cti directory:

   a. Expand the **Software.cti** directory.

   b. Click the **WP** subdirectory to display all the .frm files.

5. Right-click the **Bid.frm** file, and then click **Properties** on the shortcut menu.

6. Click the **Facts** tab to display the file size, owner, and access date information. Try changing any of the information fields. On your student answer sheet, record the owner and creation date information and any facts you can change. Information fields that are grayed out indicate that you cannot change them because you do not have Supervisor rights to the files in the SYS volume. (You will learn more about file system access rights in Chapter 5.)

7. Click the **Cancel** button to return to the ConsoleOne window.

8. Copy all files in the WP subdirectory that have an .frm extension to your Clipboard by following these steps:

   a. Click the first filename with an .frm extension.

   b. Hold down the **Ctrl** key while you click each file with an .frm extension, or hold down the **Shift** key and click the last file to highlight all files.

    c. Right-click the highlighted files, and then click **Copy**.

  9. Paste the files into the Forms directory located under your ##CORP volume:

    a. Expand your **UASHOST_CORP** volume, and click the **Forms** directory to highlight it.

    b. Right-click your **Forms** directory in the Navigation frame, and then click **Paste** to open the Copy Trustees dialog box.

    c. Record the contents of the Copy Trustees dialog box on your student answer sheet.

    d. Click **No** in the Copy Trustees dialog box. A window showing that the files are being copied to the destination is displayed.

  10. Your copied files should now appear in the Object frame.

  11. To check the properties of the Bid.frm file, follow these steps:

    a. Right-click the **Bid.frm** file in your Forms directory, and then click **Properties** on the shortcut menu.

    b. Click the **Facts** tab to display file information. On your student answer sheet, record any facts that you can now change. Being able to change owner information can be important if one user creates a large shared file and you do not want the space that file uses to be accumulated against that user's total disk space allotment.

    c. Click the **Cancel** button to return to the ConsoleOne window.

  12. Exit ConsoleOne, and log out.

Activity 3-10: Uploading Files Using Remote Manager

Time Required: 15 minutes

Objective: Use Remote Manager to work with files and directories in the NetWare file system.

Description: In Activity 3-6, you learned how to use Remote Manager to create directories from your Web browser, but it's also useful for copying files to the network file system from a remote location. In this activity, you use Remote Manager to upload files from your workstation to your CAD directory.

  1. If necessary, start your computer to open the Novell Login window. To simulate being at home without Novell Client, when you see the Novell Login window, click the **Workstation only** check box, and then log on to your local computer using your Windows user name and password.

  2. Start your Web browser software.

  3. Start Remote Manager:

    a. Enter the following URL for your server, replacing *ip_address* with the IP address of your assigned server: **https://ip_address:2200**.

As a shortcut, you can use the list arrow to the right of the Address text box to select this address, which you used in Activity 3-6.

    b. When you see the security alert message boxes, click **OK** or **Yes** to proceed and open the NetWare Web Manager dialog box.

    c. To start Remote Manager, click your **UASHOST** server name under the NetWare Remote Manager title.

    d. If you see any security alert message boxes informing you that you are about to view pages over a secure connection, click **OK** or **Yes** to proceed.

3

4. Log in to Remote Manager by following these steps:

   a. When the Enter Network Password dialog box opens, enter the typeless distinguished name of your ##Admin user (for example, on the classroom server use either .##Admin.##UAS, or .##Admin.##UAS.CLASS depending on the tree structure in use).

   b. Enter your password, and then click **OK** to log in.

   c. If you see a security alert message box, click **OK** or **Yes** to proceed and open the Remote Manager window.

5. Browse to your CAD subdirectory:

   a. Click your **##CORP** volume (## represents your assigned student number) to display your existing file system structure.

   b. Click your **Apps** directory to display the CAD subdirectory.

   c. Click your **CAD** subdirectory to display any existing files. Currently, the file listing should be empty.

6. Upload the MS Paint application from your workstation:

   a. Click the **Upload** icon at the top of the /##CORP/Apps/CAD window on the right.

   b. Click the **Browse** button.

   c. Navigate to the C:\WINNT\System32 folder.

   d. Double-click the **Mspaint.exe** program to insert the filename into the File name text box.

   e. Click the **OK** button.

7. Verify that the files are listed in the CAD subdirectory.

8. On your student answer sheet, record an advantage and a disadvantage of using Remote Manager to upload files to network directories.

9. Click your **##CORP** volume in the left-hand frame to display your file system structure.

10. Delete three files from the Forms directory (you will salvage these files in the next activity):

    a. Click the **Forms** directory to display the files in the right-hand frame.

    b. Click the **?** icon to the left of the Bid.frm file to display a file information window.

    c. Click the **Delete File** button, and then click **Yes** to confirm.

    d. Repeat this procedure to delete the Order.frm file.

    e. Repeat this procedure to delete the Memo.frm file.

11. Exit Remote Manager by clicking the **Exit** button on the toolbar.

12. If necessary, click **Yes** to close the browser software.

13. Log off your Windows workstation.

Activity 3-11: Salvaging Deleted Files

Time Required: 10 minutes

Objective: Salvage network files.

Description: With Novell Client software, you can use Windows to salvage files as long as a drive letter is assigned to the physical volume containing the files to be salvaged. In this activity, you learn how to use NetWare's Salvage Files option to recover deleted files.

1. If necessary, start your computer, and log in with your assigned ##Admin user name.

2. Double-click your **My Network Places** desktop shortcut, and then follow these steps to browse to your ##CORP volume:

   a. Double-click **Novell Connections** to open the Novell Connections dialog box.

   b. Double-click the **UASHOST** server to display all available volumes.

   c. Double-click your **##CORP** volume.

3. Double-click your **Forms** directory, and record the existing filenames on your student answer sheet.

4. Return to your ##CORP directory window by clicking the **back arrow**.

5. Right-click your **Forms** directory, and then click **Salvage Files** to open the Salvage Network Files dialog box.

6. Record the salvageable files on your student answer sheet. In this dialog box, you can salvage all files or select certain files to salvage.

7. To salvage the Bid.frm file, click the **Bid.frm** file, and then click the **Salvage File** button.

8. Salvage all remaining files by clicking the **Salvage All** button.

9. Click **Close** to close the Salvage Network Files dialog box.

10. To verify that the files now exist in the Forms directory, double-click the **Forms** directory.

11. Record the filenames in the Forms directory on your student answer sheet.

12. Close the Forms directory window.

13. Close all windows, but stay logged in if you're continuing to the next activity.

Activity 3-12: Purging Deleted Files

Time Required: 10 minutes

Objective: Purge network files.

Description: As discussed earlier, Eric sometimes purges deleted files from a folder to make the space immediately available and prevent sensitive documents from being salvaged for security reasons. For example, Eric installed some utility programs but found a newer version of them, so he decided to delete his existing utilities and install the new program. By deleting the files from the Utility directory and then purging the files, Eric made their space immediately available for the new program. In this activity, you simulate this process by copying files to your Utility directory and then purging them. To reduce the time it takes to access your ##CORP volume through My Network Places, in this activity you use Windows to map a drive letter to your ##CORP volume and then use the drive letter to access the Utility folder.

1. If necessary, start your computer, and log in with your assigned ##Admin user name.

2. To make accessing network files more convenient, follow these steps to map a drive to your ##CORP volume:

   a. Right-click your **My Network Places** shortcut, and then click **Novell Map Network Drive**.

   b. Select any available drive letter (except G:) in the Choose the drive letter to map text box. Record the drive letter on your student answer sheet.

   c. In the Enter the network path to the resource text box, enter the UNC name **\\UASHOST\##CORP** (replacing ## with your assigned student number).

   d. Verify that the drive letter will not be mapped each time you log in.

3

    e. Click the **Map** button to map the drive letter.

    f. Close the ##Corp on Uashost window.

3. Copy files from the SYS:\Software.cti\Utility directory to your Utility directory:

    a. Double-click your **My Computer** desktop shortcut, and browse to the Software.cti directory on the drive mapped to your SYS volume (usually drive letter F:).

    b. Double-click the **Software.cti** folder to open it.

    c. Double-click the **Utility** directory to display all files.

    d. Click **Edit** on the menu bar, and then click **Select All**.

    e. Click **Edit** on the menu bar, and then click **Copy**.

    f. Close the Utility directory window.

    g. Double-click **My Computer**, and then double-click the drive letter you recorded in Step 2 to open a window to your ##CORP volume.

    h. Double-click the **Apps** directory.

    i. Right-click your **Utility** directory, and then click **Paste** to copy the files.

4. Double-click your **Utility** directory to display the files.

5. Delete all files in your Utility directory:

    a. Click **Edit**, **Select All** on the menu bar.

    b. Press the **Delete** key, and then click **Yes** to confirm the deletion.

6. Close your Utility directory window.

7. Verify that the deleted files can be salvaged:

    a. Double-click **My Computer**, and then double-click the drive letter you recorded in Step 2 to open a window to your ##CORP volume.

    b. Open your Apps directory by double-clicking it.

    c. Right-click your **Utility** directory, and click **Salvage Files** on the shortcut menu.

    d. On your student answer sheet, record the number of files that can be salvaged.

    e. Click **Close** to return to the Apps directory window in My Computer.

8. Purge all files from the Utility directory:

    a. Right-click your **Utility** directory, and then click **Purge Files**.

    b. Click the **Purge All** button, and then click **Yes** to purge the files.

    c. Click **Close** to close the Purge Network Files dialog box.

9. Verify that the files are no longer available for salvaging:

    a. Right-click your **Utility** directory, and then click **Salvage Files**.

    b. On your student answer sheet, record the number of files that can be salvaged.

    c. Click **Close** to return to the Apps directory window in My Computer.

10. Close the Apps directory window.

11. Repeat Step 3 to copy the files back to your Utility directory.

12. Close all windows and log out.

PLANNING DRIVE POINTER USAGE

As described in the previous section, drive pointers play an important role in the accessing of files located on different volumes and directories. A **drive pointer** is a letter of the alphabet used to reference storage areas in the file system. By default, DOS reserves the first five drive pointers (A: through E:) to reference storage devices on the local workstation, so these letters are often referred to as the **local drive pointers**. For example, letters A and B are reserved for floppy disk drives, C and D are normally used for hard disks, and E is often reserved for a CD-ROM or other external storage device.

Network drive pointers are letters of the alphabet (usually F: through Z:) that represent directory paths and volumes in the network file system. Establishing network drive pointers is important for two major reasons:

- They make it easier to access data files without needing to specify a complete path. For example, if the G: drive pointer is assigned to your ##UAS directory on the CORP volume, you can specify a path to your Apps directory by typing G:Apps rather than UAS_HOST_CORP:##UAS\Apps.

- They allow applications and DOS commands that do not recognize volume names to access data and programs on multiple volumes and servers.

Network drive pointers can be one of two types: regular or search. Regular drive pointers are usually assigned to directories containing data files, whereas search drive pointers are assigned to network software directories. A **regular drive pointer** is assigned to a directory path and shows all directories and subdirectories leading to the storage area. In addition to commonly used directories, a regular drive pointer should be assigned to each volume so that applications that cannot use NetWare complete paths are able to access the data on any volume. Figure 3-30 illustrates dividing drive pointers between local, regular, and search.

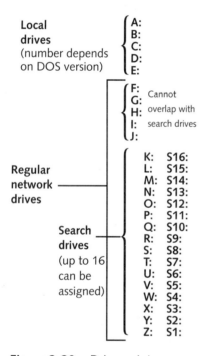

Figure 3-30   Drive pointers

Drive pointers can be made to appear to the user or application as though the directory path were at the beginning of the drive or volume by making the drive pointer a **root drive pointer**. Figure 3-31 shows an example of using two drive pointers, I: and J:, to access the same directory area. Notice that the J: drive pointer is a regular pointer because it shows the entire path leading to the directory, but I: is a root drive pointer that appears as though it were the first level in the directory structure.

3

On the root drive, the path does not
appear on the DOS path

```
I:\>dir
 Volume in drive I is CTS
 Directory of I:\
INV      DAT          6    12-03-01   6:14p
INVAPP        <DIR>        12-03-01   6:20p
        1 file(s)            6 bytes
        1 dir(s)     14,417,920 bytes free

I:\>j:

J:\INVENTRY>dir

 Volume in drive J is CTS
 Directory of J:\INVENTRY

INV      DAT          6    12-03-01   6:14p
INVAPP        <DIR>        12-03-01   6:20p
        1 file(s)            6 bytes
        1 dir(s)     14,417,920 bytes free
J:\INVENTRY>
```

In regular drive mapping, the path is displayed
and can be changed from the application

Figure 3-31   Regular and root drive pointers

Both drive pointer I: and J: are assigned (or mapped) to the Inventry directory and, as you can see in the figure, have access to the same file. The advantage of using the root drive pointer is that it helps prevent an application or DOS command from changing the drive pointer's mapping to some other location in the directory structure. Root drive pointers are normally used to access user home directories along with the starting path to shared data directories. For example, mapping drive letter I: as a root pointer to the Inventry directory enables users to access files and software in the Inventory system without the risk of changing the drive pointer to a different path.

A **search drive pointer** is a drive pointer that has been added to the DOS **path**, which specifies a sequence of locations in which DOS and the NetWare shell look for program files that are not in the current directory. Search drive pointers play an important role in accessing the file system from DOS because they allow a network administrator to place data files in separate directories from the application software. Search drive pointers act like a Windows shortcut, enabling a user or an application in one directory path to access software and data located elsewhere in the directory structure.

As illustrated in Figure 3-32, when you enter a command in the command-prompt window, Windows first determines that it is not one of its internal commands and looks in the current directory for a program or batch file with the name you specified. If no program or batch file exists in the current directory, each search drive specified in the path is searched, starting with S1: until the program is found or the message "Bad command or filename" is displayed. By assigning a search drive to the SYS:Public directory, NetWare enables you to run utilities such as FILER, NDIR, and LOGOUT from any directory in the file system.

Search drives are assigned the letter *S*, followed by a sequential number from 1 to 16, and each search drive can point to only one directory location. Subdirectories of that directory location are not searched unless they are assigned to separate search drives. In addition to being assigned a sequence number from S1 through S16, search drives are also given a drive pointer. It starts with Z being assigned to S1, Y assigned to S2, X to S3, and so on. Drive pointers are kept in a table stored in each workstation's RAM, and any changes made are effective as long as the user is logged in to the network. Because each workstation keeps track of its own drive pointers in memory, each user can assign the same drive pointer to different directory locations. For example, your workstation can have the F: drive pointer mapped to the SYS:Public directory, and its S3: search drive mapped to SYS:Software.cti\WP, while the user next to you might have the F: drive pointer on his or her workstation mapped to the CORP volume, and the S3: search drive mapped to the SYS:Software.cti\WP directory.

Planning Drive Mappings for Universal AeroSpace

In a NetWare environment, the network administrator is responsible for establishing drive pointers to reference software and data locations in the directory structure. These drive pointers need to be assigned correctly so that Windows and DOS applications can access network files and directories as though they were on a local hard disk. In this section, you learn how to plan a set of drive pointers for an organization and assign those pointers by using Windows and NetWare utilities.

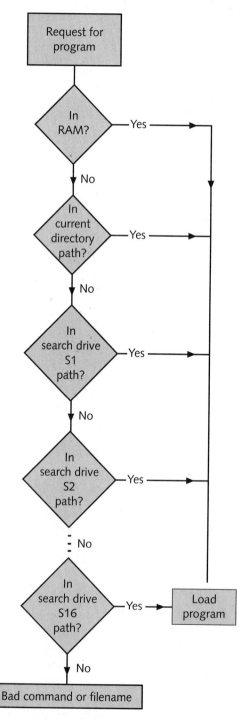

Figure 3-32   Using search drive pointers

3

As a CNA, you'll need to plan how to assign the regular and search drive pointers for users who want access to the information and software in your file system's directory structure. If each workstation had an unlimited number of drive pointers available, you could assign a regular or root drive pointer to each data directory to be accessed, along with a search drive for each software package. However, even if this were the case, having so many drive pointers would be confusing to track, and too many search drives would slow the workstation's performance because of the number of directories it would need to search through when loading software. Therefore, you need to come up with a plan for a minimum set of standard drive pointers that will enable the workstation to run the necessary software and give users convenient access to data. You should first determine which regular and root drive pointers are necessary to allow easy access to shared and private files with a drive letter rather than a lengthy NetWare path. Try to keep these drive pointers to a minimum, as most users cannot keep track of more than five different drive pointers. Typical drive pointers for each user should include the following:

- *A drive pointer to the root of each volume*—These drive pointers give users easy access to data and software stored on volumes. A drive pointer to each volume also provides a standard path for running applications because some application packages require that a drive letter and path be assigned to reference configuration and data file locations. Having the same drive letter mapped to each volume for all users is necessary to run this software. When using a two-volume structure, many network administrators map drive letter F: to the SYS volume and then use another drive letter, such as G:, to access the CORP volume. Another use for the volume drive pointer is accessing shared work directories that are available to all users. For example, if a shared work directory for all users named Work is created on the root of the CORP volume, any user could access files in this directory by using the path G:\Work. Similarly, because the shared word-processing forms directory named Forms is located on the root of the CORP volume, any user can access a common word-processing form by using the path G:\Forms.

- *A root drive pointer mapped to the user's home directory*—This drive letter is the starting point for users' personal data storage, and each user has a different path. Making this drive letter a root drive is important because it prevents the user from accidentally changing the H: drive pointer, for example, to a different directory location. Each user can create subdirectories within his or her home directory, and then move around in those subdirectories using the CD command to return to the beginning of his or her home directory instead of changing to the root of the volume.

- *A root drive pointer mapped to the user's workgroup directory*—This drive pointer allows users to access shared files within their workgroups. For example, users in the Engineering department could have their L: drive mapped to CORP:Engineer, but the IS department has its L: drive mapped to the CORP:IS directory. If a Shared directory is created for each department, any user in the system can get to his or her workgroup's shared work directory by using the path L:\Shared.

- *Application drive pointers*—Additional drive pointers might be necessary for installing and accessing certain application packages, depending on the installation instructions. When planning these drive pointers, all users who will run the application must use the same drive pointer letter because the software will be installed using this drive letter to access its data and work files. For example, if an application is installed using the L: drive mapped to the Apps directory of the CORP volume, a workstation with drive letter M: mapped to the Apps directory of the CORP volume could not install and run the program.

In addition to regular drive pointers, the network administrator needs to plan search drive pointers so that users can access utilities or applications that are run from the command prompt. When planning search drive usage, you should keep the total number of search drives to fewer than eight for better performance and less chance of conflicts with regular drive pointers. Windows applications do not need search drives mapped to their software directories because the path to these directories is stored in the properties of the Windows icons and shortcuts. As a minimum, most network administrators set up the following search drive mappings:

- Search drive S1: to the SYS:Public directory

- Search drives S2: through S6: to DOS-based applications and utilities

A well-planned set of drive pointers should include a standard set of drive pointers that give users easy access to data volumes containing the files and applications they need. Table 3-5 illustrates the drive pointer usage Eric planned for accessing the UAS file system.

Table 3-5   Universal AeroSpace Drive Pointer Usage

Drive Letter	Path
F:	Root of the SYS volume
G:	Root of the CORP volume (CORP:##CORP)
H:	Root drive to user's home directory
L:	Root drive to user's department directory, as follows: • IS users: CORP\##CORP\IS • Engineering users: CORP\##CORP\Engineer • Marketing users: CORP\##CORP\Sales
S1:	SYS:Public
S2:	Utility directory for IS department

In his plan, Eric has identified drive pointers for the following purposes:

- The F: drive pointer to the SYS volume is used to give certain administrative users access to applications or utilities stored on the SYS volume. Standard users should not need a regular drive letter mapped to the SYS volume because their applications and data should be stored on separate data volumes, such as CORP. Most users should not have a regular drive letter mapped to the SYS volume, but a drive letter should be reserved for administrative users.

- The G: drive pointer mapped to the root of the CORP volume gives each user access to the global data structure for the organization. For example, to access the organization's global work directory, a user can use the path G:\Shared or access the organization's shared forms directory with the path G:\Forms.

- The H: drive pointer to the user's home directory allows users to easily access their own private data.

- The L: drive pointer mapped to each user's local department or workgroup enables users to access their department's shared work files by using the path L:\Shared. In the future, if a department wants its own Forms directory, it could be accessed with the path L:\Forms.

- Search drive pointer S1: will be used for the SYS:Public directory, and S2: will be used for utility programs used by the administrator. Additional search drive pointers may need to be established based on applications installed in the future.

Planning a good set of drive pointers makes it easier to establish login scripts, install software, and work with applications, and provides a standard user environment that is convenient for users to access and for you to troubleshoot and maintain.

Establishing Drive Pointers

Drive pointers can be assigned to the network file system through Windows, with DOS commands, or from a login script. When a user logs out, all network drive pointers are disconnected from their assigned paths. When mapping drives from My Network Places, you can use the Always map this drive letter when you start Windows option to reconnect a drive letter to the specified network path the next time you log on from that workstation. When you use this option, Windows 2000 keeps track of the drive mapping in the user's profile. When that user logs on to the local workstation, Windows 2000 attempts to map the selected drive letter to the specified network directory. If another user logs on from the workstation, the drive letter will not be mapped, however. One solution to this problem is to use NetWare user login scripts to assign drive pointers. Login scripts can map drive letters to network directory paths by using MAP commands that the workstation processes when a user logs in. The MAP command can be used in login scripts or from the DOS prompt to assign drive letters to network paths. In Chapter 7, you learn how to create and manage MAP commands from login scripts. Because of the importance of drive pointers, as a CNA you are required to use both Windows and the MAP command to work with drive mappings.

The MAP Command

The MAP command is a versatile command-line utility that network administrators use to create, modify, and delete regular and search drive pointers from the DOS prompt or login scripts. A Novell CNA must be familiar with the MAP command to perform several different types of tasks, such as creating regular and root drive pointers by assigning a NetWare path to a drive letter. This is the syntax of the MAP command needed to create a new drive letter:

```
MAP [root] drive:=[path]
```

You use the [root] option to make the drive pointer a root mapping. The drive: parameter can be any letter of the alphabet. You can replace the [*path*] option with a complete or relative NetWare path leading to the directory, as described in the previous section. If you do not include a path on the MAP command, the MAP command assigns the drive pointer specified to the current path. In the following activity, you learn how to use the MAP command.

Activity 3-13: Using the MAP Command

Time Required: 10 minutes

Objective: Plan and implement network drive pointers.

Description: You have just logged in to Kellie's workstation and need to revise the drive mappings to access your directories. In this activity, you learn how to use the MAP command to create, view, and remove regular and root drive pointers.

1. If necessary, start your computer, and log in with your ##Admin user name.

2. Click **Start**, **Run**, type **command** in the Open text box, and click **OK** to open a command-prompt window.

3. Change to drive F: by typing **F:** at the command prompt and pressing **Enter**.

4. Enter the **MAP** command to display your current drive mappings.

5. Record the regular drive mappings on your student answer sheet, and then press **Enter**.

6. Enter the following MAP command, and then press **Enter** to create a drive pointer to the IS directory on your CORP volume:

    F:\>MAP G:=UASHOST_CORP:

7. After you have mapped the G: drive to your CORP volume, you can use relative paths that include the G: drive letter to access other directories in your Universal AeroSpace structure. Use the following command (pressing **Enter** after each line) to map drive letters to each department directory:

    F:\>MAP ROOT I:=G:INVENTRY
    F:\>MAP ROOT L:=G:IS

8. The MAP NEXT [path] command can be used to assign the specified path to the first available drive letter, proceeding from F: through Z:. This command is useful when you want to map an unused drive letter to a directory path and you don't care what letter is used. To map the next available drive letter to the Shared directory on the SYS volume using a physical volume name, enter the following command, and then press **Enter**:

    F:\>MAP NEXT SYS:SHARED

9. Record the drive letter used for the Shared directory on your student answer sheet.

10. To delete drive mappings, use the MAP DEL drive: command, replacing "drive" with the drive letter you want to delete. To delete the drive letters created in Step 7, enter the following commands, and then press **Enter**:

```
F:\>MAP DEL I:
F:\>MAP DEL L:
```

11. Enter the **MAP** command, and record your regular drive pointers on your student answer sheet.

12. Enter the **EXIT** command to return to Windows, and then log out.

Activity 3-14: Mapping Search Drives

Time Required: 10 minutes

Objective: Plan and implement network drive pointers.

Description: In this activity, you remove all existing search drives for Kellie and then use various MAP commands to establish a set of search drive pointers to software directories on your network.

1. If necessary, start your computer, and log in with your assigned ##Admin user name.

2. Click **Start**, **Run**, and type **command** to open a DOS command-prompt window. (Typing the usual "cmd" opens a Windows 2000 command-prompt window that doesn't support mapping search drives.) Change to your F: drive letter.

3. Enter the **MAP** command, and then record your search drives on the student answer sheet.

4. Try running the DB program without a search drive by typing the command **DB**, and then pressing **Enter**. Record the message you see on your student answer sheet.

5. To use the DB program, enter the following command to map search drive S2: to the DB software directory, and then press **Enter**:

```
F:\>MAP S16:=SYS:SOFTWARE.CTI\DB
```

Mapping a search drive to S16: adds the search drive mapping to the end of the existing search drives and prevents overwriting an existing path.

6. Test your search drive by repeating the DB command you entered in Step 4, and then press **Enter**. Record the results on your student answer sheet. If your new search drive works, the program will display the database test screen.

7. When inserting a search drive between two existing drives, include the **INS** option and replace the search drive number with the number of the existing search drive you want the new drive to be placed before. When setting up search drives, the most commonly used paths should be given lower search drive numbers. This makes the system more efficient by reducing the number of directories NetWare has to search through when looking for a program file. To insert a search drive mapping between the existing S1: and S2: search drives and then view your drive mappings, enter the following commands, pressing **Enter** after each line:

```
F:\>MAP INS S2:=SYS:SOFTWARE.CTI\SP
F:\>MAP
```

8. Sometimes it's convenient to add a new search drive to the beginning of the list and then delete it when it's no longer needed. To add a search drive to the WP directory before the existing S1: search drive, enter the following commands, pressing **Enter** after each line:

```
F:\>MAP INS S1:=SYS:SOFTWARE.CTI\WP
F:\>MAP
```

Notice that drive letter W: was assigned to the S1: search drive, and that although the other search drives were renumbered, they retained their drive letter assignments. NetWare keeps track of search drive numbers by their sequence in the DOS path; because drive W: is now the first drive in the path, it becomes search drive one.

9. To verify the sequence of search drive letters in your DOS path, enter the following command, and then press **Enter**:

   ```
   F:\>PATH
   ```

10. To remove the search drive to the WP directory and resequence the search drives, enter the following commands, pressing **Enter** after each line. Notice that the search drive letters (X:, Y:, Z:) appear in the path sequence based on their search number.

    ```
    F:\>MAP DEL S1:
    F:\>PATH
    ```

11. Because search drives are really the sequence of the drive letter in the DOS path, NetWare does not skip search drive numbers. As a result, you can use the command MAP S16:=[path] if you want to add a search drive to the end of the search list but don't know the number of the last search drive. To add a search drive to the end of your list and then verify your results, enter the following commands, pressing **Enter** after each line:

    ```
    F:\>MAP S16:=SYS:SOFTWARE.CTI\WP
    F:\>MAP
    ```

12. Enter **EXIT** at the command prompt to return to Windows, and then log out.

Using Directory Map Objects

For users or network administrators to set up drive pointers, they must know the physical location of the directory being mapped to the drive letter. Maintaining drive pointers for many users can become a problem if certain files or directories are moved from one volume to another. Although not an essential part of the network file system, the Directory Map object simplifies accessing network data and maintaining drive pointers. A **Directory Map object** is an object created in the eDirectory tree that contains the path to a volume and directory in the network file system. Map commands can then establish drive pointers by simply specifying the Directory Map object instead of entering the complete path to the data. Because drive pointers can be relative to the value specified in the Directory Map object's Path property, when a directory's location is moved, only the path in the Directory Map object needs to be changed. MAP statements in login scripts and batch files that use the Directory Map object won't need to be modified.

Eric established Directory Map objects, shown in Table 3-6 for each department's directory.

Table 3-6   Universal AeroSpace Directory Map Objects

Name	Context	Path
EngData	.Engineering.UAS	UASHOST_Corp:Engineer
ISData	.IS.UAS	UASHOST_Corp:IS
MgmtData	.Mgmt.UAS	UASHOST_Corp:Mgmt
MfgData	.Mfg.UAS	UASHOST_Corp:Engineer\MfgData

Drive letter L: will point to each department's work directory (refer back to Table 3-5). Currently, the Engineer directory is planned for storage on the CORP volume. However, UAS is planning to add a server to the network for the Engineering department's use. Using a Directory Map object when mapping drive letters for the Engineer directory means the system can be expanded by simply changing the path to include the new server in the Directory Map object. In the following activity, you create Directory Map objects in your ##UAS Organization.

Activity 3-15: Creating Directory Map Objects

Time Required: 10 minutes

Objective: Create Directory Map objects.

Description: In this activity, you create the Directory Map objects in Table 3-6, and then test the objects by using them with the MAP command to map drive letters.

1. If necessary, start your computer, and log in with your ##Admin user name.

2. Start ConsoleOne, and expand **UAS_Tree** and your **##UAS** Organization.

3. Create a Directory Map object named EngData in the Engineering container, as follows:

   a. Click the **Engineering** container, and press **Insert** to open the New Object dialog box.

   b. Double-click the **Directory Map** object to open the Create Directory Map dialog box.

   c. Enter **EngData** in the Directory Map Name text box, and press **Tab**.

   d. To enter the volume name, click the **Browse** button to the right of the Volume text box. The Select Object dialog box opens.

   e. Click the **UASHOST_CORP** volume object, and then click **OK** to place the UASHOST_CORP volume in the Volume text box.

   f. Click in the **Path** text box, and then click the **Browse** button.

   g. Double-click the **UASHOST_CORP** volume to expand it.

   h. Click the **Engineer** directory, and then click **OK** to place Engineer in the Path text box.

   i. Click the **OK** button to create the new Directory Map object in the Engineering container.

4. Follow the procedure in Step 3 to create a Directory Map object named ISData in the IS Organizational Unit that points to your ##CORP:IS directory.

5. Follow the procedure in Step 3 to create a Directory Map object named MgmtData in the Mgmt Organizational Unit that points to your ##CORP:Mgmt directory.

6. Follow the procedure in Step 3 to create a Directory Map object named MfgData in the Mfg Organizational Unit that points to the ##CORP:Engineering\MfgData subdirectory.

7. Test the newly created Directory Map objects:

   a. Click **Start**, **Run**, enter **command** in the Open text box, and then click **OK** to open a command-prompt window.

   b. Map drive letter L: to the IS directory by typing **F:**, pressing **Enter**, typing **MAP ROOT L:=ISData.IS**, and then pressing **Enter** again.

   c. Map drive letter N: to the Engineering directory by typing **MAP ROOT N:=ENGData.Engineering,** and then pressing **Enter**.

   d. Type **MAP**, and then press **Enter** to confirm that the drive letters now point to your Engineer and IS directories.

   e. Type **EXIT**, and then press **Enter** to close the command-prompt window and return to your Windows desktop.

8. Double-click the **My Computer** icon, and record your network drive mappings on your student answer sheet.

9. Close all windows, and log out.

BACKING UP NETWORK DATA

An organization's data plays a critical role in today's highly competitive and rapidly changing world of business and industry. A company robbed of its information would certainly suffer major losses and could even be forced out of business. Therefore, as a network administrator in an organization that relies on the network for data storage and retrieval, you become the "keeper of the flame," in that you're responsible for much, if not all, of your organization's critical data files. As a result, management counts on your knowledge to provide a reliable storage system, secure from unauthorized access and protected from accidental loss caused by equipment failure, operator error, or natural disaster.

The Storage Management System

NetWare includes the **Storage Management System (SMS)** for backing up even complex networks consisting of data residing on multiple file servers and on DOS and OS/2 workstations. The NetWare server that runs the backup program and has the attached tape or other backup media is referred to as the **host server**. Other servers and client workstations being backed up are referred to as **target servers**. When using the SMS system, the term "parent" refers to a data set, such as a directory or subdirectory, and the term "child" refers to a specific subset of a data set, such as a file or program. SMS uses NetWare Loadable Modules on the host server to communicate with modules on target devices, read the information from the target devices, and send it to the backup media, as shown in Figure 3-33.

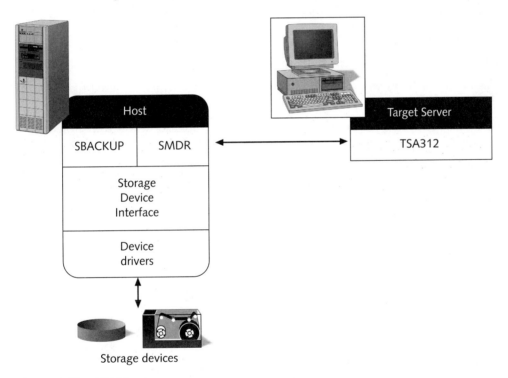

Figure 3-33   SMS backup process

The NetWare SMS consists of the following software components that can be run on NetWare servers as well as DOS or OS/2 workstations:

- Storage device drivers are loaded on the host server and control the mechanical operation of various storage devices and media, such as tape drives.

- The Target Server Agents (TSAs) are loaded on the target servers and communicate with the SBACKUP program running on the host server. The purpose of the TSA is to get information from the target server's volumes and send it to the SBACKUP program running on the host server. A server can act as host *and* target by running both the SBACKUP and TSA software.

- Workstation TSAs are run on the DOS or OS/2 workstations to back up data on the local drives across the network.

- The enhanced SBACKUP utility is the main NetWare-provided software, which runs on the host server or Windows workstation. It works with the SMS architecture to control the backup process and transfer data to and from the host server.

- In addition to the SBACKUP software that runs from the server console, NetWare includes the NWBACK32 program, which runs on a Windows workstation. It is used to create backup jobs that are processed by the Backup/Restore NLMs running on the NetWare server.

Other Backup Software Packages

In addition to the SMS backup software that ships with NetWare 6, a number of other companies offer specialized backup software packages with several features and benefits. The most common third-party backup systems are ARCserve and Backup Exec. As a CNA, you should be aware of their basic features, described in the following sections.

ARCserve for NetWare   ARCserve for NetWare (currently marketed as Brightstor ARCserve Backup for NetWare) fully supports eDirectory and the NSS storage system to provide enterprise-wide backups. ARCserve has the following features:

- *Cross-platform capability*—Enables ARCserve to back up data from and restore data to computers connected to the NetWare network.

- *Backup storage selection*—Lets you protect your data by storing it in more than one location.

- *File interleaving*—Enables you to back up several servers at one time.

- *Media pooling*—Allows you to separate media into groups, which are used to create certain backup jobs

- *Server-to-server copying*—Gives you the advantage of a duplicate server to help reduce downtime; also called "server mirroring."

- *User-defined scripts*—Enable you to configure backups once and reuse them when needed.

- *Databases*—Give you quick access to data on the backup media and information about jobs performed by ARCserve.

- *Reports and logs*—Provide a complete history of operations.

ARCserve consists of both server and client components. The client component, ARCserve Manager, runs on the Windows workstation and handles all backup and restore sessions. ARCserve Manager also performs such tasks as copying files from one server to another, accessing the ARCserve utilities, and viewing information about past and current jobs.

The server component of ARCserve, called ARCserve Server, runs on the NetWare server console and processes all unattended jobs scheduled by ARCserve Manager and all jobs submitted from the ARCserve server. ARCserve Server has the following subcomponents:

- The Schedule component manages jobs you schedule through ARCserve Manager.

- Job Processing Modules scan the queue and, when a job is ready to print, dynamically load the NLMs required for the print job.

- Tape Server Modules communicate with your tape drives and enable you to view the tape server log and current activities.

- Databases keep track of workstations and servers on the network, the jobs you have run, and all the files backed up, copied, or restored.

ARCserve client agents run on Windows workstations and allow you to back up and restore Windows, DOS, and OS/2 workstations. Optional client agents are available for Macintosh, Windows NT, and Unix workstations.

VERITAS Backup Exec for NetWare   Like ARCserve, Backup Exec supports NSS and eDirectory and lets you back up and restore NetWare server volumes, workstation drives, and non-volume objects, such as binderies and registries. Backup Exec offers the following features and benefits:

- The ability to act as a data management system for Novell networks.

- An administrative console for NetWare servers.

- A Java-based administrative console so that you can access your NetWare server from any Windows workstation. This console provides the following functions:
  - Configuring default options for your media server
  - Managing your devices and media
  - Viewing scheduled and active jobs
  - Obtaining histories of completed jobs
  - Running general reports

- Back up and restore Windows 2000/XP systems.

- Policy-based backup allows you to store all settings for a job in a policy that can be viewed and reused. With this feature, you can save all backup job settings, except files and target devices, as a policy that you then apply to specific resources, making it easier to create new backup jobs.

- Enhanced device management simplifies how you organize and allocate storage devices attached to your media server.

- Multiple catalog views give you the choice of a catalog-based (tape) view or a volume-based view of the backed-up data. Volume-based views make it easier to locate and identify damaged or deleted files for restoring.

- Backup jobs can be submitted from the Administrative Console program running on a Windows workstation or Administrative Console for NetWare running on a server.

As with ARCserve, Backup Exec uses both server and workstation components. The Bestart.ncf file in the SYS:System directory is used to load the Backup Exec job engine software on the media server (the server that hosts a backup device, such as a tape drive). The job engine then processes jobs submitted from the Administrative Console running on a workstation.

 Backup Exec is designed to work with earlier NetWare versions as well as NetWare 6. When Backup Exec is installed, it determines the NetWare version running on the media server and then adds the necessary lines to the Bestart.ncf file.

The Bestop.ncf file removes the Backup Exec job engine from the media server's memory. You should run this file before shutting down your server. If you are running Administrative Console for NetWare on the server, you need to manually exit this program before shutting down the server.

Establishing a Backup System

Having a reliable and tested backup system is one of the best medicines a network administrator can have to ensure a good night's sleep, so spending some extra time planning and testing the backup system is well worth it. Establishing a successful backup system involves six steps:

- Determine your network's storage needs
- Determine a backup strategy
- Assign a backup user
- Run the backup software on a scheduled basis
- Test the backup
- Develop a disaster recovery procedure

In the following sections, you learn how Eric applied these steps to setting up the backup system for Universal Aerospace.

Determining Storage Needs

The first step in establishing a backup system for your network is to calculate how much data needs to be copied to the backup tape on a daily basis by determining which volumes and directories you plan to back up. If possible, you should try to obtain an SMS-compatible tape backup system with enough capacity to store your daily backup on one tape cartridge. In a single-file server environment, the file server acts as both the host and target devices, requiring you to load the SBACKUP and TSA modules on the same server. An advantage of having a file server as both host and target devices is that a file server backing up its own data runs almost four times faster than a host file server backing up data across the network from another target file server. As a result, when implementing SMS in a multiple-file server environment, you should plan on making the server that stores the most data the host system.

Determining a Backup Strategy

Depending on the backup storage needs, one of the three backup strategies shown in Table 3-7 are normally used.

Table 3-7   Backup Strategies

Type of Backup	Data to Back Up	Status of Archive Attribute
Full	All data, regardless of when or if it has been previously backed up	Cleared
Incremental	Files created or modified since the last full or incremental backup	Cleared
Differential	All data modified since the last full backup	Not cleared

With the **full backup** strategy, all data is copied to the backup tape each night. This backup strategy will work well for Universal AeroSpace because the current size of files to be included on the backup does not exceed one tape cartridge. The advantage of the full backup strategy is that if a crash occurs, only the previous day's backup needs to be restored. The disadvantage is the need for a large tape capacity and the time required to perform backups.

The **incremental backup** strategy takes the least amount of time for each backup because only the data files that have changed that day are copied to the backup tape. When using the incremental backup strategy, a full backup is made at the beginning of the week and an incremental backup is made each day. The disadvantage of this strategy is that all incremental backup tapes must be restored if data is lost. For example, if a crash occurs on Thursday, you need to restore the Monday full backup first, followed by the Tuesday and Wednesday incremental backups.

3

A compromise between the full backup and the incremental backup is the **differential backup** strategy, in which all files that have changed since the last full backup are copied to the backup tape. That means the size of the tape backup increases as the week progresses. The advantage of the differential strategy is that if a crash occurs later in the week, only the full backup and the last day's differential backup need to be restored.

Currently, Eric is using the full backup strategy for UAS to make a complete backup of all data and the eDirectory database each day. In the future, as UAS's data storage requirements grow beyond the space of one tape cartridge, Eric recommends implementing a differential backup strategy to reduce the backup time and eliminate the need for someone to change tapes in the middle of the night.

Assigning a Backup User

Although you can log in as Admin to perform the backup, most network administrators prefer to create a separate user name for backups. Creating a separate user name has the advantage of allowing you to assign other people to perform the backup and limits the number of times you need to log in to the network as Admin. The user name you create to perform the backup must have the following access rights and privileges:

- To back up the file system, the user name needs to have Read, File Scan, and Modify rights to the volumes and directories included in the backup. The Modify right is necessary for the backup program to reset the Archive attribute after backing up data files. When assigning these rights to the directory, you need to be aware of any IRFs (Inherited Rights Filters) that might block these rights from a subdirectory you want to back up.

- To back up the eDirectory database, the backup user name needs to have the Browse Entry and Read Attribute rights to the containers included in the backup.

- The person performing the backup needs to know the password used on the host server and the passwords assigned to any target servers or clients.

Running the Backup Software

After you have decided on a backup strategy and created any necessary user names, your next step is to test the SMS installation by backing up your server data and then testing the backup by restoring selected files from the backup tape. In the following steps, Eric leads you through the backup process using the SMS from the server console screen. If you have access to the server console, you can follow along with Eric to back up your network data:

1. To load the enhanced SBACKUP utility, Eric first loaded the Storage Manager Device Redirector software by entering the command LOAD SMDR.

2. Next, Eric entered the full context of the Admin user name and password.

3. After the SMDR software was loaded, Eric loaded the target agents for backing up NetWare 5 server data and the eDirectory database with these commands:

```
LOAD TSA500
LOAD TSANDS
```

4. After loading the target service agents, Eric completed the initialization by loading the Storage Management System Device Interface software with this command:

```
LOAD SMSDI
```

5. The SMS uses job queues to enable backup and restore jobs to be stored until they are to be run. Just as a print queue enables a print job to wait for a printer to be available, the job queue enables you to enter a job and have it run later that night or when the backup device is available. To load the job queue software, Eric entered this command:

```
LOAD QMAN
```

6. To load the enhanced SBACKUP software on the server, Eric entered the following two commands to display the backup options shown in Figure 3-34:

```
LOAD SBSC
LOAD SBCON
```

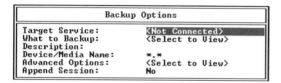

Figure 3-34 SBACKUP options

7. Next, Eric selected the Target Service option to choose the NetWare server running the Target Service Agent.

8. When prompted for the target server's user name, he entered the Admin user name and password for the UASHOST server. The enhanced SBACKUP utility then took a few moments to attach to that target. Next, the Backup Options form appeared. To perform a full backup, Eric selected the default values. Other options include incremental and differential backups.

9. Next, Eric selected what he wanted to back up from the List of Resources and entered a descriptive name for the backup session.

10. Finally, he selected the backup media to start the backup process.

Testing the Backup

After completing a successful backup, the next step in testing your backup system is to try restoring selected files from the backup media. Doing a complete restore is often not feasible because of time constraints and the possible loss of data if the restore process fails. As a result, before doing a major restore, you should restore test files that are not needed or files that have been copied to another disk storage device. To restore selected files, select the Restore option from the main SBCON menu and then enter the path to the working directory you used when the backup tape was created. Next, select the option Restore from session files, and select the session you named previously when the backup was created.

After the restore screen has been completed, start the restore process. The selected files should then be copied back to their appropriate directories. When the restore process is finished, log in from a user workstation and verify that the files have been correctly restored.

Developing a Disaster Recovery Procedure

After the backup system has been tested, the next step in implementing a reliable disaster recovery plan is to develop a tape rotation procedure and backup schedule. Having a multiple-tape rotation procedure that enables you to save certain backups for a long time is an important part of a disaster recovery plan because it gives you a way to go back to an earlier backup to recover files and to be able to store backup tapes outside the building. Sometimes you must be able to recover a file from an earlier backup if it becomes corrupted by a software virus, an operator error, or a software bug, and the damage to the file is not discovered for several days or weeks. If you were rotating your backups between just a few tapes, by the time the error was discovered, the original backup with the valid file would have been overwritten by a backup copy of the corrupted file. To help prevent this problem, Eric has recommended a tape rotation system consisting of 20 tapes, as shown in Figure 3-35.

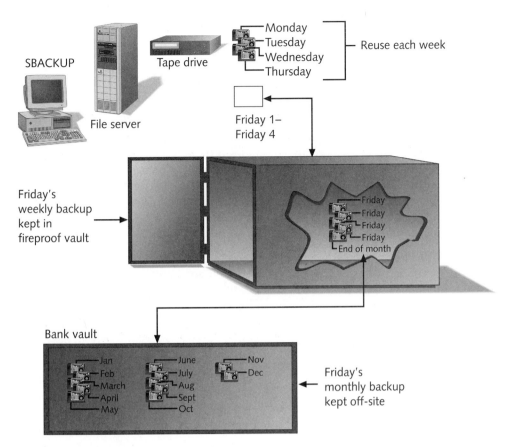

Figure 3-35   Tape rotation procedure

Four tapes are labeled Monday through Thursday and are rotated each week. Four tapes are labeled Friday1 through Friday4, with Friday1 used on the first Friday of the month, Friday2 on the second, Friday3 on the third, and Friday4 on the fourth. In addition, 12 tapes are labeled January through December. These tapes are rotated each year and can be used on the last Friday of each month by replacing the Friday# tape with the correct monthly backup. Another alternative, if someone is available to change the tape, is to make the monthly backup on the last Saturday of each month. Storage for backup tapes is also important in case of a fire or damage to the building; many administrators store weekly backups in a fireproof vault and keep monthly backup tapes off-site in a secure location, such as a safety-deposit box.

The final step in implementing the backup system is to set up a time for the backup to be performed and ensure that no users are logged in during the backup process. To prevent interference with user work schedules, many network administrators like the backup to start each night at about 12:00 a.m. To keep night owls from working late and to prevent users from leaving their workstations logged in during the backup, all user accounts, except the user name used to back up the system, should have a time restriction to prevent accessing the network between 12:00 a.m. and 5:00 a.m. This five-hour interval should be enough time to create your backup. If you need extra time, you can set the backup to begin at 11:00 p.m. or perhaps to end at 6:00 a.m., as long as the user time restrictions are also set for the longer backup period.

Congratulations! You have set up a basic file system for the Universal AeroSpace company. In the following chapters, you will learn more efficient ways to create and secure user accounts and give users access to the data and applications they need to work with.

CHAPTER SUMMARY

❑ The basic components of Novell Storage Services (NSS) include partitions, pools, volumes, directories, and files. Storage pools are made up of one or more physical disk partitions; a volume is the logical division of the storage pool, holding folders and files. Each server must have a minimum of one NSS volume named SYS.

❑ During installation, NetWare creates a number of system directories on the SYS volume, including Login, Public, and System. The Login directory contains programs and files necessary to log a user into the network. The Public directory contains program commands and utilities that users can run after logging in to the network. The System directory contains operating system files and utilities available only to the network administrator. Because running out of space on the SYS volume can bring down the server, network administrators usually plan one or more data volumes to contain the organization's files and applications.

❑ Files are used to store network data and software. In addition to a file's name and size, NetWare stores information about each file, such as owner, access dates, and attributes, in the directory entry table (DET) located at the beginning of each volume. In addition to ConsoleOne and NetWare Administrator, administrators can use the new NetWare 6 Remote Manager utility from a Web browser to manage the network file system.

❑ Network administrators should plan and implement a structure for the network file system that supports the organization's processing needs. When planning the directory structure, Novell suggests that you set aside private home directories for each user, shared directories to store files that are needed by multiple users, and application software directories. To provide space for these directories, many network administrators use multiple volumes. The SYS volume is reserved for operating system files; one or more data volumes are usually designated to store print queues, user files, and applications.

❑ After the directory structure has been designed, any necessary volumes are created with ConsoleOne or Remote Manager. After all volumes are created and mounted, the network administrator can log in as Admin and create the necessary directories and subdirectories by using Windows, ConsoleOne, or Remote Manager.

❑ To work efficiently with the newly created directory structure, you need to establish drive pointers to strategic locations in the directory structure. Drive pointers are alphabetical letters assigned to local drives and network directories that make it easier to work with the file system and to access software stored in other directories. Regular drive pointers are assigned to directories that contain data files, and search drive pointers are assigned to application directories to run command-line utilities not located in the Windows directory. Root drive pointers appear to applications as though the directory path were the beginning of a drive or volume, enabling the network administrator to make it more difficult for users or applications to move out of the assigned directory path.

❑ Because drive pointers play a major role in how users and applications access the NetWare file system, network administrators should establish standards for drive pointer usage to prevent conflicts and software configuration problems. A drive pointer planning form similar to the one in this chapter can help establish a standard set of drive pointers for your network. A drive pointer usage plan makes accessing and maintaining the network file system easier for users and network administrators.

❑ Backing up data is a critical function that needs to be performed daily on any network system. NetWare 6 includes the Storage Management System (SMS) for backing up data and eDirectory objects with a full, differential, or incremental backup strategy. The backup software is loaded and run at the host server with Target Service Agents (TSAs) running on the server and workstations to be backed up. The TSA600 agent is used to back up network data to the host, and the TSANDS agent backs up eDirectory objects.

KEY TERMS

balanced tree (B-tree) — An indexing system used with the NSS file system that enables NSS volumes to be mounted more quickly and with less RAM than traditional volumes.

block — The smallest unit of disk storage on a NetWare volume. NSS volumes use a block size of 4 KB, but the block size in traditional volumes can be set from 4 KB to 64 KB.

differential backup — A backup strategy in which only files that have changed since the last full backup are copied to the backup tape. When performing a differential backup, the SBACKUP program backs up all files that have the Archive attribute enabled but does not reset the Archive attribute, thus making it easier to restore all data after a disaster.

directory entry table (DET) — A storage location at the beginning of each volume for storing information on files and directories, including name, size, location, owner, and access dates.

Directory Map object — An object in the eDirectory tree that contains the path to a volume and directory in the network file system.

disk partition — An area of hard disk storage formatted for a specific operating system. NetWare 6 uses NSS-formatted disk partitions to form storage pools.

drive pointer — A letter used to reference storage areas in the file system.

duplexing — A technique to increase file service reliability by keeping two disks attached to separate controller cards synchronized on the server.

failover — The process of switching from a failed server to an operational server.

file compression — A NetWare technique to save disk space by automatically compressing files that have not been accessed for a specified time period.

full backup — A backup strategy in which all data is copied to the backup tape daily, regardless of when it changed.

home directory — A directory created for each user for storing his or her own files and documents.

host server — The NetWare server that runs the backup program and has the attached tape or other backup media.

incremental backup — A backup strategy that backs up only the files that have changed (the Archive attribute is on) that day, and then resets the Archive attribute on all files that are backed up.

local drive pointer — Drive letters that point to physical devices on the local computer, such as the floppy drive, hard drive, or CD-ROM drive.

Login directory — A required NetWare operating system directory that contains files and programs needed by DOS clients to log in to the network.

login script — A list of commands performed when you first log in to the network. An important use of the login script is establishing the initial drive pointer mappings.

mirroring — The process of automatically synchronizing the information on two partitions located on different disk drives attached to the same controller.

network drive pointer — A letter, usually F: through Z:, used to represent directory paths and volumes in the network file system.

Novell Storage Services (NSS) — The file system used primarily by NetWare 6. In NSS, logical volumes are created from storage pools that consist of one or more disk partitions.

path — The location of a file or directory in the network file system.

Public directory — A required NetWare operating system directory that contains NetWare utility programs and commands available to all users.

regular drive pointer — A drive pointer that is assigned to a data directory on each volume.

root drive pointer — A regular drive pointer that acts as though it were the root of the volume.

search drive pointer — A drive pointer that is used to reference executable files and application directories by using a DOS path.

server clustering — A setup in which two or more servers can share a common disk system, making the data available in case one of the servers has a hardware failure.

Storage Management System (SMS) — The NetWare backup service that includes several NetWare Loadable Modules, along with workstation software that enables the host server to back up data from one or more target devices by using the SBACKUP NLM.

storage pool — An NSS file system component used to group one or more partitions into a storage area that can be divided into one or more volumes.

suballocation — A feature of traditional volumes that divides blocks into smaller 512-byte increments so that multiple files can share the same block, thus saving disk space.

System directory — A required NetWare-created operating system directory that contains system software and commands available only to the server and Admin user, not to other users.

target server — A server whose data is backed up by a host server.

REVIEW QUESTIONS

1. The logical divisions of NSS storage pools are called _____.

2. List the three major components of the NSS file system:

   _____

   _____

   _____

3. The _____ volume is required on all NetWare 6 servers.

4. List three required NetWare directories that are created when NetWare is installed on a server:

   _____

   _____

   _____

5. Which of the following directories contains files and programs that can be accessed and run before logging in to the network?

   a. Public

   b. System

   c. Login

   d. Etc

6. Which of the following directories contains NetWare utility programs that are available to all users?

   a. Public

   b. System

   c. Login

   d. Etc

7. Which of the following directories contains operating system files that are not available to users?

   a. Public

   b. System

   c. Login

   d. Etc

3

8. List three types of directories that Novell suggests you create in the file system:

_____

_____

_____

9. Large file systems are easier to manage when using a departmental directory structure design. True or false?

10. What is the advantage of leaving some unallocated disk space when creating partitions for a NetWare 6 server?

11. Which of the following eDirectory objects is used to access the file system from eDirectory?

  a. [Root]

  b. storage pool

  c. volume

  d. partition

12. Which of the following drive pointers appears to the user or application as though the default path is at the beginning of the volume?

  a. search

  b. root

  c. regular

  d. system

13. Which of the following drive pointers is added to the DOS path?

  a. search

  b. root

  c. regular

  d. system

14. List three drive pointers that you should include for each user:

_____

_____

_____

15. Which of the following utilities can be used to create a new partition? Choose all that apply.

  a. NetWare Administrator

  b. ConsoleOne

  c. iManager

  d. Remote Manager

16. Purged files are placed in the Deleted.sav folder until NetWare needs their space. True or false?

17. Which of the following utilities can be used to salvage deleted files? Choose all that apply.

  a. My Computer

  b. Remote Manager

  c. iManager

  d. ConsoleOne

18. NSS volumes are created inside which of the following?

    a. partitions

    b. storage pools

    c. containers

    d. clusters

19. Which of the following options is not found on NSS volumes?

    a. block suballocation

    b. clustering

    c. file compression

    d. data shredding

20. Mirroring involves synchronizing data on two different _____.

    a. storage pools

    b. partitions

    c. volumes

    d. controller cards

21. Which of the following backup strategies backs up only files that have been created or modified since the last full backup?

    a. full

    b. incremental

    c. differential

    d. system

22. Other servers or client workstations that are being backed up are referred to as which of the following?

    a. child servers

    b. host servers

    c. target servers

    d. parent servers

23. Which of the following Target Service Agents must be loaded on a server to back up the data files?

    a. TSANDS

    b. TSA600

    c. SBCON

    d. SMS

24. To back up the file system, the user name for logging in to the network must have which of the following rights?

    a. Full Control

    b. Read and File Scan

    c. Read, File Scan, and Modify

    d. All rights except Supervisor and Access Control

25. In the Storage Management System, which of the following terms refers to a data set such as a directory or subdirectory?

    a. host

    b. target

    c. parent

    d. child

3

UNIVERSAL AEROSPACE CASE PROJECTS

Your next step in implementing the file system for your version of the UAS network is to design and create a directory structure for the Business office, which consists of the Accounting, Marketing, and Desktop Publishing departments.

Case Project 3-1: Identifying Storage Requirements

Given the Business office processing needs defined by Eric in Figure 3-36, fill out a Storage Requirements Form (copy a blank one from Appendix D) that includes the following information for each directory: description, users, name, and estimated size.

Case Project 3-2: Designing the Directory Structure

Use the existing UAS directory structure along with the Storage Requirements Form you have completed to design a directory structure for each of the following departments and record them on a separate directory worksheet:

❐ Accounting department

❐ Marketing department

❐ Desktop Publishing department

Case Project 3-3: Creating the Remaining UAS Directory Structure

In this project, you create the remainder of the UAS directory structure in your ##CORP directory using the directory worksheet from Case Project 3-2. You can use NetWare Administrator, ConsoleOne, or Remote Manager to create the directory structure. When you're done, create a printout of your newly created directory structure.

Case Project 3-4: Setting Directory Space Limitations

Use NetWare Administrator to enter the directory space limitations you defined on the Storage Requirements Form.

Case Project 3-5: Planning Drive Mappings

Using the Universal AeroSpace Drive Pointer Usage Form (refer to Table 3-5 for an example), plan drive mappings for users in the Business office.

Case Project 3-6: Creating Directory Map Objects

Each department should have a Directory Map object that points to that department's directory. Identify a Directory Map object for each department and write down the object names, along with their path and location in the eDirectory tree. Use ConsoleOne or NetWare Administrator to create the directory objects you defined. Create a printout of the objects for your instructor to check.

Case Project 3-7: Backing Up the Server

After the network is operational, network administrators must be able to establish and test a backup system to provide disaster recovery capability for organizations. In this project, you use the SBACKUP utility to back up your Universal AeroSpace file system and eDirectory containers to a backup media. Depending on your server hardware and accessibility, your instructor will give you instructions on how to perform the backup by loading the necessary device drivers and then running the SBACKUP software as described in this chapter.

Business Office Processing Needs

The Business office uses a DOS-based software package that includes general ledger and payroll applications. Currently, Terry Blackwell, George Perez, and Amy Pan in the Accounting department are using this package. However, to improve performance, security, and reliablity, a new Windows accounting package has been purchased and will be installed on the NetWare 6 server in a single directory structure named AcctApp within the Business directory. The storage requirements for the accounting packages and data should not exceed 5 GB. In addition to the accounting applications, all business staff use the Excel spreadsheet program to create and update budget data. Because Terry, George, and Amy need access to the budget accounting data, it should be stored in a shared Budget subdirectory within the Business directory. Currently, the projected storage needs for the Budget directory do not exceed 3 GB.

In addition to having access to the new inventory system, the Marketing users use Microsoft Access to keep a database of the customers and vendors they work with on their notebook computers. Because the Marketing staff often work with the same customers and vendors, sometimes they have conflicting information on their notebook computers. To solve this problem, separate directories for the customer and vendor databases will be stored in the Marketing directory structure on the NetWare 6 server. These directories should not exceed 3 GB each. The department secretary, Laura Hiller, will maintain the customer and vendor database files by entering new data from the Marketing staff. When in the office, the database files will be accessed directly from the network. Initially, the Marketing staff members need to be able to copy the database files to their notebook computers before going on the road. In the future, they would like to have direct access to the server database from a dial-up phone connection. In addition, the Marketing staff use word-processing software for correspondence and work on promotional material. The Marketing staff will need a 5 GB shared document directory to exchange promotional material in their department and with the Desktop Publishing users.

The Desktop Publishing department is responsible for working with the Engineering and Marketing departments to create operation and installation manuals for the NASA and Mars Rover projects. As a result, shared directories for up to 10 GB need to be created for these projects within the Desktop directory structure.

Figure 3-36   Business and Marketing processing needs

4

MANAGING USER ACCESS

> **After reading this chapter and completing the exercises, you will be able to:**
>
> ♦ Use ConsoleOne to establish login security by setting user login, password, and account restrictions
> ♦ Use ConsoleOne, NetWare Administrator, and iManager to create and manage user accounts, and use ConsoleOne's Import option to create user accounts from Lightweight Directory Interchange Format files
> ♦ Use ConsoleOne to create and manage Organizational Role objects
> ♦ Use ConsoleOne to move container objects

As you learned in Chapter 1, each network user must be assigned a user name and password to access network resources and services. In Chapter 2, you learned that Novell's eDirectory uses a global database to store information on network objects such as users, groups, printers, and volumes so that they are accessible to all NetWare servers; you also used ConsoleOne to build a tree structure for your user accounts consisting of container objects for each department. In Chapter 3, you established the file system structure with directories for network files and locations for user home directories. In this chapter, you learn how to use NetWare 6 utilities to set up login restrictions and create user accounts for your version of the Universal AeroSpace network. You also learn how to secure user accounts against intruders, how to use templates and the NDS Import/Export Wizard to create user accounts more efficiently, and how to move user and container objects to other locations in your eDirectory tree. Delegating tasks to other users is also an important task for network administrators, so you'll learn how Organizational Role objects can be used to delegate privileges to certain user accounts.

ESTABLISHING LOGIN SECURITY

In addition to establishing a network file system and eDirectory structure, a network administrator must secure the network so that users can access only the network resources and services they have been authorized to use. NetWare 6 security consists of several systems: login security, file system security, eDirectory security, printer security, and server console security. Login security provides the basis for all security systems by ensuring that only authorized users have access to network resources. In this chapter, you learn how to set up login security to protect user accounts from unauthorized access. Later chapters will cover the other security systems in NetWare 6.

NetWare login security relies on NetWare **authentication**, which validates each network request to guarantee the following:

- The authorized user sent the message.

- The message was sent from the client computer where the authorized user logged in.

- The message pertains to the user's current login session.

- The message has not been corrupted or modified.

Because the authentication security process occurs in the background, it is not visible to the user or network administrator. The authentication process starts when the user is issued a private key from the Certificate Authority service running on the NetWare server. The Novell client then creates a signature using the private key, along with information identifying the user, workstation, and session. The client uses the signature to uniquely code the data in each packet sent from the workstation. When the server receives a packet, it uses the packet's signature to validate that the packet came from the authorized user's workstation.

Authentication is an ongoing process that prevents an intruder from building message packets that appear to the network to have come from an authorized user. For example, suppose an intruder were able to capture packets from your client. Without authentication, it would be possible for the intruder to create a message in a packet that seems to come from your client computer, thus giving the intruder access to any information or services you have rights to when you're logged in. Authentication prevents packet capturing because each packet has a unique signature, created by applying the user's private key to the information in the message. Without the user's password and signature, the intruder is unable to fool the system into accepting falsified packets.

Creating user objects and assigning passwords are only part of implementing login security, which also consists of user account restrictions, intruder detection, and administrative roles. In the following sections, you learn what a CNA needs to know about these security measures and how to apply them to Universal AeroSpace Corporation.

Implementing User Account Restrictions

User account restrictions help ensure that the user logging in is actually the authorized person by allowing the network administrator to establish password restrictions, time restrictions, and station restrictions. In this section, you learn how these account restrictions can be used to increase network security.

As you learned in Chapter 1, passwords that are known only to the user are a necessary part of login security to authenticate the person logging in as a valid user. However, passwords have a way of becoming common knowledge among other users and thus lose their effectiveness at authenticating specific users. To help keep passwords secret, they need to be changed periodically. Because users often neglect this task, administrators can use NetWare password restrictions to require users to change passwords within a given time period. In addition, NetWare password restrictions include a unique option for making sure users come up with a different password each time they change instead of rotating between a few favorite passwords.

Despite all your efforts, you cannot prevent users from revealing their passwords to other people or keep them from writing down their passwords and leaving slips of paper with the password on desks or in wastebaskets. To increase security in case someone detects a user's password, NetWare offers the option to set time and station restrictions on user accounts. With these restrictions, you can keep users who work with highly secure data, such as payroll information and customer lists, from logging in except during specified time periods or from certain workstations. By using time and station restrictions on a user's account, a potential intruder who knows a user's password would have to enter the building during normal business hours to log in as that user. For example, Eric Kenton set up Lynn Dai's user account with the restriction of logging in only on her workstation from 8:00 a.m. until 4:00 p.m. If an intruder learned Lynn's password and tried to log in from any other workstation on the network, the login request would be denied. To log in, the intruder would have to go to Lynn's office and use her computer between 8:00 and 4:00, and others would likely notice this suspicious behavior. Another way to increase user account security is by limiting the number of stations from which a user can be logged in. By default, a user can be logged in concurrently from multiple stations. This can be a security problem for mobile users if they forget to log out before moving to another station. As a result, you should normally restrict user accounts to logging in from only one station at a time.

As a network administrator, you can use ConsoleOne to set password restrictions along with time and station restrictions on existing users or use templates to apply standard restrictions for new users. Using account restriction templates saves time by automatically applying these restrictions to all users who are created with that template. In Activities 4-1 and 4-2, you learn how to establish account restrictions on existing users. In later activities, you will learn how to create templates with a set of standard login restrictions.

Activity 4-1: Setting User Account Restrictions

Time Required: 10 minutes

Objective: Use ConsoleOne to establish user login restrictions.

Description: Because the Admin user account has all rights to manage the network, one of the most important security needs on your network is login security for the Admin user. To help secure the Admin user account, Eric placed restrictions on the Admin user to limit the account to only one connection at a time from one of two workstations. In addition, Eric required the Admin user account to be given a unique password of at least eight characters every 60 days. In this activity, you will secure the user account you created for yourself in Activity 2-14 by using ConsoleOne to set up account and password restrictions.

While you could also secure your ##Admin user account, doing so may cause problems for you in future activities.

1. If necessary, start your computer, and log in with your assigned ##Admin user name.

2. If necessary, log on to your Windows 2000 workstation.

3. Start ConsoleOne.

4. In the Navigation frame, expand **UAS_Tree** and your **##UAS** Organization by clicking the **+** symbol to the left of each object.

5. Click your **##UAS** Organization to display the objects in the Object frame.

6. Determine your workstation's IP address:

   a. Click **Start**, **Run**, enter **cmd**, and then press **Enter** to open a command-prompt window.

   b. Enter the command **IPCONFIG**, and then press **Enter**.

   c. On your student answer sheet, record your workstation's IP address and the IP address of another student's workstation.

   d. Type **exit**, and then press **Enter** to close the command-prompt window.

7. Create an address restriction to allow the user name you created for yourself in Activity 2-14 to log in only from your workstation.

   a. Right-click on your username, and then click **Properties** to open the Properties of your-user-name dialog box. Click the **down arrow** on the Restrictions tab.

b. Click the **Address Restrictions** option to open the Network address restrictions dialog box.

c. Click the **Add** button to open the Create Network Address dialog box.

d. If necessary, click **IP** in the NetAddress Type list box to select this option.

e. Enter the IP address you recorded in Step 6.

f. Click **OK** to save your entry and return to the Network address restrictions dialog box.

8. Repeat the preceding steps to enter the IP address of a second workstation from which your user can log in, in case your primary computer is down. Record the IP address on your student answer sheet.

9. Set password restrictions on your user to require a new unique password of at least eight characters every 60 days.

a. Click the **down arrow** on the Restrictions tab, and then click the **Password Restrictions** option to open the Password Restrictions dialog box.

b. Click the **Require a password** check box, and then enter **8** in the Minimum password length text box to change the default of five characters.

c. Click the **Force periodic password changes** check box, and then enter **60** in the Days between forced changes text box.

Note that the entry in the Date and time password expires text box will not reflect the number of days entered in the Days between forced changes text box.

d. On your student answer sheet, record the date and time your password will expire.

e. Click the **Require unique passwords** check box to require a different password each time.

f. Click the **Limit grace logins** check box, and accept the default of allowing the user six logins after the password expires.

g. Verify that your Password Restrictions dialog box looks similar to the one shown in Figure 4-1.

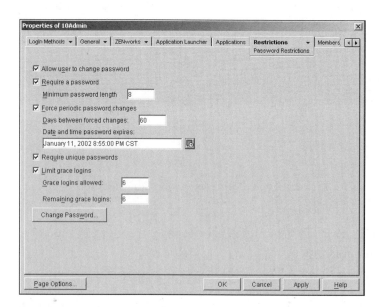

Figure 4-1   The Password Restrictions dialog box in ConsoleOne

10. Click **OK** to save the account restrictions.

11. Exit ConsoleOne, and log off.

12. Attempt to log in using your user name from another station. On your student answer sheet, record any message you see.

Activity 4-2: Establishing Time Restrictions

Time Required: 10 minutes

Objective: Use ConsoleOne to establish user login restrictions.

4

Description: In addition to the password and station restrictions, Eric wanted to secure the Admin user account so that it was active only from 6:00 a.m. until 11:30 p.m. on the two workstations he normally uses. In this activity, you follow Eric's example and secure your ##Admin user account by allowing its use only from 6:00 a.m. through 11:30 p.m. on your assigned workstation.

1. If necessary, start your computer, and log in with your assigned ##Admin user name.

2. If necessary, log on to your Windows 2000 workstation.

3. Start ConsoleOne.

4. In the Navigation frame, expand **UAS_Tree** and your **##UAS** Organization.

5. Click your **##UAS** Organization to display the objects in the Object frame.

6. Right-click your **##Admin** user name, and then click **Properties** to open the Properties of ##Admin dialog box.

7. Set the Login Time restriction to allow your ##Admin to log in only between 6:00 a.m. and 11:30 p.m.:

   a. Click the **down arrow** on the Restrictions tab, and then click the **Time Restrictions** option to open the Time Restrictions dialog box.

   b. To restrict the ##Admin account to accessing the network any day of the week between 6 a.m. and 11:30 p.m., move your mouse pointer to the upper-left position in the time chart. Notice that the current location of the cursor, including day and time, is displayed beneath the time chart. After you have pointed to Sunday, 12:00 a.m., click and drag the cursor to the right until you reach the 6:00 column and then continue to drag down to the Saturday row. Release the mouse button to highlight the selected area.

When setting time restrictions, the highlighted area represents the times the user is excluded from logging in.

   c. Repeat this process to highlight the 11:30 p.m. column for all days of the week, as shown in Figure 4-2.

8. To save the new login security restrictions, click the **OK** button at the bottom of the dialog box.

9. Exit ConsoleOne, and log out.

Implementing Intruder Detection Limits

Another potential login security problem is an intruder who is able to successfully guess user passwords. Forcing user passwords to be longer than four characters and training users to create nonobvious passwords that contain numbers as well as characters can go a long way toward preventing password guessing. Having nonobvious passwords is critical because intruders could get lucky with guesses, or, even more frightening, they might have a password-guessing program that can send hundreds of password combinations into a computer in just a few seconds. An effective way to deter password guessing is to implement the NetWare Intruder Detection feature in each Organizational Unit container.

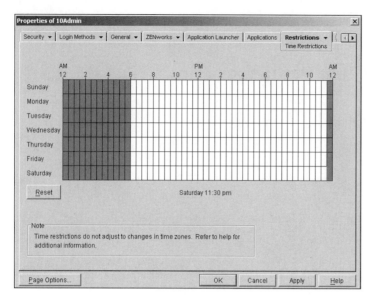

Figure 4-2   Setting a range of excluded login times in the Time Restrictions dialog box

Intruder detection works at the container level by setting a limit on the number of incorrect login attempts that can be made on a user account in that container during a specified time period. When a potential intruder reaches the maximum number of incorrect login attempts in the established time period, the user's account is locked for a specified time period and the time and station address of the login attempt is recorded on the user's account. The user account will become available again at the end of the lockout time period, or the Admin user can free the account at any time. In the following activities, you use NetWare Administrator to set the Intruder Detection option for your UAS network, and then test your security by locking your ##Admin user account and attempting several invalid passwords.

Activity 4-3: Enabling Intruder Detection

Time Required: 10 minutes

Objective: Establish user login restrictions.

Description: Because they are working on secure government contracts, some UAS engineers and IS staff have had to sign nondisclosure agreements stating that they will not reveal information about the projects they're working on. To help secure user accounts from unauthorized access, Eric has enabled the Intruder Detection option on the UAS, Engineering, and IS containers. In this activity, you use NetWare Administrator to enable intruder detection to lock out a user's account for five minutes when more than five incorrect login attempts have been made in a 10-minute period.

1. If necessary, start your computer, and log in with your assigned ##Admin user name.

2. If necessary, log on to your local Windows 2000 workstation.

3. Double-click the **nwadmn32** shortcut to start NetWare Administrator. If you see the Welcome to NetWare Administrator window, read the tip, and then click **Close** to continue.

4. If necessary, open a browse window:

    a. Click **Tools**, **NDS Browser** on the NetWare Administrator menu bar to open the Set Context dialog box.

    b. In the Context text box, enter the context of your UAS organization (for example, if using the classroom server enter either **.UAS** or **.UAS.CLASS** depending on the classroom tree structure).

    c. Click **OK** to open a browse window showing all objects in your ##UAS Organization.

5. Set intruder detection on your ##UAS container:

a. Right-click your container, and then click **Details** to open the dialog box.

b. Click the **Intruder Detection** button to open the Intruder Detection dialog box.

c. Click the **Detect intruders** and **Lock account after detection** check boxes to enable these options.

d. Record the default reset and lockout times on your student answer sheet.

e. In the Incorrect login attempts text box, enter **5** to change the default from 7 attempts.

f. Enter **10** in the Minutes text box.

g. Record the new reset and lockout times on your student answer sheet.

h. In the Intruder lockout reset interval section, enter **2** in the Minutes text box to change the default time, as shown in Figure 4-3.

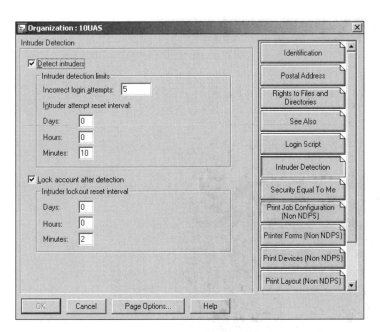

Figure 4-3   Configuring settings in the Intruder Detection dialog box

i. Click the **OK** button to save the intruder detection settings for the ##UAS Organization.

6. Set intruder detection on your Engineering container:

a. Right-click your **Engineering** OU, and then click **Details** to open the Organization Unit: Engineering dialog box.

b. Click the **Intruder Detection** button to open the Intruder Detection dialog box.

c. Click the **Detect intruders** check box.

d. In the Incorrect login attempts text box, enter **5** to change the default from 7 attempts.

e. Enter **10** in the Minutes text box.

f. Click the **Lock account after detection** check box, and change the default minutes to **2**.

g. Click the **OK** button to save the intruder detection settings for the Engineering OU.

7. Repeat Step 6 to set intruder detection on your IS container.

8. Repeat Step 6 to set intruder detection on your Mgmt container.

9. To test intruder detection, exit NetWare Administrator and log out.

Setting intruder detection on the container that holds the Admin user name could result in the user name being locked out for the specified time period, causing you to temporarily lose administrative access to the network. To help prevent this problem, you should create a backup Admin account that you can use to manage the network and rename the Admin user, as described in "Increasing Admin User Security," later in this chapter.

Activity 4-4: Testing Intruder Detection

Time Required: 10 minutes

Objective: Test user login restrictions.

Description: The next step in implementing your intruder detection system is to test the system and practice unlocking a user account. In this activity, you attempt to lock out your ##Admin user account and then wait for the account to clear before logging back in. In addition, you lock out your user name account and then log in using your ##Admin user name and unlock the account.

1. Attempt to log in with your ##Admin user name in the ##UAS context, using incorrect passwords and counting each unsuccessful login attempt. After several unsuccessful attempts, you see a NetWare security message box stating that your login is denied because of a possible intruder attack. Record the message, along with the number of login attempts, on your student answer sheet.

2. Now try logging in with the correct password. Record the error message on your student answer sheet.

3. Wait at least 3 minutes to allow NetWare to unlock your ##Admin user account.

4. Log in with your ##Admin user name and correct password.

5. If necessary, log on to your local Windows 2000 workstation.

6. Log out to display a new login window.

7. Attempt to log in as the user name you created for yourself in Chapter 2 by using incorrect passwords until the account is locked out.

8. Log in with your ##Admin user name and correct password.

9. Start ConsoleOne, and expand **UAS_Tree** and your **##UAS** container.

10. Right-click your **##Admin** user name, and then click **Properties** to open the Properties of ##Admin dialog box.

11. Click the **down arrow** on the Restrictions tab, and then click the **Intruder Lockout** option to display the Account Locked information. On your student answer sheet, record the Account reset time and Last intruder address.

12. Click the **Account Locked** check box to remove the check mark.

13. Click **OK** to save your change and return to the main ConsoleOne window.

14. Exit ConsoleOne, and log out.

CREATING AND MANAGING USERS AND GROUPS

After establishing password restrictions and setting an intruder detection policy for the Engineering, IS, and Mgmt OUs, your next task in creating your UAS network is increasing security for your Admin user and then creating the user and group accounts needed for each department. Group objects play an important role in network administration because they make it possible for network administrators to give similar privileges to several users at once, instead of assigning rights separately to each user. In NetWare 6, you can use ConsoleOne, NetWare Administrator, or the new iManager Internet utility to create and manage user and group objects. Which utility you use depends on your personal preference and needs. If you're working from a LAN using a computer with Novell Client software, you'll find that ConsoleOne and NetWare Administrator have more options and are easier to use. As an essential part of Novell's OneNet strategy, the iManager utility enables network management functions to be performed on any computer, regardless of how it's attached to the network or its installed client. For example, if you're logging in to your company's network via the Internet, or working from a local computer that does not have Novell Client installed, you need to use the iManager utility to manage the eDirectory system and create new user accounts.

In previous chapters, you learned how to use Novell's ConsoleOne utility to create and manage objects in the eDirectory database. This section will enhance your ability to use ConsoleOne by explaining what a CNA needs to know to create user and group objects and manage multiple user accounts. Later in the chapter, you learn how iManager can be used to create and manage user and group accounts from any computer with Internet access.

Increasing Admin User Security

Securing access to the network is an important responsibility of the network administrator, and Novell has provided NetWare with many features you can use to meet this responsibility. As a CNA, you'll need to know how to set up NetWare security options that meet the security needs of your users. As you learned in the previous section, attempting to log in as the network administrator without the correct authentication credentials can lock out the Admin user account, making it unavailable for the lockout duration you established. Some network administrators rename their Admin user accounts to make it harder to hack and to help prevent locking out the Admin user, but this method makes it harder to use certain utilities that default to using the Admin user name. However, if your server will be attached to the Internet, the additional security of renaming the Admin user can be worth the inconvenience. For this reason, the UAS IS director, Luke McMann, recommended renaming the Admin user before connecting the UAS server to the Internet.

Another security concern is having a backup administrator account that you can use to administer the network if your primary Admin user name becomes disabled or deleted. You can also use this backup account if the network administrator leaves the company, taking the Admin user name and password with him or her, or if he or she is incapacitated for any reason. When creating a backup administrator account, the CEO or office manager should keep the name and password secure. In the following activity, you create a backup user account and rename your existing ##Admin user name to help prevent hacking and account lockouts.

Activity 4-5: Securing the Admin User Account

Time Required: 10 minutes

Objective: Use ConsoleOne to create and manage user accounts.

Description: When planning the network, Luke asked Eric to create a backup administrator account named Clark Kent. Luke plans to have the company's administrative assistant, Lynn Dai, keep the backup administrator's user name and password locked up in a safe place in case they're needed to recover the main Admin user account and Eric is unavailable. In addition, before connecting the UASHOST server to the Internet, Luke asked Eric to rename the Admin user account to help prevent unauthorized access. In this activity, you create a backup administrator account named CKent and then rename your ##Admin user name. In Chapter 6, you will learn how to empower your CKent user to have Supervisor rights for your ##UAS Organization.

1. If necessary, start your computer, and log in with your assigned ##Admin user name.

2. If necessary, log on to your local Windows 2000 workstation.

3. Start ConsoleOne.

4. In the Navigation frame, expand **UAS_Tree** and your **##UAS** container.

5. Click your **IS** OU to display the objects in the Object frame.

6. Create a new user account for Clark Kent:

   a. Click the **New User** button on the ConsoleOne toolbar.

   b. In the Name text box, type **CKent**.

   c. In the Surname text box, type **Kent**.

   d. Leave all other fields and options blank, and click **OK** to open the Set Password dialog box.

   e. Enter **password** in both the New Password and Retype Password text boxes.

   f. Click the **Set Password** button to create the CKent user.

7. Rename your ##Admin user name as UasAdmin:

   a. Click your **##UAS** container to display the objects in the Object frame.

   b. Right-click your **##Admin** user name, and then click the **Rename** option.

   c. Enter **UasAdmin** in the New name text box, and click **OK**. Your ##Admin user name should now appear as UasAdmin in the Object frame.

8. Exit ConsoleOne by clicking the **Exit** button on the ConsoleOne toolbar, log out, and on your student answer sheet, record an advantage of renaming your Admin user account.

From now on, you'll need to log in using the name UasAdmin instead of using your ##Admin user name.

Defining and Creating Groups

Often, it's convenient to establish groups to give two or more users access to shared resources and services. Instead of assigning rights directly to user accounts, many network administrators would rather assign rights to groups and then make a user a member of the groups that have the necessary rights. For example, in UAS's Engineering department, only design engineers are given access to certain software and files they need for their work. Instead of repetitively giving access rights to each of the design engineer user accounts, it's more efficient to create a Design group and then add the design engineers as members. This group can then be given the rights and privileges necessary to access the restricted resources and services. In addition to reducing the redundancy of assigning the same rights to multiple users, groups are a convenient way to change user job responsibilities. For example, Kellie Thiele and Julie Damrau currently have responsibility for the UAS Web site, so Eric created a group called WebMgrs and made both Julie and Kellie members to give them rights to maintain the Web site files. (You'll be adding Julie in the end-of-chapter projects.) In the future, if Kellie gets too busy programming, another user could be assigned the responsibility by simply removing Kellie and then adding the new user to the WebMgrs group. Table 4-1 contains a Group Planning Form that lists the groups and members Eric implemented in the UAS Engineering and IS departments.

Table 4-1   Group Planning Form

Group Name	Members	Context	Description
Design	Lianne Jarka, Tony Rucci, Paul Alm, Kellie Thiele, Kari Means	Engineering.##UAS	Design engineers who will be working with CAD software to create and maintain engineering design files (as the programmer in charge of CAD applications, Kellie Thiele needs to be a member to test CAD software)
ISMgrs	Kellie Thiele, your_user_name, Luke McMann, Bernie Muelner	IS.##UAS	IS staff who have rights to install, configure, and manage software and workstation environments
Production	Russ Pence, Receiving terminals, Shipping terminals	Mfg.Engineering.##UAS	Users who need access to the inventory system to record shipments and receipts, and those who need access to read information from the RPS system
WebMgrs	Kellie Thiele	.##UAS	Users who are responsible for the design and maintenance of the UAS home page
Mgrs	David Heise, Lynn Dai, Maria Frias	Mgmt.##UAS	Upper management group with access to certain company policies and contracts

4

Because user accounts can be assigned group membership when they are initially created, when setting up the UAS network, Eric simplified the task of assigning users to groups by creating the group objects first, and then assigning each user to his or her appropriate groups when the user account was created. If you create group objects after the user accounts have been created, you need to perform another step to assign users to their appropriate groups. The hands-on activities in this section walk you through defining and creating the group accounts you'll need for your version of the UAS network. Later in the chapter, you'll use iManager and ConsoleOne to create the users defined in Chapter 2 for the IS, Engineering, and Manufacturing departments. The UAS projects at the end of the chapter will allow you to apply what you have learned to create and secure the remainder of the UAS user objects.

Novell's OneNet strategy is to move more functionality into Internet tools such as iManager and eventually phase out utilities, such as ConsoleOne and NetWare Administrator, that must be run from a LAN using the Novell client. In Activity 4-6, you practice using ConsoleOne to create group and user accounts. In a later activity, you'll learn how to use iManager to create group and user accounts for the Mgmt department.

Activity 4-6: Creating Groups with ConsoleOne

Time Required: 10 minutes

Objectives: Use ConsoleOne to create and manage group objects.

Description: In this activity, you create the groups shown on the Group Planning Form in Table 4-1.

1. If necessary, start your computer, and log in with your assigned UasAdmin user name.

2. If necessary, log on to your Windows 2000 workstation.

3. Start ConsoleOne.

4. In the Navigation frame, expand **UAS_Tree** and your **##UAS** container.

5. Create the ISMgrs group within your IS Organizational Unit and make your user name a member:

   a. Click your **IS** OU in the Navigation frame, and click the **New Group** button on the ConsoleOne toolbar (see Figure 4-4).

   b. In the New Group dialog box, enter the group name **ISMgrs** in the Name text box, and click the **Define additional properties** check box.

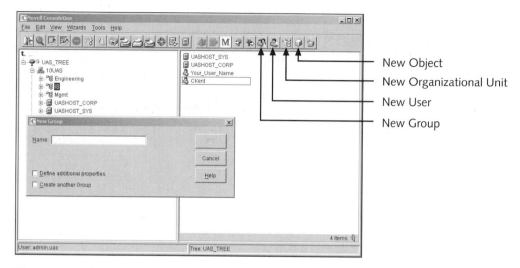

Figure 4-4 Creating a new group

   c. Click **OK** to create the group and open the Properties of ISMgrs dialog box.

   d. Click the **Members** tab, and click the **Add** button to open the Select Object dialog box.

   e. Click your user name, and then click **OK** to add this user to the ISMgrs group.

   f. Click **OK** to save your changes and return to the ConsoleOne window.

6. Create the WebMgrs group within your ##UAS Organization, but do not add any users at this time:

   a. Click your **##UAS** Organization, and click the **New Group** button on the ConsoleOne toolbar.

   b. Enter the group name **WebMgrs** in the Name text box.

   c. Click **OK** to create the group.

7. Create the Design group within your Engineering Organizational Unit, but do not add any users at this time:

   a. Click your **Engineering** OU, and click the **New Group** button on the ConsoleOne toolbar.

   b. Enter the group name **Design** in the Name text box.

   c. Click **OK** to create the group.

8. Create the Production group within the Mfg Organizational Unit, but do not add any users at this time:

   a. Expand your **Engineering** OU.

   b. Click your **Mfg** OU, and click the **New Group** button on the ConsoleOne toolbar.

   c. Enter the group name **Production** in the Name text box.

   d. Click **OK** to create the group.

9. Do not create the Mgrs group at this time; you will use the iManager utility to create this group and its users later in the chapter. Exit ConsoleOne, and log out.

Creating User Templates

Now that the necessary groups have been created, you need to create accounts for all your users. Although you could create each user individually as you did in Activity 4-5, this method is time consuming, and it's easy to miss a setup task, such as forgetting to add the new user to a group or omitting certain account restrictions. Missing setup steps can result in the user being unable to access certain data files or having nonstandard login restrictions. Therefore, establishing user templates to simplify and standardize creating user accounts is an efficient method for network administrators to use. A **user template** defines certain standard settings you want to establish for users. For example, users in most organizations have certain account restrictions, along with a home directory where they can create and manage their own files; with user templates, network administrators can easily define these restrictions and the location of home directories for all users created in that container.

Another practical use of templates is changing the default file system and eDirectory rights NetWare provides to new users. In Chapters 5 and 6, you'll learn about file system and eDirectory security and how users are granted rights to work with and manage files and eDirectory information. For example, when you create new users, NetWare grants them all rights to their home directories as well as rights to change their personal login scripts. As you'll learn in Chapter 7, login scripts contain commands that run each time a user logs in. Because Kellie will be responsible for maintaining all login scripts, Luke does not want users to be able to change the login scripts Kellie sets up for them.

In addition, new users, by default, can give other users authority in their home directories. To maintain better security, Luke does not want users to be able to change the security assignments to their home directories. By using templates, Eric can change the default file system and eDirectory security settings for new users to ensure the file system and eDirectory security Luke has deemed necessary. Table 4-2 contains a worksheet showing the template requirements Eric created for the Engineering, IS, and Mgmt departments. By removing Supervisor and Access Control rights from the user home directories, users will not be able to grant rights to others. In addition, granting only Read rights to the Login Script property will prevent users from changing their login script commands. Using the "T_" prefix before each template name helps identify the object as a template and makes the name different from corresponding group names.

In the following activity, you use ConsoleOne to create the templates Eric defined in Table 4-2 for your UAS network.

Table 4-2   User Template Planning Form

Template name	T_IS
Context	.OU=IS.O=##UAS
Home directory path	UASHOST_CORP:IS
Minimum password length	6
Require unique passwords	No
Days between password changes	90
Grace logins	6
Valid login times	5:00 a.m. until 11:59 p.m. Monday through Saturday
Concurrent connections	1
Groups	ISMgrs
Users	Kellie Thiele, Luke McMann, your_user_name
Rights to Login Script	Read
Rights to home directory	All rights except Supervisor and Access Control
Template name	T_Engineering
Context	OU=Engineering.O=##UAS
Home directory path	UASHOST_CORP:Engineer\Users
Minimum password length	6
Require unique passwords	Yes
Days between password changes	90
Grace logins	6
Valid login times	5:00 a.m. until 11:59 p.m. Monday through Saturday

Table 4-2   User Template Planning Form (continued)

Concurrent connections	1
Groups	Design
Users	Kari Means, Tony Rucci, Lianne Jarka, Paul Alm, Kellie Thiele, Russ Pence
Rights to Login Script	Read
Rights to home directory	All rights except Supervisor and Access Control

Activity 4-7: Creating User Templates

Time Required: 20 minutes

Objective: Use templates to help create user accounts.

Description: Before creating the users for the IS and Engineering departments, Eric defined and created templates for these departments, as shown in Table 4-2. In this activity, you use ConsoleOne to create user templates for the users in the Engineering and IS departments, as defined in the User Template Planning Form.

1. If necessary, start your computer, and log in with your assigned UasAdmin user name.

2. If necessary, log on to your Windows 2000 workstation.

3. Start ConsoleOne.

4. In the Navigation frame, expand **UAS_Tree** and your **##UAS** Organization.

5. Click your **IS** OU, and create the T_IS template for your IS department by following these steps:

   a. Click **File** on the menu bar, point to **New**, and click **Object** to open the New Object dialog box.

   b. Scroll down and double-click the **Template** object to open the New Template dialog box.

   c. Enter **T_IS** in the Name text box, and then click the **Define additional properties** check box.

   d. Click **OK** to create the template and open the Properties of T_IS dialog box.

6. Set the home directory path for your IS users:

   a. Click the **down arrow** on the General tab, and click the **Environment** option to display the Home Directory section.

   b. Click in the **Volume** text box, and then click the **Browse** button to open the Select Object dialog box.

   c. Double-click the **UASHOST_CORP** volume object to display all the directories in your CORP volume.

   d. To create home directories in the IS directory, click the **IS** object, and then click **OK**. Your dialog box should look similar to Figure 4-5.

Figure 4-5   Specifying the home directory for the user template

7. Set the password restrictions for your IS users as specified on the User Template Planning Form:

   a. Click the **down arrow** on the Restrictions tab, and click the **Password Restrictions** option to open the Password Restrictions dialog box.

   b. Verify that the Allow user to change password check box is selected.

   c. Click the **Require a password** check box, and change the minimum password length, as shown in the User Template Planning Form.

   d. Click the **Force periodic password changes** check box, and enter the number of days between forced password changes, as defined in the User Template Planning Form.

   e. Click the **Require unique passwords** check box if the User Template Planning Form requires new users to use a different password each time they change it.

   f. Click the **Limit grace logins** check box to allow new users a maximum number of logins after their password expires, as specified in the User Template Planning Form.

8. Set the login restrictions specified in the User Template Planning Form:

   a. Click the **down arrow** on the Restrictions tab, and click the **Login Restrictions** option to open the Login Restrictions dialog box.

   b. Click the **Limit Concurrent Connections** check box to restrict new user accounts to being logged in from only one computer at a time.

9. If necessary, set time restrictions, as shown in the User Template Planning Form:

   a. Click the **down arrow** on the Restrictions tab, and then click the **Time Restrictions** option to open the Time Restrictions dialog box.

   b. Block out 12:00 a.m. until 5:00 a.m. for Monday through Saturday, and block out Sunday completely, as shown in Figure 4-6.

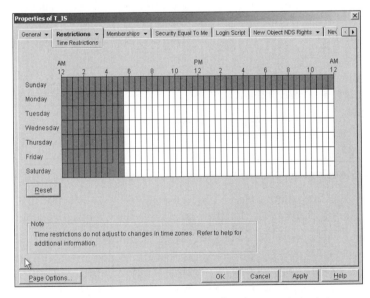

Figure 4-6   Setting time restrictions for the user template

10. Click the **Memberships** tab to open the Memberships dialog box and follow these steps to add groups to this template:

    a. Click the **Add** button to open the Select Object dialog box.

    b. Double-click the **ISMgrs** group to add it to the Memberships dialog box.

11. Change the Login Script property rights to Read:

   a. Click the **down arrow** on the New Object NDS Rights tab, and then click the **Rights to Other Objects** option.

   b. Click **<New Object>**, and then click the **Assigned Rights** button.

   c. Click the **Add Property** button to display the Property list box.

   d. Scroll down the list, click **Login Script**, and click **OK** to add it to the Property list box.

   e. Verify that the Write check box is not selected, and then click **OK** to save the assignment and return to the Rights to Other Objects dialog box.

12. Remove the Supervisor and Access Control rights from the user home directories:

   a. Click the **New Object FS Rights** tab to display existing trustee assignments.

   b. Click the **Supervisor** and **Access Control** check boxes to remove these rights.

13. Click **OK** to save your changes and return to the main ConsoleOne window.

14. Click your **Engineering** OU, and repeat Steps 5 through 13 to create the T_Engineering user template, using Table 4-2 as a reference.

15. Exit ConsoleOne, and log out.

Creating User Objects from Templates

In NetWare, network users are given login names by creating a user object in an eDirectory container. In addition to login names, you can use eDirectory to keep track of many other fields of information, called properties, about each user. As you learned in previous activities, at a minimum, user objects must be assigned a login name and a last name; other properties, such as title, address, home directories, passwords, and time restrictions, are optional. Because certain properties, such as the location of the user's home directory or password requirements, are often the same for several users, using templates can make creating user objects easier and more standardized. Before creating users, you should develop a user naming convention and identify which information properties you want to enter on each user account. Popular naming conventions include the following:

- The user's last name followed by the first initial of the first name (for example, Kellie Ann Thiele would have the user login name ThieleK)

- The first letter of the user's first name followed by the last name (for example, Kellie Ann Thiele would have the user login name KThiele)

- The user's first name followed by the first letter of the last name (for example, Kellie Ann Thiele would have the user login name KellieT)

- The first three characters of the first name followed by the middle initial and the first three letters of the last name (for example, Kellie Ann Thiele would have the user login name KelAThi)

For the UAS network, Luke decided to have user login names consist of the first letter of the first name followed by the user's last name. Another important consideration is what to do when your network has two users with the same login name. NetWare can support multiple user accounts with the same login name as long as the users' accounts exist in different OUs. For example, if you have the user Kellie Ann Thiele in the IS department and the user Ken Locke Thiele in the Engineering department, you could create a user account named KThiele in the IS OU for Kellie and create another KThiele account in the Engineering OU for Ken. Novell's eDirectory system can keep each user separate because they exist in different contexts. Although NetWare will work with two or more users having the same user login name, this setup can create conflicts when accessing the network from other environments, so you should select a naming convention that creates user login names that are unique throughout the entire tree. For example, Luke and Eric plan to add a number to the end of any duplicate user names to keep them unique. In the preceding example, Ken's login name would become KThiele2.

To define the user accounts, Luke developed the User Planning Form shown in Table 4-3, which lists the users in the IS, Engineering, and Manufacturing departments along with their context and template requirements. In the following activities, you learn how to use the templates you established in Activity 4-7 to create the user accounts defined in Table 4-3.

Table 4-3   User Planning Form

Company: Universal AeroSpace
Created by: Eric Kenton

User Name	Login Name	Initial eDirectory and Simple Password	Context	Template Name	Home Directory	Groups	Additional Properties
Kari Means	KMeans	password	Engineering.##UAS	T_Engineering	Yes	Design	Title: AdmAsst
Lianne Jarka	LJarka	password	Engineering.##UAS	T_Engineering	Yes	Design	Title: Engineer
Paul Alm	PAlm	password	Engineering.##UAS	T_Engineering	Yes	Design	Title: Engineer
Russ Pence	RPence	password	Engineering.##UAS	T_Engineering	Yes	Production	Title: Production Manager Home Dir: ##CORP\Engineer Security same as Engineering
Tony Rucci	TRucci	password	Engineering.##UAS	T_Engineering	Yes	Design	Title: Engineer
Bradley Dahl	BDahl	password	Engineering.##UAS	T_Engineering	Yes	Design	Title: Engineer
Eric Kenton	EKenton	password	IS.##UAS	No template; created separately	Yes	ISMgrs	Title: Network Administrator
Kellie Thiele	KThiele	password	IS.##UAS	T_IS	Yes	Design ISMgrs WebMgrs	Password required every 90 days
Luke McMann	LMcMann	password	IS.##UAS	T_IS	Yes	ISMgrs	Password required every 90 days
Bernie Muelner	BMuelner	password	IS.##UAS	T_IS	Yes	ISMgrs	Title: Network administrator for the AeroDyn division; needs to be able to log in and manage the AeroDyn OU; Password required every 90 days
Your name	Your-user-name	password	IS.##UAS	No template; created separately	Yes	ISMgrs	Password required every 90 days
Receiving 1	Receiving1	password	Mfg.Engineering.##UAS	No template; created with LDIF	No	Production	Title: Enter Receipts
Receiving 2	Receiving2	password	Mfg.Engineering.##UAS	No template; created with LDIF	No	Production	Title: Enter Receipts
Shipping 1	Shipping1	password	Mfg.Engineering.##UAS	No template; created with LDIF	No	Production	Title: Enter Shipments

Table 4-3   User Planning Form (continued)

Company: Universal AeroSpace
Created by: Eric Kenton

User Name	Login Name	Initial eDirectory and Simple Password	Context	Template Name	Home Directory	Groups	Additional Properties
Shipping 2	Shipping2	password	Mfg. Engineering.##UAS	No template; created with LDIF	No	Production	Title: Enter Shipments
David Heise	DHeise	password	Mgmt.##UAS	No template; created with iManager. Home directory path: Corp:Mgmt	Yes	Mgrs	Password required every 90 days
Lynn Dai	LDai	password	Mgmt.##UAS	No template; created with iManager. Home directory path: Corp:Mgmt	Yes	Mgrs	Password required every 90 days
Maria Frias	MFrias	password	Mgmt.##UAS	No template; created with iManager. Home directory path: Corp:Mgmt	Yes	Mgrs	Password required every 90 days

Activity 4-8: Creating User Accounts with ConsoleOne

Time Required: 15 minutes

Objective: Use templates to help create user accounts.

Description: In this activity, you use the templates you created in Activity 4-7 to create user objects for your Engineering and IS departments. In Activity 4-9, you'll use iManager to create the users in the Mgmt department.

1. If necessary, start your computer, and log in with your assigned UasAdmin user name.

2. If necessary, log on to your Windows 2000 workstation.

3. Start ConsoleOne.

4. In the Navigation frame, expand **UAS_Tree** and your **##UAS** Organization.

5. Create a user account for Kari Means in the Engineering Organizational Unit:

   a. Click your **Engineering** OU, and then click the **New User** button on the ConsoleOne toolbar to open the New User dialog box.

   b. Enter **KMeans** in the Name text box.

   c. Press the **Tab** key to advance to the Surname text box, and enter **Means**.

   d. To allow users to use NFAP to access the NetWare 6 server without Novell Client, as described in Chapter 2, Eric gave each user a simple password. To enable your users to log in using only the Windows client, click the **Assign Simple Password** check box.

e. To keep it easier for the users, Eric initially made the simple password the same as the NetWare password and required users to change the password when they first log in. To do the same for your users, click the **Force Password Change** check box, and then enter the initial password shown in the User Planning Form (Table 4-3) in the Assign Simple Password text box.

f. To use the T_Engineering template, click the **Use template** check box, click the **Browse** button to the right of the Use template text box, and then double-click the **T_Engineering** template.

g. Click the **Create another User** check box.

h. After completing your entries, verify that your New User dialog box looks similar to the one in Figure 4-7 (you might need to scroll over to see the entire pathname), and then click **OK** to create Kari's user account and open the Set Password dialog box.

i. Enter the initial password shown in your User Planning Form in both the New password and Retype password text boxes, and then click the **Set Password** button to create the new user and return to the New User dialog box.

6. Create additional Engineering user accounts:

a. Enter the name and surname for the next Engineering user, as shown in the User Planning Form.

b. Click **OK** to create the new user and open the Set Password dialog box.

c. Enter the user's initial password in both the New password and Retype password fields, and then click the **Set Password** button to create the new user.

d. Repeat Steps 6a through 6c to create the remaining Engineering user accounts in the User Planning Form. When creating the last user in the Engineering context, click the **Create another User** check box to disable this option. If you forget to remove the check mark, you can click **Cancel** after creating the final Engineering user.

e. After creating all the Engineering users, your ConsoleOne window should look similar to the one in Figure 4-8.

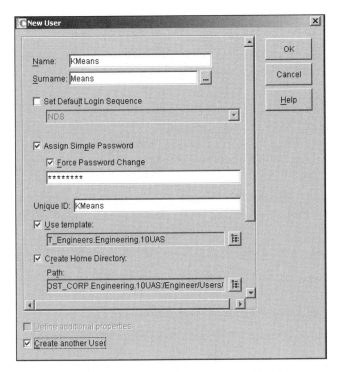

Figure 4-7   The New User dialog box for Kari Means

Later in this chapter, you'll move Russ's user account from the Engineering OU to Mfg.

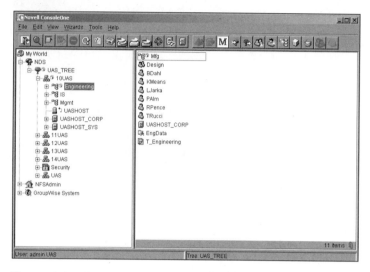

Figure 4-8   Engineering users in the ConsoleOne window

7. Create a user account for KThiele in the IS Organizational Unit:

   a. Click your **IS** OU to highlight it.

   b. Click the **New User** button on the ConsoleOne toolbar to open the New User dialog box.

   c. Enter **KThiele** in the Name text box.

   d. Press the **Tab** key to advance to the Surname text box, and enter **Thiele**.

   e. Click the **Assign Simple Password** check box.

   f. Click the **Force Password Change** check box, and then enter the initial password shown in the User Planning Form in the Assign Simple Password text box.

   g. To use the T_IS template, click the **Use template** check box, click the **Browse** button next to the Use template text box, and then double-click the **T_IS** template.

   h. Click the **Create another User** check box.

   i. Click **OK** to create Kellie's user account and open the Set Password dialog box.

   j. Enter the password shown in your User Planning Form in both the New password and Retype password text boxes, and click the **Set Password** button to create the new user and return to the New User dialog box.

8. Bernie Muelner, the network administrator for the AeroDyn division, will need a user account to log in and manage the AeroDyn OU. Repeat Step 7 to create a user account in the IS OU for Bernie Muelner.

9. Repeat Step 7 to create a user account for Luke McMann. Remember to click the **Create another User** check box to disable this option before creating the account. After creating the account for Luke, the main ConsoleOne window should be displayed.

10. Make Kellie Thiele a member of the Design and WebMgrs group:

   a. Right-click **KThiele**, and then click **Properties** to open the Properties of KThiele dialog box.

   b. Scroll to the right and click the **Memberships** tab.

c. On your student answer sheet, record the groups that Kellie is currently a member of and how she obtained the group memberships.

d. Click the **Add** button.

e. Click the **up arrow** to display the objects in your ##UAS organization.

f. Double-click the **Engineering** OU to display all objects in your Engineering container.

g. Double-click the **Design** group to add it to Kellie's Memberships dialog box.

h. Click the **Add** button.

i. Click the **up arrow** to display the objects in your ##UAS organization.

j. Double-click the **WebMgrs** group to add it to Kellie's Memberships dialog box.

k. Click **OK** to save your changes and return to the ConsoleOne window.

11. Verify that all users in the Engineering department are members of the Design group:

a. Expand your **Engineering** OU, and then click the **Mfg** container to display its objects in the Object frame.

b. Right-click the **Design** group, and then click **Properties** to open the Properties of Production dialog box.

c. Click the **Members** tab to verify that the current members include all the engineers.

d. Record the members on your student answer sheet.

e. Click **Cancel** to return to the ConsoleOne window.

12. Exit ConsoleOne, and log out.

Using iManager to Create Users and Groups

One of Novell's objectives in the OneNet strategy is to make it easier to manage and maintain the organization's network from any computer, regardless of the type of computer you're working on or the network system it is attached to. The iManager utility is one of the new utilities that make managing and maintaining eDirectory possible from an Internet browser. To run iManager, you start your Web browser and then enter the URL for your server, followed by port number 2200. For example, if your server were assigned the IP address 172.20.0.60, you would enter "https://172.20.0.60:2200" in the Address field. The "https" tells the browser to use the Secure Socket Layer (SSL) for a secure connection, and the port number 2200 tells the NetWare Web server to open the Web Manager page, shown in Figure 4-9. Before displaying the NetWare Web Manager window, you might see a security alert message stating that you are about to view pages over a secure connection. You can click the In the future, do not show this warning check box, and then click OK to continue. You might see another security alert message informing you that the security certificate was issued by a company you have not chosen to trust. Security certificates accompany the key sent from the server to the client to encrypt data before sending it over the Internet. The certificate authorizes the key as being issued from a server in a valid organization. Many Internet companies obtain certificates from recognized Internet authorities that are included with Internet Explorer. This message is displayed because your browser software does not have your NetWare server in its trusted certification authority file. You can click the View Certificate option to view the certificate information and then install the certificate. Click Yes to accept the security certificate and display a NetWare Web Manager menu, similar to the one in Figure 4-9. (The options on the menu vary, depending on the services installed on the server.)

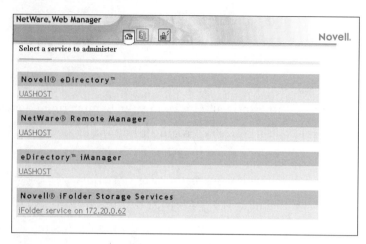

Figure 4-9 The NetWare Web Manager window
When using NetWare 6.5, you will see the NetWare 6.5 Welcome as shown in Figure D-17.

To use iManager, click the server name, UASHOST, displayed under the Novell eDirectory heading to open the iManager Login window, shown in Figure 4-10.

To use iManager to maintain eDirectory objects, you need to log in using the administrator's user name and password or be logged in as a user who has been delegated the authority to perform administrative tasks through Novell's Role Based security (in Chapter 6, you learn how to use Role Based security to assign administrative roles to other objects). Figure 4-11 shows the iManager window after logging in as the network Admin user.

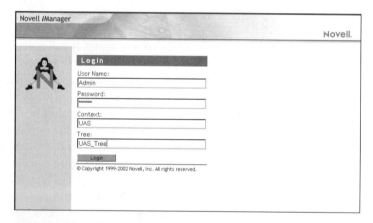

Figure 4-10 The iManager Login window

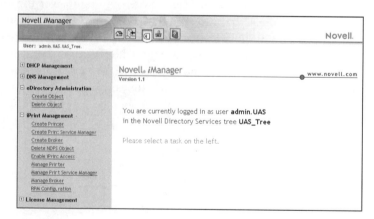

Figure 4-11 List of administrative roles in the iManager window

The roles the user can perform are displayed in the left-hand frame. Role Based security consists of groups of administrative tasks called **administrative roles** that can be assigned to certain users, enabling them to perform the tasks within a particular context in the eDirectory tree. The administrative roles in NetWare 6 include:

- *eDirectory Administration*—Basic directory administration tasks, such as creating users and groups

- *License Management*—Tasks that include maintaining and managing NetWare server licensing (see Chapter 10 for more information)

- *iPrint Management*—Tasks such as creating printer objects and enabling iPrinter access (see Chapter 8 for more information)

- *DNS Management*—Tasks necessary to set up and manage Domain Name Services on NetWare 6 servers

- *DHCP Management*—Tasks necessary to set up and manage Dynamic Host Configuration Protocol services on NetWare 6 servers

To perform the activities in this book, Role Based security was used to give your ##Admin user name the administrative roles necessary to manage users and printers in your ##UAS Organization. In addition to delegating administrative tasks to other users, roles can be used to reduce the need to log in as the network administrator. Logging in as the network administrator over the Internet can increase the likelihood of security leaks or mistakes. Delegating roles is a good way to decrease the need to log in with the network administrator user name by using a user name that has been assigned only the permissions you need. For example, if you're working on network printers, log in to the network with the user name that has only that role. Using the iPrinter role will prevent you from accidentally deleting or changing the configuration of another object. As described later in this chapter, rather than log in over the Internet using the administrator user name, Eric created special Organizational Role objects for various administrative purposes. In the following activity, you use iManager to simulate Eric's ability to manage users and groups when away from the office.

Activity 4-9: Creating User and Group Accounts with iManager

Time Required: 10 minutes

Objective: Use iManager to create user and group accounts from a Web browser.

Description: Eric finds the OneNet utilities useful for performing network management tasks, such as creating new users or adding users to a group, when he's working from home or while on the road. Last November, Eric took a vacation to Churchill, Canada, to view the polar bears that congregate there while waiting for the ice to form on Hudson Bay. Unfortunately, he had to leave for his trip before he had finished setting up user accounts for the UAS network. Luke approved his vacation request, however, because Eric would still be able to finish his work while traveling by using the Internet and Novell's OneNet strategy. While in Canada, he learned that David Heise, the president of UAS, needed a user account to log in to the network. To do this, Eric went down to the local community center and used a computer with Internet access to log in to the UAS network and create user accounts for David Heise and Lynn Dai. In this activity, you simulate Eric's process by using iManager to create user and group accounts for the Mgmt department.

1. If necessary, start your computer. Log in to the network with your UasAdmin user name and password.

2. Start Internet Explorer. In the Address text box, enter the URL **https://IP_address:2200**, and then press **Enter** (replace *IP_address* with the IP address supplied by your instructor).

3. If necessary, click **OK** or **Yes** to respond to the security alert messages and open the NetWare Web Manager window.

4. Click the **UASHOST** server link beneath the eDirectory iManager option to open the Login window.

5. Log in to iManager with your UasAdmin user name and password:

   a. Enter your **UasAdmin** user name in the User Name text box.

   b. Enter your password in the Password text box.

   c. Enter the context to your UAS container in the Context text box (for example, if using the classroom server enter either **.UAS** or **.UAS.CLASS** depending on the classroom tree structure).

   d. Verify that UAS_Tree is displayed in the Tree text box.

   e. Click the **Login** button to log in and display the iManager window.

6. Expand the eDirectory Administration role by clicking the **+** symbol to the left of that role.

7. Create a group for the Universal AeroSpace Mgmt department:

   a. Click the **Create Object** link to open the Available Classes dialog box.

   b. If necessary, click the **Group** object class, and then click the **Next** button to open the Create Group dialog box.

   c. Enter **Mgrs** in the Object Name text box.

   d. Click the **Browse** button next to the Context text box, click the **down arrow** to the left of ##UAS Organization, and then click your **Mgmt** container to enter the Mgmt.##UAS context, as shown in Figure 4-12.

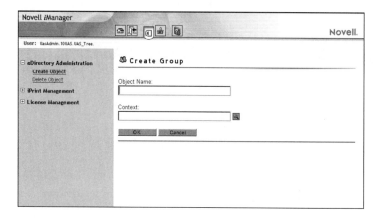

Figure 4-12   The Create Group dialog box in iManager

   e. Click **OK** to create the group.

f. Click **OK** to close the Create Object request succeeded message box and return to the iManager main window.

8. Create a user account for Lynn Dai:

a. Click the **Create Object** link under the eDirectory Administration role to open the Available Classes dialog box.

b. Click the **User** object class, and then click the **Next** button to open the Create User dialog box.

c. Enter **LDai** in the User name text box.

d. Enter **Dai** in the Last name text box.

e. Click the **Browse** button next to the Context text box to select the Mgmt context, as shown in Figure 4-13.

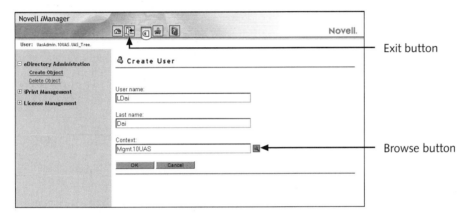

Figure 4-13   The Create User dialog box in iManager
When using NetWare 6.5, the Create User dialog box contains additional fields as shown in Figure D-26.

f. Click **OK** to create the user.

g. Click **OK** to close the Create User request succeeded message box, and return to the iManager main window.

9. Follow the procedure in Step 9 to create a user account for David Heise.

10. Follow the procedure in Step 9 to create a user account for Maria Frias.

11. Exit iManager and return to the Login window by clicking the **Exit** button on the toolbar.

12. Close Internet Explorer by clicking **File**, **Close** on the menu.

13. Log off Windows by clicking **Start**, **Shut Down**, and **Log off** *<name>*.

Updating Multiple User Accounts

As a network administrator, you'll often find that after creating user accounts, you need to make changes that affect several different users, such as preventing users from being logged in to the network between midnight and 4:00 a.m. so that you can perform a network backup. To make this job easier, you can use NetWare Administrator or ConsoleOne to simultaneously modify multiple user accounts. In ConsoleOne, to change properties common to several users, such as an address or login restriction, you can select multiple users by pressing the Ctrl key to highlight the user names, highlighting a group or template object or highlighting a container, and then selecting File, Properties of Multiple Users on the menu bar. If you highlight a group or container object, all users in that group or container will be modified. If you highlight a template object and select Properties of Multiple Users, all user accounts created with that template will be modified. In the following activities, you use the Properties of Multiple Objects dialog box to update home directories and login restrictions for the Mgmt users Lynn Dai, Maria Frias, and David Heise, and update information on the Engineering user accounts.

Activity 4-10: Updating All Users in a Container

Time Required: 10 minutes

Objectives: Use ConsoleOne to create and manage user accounts.

Description: After returning from his vacation, Eric needed to create home directories and apply password and login restrictions he defined on the User Planning Form for the accounts he created from iManager. In this activity, you use the Properties of Multiple Users option in ConsoleOne to add home directories and password restrictions for your Mgmt user accounts.

1. If necessary, start your computer, and log in with your assigned UasAdmin user name and password.

2. If necessary, log on to your Windows 2000 workstation.

3. Start ConsoleOne.

4. In the Navigation frame, expand **UAS_Tree** and your **##UAS** container.

5. Select all users in your Mgmt Organizational Unit:

   a. Click your **Mgmt** OU container.

   b. Click **File**, **Properties of Multiple Objects** on the menu bar to open the Properties of Multiple Objects Available Classes dialog box. On your student answer sheet, record the available object classes.

   c. Click the **User** object class, and then click **OK** to open the Properties of Multiple Users dialog box.

6. Create user home directories for the Mgmt user accounts:

   a. Click the **down arrow** on the General tab, and then click the **Environment** option to display the Home Directory section.

   b. Click the **Browse** button next to the Volume and Path text boxes, and then double-click your **UASHOST_CORP** volume to expand it.

   c. Click your **Mgmt** folder, and then click **OK** to display the Home Directory path, as shown in Figure 4-14.

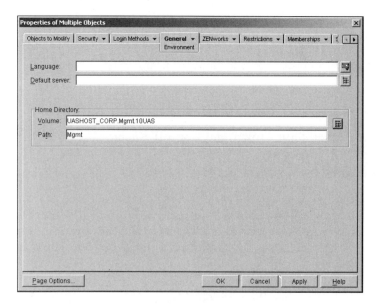

Figure 4-14   The Properties of Multiple Objects dialog box in ConsoleOne

d. Click the **Apply** button to create the user home directories.

7. Add all users to the Mgrs group:

   a. Click the **Memberships** tab to open the Memberships dialog box.

   b. Click the **Add** button to open the Select Object dialog box.

   c. If necessary, click the **Mgrs** group, and then click **OK** to add the group to the Memberships dialog box.

8. Set password restrictions for the Mgmt users:

   a. Click the **Restrictions** tab to open the Password Restrictions dialog box.

   b. Enter the password restrictions for the Mgmt users, referring to the Additional Properties column in Table 4-3.

9. Click **OK** to save your changes and return to the main ConsoleOne window.

10. If you're continuing to the next activity, leave the ConsoleOne window open and stay logged; if not, exit ConsoleOne, and log out.

Activity 4-11: Updating Selected Users

Time Required: 10 minutes

Objectives: Use ConsoleOne to create and manage user accounts.

Description: The engineers share a fax machine, and management would like to have that fax number set up on the Engineering user accounts. To make all engineers members of the Design group and give them the new fax number, Eric used the Details on Multiple Users option. In this activity, you learn how to use this option to update just the Engineering user accounts with fax numbers and group membership.

1. If necessary, start your computer, log in with your UasAdmin user name and password, start ConsoleOne, and expand **UAS_Tree** and your **##UAS** container.

2. Give the design engineers the fax number of (715) 555-7223:

   a. Click your **Engineering** OU to display all user accounts.

   b. Hold down the **Ctrl** key, and click the **LJarka**, **TRucci**, **PAlm**, and **BDahl** Engineering user accounts to select them.

   c. Click **File**, **Properties of Multiple Objects** on the menu bar to open the Properties of Multiple Objects dialog box.

   d. On your student answer sheet, record the user objects to be modified.

   e. Click the **Memberships** tab, and then click the **Add** button. Click **Design** in the Select Object dialog box, and click **OK** to add the Design group to the Groups list box.

   f. Click the **General** tab, and enter **(715) 555-7223** in the Fax number text box.

   g. Click the **down arrow** on the Restrictions tab, and then click the **Time Restrictions** option.

   h. Restrict users from logging in on Sunday, and on your student answer sheet, record the process you used.

   i. Click **OK** to save the changes and return to the ConsoleOne main window.

3. Verify that the changes were made by following these steps:

   a. Right-click **TRucci**, and then click **Properties** to open the Properties of TRucci dialog box.

   b. Click the **General** tab, and verify that the Fax number text box contains (715) 555-7223.

   c. Click the **down arrow** on the Restrictions tab, and then click the **Time Restrictions** option.

      d. Verify that Sunday is blocked out.

      e. Click the **Memberships** tab, and verify that Tony is a member of the Production and Design groups.

      f. Click **Cancel** to return to the ConsoleOne main window.

4. Repeat Step 3 to verify changes for LJarka, PAlm, and BDahl.

5. Exit ConsoleOne, and log out.

Using LDAP to Import Objects

As described in Chapter 1, eDirectory uses the industry-standard X.500 naming system to store information on network objects. Because eDirectory is based on an industry-standard system, information can be exported or imported from other directory systems, such as Windows 2000 Active Directory, that are also based on X.500. The **Lightweight Directory Access Protocol (LDAP)** is a simplified version of X.500 that makes it easier for compatible systems to exchange directory information. NetWare 6 includes an LDAP import and export wizard with ConsoleOne that network administrators can use to transfer information to and from eDirectory with **Lightweight Directory Interchange Format (LDIF)** files, which are simple ASCII text files that use a standardized syntax to add, change, or delete objects. The basic syntax of an LDIF file consists of a distinguished name, a change type, an object class, and attribute values, as shown in Table 4-4.

Table 4-4   LDIF Command Syntax

Command Line	Purpose
dn: *distinguished name*	Distinguished name of object to be created, modified, or deleted
changetype: *Add*	Specifies the type of change: add, modify, or delete
ObjectClass: *object class*	Specifies an object class to be used with this entry; an object can have multiple object classes defined for it
uid: *username*	The user's login name
cn: *common name*	The user's last name
ACL: *access control list (rights to eDirectory)*	Multiple ACL entries are used to assign the new user object rights to certain properties, as described in Chapter 6
groupMembership: *groups*	Distinguished name of group objects the user will be added to
securityEquals	Identifies other objects with the same rights that the new object will have; usually specifies group the new user account will belong to

LDAP distinguished names use a typeful format with commas to separate the components instead of periods, which are used with eDirectory distinguished names. In addition, unlike eDirectory distinguished names, LDAP distinguished names do not start with a period. For example, when using LDAP, Kellie Thiele's distinguished name would be specified as follows:

```
cn=KThiele,ou=is,o=uas
```

The changetype field specifies the action: Add, Modify, or Delete. The object class specifies the type of object being created or modified, such as a user, container, or printer. The attribute fields specify information properties that are unique to the specified object class. Examples of attributes for a user object include givenName, fullName, and title. UAS has several computers in the Manufacturing department that are used mostly for entering shipping and receiving data. Instead of creating user accounts for each user who can enter data on these stations, Russ Pence has recommended having a generic account for each station based on its function. Although Eric could use ConsoleOne to create the accounts for the computer stations in the Shipping and Receiving areas, because these accounts will be very similar, he decided to use an LDIF file to create the accounts. Using an LDIF file makes it easy to add stations in the future because the file can simply be edited to insert the new station name and location. Figure 4-15 shows an example of an LDIF file Eric used to create two of the computer station accounts named Receiving1 and Shipping1 in the Mfg OU.

In Activity 4-12, you use Eric's LDIF file as a model to create your own LDIF file containing the station accounts identified earlier in Table 4-3. You then learn how to use ConsoleOne to import the users from your LDIF file into your Mfg OU.

```
Scr04-19 - Notepad                                                    _|□|×|
File  Edit  Format  Help
#The following lines create the Receiving 1 station in the Mfg container
dn: cn=Receiving1,ou=Mfg,ou=Engineering,o=UAS
changetype: add
uid: Receiving1
Language: ENGLISH
title: Receiving Department Computer
sn: Receiving
securityEquals: cn=Production,ou=Mfg,ou=Engineering,o=UAS
objectClass: inetorgPerson
objectClass: organizationalPerson
objectClass: person
objectClass: ndsLoginProperties
objectClass: top
groupMembership: cn=Production,ou=Mfg,ou=Engineering,o=UAS
cn: Receiving1
ACL: 2#subtree#cn=Receiving1,ou=Mfg,ou=Engineering,o=UAS#[All Attributes Rights]
ACL: 2#entry#cn=Receiving1,ou=Mfg,ou=Engineering,o=UAS#loginScript
ACL: 1#subtree#[Root]#[Entry Rights]
ACL: 2#entry#[Public]#messageServer
ACL: 2#entry#[Root]#groupMembership
ACL: 6#entry#cn=Receiving1,ou=Mfg,ou=Engineering,o=UAS#printJobConfiguration
ACL: 2#entry#[Root]#networkAddress

#The following lines create the Shipping 1 station in the Mfg container
dn: cn=Shipping1,ou=Mfg,ou=Engineering,o=UAS
changetype: add
uid: Shipping1
Language: ENGLISH
title: Machine tool supervisor
sn: Shipping
securityEquals: cn=Production,ou=Mfg,ou=Engineering,o=UAS
objectClass: inetorgPerson
objectClass: organizationalPerson
objectClass: person
objectClass: ndsLoginProperties
objectClass: top
groupMembership: cn=Production,ou=Mfg,ou=Engineering,o=UAS
cn: Shipping1
ACL: 2#subtree#cn=Shipping1,ou=Mfg,ou=Engineering,o=UAS#[All Attributes Right
s]
ACL: 2#entry#cn=Shipping1,ou=Mfg,ou=Engineering,o=UAS#loginScript
ACL: 1#subtree#[Root]#[Entry Rights]
ACL: 2#entry#[Public]#messageServer
ACL: 2#entry#[Root]#groupMembership
ACL: 6#entry#cn=Shipping1,ou=Mfg,ou=Engineering,o=UAS#printJobConfiguration
ACL: 2#entry#[Root]#networkAddress
```

Figure 4-15   Eric's LDIF file

Activity 4-12: Importing Users from an LDIF File

Time Required: 20 minutes

Objective: Use ConsoleOne to import users from an LDIF file.

Description: In this activity, you edit the LDIF file Eric used to create his users, and then use ConsoleOne to create your additional Mfg users by importing your modified LDIF file.

1. If necessary, start your computer, and log in with your assigned UasAdmin user name and password.

2. If necessary, log on to your Windows 2000 workstation.

3. If necessary, map a drive to your ##CORP volume:

    a. Right-click **My Network Places**, and then click **Novell Map Network Drive** to open the Map Drive dialog box.

    b. Click the **Choose the drive letter to map** list arrow, and then click **L:** in the list of options.

    c. Enter **\\UASHOST\##CORP** in the Enter the network path to the resource text box.

    d. Click the **Map** button to display all directories on your volume.

4. Open the Stations.ldif file in your Utility folder:

    a. Browse to the Apps\Utility directory.

    b. Right-click the **Stations.ldif** file, and then click **Open with**.

    c. Double-click **Notepad** to display the contents of the Stations.ldif file.

5. Use Notepad to edit the existing LDIF file to create your Shipping and Receiving stations:

    a. Check each line and change the name of the Organization from UAS to **##UAS** (## represents your assigned student number).

    b. To enter the lines needed to create an account for a second Receiving station, copy the lines for creating the Receiving1 station and paste them to the end of your LDIF file. In the copied lines, replace the name Receiving1 with **Receiving2**.

    c. To enter the lines needed to create an account for a second Shipping station, copy the lines for creating the Shipping1 station and paste them to the end of your LDIF file. In the copied lines, replace the name Shipping1 with **Shipping2**.

    d. Click **File**, **Exit** on the menu bar, and then click **Yes** to save your changes and exit Notepad.

6. Import the LDIF file from ConsoleOne:

    a. Start ConsoleOne, and expand **UAS_Tree** and your **##UAS** Organization.

    b. Expand your **Engineering** container, and click the **Mfg** OU.

    c. Click **Wizards**, **NDS Import/Export** on the menu bar to open the NDS Import/Export Wizard.

    d. In the Select Task dialog box of the wizard, verify that the **Import LDIF File** radio button is selected, and then click the **Next** button to open the Select Source LDIF File dialog box.

    e. Click the **Browse** button, and select the **L:** drive from Step 4. Navigate to your Apps\Utility directory.

    f. Double-click your **Stations.ldif** file to include it in the Select Source LDIF File text box.

    g. Click the **Next** button to open the Select Destination LDAP Server dialog box.

    h. In the Server DNS Name/IP Address text box, enter the IP address of your UASHOST server.

    i. Enter **389** in the Port text box.

    j. Click the **Authenticated Login** button, and enter **cn=UasAdmin,o=##UAS** in the User DN text box. (Be sure to separate the entries with commas.)

    k. Enter your password in the Password text box.

    l. Click the **Advanced** button to open the Advanced Options dialog box. Record the four advanced options on your student answer sheet.

    m. To allow the LDAP server to create objects in the sequence it needs them, click to place a check mark in the **Allow forward references** check box. Leave the Use LBURP check box selected, and click **OK** to return to the NDS Import/Export Wizard dialog box (see Figure 4-16).

    n. Click the **Next** button to display summary information.

    o. Verify your entries, and then click the **Finish** button to import the users.

    p. Record the results of your operation on your student answer sheet.

    q. Click **Close** to return to ConsoleOne.

7. If you have any errors, correct your Stations.ldif file, delete any users created in Step 6, and then repeat Step 6.

8. Use ConsoleOne to verify that the new station accounts exist.

9. Exit ConsoleOne, and log off.

4

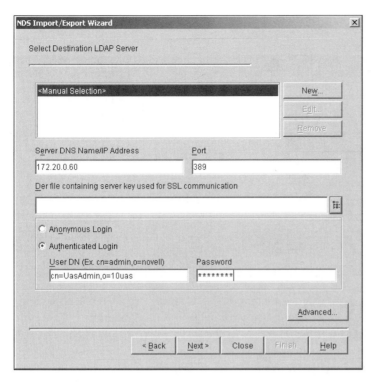

Figure 4-16 The NDS Import/Export Wizard

ESTABLISHING ORGANIZATIONAL ROLE OBJECTS

In addition to reducing the need to assign rights to multiple users, group objects are a convenient way to give users the rights they need for certain job responsibilities. However, normally you would not want to create groups that represent positions within the company. For example, David Heise wanted the IS department to set up a manager for each department's data and user accounts. Currently, Kari Means is assigned to act as the manager for the Engineering department's data and user accounts, Russ Pence is responsible for the Mfg data and users, and the administrative assistant, Lynn Dai, acts as the manager for the Mgmt department. Because the network administrator for the AeroDyn division, Bernie Muelner, has a lot of experience working with AeroDyn's Manufacturing department, he will work with Russ Pence to maintain Mfg users and resources for both Universal AeroSpace and AeroDyn.

However, David wants only Bernie to be able to manage the objects in the AeroDyn OU. In addition, to increase security by limiting the use of the network administrative user name, Luke wanted Eric to create separate accounts to perform iManager administrative roles, such as eDirectory management and printer management. Because the user accounts assigned to these positions will change and could include multiple users, Eric didn't want to assign the rights to individual users. Instead of having to create group objects for these types of positions, Novell has another object type called an **Organizational Role object**, which enables you to assign rights to an object rather than a specific user. You can then make any user an occupant of the organizational role to gain the associated rights and privileges given to the object. If the job duties are given to another employee, you simply need to make the new employee an occupant of the Organizational Role object. For example, to give Bernie and Russ rights to manage the Mfg data and users, Eric made them occupants of the MfgMgr Organizational Role object. Only Bernie will currently manage the AeroDyn objects, so Eric made him the only occupant of the AeroMgr organizational role. Another good use for an Organizational Role object is to assign rights to a backup administrator account that can be used in case your Admin user name is disabled. Table 4-5 contains a list of all the Organizational Role objects Eric defined and created for the UAS network.

Table 4-5   Organizational Role Planning Form

Created by: *Eric Kenton*   Date: _____

Role Name	Context	Purpose	Primary Occupant
SysOp	.IS.##UAS	Backup system operator	Clark Kent
eDirAdm	.IS.##UAS	Administrative role for maintaining eDirectory	Your-user-name
PrintAdm	.IS.##UAS	Administrative role for maintaining Internet printing	Your-user-name
EngMgr	.Engineering.##UAS	Engineering department data manager	Kari Means
ISSEng	.Engineering.##UAS	Primary engineer assigned to the International Space Station	Tony Rucci
RoverEng	.Engineering.##UAS	Primary engineer assigned to the Mars Rover project	Lianne Jarka
MfgMgr	.Mfg.Engineering.##UAS	Manufacturing department data manager	Russ Pence, Bernie Muelner
AdmAsst	.Mgmt.##UAS	UAS administrative assistants	Lynn Dai, Kari Means
AeroMgr	.Mfg.Engineering.##UAS	Manager of AeroDyn division network objects	Bernie Muelner

In Chapters 5 and 6, you'll learn how to assign the rights these Organizational Role objects need to perform their required functions. In the following activity, you create the Organizational Role objects shown in Table 4-5 and then assign the users listed in the table as the occupants.

Activity 4-13: Creating Organizational Role Objects

Time Required: 10 minutes

Objectives: Use ConsoleOne to create and manage user accounts.

Description: To meet the directive of having a manager for each department's data, Eric created an Organizational Role object for each department manager and then made the designated user the occupant. In this activity, you create the Organizational Role objects that Eric identified in Table 4-5 for your UAS network.

1. If necessary, start your computer, and log in with your assigned UasAdmin user name and password.

2. Start ConsoleOne.

3. In the Navigation frame, expand **UAS_Tree**.

4. Create an Organizational Role object named SysOp:

   a. Expand your **##UAS** container, and then click the **IS** OU.

   b. Click the **New Object** button on the toolbar to open the New Object dialog box.

   c. Scroll down and double-click the **Organizational Role** object to open the New Organizational Role dialog box.

   d. Enter **SysOp** in the Name text box, and then click the **Define additional properties** check box.

   e. Click the **OK** button to create the SysOp object and open the Properties of SysOp dialog box.

   f. Click the **Browse** button next to the Occupant text box to open the Select Object dialog box.

   g. Double-click **CKent** to make Clark the occupant of the SysOp organizational role.

   h. Click **OK** to save the changes and return to ConsoleOne.

5. Create the remaining Organizational Role objects in Table 4-5 by clicking the specified container context and then following the procedure in Step 4.

6. After all Organizational Role objects are created, exit ConsoleOne, and log out.

DELETING, RENAMING, AND MOVING OBJECTS

When working with the eDirectory tree, you might need to rename, delete, or move an object from one location to another to better organize the structure. As you'll learn in Chapters 5 and 6, users often obtain rights to access files and use eDirectory objects by being a member of an OU. In addition, login scripts are usually associated with OUs to provide drive mappings and workstation setups for all users in an OU. As a result, when moving objects, keep in mind that moving an object to a different location can change the drive mappings and computer setups users have when they log in, and affect users' rights to access files and other network objects, such as printers.

Renaming an object simply involves using ConsoleOne or NetWare Administrator to right-click the object, select the Rename option, and then type a new name. Deleting leaf objects, such as user accounts and groups, is as easy as clicking on the object and pressing the Delete key; when deleting container objects, however, you need to remove all objects from the container before deleting it. The complex part of renaming, deleting, or moving objects is understanding how the change affects other objects in the tree. For example, deleting a group object that has been given rights to a directory or printer could prevent users from accessing network information or resources. In the following activity, you practice renaming and deleting eDirectory objects.

To move a leaf object, such as a user, group, or volume, in ConsoleOne, you simply need to select the object and choose File, Move on the menu bar. Moving container objects is more difficult because NetWare will move only partitions. To move an OU from one location to another, you must first make the container a separate partition, as described in Chapter 2. You can then move the container's partition to another location and merge it back into the tree. In the following sections, you learn how to use ConsoleOne to move user and container objects.

Activity 4-14: Moving, Deleting, and Renaming Objects

Time Required: 5 minutes

Objectives: Use ConsoleOne to create and manage user accounts.

Description: Although Eric originally placed Russ Pence in the Engineering OU, because Russ is the Manufacturing manager, Luke decided that Russ's user account should be in the Mfg container. In this activity, you use ConsoleOne to move the user object RPence from the Engineering OU to the Mfg OU. You then practice deleting and renaming objects.

1. If necessary, start your computer, and log in with your assigned UasAdmin user name and password.

2. If necessary, log on to your Windows 2000 workstation.

3. Start ConsoleOne.

4. In the Navigation frame, expand **UAS_Tree** and your **##UAS** container.

5. Click your **Engineering** container to display all users in the Object frame.

6. Right-click **RPence**, and then click **Move** to open the Move dialog box.

7. Click the **Browse** button to the right of the Destination text box to open the Select Object dialog box.

8. Click **Mfg**, and then click **OK** to insert Mfg.Engineering.## UAS in the Destination text box.

9. Click **OK** to move the user object.

10. Expand the **Engineering** OU, if necessary, and then click the **Mfg** container to verify that the user object RPence has been moved.

11. Create an OU named Temp in the Engineering container:

    a. Click your **Engineering** OU to display all objects in the Object frame.

b. Click the **New Object** button on the ConsoleOne toolbar to open the New Object dialog box.

c. Scroll down and click **Organizational Unit**, and then click **OK** to open the New Organizational Unit dialog box.

d. Enter **Temp** in the Name text box, and then click **OK** to create the Temp OU and return to the main ConsoleOne window.

12. Create a user named Guest in the Temp OU:

a. Click the new **Temp** OU, and then click the **New User** button to open the New User dialog box.

b. Enter **Guest** in both the Name and Surname text boxes, and then click **OK** to open the Set Password dialog box. Enter **password** in the New Password and Retype Password text boxes, and then click the **Set Password** button to create the new user and return to the ConsoleOne main window.

13. Attempt to delete the Temp OU:

a. Click the **Temp** OU, and then press the **Delete** key.

b. Click **Yes** to confirm the deletion.

c. On your student answer sheet, record the message you see.

d. Click **OK** to return to the ConsoleOne main window.

14. Change the name of the Temp OU:

a. Right-click the **Temp** OU, and then click **Rename** to open the Rename dialog box.

b. Enter the name **Temporary**, and then click **OK** to save your change and return to the main ConsoleOne window.

15. Delete the Guest user account:

a. If necessary, click the **Temporary** OU to display all objects in the Object frame.

b. Right-click the **Guest** user, and then click **Delete NDS Object** to open the Delete confirmation message box.

c. Click **Yes** to confirm the deletion and return to the main ConsoleOne window.

16. Delete the Temporary OU:

a. Click the **Temporary** OU, and press the **Delete** key (or right-click the **Temporary** OU and click **Delete NDS Object**) to display the Delete confirmation message box.

b. Click **Yes** to confirm the deletion.

c. Record the results on your student answer sheet.

17. Exit ConsoleOne, and log out.

Moving a Container Object

When managing the structure of the eDirectory database, sometimes you need to move a container object from one location to another within the eDirectory hierarchy to make access to resources easier, for example. As you'll learn in Chapter 6 on eDirectory security, when a container becomes a subcontainer of another container, the subcontainer has access rights to objects in the parent container. For example, the Mfg container is currently a subcontainer of the Engineering container, but David Heise has suggested that the Mfg container be made a separate container to prevent accidental access to Engineering department resources.

Moving a container object is more complex than moving a leaf object because it changes the hierarchy of the eDirectory tree, thereby reorganizing the eDirectory database. In Chapter 2, you learned that the eDirectory database is divided into one or more partitions, starting with the [Root] partition. Each partition is a separate file or replica located on one or more NetWare servers. The main reason for creating additional partitions is to divide a large eDirectory database into smaller files or replicas for more efficient access. However, partitioning eDirectory also makes it easier to move containers. By making a container a separate partition, it becomes a separate file that can be moved and synchronized to another location in the hierarchical structure of the eDirectory database. As a result, to move a container object to another location in the eDirectory tree, you need to perform only these three steps:

1. Use ConsoleOne to create a partition that starts with the container to be moved (the Mfg OU, in this example).

2. After a partition has been created for the container, use ConsoleOne to move the container's partition to the new location.

3. Complete the move by merging the Mfg container's partition back into the [Root] partition.

Another consideration when moving container objects is that creating and merging partitions requires changes to the [Root] partition of the eDirectory tree. As a result, to move container objects, NetWare requires that your user name have the Supervisor right to the root of the eDirectory tree, as described in Chapter 5. In Activity 4-15, you perform a three-part procedure to move one of your OUs to a new location.

Activity 4-15: Moving an Organizational Unit

Time Required: 10 minutes

Objectives: Use ConsoleOne to create and manage user accounts.

Description: This activity consists of three parts. In Part I, you create a separate partition for the Mfg container. In Part II, you move the Mfg container to your ##UAS organization, and in Part III, you merge the Mfg partition into your ##UAS [Root] partition. If necessary, log in and start ConsoleOne to begin this activity.

Part I: Creating a New Partition   Before you can move a container object, you need to make the container a separate partition. Follow these steps to make the Mfg container a separate partition:

1. To display partition information in your ConsoleOne window, click your **##UAS** Organization, and then click **View**, **Partition and Replica View** on the menu bar.

2. If necessary, expand your **Engineering** OU to display the Mfg container.

3. Click your **Mfg** OU to select it.

4. Click **Edit**, **Create Partition** on the menu bar to open the Create Partition dialog box.

5. Click **OK** to create a new partition and return to the ConsoleOne Partition and Replica view. On your student answer sheet, record the change to your Mfg container icon.

Part II: Moving the Container   After the container is a separate partition, you can use ConsoleOne to move the Mfg container beneath your ##UAS Organization by following these steps:

1. Right-click the **Mfg** partition, and then click **Move** to open the Move dialog box.

2. Click the **Browse** button next to the Destination text box to open the Select Object dialog box.

3. Click the **up arrow** twice to display your ##UAS Organization.

4. Click your **##UAS** container, and then click **OK**. Your Move dialog box should look similar to the one in Figure 4-17.

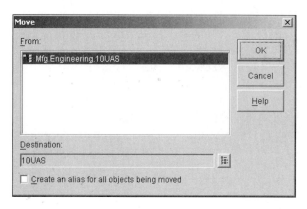

Figure 4-17   Moving a partition to a new container

5. Click the **OK** button to move the Mfg OU.

6. The ConsoleOne view should automatically change back to the normal tree view, with your Mfg OU appearing directly under your ##UAS Organization along with the Engineering, IS, and Mgmt containers. If you need to update the view, press **F5**.

Part III: Merging the Mfg Partition Back into the [Root] Partition   Although he could have left Mfg as a separate partition, Eric wanted to keep the number of partitions to a minimum to reduce administrative overhead. In this part of the activity, you merge the Mfg partition back into the [Root] partition by performing these steps:

1. Click the **Mfg** partition to select it.

2. Change to the Partition and Replica view by clicking **View**, **Partition and Replica View** on the menu bar.

3. Click **Edit**, **Merge Partition** on the menu bar to open the Merge Partition dialog box, similar to the one in Figure 4-18.

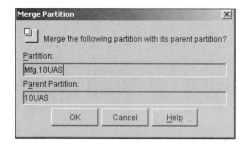

Figure 4-18   The Merge Partition dialog box

4. Click **OK** and wait for the Mfg partition to be merged back into your parent ##UAS partition. After the merge is complete, the partition icon will be removed from your Mfg OU.

5. Change your view back to the Console view by clicking **View**, **Console View** on the menu bar.

6. Click the **Mfg** OU to confirm that all objects have been moved along with the Mfg container to be placed under your ##UAS Organization, as shown in Figure 4-19.

7. Exit ConsoleOne, and log out.

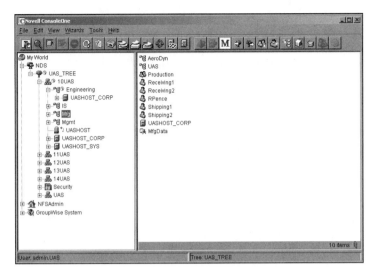

Figure 4-19 Confirming the Mfg container's move in the ConsoleOne window

Congratulations! You're well on your way to setting up your UAS network system. Now that you've established your login security by creating user, group, and Organizational Role objects for the Engineering and IS departments, you can apply what you've learned to complete your login security for the other UAS departments by performing the end-of-chapter projects. In Chapter 5, you will secure the file system by granting users the rights they need to access files and applications.

CHAPTER SUMMARY

- The eDirectory tree is the skeleton of the NetWare 6 network system, providing the structure that contains all network objects. As a result, network administrators must know how to implement the eDirectory system by creating the necessary objects and establishing a login security system. ConsoleOne is a powerful and easy-to-use Windows-based utility that Novell CNAs use when setting up and securing the network. The iManager utility can also be used to create and maintain user and group objects from an Internet browser.

- Login security consists of account restrictions, intruder detection, and authentication. Account restrictions include password, time, and station restrictions and can be set for user and user template objects. Intruder detection, enabled on a container-by-container basis, helps protect against intruders guessing user passwords by locking user accounts after the specified number of incorrect login attempts have been made in a given time period.

- User templates make creating user objects more efficient. You can use them to define the path to users' home directories and set common account and password restrictions.

- LDAP provides a way to exchange directory information between systems that are X.500 compatible, such as eDirectory and Microsoft ActiveDirectory, by using LDIF files. You can use LDIF files as a quick way to create user objects.

- Novell supplies an Organizational Role object that's useful when assigning special privileges to certain user accounts. Organizational Role objects are similar to groups, except that they usually represent positions in the organization. If another user is assigned the responsibilities, you simply need to change the occupant of the organizational role to give him or her the required privileges.

- When managing an eDirectory system, you often need to move objects from one container to another. Although moving leaf objects is fast and easy, moving a container from one location to another requires the administrator to create a partition starting at the container to be moved, move the partition to the new location, and then merge the new partition with the parent partition of the container it has been moved into.

KEY TERMS

administrative role — A group of administrative tasks that can be assigned to Admin users so that they can perform administrative functions, such as managing eDirectory, printing, licensing, and DHCP/DNS services.

authentication — The part of NetWare security that helps protect against hackers by validating each network packet to guarantee that it was sent from the authorized user.

intruder detection — A part of login security that works at the container level by setting a limit on the number of incorrect login attempts that can be made on a user account in that container during a specified time period.

Lightweight Directory Access Protocol (LDAP) — A simplified version of X.500 that makes it easier for compatible systems to exchange directory information.

Lightweight Directory Interchange Format (LDIF) — An ASCII text file format that uses a standardized syntax to add, change, or delete objects in LDAP-compatible directory systems.

Organizational Role object — An object type that enables you to assign rights to an object rather than a specific user.

user template — A property that defines standard settings and configures restrictions for each user in a particular container.

REVIEW QUESTIONS

1. List five security systems used in setting up a NetWare 6 network.

_____

_____

_____

_____

_____

2. Which of the following allows the network administrator to define standard settings, such as the location of home directories and password restrictions for new users?

   a. groups

   b. templates

   c. organizational roles

   d. LDIF files

3. List the three steps for moving the Production container from the Engineering container to the Business container:

_____

_____

_____

4. Which of the following is not a component of login security?

   a. password restriction

   b. intruder detection

   c. administrative role

   d. station restriction

5. List three types of account restrictions:

_____

_____

_____

6. Which of the following security measures allows you to set the maximum number of times a user can enter an incorrect password?

   a. password restriction

   b. account restriction

   c. intruder detection

   d. authorization

7. Authentication involves validating a user's login request. True or false?

8. Which of the following involves validating each network packet to make sure it has come from an authorized user?

   a. authorization

   b. authentication

   c. password security

   d. intruder detection

9. Which of the following NetWare 6 utilities can be used to move a container to another location in the eDirectory tree?

   a. ConsoleOne

   b. NDSMgr

   c. NetWare Administrator

   d. iManager

10. Which of the following objects should be used to provide a backup administrator account?

   a. group

   b. Organizational Role

   c. Organizational Unit

   d. administrative role

11. Using the naming conventions identified in this chapter, write four possible user names for Kari Means.

_____

_____

_____

_____

12. Which of the following defines certain standard settings you want to establish for multiple users?

   a. Organizational Role object

   b. user template

   c. administrative role

   d. import

13. Which of the following is *not* an administrative role?

   a. eDirectory Management

   b. Printer Management

   c. DNS/DHCP Management

   d. Disk Storage Management

14. Which of the following protocols can be used to transfer objects between X.500–compatible directories?

    a. LDIF

    b. LDAP

    c. TCP

    d. IP

15. Which of the following utilities can be used to import an LDIF file?

    a. LDAP

    b. ConsoleOne

    c. iManager

    d. Both b and c

16. Intruder detection works at which of the following levels by setting a limit on the number of incorrect login attempts that can be made on a user account in that container during a specified time period?

    a. user

    b. [Root]

    c. container

    d. Organization

17. A user is granted rights to use iManager to create eDirectory objects through which of the following?

    a. eDirectory security

    b. Role Based security

    c. membership in the Admin group

    d. login security

18. Which of the following object types is best suited for giving users the rights needed for a particular position in the company?

    a. Organizational Unit

    b. group

    c. Organizational Role

    d. security equivalent

19. In an LDIF file, which of the following fields specifies information properties that are unique to the specified object class?

    a. attribute

    b. property

    c. name

    d. entry

20. Which of the following utilities can be used to add users from a Web browser?

    a. Remote Manager

    b. ConsoleOne

    c. iManager

    d. Both a and c

UNIVERSAL AEROSPACE CASE PROJECTS

Now that you've finished establishing user accounts for the Engineering, IS, Mfg, and Mgmt departments, you'll apply what you've learned to finish the user account setup for the remainder of your UAS network. After the user setup is finished, you can give users access to the file system by proceeding to the material in Chapter 5.

Case Project 4-1: Creating the Groups

Using the Business container you created in the Chapter 2 case projects, create the Business group accounts shown in Table 4-6.

Table 4-6   Business Group Planning Form

Group Name	Users	Context	Description
Marketing	Michael Horowitz, Darrell Minick, Laura Hiller	Business.##UAS	Maintain customer data, access the inventory, and work with orders
Publishing	Diana Brady, Julie Damrau, Bradley Dahl	Business.##UAS	Design marketing literature and the UAS home page and develop operation instruction manuals
Accounting	Terry Blackwell, George Perez, Amy Pan	Business.##UAS	Access accounting software and data and maintain the inventory
Guests	Guest1 and Guest2	Business.##UAS	Give visitors to the company access to certain public files and the company Web site

Case Project 4-2: Creating User Templates for Business and Marketing

To make creating users easier and more standardized, the first step in setting up the Business office is to create the user templates. In this project, you use NetWare Administrator or ConsoleOne to create the remaining templates shown in Table 4-7.

Table 4-7   Business Templates Planning Form

Template name	T_Account
Context	Business.##UAS
Home directory path	UASHOST_CORP:Accting
Minimum password length	6
Require unique passwords	Yes
Days between password changes	90
Grace logins	6
Valid login times	7:00 a.m. until 10:00 p.m.
Concurrent connections	1
Groups	Accounting
Users	Terry Blackwell, George Perez, Amy Pan
Rights to user home directory	All rights except Supervisor and Access Control
Rights to Login Script	Read
Template name	T_Marketing
Context	Business.##UAS
Home directory path	UASHOST_CORP:Mrkting
Minimum password length	6
Require unique passwords	No

Table 4-7   Business Templates Planning Form (continued)

Days between password changes	90
Grace logins	6
Valid login times	5:00 a.m. until 11:59 p.m.
Concurrent connections	1
Groups	Marketing
Users	Michael Horowitz, Darrell Minick, Laura Hiller
Rights to user home directory	All rights except Supervisor and Access Control
Rights to Login Script	Read
Template name	T_Publish
Context	Business.##UAS
Home directory path	UASHOST_CORP:Publish
Minimum password length	6
Require unique passwords	No
Days between password changes	90
Grace logins	6
Valid login times	5:00 a.m. until 11:59 p.m.
Concurrent connections	1
Groups	Publishing
Users	Diana Brady, Bradley Dahl, Julie Damrau
Rights to user home directory	All rights except Supervisor and Access Control
Rights to Login Script	Read

Case Project 4-3: Creating the Users

Using the appropriate templates, create the Business office user accounts shown in Table 4-8. Add Julie Damrau to the WebMgrs group you created in the chapter activities. If necessary, add other users to the groups you created in Project 4-1.

Table 4-8   Business User Planning Form

Company: Universal AeroSpace
Division: Business Office

User Name	Login Name	Context	Template Name	Home Directory	Groups	Additional Properties
Michael Horowitz	MHorowitz	Business.##UAS	T_Marketing	Yes	Marketing	
Darrell Minick	DMinick	Business.##UAS	T_Marketing	Yes	Marketing	
Laura Hiller	LHiller	Business.##UAS	T_Marketing	Yes	Marketing	
Diana Brady	DBrady	Business.##UAS	T_Publish	Yes	Publishing	
Julie Damrau	JDamrau	Business.##UAS	T_Publish	Yes	Publishing, WebMgrs	
Terry Blackwell	TBlackwell	Business.##UAS	T_Account	Yes	Accounting	
George Perez	GPerez	Business.##UAS	T_Account	Yes	Accounting	
Amy Pan	APan	Business.##UAS	T_Account	Yes	Accounting	

Case Project 4-4: Enabling Intruder Detection

Enable intruder detection on the Business OU so that a user account will be locked for 15 minutes after five invalid login attempts are made within a 10-minute period. If requested by your instructor, print the screen showing your Business container's intruder detection settings.

4

Case Project 4-5: Creating Organizational Role Objects

Organizational Role objects can simplify network administration. For example, Terry Blackwell is currently responsible for managing the data in the Accounting department, Julie Damrau is the data manager of the Desktop Publishing department, and Laura Hiller is the manager for the Marketing department's data. In this project, you should copy the Organizational Role Planning Form in Appendix D to identify the necessary organizational roles and their occupants, and then use ConsoleOne to create Organizational Role objects for the Business office managers and make the appropriate users the occupant.

Case Project 4-6: Modifying Multiple User Accounts

Luke wants all users to have their department's phone and fax numbers included in their user accounts. In this project, you use ConsoleOne's Multiple Objects option to add the phone and fax numbers shown in Table 4-9 to the user accounts in the Business office.

Table 4-9   Business Office Phone and Fax Numbers

Department	Phone	Fax
Accounting	715-555-1231	715-555-1241
Marketing	715-555-1232	715-555-1242
Desktop Publishing	715-555-1233	715-555-1243
Engineering	715-555-1234	715-555-1244

Case Project 4-7: Using an LDIF File to Create Guest User Accounts

Luke recently purchased two computers to be used in the reception area to access the company Web site. These computers should be used similarly to the ones in the Shipping and Receiving departments, and visitors will be able to automatically log in using accounts named Guest1 and Guest2. In this project, use the specifications in Table 4-10 to modify the LDIF file you used to create the Mfg department users. Change the user name to Guest1 or Guest2 in the dn, uid, sn, cn, and ACL statements. Change the group name to Guests in the securityEquals and groupMembership statements. In the dn, securityEquals, groupMembership, and ACL statements, change the context to ou=Business, o=##UAS (remember to replace ## with your student number).

Follow these steps to create guest user accounts with an LDIF file:

1. Use Notepad to open the Stations.ldif file.
2. Make the necessary modifications.
3. Use the Save as option to save the changes in a file named Guests.ldif.
4. Use ConsoleOne to create a group named Guests in your Business OU.
5. Use the ConsoleOne NDS Import/Export Wizard to import the users from the Guests.ldif file.
6. Verify that your Business OU contains the Guest1 and Guest2 user accounts.

Table 4-10   Planning Form for Guest Users

Company: Universal AeroSpace
Division: Business Office

User Name	Login Name	Context	Template Name	Home Directory	Groups	Additional Properties
Guest 1	Guest1	Business.##UAS	No template needed	No	Guests	
Guest 2	Guest2	Business.##UAS	No template needed	No	Guests	

5

SECURING THE FILE SYSTEM

> **After reading this chapter and completing the exercises, you will be able to:**
>
> ♦ Identify the access rights used with NetWare file system security and use ConsoleOne, Windows, and the RIGHTS command to assign and list rights for users, groups, and containers
>
> ♦ Calculate the effective rights obtained from a combination of trustee assignments, group rights, and inherited rights, and describe how the Inherited Rights Filter is used to selectively block inherited rights
>
> ♦ Apply file system security concepts to creating a file system security plan for an organization
>
> ♦ Identify directory attributes and use ConsoleOne, Windows, and the FLAG utility to implement directory attributes for an organization

In Chapter 4, you learned how to create user accounts with ConsoleOne and iManager. Now that you have created your users, by default they have rights to access and save files only in their home directories. To enable them to fully use the network file system, you need to use file system security so that they have the necessary rights to access and maintain network files they are responsible for, and you can still protect sensitive network information from unauthorized access. In this chapter, you learn how to plan and implement file system security for your version of the Universal AeroSpace Corporation.

ACCESS RIGHT SECURITY

NetWare file system security consists of two levels: access right security and attribute security. **Access rights** are like a set of keys given to users to allow them to work in certain areas. Just as keys give employees access to specific rooms in a building, access rights ensure that users can work with data only in certain files and directories. A user gains access rights through direct assignment or by being a member of a group or container. In this section, you learn how to apply the eight NetWare access rights to give users the rights they need to work with the network file system. **Attributes** are flags attached to files and directories to limit the functions that can be performed in those files or directories. For example, placing the Read Only attribute on a file prevents its contents from being modified even by users who have rights to change data in the directory where the file is stored. Later in the chapter, you'll learn about NetWare file and directory attributes and how to use ConsoleOne and Windows to implement attribute security.

NetWare Access Rights

File system security is based on the concept of making an eDirectory object, such as a user, group, or container, a trustee of a file or directory with certain assigned access rights. File system security consists of a single group of eight access rights that are used to control the operations a trustee can perform in the file system. Each network directory and file has an entry in the directory entry table (DET) that contains information about it, including the file or directory name and the access control list (ACL). The ACL lists each trustee assignment for the directory or file along with the access rights associated with that trustee assignment. Table 5-1 lists the NetWare file system access rights along with their effect in files or directories.

Table 5-1   NetWare Access Rights

Access Right	Effect in Directory	Effect in File
Supervisor [S]	Grants all rights to the directory and all subdirectories; cannot be blocked or reassigned at a lower subdirectory or file level.	Grants all rights to the specified file.
Read [R]	Allows users to read files or run programs in the directory.	Allows users to read or run the file or program when they do not have Read rights at the directory level.
Write [W]	Allows users to change or add data to files in the directory.	Allows users to change or add data to the specified file when they do not have Write rights at the directory level.
Create [C]	Allows users to create files and subdirectories.	Allows users to salvage the specified file if it's deleted.
Erase [E]	Allows users to delete files and remove subdirectories.	Allows users to delete the specified file when they have not been granted Erase rights at the directory level.
Modify [M]	Allows users to change file and subdirectory names and use the FLAG command to change attribute settings on files or subdirectories.	Allows users to change the name or attribute settings of the specified file when they do not have Modify rights at the directory level.
File Scan [F]	Allows users to view a directory of file and subdirectory names.	Allows users to view the specified filename or a directory listing when they do not have File Scan rights at the directory level.
Access Control [A]	Allows users to grant access rights to other users for the directory.	Allows users to grant access rights to the specified file when they do not have Access Control rights at the directory level.

The **Read [R] right** and the **File Scan [F] right** are often used together when you want the trustee to be able to call up files or run programs in a specified directory. For example, by default, any container with a server object is given [R] and [F] rights to the SYS:Public directory so that users in that container can run NetWare commands and utilities in the Public directory.

With the **Create [C] right** to a directory, users can create new files and subdirectories in that directory. Having only the Create right to a directory enables users to copy files into the directory as long as no other file in the directory has the same name, and having the Create right to a *shared* directory allows users to copy or create new files in the directory and create subdirectories. Having the Create right to an existing file might seem redundant, but it means that users can salvage the file if it's deleted.

In addition to erasing files, the **Erase [E] right** to a directory allows users to remove the entire directory and its subdirectories. Notice the difference between the Write and Modify rights: The **Write [W] right** grants the privilege of changing or adding data to an existing file, but the **Modify [M] right** allows users to change only a file's name or attributes, not its contents.

As its name implies, the **Access Control [A] right** allows users to grant access rights to other users to control which users have access to a certain directory or file. However, allowing users to grant rights to other users can make it difficult for the network administrator to keep track of file system security, so the Access Control right shouldn't normally be given to other users.

Having the **Supervisor [S] right** is different from having all rights because it cannot be changed or blocked at a lower-level directory or file, and it can be assigned only by another user who has the Supervisor right to the directory. Having the Access Control right does not allow users to assign the Supervisor right to themselves or to another user. The Supervisor right is often granted to workgroup managers so that they can control some section of the file system's directory structure. For example, if Kari Means is the workgroup manager for the Engineering department, she could be granted the Supervisor right to the CORP:Engineer directory structure.

If users have the Access Control right, but not the Supervisor right, in a directory, they could restrict themselves from working in the directory by accidentally assigning their user names fewer rights than they need to the directory or subdirectory. For that reason, the Access Control right usually shouldn't be granted to a user unless it's absolutely necessary for the user to assign rights to others.

To help you better understand which access rights are necessary for performing functions in the network file system, Table 5-2 contains a list of typical operations that users need to perform on files and directories, along with the access rights required to perform those operations.

Table 5-2   Rights Required for Common Functions

Task	Rights Required
Read a file	Read
View a directory listing	File Scan
Change the contents of a file	Write
Write to a closed file using a text editor that creates a backup file	Write, Create, Erase, Modify (not always required)
Run a program file	Read
Create and write to a new file	Create
Copy a file from a directory	Read, File Scan
Copy a file into a directory	Create
Copy multiple files to a directory with existing files	Create, File Scan
Create a subdirectory	Create
Delete a file	Erase

Table 5-2 Rights Required for Common Functions (continued)

Task	Rights Required
Salvage deleted files	Read and File Scan on the file, and Create in the directory or on the file
Change attributes	Modify
Rename a file or subdirectory	Modify
Change the Inherited Rights Filter	Access Control
Make or change a trustee assignment	Access Control

Trustee Assignments

Trustee assignments give users, groups, or containers rights to access and maintain the file system and can be made to directories or individual files. A **directory trustee** is a user, group, or container object that has been granted access rights to a directory, and directory trustees are kept track of in each volume's DET. A DET entry can hold up to six trustee assignments. If more than six trustees are assigned to a directory, an additional entry is made in the DET for that directory's name. For this reason, you should keep trustee assignments to six or fewer for each directory. This is usually done by making a group a trustee of a directory and then adding users to the group if they need access to that directory. A **file trustee** is a user or group that has been granted access rights to a file. As with directory trustees, file trustees are kept track of in the DET. If more than six trustees are assigned to a file, the filename needs an additional entry in the DET.

The term **effective rights** is used to define which access rights a user has in a specific directory or file. Effective rights are a combination of the access rights a user has from his or her trustee assignment, plus any access rights obtained from being a member of a group or container. In the UAS network, for example, the Design group was made a trustee of the NASA directory with Read and File Scan rights. Paul Alm, a member of the Design group, is made a trustee of NASA with Create and Write rights. In this case, Paul's effective rights would be [R W C F], a combination of Paul's individual trustee assignment—[W C]—plus his rights from being a member of the Design group—[R F]. Basically, a user's effective rights to a directory or file are the result of one or more of these five factors:

- A trustee assignment is made directly to the user name.
- A trustee assignment is made to a group of which the user is a member.
- A trustee assignment is made to a container where the user or the user's group resides.
- A file or directory inherits container, group, and user rights from a higher-level directory.
- Inherited rights are blocked by an Inherited Rights Filter applied to a directory or file.

In this chapter, you learn the five ways a user can acquire effective rights and how to apply this knowledge to establish file system security on your UAS network.

User Trustee Assignments

The simplest and most straightforward way for a user to get effective rights to a directory or file is by being granted a direct trustee assignment, consisting of a specific set of access rights to the directory or file. The user's name and assigned access rights are then stored in the ACL property of the DET for that directory or file. This process is called a **trustee assignment** because it makes the user a trustee of the directory or file with certain access privileges. Provided no trustee assignments have been made to any groups or containers of which the user is a member, the user's effective rights will always be equal to his or her trustee assignment. When specifying trustee assignments, access rights are usually indicated with the first letter of each access right enclosed in brackets. For example, [R C F] indicates that a user has Read, Create, and File Scan rights. [All] is often used to represent all access rights, including Supervisor, and is easier than specifying each right individually.

The most common application of user trustee assignments is granting users all rights to their home directories. When you created home directories for users in Chapter 4, each user was given a trustee assignment based on the access rights you defined in the user template. By default, a new user gets [R W C E M F A] rights to his or her home directory; however, the UAS network administrator, Eric Kenton, believes that giving users Access Control or Supervisor rights to their home directories creates possible security problems. First, with the Access Control or Supervisor right, users can make other objects trustees of their directories. In addition to making it harder for you to manage file system security, it increases the probability of intruders accessing or destroying data. Second, having the Access Control right without the Supervisor right enables users to accidentally reassign their own rights to a file or subdirectory, possibly locking themselves out of a portion of their directories and eventually requiring your assistance to bail them out. For those reasons, the templates you used when creating the user accounts in Chapter 4 were modified to remove the Supervisor and Access Control rights from each new user's home directory trustee assignment.

By default, ConsoleOne gives new users a trustee assignment of [R W C E M F A] to their home directories.

When the Novell client is installed on a workstation, you can use My Computer, My Network Places, or Windows Explorer to make and change trustee assignments. Making trustee assignments in Windows is often convenient, but ConsoleOne and NetWare Administrator offer additional capabilities for making and maintaining trustee assignments. For example, you need to use ConsoleOne or NetWare Administrator to assign the Supervisor right, make multiple trustee assignments to a user, or view a user's effective rights. In the following activities, you practice using ConsoleOne and My Computer to make and modify trustee assignments.

Activity 5-1: Modifying User Trustee Assignments

Time Required: 10 minutes

Objective: Use ConsoleOne to assign rights to users, groups, and containers.

Description: To manage their files and documents when they are away from the office, Luke McMann wants Eric Kenton and Kellie Thiele to be able to give him Supervisor rights to their home directories when they are away from the office. To do this, Eric decided to make all users in the IS department supervisors of their own home directories. In this activity, you perform this task on your file system by using ConsoleOne to make each of your IS department users a supervisor of his or her own home directory. In Activity 5-2, you'll test the system by logging in as Kellie and using Windows to grant Luke rights to Kellie's home directory.

1. If necessary, start your computer, and log in with your UasAdmin user name.

2. Start ConsoleOne, and expand the **UAS_Tree** and your **##UAS** container.

3. Display the subdirectories of your IS directory in the Object frame:

   a. Expand the **IS** OU, and then expand your **UASHOST_CORP** volume object to display all directories in the Navigation frame.

   b. Click your **IS** directory to display all subdirectories in the Object frame.

4. Give your user name Supervisor rights to your home directory:

   a. Right-click your user name's home directory, and then click **Properties** to open the Properties dialog box.

   b. Click the **Trustees** tab and record your default rights on your student answer sheet.

   c. If necessary, click the **Supervisor** check box to enable this access right.

   d. Click **OK** to save your assignment.

5. Repeat Step 4 to give Kellie Supervisor rights to her home directory.

6. Repeat Step 4 to give Luke Supervisor rights to his home directory.

7. Exit ConsoleOne, and log out.

Activity 5-2: Making User Trustee Assignments in Windows

Time Required: 10 minutes

Objective: Use Windows to assign rights to users, groups, and containers.

Description: Kellie is taking a vacation, and before leaving, she wants to grant Luke the rights needed to manage files in her home directory. In this activity, you log in using the account you created for Kellie in Chapter 4, and then use My Computer to add Luke as a trustee of Kellie's home directory with Read and File Scan rights.

1. Log in with the user name you created for Kellie in Chapter 4:

   a. Enter **KThiele** in the Username text box and the password you defined for Kellie in the Password text box.

   b. Click the **Advanced** button, click the **Context** browse button, navigate to your ##UAS container, click the **IS** OU, and then click **OK** to place IS.##UAS in the Context text box.

   c. Click **OK** to log in.

2. If necessary, log on to your Windows 2000 computer using your local user name and password.

3. Map drive letter L: to the IS directory:

   a. Right-click **My Network Places**, and then click **Novell Map Network Drive** to open the Map Drive dialog box.

   b. Click the **Choose the drive letter to map** list arrow, and then click **L:** in the list of options.

   c. Enter **\\Uashost\##Corp\IS** in the Enter the network path to the resource text box, and then click the **Map** button to open a window for the IS directory.

4. Add Luke as a trustee of Kellie's home directory:

   a. Right-click Kellie's home directory, and click **Properties** to open the KThiele Properties dialog box.

   b. Click the **NetWare Rights** tab to display the Trustees list box shown in Figure 5-1.

   c. If necessary, expand the **IS** container in the lower pane.

   d. Click **LMcMann**, and then click the **Add** button to add Luke to the Trustees list box. Record Luke's default rights on your student answer sheet.

   e. If necessary, change LMcMann's rights to only Read and File Scan access rights.

   f. Click **OK** to save the assignment.

5. Close the IS directory window, and log out.

Viewing Effective Rights

When working with file system security, often you need to verify a specific user's effective rights to a directory. Although you can use Windows Explorer or My Computer to set and view trustee assignments and inherited rights, you cannot view another user's effective rights in a directory with these utilities. To verify effective rights in the file system, you should use ConsoleOne or NetWare Administrator. In the following activity, you use ConsoleOne to view a user's effective rights in a directory.

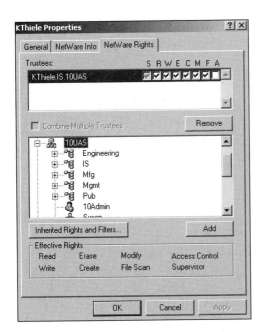

Figure 5-1   Viewing the current trustees in the KThiele Properties dialog box

Activity 5-3: Viewing Effective Rights

Time Required: 5 minutes

Objective: Be able to use ConsoleOne to list rights for users.

Description: In this activity, you use ConsoleOne to view Luke's effective rights to Kellie's home directory.

1. Log in with your UasAdmin user name.

2. Start ConsoleOne, and expand the **UAS_Tree** and your **##UAS** container.

3. Navigate to the correct directory:

   a. Expand the **IS** OU, and then expand your **UASHOST_CORP** volume object to display all directories in the Navigation frame.

   b. Click your **IS** directory to display all subdirectories in the Object frame.

4. Display the trustees of Kellie's home directory:

   a. Right-click your **KThiele** directory, and then click **Properties** to open the KThiele Properties dialog box.

   b. Click the **Trustees** tab to display all trustees of Kellie's home directory. Record the trustees on your student answer sheet.

5. Check Luke's effective rights to Kellie's home directory:

   a. Click the **Effective Rights** button to open the Effective Rights dialog box, shown in Figure 5-2.

   b. Click the **Browse** button to the right of the Trustee text box to open the Select Object dialog box.

   c. Click the **up arrow** to display all users in the IS department.

   d. Click **LMcMann**, and then click **OK** to display effective rights for Luke.

   e. Record the effective rights on your student answer sheet.

   f. Click **Close** to close the Effective Rights dialog box.

Figure 5-2   The Effective Rights dialog box

    6. Click **Cancel** to close the KThiele Properties dialog box.

    7. Exit ConsoleOne, and log out.

Group Trustee Assignments

As described in Chapter 4, groups are network objects that help organize users with common network requirements and are particularly useful in simplifying trustee assignments; when a group is made a trustee of a directory or file, all members of that group are also considered trustees of the directory or file, with the same rights assigned to the group. When users are members of a group, their effective rights in a directory are a combination of any personal trustee assignments they have, plus any rights they have from being members of the group. For example, all IS users in the UAS network need to have Read and File Scan rights to the Apps\Utility directory to run the utility software. One way to do this is to make the ISMgrs group you created in Chapter 4 a trustee of the Apps\Utility directory with Read and File Scan rights. Because you, Kellie, and Luke are members of the ISMgrs group, you all get Read and File Scan rights to the Apps\Utility directory. If you wanted your user name to be responsible for changing data, you could also make your user name a trustee of the Utility directory with Create, Write, Erase, and Modify rights, as shown in Figure 5-3. Your effective rights would then be [R W C E M F]; the [R F] rights come from your membership in the ISMgrs group, and the [W C E M] rights come from the trustee assignment made to your user name. Kellie's effective rights would be [R F] from being a member of the ISMgrs group. In the following activity, you use Windows to implement the trustee assignments shown in Figure 5-3, and then use NetWare Administrator to check effective rights for you and Kellie.

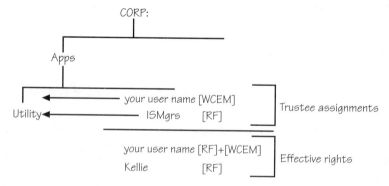

Figure 5-3   Group trustee assignment

Activity 5-4: Making Group Trustee Assignments

Time Required: 5 minutes

Objective: Use Windows and NetWare Administrator to assign and check rights to users and groups.

Description: In this activity, you use Windows to make the ISMgrs group a trustee of the Utility directory with Read and File Scan rights. In addition, you give your user name [W C E M] rights and then use NetWare Administrator to verify effective rights for Kellie and your user name.

1. If necessary, start your computer, and log in with your UasAdmin user name.

2. If necessary, map drive letter G: to your ##CORP directory:

   a. Right-click **My Network Places**, and then click **Novell Map Network Drive** to open the Map Drive dialog box.

   b. Click the **Choose the drive letter to map** list arrow, and then click **G:** in the list of options.

   c. Enter **\\Uashost\##Corp\Apps** in the Enter the network path to the resource text box, and then click the **Map** button to open a window for the Apps directory.

3. Use Windows to add ISMgrs as a trustee of the Utility directory with Read and File Scan rights:

   a. Right-click your **Utility** directory, and then click **Properties** to open the Utility Properties dialog box.

   b. Click the **NetWare Rights** tab to view the trustee assignments.

   c. Record any existing trustee assignments on your student answer sheet.

   d. Expand the **IS** OU in the lower pane.

   e. Click the **ISMgrs** group, and then click the **Add** button. The ISMgrs group should now appear in the Trustees list box with Read and File Scan rights.

4. Add your user name as a trustee of the Utility directory with [W C E M] rights:

   a. Click your user name, and then click the **Add** button.

   b. To change your rights to [W C E M], click to remove the check marks from the Read and File Scan rights. You do not need these access rights because you'll get them by being a member of the ISMgrs group.

   c. Click the **W**, **C**, **E**, and **M** check boxes of your user name's trustee assignment to enable these rights.

5. Click **OK** to close the Utility Properties dialog box.

6. Close the Apps directory window.

7. Double-click the **NetWare Administrator** icon on your desktop.

8. If necessary, open a browse window for your ##UAS Organization.

9. Double-click your **UASHOST_CORP** volume to display all directories.

10. Double-click the **Apps** directory to show all subdirectories.

11. Check the effective rights for Kellie and your user name in the Utility directory:

   a. Right-click the **Utility** directory, and then click **Details** to open the Directory: Utility dialog box.

   b. Click the **Trustees of this Directory** button to display the current trustees of the Utility directory.

   c. Record the trustees and their access rights on your student answer sheet.

   d. Click the **Effective Rights** button to open the Effective Rights dialog box.

   e. Click the **Browse** button, and then double-click the **IS** container in the Browse context pane.

   f. In the Available objects pane, double-click Kellie's user name. Record her effective rights on your student answer sheet.

g. Click the **Browse** button, and double-click your user name. Your effective rights should be everything except Supervisor and Access Control.

h. Click the **Close** button, and then click **Cancel** to return to the NetWare Administrator window.

12. Exit NetWare Administrator, and log out.

Container Trustee Assignments

As with a group, when a container object is made a trustee of a file or directory, all users in the container, as well as any subcontainer objects, share the rights made in the trustee assignment. When working with container trustee assignments, remember that a child container has the same effective rights as its parent. For example, rights granted to your ##UAS container also belong to the Mgmt, Engineering, Mfg, and IS containers. In the following activity, you use ConsoleOne to make your ##UAS Organization a trustee of a directory and then verify effective rights for users throughout your organization.

Activity 5-5: Making a Container Trustee Assignment

Time Required: 5 minutes

Objective: Use ConsoleOne to assign rights to containers.

Description: Eric wanted all users to have rights to save and delete files in the Temp directory located off the [Root] of the CORP volume. To do this efficiently, he made the UAS Organization a trustee of the Temp directory with all rights except Supervisor and Access Control. In this activity, you use ConsoleOne to make your ##UAS Organization a trustee of your Temp directory, and then check effective rights for your users.

1. If necessary, start your computer, and log in with your UasAdmin user name.

2. Start ConsoleOne, and expand the **UAS_Tree** and your **##UAS** container.

3. Expand your **UASHOST_CORP** volume object.

4. Right-click your **Temp** directory, and then click **Properties** to open the Properties of Temp dialog box.

5. Add your ##UAS container as a trustee of Temp with all rights except Supervisor and Access Control:

   a. Click the **Trustees** tab to display current trustees of the Temp directory.

   b. Click the **Add Trustee** button to open the Select Object dialog box.

   c. Click the **up arrow** to display all Organizations.

   d. Click your **##UAS** Organization, and then click **OK** to add it to the Trustees list box.

   e. Record the default trustee rights of your ##UAS Organization on your student answer sheet.

   f. Grant all rights except Supervisor and Access Control by clicking to place check marks in the appropriate access right check boxes.

   g. Click the **Apply** button to save your trustee assignment.

6. Check effective rights for Kari Means in the Temp directory:

   a. Click the **Effective Rights** button to open the Effective Rights dialog box.

   b. Click the **Browse** button to the right of the Trustee text box to open the Select Object dialog box.

   c. Click the **up arrow** until you see your Engineering OU.

   d. Double-click the **Engineering** OU to display all users in Engineering.

   e. Click **KMeans**, and then click **OK** to display Kari's effective rights.

5

f. Record Kari's effective rights on your student answer sheet.

g. Click **Close** to return to the Properties of Temp dialog box.

h. Click **Close** to close the Properties of Temp dialog box.

7. Repeat Step 6 to record effective rights for another user. Record that user's name and effective rights on your student answer sheet.

8. Close any open windows, and log out.

Inherited Rights

Inherited rights are the NetWare feature that allows a user, group, or container's effective rights to a directory to "flow down" into files and other subdirectories. Inheritance is an essential concept in making file system security efficient by eliminating an excessive number of trustee assignments. For example, Eric wanted all users to have Read and File Scan rights in the Office, Desktop, and Utility subdirectories of Apps to install and run the software stored in these directories. Eric could have assigned rights to all users by making the UAS container a trustee of each subdirectory with Read and File Scan rights. However, with inherited rights you can simply assign your ##UAS container Read and File Scan rights to the CORP:Apps directory and then let the effective rights flow down to the subdirectories, as shown in Figure 5-4. In the following activity, you use Eric's method to give all your users rights to the software directories in the Apps directory structure.

 In the following diagram, a box for each user and group is included under each directory to indicate the user or group's trustee assignment and effective rights. A vertical arrow above a trustee assignment indicates that the rights are inherited from a higher directory. When calculating the inherited rights for a specific object, be sure to remove any rights that will be blocked by an Inherited Rights Filter on that subdirectory or file. A horizontal arrow indicates that a direct trustee assignment has been made to that directory. A user's effective rights consist of the sum of the rights in the user's box combined with the rights in any group or container box to which he or she belongs.

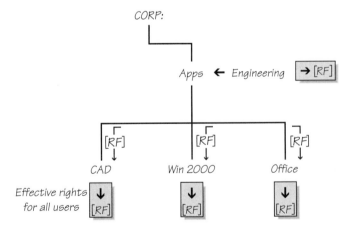

→ Indicates trustee assignment

↓ Indicates inherited rights

Figure 5-4   Inherited rights

Activity 5-6: Applying Inherited Rights

Time Required: 5 minutes

Objective: Use ConsoleOne to assign rights to containers and check effective rights.

Description: The simplest way to give all users in your organization rights to run software from application directories is to give your ##UAS container Read and File Scan rights to the Apps directory. Through inheritance, users in your ##UAS Organization will then acquire Read and File Scan rights to each of the application subdirectories. In this activity, you use ConsoleOne to make your ##UAS Organization a trustee of the Apps directory and then check users' effective rights in the application subdirectories.

1. If necessary, log in with your UasAdmin user name and password, start ConsoleOne, and expand your **UASHOST_CORP** volume.

2. Make your ##UAS container a trustee of the Apps directory with Read and File Scan rights:

    a. Right-click your **Apps** directory, and then click **Properties**.

    b. Click the **Trustees** tab to display all trustees of Apps.

    c. Click the **Add Trustee** button to open the Select Object dialog box.

    d. Click the **up arrow** until you can see your ##UAS Organization.

    e. Click your **##UAS** Organization, and then click **OK** to add it to the Trustees list box.

    f. Click **OK** to save your trustee assignment and return to the ConsoleOne window.

3. View trustees of the Utility directory:

    a. Expand your **Apps** directory.

    b. Right-click the **Utility** subdirectory, and then click **Properties** to open the Properties of Utility dialog box.

    c. Click the **Trustees** tab to display existing trustees.

    d. Record any existing trustees on your student answer sheet.

    e. Click the **Effective Rights** button to open the Effective Rights dialog box.

4. Check effective rights for Tony Rucci to the Utility directory:

    a. Click the **Browse** button to open the Select Object dialog box.

    b. Click the **up arrow** until your Engineering OU is displayed.

    c. Double-click the **Engineering** OU, and then click **TRucci**.

    d. Click **OK** to display the effective rights for TRucci.

    e. Record TRucci's effective rights on your student answer sheet.

5. Repeat Step 4 to record the effective rights to the Utility directory for a user in the Mfg department.

6. Click **Close** to return to the Properties of Utility dialog box, and then close the Properties of Utility dialog box.

7. Click **Cancel** to return to the ConsoleOne window, exit ConsoleOne, and log out.

The Inherited Rights Filter

In some cases, you might not want user, group, or container rights to be inherited by a lower-level directory. For example, Eric first placed the CAD software folder in the Apps directory and gave all users Read and File Scan rights to the Apps directory. Through inheritance, all users will get Read and File Scan rights to all subdirectories of Apps, including the CAD subdirectory. Because only the engineers should be able to run the CAD software, Eric wants to prevent other users from inheriting rights to run the CAD software. With NetWare 6, you can prevent a subdirectory from inheriting rights by adding an **Inherited Rights Filter (IRF)** to it. An IRF acts as a block to keep selected rights from passing into the subdirectory structure or files. Each directory or file has an IRF field stored in the DET and can inherit any rights specified in the IRF. By default, when you create a directory or file, all rights are included in its IRF. You can then block a directory or file from inheriting rights by removing the rights from the IRF.

The exception to using an IRF to block rights is the Supervisor right. In file system security, the Supervisor access right cannot be removed from an IRF, and an IRF cannot be used to block the Supervisor right. Because the IRF filters only inherited rights from the parent directory, it has no effect on the direct trustee assignments made to the directory or file. For example, Kari has enough CAD software licenses for just the design engineers. However, because the CAD software is located in the Apps directory, currently all users could run the CAD software, thereby violating the license agreement. To fix this problem, Eric used an IRF on the CAD subdirectory to block it from inheriting rights granted to the UAS Organization. In the following activity, you set up an IRF on your Utility directory and then check users' effective rights.

Activity 5-7: Using an Inherited Rights Filter

Time Required: 5 minutes

Objective: Use ConsoleOne to set an Inherited Rights Filter.

Description: Only users in the IS department should be able to run programs from the Utility directory. However, through inheritance, all users get Read and File Scan rights to each of the application subdirectories, including the Utility directory. In this activity, you use ConsoleOne to set up an IRF on your Utility directory and then check effective rights to verify that rights have been removed for all users except members of the ISMgrs group.

1. If necessary, start your computer, log in with your UasAdmin user name, and start ConsoleOne. Expand the **UAS_Tree**, and then expand your **##UAS** container.

2. If necessary, expand your **UASHOST_CORP** volume, and then expand the **Apps** directory.

3. Right-click the **Utility** directory, and then click **Properties** to open the Properties of Utility dialog box.

4. Click the **Trustees** tab, and record the current trustees on your student answer sheet.

5. Remove all rights except Supervisor from the Utility directory's IRF:

   a. Click the **Inherited Rights Filter** tab to display the existing IRF, as shown in Figure 5-5. The check mark in front of each right indicates that the right can be inherited from the parent directory.

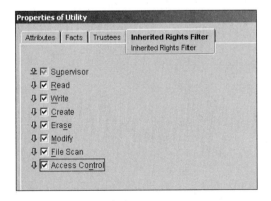

Figure 5-5   The Inherited Rights Filter tab

   b. Click to remove the check marks from all rights in the IRF. Notice that you cannot remove the check from the Supervisor check box. Because the Supervisor right cannot be removed from an IRF, a user who has been granted the Supervisor right to a higher-level directory is not affected by the IRF.

    c. Click the **Apply** button to save your changes.

    d. Click the **Trustees** tab.

    e. Click the **Effective Rights** button to open the Effective Rights dialog box.

6. Check the effective rights for Kellie:

    a. Click the **Browse** button, click the **up arrow**, and then double-click your **IS** OU.

    b. Click **KThiele**, and then click **OK**.

    c. Record Kellie's effective rights on your student answer sheet, and explain how she received these rights.

7. Repeat Step 6 to record the effective rights for a user in the Engineering department on your student answer sheet.

8. Repeat Step 6 to record the effective rights for a user in the Mfg department on your student answer sheet.

9. Click **Close** to return to the Properties of Utility dialog box.

10. Click **Close** to close the Properties of Utility dialog box and return to the ConsoleOne window.

11. Exit ConsoleOne, and log out.

Combining Trustee Assignments and Inherited Rights

As described earlier, a user's effective rights in a directory are a combination of the user object's trustee assignment or inherited rights (minus rights blocked by an IRF), along with the effective rights the user has from any container or group memberships. As a network administrator, you can reduce the number of rights granted to a user by taking group or container rights into consideration. For example, Kellie has recently written a software package for maintaining quality standards in the manufacturing process. To install this package, Eric created a subdirectory structure named Quality in the Apps directory, as shown in Figure 5-6.

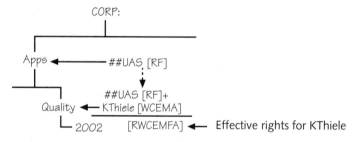

Figure 5-6　Combining inherited rights

To install and test the package, Kellie needed all rights except Supervisor to the Quality subdirectory. Through inheritance, Kellie automatically gets Read and File Scan rights by being part of the UAS Organization. The remaining rights can be provided by making Kellie a trustee of the Quality subdirectory with [W C E M A] rights. As shown in Figure 5-6, Kellie's effective rights will then become [R W C E M F A]. The [R F] rights are inherited from the UAS Organization, and the [W C E M A] rights come from the trustee assignment made to Kellie's user name. In the following activity, you practice combining inherited and user rights in your UAS network.

Activity 5-8: Combining Inherited Rights with Trustees

Time Required: 5 minutes

Objective: Use ConsoleOne to assign rights to users, groups, and containers.

Description: In this activity, you create a Quality subdirectory and then give Kellie all rights to it, as shown in Figure 5-6. Because your ##UAS Organization will inherit Read and File Scan rights as a result of the trustee assignment you made previously, Kellie will need to be assigned only the [W C E M A] rights to have all effective rights in the Quality subdirectory.

1. If necessary, start your computer, log in with your UasAdmin user name, and start ConsoleOne.

2. If necessary, expand the **UAS_Tree**, and then expand your **##UAS** container.

3. If necessary, expand your **UASHOST_CORP** volume, and then expand the **Apps** directory.

4. Create a Quality subdirectory:

   a. Right-click your **Apps** directory, point to **New**, and then click **Object** to open the New Object dialog box.

   b. Click **Directory**, and then click **OK** to open the New Directory dialog box.

   c. Enter the name **Quality**, and then click **OK** to create the Quality subdirectory.

   d. Right-click the newly created **Quality** subdirectory, point to **New**, and then click **Object** to open the New Object dialog box.

   e. Click **Directory**, and then click **OK** to open the New Directory dialog box.

   f. Enter the name **2002**, and then click **OK** to create the 2002 subdirectory.

5. Assign Kellie [W C E M A] rights to the Quality subdirectory:

   a. Right-click the **Quality** directory, and then click **Properties** to open the Properties of Quality dialog box.

   b. Click the **Trustees** tab to display the Trustees list box.

   c. Click the **Add Trustee** button to open the Select Object dialog box.

   d. If necessary, double-click your **IS** OU to view all IS department users.

   e. Click **KThiele**, and then click **OK** to add Kellie to the Trustees list box.

   f. Click to remove the check marks from the **R** and **F** check boxes to disable the Read and File Scan rights. (Kellie will receive Read and File Scan rights from the ##UAS Organization.)

   g. Click the **W**, **C**, **E**, **M**, and **A** check boxes to give Kellie the corresponding rights.

   h. Click the **Apply** button to save your changes.

6. Check Kellie's effective rights in the Quality subdirectory:

   a. Click the **Effective Rights** button to open the Effective Rights dialog box.

   b. Click the **Browse** button to open the Select Object dialog box, and navigate to the IS OU, if necessary.

   c. Double-click **KThiele**, record Kellie's effective rights on your student answer sheet, and then click **Close** twice to return to the main ConsoleOne window.

7. Check Kellie's effective rights in the 2002 subdirectory:

   a. If necessary, expand your **Quality** directory.

   b. Right-click the **2002** subdirectory, and then click **Properties** to open the Properties of 2002 dialog box.

   c. Click the **Trustees** tab, and record any trustees on your student answer sheet.

   d. Click the **Effective Rights** button to open the Effective Rights dialog box.

   e. Click the **Browse** button to open the Select Object dialog box.

f. Click the **up arrow**, and then double-click your **IS** OU to display all users.

g. Click **KThiele**, and then click **OK**; record Kellie's effective rights on your student answer sheet.

8. Close the Effective Rights dialog box, and then click the **Cancel** button to return to the ConsoleOne window.

9. Exit ConsoleOne, and log out.

Calculating Effective Rights

When calculating effective rights for a user, you should know that NetWare tracks inherited rights separately for each type of object. That means a user object's inherited rights in a directory are kept separate from the inherited rights for containers or groups. At the directory or subdirectory level, users' effective rights are calculated by combining their individual effective rights with the effective rights of any groups or containers to which they belong. You can use Windows to view inherited rights for objects in a directory by clicking the Inherited Rights and Filters button (shown previously in Figure 5-1) in the NetWare Rights tab. Notice in Figure 5-6 that KThiele is inheriting [W C E M A] rights, and the ##UAS organization is inheriting [R F] rights. You can calculate Kellie's effective rights by simply combining the ##UAS rights with the rights KThiele inherited.

Making a new trustee assignment to a user, group, or container overrides the inherited rights for that object. For example, Kellie's effective rights in the Apps\Quality\2002 directory are [R W C E M F A]. If Kellie is given a new trustee assignment of [W A] in the 2002 directory, her effective rights will be changed to [R W F A], with [R F] coming from the ##UAS Organization and [W A] coming from her trustee assignment. In the following activity, you change Kellie's effective rights in the 2002 directory by giving her a new trustee assignment and then using ConsoleOne to check inherited and effective rights.

Activity 5-9: Reassigning Inherited Rights

Time Required: 5 minutes

Objectives: Use ConsoleOne and Windows to view inherited and effective rights.

Description: In this activity, you see how Kellie's effective rights can be modified through a new assignment of Write and Access Control rights to her user name in the Quality\2002 subdirectory. You then use Windows and ConsoleOne to view inherited and effective rights for all objects in the Quality\2002 subdirectory.

1. If necessary, start your computer, log in with your UasAdmin user name, and start ConsoleOne.

2. If necessary, expand the **UAS_Tree**, and then expand your **##UAS** container.

3. If necessary, expand your **UASHOST_CORP** volume, **Apps** directory, and **Quality** subdirectory.

4. Assign Kellie's Write and Access Control rights to the Quality\2002 subdirectory:

a. Right-click the **2002** directory, and then click **Properties** to open the Properties of 2002 dialog box.

b. Click the **Trustees** tab to display the Trustees list box.

c. Click the **Add Trustee** button to open the Select Object dialog box.

d. If necessary, double-click your **IS** OU to view all IS department users.

e. Click **KThiele**, and then click **OK** to add Kellie to the Trustees list box.

f. Click the **R** and **F** check boxes to remove the check marks for Read and File Scan rights. (Kellie will inherit these rights from the ##UAS Organization.)

g. Click the **W** and **A** check boxes to give Kellie the corresponding rights.

h. Click **OK** to save your changes and return to the main ConsoleOne window.

i. Minimize the ConsoleOne window.

5. Map drive letter G: to your ##Corp directory:

   a. Right-click **My Network Places**, and then click **Novell Map Network Drive** to open the Map Drive dialog box.

   b. Click the **Choose the drive letter to map** list arrow, and then click **G:** in the list of options.

   c. Enter **\\Uashost\##Corp\Apps** in the Enter the network path to the resource text box.

   d. Click the **Map** button to map the drive and open a window for the Apps directory.

6. Use Windows to check the inherited rights for all objects in the 2002 subdirectory:

   a. Double-click the **Quality** subdirectory to open a window for the Quality subdirectory.

   b. Right-click the **2002** subdirectory, and then click **Properties** to open the 2002 Properties dialog box.

   c. Click the **NetWare Rights** tab to display the Trustees list box, shown in Figure 5-7.

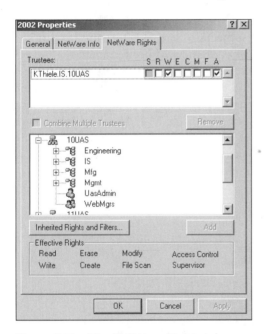

Figure 5-7   The NetWare Rights tab

   d. Click the **Inherited Rights and Filters** button to open the Inherited Rights and Filters dialog box. Record each object and its inherited rights on your student answer sheet.

   e. Calculate Kellie's effective rights, given that she is part of your ##UAS Organization, and record your calculations on your student answer sheet.

   f. Click **Cancel** to close the Inherited Rights and Filters dialog box.

   g. Click **OK** to close the 2002 Properties dialog box.

   h. Close the window for the Quality subdirectory.

7. Use ConsoleOne to check Kellie's effective rights in the 2002 subdirectory:

   a. Maximize the main ConsoleOne window.

   b. If necessary, expand your **UASHOST_Corp** volume, and then expand the **Apps** directory.

c. Click the **Quality** subdirectory to display its contents in the Objects frame.

d. Right-click the **2002** subdirectory in the Objects frame, and then click **Properties** to open the Properties of 2002 dialog box.

e. Click the **Trustees** tab, and record any trustees on your student answer sheet.

f. Click the **Effective Rights** button to open the Effective Rights dialog box.

g. Click the **Browse** button to open the Select Object dialog box.

h. Click the **up arrow**, and then double-click your **IS** OU to display all users.

i. Click **KThiele**, and then click **OK**; record Kellie's effective rights on your student answer sheet. Explain the change between effective rights in this activity and the effective rights to the 2002 subdirectory in the previous activity.

8. Close the Effective Rights dialog box, and then click the **Cancel** button to return to the main ConsoleOne window.

9. Exit ConsoleOne, and log out.

Working with Supervisor Rights

When combining inherited rights and trustee assignments, you must remember that a new trustee assignment for a user, group, or container object overrides the object's inherited rights and becomes the object's effective rights with one exception: When a user, group, or container has been granted the Supervisor right to a directory, new trustee assignments made to subdirectories or files will not override the inherited Supervisor right. For example, to help limit the use of the Admin account, Eric has recommended giving your user name rights to manage certain directory structures, such as the Apps and IS directories. You could do this in one of two ways: Grant your user name all rights [R W C E M F A] to the Apps and IS directories, or grant the Supervisor right. If you grant your user name all rights, the rights can be redefined in a subdirectory. However, if you grant the Supervisor right to a directory, your rights cannot be reduced by another trustee assignment or IRF, as illustrated in Figure 5-8.

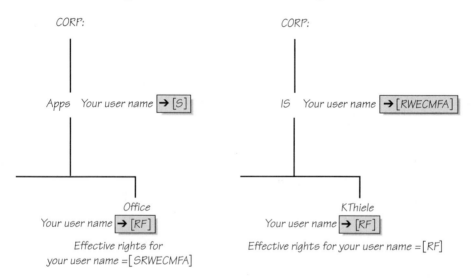

Figure 5-8   Granting Supervisor rights

When the Supervisor right is assigned to a directory, it cannot be changed or blocked in one of the subdirectories; it can be changed only at the point of origin. Therefore, the user with Supervisor rights can manage an entire directory structure without being blocked by another user or incorrect trustee assignment. In the following activities, you practice assigning the Supervisor right to your user name for a directory and then attempt to change your effective rights in the subdirectories.

Activity 5-10: Granting Supervisor Rights

Time Required: 5 minutes

Objective: Use ConsoleOne to assign rights to users.

Description: To manage information in the IS and Apps directory structures without having to log in as the Admin user, Eric made his user name a trustee of the IS and Apps directories with Supervisor rights. In this activity, you use ConsoleOne to grant your user name Supervisor rights to the Apps and IS directories and then verify your effective rights in each location.

1. If necessary, start your computer, log in with your UasAdmin user name, and start ConsoleOne.
2. If necessary, expand **UAS_Tree**, and then expand your **##UAS** container.
3. If necessary, expand your **UASHOST_CORP** volume.
4. Add your user name as a trustee of your IS directory with Supervisor rights:
   a. Right-click the **IS** directory, and then click **Properties** to open the Properties of IS dialog box.
   b. Click the **Trustees** tab to display the existing trustees of the IS directory.
   c. Click the **Add Trustee** button to open the Select Object dialog box.
   d. If necessary, click the **up arrow** to navigate to your IS OU.
   e. Click your user name, and then click **OK** to add it to the Trustees list box.
   f. Click the **Supervisor** right, and then click **OK** to save the assignment.
5. Repeat Step 4 to add your name as a trustee of the Apps directory with Supervisor rights.
6. Check your effective rights in the KThiele subdirectory:
   a. If necessary, expand your **IS** directory.
   b. Right-click the **KThiele** subdirectory, and then click **Properties** to open the Properties of KThiele dialog box.
   c. Click the **Trustees** tab, and then click the **Effective Rights** button to open the Effective Rights dialog box.
   d. Click the **Browse** button to open the Select Object dialog box.
   e. Click the **up arrow** to navigate to your IS OU, click your user name, and then click **OK** to display your effective rights in Kellie's subdirectory.
   f. Record your effective rights on your student answer sheet.
   g. Click the **Close** button, and then click **Cancel** to return to the ConsoleOne window.
7. Repeat Step 6 to record your effective rights in the Apps\CAD subdirectory.
8. If you're continuing to the next activity, leave ConsoleOne open and stay logged in. If not, exit ConsoleOne, and log out.

Activity 5-11: Changing Supervisor Rights

Time Required: 5 minutes

Objective: Use ConsoleOne to assign rights to users.

Description: Kellie was not very happy with the idea of Eric having Supervisor rights to her home directory. She would rather he had only Read and File Scan rights. In this activity, you learn how Eric used ConsoleOne to reduce his Supervisor right in Kellie's home directory by experimenting with different trustee assignments and checking his effective rights.

1. If necessary, start your computer, log in with your UasAdmin user name, and start ConsoleOne.

2. If necessary, expand the **UAS_Tree**, and then expand your **##UAS** container.

3. If necessary, expand your **UASHOST_CORP** volume, and then expand the **IS** directory.

4. Add your user name as a trustee of Kellie's home directory with only Read and File Scan rights:

   a. Right-click the **KThiele** subdirectory, and then click **Properties** to open the Properties of KThiele dialog box.

   b. Click the **Trustees** tab, and then click the **Add Trustee** button to open the Select Object dialog box.

   c. If necessary, click the **up arrow** to navigate to your IS OU.

   d. Click your user name, and then click **OK** to add it to the Trustees list box with Read and File Scan rights.

   e. Click the **Apply** button to save the assignment.

5. Check your user name's effective rights in Kellie's home directory:

   a. Click the **Effective Rights** button to open the Effective Rights dialog box.

   b. Click the **Browse** button to open the Select Object dialog box.

   c. Click the **up arrow** to navigate to your IS OU.

   d. Double-click the **IS** OU, click your user name, and then click **OK** to display your effective rights.

   e. On your student answer sheet, record your effective rights and how you obtained them.

   f. Click **Close** twice to return to the ConsoleOne window.

6. For your user name's trustee assignment to work in Kellie's directory, you need to remove the Supervisor right from your trustee assignment in the IS directory at the point of origin and replace it with all rights by following these steps:

   a. Right-click your **IS** directory, and then click **Properties** to open the Properties of IS dialog box.

   b. Click the **Trustees** tab to display the trustee assignments.

   c. Click your user name's trustee assignment, change the access rights to remove the Supervisor right, and then select all other rights.

   d. Click the **Apply** button to save the trustee assignment changes.

7. Right-click the **KThiele** subdirectory, repeat Step 5, and record your user name's effective rights in Kellie's home directory on your student answer sheet.

8. Click **Close** and then click **Cancel** to return to the ConsoleOne window.

9. Exit ConsoleOne, and log out.

PLANNING FILE SYSTEM SECURITY

NetWare file system security is a sophisticated, complex system with many options for ensuring the necessary access to network data. Giving users the effective rights needed to perform their work, while protecting data from unauthorized access, requires careful thought and planning by the network administrator. To make file system security simpler and easier to maintain with multiple group and user trustee assignments, you should plan the security system to keep trustee assignments and IRFs to a minimum. The following sections offer several guidelines and suggestions that will help you design a secure network file system. You'll also learn how these guidelines can be applied to defining the trustee assignments for the Engineering department.

File System Security Guidelines

To help keep file system security as simple and effective as possible, Novell suggests that CNAs follow certain guidelines when planning file system security. In this section, you learn how the Novell-recommended guidelines can be used to improve your file system security plan.

Identify Rights Needed for Each User

The first guideline in successfully establishing file system security is to analyze each user's processing needs and then determine and document the access rights needed for each directory to meet the processing requirements. An advantage of this analysis is that you can identify processing needs that are common to multiple users, which reduces and simplifies the number of trustee assignments you need to make. When several users need the same rights to a set of files, it's much easier to keep track of and maintain a single trustee assignment to a group or container than to make redundant trustee assignments for several users.

Proper Directory Structure Design

A proper directory design takes advantage of the principle that lower-level directories and files inherit rights from higher-level directories—a top-down inherited rights strategy. Planning a directory structure is the key to taking advantage of this top-down strategy and preventing users from inheriting rights to directories in which they do not belong. The following list of suggestions will help you implement a top-down strategy:

- Design a directory structure that has directories requiring the most security near the top of the structure, separated from the directories that allow general user access. A well-designed directory structure can help reduce the number of trustee assignments by using the inherited rights principle, so that a common set of rights flows down to subdirectories. A good example of this is the UAS Apps directory structure, with subdirectories for all application software packages that are available to users.

- Directories that limit access to only specific users or access rights should not be included in a directory structure that has a trustee assignment for other users. For example, a document directory should not be included in an application directory unless you want all application users to be able to read the documents.

- Use IRFs to protect high-security directories against accidentally inheriting unwanted trustees. An IRF is a good way to prevent effective rights from accidentally flowing into the directory from a parent directory.

Reduce Use of IRFs

The need for an IRF as part of your security plan might indicate that you have placed a directory needing more security within a general-purpose directory and that you need to rethink your directory structure design. For example, the file system on one of the servers in your company has a directory structure like the one in Figure 5-9. Notice that the budget files are stored in a subdirectory of the Apps\SP directory and that the [Root] of the tree has been made a trustee of Apps with Read and File Scan rights. Because [Root] is a trustee of Apps with [R F] rights, all users inherit the [R F] rights to the Budgets subdirectory, creating a potential security problem in which all users have rights to read the budget data.

To prevent this, you could block inherited rights by removing all rights from the Budgets subdirectory's IRF, giving rights to only the Accting group, which is a trustee of the Budgets subdirectory. Although this solution works, it does not address the real problem of placing a subdirectory with higher security needs within a general-purpose directory. A better solution in this case is to move the Budgets subdirectory to a secure location in the file system and then make the appropriate trustee assignments, as shown in Figure 5-10.

Another method many network administrators use is reducing the number of IRFs whenever possible to use an explicit trustee assignment to reduce a user or group's effective rights. In addition, it's usually easier to troubleshoot explicit trustee assignments than trace the use of IRFs.

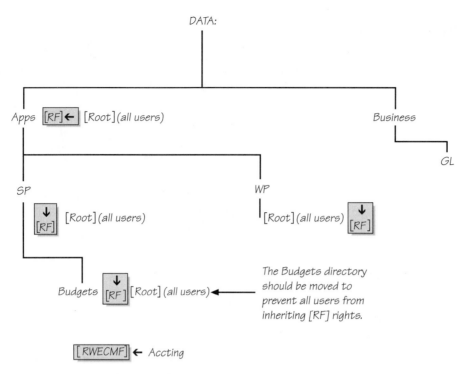

Figure 5-9   Poor directory design

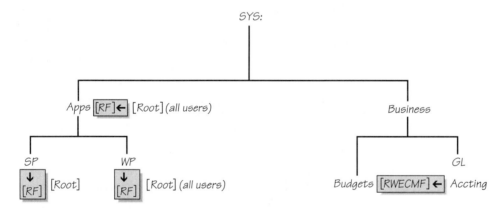

Figure 5-10   Proper directory design

Minimize Trustee Assignments

When planning trustee assignments, you can often keep user trustee assignments to a minimum by assigning rights to the containers or groups that have the most users, and then proceeding to user trustee assignments. Some network administrators go to the extreme of never making trustee assignments to users; instead, they make the trustee assignment to a group name and then make the users who need access rights members of the appropriate group. Although it might mean having to create and maintain additional group names, this approach makes it easier for the network administrator to deal with several users changing job functions, which can happen during a company reorganization, for example.

A similar technique you can use with NetWare 6 is to create an Organizational Role object (discussed in Chapter 4) and then make it, not a user object, the trustee of a directory or file. The Organizational Role object can then be assigned to users who need access to the directory or file information. If your company does a lot of reorganizing, you might want to consider using groups or Organizational Role objects instead of assigning rights to individual users. An effective way to minimize the number of trustee assignments you need is to make trustee assignments in the following order:

1. Assign rights to containers.

2. Assign rights to departmental groups.

3. Assign rights to Organizational Role objects.

4. Assign rights to individual users.

Avoid Complex Combinations

The last guideline in planning file system security is to avoid combinations of assignments to groups, containers, and individual users within the same directory structure. To keep things as simple as possible, do not rely on users inheriting certain rights because of membership in certain groups and containers; instead, make users explicit trustees of a directory or file with just the rights needed for access.

Universal AeroSpace File System Security

As described previously, the first step in planning file system security for an organization is to define the processing functions each user needs to perform in the file system. Table 5-3 contains file system usage information Eric documented for each user in the Management, Engineering, and Manufacturing departments.

Table 5-3   Universal AeroSpace File System Usage

User	File System Usage
All Users	Read files in the Forms directory. Run all applications except the Utility and CAD software. Read files in the Web directory. Have rights to create and update files in the ##CORP\Shared and Temp directories.
Management	
Lynn Dai	Updates and maintains files in the ##CORP\Forms directory. Maintains the ##CORP\Mgmt directory structure.
Engineering	Create and update files in the Engineer\Shared directory. Read files in the NASA and Aircraft directories. Run CAD software.
Kari Means (EngMgr Organizational Role)	Maintains the Engineer directory structure, but should have only Read access to the user home directory files. Also needs to be able to update engineering files in the Web\Engineer directory.
Lianne Jarka (RoverEng Organizational Role)	Currently the lead engineer responsible for the Rover project (ISS), but this could change if engineers are moved on and off the project.
Tony Rucci (IISEng Organizational Role)	Currently the lead engineer assigned to the IIS project, but as needs for this project change, additional engineers might be moved on or off the project.
Paul Alm	Senior engineer; works on all projects.
Bradley Dahl (AeroMgr Organizational Role)	Responsible for the Aircraft and AeroDyn projects.
Manufacturing	Work with files in the Engineer\Shared directory. Read and File Scan rights to the Requirements Planning System (RPS) software. Read, File Scan, and Write rights to the Inventry directory.
Russ Pence (MfgMgr Organizational Role)	As head of the Manufacturing department, will be given rights to maintain the RPS and Manufacturing data.

After identifying each user's processing needs, the next step in implementing file system security is to review the directory structure to determine whether it meets the directory structure guidelines described previously. In the UAS directory structure, the CAD software is currently located in a subdirectory of the

Apps directory. Because your ##UAS Organization is a trustee of Apps with [R F] rights, all users inherit [R F] rights to the CAD subdirectory, creating a potential licensing problem because the company currently has software licenses only for the Engineering users. You could prevent other users from accessing the CAD software by removing all rights from the CAD subdirectory's IRF, and then grant [R F] rights only to the Design group by making the group a trustee of the CAD directory. Although this solution works, it doesn't address the real problem of placing a subdirectory with higher security needs in a general-purpose directory. A better solution is moving the CAD subdirectory to the Engineer directory and then making the appropriate trustee assignments. To facilitate file system security, you should also create a subdirectory in the Web directory for engineering files. This would allow Kari to update engineering Web-based files without affecting other Web documents that Julie and Kellie maintain. In the following activity, you learn how to use ConsoleOne and My Computer to modify the directory structure.

Activity 5-12: Modifying the Directory Structure

Time Required: 10 minutes

Objectives: Use ConsoleOne and My Computer to assign rights to users, groups, and containers.

Description: After analyzing the UAS file system usage plan, Eric decided to reduce the number of IRF changes by moving the MfgData and CAD directories to the departments that own them. In this activity, you follow Eric's plan by making these changes to improve file system security: Use My Computer to move the CAD subdirectory to the Engineer directory, and create an Engineer subdirectory in the Web directory.

1. If necessary, start your computer, and log in with your UasAdmin user name.

2. If necessary, map drive letter G: to your ##CORP\Apps directory:

   a. Right-click **My Network Places**, and then click **Novell Map Network Drive** to open the Map Drive dialog box.

   b. Click the **Choose the drive letter to map** list arrow, and then click **G:** in the list of options.

   c. Enter **\\Uashost\##Corp\Apps** in the Enter the network path to the resource text box.

   d. Click the **Map** button to map the drive and open a window for the Apps directory.

3. Check the objects inheriting rights to the CAD directory:

   a. Right-click your **CAD** subdirectory, and then click **Properties** to open the CAD Properties dialog box.

   b. Click the **NetWare Rights** tab, and then click the **Inherited Rights and Filters** button.

   c. On your student answer sheet, record all objects inheriting rights to the CAD subdirectory.

   d. Click **Cancel** twice to return to the Apps directory window.

4. Use My Computer to move your CAD subdirectory to the Engineer directory:

   a. Right-click the **CAD** subdirectory, and then click **Cut**.

   b. Click the **up arrow** to return to your ##Corp dialog box.

   c. Double-click the **Engineer** directory.

   d. Click **Edit**, and then click **Paste** to place the CAD subdirectory in the Engineer directory.

5. Move the MfgData directory to the [Root] of your ##CORP volume:

   a. Right-click the **MfgData** directory, and then click **Cut**.

   b. Click the **up arrow** to open the directories in your ##CORP volume dialog box.

   c. Click **Edit**, and then click **Paste** to place the MfgData directory in your ##CORP volume dialog box.

6. Create an Engineer subdirectory in the Web directory:

   a. Double-click the **IS** directory, and then double-click the **Web** directory.

   b. Click **File** on the menu bar, point to **New**, and then click **Folder**.

   c. Type **Engineer**, and then press **Enter**.

7. Exit My Computer by closing the Engineer subdirectory dialog box.

After the directory structure meets the file system security guidelines, the next step in implementing file system security is to plan your trustee assignments. When planning trustee assignments, you should minimize the number of trustee assignments you need by following the guidelines described in the previous section. To help perform this task, Eric designed a Directory Trustee Worksheet, shown in Table 5-4. Using the previously described guidelines, Eric filled in the worksheet to show trustee assignments made to each directory and any changes made to the directory's IRF. Each row on the form represents the trustee assignments for the directory path designated in the first column. The second column indicates the rights allowed by the IRF. The remaining columns designate trustee assignments for the objects in the column headings. Eric placed each object that needs a trustee assignment in a Trustee column. On the first page, he listed the container objects followed by the groups. On the second page, he listed the Organizational Role objects (created in Chapter 4) and any individual user names. He identified each directory's trustee assignment by placing the directory path in the leftmost column and listing the access rights in the appropriate container, group, or Organizational Role column. Because some directories have trustee assignments from container, group, and Organizational Role objects, the second page repeats certain directory paths with the additional trustee assignments. Notice that Eric used Organizational Role objects to reduce the trustee assignments made to individual users.

Table 5-4   Directory Trustee Worksheet

Directory Path	IRF	Trustee: ##UAS container	Trustee: Engineering container	Trustee: Mfg container	Trustee: Mgmt container	Trustee: Design group	Trustee: ISMgrs group	Trustee: WebMgrs group	Trustee: Production group
Page 1									
Apps	All	RF							
Forms	All	RF							
Shared	All	RWECMF							
Temp	All	RWECMF							
Inventry	All	RF		RWF					
Apps\Utility	None						RF		
Mgmt\Shared					RWECMF				
IS\Web	All	RF						RWECMF	
IS\Shared	All						RWECMF		
Engineer	All								
Engineer\CAD	All					RF			
Engineer\RPS	All			RF					
Engineer\Shared	All		RWECMF	RWECMF					
Engineer\Aircraft	All		RF						
Engineer\NASA	All		RF						
MfgData\Shared	All								RWECMF
Apps\Quality	All			RWF					

Table 5-4 Directory Trustee Worksheet (Page 2)

Directory Path	IRF	Trustee: SysOp org role	Trustee: AdmAsst org role	Trustee: ISSEng org role	Trustee: RoverEng org role	Trustee: EngMgr org role	Trustee: AeroMgr org role	Trustee: MfgMgr org role	Trustee: PAlm user
CORP volume	All	SRF							
Mgmt	All		SRF						
Forms	All		RWECMF						
IS\Web\ Engineer	All					RWECMF			
Engineer	All					RWECMFA			
Engineer\ Aircraft	RF						RWECMF		RWECMF
Engineer\ NASA	RF								RWECMF
Engineer\ NASA\ISS	All			RWECMF					
Engineer\ NASA\Rover	All				RWECMF				
Engineer\ user name	RF								
MfgData	All						RWECMF	RECMF	

In the Directory Path column, Eric placed the directories starting from the highest level down to the lower levels. Making trustee assignments in the higher-level directories first helps reduce the number of trustee assignments through inheritance. Eric arranged the columns with containers and groups on the left, followed by Organizational Role objects, and finally individual user assignments. Making assignments to containers and groups first helps reduce the number of trustee assignments and simplifies maintaining file system security. The access rights to be granted to each directory are then listed in the corresponding row under the Trustee column. In this example, the top-level container, ##UAS, is listed in the first column and given a trustee assignment to the Apps, IS\Web, Forms, Temp, Inventry, and Shared directory structures. Next, the Engineering container is listed in the second column and given a trustee assignment to the Engineer\Shared, Engineer\NASA, and Engineer\Aircraft directories.

After rights have been assigned to the containers and groups, Organizational Role objects and individual users who need special rights are made trustees of the appropriate directories. As the occupant of the EngMgr Organizational Role object, for example, Kari Means will have rights to maintain the Engineer directory structure and work with files in the Web\Engineer directory. Also, the IRF of the Engineer\Users directory has been modified to allow only [R] and [F] rights to pass to the users' home directories. Although Eric set most of the rights needed for the Engineering department, in the end-of-chapter projects, you'll fill out the Directory Trustee Worksheet to include the Business users and grant appropriate access to their directories.

Implementing Trustee Assignments

After you have defined the trustee assignments in the Directory Trustee Worksheet, you can begin using NetWare utilities to implement those assignments. NetWare 6 has four ways of making a trustee assignment or changing an IRF:

- Windows Explorer, My Computer, or Network Neighborhood
- ConsoleOne

- NetWare Administrator
- The RIGHTS command-line utility

In this chapter, you have used Windows, ConsoleOne, and NetWare Administrator to practice making trustee assignments and checking effective rights for some of the directories listed in Table 5-4. In the activities in this section, you continue using these utilities to implement the trustee assignments and IRFs defined in the table. You'll use Windows to make the container trustee assignments, and then use ConsoleOne to make the group trustee assignments and set the directory IRFs. Next, you'll use NetWare Administrator to assign rights to the Organizational Role objects and individual users and to check effective rights. Finally, you'll use the RIGHTS command-line utility to document trustee assignments and directory IRFs.

Before performing the activities in this section, compare the directories in your structure to be sure you have created all the directories in the paths shown in Figure 5-11. If necessary, log in to the network with your administrator user name and create the directories. Also, if you have completed the end-of-chapter projects in previous chapters, you might have additional items in your tree that aren't shown in Figure 5-11.

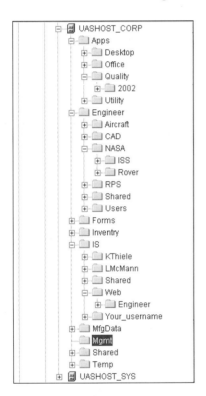

Figure 5-11   Revised UAS directory structure

Activity 5-13: Trustee Assignments with Windows

Time Required: 5 minutes

Objective: Use Windows to assign rights to containers.

Description: The Windows utilities offer convenient ways to make trustee assignments and check effective rights when working in the Windows environment. In this activity, you use Windows utilities to make trustee assignments for the containers identified in Page 1 of the Directory Trustee Worksheet (refer to Table 5-4).

1. If necessary, start your computer, and log in with your UasAdmin user name.

2. If necessary, map a drive to your ##Corp directory:

   a. Right-click **My Network Places**, and then click **Novell Map Network Drive** to open the Map Drive dialog box.

   b. Click the **Choose the drive letter to map** list arrow, and then click **G:** in the list of options.

   c. Enter **\\Uashost\\##Corp** in the Enter the network path to the resource text box.

   d. Click the **Map** button to map the drive and open a ##Corp dialog box.

3. Use Windows to make your ##UAS container a trustee of the Forms directory with Read and File Scan rights (refer to Table 5-4):

   a. Right-click **Forms**, and then click **Properties** to open the Forms Properties dialog box.

   b. Click the **NetWare Rights** tab to display any existing trustee assignments.

   c. Click your **##UAS** container in the lower pane, and then click the **Add** button to add your ##UAS Organization as a trustee.

   d. Verify that the Read and File Scan Rights are selected.

   e. Click **OK** to save the trustee assignment and return to the ##Corp directory window.

4. Repeat Step 3 to make your ##UAS container a trustee of the other directories in the ##Corp directory window, with the rights shown in Table 5-4.

5. Make your ##UAS Organization a trustee of the IS\\Web subdirectory:

   a. Double-click your **IS** directory to expand it.

   b. Right-click the **Web** subdirectory, and then click **Properties** to open the Web Properties dialog box.

   c. Click the **NetWare Rights** tab to display any existing trustee assignments.

   d. Click your **##UAS** container in the lower pane, and then click the **Add** button to add your ##UAS Organization as a trustee.

   e. Click **OK** to save the trustee assignment and return to the IS directory window.

   f. Click the **up arrow** to return to the ##Corp directory window.

6. Repeat Steps 4 and 5 to make your Engineering container a trustee of the directories shown in Table 5-4.

7. Repeat Steps 4 and 5 to make your Mfg container a trustee of the directories shown in Table 5-4.

 In Activity 5-15, you use ConsoleOne to make the Mgmt container a trustee of the directories shown in Table 5-4.

8. Close the My Computer window.

9. If you're continuing to the next activity, stay logged in. If not, log out.

Activity 5-14: Trustee Assignments with NetWare Administrator

Time Required: 10 minutes

Objective: Use NetWare Administrator to assign rights to groups.

Description: As a network administrator, sometimes you'll find it faster or more convenient to use NetWare Administrator rather than ConsoleOne or Windows to perform such functions as making directory trustee assignments, changing an IRF, and checking effective rights. In this activity, you use NetWare Administrator to make the group trustee assignments on Page 1 of the Directory Trustee Worksheet (see Table 5-4).

1. If necessary, start your computer, and log in with your assigned UasAdmin user name.

2. Start NetWare Administrator.

3. If necessary, open a browse window for your ##UAS container.

4. Double-click your **UASHOST_CORP** volume to display all directories.

5. Double-click the **Engineer** directory to display all subdirectories.

6. Make the Design group a trustee of the Engineer\CAD software directory with Read and File Scan rights:

   a. Right-click the **CAD** subdirectory, and then click **Details** to open the Directory: CAD Identification dialog box.

   b. On your student answer sheet, record the option buttons at the right of the Identification section.

   c. Click the **Trustees of this Directory** button to open the Trustees of this Directory dialog box.

   d. Click the **Add Trustee** button to open the Select Object dialog box.

   e. Double-click the **Engineering** container in the Browse context pane to display all Engineering objects in the Available objects pane.

   f. Click the **Design** group in the Available objects pane, and then click **OK** to place the Design group in the Trustees list box.

   g. Verify that the correct rights are listed, and then click **OK** to return to the NetWare Administrator browse window.

7. Double-click the **MfgData** directory to display the Shared subdirectory.

8. Repeat Step 6 to make the Production group a trustee of the MfgData\Shared directory with all rights except Supervisor and Access Control.

9. Double-click the **IS** directory to show all subdirectories.

10. Repeat Step 6 to make the WebMgrs group a trustee of the IS\Web subdirectory with all rights except Supervisor and Access Control.

11. Repeat Step 6 to make the ISMgrs group a trustee of the IS\Shared subdirectory with all rights except Supervisor and Access Control.

12. Exit NetWare Administrator.

13. If you're continuing to the next activity, stay logged in. If not, log out.

Activity 5-15: Trustee Assignments with ConsoleOne

Time Required: 15 minutes

Objective: Use ConsoleOne to assign rights to users, groups, and containers.

Description: As a CNA, you'll be required to use ConsoleOne to perform functions such as making directory trustee assignments, changing an IRF, and checking effective rights. In this activity, you use ConsoleOne to make the group and user trustee assignments on Page 2 of the Directory Trustee Worksheet (see Table 5-4) and then set all the directory IRFs.

1. If necessary, start your computer, and log in with your UasAdmin user name.

2. Start ConsoleOne, expand the **UAS_Tree**, and then expand your **##UAS** container.

3. Expand your **UASHOST_CORP** volume to display all directories.

4. Make your Mgmt container a trustee of the Mgmt\Shared subdirectory:

   a. Expand the **Mgmt** directory.

   b. Right-click the **Shared** subdirectory, and then click **Properties** to open the Properties of Shared dialog box.

   c. Click the **Trustees** tab to display the Trustees list box.

   d. Click the **Add Trustee** button to display the Select Object dialog box.

   e. If necessary, click the **up arrow** to navigate to your Organizational Units. Click your **Mgmt** container, and then click **OK** to add Mgmt to the Trustees list box.

   f. Click to enable all rights except Supervisor and Access Control.

   g. Click **OK** to save the assignment and return to the main ConsoleOne window.

5. Make the SysOp Organizational Role object a trustee of the UASHOST_CORP volume with Supervisor rights:

   a. Right-click the **UASHOST_Corp** volume, and then click **Properties** to open the Properties of UASHOST_CORP dialog box.

   b. Click the **Trustees** tab to display the Trustees list box.

   c. Click the **Add Trustee** button to open the Select Object dialog box.

   d. If necessary, browse to your ##UAS\IS container, and click the **SysOp** Organizational Role object.

   e. Click **OK** to add this object to the Trustees list box.

   f. Click the **Supervisor** check box to enable this access right.

   g. Click **OK** to save the assignment and return to the main ConsoleOne window.

6. When you have multiple trustee assignments for a single object, it's faster to select that object and then add the trustee assignments. In this step, you'll make all the trustee assignments for the AdmAsst Organizational Role object shown in Table 5-4:

   a. If necessary, expand your **##UAS** organization.

   b. Click the **Mgmt** OU to display all objects in the Objects frame.

   c. Right-click **AdmAsst**, and then click **Properties** to open the Properties of AdmAsst dialog box.

   d. Click the **Rights to Files and Folders** tab to display the Files and Folders section shown in Figure 5-12. Click the **Show** button to view the current information.

   e. Click the **Add** button to open the Select Object dialog box.

   f. Double-click the **UASHOST_CORP** volume to expand it.

   g. Click the **Mgmt** directory, and then click **OK** to add it to the Files and Folders pane.

   h. Click the **Supervisor** check box.

   i. To make another assignment, click the **Add** button to open the Select Object dialog box.

   j. Double-click the **UASHOST_CORP** volume to expand it.

   k. Click the **Forms** directory, and then click **OK** to add it to the Files and Folders section.

   l. Click all check boxes except Supervisor and Access Control to give occupants of the AdmAsst Organizational Role object rights to manage the Forms directory.

   m. Now that all assignments have been made for AdmAsst, click **OK** to save the changes and return to the main ConsoleOne window.

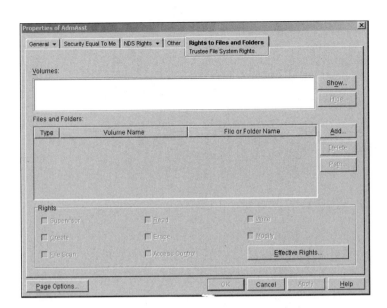

Figure 5-12   Adding trustee assignments to an object

For the remaining trustee assignments, remember to refer to Table 5-4 for the information you need to make the assignments.

7. Repeat Step 5 to make trustee assignments for your ISSEng Organizational Role object. Document the steps on your student answer sheet.

8. Repeat Step 5 to make trustee assignments for your RoverEng Organizational Role object.

9. Repeat Step 6 to make trustee assignments for your EngMgr Organizational Role object. Document the steps on your student answer sheet.

10. Repeat Step 6 to make trustee assignments for your AeroMgr Organizational Role object.

11. Repeat Step 5 to make trustee assignments for your MfgMgr Organizational Role object.

12. Repeat Step 5 to make trustee assignments for the user PAlm.

13. Change the IRF on the Engineer\Users subdirectory to block all rights except Read and File Scan:

    a. If necessary, expand your **UASHOST_CORP** volume, and then expand your **Engineer** directory.

    b. Right-click the **Engineer\Users** subdirectory, and then click **Properties** to open the Properties of Users dialog box.

    c. Click the **Inherited Rights Filter** tab to display the existing filter settings.

    d. Click to remove the check mark from all rights except Supervisor, Read, and File Scan (see Figure 5-13).

    e. Click **OK** to save your IRF changes and return to the main ConsoleOne window.

14. Repeat Step 13 to change the IRF on the Engineer\NASA directory to block all rights except Supervisor, Read, and File Scan.

15. Repeat Step 13 to change the IRF on the Engineer\Aircraft subdirectory to block all rights except Supervisor, Read, and File Scan.

16. Exit ConsoleOne, and log out.

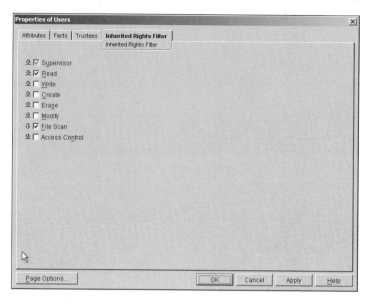

Figure 5-13   Setting the directory IRF

Documenting Trustee Assignments

Luke requested that Eric document the trustee assignments for future reference. Eric could have used NetWare Administrator or ConsoleOne to print each directory's Trustee dialog box, but to save time, he used the NetWare RIGHTS command-line utility. In addition to printing lists of trustee assignments, the RIGHTS command is convenient for working at the command prompt, creating a batch file or script to assign rights, or accessing the network from a station that does not have Windows installed. Because the RIGHTS command has several different options, Novell included a Help function so that you can review the syntax for a specific function. By doing the hands-on activities in this section, you learn how to use the RIGHTS command to get help information, view and print trustee assignments, view and print directory IRFs, and make a simple trustee assignment.

Activity 5-16: Using the RIGHTS Command

Time Required: 5 minutes

Objective: Use the RIGHTS command to list and document trustee assignments.

Description: In this activity, you use the RIGHTS command to view help information and print a report for Luke showing the current directory trustee assignments and IRFs.

1. If necessary, start your computer, and log in with your UasAdmin user name.

2. Open a command-prompt window (click **Start**, **Run**, enter **command**, and click **OK**), and change to your F: drive.

3. To view help information, type **RIGHTS /?**, and then press **Enter**. If you see the "Bad command or file name" message, enter the command **CD SYS:PUBLIC**, and then repeat this step.

4. To view the trustees of all directories in your ##Corp directory, enter the command **RIGHTS ##CORP:*.* /T**, and then press **Enter**. After each screen, the system will halt and wait for you to press the Enter key.

5. To view trustee assignments for all directories and subdirectories, you need to include the /S option. To see these trustee assignments, enter the command **RIGHTS *.* /S /T**.

6. You can print this information by including >PRN at the end of the command to redirect output to the printer assigned to your LPT1 printer port. To print your trustee assignments, enter the command **RIGHTS *.* /S /T > PRN**, and then press **Enter**.

7. Retrieve your printout, and then close your command-prompt window.

8. Log out.

Congratulations! You have finished setting up trustee rights for the users in your Engineering, IS, Mfg, and Mgmt departments. In the next section, you learn how Eric used attributes to enhance file system security for the UAS network.

ATTRIBUTE SECURITY

5

Attributes are flags or codes that you can associate with files and directories so that the network operating system can determine what type of processing can be performed on the associated file and directory. The network administrator often places attributes on directories and files as additional protection against accidental change or deletion or to specify special processing, such as controlling file compression, making a file sharable, or purging files immediately after they are deleted. As a CNA, you'll need to know the file and directory attributes, what they are used for, and how to use NetWare utilities to work with attributes.

File and Directory Attributes

Attributes placed on files and directories override a user's effective rights in that file or directory. If a file is flagged with the Read Only attribute, for example, no matter what the effective rights are, the only operations you can perform on the file are Read and File Scan. For example, Kari has all rights to the Engineer directory and, therefore, would inherit all rights to the files and subdirectories in the Engineer directory structure. If a file named Partlist.dat stored in the NASA directory is flagged with the Read Only attribute, even though Kari has all effective rights as a result of the trustee assignment, she still has only Read and File Scan access to the Partlist.dat file. However, because Kari has inherited the Modify right to the directory as a result of her trustee assignment to the Engineer directory, the Modify right enables her to remove the Read Only attribute and then change or even delete the Partlist.dat file.

File Attributes

Table 5-5 lists the file attributes used in NetWare, along with their corresponding abbreviations. In the following sections, each of these attributes is described briefly.

Table 5-5   File Attributes

Attribute	Abbreviation	Attribute	Abbreviation
Archive Needed	A	Migrated	M
Can't Compress	Cc	Purge	P
Copy Inhibit	Ci	Read Only	Ro
Delete Inhibit	Di	Read Write	Rw
Don't Compress	Dc	Rename Inhibit	Ri
Don't Suballocate	Ds	Sharable	Sh
Execute Only	X	System	Sy
Hidden	H	Transactional	T
Immediate Compress	Ic		

Archive Needed (A)   The **Archive Needed (A)** attribute is automatically assigned to files when the file contents are modified. Copy or backup utilities can remove this attribute after copying the file to another storage location. This attribute controls which files are copied to a backup disk, making it possible to back up only the files that have been changed since the last backup.

Can't Compress (Cc)   The network system sets the **Can't Compress (Cc)** attribute on files that cannot be compressed. A user or network administrator is not allowed to change this attribute setting.

Copy Inhibit (Ci)   The **Copy Inhibit (Ci)** attribute is used only to prevent Macintosh users from copying specified files, such as software programs that won't work on Macintosh computers. Setting this attribute prevents Macintosh computers running AppleTalk Filing Protocol 2.0 and above from copying the file.

Delete Inhibit (Di)   The **Delete Inhibit (Di)** attribute prevents a file from being deleted, but still allows the file to be renamed or have changes made to its content. To delete the file, a user must first be granted the Modify right to remove the Delete Inhibit attribute. The Delete Inhibit attribute is often useful to protect an important data file from accidentally being deleted, yet still allow its contents to be changed. You should consider setting the Delete Inhibit attribute on many of your organization's permanent files, such as customer, payroll, inventory, and accounting.

Don't Compress (Dc)   Users or network administrators can set the **Don't Compress (Dc)** attribute to prevent a file from being automatically compressed, as described in Chapter 3. Preventing file compression can produce a minor improvement in performance when that file is accessed because the file doesn't need to be decompressed.

Don't Suballocate (Ds)   Users or network administrators can set the **Don't Suballocate (Dc)** attribute to prevent a file from being suballocated to other files. Using this attribute provides a way to run certain applications and to use a database system that will not work with files that have been suballocated.

Execute Only (X)   The major use of the **Execute Only (X)** attribute is to protect software files from being illegally copied. Execute Only can be set only on .exe and .com files by a Supervisor-equivalent user; once set, it cannot be removed, even by the network administrator. Do *not* assign Execute Only to files unless you have backup copies of those files. Certain program files will not run when they are flagged Execute Only because these programs need to copy information from their program files into the workstation's memory, and the Execute Only attribute prevents them from applying the copy functions. Because the Execute Only attribute cannot be removed, to get rid of it, you need to delete the file and reinstall it from another disk.

Hidden (H)   The **Hidden (H)** attribute is used to hide files from DOS utilities and certain application software. NetWare utilities display hidden files when the Hidden attribute is enabled. One simple way to help protect software from illegal copying is to use the Hidden attribute to hide software directories and files from normal DOS utilities, and then move the NCOPY and NDIR commands from the SYS:Public directory to the SYS:System directory or some other location where typical users will not have access to them.

Immediate Compress (Ic)   The **Immediate Compress (Ic)** attribute is usually assigned to large files that you want compressed immediately after they are closed to save disk space. As described in Chapter 3, by default, files are compressed after seven days of no activity.

Migrated (M)   The system sets the **Migrated (M)** attribute on files that have been migrated to a high-capacity storage medium, such as an optical disk drive or a tape backup system. Although migrated files are accessible to users, there might be a long delay to restore the file before it can be accessed.

Purge (P)   As described in Chapter 3, in NetWare, deleted files can be salvaged by using the SALVAGE utility until the deleted file's space is reused by the file server or the directory is purged with the PURGE command. After files have been purged, that space is no longer available to the operating system, so those files cannot be recovered with the SALVAGE utility. The **Purge (P)** attribute can be assigned to a file if you want the NetWare server to immediately reuse the space from that file when it's deleted. The Purge attribute can also be assigned for security reasons to files that contain sensitive data, thereby preventing an intruder from salvaging and then accessing information from these files after they have been deleted.

Read Only (Ro)   The **Read Only (Ro)** attribute applies only to files and can be used to protect file contents from being modified. Its function is similar to opening the write-protect tab on a disk. Files whose contents are not normally changed, such as a zip code file or a program file, are usually flagged Read Only. When you first set the Read Only attribute, the Delete Inhibit and Rename Inhibit attributes are also set by default. If you want to allow the file to be renamed or deleted but don't want its contents changed, you can remove the Rename Inhibit and Delete Inhibit attributes.

Read Write (Rw)   The **Read Write (Rw)** attribute applies only to files and is used to indicate that the contents of the file can be added to or changed. When files are created, the Read Write attribute is automatically set.

Rename Inhibit (Ri)   When assigned to a file, the **Rename Inhibit (Ri)** attribute protects the filename from being changed. During installation, many software packages create data and configuration files that might need to be updated or changed, but those filenames must remain constant for the software package to operate correctly. After installing a software package that requests certain filenames, it's a good idea to set the Rename Inhibit attribute on these files to prevent future changing of the file or directory name, which could cause the program to crash or signal an error.

Sharable (Sh)   Files are available to only one user at a time. For example, suppose you created a file called Budget95.wk1 on the file server and a co-worker opened this file with a spreadsheet program. If you or another user attempted to access the Budget95.wk1 file, an error message would inform the user that the file is in use or is not accessible. With spreadsheet files and word-processing documents, you would not want more than one user to have a copy of the file at one time, because any changes the user makes could be overwritten by another user. Program files and certain database files, however, should be made available to multiple users simultaneously. For example, you would want all licensed users to be able to run the word-processing software you have just installed or perhaps to access a common database of customers. To allow a file to be opened by more than one user at a time, the **Sharable (Sh)** attribute for that file must be set. If you want multiple users to be able to copy or run a program simultaneously, you need to flag all program files as Sharable after software installation.

System (Sy)   The **System (Sy)** attribute is often assigned to files that are part of the NetWare operating system. Like the Hidden attribute, the System attribute hides files from DOS utilities and application software packages, but also marks the file as being for operating system use only.

Transactional (T)   The **Transactional (T)** attribute can be assigned only to files and is used to indicate that the file is protected by the **Transaction Tracking System (TTS)**. TTS ensures that when changes or transactions are applied to a file, either all transactions are completed or the file is left in its original state. This system is particularly important when working with database files, when a workstation might start updating a record and then crash before the update is finished. For example, assume that a NetWare file server is used to maintain an online order entry system containing customer and inventory files. When entering an order, at least two transactions are necessary: one to update the customer's account balance and the other to record the inventory item to be shipped. Suppose that while entering the order, the workstation crashes after it updates the customer balance and therefore fails to record the item on the shipping list. In this case, the TTS would cancel the transaction and restore the customer's balance to its original amount, allowing you to re-enter the complete order. Because TTS is a feature used by application software, using the Transactional attribute does not implement TTS protection. You also need to have the proper system design and application software.

Directory Attributes

With the exception of the Don't Migrate attribute, the directory attributes shown in Table 5-6 are actually a subset of the file attributes and have similar functions. Some directory attributes affect only the directory, and others apply to all files in the directory. As a network administrator, you should know the differences between directory attributes and file attributes, as well as how directory attributes affect the files stored in the directory.

Table 5-6   Directory Attributes

Attribute	Abbreviation
Delete Inhibit	Di
Don't Compress	Dc
Don't Migrate	Dm
Normal	N
Hidden	H
Immediate Compress	Ic
Purge	P
Rename Inhibit	Ri
System	Sy

Delete Inhibit (Di)   Setting the Delete Inhibit attribute on a directory prevents the directory's name from being removed, but does not prevent the contents of the directory—its files and subdirectories—from being deleted. You might want to protect the fixed parts of your organization's directory structure from being modified by flagging all main directories with the Delete Inhibit attribute.

Don't Compress (Dc)   Setting the Don't Compress attribute on a directory prevents all files in the directory from being compressed. If disk space is not a problem, preventing file compression in a directory can result in slightly faster performance because NetWare 6 does not have to decompress the file when it's opened by a user.

Don't Migrate (Dm)   If you have data migration enabled on a volume, you can set the **Don't Migrate (Dm)** attribute on a directory to prevent files in that directory from being migrated to a high-capacity storage device. Preventing migration can be helpful if users need quick access to these archive files and don't want to wait for the data migration system to load them from the high-capacity storage medium.

Normal (N)   The **Normal (N)** directory attribute removes all directory attributes.

Hidden (H)   As with the file attribute, the Hidden directory attribute is used to hide directories from DOS utilities and certain application software. Although hidden directories can still be viewed by using NetWare utilities, DOS commands and Windows applications will not be able to see the directory structure. The Hidden directory attribute can be useful when you have Windows workstations because it's easy for users to explore the directory structure by using File Manager. By hiding directories, you can make the file structure a lot less accessible.

Immediate Compress (Ic)   The Immediate Compress attribute is usually assigned to directories containing several large files that you want compressed immediately after they are closed to save disk space.

Purge (P)   The Purge attribute can be assigned to a directory so that the NetWare file server immediately reuses the space from any files deleted in that directory. When the Purge attribute is assigned to a directory, any file deleted from the directory is automatically purged and its space reused. The Purge attribute is often assigned to directories containing temporary files so that the temporary file space can be reused as soon as the file is deleted.

Rename Inhibit (Ri)   Using the Rename Inhibit attribute on a directory prevents that directory's name from being changed, but still allows files and subdirectories in that directory to be renamed. Directories that are part of the system drive mappings and application software paths should be protected by the Rename

Inhibit attribute because changing the directory's name affects the running of software and drive mappings made to data in that directory structure.

System (Sy) The System attribute is often assigned to directories that are part of the NOS or certain client software. Print queues, described in Chapter 6, are actually subdirectories and are flagged with the System attribute. Like the Hidden attribute, the System attribute hides directories from the DOS utilities and application software packages, but also marks directories as being for operating system use only.

Planning Directory Attribute Usage at Universal AeroSpace

Users who have been granted Erase and Modify access rights to a directory can remove or rename the directory as well as the files it contains. Without adequate planning, renaming directories in a structure could cause problems with directory map commands and could prevent some applications from finding data in a predefined path. One of the important uses of directory attributes is protecting the directory structure from name changes and accidental deletion. In addition to the Delete Inhibit and Rename Inhibit attributes, some directories can be further protected by hiding them from DOS or Windows with the Hidden attribute. The Purge attribute is useful on directories containing temporary files that are frequently deleted. Using the Purge attribute on these directories results in deleted files from other directories being available for salvaging for a longer time.

Table 5-7 lists the directory attributes Eric planned for each of the directories in the UAS file system.

Table 5-7   Directory Attributes for Universal AeroSpace

Directory	Attributes
Shared	Di, Ri
Inventry	Di, Ri
Temp	P
Forms	Di, Ri
IS\Web	Di, Ri, P
Engineer	Di, Ri
Apps	Ri, P
Apps\Office	Di, Ri, P, Ic, H
Apps\Quality	Di, Ri
Apps\Utility	Di, Ri, H

The Delete Inhibit and Rename Inhibit attributes have been suggested for all major directories to prevent deletion or name changes. The Purge attribute was suggested on the Temp directory because of the number of temporary files that the UAS database software creates. By placing the Purge attribute on the IS\Web, Apps, and Apps\Office directories, the system can immediately reuse space from old deleted files when a new version of the software is copied to these directories.

Planning File Attribute Usage at Universal AeroSpace

Eric finds that the most commonly used file attributes are Read Only and Shared. As shown in Table 5-8, the software programs in the Apps\Office directory are used by multiple users and need to be flagged with the Shared attribute so that more than one user can run or copy a program simultaneously.

Table 5-8   File Attributes for Universal AeroSpace

Filename and Path	Attributes
Apps\Office*.exe	Sh
Engineer\CAD*.*	Ro
Apps\Utility*.exe	X

The Read Only attribute is another common file attribute often used on program files to prevent the software from being accidentally changed or deleted and to protect against virus infection. If users are granted only Read and File Scan rights to a software directory, protecting the program files with the Read Only attribute is not necessary. However, with some software packages, such as the UAS CAD software, users need to maintain configuration or temporary files in the same software directory as the program files. As a result, Eric needed to grant the Design users Write, Create, and Erase rights in addition to Read and File Scan rights to maintain the configuration files and to create and delete temporary files. When users have more than Read and File Scan rights in a software directory, placing the Read Only attribute on the program files becomes essential to protect them from deletion or changes by users or computer viruses. In addition to the Shared and Read Only attributes, the Execute Only attribute is important when software is used in an environment where there is a possibility of illegal copying.

Implementing Directory and File Attributes

As a network administrator, you need to be able to use NetWare utilities along with Windows to implement directory and file attributes in the network file system. Knowing how to use the Windows-based ConsoleOne utility is required for the CNA test, but as a network administrator, you'll also find it convenient to know how to use Windows utilities. In the following activities, you learn how to use ConsoleOne along with Windows Explorer or My Computer to set and view file and directory attributes.

Activity 5-17: Setting Directory Attributes

Time Required: 5 minutes

Objective: Use ConsoleOne to assign attributes to directories.

Description: In this activity, you use ConsoleOne to set directory attributes on the directories listed in Table 5-7. You'll set attributes for the Apps directory structure in Activity 5-18.

1. If necessary, start your computer, and log in with your UasAdmin user name.

2. Start ConsoleOne, expand the **UAS_Tree**, and then expand your **##UAS** container.

3. Expand your **UASHOST_CORP** volume.

4. Use ConsoleOne to set the Delete Inhibit and Rename Inhibit attributes on the Shared directory:

   a. Right-click the **Shared** directory, and then click **Properties** to open the Properties of Shared dialog box. If necessary, click the **Attributes** tab (see Figure 5-14).

   b. Click the **Delete Inhibit** and **Rename Inhibit** check boxes.

   c. Click **OK** to save your attribute assignment.

5. Repeat Step 4 to set the attributes in Table 5-7 for all directories except the Apps directories.

6. Exit ConsoleOne. If you're continuing to the next activity, stay logged in. If not, log out.

Activity 5-18: Setting Attributes from Windows

Time Required: 5 minutes

Objective: Use Windows to set directory attributes.

Description: In this activity, you use Windows to set the attributes Eric defined in Table 5-7 for the Apps directories.

1. If necessary, start your computer, and log in with your UasAdmin user name.

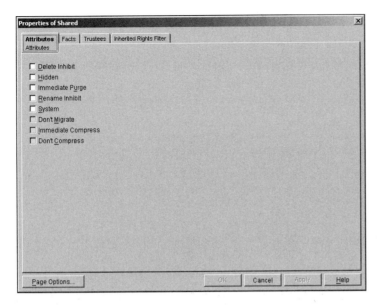

Figure 5-14   The Attributes tab

2. If necessary, map drive letter G: to your ##CORP volume by right-clicking **My Network Places** and clicking **Novell Map Drive** (refer to Step 2 in Activity 5-13 for detailed instructions, if you need a reminder). After completing this step, the ##Corp on 'Uashost' (G:) dialog box, similar to the one in Figure 5-15, opens to display all directories in your ##CORP volume.

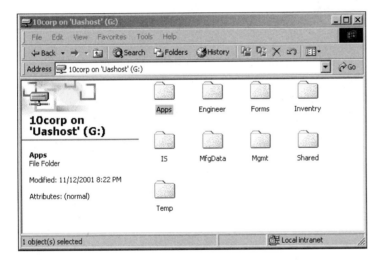

Figure 5-15   Viewing directories in your ##CORP volume

3. Use Windows to set the Rename Inhibit attribute on the Apps directory:

   a. Right-click your **Apps** directory, and then click **Properties** to open the Apps Properties dialog box.

   b. Click the **NetWare Info** tab.

   c. Click the **Rename Inhibit** and **Purge Immediate** check boxes.

   d. Click **OK** to save the attribute settings and return to the ##CORP volume dialog box.

4. Double-click the **Apps** directory to expand it.

5. Set the attributes for the subdirectories of Apps (referring to Table 5-7) by following these general steps:

    a. Right-click a subdirectory, and then click **Properties** to open the corresponding Properties dialog box.

    b. Click the **NetWare Info** tab.

    c. Click the check box corresponding to the appropriate attribute.

    d. Click **OK** to save the attribute settings and return to the Apps dialog box.

6. Click **View**, **Refresh** on the menu bar to refresh the Apps dialog box. The Utility and Office directories should no longer be displayed because they have been flagged as Hidden.

7. Configure Windows to show hidden directories:

    a. Click **Tools**, **Folder Options** on the menu to open the Folder Options dialog box.

    b. Click the **View** tab.

    c. In the Advanced settings section, click the **Show hidden files and folders** radio button, shown in Figure 5-16.

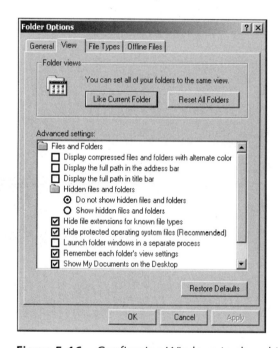

Figure 5-16   Configuring Windows to show hidden directories

    d. Click **OK** to save the settings.

    e. Your Office and Utility folders should now be listed in the Apps dialog box. Notice that the folder icons are lighter to indicate that the folders are hidden.

8. Close your Apps directory window.

9. If you're continuing to the next activity, stay logged in. If not, log out.

Activity 5-19: Working with File Attributes

Time Required: 5 minutes

Objective: Use Windows to set file attributes.

Description: To prevent accidental changes or corruption to files in the CAD directory, Eric set the Read Only attribute on all files in the directory. In this activity, you protect the CAD software files in your CAD directory by using Windows to set all file attributes to Read Only.

1. If you logged out after the last activity, log in with your UasAdmin user name, and follow the procedure in Step 2 of Activity 5-13 to map drive letter G: to your ##CORP volume. After completing this step, the ##Corp on 'Uashost' (G:) dialog box opens to display the directories on your ##CORP volume, and you can skip to Step 3.

2. If you're still logged in from the previous activity, double-click **My Computer**, and then double-click the **G:** drive to open the ##Corp on 'Uashost' (G:) dialog box.

3. Double-click your **Engineer** directory, and then double-click the **CAD** subdirectory to open the CAD dialog box showing all files in the CAD subdirectory.

4. Right-click the **mspaint.exe** file, and then click **Properties** to open the Properties dialog box.

5. Click the **NetWare Info** tab to display information about the selected file.

6. Click the **Read-only** check box.

7. Click **OK** to save your changes and return to the CAD dialog box.

8. Close your CAD dialog box and log out.

The FLAG Command-Line Utility

Just as the RIGHTS command is useful for documenting or setting access rights from the DOS prompt, the NetWare FLAG command-line utility is useful for documenting and setting directory and file attributes. The FLAG command has two different options to work with file or directory attributes. As a network administrator, you should know how to use the FLAG command's directory and file options to work with attributes.

Setting and Documenting Directory Attributes

The FLAG command uses the /DO parameter to set and view directory attributes:

```
FLAG [path] [+/-] [attribute_list] /DO
```

You can replace [*attribute_list*] with one or more of the directory attributes shown previously in Table 5-6. Use the + operator if you want to add the attribute to the directory, or the - operator to remove the attribute from the directory. The [*path*] parameter is optional, and if you enter only the FLAG /DO command, you'll see a list of the attribute settings for all subdirectories of the current directory. In the following activity, you get a chance to practice using the FLAG command to view attribute settings.

Activity 5-20: Documenting Attribute Settings with the FLAG Command

Time Required: 5 minutes

Objective: Use the FLAG command to document attribute settings.

Description: In this activity, you use the FLAG command to document your directory attributes and then set attributes for the Office subdirectory.

1. If necessary, start your computer, and log in with your UasAdmin user name.

2. Open a command-prompt window (click **Start**, **Run**, enter **Command**, and click **OK**), and change to drive F:.

3. View help information on the FLAG command by entering the command **FLAG /?** and pressing **Enter**. If you see the "Bad command or file name" message, enter the command **CD SYS:\PUBLIC**, press **Enter**, and repeat the FLAG command.

4. To view help information on setting directory attributes, enter the command **FLAG /? DO**, and then press **Enter**.

5. To view all your directory attribute settings, enter the command **FLAG ##CORP:*.* /DO**, and then press **Enter**.

6. To view attribute settings for all subdirectories, enter the command **FLAG *.* /DO /S**, and then press **Enter**.

7. To set the Delete Inhibit, Rename Inhibit, and Hidden attributes on your Apps\Office subdirectory, enter the FLAG command **FLAG ##CORP:APPS\OFFICE +Di +Ri +H /DO**, and then press **Enter**.

8. Exit the command-prompt window.

9. Use My Computer to verify the attribute settings for the Office subdirectory:

   a. Double-click **My Computer**, and then double-click the **G:** drive to open the ##Corp on 'Uashost' (G:) dialog box.

   b. Double-click the **Apps** directory to expand it.

   c. Right-click the **Office** subdirectory, and then click **Properties** to open the Office Properties dialog box.

   d. Click the **NetWare Info** tab to display attribute settings. Verify that the attributes set in Step 7 have been enabled.

   e. Click **Cancel** to close the Office Properties dialog box.

   f. Close the Apps directory window.

10. Log out.

Setting and Documenting File Attributes

To view or set attributes on files, the FLAG command uses the /FO (Files Only) parameter to set and view file attributes:

```
FLAG [path] [+/-] [attribute_list] /FO
```

You can replace [attribute_list] with one or more of the file attributes shown in Table 5-5. Use the + operator if you want to add the attribute to the files, or the - operator to remove the attribute from the files. The [path] parameter is optional, and if you enter only the FLAG /FO command, you'll see a list of attribute settings for all files in the current directory. You can also use a global parameter, such as *.exe, in the [path] parameter to specify a group of filenames that have the same extension. In the following activity, you get a chance to practice using the FLAG command with file attributes.

Activity 5-21: Setting and Documenting File Attributes

Time Required: 10 minutes

Objective: Use the FLAG command to set file attributes.

Description: In case you run a utility program from a computer that's infected with a virus, Eric has suggested making all the files in the Utility directory Read Only, and then removing the Modify right from your user name's trustee assignment; these measures will help make sure viruses don't modify files in your Utility directory. In this activity, you use the FLAG command to set the Read Only attribute on all files in the Utility directory.

1. If necessary, start your computer, and log in with your UasAdmin user name.

2. Open a command-prompt window, and change to drive F:.

3. To view help information on setting file attributes, enter the command **FLAG /? FO**, and press **Enter**. If you see the "Bad command or file name" message, enter the command **CD SYS:\PUBLIC**, press **Enter**, and repeat the FLAG command.

4. To view file attribute settings in your Utility directory, enter the command **FLAG ##CORP:Apps\Utility*.* /FO**, and then press **Enter**.

5. To set the Read Only attribute on all files in your Utility directory, enter the FLAG command **FLAG ##CORP:APPS\Utility*.* +RO   /FO**, and then press **Enter**.

6. Use the command in Step 5 to view the file attributes in your Utility directory. Notice that the Delete Inhibit and Rename Inhibit attributes are enabled by default when you use the Read Only attribute.

7. Exit the command-prompt window, and log out.

In a recent department meeting with David Heise and other department managers, Eric reported that he had established file system security in the Engineering and Manufacturing departments that enabled users to take advantage of the network's file system. Of course, the Business and Marketing managers were anxious to know when their departments would be ready to go. Eric explained that he had documented their processing needs, and you would be working with him to implement their file system access rights (see the case projects at the end of this chapter).

CHAPTER SUMMARY

❏ Just as a building needs to be secured by using locks and keys, the NetWare file system must be secured by using trustee assignments to provide access rights that allow users to access the storage areas they need. NetWare has eight access rights: Read, File Scan, Write, Create, Erase, Modify, Access Control, and Supervisor.

❏ The Access Control right allows users to assign other rights, except Supervisor, to other users. The Supervisor right can be assigned only by a Supervisor-equivalent user and gives users all rights to a directory and its subdirectories, including the right to assign the Supervisor right to other users. In addition, because the Supervisor right cannot be revoked or blocked at lower levels, assigning the Supervisor right is a good way to make a user act as a supervisor of a portion of the directory structure.

❏ Trustee assignments are used to grant rights to users or groups for a directory. Effective rights for a user are a combination of the user object's rights and the rights given to any groups of which the user is a member. A user or group's trustee assignments for a directory are then inherited by all the subdirectories and files in the directory where the trustee assignment was made. A user's effective rights often include inherited rights from a trustee assignment made to a group or user in a higher-level directory.

❏ Each directory and file has an Inherited Rights Filter (IRF) to control which rights it can inherit from higher-level directories. When a file or directory is first created, the IRF allows all rights to flow down to that directory or file. You can optionally use the IRF to block the directory or file from inheriting those rights.

❏ You can use ConsoleOne, NetWare Administrator, Windows Explorer, or the RIGHTS command to set and view trustee assignments.

❏ Attributes play a vital role in file system security because they enable you to protect files and directories from certain operations, such as deleting, renaming, and copying.

❏ You can use the Windows-based ConsoleOne utility along with the FLAG command-line utility to set attributes on files and directories.

KEY TERMS

Access Control [A] right — An access right that allows the user to grant access rights for a directory to other users.

access right — A file system permission that can be granted to users, groups, or containers. Access rights include Supervisor, Read, Write, Create, Erase, Modify, File Scan, and Access Control.

Archive Needed (A) — A file attribute that indicates the file has been changed since it was last backed up.

attribute — A flag or code associated with files and directories to control what type of processing can be performed on them.

Can't Compress (Cc) — A file attribute indicating that the operating system was unable to compress the file.

Copy Inhibit (Ci) — A file attribute that prevents Macintosh computers from copying the file.

Create [C] right — An access right that allows users to create files and subdirectories.

Delete Inhibit (Di) — An attribute that protects a file or directory from being deleted.

directory trustee — A user, group, or container object that has been granted access rights to a directory.

Don't Compress (Dc) — A file attribute that tells the operating system not to compress the file. When applied to a directory, none of the files in the directory will be compressed.

Don't Migrate (Dm) — An attribute that prevents files or directories from being migrated to a high-capacity storage device.

Don't Suballocate (Ds) — A file attribute that tells the operating system not to use block suballocation on the file.

effective rights — A subset of access rights that controls which functions a user can perform in a directory or file.

Erase [E] right — An access right that allows the user to delete files and remove subdirectories.

Execute Only (X) — A file attribute that can be applied to .com and .exe files to prevent them from being copied. Once applied, the Execute Only attribute cannot be removed.

File Scan [F] right — An access right that allows the user to view a directory of file and subdirectory names.

file trustee — A user, group, or container object that has been granted access rights to a file.

Hidden (H) — A file or directory attribute that prevents standard DOS and Windows applications from seeing the associated file or directory.

Immediate Compress (Ic) — A file or directory attribute that tells the system to compress a large file immediately after it has been used.

Inherited Rights Filter (IRF) — A method of reducing inherited rights in a subdirectory or file by allowing only the access rights specified in the filter to be inherited.

Migrated (M) — A file attribute set by the system indicating that a file has been moved to an archive data medium.

Modify [M] right — An access right that allows the user to change file and directory names—without changing the file contents—and use the FLAG command to change attribute settings on files or subdirectories.

Normal (N) — A directory attribute that removes all other directory attributes.

Purge (P) — A file or directory attribute that prevents a file or all files in a directory from being salvaged after deletion.

Read [R] right — An access right that allows the user to read files or run programs in a directory.

Read Only (Ro) — A file attribute that prevents the contents of a file from being modified.

Read Write (Rw) — A default file attribute that allows the contents of a file to be changed.

Rename Inhibit (Ri) — A file or directory attribute that prevents the name of a file or directory from being changed.

Sharable (Sh) — A file attribute that allows multiple users to use a file at the same time.

Supervisor [S] right — An access right that grants all rights to a directory and its subdirectories; this right cannot be blocked or reassigned at a lower subdirectory or file level.

System (Sy) — A file or directory attribute that flags a file or directory for operating system use.

Transaction Tracking System (TTS) — A system that protects the Transactional attribute, ensuring that all transactions are completed or left in the original state.

Transactional (T) — A file attribute used on database files to enable the system to restore the file to its previous state if a transaction is not completed.

trustee assignment — An entry in the ACL for a file or directory that makes the user a trustee of a directory or file.

Write [W] right — An access right that allows the user to change or add data to files in a directory.

REVIEW QUESTIONS

1. Which of the following defines file system functions that can be performed by users in the NetWare file system?

   a. attributes

   b. access rights

   c. eDirectory

   d. NSS

2. Which of the following rights allows a user to change data in an existing file?

   a. Modify

   b. Write

   c. Create

   d. Access Control

3. Which of the following rights allows a user to assign rights to other users?

   a. Modify

   b. Write

   c. Create

   d. Access Control

4. Which of the following rights cannot be revoked or blocked within the directory structure it defines?

   a. Modify

   b. Supervisor

   c. Create

   d. Access Control

5. Which of the following are flags that control directory and file characteristics?

   a. attributes

   b. properties

   c. rights

   d. permissions

6. You are a member of the Admin group that has been granted [R W F] rights to a directory called Business, and you have a trustee assignment of [R C F] to the Business directory. What are your effective rights in the Business directory?

   _____

7. You have been given a trustee assignment of [R C F] to the Business directory and a trustee assignment of [W E] to the Business\Spdata\Budgets subdirectory. What are your effective rights in the Business\Spdata subdirectory?

   _____

For Questions 8 through 11, use the following file system information:

You have a trustee assignment of [W E C] to the Business directory along with a trustee assignment of [W E] to the Business\Spdata\Budgets subdirectory. In addition, you belong to a group that was granted [R F] rights to the Business directory.

5

8. What are your effective rights in the Business\Spdata\Budgets subdirectory?

   _____

9. Assume that all rights except [R] and [F] are removed from the IRF of the Business\Spdata subdirectory. What are your rights in the Business\Spdata subdirectory?

   _____

10. What are your rights in the Business\Spdata\Budgets subdirectory?

    _____

11. Write the command to list all trustee assignments in the Business directory structure.

    _____

12. The user Joeman was given a trustee assignment of [R W E C M F] to the Business\Spdata directory and a trustee assignment of [R W F] to the Business\Spdata\Budgets subdirectory. What are Joeman's effective rights in the Business\Spdata\Budgets subdirectory after deleting his trustee assignment to the Budgets directory?

    _____

13. Did Joeman gain or lose rights in the Budgets directory? Why?

    _____

14. If you're using Windows, which of the following utilities could you use to make the user Billsim a trustee of the following three directories: Business\AR, Sales\Inventry, and Data\Projects? (Choose all that apply.)
    a. NetWare Administrator
    b. My Computer
    c. iManage
    d. ConsoleOne

15. When you set the Read Only attribute, what other attributes are also set by default? (Choose all that apply.)
    a. Delete Inhibit
    b. Copy Inhibit
    c. Rename Inhibit
    d. Execute Only

16. Which of the following attributes are used with directories? (Choose all that apply.)
    a. Purge
    b. Shared
    c. Read Only
    d. Delete Inhibit
    e. Copy Inhibit
    f. Hidden
    g. System
    h. Don't Migrate

17. Which of the following attributes would prevent deleted files in the SYS:Software\Temp directory from being salvaged?
    a. Purge
    b. Shared
    c. Read Only
    d. Delete Inhibit

18. Which of the following DOS-based commands or utilities can be used to set NetWare file attributes?

a. RIGHTS

b. FLAG

c. NDIR

d. ATTRIB

19. Which of the following is the minimum right you need in a directory to change trustee assignments?

a. Supervisor

b. Modify

c. Access Control

d. Full Control

20. Which of the following is the minimum right you need in a directory to flag all files as Delete Inhibit?

a. Supervisor

b. Modify

c. Access Control

d. Full Control

21. When a user is first added as a trustee of a directory, which of the following rights is he or she given by default?

a. Supervisor

b. Read Only

c. Read and File Scan

d. File Scan

22. If no template is used, what rights do new users created with ConsoleOne have to their home directories?

UNIVERSAL AEROSPACE CASE PROJECTS

You were pleased to learn in the department meeting that Eric and your instructor are happy with your progress as a student intern. Now that you understand the steps Eric used in setting up file system security for the Engineering, Manufacturing, Management, and Information Systems departments, your next step is to apply what you have learned to implementing the processing needs Eric defined in Table 5-9.

Table 5-9 Business Office File System Usage

Marketing	**Create and update files in the Mktg\Shared directory.** **Read information from Inventry and enter new orders by writing to the database.**
Michael Horowitz	Reads the **customer** and **vendor** database files.
Darrell Minick	Reads the **customer** and **vendor** database files.
Laura Hiller	Updates the **customer** and **vendor** database files.
Desktop Publishing	**Create and update files in the Publish\Shared directory.** **Read files from the Engineering department's Shared directory.**

Table 5-9   Business Office File System Usage (continued)

Diana Brady	Responsible for working on promotional materials in the **Publish** directory. Reads information from the **Publish\Manuals** directory maintained by Bradley Dahl.
Julie Damrau	Works with Diana to maintain the Publish\Promote directory files. Responsible for Web site design and development and belongs to the WebMgr group.
Accounting	**Create and update files in the Accounting\Shared directory.** **Needs all rights to run the Accounting software package and update files.**
Terry Blackwell	Maintains the files in the Inventry directory. Maintains the **Accounting\Budget** files.
Amy Pan	Performs weekly payroll and updates the files in the Accounting software directory. Works with Terry Blackwell to maintain the **Accounting\Budget** files.
George Perez	Performs monthly general ledger processing and maintains files in the Accounting software directory.

Case Project 5-1: Planning Access Rights

In this chapter, you learned how Eric incorporated users' processing requirements to define directory trustee assignments for the Engineering and Manufacturing departments. Before completing the trustee assignments for UAS, you need to apply the guidelines described in this chapter to finish defining the access rights required for users or groups to perform the processing functions Eric defined. To do this, you need to copy the Directory Trustee Worksheet from Appendix D and then plan trustee assignments for the Accounting, Marketing, and Desktop Publishing departments, using the requirements shown in Table 5-9. Before continuing to Project 2, have your instructor check the trustee assignments against the recommendations on your student answer sheet. Although you can write trustee assignments in many different ways, you must define the ones indicated on the answer sheet to make future assignments work correctly.

Case Project 5-2: Implementing Trustee Assignments

Log in to the network with your assigned UasAdmin user name and then use Windows or ConsoleOne to implement the trustee assignments defined on your finalized Directory Trustee Worksheet.

Case Project 5-3: Documenting Trustee Assignments

In this project, you need to use the appropriate option of the RIGHTS command to print reports documenting trustee assignments and the IRF for each of the following directories:

- Publish
- Mktg
- Accounting

Print the IRFs for each of these directory structures. Use the RIGHTS command with the > PRN option to print your results, or use the > FILE.TXT option to save the results to a disk file for use in a word processor or text editor.

Case Project 5-4: Defining Attributes

In this chapter, you learned the importance of using directory attributes to enhance file system security. To implement attribute security, you need to copy the Directory Attribute Form from Appendix D and then use it to identify the attributes you think are necessary for the Accounting, Publish, and Mktg directory structures. At a minimum, you should define attributes that will protect the directory structures from being renamed or deleted. Define additional attributes that you think are important to the system's security and operation.

Case Project 5-5: Setting Attributes

Use Windows, ConsoleOne, or NetWare Administrator to set the attributes you identified in Project 5-4. Use the FLAG command to flag all files in the Forms directory with the Delete Inhibit and Rename Inhibit attributes. Write down the command you used. Next, use the FLAG command along with the > PRN option to print your results, or use the > FILE.TXT option to save the results to a disk file for use in a word processor or text editor.

5

WORKING WITH eDirectory SECURITY

After reading this chapter and completing the exercises, you will be able to:

♦ Describe eDirectory security and identify its similarities and differences with system security

♦ Identify and assign Entry and Attribute rights for the eDirectory system

♦ Define and implement the eDirectory security needs for Universal AeroSpace

♦ Describe how iManager administrative roles are used to delegate rights to other users

In Chapter 5 on file system security, you learned that users, groups, and containers are made trustees of directories or files and then granted certain access rights. In a similar way, to access or manage network objects, you can use eDirectory security to make users, groups, or containers trustees of other objects in the eDirectory tree. In this chapter, you learn how to set up eDirectory security so that users can access and maintain network objects and learn how to delegate administrative tasks to other users.

Introduction to eDirectory Security

Just as file system security gives users rights to access and manage files in the NetWare file system, eDirectory security gives users rights to access and manage objects in the eDirectory tree. NetWare, by default, provides most of the eDirectory security rights users need to work with objects in their containers. However, a network administrator sometimes needs to modify the default eDirectory security assignments to grant users the rights they need to access certain objects, such as the Directory Map objects you created in Chapter 3, or objects located in other containers. Conversely, an administrator might want to reduce the default eDirectory rights to prevent users from performing certain tasks, such as modifying their personal login scripts or changing their print job configuration data. Another use of eDirectory security is to delegate work by giving users the rights needed to manage other users and objects in certain containers. In addition, an organization can use eDirectory security to establish an exclusive administrator for certain containers; an exclusive administrator is a user account with Supervisor rights to manage all objects in the container. Establishing an exclusive administrator for a container allows the main network administrator's rights to be blocked in that container. Having exclusive container administrators can be beneficial for large organizations and government agencies that do not want to put the entire network under the control of one all-powerful network administrator that has Supervisor rights to all data and objects in the eDirectory tree. In the following sections, you learn what a CNA is required to know about eDirectory security rights and inheritance, and how to use ConsoleOne to view, assign, or modify these rights.

As you learned in Chapter 2, each object in the eDirectory database contains fields of information called properties, and all objects have a property called the access control list (ACL), a multivalued property containing the names of users, groups, or containers that have been given rights to the object. In addition to user, group, and container objects, NetWare includes two special objects named [Root] trustee and [Public] trustee that can be made trustees of another object. The **[Public] trustee object** represents all client computers attached to the network and running the Novell client. An example of [Public] rights is the ability to use the Contexts browse button in the Novell Login window to locate a context to log in to. If the [Public] trustee is not given rights to browse the eDirectory tree, you need to type the distinguished context of the Organizational Unit the user account is located in, instead of browsing to it. The **[Root] trustee object** represents all users defined in the eDirectory tree. To gain the access rights granted to the [Root] trustee, a user must first be authenticated by successfully logging in to the eDirectory tree.

 Remember that when you're assigning rights, any rights granted to the [Root] trustee object are effective for all users in the eDirectory tree. As a result, you should be careful when making [Root] a trustee of another object.

Any user or other object placed in the ACL property of another object becomes a trustee of that other object with certain rights. In Chapter 5, you learned that file system security consists of a single group of eight access rights that control which operations a user can perform in a directory or file. Instead of having a single group of rights, in eDirectory security the rights are divided into two categories: Entry (or Object) rights and Attribute (or Property) rights.

 Although NetWare Administrator uses the terms "Object rights" and "Property rights," ConsoleOne uses the term "Entry rights" to describe a trustee's Object rights and the term "Attribute rights" to describe a trustee's rights to an object's properties. In this chapter, the term "Entry rights" is used to describe the rights given to an object, and the term "Attribute rights" is used to describe the rights given to individual properties.

Entry rights control what a trustee can do to an object, such as renaming, creating, or deleting it. Figure 6-1 shows an example of the default Entry rights that [Public] is given to the [Root] of the eDirectory tree. Having Browse rights enables users to find the context for their user name when logging in from the Novell client. **Attribute rights** determine whether a user is allowed to view or change information fields in the object. Figure 6-2 illustrates the Attribute rights assigned to the Students group for the UAS Organization. Having Read and Compare rights means that all student accounts can view information about objects in the UAS Organization, but cannot make any changes.

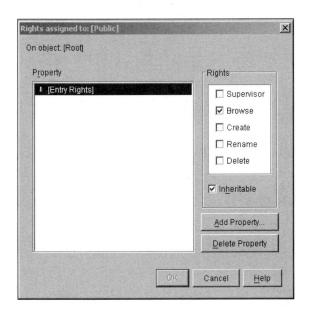

Figure 6-1   Entry rights

Figure 6-2   Attribute rights

As shown in Table 6-1, Entry rights consist of Supervisor, Browse, Create, Delete, Rename, and Inheritable.

Table 6-1   eDirectory Entry Rights

Right	Description	Comparable File System Right
Supervisor	Grants all access privileges, including Supervisor right to All Properties.	Comparable to the Supervisor right in the file system, except that the eDirectory Supervisor right can be blocked or reassigned at a lower level; the Supervisor right in file system security cannot be blocked or reassigned.
Browse	Grants the right to view network objects in the eDirectory tree.	Comparable to the File Scan right in the file system, which allows users to see file and directory names.
Create	Grants the right to create objects in a container.	Performs the same function as in file system security.
Delete	Grants the right to delete the object or leaf objects from a container.	Performs the same function as in file system security.

Table 6-1   eDirectory Entry Rights (continued)

Right	Description	Comparable File System Right
Rename	Grants the right to change the name of the object.	Performs the same function as in file system security.
Inheritable	Allows leaf objects and subcontainers to inherit trustee assignments.	No comparable right in file system security.

As in the file system, the **Supervisor Entry right** includes all other rights. When you assign the Supervisor Entry right, the trustee is automatically given Supervisor rights to all the object's attributes or properties. Unlike file system security, however, the Supervisor right in eDirectory security can be reassigned or blocked by an Inherited Rights Filter (IRF) in a subcontainer or leaf object. Later in this chapter, you'll practice blocking and reassigning Supervisor Entry rights. The **Browse Entry right** is similar to the file system's File Scan right in that it allows a user to find the object, and most users need only this right to access objects in a container. If one user is supposed to control other users or manage a container, the network administrator will need to make that user a trustee of the other users or container by assigning additional rights. The **Create Entry right** applies only to container objects and allows the trustee to create new subcontainer or leaf objects. Having the **Rename Entry right** and the **Delete Entry right** enables trustees to change an object name, delete an object, or move an object to another location. The **Inheritable Entry right** allows leaf objects and other subcontainers to inherit the trustee's assignment.

Attribute rights control access to an object's information fields (its attributes or properties) and include the six rights described in Table 6-2.

The two major Attribute rights are Read and Write. The **Read Attribute right** includes the Compare right and allows the trustee to view and compare values in the attribute fields. The **Compare Attribute right**, a limited version of the Read right, enables trustees to find an object based on information in the property field without allowing them to actually view the attribute information. For example, the UAS administrative assistant, Lynn Dai, needs to be able to find users by their social security numbers. By giving Lynn the Compare right to the Social Security attribute, Lynn can use the search feature to find users by entering their social security numbers, but she can't browse the eDirectory tree to view users' social security numbers. The **Write Attribute right** includes the Add Self right and allows trustees to change the information in attribute fields. The **Add Self Attribute right**, a special case of the Write right, can be used to enable trustees to make themselves members of a group or remove their user names from a group. For example, if you give all users the Add Self right to a mail group, they can make their user names members of a group that receives copies of all e-mail messages, or remove their user names from the group when they no longer want to receive these messages. The **Supervisor Attribute right** assigns all attribute rights and is normally assigned only to administrative user accounts. Much like the Inheritable Entry right, the **Inheritable Attribute right** enables leaf objects and subcontainers to inherit Attribute rights in a container trustee assignment. You'll learn more about inheriting Attribute rights later in this chapter.

Table 6-2   eDirectory Attribute Rights

Right	Description	Comparable File System Right
Supervisor	Grants all rights to the property unless blocked by an object's Inherited Rights Filter.	Comparable to the Supervisor right in the file system in that it grants all other rights; however, unlike the Supervisor right in file system security, it can be blocked or reassigned at a lower level.
Read	Grants the right to view the values stored in the object's property fields. Includes the Compare right.	Comparable to the Read right in the file system, which allows a trustee to view or copy the contents of a file.
Compare	A special case of the Read right that allows the trustee to compare the value of a property field to a fixed value returning true or false, without being able to view a property's contents.	No comparable right in the file system.

Table 6-2   eDirectory Attribute Rights (continued)

Right	Description	Comparable File System Right
Write	Grants the right to add, change, or remove any value of a property field. Includes the Add Self right.	Comparable to the Write right in the file system, which allows a trustee to change the contents of a file. Having the Write right to the ACL attribute enables the trustee to change an object's trustee assignments in much the same way as having the Access Control right allows a trustee in the file system to add, change, or remove trustee assignments to a file or directory. In addition, having the Write right to the server object's ACL attribute gives the trustee Supervisor file system rights to all the server's volumes.
Add Self	A special case of the Write right that allows trustees to add or remove themselves as a value of the property field. This right is applicable for properties that contain object lists, such as group membership and mailing lists.	No comparable right in the file system.
Inheritable	Allows leaf objects and subcontainers to inherit trustee assignments.	No comparable right in the file system.

Attribute rights can be assigned to all of an object's attributes or just to specific attributes. Notice in Figure 6-2 that the All Attributes Rights option is selected, a blanket way of granting rights to all the object's attributes. Selecting this option means that the Students group has been given the Compare right to view all information attributes in the UAS Organization. In addition, because the Inheritable right is selected, the Students group will be able to read attribute information for the objects in all subcontainers of the UAS Organization.

Be careful when assigning the Write Attribute right to the All Attributes Rights option. If users have the Write Attribute right to the ACL property, for example, they can modify their trustee assignments, even to the point of making themselves a Supervisor of the object. In addition, having the Write Attribute right to the server object's ACL property gives the trustee Supervisor rights to all volumes on that server—the one exception when assigning eDirectory rights affects file system security. Making users a Supervisor of a server object grants them all rights to the file system, which cannot be blocked or overridden in any subdirectories or files.

You can also add selected Attribute rights to give a trustee special rights to a specific property. Rights assigned to selected Attribute rights override the rights assigned through the All Attributes Rights option. For example, in Figure 6-3, the Students group has been assigned no rights to the selected Account Balance property. This assignment overrides the Read and Compare rights granted through the All Attributes Rights option and prevents users in the Students group from viewing the account balance information of other objects.

Assigning eDirectory Rights

As you learned in Chapter 5, effective rights are the actual rights a user has to an object and dictate what actions a user can perform with eDirectory objects. A user's effective rights are the result of one or more of the following factors:

- A trustee assignment made directly to the user name
- A trustee assignment made to a group (that the user is a member of) or an Organizational Role object (that the user is an occupant of)
- A trustee assignment made to the user's parent container
- Container, group, and user rights inherited from a trustee assignment made to a parent container
- Inherited rights blocked by an IRF applied to a container or leaf object

Figure 6-3   Adding a specific Attribute right

Because effective rights are determined by a combination of factors, sometimes it's difficult to know what effective rights a user has in a container or leaf object. To make it easier to determine effective rights, Novell includes an Effective Rights option in both ConsoleOne and NetWare Administrator that you can use to determine a user's effective rights to another object. In the following sections, you learn how to use ConsoleOne and NetWare Administrator to make trustee assignments in your ##UAS Organization using each of the preceding factors. In the "eDirectory Security for Universal AeroSpace" section, you'll learn how to plan and implement the remaining trustee assignments to complete your eDirectory security setup.

Trustee Assignment to a User

The most direct way to give a user effective rights to an object is by making the user a trustee of the object and then granting the necessary access rights. For example, when Kellie Thiele temporarily needed rights to manage objects in the Mfg container to test and implement a new software package, Eric Kenton used ConsoleOne to grant her the Supervisor Entry right to the Mfg OU, which automatically gave her Supervisor rights to all properties. In the following activity, you practice making a user a trustee of an OU and then check his or her effective rights.

Activity 6-1: Making User Trustee Assignments

Time Required: 10 minutes

Objective: Use ConsoleOne to assign eDirectory rights and check effective rights.

Description: In this activity, you make Kellie a supervisor of the Mfg container, and then check her effective rights.

1. If necessary, start your computer, and log in with your UasAdmin user name.

2. Start ConsoleOne, and then expand **UAS_Tree** and your **##UAS** container.

3. Right-click your **Mfg** OU, and then click **Properties** to open the Properties of Mfg dialog box.

4. Click the **NDS Rights** tab to display the trustees of the Mfg OU. Record the existing trustee on your student answer sheet.

5. Click the existing trustee, and then click the **Assigned Rights** button to open the Rights assigned to: Mfg.##UAS dialog box, similar to the one in Figure 6-4.

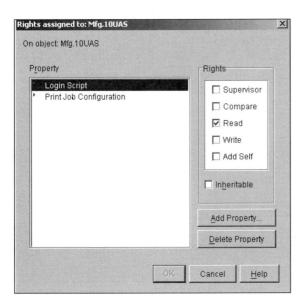

Figure 6-4   Rights assigned to the Mfg Organizational Unit

6. Click each property in the Property list box, and record the rights on your student answer sheet.

7. Click the **Cancel** button to return to the Properties of Mfg dialog box.

8. Make Kellie a trustee of the Mfg OU with the Supervisor Entry right:

   a. Click the **Add Trustee** button to open the Select Object dialog box.

   b. If necessary, click the **up arrow** to navigate to your IS container. Expand the **IS** container, click **KThiele**, and then click **OK** to open the Rights assigned to selected objects dialog box, shown in Figure 6-5.

Figure 6-5   Checking rights assigned to a selected object

   c. Click the **Supervisor** check box in the Rights section.

   d. Verify that the Inheritable check box is selected, and then click **OK** to save the trustee assignment and add KThiele to the Trustees list box.

e. Click the **Assigned Rights** button to open the Rights assigned to: KThiele.IS.##UAS dialog box, shown in Figure 6-6. Notice that Kellie has been assigned Read and Compare rights to all attributes.

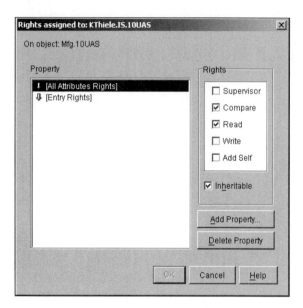

Figure 6-6   Making trustee assignments for the KThiele user

f. Click **[Entry Rights]**, and record the Entry rights on your student answer sheet.

g. Because you did not make any changes, click **Cancel** to return to the Properties of Mfg dialog box.

9. Click the **Apply** button to save the trustee assignment.

10. Check Kellie's effective rights in the Mfg container:

a. In the Properties of Mfg dialog box, click **KThiele**, and then click the **Effective Rights** button to open the Effective Rights dialog box.

b. Click the **[All Attributes Rights]** object, and record Kellie's effective Attribute rights on your student answer sheet.

c. Click the **[Entry Rights]** object, and record Kellie's effective Entry rights on your student answer sheet.

d. Click **Close** to return to the Properties of Mfg dialog box.

11. Click the **Close** button to return to the ConsoleOne window.

12. After Kellie finished her work, Eric removed her user name as a trustee of the Mfg OU. Follow these steps to remove KThiele from the trustees of your Mfg OU:

a. Right-click your **Mfg** OU, and then click **Properties** to open the Properties of Mfg dialog box.

b. Click the **NDS Rights** tab to display the Trustees list box.

c. Click **KThiele**, and then click the **Delete Trustee** button to open the Delete Trustee dialog box.

d. Click **Yes** to delete Kellie's trustee assignment and return to the Properties of Mfg dialog box.

e. Click **OK** to save your change and return to the main ConsoleOne window.

13. Exit ConsoleOne, and log out.

Trustee Assignment to a Group

As in file system security, a better way for users to gain effective rights is through membership in a group or by being an occupant of an Organizational Role object. Giving rights to Organizational Role objects makes it easier to maintain security when users change job responsibilities. When multiple users need effective rights to an object, you can reduce the number of trustee assignments and thereby simplify your eDirectory security by implementing a group trustee assignment. In the following activity, you practice making a group a trustee of an object and then checking the group members' effective rights.

Activity 6-2: Making Group Trustee Assignments

Time Required: 10 minutes

Objective: Use ConsoleOne to assign eDirectory rights.

Description: Luke McMann wanted Eric to set up eDirectory security so that the IS users could create and modify objects in the UAS Organization. To do this, Eric made the ISMgrs group a trustee of the UAS Organization with Create and Rename Entry rights along with the Write Attribute right to all attributes except the ACL property. In this activity, you give the ISMgrs group a trustee assignment to your ##UAS Organization and then check effective rights for Kellie and your user name.

1. If necessary, start your computer, and log in with your UasAdmin user name.

2. If necessary, start ConsoleOne, and expand **UAS_Tree** and your **##UAS** container.

3. Make the ISMgrs group a trustee of your ##UAS Organization with Create and Rename Entry rights and the Write Attribute right:

   a. Right-click your **##UAS** container, and then click **Properties** to open the Properties of ##UAS dialog box.

   b. Click the **NDS Rights** tab to display the Trustees list box.

   c. As you click each trustee, click the **Effective Rights** and **Assigned Rights** buttons, and record the trustee's Entry and Attribute rights on your student answer sheet. After recording the rights, click **Close** to return to the Properties of ##UAS dialog box.

   d. Click the **Add Trustee** button to open the Select Object dialog box.

   e. Expand the **IS** OU, click your **ISMgrs** group, and then click **OK** to open the Rights assigned to selected objects dialog box.

   f. Verify that the [Entry Rights] object is selected, and then click the **Create** and **Rename** check boxes to assign these rights.

   g. Verify that the Inheritable check box is selected, and then click to select the **[All Attributes Rights]** object.

   h. Click the **Write** check box to assign this Attribute right.

   i. Verify that the Inheritable check box is selected.

4. Remove the Write Attribute right from the ACL property:

   a. Click the **Add Property** button to open the Add Property dialog box.

   b. Click the **ACL** property, and then click **OK** to add it to the Property list box in the Rights assigned to selected objects dialog box.

   c. Verify that only the Compare and Read Attribute rights are selected, and then click **OK**. Click **OK** to save the trustee assignment and return to the Properties of ##UAS dialog box.

   d. Click the **Apply** button to save the trustee assignments.

5. Check Kellie's effective rights in your ##UAS containers:

    a. Click the **Effective Rights** button to open the Effective Rights dialog box.

    b. Click the **Browse** button next to the For Trustee text box to open the Select Object dialog box.

    c. Expand the **IS** OU, click **KThiele**, and then click **OK** to open the Effective Rights for KThiele dialog box.

    d. Click the **[All Attributes Rights]** object, and record Kellie's effective Attribute rights on your student answer sheet.

    e. Click the **[Entry Rights]** object, and record Kellie's effective Entry rights on your student answer sheet.

    f. Click the **ACL** property, and verify that Kellie has only Read and Compare rights.

6. Check your user name's effective rights to the ##UAS container:

    a. Click the **Browse** button next to the For Trustee text box to open the Select Object dialog box.

    b. If necessary, expand the **IS** OU. Click your user name, and then click **OK** to open the Effective Rights for <*your user name*> dialog box.

    c. Click the **[All Attributes Rights]** object, and record your user name's effective Attribute rights on your student answer sheet.

    d. Click the **[Entry Rights]** object, and record your user name's effective Entry rights on your student answer sheet.

    e. Click **Close** to return to the Properties of ##UAS dialog box.

7. Click the **Close** button to close this dialog box and return to ConsoleOne.

8. Exit ConsoleOne, and log out.

Trustee Assignment to a Container

When all users in a container need the same effective rights to an object, the best solution is to make the container a trustee of that object and assign it the necessary rights. As in the file system, when a container is made a trustee of an object, all users in that container have the Entry and Attribute rights that were granted to the container added to their effective rights. In addition, when a container is made a trustee of another object, all subcontainers of that container inherit the same Entry and Attribute rights as their parent container. As you learned in Chapter 3, a Directory Map object contains a Path property that points to a directory in the file system. By reading the directory path from the Path property, MAP commands can use a Directory Map object to map a drive letter to a specific directory in the file system. As a result, to use a Directory Map object, users must have rights to read the Directory Map object's Path property. In the following activity, you assign Attribute rights to an object for all users by making your Engineering OU a trustee of the EngData Directory Map object.

Activity 6-3: Making Trustee Assignments to a Container

Time Required: 10 minutes

Objective: Use NetWare Administrator to assign eDirectory rights.

Description: Before users in the Engineering department could use the EngData Directory Map object, Eric needed to grant them Read rights to the Path property. Instead of making multiple assignments or creating another group, Eric made the Engineering container a trustee of the EngData object with Read Attribute rights. In this activity, you learn how to use NetWare Administrator to grant all users in your Engineering department Read rights to the EngData object, and then check effective rights for an Engineering user.

1. If necessary, start your computer, and log in with your UasAdmin user name.

2. Double-click the **NetWare Administrator** desktop icon.

3. If necessary, open a browse window to display your ##UAS container, and then double-click the **Engineering** container to display all Engineering objects (see Figure 6-7).

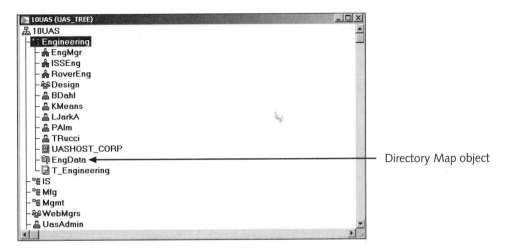

Directory Map object

Figure 6-7   Using NetWare Administrator to view objects in the Engineering container

4. To make your Engineering container a trustee of the EngData Directory Map object with Read rights to only the Path property, follow these steps:

a. Click the **Engineering** container, and hold the mouse button down while you drag and drop it onto the **EngData** Directory Map object.

The Engineering container should now be added to the Trustees list box (see Figure 6-8). Notice that by default the Engineering container has been given the Browse Object right (Entry right) and the Read and Compare Property rights (Attribute rights) to all properties.

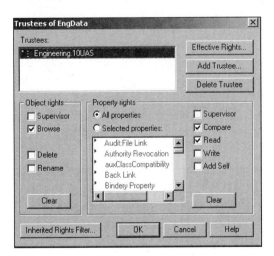

Figure 6-8   Making the Engineering container a trustee

b. Click the **Read** check box to remove this Attribute right.

c. Click the **Selected properties** radio button.

d. Scroll down the list of properties, and click the **Path** property to select it.

    e. Click the **Read** check box to assign this right.

    f. Click the **OK** button to save the trustee assignment and return to the NetWare Administrator browse window.

5. Use NetWare Administrator to determine the effective rights that users now have to the EngData Directory Map object:

    a. Right-click **EngData**, and then click **Trustees of this Object** to open the Trustees of EngData dialog box.

    b. Click the **Effective Rights** button to open the Effective Rights dialog box.

    c. Click the **Browse** button next to the Object name text box to open the Select Object dialog box.

    d. Double-click the user object **TRucci** in the Available objects section. Tony's effective rights to the EngData Directory Map object are then highlighted in the Effective Rights dialog box. Record Tony's effective rights on your student answer sheet.

    e. Click the **Selected Properties** radio button.

    f. Scroll down the list of properties, and click the **Path** property.

    g. Record Tony's effective rights on your student answer sheet, and describe how he obtained rights to the Path property.

6. Click the **Close** button to close the Effective Rights dialog box.

7. Click the **Cancel** button to return to the NetWare Administrator browse window.

8. Exit NetWare Administrator, and log out.

Inherited Rights

To decrease the number of trustee assignments you need to make, NetWare allows trustee Entry and Attribute rights granted in a container to flow down to any subcontainers or leaf objects. The process of rights flowing down the tree structure is referred to as **inherited rights**. For example, the occupant of the AeroMgr Organizational Role object needs to be able to maintain Manufacturing users and resources for the entire Mfg.UAS OU, which includes the UAS and AeroDyn subcontainers. To grant the AeroMgr Organizational Role rights to manage the UAS and AeroDyn containers, Eric gave the AeroMgr object Supervisor Entry rights to the Mfg container. Because UAS and AeroDyn are subcontainers of Mfg, they will inherit the trustee assignments Eric made for the AeroMgr object. Without inheritance, Eric would have needed to make at least three trustee assignments granting the AeroMgr object Entry rights to the Mfg, UAS.Mfg, and AeroDyn.Mfg containers. Although assigning the Supervisor Entry right gives the trustee all Entry and Attribute rights, Eric also assigned AeroMgr all the other Entry and Attribute rights. This way, should the manager's rights be accidentally reassigned or blocked by an IRF, the AeroMgr occupants could still manage the container and even restore their Supervisor rights because they would have the Write right to the ACL property.

As in the file system, inherited Entry and Attribute rights can be blocked by using an IRF. In addition, each property has its own IRF that can be used to block rights to just that property. A difference between eDirectory security and file system security is that with eDirectory security, you can block a container or leaf object from inheriting Supervisor rights. You'll use this feature later in the "eDirectory Security for Universal AeroSpace" section. In the following activity, you use ConsoleOne and an IRF to make trustee assignments to your ##UAS Organization.

Activity 6-4: Working with Inherited Rights

Time Required: 10 minutes

Objective: Use ConsoleOne to assign eDirectory rights.

Description: In this activity, you observe inherited Entry rights in action by using ConsoleOne to check the effective rights that ISMgrs group members inherit as a result of having the Create and Rename rights granted to the UAS container. You then use an IRF to block the Mfg container from inheriting all rights except Supervisor.

1. If necessary, start your computer, and log in with your UasAdmin user name.

2. Start ConsoleOne, and expand **UAS_Tree** and your **##UAS** container.

3. Check Kellie's effective rights to the Mfg OU:

   a. Right-click **Mfg**, and then click **Properties** to open the Properties of Mfg dialog box.

   b. Click the **NDS Rights** tab to display the existing trustees of Mfg.

   c. Click the **Effective Rights** button to open the Effective Rights dialog box.

   d. Click the **Browse** button to open the Select Object dialog box.

   e. If necessary, click the **up arrow** to navigate to your IS OU. Expand the **IS** OU, click **KThiele**, and then click **OK** to open the Effective Rights to: MFG.##UAS dialog box.

   f. Click the **[All Attributes Rights]** object, and record Kellie's effective Attribute rights on your student answer sheet.

   g. Click the **[Entry Rights]** object, and record Kellie's effective Entry rights on your student answer sheet.

   h. Click **Close** to return to the Properties of Mfg dialog box.

4. Set up an IRF to block all rights except Supervisor from the Mfg container:

   a. Click the **down arrow** on the NDS Rights tab, and record the three options on your student answer sheet.

   b. Click the **Inherited Rights Filters** option to display the Property list box.

   c. Click the **Add Filter** button to open the Add Property dialog box.

   d. Click the **[Entry Rights]** object, and click **OK** to add [Entry Rights] to the Property list box in the Properties of Mfg dialog box.

   e. In the Rights section, click the **Create**, **Rename**, and **Delete** check boxes to remove these rights, as shown in Figure 6-9.

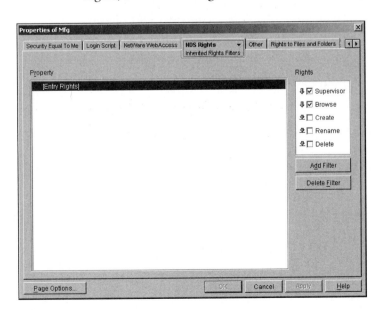

Figure 6-9   Setting up an IRF in ConsoleOne

    f. Click **OK** to save the modified IRF and return to the main ConsoleOne window.

5. Repeat Step 3 to record Kellie's effective rights in the Mfg container on your student answer sheet.

6. Click the **Cancel** button to return to the ConsoleOne window.

7. Exit ConsoleOne, and log out.

Using the Inheritable Right

A powerful feature of NetWare 6 eDirectory security is that you can use the Inheritable right to specify whether subcontainers or leaf objects can inherit the Entry and Attribute rights you give a trustee. For example, you want a trustee to have Supervisor rights in a container but not in the subcontainers. Using the IRF to block the Supervisor right in subcontainers would prevent the Admin user from managing the subcontainers. In NetWare 6, however, you can easily solve this problem by simply removing the object's Inheritable right. The trustee will then be limited to having Supervisor rights in just the container where the right is assigned. In Activity 6-5, you use the Inheritable Entry right to assign the Supervisor right to your user name in only the ##UAS Organization.

In versions before NetWare 5, subcontainers could inherit only the assignments to the All Properties rights. This created a lot of work if you wanted to give a user rights to administer only certain properties, such as addresses or phone numbers. With NetWare 6, you can set the Inheritable right to allow OUs and leaf objects to inherit selected Attribute rights from their parent containers. For example, Lynn is in charge of changing user address and phone number information for the entire company, so Eric gave her only the Attribute rights she needed to maintain these information fields. Because Eric used the Inheritable option for these rights, Lynn will be able to change address and phone information for all user accounts in the entire organization. In Activity 6-6, you practice troubleshooting eDirectory security, and in Activity 6-7, you practice using the Inheritable Attribute right to allow a user to manage address information in your ##UAS Organization.

Activity 6-5: Using the Inheritable Entry Right

Time Required: 10 minutes

Objective: Use ConsoleOne to assign eDirectory rights.

Description: To reduce the number of times he needed to log in with the Admin user name when maintaining objects in the UAS container, Eric wanted to assign his user name the Supervisor Entry right in the UAS Organization, but not in the OUs. Eric solved this problem by removing the Inheritable Entry right from his trustee assignment to the UAS Organization. In this activity, you use Eric's method to grant your user name the Supervisor Entry right to your ##UAS container and then remove the Inheritable Entry right to prevent the Mfg, Engineering, or IS OUs from inheriting the Supervisor right.

1. If necessary, start your computer, and log in with your UasAdmin user name.

2. If necessary, start ConsoleOne, and then expand **UAS_Tree** and your **##UAS** container.

3. Make your user name a trustee of the ##UAS Organization with the Supervisor right:

    a. Right-click your **##UAS** Organization, and then click **Properties** to open the Properties of ##UAS dialog box.

    b. Click the **NDS Rights** tab to display all existing trustees of the ##UAS Organization.

    c. Click the **Add Trustee** button to open the Select Object dialog box.

    d. If necessary, click the **up arrow** to navigate to your IS OU. Expand the **IS** OU, click your user name, and then click **OK** to open the Rights assigned to selected objects dialog box.

    e. Verify that the [Entry Rights] object is selected, and then click the **Supervisor** check box to assign this right.

f. Click the **Inheritable** check box to remove this right.

g. Click **OK**, and then click the **Apply** button to save your trustee assignment.

4. Check your user name's effective rights in the ##UAS Organization:

a. If necessary, click your user name in the Trustees list box to select it.

b. Click the **Effective Rights** button to open the Effective Rights dialog box.

c. Click the **[All Attributes Rights]** object, and record your effective Attribute rights on your student answer sheet.

d. Click the **[Entry Rights]** object, and record your effective Entry rights on your student answer sheet.

e. Click the **Close** button to close the Effective Rights dialog box.

f. Click the **Close** button to return to the main ConsoleOne window.

5. Check your user name's effective rights in the Mfg container:

a. Right-click **Mfg**, and then click **Properties** to open the Properties of Mfg dialog box.

b. Click the **NDS Rights** tab to display the existing trustees of Mfg.

c. Click the **Effective Rights** button to open the Effective Rights dialog box.

d. Click the **Browse** button next to the For Trustee text box to open the Select Object dialog box.

e. If necessary, click the **up arrow** to navigate to your IS OU. Expand the **IS** OU, click your user name, and then click **OK** to view your effective rights.

f. Click the **[All Attributes Rights]** object, and record your effective Attribute rights on your student answer sheet. Explain why you have these rights.

g. Click the **[Entry Rights]** object, and record your effective Entry rights on your student answer sheet. Explain why you have these rights.

h. Click the **Close** button to close the Effective Rights dialog box.

6. Click the **Cancel** button to return to the main ConsoleOne window.

7. Exit ConsoleOne and log out.

Activity 6-6: Troubleshooting eDirectory Security

Time Required: 10 minutes

Objective: Troubleshoot eDirectory rights.

Description: Eric was surprised when Kellie informed him that she could change trustee assignments in the Engineering and Mgmt containers. As described in Activity 6-2, Eric had intended members of the ISMgrs group to have only the rights to create, rename, and modify existing objects in the UAS organization. In this activity, you verify that Kellie has the right to change trustee assignments in the OUs. Then you determine where these rights are coming from and make a modification to correct the problem.

1. If necessary, start your computer, and log in with your KThiele user name and password.

2. Verify Kellie's rights to modify trustee assignments in the Mgmt OU:

a. Start ConsoleOne, and expand **NDS_Tree** and your **##UAS** container.

b. Right-click the **Mgmt** OU, and then click **Properties** to open the Properties of Mgmt dialog box.

    c. Click the **NDS Rights** tab, and then click **Add Trustee** button.

    d. Click **LDai**, and then click **OK** to open the Rights assigned to selected objects dialog box.

    e. Click **OK** to verify that Kellie can add LDai to the Trustees list box.

    f. Verify that LDai is highlighted, click the **Delete Trustee** button, and then click **Yes** to remove LDai from the Trustees list box.

    g. Click the **OK** button to close the Properties of Mgmt dialog box.

    h. Exit ConsoleOne, and log out.

3. When troubleshooting the eDirectory security problems, Eric started by checking trustee assignments and effective rights in the container where Kellie had the incorrect rights and then worked his way up the tree until he found where the rights in question were defined. In this step, you document trustee assignments for the Mgmt, #UAS, and [Root] objects:

    a. Log in with your UasAdmin user name and password.

    b. Start ConsoleOne, and expand **UAS_Tree** and your **##UAS** Organization.

    c. Right-click the **Mgmt** OU, and then click **Properties** to open the Properties of Mgmt dialog box.

    d. Click the **NDS Rights** tab, and record any trustee assignments on your student answer sheet.

    e. Click the **Cancel** button to return to the main ConsoleOne window.

    f. Right-click your **##UAS** Organization, and then click **Properties** to open the Properties of ##UAS dialog box.

    g. Click the **NDS Rights** tab, and on your student answer sheet, record any trustee assignments that would affect Kellie's effective rights.

    h. Click the **Cancel** button to return to the main ConsoleOne window.

    i. Right-click **UAS_Tree**, and then click **Properties** to open the Properties of UAS_Tree dialog box.

    j. Click the **NDS Rights** tab, and on your student answer sheet, record any trustee assignments that would affect Kellie's effective rights.

    k. Click the **Cancel** button to return to the main ConsoleOne window.

4. To change trustee assignments, a user needs to have Write rights to the ACL property. On your student answer sheet, identify any trustee assignments that would affect Kellie's rights to the ACL property.

5. Check Kellie's effective rights to the ACL property in the Mgmt and ##UAS containers:

    a. Right-click the **Mgmt** OU, and then click **Properties** to open the Properties of Mgmt dialog box.

    b. Click the **down arrow** on the NDS Rights tab, and then click the **Effective Rights** option.

    c. Click the **Browse** button next to the Look in text box to open the Select Object dialog box.

    d. Click the **up arrow** to navigate to your IS OU, and then double-click **KThiele**.

    e. Click the **ACL** property, and on your student answer sheet, record Kellie's effective rights.

    f. Click the **Cancel** button to return to the main ConsoleOne window.

6. Repeat Step 5 and record Kellie's effective rights to the ACL property of your ##UAS container.

7. On your student answer sheet, describe the reason Kellie has Write rights to the ACL property of the Mgmt OU, but not the ##UAS Organization.

8. After Eric identified the trustee assignment that gave Kellie Write rights to the user attributes, he made some modifications to correct the problem. In this step, you assign the Inheritable right to the ACL property to the ##UAS Organization:

   a. Right-click your **##UAS** Organization, and then click **Properties** to open the Properties of ##UAS dialog box.

   b. Click the **NDS Rights** tab to display the existing trustee assignments.

   c. Click the **ISMgrs** trustee assignment, and then click the **Assigned Rights** button.

   d. Verify that the ACL property is selected, and then click the **Inheritable** check box to assign this right.

   e. Click **OK** twice to save the assignment and return to the Properties of ##UAS dialog box.

9. To test your correction, repeat Step 5 and on your student answer sheet, record Kellie's effective rights to the ACL property of the Mgmt OU.

Activity 6-7: Setting the Inheritable Option on Selected Attribute Rights

Time Required: 15 minutes

Objective: Use ConsoleOne to assign eDirectory rights.

Description: In this activity, you work with the Inheritable Attribute right for selected properties to make Lynn a trustee of your ##UAS container with rights to change only user postal information for all users except those in the AeroDyn OU.

1. If necessary, start your computer, and log in with your UasAdmin user name.

2. If necessary, start ConsoleOne, and expand **UAS_Tree** and your **##UAS** container.

3. Make Lynn Dai a trustee of your ##UAS container with the Browse Entry right and Read and Write Attribute rights to the postal properties:

   a. Right-click your **##UAS** Organization, and click **Properties** to open the Properties of ##UAS dialog box.

   b. Click the **NDS Rights** tab to display the existing trustees of ##UAS.

   c. Click the **Add Trustee** button to open the Select Object dialog box.

   d. If necessary, click the **up arrow** to navigate to your Mgmt OU. Expand the **Mgmt** OU, click **LDai**, and click **OK** to open the Rights assigned to selected objects dialog box. Verify that LDai has the Browse Entry right along with Read and Compare rights for All Attributes in the default assignment.

   e. Click the **Add Property** button to open the Add Property dialog box.

   f. Scroll down the list of properties, click the **Postal Address** property, and then click **OK** to add it to the Property list box.

   g. Click the **Write** and **Inheritable** check boxes to assign these rights.

   h. Repeat Steps 3e through 3g to add the Postal Code and Postal Office Box properties to the Property list box, as shown in Figure 6-10.

   i. Click **OK** to return to the Properties of ##UAS dialog box.

   j. Click **OK** to save your assignment and return to the main ConsoleOne window.

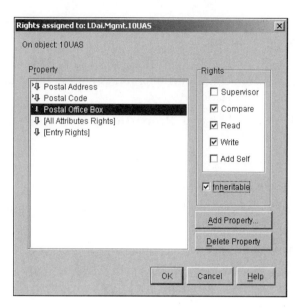

Figure 6-10   Assigning selected properties in ConsoleOne

4. Check Lynn's effective rights to the postal properties for a user in the Mfg OU:

   a. Click the **Mfg** OU to display all users in the Object frame.

   b. Right-click the **RPence** user, and then click **Properties** to open the Properties of RPence dialog box.

   c. Click the **NDS Rights** tab, and then click the **Effective Rights** button to open the Effective Rights to RPence dialog box.

   d. Click the **Browse** button next to the For Trustee text box to open the Select Object dialog box.

   e. If necessary, click the **up arrow** to navigate to your Mgmt OU. Expand the **Mgmt** OU, click **LDai**, and then click **OK** to display Lynn's effective rights.

   f. On your student answer sheet, record Lynn's Attribute and Entry rights.

   g. Scroll down the list of postal properties, click each postal property, and record Lynn's effective rights on your student answer sheet.

   h. Click the **Close** button to close the Effective Rights dialog box.

   i. Click **Cancel** to return to the main ConsoleOne window.

5. Use an Inherited Rights Filter to block Lynn's inherited rights in the AeroDyn.Mfg container:

   a. If necessary, expand your **Mfg** OU.

   b. Right-click the **AeroDyn** container, and then click **Properties** to open the Properties of AeroDyn dialog box.

   c. Click the **down arrow** on the NDS Rights tab, and click the **Inherited Rights Filters** option to display a blank Property list box.

   d. Click the **Add Filter** button to open the Add Property dialog box.

   e. Scroll down to the postal properties, click the **Postal Address** property, and click **OK** to add it to the Property list box.

   f. Click the **Write** and **Add Self** check boxes to remove these rights (see Figure 6-11).

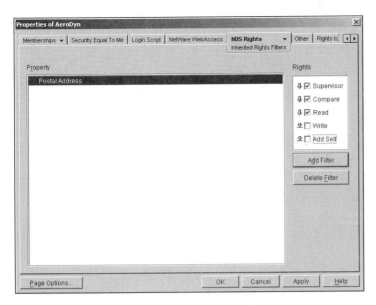

Figure 6-11   Setting the IRF on a selected property

     g. Repeat Steps 5d through 5f for the remaining postal properties.

     h. Click **OK** to save your filter and return to the main ConsoleOne window.

  6. Check Lynn's effective rights to the selected postal properties of users in the AeroDyn.Mfg OU:

     a. Right-click the **AeroDyn.Mfg** OU, and then click **Properties** to open the Properties of AeroDyn.Mfg dialog box.

     b. Click the **NDS Rights** tab, and then click the **Effective Rights** button to open the Effective Rights to AeroDyn dialog box.

     c. Click the **Browse** button next to the For Trustee text box to open the Select Object dialog box.

     d. Expand the **Mgmt** OU, click **LDai**, and then click **OK** to display Lynn's effective rights.

     e. On your student answer sheet, record Lynn's Attribute and Entry rights.

     f. Scroll down to the postal properties, click each postal property, and record Lynn's effective rights on your student answer sheet.

     g. Click the **Close** button to close the Effective Rights dialog box.

  7. Click **Cancel** to return to the main ConsoleOne window.

  8. Exit ConsoleOne, and log out.

eDirectory Default Rights

The eDirectory security system is very powerful and flexible, allowing network administrators to tailor their systems to meet special needs. Knowing what rights are available by default and where they come from is important in planning for eDirectory security needs and troubleshooting the eDirectory security system. When eDirectory is installed on the first server, the [Public], [Root], and Admin objects are created. The Admin object is assigned the Supervisor Entry right to the root of the new eDirectory tree, thereby making Admin a supervisor of the entire network, including all servers. Giving the Supervisor Entry right to a server object automatically gives that user Supervisor file system rights to the server's volumes and file system, as described in Chapter 5. In addition to the Admin user assignment, during installation the [Public] trustee is given the Browse Entry right all the way to the root of the tree, so users can view all objects in the tree by using the CX /T /A /R command before logging in. If this creates a security problem in your organization, you'll need to remove [Public] as a trustee of the root of the tree, and then assign the Browse Entry right to individual users, groups, or containers. You can give all users who have logged in to the network rights to browse the entire tree by making the [Root] object a trustee of the tree with Browse Entry rights. In the following activities, you learn what a CNA needs to know about the eDirectory default assignments by using NetWare Administrator to view and record the default trustees for the root of the eDirectory tree, a new container, and a new user.

Activity 6-8: Default Trustees of the eDirectory Tree

Time Required: 5 minutes

Objective: Identify the default Entry and Attribute rights for the eDirectory system.

Description: In this activity, you use NetWare Administrator to record the trustees of the root of the tree along with their Entry (Object) and Attribute (Property) rights.

1. If necessary, start your computer, and log in with your UasAdmin user name.

2. Double-click the **NetWare Administrator** desktop icon.

3. Open a browse window showing the root of the tree:

    a. Click **View**, **Set Context** on the menu bar.

    b. Enter **[Root]** in the Context text box, and then click **OK**.

4. To check the trustees of the [Root] object, right-click the **[Root]** object, and then click **Trustees of this Object**.

5. Record the trustees of the [Root] object along with their assigned Entry and Attribute rights on your student answer sheet.

6. Click the **Cancel** button to return to the NetWare Administrator browse window.

7. If you're continuing to the next activity, leave NetWare Administrator open and stay logged in. If not, exit NetWare Administrator, and log out.

Activity 6-9: Default Rights Assigned to the Server Object

Time Required: 5 minutes

Objective: Identify the default Entry and Attribute rights for the eDirectory system.

Description: When a server object is installed in the eDirectory tree, default rights are given to the server object and the [Public] trustee object. In this activity, you use NetWare Administrator to record the default trustees and rights assigned to the server.

1. If necessary, start your computer, log in with your UasAdmin user name, and start NetWare Administrator.

2. Open a browse window to the UAS container.

3. To check the trustees of the UASHOST server object, right-click the **UASHOST** server object, and then click **Trustees of this Object**.

4. On your student answer sheet, record the trustees of the server object along with their assigned Entry and Attribute rights.

5. Click the [Public] trustee object, and then click the **Selected properties** radio button.

6. Scroll down the Selected properties list box, and click any property right assignments that are marked with a check. On your student answer sheet, record the rights assignment for each property you select.

7. Click the **Cancel** button to return to the NetWare Administrator browse window.

8. If you're continuing to the next activity, leave NetWare Administrator open and stay logged in. If not, exit NetWare Administrator, and log out.

Activity 6-10: Documenting the Default Trustees of a New User

Time Required: 5 minutes

Objective: Identify the default Entry and Attribute rights for the eDirectory system.

Description: When a new user object is created in eDirectory, certain Attribute rights are granted automatically to give the user access to basic resources on the network. Knowing the default rights assignments for a new user can help plan and implement an eDirectory security system that meets the needs of the organization and the users. In this activity, you use NetWare Administrator to document the default trustees of a new user by checking the trustees of your user name.

1. If necessary, start your computer, log in with your UasAdmin user name, and start NetWare Administrator.

2. If necessary, open a browse window for your ##UAS container:

    a. Click **View**, **Set Context** on the menu bar.

    b. Click the **Browse** button next to the Context text box.

    c. Double-click your **##UAS** container in the Available objects section.

    d. Click **OK** to open a ##UAS browse window.

3. Check the trustees of your user name:

    a. Double-click your **IS** OU to expand it.

    b. Right-click your user name, and then click **Trustees of this Object**.

4. Record the trustees of your user name along with their assigned Entry and Attribute rights on your student answer sheet. Click the **Selected properties** radio button to include any selected Attribute rights.

5. Click the **Cancel** button to return to the NetWare Administrator browse window.

6. Exit NetWare Administrator, and log out.

eDIRECTORY SECURITY FOR UNIVERSAL AEROSPACE

As with file system security, when setting up eDirectory security, you should first identify and document the effective rights users need for accessing their resources or performing their management responsibilities. After meeting with the department managers, Luke sent a memo to Eric, shown in Figure 6-12, that documents the UAS eDirectory security requirements to be implemented.

MEMO

To: Eric Kenton

From: Luke McMann

Date: Yesterday

Subject: eDirectory security meeting notes

1. Kellie Thiele will be responsible for maintaining user login scripts for all users except those in the AeroDyn OU. Users should not be able to change their own login scripts.
2. To reduce the number of times Eric has to log in as Admin, his user name should be given Supervisor rights to objects in only the UAS Organization.
3. All users in the ISMgrs group should have rights to create and rename objects in all containers except the AeroDyn.Mfg OU.
4. Lynn Dai will be responsible for maintaining user postal address information for all users except those in the AeroDyn OU.
5. All users in the Engineering OU need rights to use the EngData Directory Map object.
6. All users in the IS OU need rights to use the ISData Directory Map object.
7. All users in the Mgmt OU need rights to use the MgmtData Directory Map object.
8. The MfgMgr Organizational Role object should have Supervisor rights to all objects in the Mfg OU structure except the AeroDyn.Mfg OU. The occupant of the MfgMgr Organizational Role should be able to create objects only in the AeroDyn.Mfg OU.
9. The occupant of the AeroMgr Organizational Role object, the network administrator, and the backup administrator should be the only users with Supervisor rights to the AeroDyn.Mfg OU.
10. The occupant of the SysOp Organizational Role object should have Supervisor rights to the entire UAS Organization.

Figure 6-12   UAS eDirectory security needs

Defining Trustee Assignments

After defining the organization's special security needs, the next step in implementing eDirectory security is to define the trustee assignments you'll need to implement the security plan. To help with this task, Eric started with a list of Novell recommendations, shown in Figure 6-13.

6

Novell Security Guidelines

- **Start with the default trustee assignments.**
  With the exception of certain objects, such as Directory Map objects, eDirectory's defaults enable users to access basic network resources and services in their default container. To keep eDirectory security assignments to a minimum, attempt to place objects that users need to access, such as volumes and printers, in the user's default context.

- **Minimize trustee assignments.**
  As with file system security, you can often keep user trustee assignments to a minimum by assigning rights to containers first. Assign rights to groups when you don't want to include all users in a container, or if you want to include selected users from multiple containers. Instead of assigning rights to individual users, consider using Organizational Role objects.

- **Use caution when assigning a trustee the Write Attribute right to the ACL property of another object.**
  If users have the Write Attribute right to another object's ACL property, they can create and remove trustees of the object and change their own trustee assignments. This includes making themselves or another user a Supervisor of the object as well as modifying the object's IRF. In a worst-case scenario, trustees with the Write Attribute right to a container's ACL property could make their user names the Supervisor of the container and lock out the Admin user by removing the Supervisor right from the container's IRF.

- **Avoid using the All Properties option when assigning the Write Attribute right.**
  Use caution when assigning a trustee the Write Attribute right for all properties, as this gives the trustee the ability to change any property values, including the ACL property. Through inheritance, the All Properties rights assigned to a container flow down to all subcontainer and leaf objects. As a general rule, it's better to assign only the Read Attribute right in All Properties and use the Selected Properties option when assigning the Write Attribute right.

- **Use caution when granting a trustee the Supervisor Entry right to a container with a server object.**
  When a user has the Supervisor Entry right to a server object, he or she also becomes a Supervisor of the server's file system by gaining the Supervisor access right to the root of all volumes. Usually, this problem happens when another user is made the manager of a container by being assigned the Supervisor Entry right to that container. If the container happens to contain a server object, the new trustee will have all rights to the file system on the server. To prevent a user from accidentally inheriting Supervisor rights to the

---

server object, you can make the Admin user a Supervisor of the server object by adding an explicit trustee assignment for Admin, and then removing the Supervisor rights from the server object's IRF.

- **Use caution when filtering Supervisor rights with an IRF.**
  NetWare will not allow you to remove the Supervisor rights from an object's IRF until you have added an explicit trustee assignment that has been granted the Supervisor Entry right for that object. However, it's still possible to lose administrative control of a section of the tree by adding a user as a trustee with Supervisor rights, removing the Supervisor rights from the IRF, and then accidentally deleting the user who has the Supervisor trustee assignment. If this happens, essentially you would lose control of the container or leaf object because it would have no supervisor.

Figure 6-13   eDirectory security guidelines

Using these guidelines, Eric created the worksheet shown in Table 6-3 to make trustee assignments for the UAS network. Each row in the eDirectory Security Worksheet contains the name and object type of an object that needs a special trustee assignment. The Trustee columns contain the trustee name along with the rights to be assigned. The Inherit Right columns contain the settings for the inherited rights associated with that object or property.

Table 6-3   eDirectory Security Worksheet

Developed by: *Eric Kenton*		Tree Name: *UAS_Tree*					
Object		**Trustee**			**Property**		
Name	**Type**	**Name/Type**	**Entry Rights**	**Inherit Right***	**Name**	**Attribute Rights**	**Inherit Right***
1 ##UAS	Organization container	ISMgrs.IS.##UAS	BCR	I	All ACL	CRW CR	I
2 ##UAS	Organization container	Your_user_name	S		All	S	
3 ##UAS	Organization container	Lynn Dai	B	I	Postal Code, Postal Address, Postal Office Box	W	I
4 EngData. Engineering. ##UAS	Directory Map object	.Engineering.##UAS/ container	B	I	Path	R	I
5 ISData. ##UAS	Directory Map object	.IS.##UAS/ container	B	I	Path	R	I
6 MfgData	Directory Map object	Mfg.##UAS/ container	B	I	Path	R	I
7 MgmtData	Directory Map object	Mgmt.##UAS/ container	B	I	Path	R	I
8 ##UAS	Organization container	.KThiele.##UAS	B	I	Login Script	RW	I
9 ##UAS	Organization container	SysOp.IS.##UAS	S	I	All	S	I
10 All users	User object	The user's name		I	Login Script	R	I
11 Mfg.##UAS	OU container	.MfgMgr.Mfg .##UAS/org role	SBCR D	I	All	S	I
12 AeroDyn. Mfg.##UAS	OU container	AeroMgr.Mfg.##UAS /org role	SBCR D	I	All	S	I
13 AeroDyn. Mfg.##UAS	OU container	MfgMgr.Mfg.##UAS /org role	BC	I	All	R	I

* The Inherit Right column indicates whether subcontainers will inherit the assigned right.

Eric also developed the eDirectory IRF Worksheet shown in Table 6-4, which contains the names and contexts of containers or leaf objects whose IRF settings will change. Notice that the Mfg container will have all rights except Supervisor removed from the Entry IRF, and the AeroDyn container will have all rights except Supervisor removed from its Entry and All Attributes IRFs. In addition, the AeroDyn container will have all rights except Read removed from the IRF of the postal properties.

After creating the eDirectory security assignment plan, Eric's next step was to implement the trustee assignments and check user effective rights. The first four rows in Table 6-3 contain the trustee assignments you made in previous activities. The activities in the following sections correspond to the trustee assignments and IRF settings Eric defined on the worksheets in Table 6-3 and Table 6-4. By doing these activities, you'll learn how to use ConsoleOne to make the eDirectory trustee assignments shown in the worksheet and apply IRFs to modify users' effective rights.

Table 6-4   eDirectory IRF Worksheet

Object Name	Type	Entry Rights IRF	All Attributes IRF	Property Name	Property IRF
Mfg	OU	S	All		
AeroDyn.Mfg	OU	S	S	Postal Code	R
				Postal Address	R
				Postal Office Box	R
				Login Script	R

Existing Trustee Assignments

In the previous activities, you implemented several of the eDirectory security requirements for your version of the UAS network. These security settings are summarized in the following list (refer to Table 6-3 to check the row numbers):

- Notice in Row 1 that the ISMgrs group is identified as needing Create and Rename rights to the ##UAS Organization so that Kellie, Luke, and Eric can create other objects, such as users, printers, or volumes. You made this trustee assignment to your UAS network in Activity 6-2.

- Row 2 identifies the trustee assignment you made in Activity 6-5 to grant your user name Supervisor rights to only the ##UAS Organization. Notice that the Inheritable right has been removed from the assignment.

- Row 3 identifies the assignment you made for Lynn Dai in Activity 6-7 to enable her to maintain name and address information for the ##UAS Organization.

- In Row 4, the Engineering OU is identified as a trustee of the EngData Directory Map object with Browse Entry rights and Read rights to only the Path property (the assignments you made in Activity 6-3).

Assigning Rights to Directory Map Objects

In addition to the EngData Directory Map object, Rows 5–7 in Table 6-3 contain the names of other Directory Map objects you created in Chapter 3:

- Row 5 identifies the IS OU as the trustee of the ISData Directory Map object.

- Row 6 identifies the Mfg OU as the trustee of the MfgData Directory Map object with Read rights to the Path property.

- Row 7 identifies the Mgmt OU as the trustee of the MgmtData Directory Map object with Read rights to the Path property.

In the following activity, you finish assigning rights to your Directory Map objects by completing the trustee assignments in Rows 5–7 of the eDirectory Security Worksheet.

Activity 6-11: Assigning Rights to Directory Map Objects

Time Required: 10 minutes

Objective: Use ConsoleOne to assign eDirectory rights.

Description: In this activity, you use ConsoleOne to make the trustee assignments specified in Table 6-3 for the Directory Map objects.

1. If necessary, start your computer, and log in with your UasAdmin user name.

2. Start ConsoleOne, and expand **UAS_Tree** and your **##UAS** container.

3. Make the IS OU a trustee of the ISData Directory Map object with Read rights to the Path property:

    a. Click your **IS** OU to display all objects in the Object frame.

    b. Right-click the **ISData** Directory Map object, and then click **Properties** to open the Properties of ISData dialog box.

    c. Click the **NDS Rights** tab to display the Trustees list box.

    d. Click the **Add Trustee** button to open the Select Object dialog box.

    e. Click the **up arrow**, and then click your **IS** OU.

    f. Click **OK** to open the Rights assigned to selected objects dialog box. Click the **All Attributes Read** check box to remove the check mark.

    g. Click the **Add Property** button to open the Add Property dialog box.

    h. Scroll down the list of properties, click the **Path** property, and then click **OK** to add the Path property to the Property list box.

    i. Record the default rights assigned to the Path property on your student answer sheet.

    j. Click **OK** to return to the Properties of ISData dialog box.

    k. Click **OK** to save your trustee assignment and return to the main ConsoleOne window.

4. Repeat Step 3 to make the Mfg OU a trustee of the MfgData Directory Map object with Read rights to the Path property.

5. Repeat Step 3 to make the Mgmt OU a trustee of the MgmtData Directory Map object with Read rights to the Path property.

6. Exit ConsoleOne, and log out.

Delegating Rights to Manage the UAS Organization

As described in Chapter 2, the occupant of the SysOp Organizational Role object will be a backup administrative user whose account can be used if the main NetWare Admin user account is disabled or its password becomes compromised. Notice in Row 9 of Table 6-3 that the SysOp Organizational Role object is granted the Supervisor Entry right to the UAS Organization with all Entry and Attribute rights. Another administrative task that Eric wanted to delegate was maintaining login scripts. As you'll learn in Chapter 7, creating login scripts has a lot in common with writing programs or batch files. Because Kellie is a programmer, Luke wants her to be in charge of writing and maintaining login scripts for all users, so in Row 8 of Table 6-3, Eric identified Kellie as needing the Read, Write, and Inheritable rights to the selected Login Script property of the UAS Organization. This assignment will allow her to maintain login scripts for all users through inheritance. In Activity 6-12, you make Kellie and the SysOp Organizational Role object trustees of your ##UAS Organization.

When a user logs in, login script files are used to automatically map network drive letters and perform other setup functions, as described in Chapter 7. By default, users are given rights to create and modify their own login script files. However, Kellie does not want users to be able to modify the login script commands she sets up for them. Notice that in Row 10 of Table 6-3, Eric is planning to remove the Write right from each user's Login Script property. To prevent users from modifying their login scripts, in Chapter 2 you learned how to remove the Login Script right from the user template. In Activity 6-13, you learn how to verify that users do not have rights to change their individual login scripts, and if necessary, remove the Write right from all users except those in the IS department.

Activity 6-12: Delegating Rights to Manage an Organization

Time Required: 10 minutes

Objective: Use ConsoleOne to assign eDirectory rights.

Description: In this activity, you complete the trustee assignments Eric specified for the UAS network in Rows 8 and 9 of Table 6-3 by assigning the Supervisor right to the SysOp organizational role and making Kellie a trustee of the UAS container with Write rights to the Login Script property. You then use ConsoleOne to check Kellie's effective rights to the Login Script property of OUs and users.

1. If necessary, start your computer, and log in with your UasAdmin user name.

2. If necessary, start ConsoleOne, and expand **UAS_Tree** and your **##UAS** container.

3. Make your SysOp Organizational Role object a Supervisor of your ##UAS Organization:

    a. Right-click your **##UAS** Organization, and then click **Properties** to open the Properties of ##UAS dialog box.

    b. Click the **NDS Rights** tab, and record the existing trustees on your student answer sheet. Click each trustee assignment, and then click the **Assigned Rights** button to record the trustee assignments on your student answer sheet. Verify that the trustee assignments match those on the eDirectory Security Worksheet in Table 6-3.

    c. Click the **Add Trustee** button to open the Select Objects dialog box.

    d. If necessary, click the **up arrow** to navigate to your IS OU, and expand the **IS** OU. Click your **SysOp** Organizational Role object, and click **OK** to open the Rights assigned to selected objects dialog box.

    e. Verify that the [Entry Rights] object is selected, and then click the check boxes corresponding to all the rights, including the Supervisor right and the Inheritable right.

    f. Click the **[All Attributes Rights]** object, and then click the check boxes corresponding to all the rights, including the Supervisor right and the Inheritable right.

    g. Click **OK** to save the trustee assignment and return to the Properties of ##UAS dialog box.

    h. Click **OK** to close the Properties of ##UAS dialog box and return to the main ConsoleOne window.

4. Check Clark Kent's effective rights in the AeroDyn.Mfg OU:

    a. If necessary, expand your **Mfg** OU.

    b. Right-click the **AeroDyn** OU, and then click **Properties** to open the Properties of AeroDyn dialog box.

    c. Click the **down arrow** on the NDS Rights tab, and then click the **Effective Rights** option.

    d. Click the **Browse** button next to the For Trustee text box to open the Select Object dialog box.

    e. If necessary, click the **up arrow** to navigate to the IS OU. Expand the **IS** OU, and click your **CKent** user name.

    f. Click **OK** to display Clark's effective rights, as shown in Figure 6-14.

    g. Click **Cancel** to return to the main ConsoleOne window.

5. Make Kellie a trustee of ##UAS with Write rights to the Login Script property:

    a. Right-click your **##UAS** organization, and then click **Properties** to open the Properties of ##UAS dialog box.

    b. Click the **NDS Rights** tab to display the existing trustees.

    c. Click the **Add Trustee** button to open the Select Object dialog box.

    d. Expand the **IS** OU, click **KThiele**, and click **OK** to open the Rights assigned to selected objects dialog box.

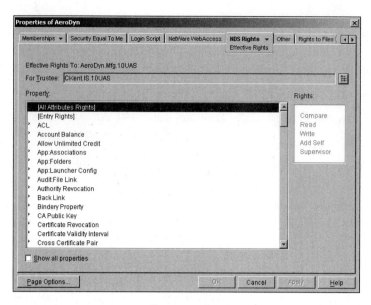

Figure 6-14 Viewing effective rights for CKent

    e. Click the **Add Property** button to open the Add Property dialog box.

    f. Scroll down the list of properties, click **Login Script**, and then click **OK** to add the Login Script property to the Property list box.

    g. Click the **Write** and **Inheritable** check boxes to assign these rights.

    h. Click **OK** to save the trustee assignment and return to the Properties of ##UAS dialog box.

    i. Click **OK** to close the Properties of ##UAS dialog box and return to the main ConsoleOne window.

6. Check Kellie's effective rights to the Login Script property of the Engineering container. Record her effective rights on your student answer sheet.

7. Check Kellie's effective rights to the Login Script property of the AeroDyn.Mfg container. Record her effective rights on your student answer sheet.

8. If you're continuing to the next activity, leave ConsoleOne open and stay logged in. If not, exit ConsoleOne, and log out.

Activity 6-13: Checking User Login Script Rights

Time Required: 10 minutes

Objective: Use ConsoleOne to assign eDirectory rights.

Description: Because Kellie will be managing login scripts, it's important that users be prevented from making changes to their personal login scripts that could interfere with system operations. In the activities in Chapter 4, you removed the Login Script rights from the template for creating new users. In this activity, you verify that users have only Read rights to their Login Script properties.

1. If necessary, start your computer, and log in with your UasAdmin user name.

2. If necessary, start ConsoleOne, and expand **UAS_Tree** and your **##UAS** container.

3. Check the Login Script property right for Kari Means in the Engineering container:

    a. Click your **Engineering** container to display all user objects.

    b. Right-click the user **KMeans**, and then click **Properties** to open the Properties of KMeans dialog box.

c. Click the **down arrow** on the NDS Rights tab, and then click the **Effective Rights** option.

d. Click the **Browse** button next to the For Trustee text box to open the Select Object dialog box.

e. If necessary, click the **up arrow** to navigate to the Engineering OU. Expand the **Engineering** OU, click **KMeans**, and then click **OK** to display the effective rights for KMeans.

f. Scroll down the list of properties, and click the **Login Script** property. Verify that Kari has only Read and Compare rights to her Login Script property.

g. Click **Cancel** to return to the main ConsoleOne window.

4. Repeat Step 3 to check the Login Script property right for one other user in each of your OUs, and record the user name and Login Script Attribute rights on your student answer sheet.

5. If necessary, remove the Write right from the Login Script property of all users except those in the IS OU.

6. Exit ConsoleOne, and log out.

Managing the Mfg Organizational Unit

To allow users occupying the MfgMgr organizational role to manage the Manufacturing division, in Row 11 of Table 6-3, Eric has identified the MfgMgr object as a trustee of the Mfg.UAS OU with Supervisor Entry rights. Because of inheritance, the Supervisor rights assigned to the MfgMgr object in the Mfg container will be inherited by both the UAS and AeroDyn OUs. Although assigning the Supervisor Entry right also gives Supervisor rights to all properties, Eric included all other Entry and Attribute rights in the assignment so that the occupant of the MfgMgr organizational role could continue managing the Mfg container if the Supervisor Entry right is deleted or blocked.

Unlike file system security, in eDirectory security, the Supervisor right can be reassigned or blocked in a sub-container. Luke wants the occupant of the AeroMgr organizational role to be the only user who can delete objects in the AeroDyn Manufacturing division. To accomplish this, in Row 12 of Table 6-3, Eric identified the AeroMgr object as the trustee of the AeroDyn.Mfg OU with Supervisor rights. To prevent the MfgMgr object from supervising objects in the AeroDyn container, in Row 13 Eric reassigned rights to the MfgMgr object in the AeroDyn OU to Browse and Create. This assignment will also prevent occupants of the MfgMgr organizational role from deleting or renaming objects in the AeroDyn container, but allow the network administrator and SysOp object to inherit Supervisor rights. Notice in the Attribute Rights column of Row 13 that Eric reassigned the MfgMgr object only the Read right to All Properties. Because the MfgMgr object will inherit Supervisor rights for the assignment in Row 11, reassigning the MfgMgr object only Read rights to All Properties will prevent an occupant of MfgMgr from changing Entry properties. In addition, having the Write right to the ACL property enables occupants of the MfgMgr organizational role to change their trustee assignment and have Supervisor rights to all volumes of any server objects in the OU. Because AeroDyn is planning to install another server in the future, Luke doesn't want the occupant of the MfgMgr organizational role to have Supervisor rights to all its volumes. In the following activities, you use Eric's method to create an Organizational Unit manager for your Mfg container and reassign the Supervisor right in a subcontainer.

Activity 6-14: Creating an Organizational Unit Manager

Time Required: 10 minutes

Objective: Use ConsoleOne to assign eDirectory rights.

Description: In this activity, you use ConsoleOne to assign the MfgMgr object all Entry rights to the Mfg container. You then use ConsoleOne to check the effective rights Russ Pence has in the Mfg and AeroDyn containers as a result of being the occupant of the MfgMgr object.

1. If necessary, start your computer, and log in with your UasAdmin user name.

2. If necessary, start ConsoleOne, and expand **UAS_Tree** and your **##UAS** container.

3. Make the MfgMgr Organizational Role object a trustee of the Mfg container with all rights, including Supervisor:

    a. Right-click your **Mfg** container, and click **Properties** to open the Properties of Mfg dialog box. Click the **NDS Rights** tab to display all existing trustees.

    b. Click the **Add Trustee** button to open the Select Object dialog box.

    c. If necessary, expand the **Mfg** OU, and click the **MfgMgr** object.

    d. Click **OK** to open the Rights assigned to selected objects dialog box.

    e. Click the **[Entry Rights]** object, and then click any check boxes, including **Supervisor**, that are not selected to make sure all rights are assigned.

    f. Click **OK**, and then click **Apply** to save the trustee assignment.

4. Check effective rights for Russ Pence in the Mfg OU:

    a. Click the **Effective Rights** button to open the Effective Rights dialog box.

    b. Click the **Browse** button to open the Select Object dialog box.

    c. If necessary, expand the **Mfg** container, click **RPence**, and then click **OK** to display Russ's effective rights.

    d. Record Russ's effective rights on your student answer sheet, and then click the **Close** button twice.

5. Right-click the **AeroDyn** OU, and then click **Properties** to open the Properties of AeroDyn dialog box. Repeat Step 4 to check the effective rights for Russ Pence in the AeroDyn subcontainer, and record the results on your student answer sheet.

6. Click the **Cancel** button to return to the main ConsoleOne window.

7. If you're continuing to the next activity, leave ConsoleOne open and stay logged in. If not, exit ConsoleOne, and log out.

Activity 6-15: Reassigning the Supervisor Right in a Subcontainer

Time Required: 10 minutes

Objective: Use ConsoleOne to assign eDirectory rights.

Description: As with file system security, a new trustee assignment overrides an object's inherited Entry and Attribute rights. In the file system, this is true for all access rights except Supervisor. However, in eDirectory security, you can block or reassign the Supervisor right at a lower-level container or leaf object. For example, the occupant of the MfgMgr organizational role should not have the Delete right in the AeroDyn.Mfg.UAS container. Because the MfgMgr object is a trustee of Mfg with Supervisor rights, Russ is currently inheriting all rights in the Mfg and AeroDyn containers. In this activity, you reduce Russ's effective rights in the AeroDyn.Mfg container by making a new trustee assignment to the MfgMgr object.

1. If necessary, start your computer, and log in with your UasAdmin user name.

2. If necessary, start ConsoleOne, and expand **UAS_Tree** and your **##UAS** container.

3. Make the MfgMgr Organizational Role object a trustee of the AeroDyn OU container with Browse, Create, and Rename Entry rights and Read rights to All Properties:

    a. If necessary, expand your **Mfg** OU.

    b. Right-click the **AeroDyn** container, and then click **Properties** to open the Properties of AeroDyn dialog box.

    c. Click the **NDS Rights** tab to display existing trustees of the AeroDyn container.

d. Click the **Add Trustee** button to open the Select Object dialog box.

e. Click the **up arrow** to navigate to the Mfg OU.

f. Click the **MfgMgr** object, and then click **OK** to open the Rights assigned to selected objects dialog box.

g. Verify that the [Entry Rights] object is selected, and then click the **Create** and **Rename** check boxes to assign these rights. If the Browse Right hasn't been assigned already, click that check box, too.

h. Click the **[All Attributes Rights]** object, and verify that Read and Compare rights are selected.

i. Click **OK**, and then click the **Apply** button to save the trustee assignment and return to the Properties of AeroDyn dialog box.

4. Check Russ's effective rights in the AeroDyn OU:

a. Click the **Effective Rights** button to open the Effective Rights dialog box.

b. Click the **Browse** button next to the For Trustee text box to open the Select Object dialog box.

c. If necessary, click the **up arrow** to navigate to your Mfg container.

d. Click **RPence**, and then click **OK** to display effective rights for Russ.

e. Record Russ's effective rights on your student answer sheet.

f. Click the **Close** button to return to the Properties of AeroDyn dialog box.

5. Click the **Close** button to return to the main ConsoleOne window.

6. Exit ConsoleOne, and log out.

Blocking Rights to the AeroDyn Container

As in file system security, a trustee's inherited rights can be changed in eDirectory security by assigning the trustee a different set of Entry and Attribute rights in a leaf or subcontainer object or by implementing an IRF. Although reassigning rights is effective for changing a single object's effective rights in a subcontainer or leaf object, it doesn't block the rights that other users or groups can inherit from the parent container. Using an IRF can be a more effective way to globally block inherited rights from giving a user effective rights in a container. As you have learned, IRFs can be applied on Entry rights as well as All Attributes and selected properties. To help him identify the IRFs to be implemented in the UAS structure, Eric added to the IRF worksheet shown previously in Table 6-4. The updated worksheet is shown in Table 6-5.

Table 6-5   eDirectory IRF Worksheet

Developed by: *Eric Kenton*		Tree Name: *UAS_Tree*			
Object Name	Type	Entry Rights IRF	All Attributes IRF	Property Name	Property IRF
##UAS	Organization	All	All		
Engineering	OU	All	All		
Mgmt	OU	All	All		
Mfg	OU	S	All		
AeroDyn.Mfg	OU	S	S	Postal Code Postal Address Postal Office Box Login Script	R R R R

Table 6-5 identifies any Entry or Attribute rights that need to be blocked from being inherited by a subcontainer. For example, to block all Entry rights except Supervisor from the AeroDyn.Mfg OU, the IRF on the AeroDyn container has been reduced to have just the Supervisor right. This assignment prevents users in the ISMgrs group who have Create rights in the UAS Organization from inheriting Create rights in the AeroDyn division. Also, reducing the IRF of All Attributes to just Supervisor doesn't prevent Kellie from changing login scripts or Lynn from changing postal address information in the AeroDyn container. To block rights, Eric used this worksheet to identify the IRF for selected rights. In the following activity, you use ConsoleOne to implement the IRFs that Eric specified.

Activity 6-16: Implementing IRFs

Time Required: 10 minutes

Objective: Use ConsoleOne to assign eDirectory rights.

Description: In this activity, you implement an IRF for the Entry rights of the AeroDyn container to block the ISMgrs group from inheriting Entry rights in the AeroDyn container.

1. If necessary, start your computer, and log in with your UasAdmin user name.

2. If necessary, start ConsoleOne, and expand **UAS_Tree** and your **##UAS** container.

3. Modify the IRF on the AeroDyn container to remove all rights except Browse and Supervisor:

   a. If necessary, expand your **Mfg** OU.

   b. Right-click the **AeroDyn** container, and then click **Properties** to open the Properties of AeroDyn dialog box.

   c. Click the **down arrow** on the NDS Rights tab, and then click the **Inherited Rights Filters** option to display the existing IRFs.

   d. Record any existing IRFs on your student answer sheet.

   e. Click the **Add Filter** button to open the Add Property dialog box.

   f. Verify that the [All Attributes Rights] object is selected, and then click **OK** to add it to the Property list box.

   g. In the Rights section, click all check boxes except Supervisor to remove these rights.

   h. Click the **Add Filter** button to open the Add Property dialog box.

   i. Click the **[Entry Rights]** object, and then click **OK** to add it to the Property list box.

   j. In the Rights section, click all check boxes except Supervisor to remove these rights.

   k. Click the **Add Filter** button to open the Add Property dialog box.

   l. Scroll down the list of properties, click **Login Script**, and then click **OK** to add the Login Script property to the Property list box.

   m. Click all check boxes except Read and Compare in the Rights section to remove these rights.

   n. Click **OK** to save your change to the IRFs and return to the main ConsoleOne window.

4. Check Kellie's effective rights in the AeroDyn container, and record them on your student answer sheet.

5. Click the **Cancel** button to return to the ConsoleOne window.

6. Exit ConsoleOne, and log out.

Setting Up an Independent Container Administrator

Because eDirectory allows you to use an IRF to block the Supervisor right, you can set up a container that's administered by a user other than the main Admin user. Of course, misuse of this capability can cause some major problems. To prevent accidentally blocking your Admin user, the NetWare operating system requires you to establish a user with Supervisor rights in a container before removing the Supervisor right from the IRF. Without this safety check, carelessly removing the Supervisor right from the IRF of a container or leaf object would mean that no one, including the network administrator, would have rights to manage that container or leaf object. As a result, before you can use an IRF to block the Supervisor right from a container, you need to use an explicit trustee assignment to grant another object or the main Admin user the Supervisor right to that container. In the next activity, you modify the trustees of the AeroDyn OU to grant the Supervisor right to the AeroMgr Organizational Role object.

Activity 6-17: Creating a Container Administrator

Time Required: 10 minutes

Objective: Establish an independent container administrator.

Description: Luke asked Eric to establish the AeroDyn OU as an independent container in the UAS_Tree that's managed by the AeroMgr occupant, not the Admin user account. As a backup in case the AeroMgr occupant account is disabled, Luke wanted the SysOp occupant to also have the Supervisor right to the AeroDyn OU. To increase security, only Luke and Lynn will know the password for the SysOp occupant. When major tree changes are necessary, the AeroMgr occupant will grant Supervisor rights to the Admin user for the time needed to complete the changes. Eric accomplished this task by making the AeroDyn and SysOp objects trustees of the AeroDyn OU with Supervisor rights, and then modifying the IRF of the AeroDyn container to block the Admin user from inheriting the Supervisor right. In this activity, you use Eric's method to make your AeroMgr and SysOp occupants exclusive administrators of your AeroDyn OU. Next, you verify the results by checking your effective rights, and then restore your UasAdmin's Supervisor right to the AeroDyn container by logging in as the occupant of the SysOp organizational role to remove the IRF and check your effective rights.

1. If necessary, start your computer, and log in with your UasAdmin user name.

2. If necessary, start ConsoleOne, and expand **UAS_Tree** and your **##UAS** container.

3. Make your AeroDyn and SysOp Organizational Role objects trustees of the AeroDyn container with Supervisor rights:

   a. If necessary, expand your **Mfg** OU.

   b. Right-click the **AeroDyn** container, and click **Properties** to open the Properties of AeroDyn dialog box.

   c. Click the **NDS Rights** tab to display the existing trustees.

   d. Record the existing trustees on your student answer sheet.

   e. Click the **Add Trustee** button to open the Select Object dialog box.

   f. Click the **up arrow** and navigate to the IS OU.

   g. Click the **SysOp** object, and then click **OK** to open the Rights assigned to selected objects dialog box.

   h. Verify that the [Entry Rights] object is selected, and then click the **Supervisor** check box to assign this right.

   i. Click the **[All Attributes Rights]** object, and then click the **Supervisor** check box to assign this right.

   j. Click **OK** to add the SysOp Organizational Role object to your Trustees list box.

4. Repeat Step 3 to make your AeroMgr Organizational Role object a trustee of the AeroDyn OU with Supervisor rights.

5. Remove all rights except Browse from the IRF of the AeroDyn container:

   a. Click the **down arrow** on the NDS Rights tab, and then click the **Inherited Rights Filters** option to display the existing IRFs.

   b. Click the **[Entry Rights]** object, and then click all check boxes except Browse to block these rights from the IRF.

   c. Click the **[All Attributes Rights]** object, and then click all check boxes except Read and Compare to block these rights from the IRF.

   d. Click **OK** to save your assignment.

6. Attempt to check your rights in the AeroDyn container. Notice that the rights are grayed out and your UasAdmin user cannot change trustee assignments.

7. Log out to display a new Novell Login window.

8. Click the **Advanced** button to change the default context to your IS.##UAS container, and then log in as CKent.

9. Start ConsoleOne, and expand **UAS_Tree** and your **##UAS** Organization.

10. Make your UasAdmin user a trustee of the AeroDyn container:

   a. If necessary, expand your **Mfg** OU.

   b. Right-click the **AeroDyn** container, and click **Properties** to open the Properties of AeroDyn dialog box.

   c. Click the **NDS Rights** tab to display existing trustees of the AeroDyn container.

   d. Click the **Add Trustee** button to open the Select Object dialog box.

   e. Click the **up arrow** and navigate to the ##UAS Organization.

   f. Click the **UasAdmin** user, and then click **OK** to open the Rights assigned to selected objects dialog box.

   g. Verify that the [Entry Rights] object is selected, and then click the **Supervisor** check box to assign this right.

   h. Click the **[All Attributes Rights]** object, and then click the **Supervisor** check box.

   i. Click **OK** to save the trustee assignment and return to the Properties of AeroDyn dialog box.

11. Click **OK** to close the dialog box. Exit ConsoleOne, and log out.

12. Log in with your UasAdmin user name.

13. Use ConsoleOne to check effective rights for your UasAdmin user in the AeroDyn container. Record the rights on your student answer sheet.

14. Exit ConsoleOne, and log out.

ASSIGNING RIGHTS THROUGH ADMINISTRATIVE ROLES

As you learned in Chapter 2, to use the iManager utility to manage the eDirectory tree, a user needs to be assigned to an administrative role. Standard administrative roles include DHCP Management, DNS Management, eDirectory Administration, iPrint Management, and License Management. In the following steps, you see how Eric granted Kellie the rights to use iManager to perform eDirectory management by adding Kellie's user name to the eDirectory Administration role. To perform these steps, you need to have access to a user name and password with Supervisor rights to the eDirectory tree of your NetWare server.

1. Eric started Internet Explorer and entered the URL https://172.20.0.60:2200 (172.20.0.60 is the IP address of the UASHOST server) to open the NetWare Web Manager window shown in Figure 6-15.

2. He then clicked the UASHOST link under the eDirectory iManager heading to open the Login window, shown in Figure 6-16.

3. After entering the Admin user name and password, Eric clicked the Login button to open the iManager home window, shown in Figure 6-17.

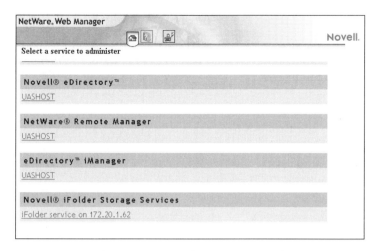

Figure 6-15 The NetWare Web Manager window

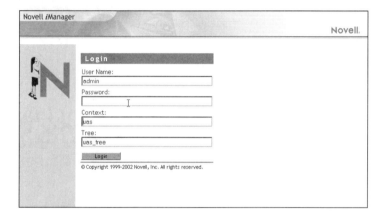

Figure 6-16 The iManager Login window

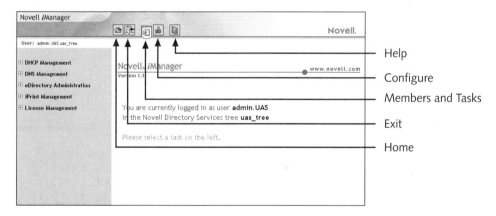

Figure 6-17 The iManager main window

4. To configure the iManager utility, Eric clicked the **Configure** button (looks like the Organizational Role object icon) on the tool bar to open the Configure window.

5. To add Kellie to the eDirectory Administration role, Eric expanded the Role Management item to display the options, shown in Figure 6-18.

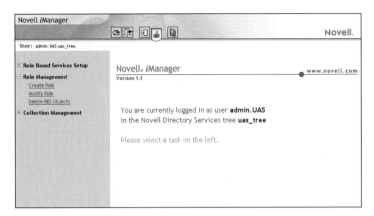

Figure 6-18   Role Management options

6. To add Kellie to an existing role, Eric clicked the Modify Role link and scrolled down to the eDirectory Administration role, shown in Figure 6-19.

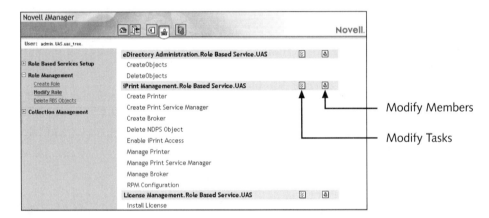

Figure 6-19   Viewing tasks in a role

The Modify Tasks button allows the administrator to add or remove tasks from the selected role. By default, the eDirectory role includes options to create and delete objects.

7. To add Kellie to the eDirectory Administration role, Eric clicked the Modify Members button to open the Modify Members window, shown in Figure 6-20.

8. Next, Eric clicked the Browse button to the right of the Name text box to open the eDirectory Object Selector window, and then navigated to the IS OU (see Figure 6-21).

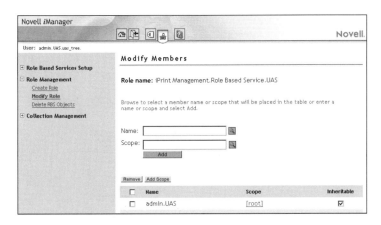

Figure 6-20 The Modify Members window

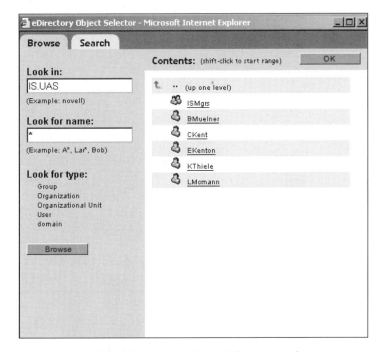

Figure 6-21 The eDirectory Object Selector window

9. He clicked the KThiele user name, and then clicked OK to add Kellie's user name to the bottom of the list in the Name column, as shown in Figure 6-22.

10. To allow Kellie to modify all objects in the UAS Organization, Eric made sure the KThiele check box was selected, and then clicked the Browse button next to the scope text box to open the eDirectory Object Selector window.

11. Eric then navigated up to the root of the UAS_Tree, and clicked the UAS Organization object to add the UAS scope to Kellie's role assigment, as shown in Figure 6-23.

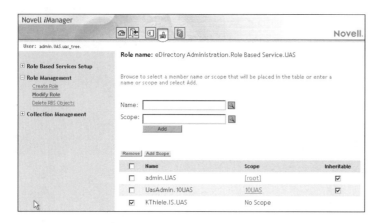

Figure 6-22   Adding Kellie to the eDirectory Administration role

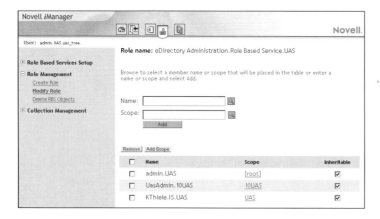

Figure 6-23   Selecting the scope

12. To complete the assignment, Eric clicked OK to return to the Modify Members window, and then clicked OK in the Modify Role Request succeeded window.

13. Eric then clicked the Exit button to exit iManager and return to the Login window.

14. He then tested the system by logging in with the user name KThiele to open the iManager window, shown in Figure 6-24.

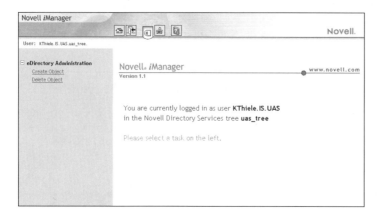

Figure 6-24   The KThiele iManager window

15. After showing Kellie how to use the iManager tool, Eric clicked the Exit button to return to the Login window and then closed Internet Explorer.

6

Congratulations! Luke is pleased with your progress as a student intern, but the work of a network administrator is never over. In the end-of-chapter case projects, you'll finish setting up eDirectory security for the Business office and then begin setting up login scripts in Chapter 7.

CHAPTER SUMMARY

- ❏ The Novell Directory Services database, or eDirectory, is the backbone of the NetWare network, providing access to all network objects. As a result, a network administrator must know how to implement the eDirectory security system to give users rights to access and manage the objects they are responsible for. eDirectory security consists of Entry and Attribute rights that are assigned to trustees. Each object in the eDirectory database has an access control list (ACL) property. An object is made a trustee of another object by placing the name of the object that is to be the trustee in the ACL property of the other object.

- ❏ Entry rights allow users to view and manage objects in the eDirectory tree, and consist of Supervisor, Browse, Create, Delete, Rename, and Inheritable.

- ❏ Attribute rights allow users to access and maintain information stored in an object, and consist of Supervisor, Read, Compare, Write, Add Self, and Inheritable.

- ❏ A trustee granted the Supervisor Entry right is automatically granted the Supervisor right to all attributes.

- ❏ Special trustee objects include [Public] and [Root]. The [Public] object represents all clients that have Novell Client loaded and are attached to the network, but have not yet logged in. The [Root] object represents all network objects, including clients, that have logged in using authorized user names.

- ❏ Entry and Attribute rights assigned to a trustee of a container can flow down from the container to leaf and subcontainer objects, unless reassigned or blocked by an Inherited Rights Filter (IRF). Effective rights consist of the actual rights a user has to an object as a result of a combination of explicit trustee assignments, inherited rights, group memberships, or rights assigned to the user's container object.

- ❏ Default rights play an important role in managing eDirectory security because they give the Admin user Supervisor rights to the eDirectory tree and give users rights to browse the network and access objects.

- ❏ In addition to default assignments, any user needing to access a Directory Map object must have the Read right to the Path property.

KEY TERMS

Add Self Attribute right — A special case of the Write Attribute right that allows trustees to add or remove their membership in a group.

Attribute rights — A group of eDirectory security rights used to define the rights granted to read and modify data in the properties of an object. Attribute rights include Read, Compare, Write, Add Self, Inheritable, and Supervisor.

Browse Entry right — An eDirectory security right that grants the right to view an object.

Compare Attribute right — A special case of the Read right that allows trustees to find an object without viewing property information.

Create Entry right — An eDirectory security right that grants the right to create objects in a container.

Delete Entry right — An eDirectory security right that grants the right to delete an object in a container.

Entry rights — A group of eDirectory security rights used to control what a user can do with an object. Consists of Browse, Create, Delete, Inheritable, Rename, and Supervisor rights.

Inheritable Attribute right — An eDirectory security right that enables leaf objects and subcontainers to inherit Attribute rights in a container trustee assignment.

Inheritable Entry right — An eDirectory security right that allows leaf objects and other subcontainers to inherit the trustee's assignments.

inherited rights — A group of Entry or Attribute rights that flow down to other containers or leaf objects.

[Public] trustee object — A special trustee object created during the NetWare installation that consists of all client computers attached to the network.

Read Attribute right — An eDirectory security right that includes the Compare right and allows the trustee to view values stored in an object's property fields.

Rename Entry right — An eDirectory security right that grants the right to change the name of an object.

[Root] trustee object — A special trustee object that represents all users defined in the eDirectory tree. All users who have logged in to the eDirectory tree are part of the [Root] trustee object.

Supervisor Attribute right — An eDirectory security right that grants all rights to a property unless blocked by an object's IRF.

Supervisor Entry right — An eDirectory security right that grants all access privileges, including the Supervisor right to all the object's attributes or properties.

Write Attribute right — An eDirectory security right that includes the Add Self right and allows the trustee to change information in property fields.

REVIEW QUESTIONS

1. When creating a Directory Map object, which of the following security assignments would allow users to use the Directory Map object?

   a. Read right to All Properties

   b. Read Entry right

   c. Browse Entry right

   d. Write right to the Path property

2. Which of the following security systems enables users to use ConsoleOne to view, access, create, and modify objects in the Directory Services tree?

   a. eDirectory

   b. file system

   c. login security

   d. eDirectory administrative role

3. Having the _____ right to the _____ property of the server object is the one exception of eDirectory security affecting file system security.

4. In the exception in Question 3, what rights would the trustee of the server object have in the SYS volume_____?

5. Any object placed in the ACL property of another object becomes a _____ of that object with certain Entry and Attribute rights.

   a. supervisor

   b. trustee

   c. manager

   d. user

6. Which of the following objects represents all users whose workstations are attached to the network?

   a. [Root]

   b. [Public]

   c. Organization

   d. network

7. Which of the following objects represents all authorized users in the network tree?

   a. [Root]

   b. [Public]

   c. Organization

   d. network

8. List the six Entry rights:

   _____

   _____

   _____

   _____

   _____

   _____

9. List the two major Attribute rights:

   _____

   _____

10. Which of the following is a special case of the Write Attribute right?

    a. Browse

    b. Create

    c. Add Self

    d. Compare

11. Which of the following is another name for Entry rights?

    a. Attribute rights

    b. Property rights

    c. Object rights

    d. Trustee rights

12. Describe one advantage of granting the Supervisor Entry right, compared to other Entry rights:

    _____

13. Which of the following describes rights flowing down the eDirectory structure?

    a. effective rights

    b. inherited rights

    c. trustee rights

    d. access rights

14. Only rights assigned with the All Attributes option will flow down from a container object to all leaf objects. True or false?

15. Which of the following is the actual eDirectory rights a user has to an object?

    a. trustee rights

    b. effective rights

    c. inherited rights

    d. attribute rights

16. Which of the following is a property of every object and contains a list of users and groups that have rights to that object?

   a. owner

   b. trustee list

   c. membership list

   d. access control list

17. Which of the following is a default right that a user has to his or her own object?

   a. Supervisor right to all properties

   b. Write right to all properties

   c. Read right to all properties

   d. Write right to the ACL property

   e. Write right to the Login Script property

18. Which of the following are tasks that can be performed by a member of the eDirectory Administrator role? (Choose all that apply.)

   a. create objects

   b. delete objects

   c. assign rights

   d. rename objects

19. By default, all clients have which of the following rights to the eDirectory tree?

   a. Read

   b. Browse

   c. Compare

   d. List

20. Assigning a user the Supervisor Entry right to which of the following objects would give a user all rights to the file system?

   a. volume

   b. server

UNIVERSAL AEROSPACE CASE PROJECTS

Your grades indicate that your instructor approves of your work. It's good to be appreciated, but the pressure is on to get your network fully operational, so your next step is to finish securing the system by applying what you have learned about eDirectory security to the Business office. In the following case projects, you define and implement the eDirectory trustee assignments necessary to give Business office users the rights they need to access and manage the resources they are responsible for.

Case Project 6-1: Defining Trustee Assignments

Figure 6-25 contains a memo Eric received from Lynn summarizing the results of the eDirectory security meetings he had with the Business office managers. Use this information to fill out an eDirectory Security Worksheet (copy the one supplied in Appendix D), showing the trustee assignments. Fill out an eDirectory IRF Worksheet (copy the one supplied in Appendix D) with any IRFs you'll need to meet these requirements. When you have completed your worksheets, have your instructor check them before continuing to Project 6-2.

6

MEMO

To: Eric Kenton

From: Lynn Dai

Date: Yesterday

Subject: Notes from the Business and Marketing security meeting

- A new container needs to be established for AeroDyn office staff.
- Only Bernie and your ##Admin user should have rights to create, rename, or delete objects in the AeroDyn office staff container.
- Lynn Dai should have rights to maintain address information on all users in the AeroDyn containers.
- Kellie Thiele has rights to maintain login scripts for all UAS users, but only Bernie Muelner should have rights to maintain login scripts in the AeroDyn staff container.
- All users in the Accounting, Desktop Publishing, and Marketing departments need rights to use their corresponding Directory Map objects.
- Both the design engineers and the desktop publishing staff need to be able to use the PubData Directory Map object.

Figure 6-25   eDirectory security memo

Case Project 6-2: Implementing Trustee Assignments

After you have verified your eDirectory trustee and IRF plans with your instructor, use NetWare Administrator and ConsoleOne to make the trustee assignments you defined on your worksheet in Project 6-1.

Case Project 6-3: Implementing IRFs

Use ConsoleOne to implement the IRFs you defined on your worksheet in Project 6-1.

7

CONFIGURING THE USER WORKSTATION ENVIRONMENT

After reading this chapter and completing the exercises, you will be able to:

♦ Identify the four types of login scripts and how they are used to map network drive letters, provide informational messages, and run special programs

♦ Identify and use login script variables and commands to write, enter, and document login scripts

♦ Plan, implement, and test login scripts to meet the access needs of users in the Universal AeroSpace organization

♦ Install and use Z.E.N.works for Desktops to help manage the user environment

After Eric Kenton finished setting up the network file system and eDirectory security, his next challenge was to make the file system easy to access and maintain. To accomplish this, he wanted to set up a consistent environment that could be managed from a central location. With NetWare 6, Novell has supplied the tools for creating a centralized and consistent environment for local workstations through the use of login scripts and Z.E.N.works. In this chapter, you learn how to use login scripts to set up a standard set of drive pointers so that you can conveniently access network directories and run applications. You also learn how to install and use Z.E.N.works for Desktops to centrally configure and manage user workstations.

LOGIN SCRIPT PROCESSING

As you learned in previous chapters, unless you select the option to reconnect drive mappings when you log in, any drive mappings you establish during a network session are effective only until you log out of the network. The next time you log in, you must reconnect each drive pointer you want to use. Requiring users to establish their drive pointers not only means they need more technical knowledge about the system, but also takes time away from productive work and can cause problems when users don't select the correct drive letters for accessing software or files. To solve these problems, Novell has provided login scripts for establishing users' network environments each time they log in. As shown in Figure 7-1, a NetWare login script consists of a set of NetWare login command statements that Novell Client processes when a user logs in.

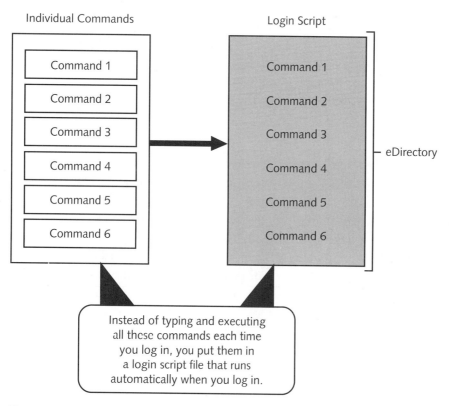

Figure 7-1   NetWare login script processing

The command statements in a login script file form a program that the client software processes after a user successfully logs in with a valid user name and password. As illustrated in Figure 7-1, the login script commands are stored in eDirectory and then sent to the user's workstation from the server. The workstation processes each command statement, one at a time, starting with the first command. As shown in Figure 7-2, the Novell Login window contains a Script tab with options for controlling how login script commands are processed.

The Run scripts check box controls whether the user's workstation processes login script commands. If you enable the Display results window option, a message is displayed for each login script command that's processed. If you want users to view messages from login scripts, you need to select this option. Selecting the Close automatically option closes the results window after all login script commands have been processed.

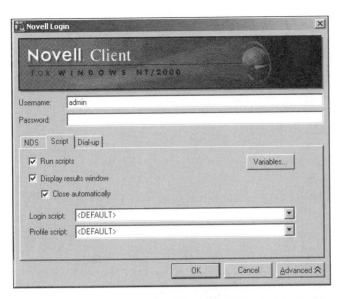

Figure 7-2   The Script tab of the Novell Login window

When testing new login scripts, you should select the Display results window option and disable the Close automatically option so that you can verify the results of your login script commands and check for any error messages. The most common problem when testing login scripts is drive mapping commands that do not work because of insufficient rights to the directory indicated in the MAP command. As a result, when implementing login script commands, you might need to review the user's file system rights, as described in Chapter 5.

If users aren't getting any network drive mappings, check to make sure the Run scripts option is enabled on their computers. If they are getting some network drive mappings but not others, check to make sure they have at least Read and File Scan rights in the directories being mapped in the login script.

Types of Login Scripts

To understand how NetWare stores and processes login scripts, you need to be aware of the types of login scripts and their purpose. For maximum flexibility, NetWare has four types of login scripts: container, profile, user, and default. Having multiple login scripts is important because it enables the network administrator to give all users a standard environment, yet allows some flexibility to meet individual user needs. A **container login script** is a property of a container that allows the network administrator to provide standard setups for all users in that container. **Profile login scripts** are special eDirectory objects that contain login commands common to multiple users, no matter in what container their user object exists. In addition to container and profile login scripts, NetWare allows for individual user requirements by supplying each user object with its own **user login script** property containing additional statements that run after the container and profile login script commands. The **default login script** is a set of commands in Novell Client used to establish a default working environment for users who don't have a user login script defined. To become a CNA, you'll need to know how these login script files work together and the sequence in which they run to set up a reliable, efficient login script system for your network. The flowchart in Figure 7-3 illustrates the relationship between the NetWare login scripts.

When a login script is created for a container, its commands are carried out when users in that container log in to the network. After all commands in the container login script run, NetWare then determines whether the user is assigned to a profile object. If the user object has a profile object assigned to it, NetWare performs any login script commands included in the profile object's Login Script property. After checking for a profile assignment, the last step is to run the commands in the user login script or the default login script. If a user does not have a user login script defined, Novell Client performs the commands in the default login script.

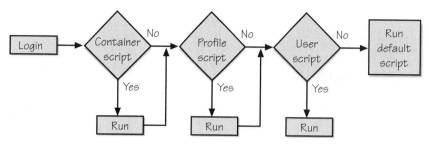

Figure 7-3   NetWare login script types

 A good way to remember the sequence of login script processing is the acronym CPU, for container, *profile*, *user* login scripts.

An important point to remember is that the login script commands that are processed last take precedence, which means drive mappings made in the user or default login script file can overwrite or replace drive mappings made by the container login script. As a result, many network administrators disable the processing of the default script and remove the rights of users to change their personal login scripts, as discussed in Chapter 6. In the following sections, you learn the purpose and processing of container, profile, user, and default login scripts and how to disable the processing of default login script commands.

Container Login Scripts

The container login script is a property of the container object, used to enter login script commands that run for each user object housed in that container. The purpose of container login scripts is to map a search drive to the Public directory and set up drive pointers that all users in a container access. When a user logs in to the network, Novell Client looks for login script commands in that user's container. Only the login script commands included in the user's home container are executed; login script commands in parent containers do not run. For example, login script commands in your ##UAS container aren't run by users in the .Engineering.##UAS or .Business.##UAS containers. That means each container's login script should include all the commands needed to set up a standard working environment for users in that container. Because your UAS tree structure has users in several different OUs, you need to create container login scripts for each container that has user accounts.

User Login Scripts

The user login script is located in the Login Script property of each user object. Unless the EXIT command is issued in the container or profile login script, Novell Client runs any login script commands in the user's Login Script property. If there are no login script commands in the user's Login Script property and the NO_DEFAULT command hasn't been issued, Novell Client runs the default login script commands.

By default, either the network administrator or the user can access and maintain the user login script by using ConsoleOne or NetWare Administrator to select the Login Script property in the user's Properties dialog box. If you don't want users to be able to modify their own login script commands, you can use the Selected properties option in ConsoleOne to remove the Write Attribute right from the user's Login Script property, as explained in Chapter 6.

Placing commands in user login scripts makes maintaining the login script environment more difficult because making changes could require accessing many separate user login script files. As a result, many network administrators prefer to place most commands in container or profile login scripts to reduce the need for user login scripts whenever possible.

Default Login Scripts

The default login script consists of several login script commands built into Novell Client. If there's no user login script file for the user who's currently logging in, Novell Client runs the default login script commands. The purpose of the default login script is to provide basic drive mappings for users until container and profile scripts have been established. The statements that make up the Novell Client default login script include the following:

- MAP *1:=SYS: (maps the first network drive to the SYS volume)

- MAP INS S1:=SYS:Public (maps the first search drive to the Public directory)

After the network administrator has established a container login script that includes the basic drive mappings for the network, it's important to prevent the default login script from running so that drive mappings in the container login script aren't overwritten or duplicated. NetWare has three basic ways to stop the default login script from running:

- Place the NO_DEFAULT statement in the container or profile login script.

- Provide a user login script for each user on the network, even if the user login script contains only the EXIT command.

- Include an EXIT command in the container or profile login script. The EXIT command ends the login script process and therefore prevents all subsequent login scripts from running. Placing the EXIT command in the container login script isn't usually a good option, however, because it also prevents profile login scripts from running.

Although some network administrators avoid large or complex login scripts, most actually prefer having one large container login script program to manage a user's network environment, instead of having lots of user and profile login scripts that require looking in many different places when problems occur. Based on your network environment and personal preference, you need to decide on the method that's best for you and your network. In the following activity, you enter a simple container login script that works with the default login script to map drives to the SYS and CORP volumes when you log in with your UasAdmin account from the ##UAS Organization.

Activity 7-1: Entering a Container Login Script

Time Required: 10 minutes

Objectives: Create and enter login script commands and variables.

Description: Currently, when you log in as UasAdmin, you have only the default login script commands, which map drive F: to the SYS volume and a search drive to the SYS:Public directory. In this activity, you create a login script for the ##UAS container that maps drive G: to your UASHOST_CORP volume. The default login script then continues to map drive F: to SYS and the search drive to SYS:Public. In this activity, you also log in using your user name in your IS.##UAS container and observe that the login script entered in the parent ##UAS container doesn't run for users logging in from accounts in subcontainers of ##UAS.

1. If necessary, start your computer, and log in with your UasAdmin user name and password.

2. Start ConsoleOne, and expand **UAS_Tree** and your **##UAS** container.

3. Right-click your **##UAS** Organization, and click **Properties** to open the Properties of ##UAS dialog box.

4. Click the **Login Script** tab to display the Login Script text box.

5. Click in the Login Script text box, enter the following command, and press **Enter**:

   ```
   MAP G:=UASHOST_Corp:
   ```

6. Click **OK** to save the login script and return to the main ConsoleOne window.

7. Exit ConsoleOne, and log out to display a new login window.

8. Log in with your UasAdmin user name and password.

9. Double-click the **My Computer** icon, and record the network drives on your student answer sheet. (If your login script worked, you should have drive G: mapped to your UASHOST_CORP volume.)

10. Close the My Computer window, and log out to display a new login window.

11. Change the default context to your IS.##UAS container, and log in as LMcMann.

12. Double-click the **My Computer** icon, and record the network drives on your student answer sheet. Does Luke have a drive mapped to the UASHOST_CORP volume? On your student answer sheet, explain why he does or does not have a drive mapped to this volume.

13. Close the My Computer window, and log out.

Profile Login Scripts

The purpose of a profile login script is to allow you to create a standard set of login commands that are performed only by selected users. Profile login scripts are set up by creating a profile object in a container and then entering the login script command in the profile object's Login Script property. Profile login scripts are independent from the container object, so they have the advantage of being available to users in any container because those users are granted Read Attribute rights to the profile object's Login Script property. A limitation of profile scripts is that users can have only one profile object associated with their user names.

In Chapter 6, Luke McMann designated Kellie Thiele as the one responsible for the company's login scripts because of her programming background. When designing the login scripts for the UAS network, Kellie felt that using profile scripts to store the MAP commands common to users in multiple containers would be easier to manage than repeating the commands in each of the IS, Engineering, Mfg, and Mgmt container login scripts. For example, all users in the WebMgrs group (currently Kellie and Julie Damrau) have access to the IS\Web directory. To make it easier to access files in the Web directory, Julie recommended assigning drive pointer W: (for Web site) to the directory for users who need to work with those files. For all members of the WebMgrs group to have the same drive mappings, Kellie created a profile object named WebProfile in the UAS Organization that contained the commands common to all users in the WebMgrs group. To enable users to use the profile login script, Kellie used ConsoleOne to give the WebMgrs group the Read Attribute right to the profile object's Login Script property. She then assigned the profile object to the Profile Login Script property of her user account in the IS container and Julie's user account in the Business container. In the future, other users can easily be added to help manage the Web site by adding their user names to the WebMgrs group and then associating their user names with the WebProfile object. In the following activity, you enter and test a profile login script object by creating a WebProfile object for your version of the UAS network.

Activity 7-2: Entering a Profile Login Script

Time Required: 10 minutes

Objectives: Create and enter login script commands and variables.

Description: The WebMgrs group contains users from several departments who need to work together on the UAS Web site. To give the group members a drive mapping to the IS\Web directory, Kellie could place a MAP command in each department's container login script. Kellie thought a better solution for UAS would be implementing a WebProfile login script that contains the necessary login commands for the WebMgrs group and then attaching the WebProfile object to each group member. In this activity, you create a WebProfile profile login script and assign it to Kellie. You then test the profile script by logging in as different users and checking your drive mappings.

1. If necessary, start your computer, and log in with your UasAdmin user name and password.

2. Start ConsoleOne, and expand **UAS_Tree** and your **##UAS** container.

3. Click your **##UAS** Organization to display all existing objects.

4. Click the **New Object** button on the ConsoleOne toolbar to open the New Object dialog box.

5. Scroll down and click to select the **Profile** object type, and then click **OK** to open the New Profile dialog box.

6. Enter WebProfile in the Name text box, and click the **Define additional properties** check box.

7. Click **OK** to create the profile object and open the Properties of WebProfile dialog box.

8. Click the **Login Script** tab.

9. Enter the following command in the Login Script text box:

```
MAP ROOT W:=UASHOST_CORP:IS\Web
```

10. Click **Apply**, and then click **Close** to save the login script and return to the main ConsoleOne window.

11. Grant the WebMgrs group the rights to read the profile login script:

    a. In the ConsoleOne window, right-click the **WebProfile** object, and then click **Properties** to open the Properties of WebProfile dialog box.

    b. Click the **NDS Rights** tab to display the trustees of the WebProfile object.

    c. Click the **Add Trustee** button to open the Select Object dialog box.

    d. Click the **WebMgrs** group, and then click **OK** to open the Rights assigned to selected objects dialog box.

    e. Click the **[All Attributes Rights]** item, and verify that the Read and Compare rights are selected.

    f. Click **OK** to place your new trustee assignment into the Trustees list box.

    g. Click **OK** to save your changes and return to the main ConsoleOne window.

12. Attach the WebProfile object to the KThiele user account:

    a. Click the **IS** OU to display all user objects.

    b. Right-click **KThiele** in the Object frame, and then click **Properties** to open the Properties of KThiele dialog box.

    c. Scroll to the right, if necessary, and click the **Login Script** tab to display the Login Script text box.

    d. Click the **Browse** button next to the Profile text box to open the Select Object dialog box.

    e. Click the **up arrow** to move up one level.

    f. Click the **WebProfile** object, and then click **OK** to place it in the Profile text box.

    g. Click **OK** to save the changes to the user login script and return to the main ConsoleOne window.

13. Exit ConsoleOne, and log out to display a new login window.

14. Log in as KThiele in your IS context.

15. Double-click the **My Computer** icon, and record the network drive mappings on your student answer sheet. Verify that your W: drive is mapped to the IS\Web directory.

If your drive mapping fails, make sure you have made Kellie a member of the WebMgrs group and that the WebMgrs group has rights to the IS\Web folder.

16. Log out to display a new login window. Change the default context to your Engineering.##UAS container, and then log in as KMeans.

17. Double-click the **My Computer** icon, and record Kari's drive mappings on your student answer sheet.

18. Close the My Computer window, and log out.

LOGIN SCRIPT PROGRAMMING

Creating login scripts is much like writing programs with any programming language. To write login scripts, you need to learn the valid commands along with the syntax, or rules, for formatting the commands. In addition, like any other programming language, login script commands can use variables so that one command can have multiple values. In the following sections, you learn how to use login script commands and variables to create sophisticated login scripts that can set up user drive mappings and display announcements and other messages to users.

Figure 7-4 illustrates a simple container login script program to map drive letters for all users in an OU. Notice that the script contains statements to display a greeting message and establish a network environment by mapping the drive pointers you identified in Chapter 3. In the following activity, you enter and test the login script commands in Figure 7-4 in your IS container. In later activities, you'll apply additional login commands to your IS container script to create the container login script Kellie developed as a model for all UAS OUs.

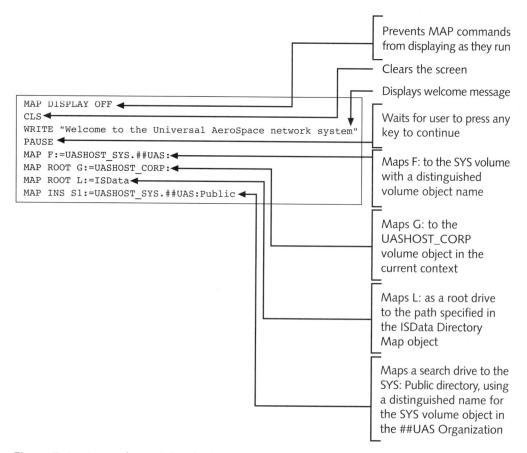

Figure 7-4 A sample container login script

Activity 7-3: Entering the IS Organizational Unit Login Script

Time Required: 10 minutes

Objectives: Create and enter login script commands and variables.

Description: In this activity, you enter the login script from Figure 7-4 for your IS OU and then practice using the client login script options to run the login script when you log in.

1. If necessary, start your computer, and log in with your UasAdmin user name and password.

2. Start ConsoleOne, and expand **UAS_Tree** and your **##UAS** container.

3. Right-click your **IS** OU, and then click **Properties** to open the Properties of IS dialog box.

4. Enter the login script shown in Figure 7-4:

    a. Click the **Login Script** tab to display the Login Script text box.

    b. Enter the login script commands shown in Figure 7-4.

    c. Click **OK** to save the login script and return to the main ConsoleOne window.

5. Exit ConsoleOne, and log out.

6. In the Novell Login window, change the context to IS.##UAS, and enter your user name and password in the Username and Password text boxes.

7. Set up Novell Client to display your login script results and not automatically close the login window:

    a. Click the **Advanced** button, and then click the **Script** tab to display the options shown previously in Figure 7-2.

    b. If necessary, click the **Close automatically** check box to disable this option.

8. Click **OK** to log in. A results window similar to the one in Figure 7-5 will be displayed with the welcome message.

Figure 7-5   The results window

9. Press the spacebar to continue. The drive mappings will be added to your results window.

10. Record the drive mappings on your student answer sheet. Identify any drive letters that are repeated.

Repeated drive letters could mean that the default login script is running or that the user has a personal user script that is changing drive mappings. You'll learn how to disable the default login script in Activity 7-5.

11. Click the **Close** button to close the results window, and log out.

12. Repeat the login process with the client set to automatically close the results window:

 a. Click the **Advanced** button, and then click the **Script** tab.

 b. Click the **Close automatically** check box.

 c. Click **OK** to log in.

13. On your student answer sheet, record the contents of the results window.

14. Close any open windows, and log out.

Login Script Variables

Login script programs consist of a limited number of command statements in the NetWare login script language. As a CNA, you'll need to know how to use this language to design and write login scripts for your organization. As with other programming languages, the NetWare login script language allows the use of variables in many of the command statements. A **login script variable** is a reserved word in the login script language whose value can change for each user logging in. By using login script variables, you can write a login script program that works for many different users and workstations. In the following sections, you learn what a CNA needs to know about login script variables and commands to design and write login script programs for the UAS network.

You may find it helpful to check Novell's Web site at *http://novell.com* for more information on login script commands and variables.

Because login script variables play an important role in writing login script programs to meet the needs of many different users, you should gain an understanding of how login script variables are used in login script command statements so that you can successfully learn the NetWare login script language. Login script variables can be divided into types based on their usage: date variables, time variables, user variables, workstation variables, and user-defined variables. The following sections discuss how each type is used and describe the specific variables associated with each type.

When placing login script variables in commands, it's important to remember to capitalize the variable and precede it with a percent sign (%). (See the section "Using Login Script Variables" later in this chapter for more information.)

Date Variables

Date variables contain information about the current day of the week, the month, and the year in a variety of formats, as shown in Table 7-1.

Date variables can be useful when displaying current date information or to check for a specific day to perform certain tasks. For example, the Engineering users need to meet at 10:00 a.m. each Monday to review weekly work projects. Using the DAY_OF_WEEK variable, you could write login script commands to display a message on Monday morning reminding them of the meeting. When using date variables, note that their values are stored as fixed-length ASCII strings. For example, the DAY variable contains the day number of the current month and ranges from 01 to 31, but the NDAY_OF_WEEK variable contains values ranging from 1 to 7.

Table 7-1   Date Variables

Variable	Description
DAY	Day number of the current month, with possible values from "01" to "31"
DAY_OF_WEEK	Name of the current day of the week, with possible values of "Monday," "Tuesday," "Wednesday," and so on
MONTH	The number of the current month, with possible values from "01" for January to "12" for December
MONTH_NAME	The name of the current month, with possible values from "January" to "December"
NDAY_OF_WEEK	The current weekday number, ranging from "1" for Sunday to "7" for Saturday
SHORT_YEAR	The last two digits of the current year, such as "02" or "03"
YEAR	The full four-digit year, such as "2002" or "2003"

7

Time Variables

The **time variables**, shown in Table 7-2, offer a variety of ways to view or check the login time.

Table 7-2   Time Variables

Variable	Description
AM_PM	Day or night (a.m. or p.m.)
GREETING_TIME	Used for displaying welcome messages, with possible values of "Morning," "Afternoon," or "Evening"
HOUR	The current hour of the day or night in the range of "01" through "12"
HOUR24	The current hour in 24-hour mode, ranging from "01" for 1 a.m. to "24" for 12 a.m.
MINUTE	The current minute, ranging from "00" to "59"
SECOND	The current second, ranging from "00" to "59"

The GREETING_TIME variable is most often used in WRITE statements to display welcome messages. The difference between the HOUR24 variable and the HOUR variable is that the HOUR variable requires using the AM_PM variable to determine whether the specified time is before or after noon. The HOUR24 variable uses a 24-hour clock, so hour 12 is noon, hour 13 is 1 p.m., and so forth. When checking for a specific time, the HOUR24 variable is often easier to use. For example, if you want all users who log in before 3:00 p.m. to be notified of a special meeting, you could write login script commands that use the HOUR24 variable to compare the current login hour to 15. If HOUR24 is less than 15, the login script commands could display a message about the meeting.

User Variables

The user variables, shown in Table 7-3, allow you to view or check the user's login name, full name, or hexadecimal user ID that's given to the user in eDirectory.

Table 7-3   User Variables

Variable	Description
FULL_NAME	The user's full name, as defined by SYSCON or USERDEF
LOGIN_NAME	The user's unique login name
USER_ID	The hexadecimal number assigned by NetWare for the user login name
HOME_DIRECTORY	The path to the user's home directory

The LOGIN_NAME and FULL_NAME variables can be used to personalize greeting messages by including the user's name. The HOME_DIRECTORY variable is useful for mapping a drive letter that points to the user's home directory. You'll use this variable in Activity 7-4 to automate the process of mapping drive letter H: to the user's home directory.

Workstation Variables

The **workstation variables** are shown in Table 7-4. The MACHINE, OS, and OS_VERSION variables are most commonly used in the system login script when mapping a search drive to the correct DOS version used on the workstation. The STATION variable contains the connection number assigned to the user's workstation; sometimes software packages use this variable to separate the user's temporary files by including the station number as part of the temporary filename. The P_STATION variable contains the actual node address of the workstation logging in and can be used in login script files to carry out certain processing tasks on specific workstations. For example, suppose only workstation address 000DC03D7D27 is used to run the new CAD software. In the login script, you could write commands to use the P_STATION variable to check for the station address 000DC03D7D27, and then set up the necessary drive mappings and start the CAD software. The NETWORK_ADDRESS variable can be used to display or check the IPX address of the cable attached to the workstation that the user is logging in from.

Table 7-4   Workstation Variables

Variable	Description
OS	The workstation's operating system; default value is "MSDOS"
OS_VERSION	The version of DOS used on the workstation processing the login script, such as "V6.20"
MACHINE	The long machine name that can be assigned in the Shell.cfg or Net.cfg file; default value is "IBM_PC"
P_STATION	The node address of the network card in the workstation, expressed as a 12-digit hexadecimal value
SMACHINE	The short machine name that can be assigned in the Shell.cfg or Net.cfg file; default value is "IBM"
STATION	The connection number of the current station
SHELL_TYPE	The workstation's shell version number
NETWORK_ADDRESS	The network address of the cabling system the user's workstation is attached to, expressed as an eight-digit hexadecimal number
FILE_SERVER	The name of the current file server

Workstation variables are most often used to allow drive mappings for software utility directories to be established according to the client computer's hardware or operating system.

User-Defined Variables

Based on the workstation or applications they need to run, more advanced network users might want to modify certain login script parameters when they log in. Novell Client offers **user-defined variables**, represented with a number preceded by a percent sign, as a way for users to enter parameters for their login scripts. To enter these variables, click the Variables button in the Script tab of the Novell Login window, and you'll see a dialog box like the one shown in Figure 7-6. Because the first variable parameter, %1, is reserved for system use, the user variables start with %2.

Figure 7-6   User-defined variables

When testing software for different departments, Kellie needs to be able to modify the drive mapping for drive letter L: to point to the departments' shared work directories. To be able to select a department's directory path when she logs in, she decides to use the %2 user-defined variable to represent the department name. She then enters the following command in her personal login script to map drive letter L: to the department name that's stored in the %2 variable:

```
MAP ROOT L:=UASHOST_CORP:\%2
```

Now when she logs in, the client computer will perform all commands in the ##UAS container login script and then perform the preceding command, substituting the department name she specified for the %2 variable. For example, if she enters "Engineer" for %2 in the Variables dialog box, the MAP command would become MAP ROOT L:=UASHOST_CORP:\Engineer.

Using Login Script Variables

As described previously, a login script variable is a reserved word that's replaced with an actual value when the login script is processed. To see how login script variables work, let's examine using a login script variable to display the current date in the greeting message and assign a drive pointer to the home directory for each user in your IS OU. To assign a drive pointer to each user's home directory without login script variables, you would have to create a separate user login script for each user that contains a MAP command to his or her home directory, as shown in Figure 7-7.

As you can see, creating a separate login script for each user involves a lot of extra work and redundancy. An alternative is creating a single login script that works for all users in the OU. Notice in Figure 7-7 that each user's directory name is the same as his or her login name. As you learned in Chapter 4, when creating new users with ConsoleOne, each user's home directory is given the same name as the user's login name by default. The path to the user's home directory is then stored as a property of the user account in the eDirectory database. When users' home directory paths are included with their user account information, you can substantially reduce the number of statements in the login script by using the HOME_DIRECTORY variable in the MAP command statement, as shown in the following example:

```
MAP ROOT H:=%HOME_DIRECTORY
```

A container login script is processed by any user in the container when he or she logs in to the network. The percent sign (%) in front of the variable name is necessary to tell Novell Client to substitute the path to the user's home directory for the HOME_DIRECTORY variable during the login process. Notice, too, that the login script variable name is entered in all uppercase letters.

 Because many login script command statements require variable names to be capitalized, it's a good practice to capitalize all login script variable names.

Therefore, when Kellie logs in, the Novell Client software running on her computer replaces the %HOME_DIRECTORY variable with the path to her home directory, and the H: drive letter is mapped to the IS\KThiele home directory. When Bernie Muelner logs in, the Novell Client software on his computer replaces the %HOME_DIRECTORY variable with the user name BMuelner, causing his H: drive letter to be mapped to the IS\BMuelner directory. In the following activity, you practice using more variables in login scripts for your version of the UAS network.

Script for Kellie

MAP DISPLAY OFF
WRITE "Welcome to the Universal AeroSpace network system"
MAP INS S1:=UASHOST_SYS:Public
MAP F:=UASHOST_SYS:
MAP G:=UASHOST_CORP:##Corp
#CAPTURE Q=IS_Q NB NT TI=5
MAP ROOT H:=UASHOST_CORP:\##Corp\IS\KThiele
DRIVE H:

Script for your user

MAP DISPLAY OFF
WRITE "Welcome to the Universal AeroSpace network system"
MAP INS S1:=UASHOST_SYS:Public
MAP F:=UASHOST_SYS:
MAP G:=UASHOST_CORP:##Corp
#CAPTURE Q=IS_Q NB NT TI=5
MAP ROOT H:=UASHOST_CORP:##Corp\IS\yourname
DRIVE H:

Script for Luke

MAP DISPLAY OFF
WRITE "Welcome to the Universal AeroSpace network system"
MAP INS S1:=UASHOST_SYS:Public
MAP F:=UASHOST_SYS:
MAP G:=UASHOST_CORP:##Corp
#CAPTURE Q=IS_Q NB NT TI=5
MAP ROOT H:=UASHOST_CORP:\##Corp\IS\LMcMann
DRIVE H:

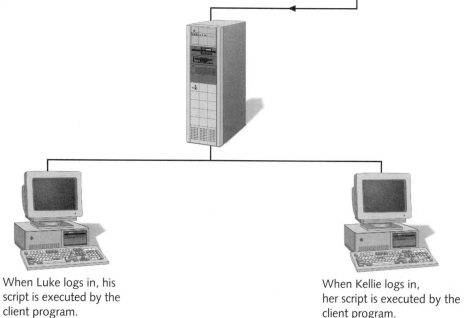

When Luke logs in, his
script is executed by the
client program.

When Kellie logs in,
her script is executed by the
client program.

Figure 7-7   Using individual user login scripts

Activity 7-4: Using Variables in Login Scripts

Time Required: 10 minutes

Objectives: Create and enter login script commands and variables.

Description: In this activity, you modify the login script for your IS container to include login script variables in commands that display a greeting message and map drive letter H: to each user's home directory.

1. If necessary, start your computer, and log in with your UasAdmin user name and password.

2. Start ConsoleOne, and expand **UAS_Tree** and your **##UAS** container.

3. Right-click your **IS** OU, and then click **Properties** to open the Properties of IS dialog box.

4. Modify your IS container script to include commands that will display a greeting message and map drive letter H: to the user's home directory:

   a. Click the **Login Script** tab.

b. Modify the login script commands to add the following greeting message before the PAUSE statement:

```
WRITE "Good %GREETING_TIME, %LOGIN_NAME"
```

c. Modify the login script to add the following command to the end of the login script:

```
MAP ROOT H:=%HOME_DIRECTORY
```

d. Verify that your login script looks like the one in Figure 7-8, and then click **OK** to save your login script changes and return to the ConsoleOne main window.

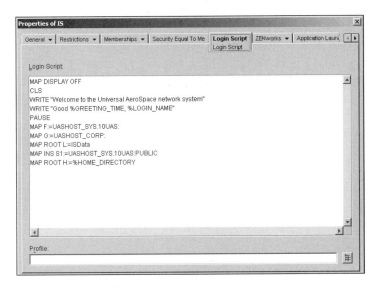

Figure 7-8 The IS container login script

5. Exit ConsoleOne, and log out to display a new login window.

6. Verify that the login script window will not close automatically:

a. Click the **Advanced** button, and then click the **Script** tab to display the login script options.

b. If necessary, click the **Close automatically** check box to disable this option.

c. Click the **NDS** tab and, if necessary, change the context to your **.IS.##UAS** container.

7. Log in as the KThiele user.

8. Verify that there are no error messages, and then click **Close** to close the results window.

9. Double-click the **My Computer** icon, and on your student answer sheet, record the path for each network drive letter.

10. Close the My Computer window, and log out.

11. Log in using your CKent user name. Record the error message when the system attempts to map drive letter H: to Clark's home directory. Because no home directory is specified in the eDirectory database, an error message is displayed. You'll learn how to correct this problem using IF statements in Activity 7-9. Close the results window.

12. Double-click the **My Computer** icon, and record Clark's drive mappings on your student answer sheet.

13. Close the My Computer window, and log out.

Writing Login Scripts

In many ways, creating login scripts is similar to writing a computer program. As in any programming language, there are specific valid commands that cause the computer to perform certain processing, and there are rules that must be followed for the commands to be processed. These rules are commonly referred to as the **syntax** of the programming language. In the following sections, you learn the valid syntax for the NetWare login script commands and examine examples of how to use the commands to perform common login functions. Before studying the login script commands, you should be aware of these general rules for their use:

- Only valid login script command statements and comments can be placed in a login script file.

- Login script command lines can be a maximum of 150 characters.

- Long commands can be allowed to "wrap" to the next line if there's not enough room on one line.

- Novell Client reads the login script commands one line at a time, and only one command is allowed on any command line.

- Commands can be entered in either uppercase or lowercase letters, except for variable values that are enclosed in quotation marks, which must be preceded by a percent sign (%) and typed in uppercase letters.

- Comments are entered by preceding the text with the command REM, an asterisk (*), or a semicolon (;).

The CLS Command

The CLS command is used simply to clear the screen. Normally, it's a good idea to precede messages to users by clearing the screen and firing multiple phaser blasts (see "The FIRE PHASERS Command," later in this chapter), which gets the user's attention and makes the message more likely to be read. You might want to follow the message with another CLS command to remove the message from the screen. If you do, be sure to follow the message with a PAUSE command, or the user will not have time to read it.

The MAP Command

The MAP command is perhaps the most important login script command because it automatically sets up both regular and search drive mappings that a user needs to access files and software in the NetWare environment. The syntax and use of the MAP login script command is very similar to the MAP command-line utility described in Chapter 3, except that you can use identifier variables and relative drive letters as part of the MAP login script command, as follows:

        MAP [option] [drive:=path;drive:=path] [variable]

 The semicolon in the MAP command is optional, used only to separate drive mappings when multiple drive letters are being mapped.

You can replace [option] with one of the parameters shown in Table 7-5.

Table 7-5   MAP Command Options

Optional Parameter	Description
ROOT	Used to make a drive appear as the root of a volume to DOS and application programs, and must be used for Windows Explorer to point to the subdirectory; including the ROOT parameter on all drive mappings is usually a good practice
INS	Used to insert a new search drive at the sequence number you specify and renumber any existing search drives
DEL	Used to remove the specified regular or search drive mapping

The [drive:] parameter must be replaced with a valid network, local, or search drive. In addition to using a specific drive letter, you can use a relative drive specification, such as *1: to indicate the first network drive, *2: for the second network drive, and so on. Then if the workstation's first network drive letter is F:, *1 will be replaced with F:, and *2: will be replaced with G:. On the other hand, if a workstation's first network drive is L:, *1: will be replaced with L:, and *2: will be replaced with J:. Replace [path] with a full directory path, beginning with a DOS drive letter or NetWare volume name.

With the login script version of the MAP command, additional drive mappings can be placed on the same line by separating them with semicolons. For example, if you wanted to map the F: drive to the SYS volume and the G: drive to the DATA volume, you could do so with this MAP command:

```
MAP F:=SYS:;G:=DATA:
```

Other special MAP command statements include MAP DISPLAY OFF and MAP ERRORS OFF. The MAP DISPLAY OFF command prevents MAP commands from being displayed on user workstations and is often included at the beginning of a login script command to reduce the amount of information displayed on users' workstations. The MAP ERRORS OFF command can be used to prevent the display of error messages generated by MAP commands that specify invalid paths. This command is useful if you include drive mapping commands in a login script that you know won't be valid for all users. Rather than have users confused by receiving error messages that don't affect them, you can include the MAP ERRORS OFF command before the MAP commands that contain the invalid drive paths. When first testing login scripts, however, you need to see the results of MAP commands and any error messages. Therefore, you should wait until after login scripts have been tested and debugged to add the MAP DISPLAY OFF and MAP ERRORS OFF commands.

The NO_DEFAULT Command

The NO_DEFAULT login script command prevents the default login script commands from running when users do not have their own login scripts. However, once you implement a login script system, running the default login script can overwrite your drive mappings and cause multiple drive mappings and error messages. As a result, it's important to include the NO_DEFAULT command at the beginning of each container's login script to prevent the default script from running. In the following activity, you use this command in your IS container to prevent the default login script from running.

Activity 7-5: Preventing Default Login Script Execution

Time Required: 10 minutes

Objectives: Create and enter login script commands and variables.

Description: In this activity, you modify your IS container login script to include the NO_DEFAULT login script command and then test the command by logging back in with your user name and observing that the extra MAP commands are no longer being displayed.

1. If necessary, start your computer, and log in with your UasAdmin user name and password.

2. Start ConsoleOne, and expand **UAS_Tree** and your **##UAS** container.

3. Right-click your **IS** OU, and then click **Properties** to open the Properties of IS dialog box.

4. Click the **Login Script** tab to display your existing login script.

5. Add the following command to the beginning of your IS container login script:

```
NO_DEFAULT
```

6. Click **OK** to save the changes and return to the main ConsoleOne window.

7. Log out to display a new Novell Login window.

8. Log in as KThiele:

   a. Enter **KThiele** in the Username text box.

   b. Enter the password for KThiele in the Password text box.

   c. Click the **NDS** tab and, if necessary, change the context to the **IS.##UAS** container.

   d. Click **OK** to log in.

   e. Read the welcome message, and then press any key to continue.

9. No additional login script commands should be displayed in the results window when the default login script is disabled. On your student answer sheet, record the contents of the results window after completing Step 8.

10. Click **Close** to close the results window.

11. Double-click the **My Computer** icon, and on your student answer sheet, record the path to each drive letter. Because the default login script doesn't run, no duplicate paths should exist.

12. Close the My Computer window, and log out.

The CONTEXT Command

As you learned in Chapter 2, accessing network resources is much easier when your current context is set to the container that holds the objects you need to use, which is usually accomplished with the Advanced button in the Novell Login window. However, if a user logs in using his or her distinguished user name, the client computer's current context isn't changed. By using the CONTEXT login script command, however, you can change the client computer's current context to another container when a user logs in. The syntax of the CONTEXT command includes the typeful distinguished name of the container that will become the default context. For example, to set the default container to the IS OU, you would enter this command:

```
CONTEXT .OU=IS.O=UAS
```

Being able to automatically change the context is important when using Directory Map objects and volume names in the login script MAP commands. If the context is not changed to the correct container, the Directory Map object might not be found or the wrong volume could be used in the MAP command. For example, to test software, Kellie often needs to log in from other users' workstations. To use her distinguished name instead of selecting the context in the Novell Login window each time she logs in, she included the CONTEXT .OU=IS.O=UAS command in the IS container login script. In the following activity, you modify your IS container login script to include a CONTEXT command.

Activity 7-6: Using the CONTEXT Command

Time Required: 10 minutes

Objectives: Create and enter login script commands and variables.

Description: In this activity, you add the CONTEXT command to your IS container login script and then test the login script to verify that the context is set to your IS OU.

1. If necessary, start your computer, and log in with your UasAdmin user name and password.

2. Start ConsoleOne, and expand **UAS_Tree** and your **##UAS** container.

3. Right-click your **IS** OU, and then click **Properties** to open the Properties of IS dialog box.

4. Click the **Login Script** tab to display the current login script commands.

5. Insert CONTEXT command immediately after the PAUSE command that will change the context to your IS OU. For example, depending on the structure of your classroom server, insert one of the following CONTEXT commands:
```
CONTEXT .OU=IS.O=.##UAS
CONTEXT .OU=IS.OU=##UAS.O=CLASS
```

6. Click **OK** to save your changes and return to the main ConsoleOne window.

7. Exit ConsoleOne, and log out to display a new login window.

8. Log in as KThiele.

9. On your student answer sheet, record the context message you see in the results window after pressing a key to continue.

10. Click **Close** to close the results window, and log out.

The WRITE Command

The WRITE command is used to display simple messages enclosed in quotation marks on users' workstations. Messages can also contain identifier variables and special control strings, as shown in the WRITE command syntax:

```
WRITE "text [control string] [%variable]"
```

Common login script variables often used with the WRITE command include %GREETING_TIME and %LOGIN_NAME. The %GREETING_TIME variable contains the current time expressed as "Morning," "Afternoon," or "Evening." For example, many network administrators include a WRITE statement such as the following, with a greeting message at the beginning of the login script to display the login time and user's full name:

```
WRITE "Good %GREETING_TIME, %LOGIN_NAME"
```

Important messages that you want to be sure all users see and acknowledge should be followed with the PAUSE statement, as shown here:

```
WRITE "File server will be coming down today, March 1, at 5:00 p.m. for
a maintenance call."
PAUSE
```

In the following activity, you modify your existing login script to use the WRITE command to display a greeting message on users' workstations.

Activity 7-7: Writing Messages with Login Scripts

Time Required: 10 minutes

Objectives: Create and enter login script commands and variables.

Description: In this activity, you modify your IS container login script to add a command that will display the greeting time before the welcome message.

1. If necessary, start your computer, and log in with your UasAdmin user name and password.
2. Start ConsoleOne, and expand **UAS_Tree** and your **##UAS** container.
3. Right-click your **IS** OU, and then click **Properties** to open the Properties of IS dialog box.
4. Click the **Login Script** tab to display the current login script commands.
5. Add the following command immediately before your current WRITE statement, and press **Enter**:

Note that the WRITE statement must appear on one line, so do not press Enter until you have typed /%YEAR" at the end of the statement.

```
WRITE "It's %HOUR:%MINUTE %AM_PM on %DAY_OF_WEEK, %MONTH/%DAY/%YEAR"
```

6. Click **OK** to save the login script change and return to the main ConsoleOne window.
7. Exit ConsoleOne, and log out.
8. Log in as KThiele, and on your student answer sheet, record the contents of your results window.

Users with no entry in the Full Name text box will have the word "Unknown" displayed in place of their full name. If necessary, you should use ConsoleOne to enter a full name for your users.

9. Close the results window, and log out.

The DISPLAY and FDISPLAY Commands

The DISPLAY and FDISPLAY (for "filtered display") commands are used to show the contents of an ASCII text file onscreen when the login script runs. This is the proper syntax for both commands:

```
DISPLAY (or FDISPLAY) [directory path] filename
```

If the [*filename*] specified is in the current directory, or if a search drive has been established to the directory containing the [*filename*], the directory path is not needed. However, in the following example, even though a search drive has been created for SYS:Public, the Welcome.msg file is in the Message subdirectory. Therefore, you need to include the FDISPLAY command as shown to make sure the message file is found:

```
MAP INS S1:=SYS:Public
FDISPLAY SYS:Public\Message\Welcome.msg
PAUSE
```

An error message will be displayed if the file specified in the DISPLAY command does not exist.

You should follow the DISPLAY or FDISPLAY command with a PAUSE statement to give the user time to read the message file. The difference between DISPLAY and FDISPLAY is that the FDISPLAY command "filters" and formats the contents of the specified filename so that only the ASCII text is displayed. FDISPLAY does not display tab characters, but converts them into spaces to make the output more readable. The DISPLAY command, on the other hand, displays the exact characters contained in the file, including "garbage" characters such as printer or word-processing edit codes. As a result, using FDISPLAY with files that have been created with word-processing packages is usually preferable; however, if you use a word-processing package, be sure to save the file in ASCII text format, or not even FDISPLAY will be able to read it.

Activity 7-8: Displaying Message Files with a Login Script

Time Required: 10 minutes

Objectives: Create and enter login script commands and variables.

Description: In this activity, you create message files for each day of the week and store them in your Shared directory. You then modify your IS container login script to add a command that will display the correct message file for the current day.

1. If necessary, start your computer, and log in with your UasAdmin user name and password.

2. Start ConsoleOne, and expand **UAS_Tree** and your **##UAS** container.

3. Create text files for Monday through Friday:

    a. Expand your **UASHOST_CORP** volume.

    b. Right-click your **Shared** directory, point to **New**, and click **Object** to open the New Object dialog box.

    c. Click **File**, and then click **OK** to open New File dialog box.

    d. Enter **Monday.txt** in the Name text box.

    e. Click the **Create another file** check box, and click **OK** to create the file.

    f. Repeat Steps 3d and 3e for the next three weekdays (Tuesday through Thursday), substituting the appropriate day name for the message filename.

    g. For the Friday message file, enter **Friday.txt** in the Name text box, click **OK**, and then click **Cancel** to return to the main ConsoleOne window.

If you're logging in on the weekend, the message file will not be found, and you'll see an error in the results window. To prevent this problem, create text files for Saturday and Sunday.

4. Right-click your **IS** OU, and then click **Properties** to open the Properties of IS dialog box.

5. Click the **Login Script** tab to display the current login script commands.

6. Enter the following command before the PAUSE command, and then press **Enter**:

   `DISPLAY UASHOST_CORP:Shared\%DAY_OF_WEEK.txt`

7. Click **OK** to save your login script changes and return to the main ConsoleOne window.

8. Exit ConsoleOne.

9. Enter a message in each day's text file:

   a. Double-click the **My Computer** icon, and then double-click your **G:** drive to display all directories in your CORP volume.

   b. Double-click the **Shared** volume to display all the day files.

   c. Double-click **Monday** to edit the file in Notepad.

   d. Enter some sample text for Monday that includes the name of the day.

   e. Click **File**, **Save** on the Notepad menu bar, and then exit Notepad.

   f. Repeat Steps 9c through 9e for each day of the week to make the files unique.

10. Close all windows, and log out.

11. Log in as KThiele.

12. On your student answer sheet, record the contents of your results window.

13. Close the results window, and log out.

The # and @ Commands (Execute a DOS Program)

The external program execution (# and @) commands are used to load and run an .exe or .com program without exiting Novell Client. The # command stops the login script from processing until the specified program has finished running, but the @ command starts the executable program and then continues processing login script commands while the executable program runs in the background. The @ command is useful if you want to load continuously running programs, such as virus detection software, into the computer's memory. Using the # command would cause the login script to "hang" because the virus detection software runs continuously in memory and does not exit back to the login script processor.

 The # command cannot be used to run a batch or script file; only executable programs, such as .exe or .com files, can be run from the login script.

When using the # command, after the program finishes, the next login script command line runs. This is the syntax for the # and @ commands:

```
@ [path] filename [parameters]
# [path] filename [parameters]
```

You can optionally replace [*path*] with a full directory path, using a DOS drive letter or NetWare volume name to specify the location of the DOS program. If a network drive letter is used, make sure a previous login script MAP command is used to map the drive letter to a valid NetWare path. You must replace *filename* with the name of the .com or .exe program you want to run. The extension is not necessary. Depending on the program you're running, you can replace [*parameters*] with any parameters that should be passed to the specified program.

The external program execution character (#) is important because it lets you run other command-line utilities or DOS commands from inside the login script. For example, a possible use of the # command is to run the CAPTURE program to establish a default network printer for DOS and Windows 3.11 clients, as described in Chapter 8. Because CAPTURE is not a login script command, the # command can be used to run the CAPTURE command with the appropriate parameters.

IF ... THEN ... ELSE Statements

Network administrators often use the IF login statement to customize a login script for specific users or groups and to perform special processing when a certain condition, such as a specific day, time, or station, exists. The syntax of a simple IF statement is as follows:

```
IF condition THEN command
```

The *condition* parameter is replaced with a conditional statement that has a value of true or false. Conditional statements usually consist of an **identifier variable** and a value enclosed in quotation marks. Examples of several common conditional statements are shown in Table 7-6.

Table 7-6   Common Conditional Statements

Condition	Description
MEMBER OF "group"	This statement is true if the user is a member of the specified group.
DAY_OF_WEEK= "Monday"	This statement is true if the name of the day is Monday. Possible values range from Sunday through Saturday. Uppercase or lowercase letters can be used.
DAY="05"	This statement is true on the fifth day of the month; valid day values range from "01" to "31." You must include the leading zero for day numbers lower than 10.
MONTH="June"	This statement is true for the month of June. You can replace "June" with any valid month name from January to December. Either uppercase or lowercase letters are accepted.
NDAY_OF_WEEK="1"	This statement is true on Sunday, which is the first day of the week. Valid weekday numbers range from "1" to "7."

The *command* parameter can be replaced with any valid login script command statement. For example, a simple IF statement with a single condition can be written as follows:

```
IF DAY_OF_WEEK="FRIDAY" THEN WRITE "Hurrah it's Friday!"
```

More complex IF statements can consist of multiple commands followed by the END statement. When using complex IF statements containing multiple commands, you should use the BEGIN command after THEN, and then place the commands after the IF statement, as shown in the following example:

```
IF condition THEN BEGIN
    command 1
    command 2
    command n
END
```

When using a multiple-command IF statement, all commands between the IF statement and the END statement are performed when the condition is true. For example, to prevent the error message created when your ##UAS Organization's login script attempts to map a home directory when the Admin user logs in, you can use an IF statement similar to the following:

```
IF MEMBER OF "Design" THEN BEGIN
MAP ROOT P:=UASHOST_CORP:\Engineer\CAD
END
```

Sometimes it's best to combine multiple conditions by using AND or OR. When using OR to connect two conditions, the login commands are performed if *either* condition is true. For example, if you wanted all members of *either* the WebMgrs or ISMgrs groups to be informed of a weekly meeting, you could use this statement:

```
IF MEMBER OF "ISMgrs" OR MEMBER OF "WebMgrs" THEN BEGIN
    WRITE "Weekly Web development meeting will be in conference room 100
    starting at 10:00 a.m."
    PAUSE
END
```

The word AND is used when you want *both* statements to be true before processing the commands. For example, suppose you wanted to remind all Marketing users of a meeting on Friday morning. Before displaying the reminder, you would want to make sure the user was a member of the Marketing department, the day was Friday, and the login time was before noon. To do this, you could use AND to connect these three conditions with the following statement:

```
IF MEMBER OF "Marketing" AND DAY_OF_WEEK="Friday" AND HOUR24 < "12" THEN
```

The optional word ELSE is a helpful feature of the IF statement because it allows you to choose between sets of commands based on a certain condition. For example, the following IF...THEN...ELSE command could be used if all members of the WebMgrs group need to have their I: drive pointer mapped to the IS\Web directory, but all other users in the IS OU should have their I: drive pointer mapped to the IS\Shared directory:

```
IF MEMBER OF "WebMgrs" THEN
    MAP I:=UASHOST_CORP:IS\Web
ELSE
    MAP I:=UASHOST_CORP:IS\Shared
END
```

The EXIT Command

The EXIT command stops execution of the login script and returns control to the client computer, so no additional login script commands are processed after the EXIT command is issued.

The FIRE PHASERS Command

The purpose of the FIRE PHASERS command is to make a noise with the PC speaker to alert the user of a message coming in or a condition encountered in the login process. You should limit the use of the FIRE PHASERS command to important messages, however; otherwise, users get used to the sound and will probably miss the message. You can control the length of the phaser blast with the following command:

```
FIRE [PHASERS] n [TIMES]
```

You can replace *n* with a number from 1 to 9 to represent how many successive times the phaser sound is made. The words PHASERS and TIMES are optional and can be omitted from the FIRE login script command. FIRE PHASERS is often used with the IF statement to notify the user of a certain condition. For example, you could use the FIRE PHASERS command in an IF statement to remind users of a special meeting time, as follows:

```
IF DAY_OF_WEEK="Tuesday" AND HOUR24 < "11" THEN
    WRITE "Department meeting at 11:30 a.m."
    FIRE PHASERS 2 TIMES
    PAUSE
END
```

The REM Command

The REM command can be used with the asterisk (*) or the semicolon (;) to place a comment line in the login script. The login process skips any line that begins with REM, REMARK, *, or ;. Using comments in your login script can make the script much easier for you or another administrator to read and understand, but placing a comment on the same line as other login script commands causes errors when the script runs. To make your work easier to identify and maintain, you should use REM statements to include your name, last modified date, and a brief description of the commands in each section in the script. The name helps other programmers identify the author in case there are questions about how the login script works. The last modified date identifies the latest version of login script command listings, and command descriptions help other programmers understand the function of command sequences in the login script. In the following activity, you document your IS container login script by using REM commands to include your name and date, and then modify the script to check for group membership.

Activity 7-9: Using IF and REM Statements in Login Scripts

Time Required: 10 minutes

Objectives: Create and enter login script commands and variables.

Description: To prevent getting error messages when she attempted to map a home directory while logging in as the CKent user, Kellie included an IF command in the IS container login script to map a home directory only for users in the ISMgrs group. Because the CKent user is not a member of the ISMgrs group, including the IF statement prevents the error message. In addition, Kellie included REM statements to make it easier for Eric to maintain the scripts in her absence. In this activity, you modify your login script to include an IF statement that prevents error messages from being generated when you log in as the CKent user. In addition, you use REM commands to identify and document your IS container login script, and test the login script by logging in as CKent and checking for any error messages.

1. If necessary, start your computer, and log in with your UasAdmin user name and password.

2. Start ConsoleOne, and expand **UAS_Tree** and your **##UAS** container.

3. Right-click your **IS** OU, and then click **Properties** to open the Properties of IS dialog box.

4. Click the **Login Script** tab to display the current login script commands.

5. Add the following REM commands to the beginning of your login script, pressing **Enter** after each command:

```
REM IS Organizational Unit login script
REM Developed by: (insert your name here)
REM Date last modified: (insert date here)
```

6. Add the following IF statement before the PAUSE command, pressing **Enter** after each line (substituting the current weekday for "current day name here"):

 In the first code line, remember not to press Enter until you have typed the THEN command. The IF statement should appear on one line.

```
IF DAY_OF_WEEK="current day name here" AND HOUR24 < "next hour here"
THEN
    WRITE "Department meeting at 11:30 a.m."
    FIRE PHASERS 2 TIMES
END
```

7. To prevent getting an error message when logging in as CKent, who has no home directory, replace your existing MAP ROOT H:=%HOME_DIRECTORY command with the following IF commands:

```
IF MEMBER OF "ISMgrs" THEN
    MAP ROOT H:=%HOME_DIRECTORY
END
```

8. Click **Apply**, and then click **Close** to save the changes and return to the main ConsoleOne window.

9. Exit ConsoleOne, and log out to display a new login window.

10. Log in using the CKent user name and password, and record the contents of your results window on your student answer sheet.

11. Close the results window, and log out to display a new login window.

12. Log in using the KThiele user name and password, and record the contents of your results window on your student answer sheet.

13. Close the results window, and log out.

Documenting Login Scripts

The best way to document your login scripts for troubleshooting and planning is to print hard copies of each container and profile login script. Unfortunately, ConsoleOne and NetWare Administrator don't have options that allow you directly print login scripts. However, you can use the NLIST command-line utility to print the login scripts to a printer attached to your computer, or highlight the login script commands and use the Ctrl+C and Ctrl+V key combinations to copy and paste the commands to Notepad or WordPad. The format of the NLIST command is as follows:

```
NLIST "object type" = context SHOW "Login Script" > PRN
```

Replace *object type* with "Organization" or "Organizational Unit" and replace *context* with the path to the container. For example, to print the contents of the UAS Organization's login script on her locally attached printer, Kellie used the following command:

```
NLIST "Organizational Unit" = .UAS SHOW "Login Script" > PRN
```

In the following activity, you learn the copy-and-paste method of saving your IS container login script as a text file and then print the script on your classroom printer.

Activity 7-10: Documenting a Login Script

Time Required: 10 minutes

Objectives: Create and enter login script commands and variables.

Description: As a programmer in charge of maintaining login scripts, Kellie needs to have hard copies of the login scripts to work with. In this activity, you log in as Kellie and use the Ctrl+C and Ctrl+V commands to paste your IS container login script into Notepad, and then print it on the classroom printer.

1. If necessary, start your computer, and log in as KThiele.

2. If necessary, click **Start**, **Settings**, **Printers**, and set the UASCLASS_P printer as your default printer.

3. Start ConsoleOne, and expand **UAS_Tree** and your **##UAS** container.

4. Right-click your **IS** OU, and then click **Properties** to open the Properties of IS dialog box.

5. Click the **Login Script** tab to display your login script commands.

6. Highlight all your login script commands in the Login Script text box, hold down the **Ctrl** key, and then press **C** to copy the selected commands to the Clipboard.

7. Start Notepad by clicking **Start**, **Programs**, **Accessories**, **Notepad**.

8. Click in the Notepad window, and then hold down the **Ctrl** key and press **V** to paste the commands into the Notepad window.

9. Click **File**, **Print** on the Notepad menu bar to print your login script to the default UASCLASS_P printer.

10. Retrieve your printout from the classroom printer, exit Notepad without saving the file, exit ConsoleOne, and log out.

IMPLEMENTING LOGIN SCRIPTS FOR UNIVERSAL AEROSPACE

Once you understand the syntax and function of login script commands and variables and how to store and run login scripts, the next task is to apply login scripts to setting up a network environment for users' workstations when they log in. Implementing a login script system for your network requires three basic steps:

1. Identify the login script requirements for each container and user.

2. Write and enter the script commands.

3. Test the login script by logging in as different users.

In the following sections, you learn how to apply these steps by implementing login scripts for users in the Engineering department.

Identifying Login Script Requirements

To design a login script system for Universal AeroSpace, Eric started by identifying the user drive mappings and messages on the Login Script Requirements Worksheet, shown in Table 7-7.

Table 7-7   Login Script Requirements Worksheet

Organization: _Universal AeroSpace_   Page _1_ of _2_

Developed by: _Eric Kenton_   Date: _____

Drive Mappings			
Users	**Drive**	**Path**	**Script**
ISMgrs	F:	UASHOST_SYS:	All containers
All	G:	UASHOST_CORP:	All containers
All	S1:	UASHOST_SYS:Public	All containers
All	H:	%HOME_DIRECTORY	All containers
Engineering	L:	EngData Directory Map object	Engineering container
IS department	L:	ISData Directory Map object	IS container
Mfg	L:	MfgData Directory Map object	Mfg container
Engineering and Mfg users	S:	UASHOST_CORP:\Engineer\Shared	EngProfile profile
Design group	P:	UASHOST_CORP:\Engineer\CAD	Engineering container
Mgmt users	H:	%HOME_DIRECTORY	Mgmt container
Mgmt users	L:	MgmtData Directory Map object	Mgmt container
WebMgrs group	W:	UASHOST_CORP:IS\Web	WebProfile profile

Table 7-7 Login Script Requirements Worksheet (continued)

Organization: _Universal AeroSpace_   Page _2_ of _2_

Developed by: _Eric Kenton_   Date: _____

Messages		
Users	**Description**	**Login Script**
All	Login greeting message	All containers
All	Daily message file for Monday through Friday	All containers
Engineering	Weekly design meeting on Monday morning at 9:00 a.m.	Engineering container
Engineering and Mfg users	Monthly meeting held at 9:00 a.m. on the first Wednesday of each month to discuss documentation and promotional needs	EngProfile
WebMgrs	Monthly Web site meeting at 8:00 a.m. on the first Monday of each month	WebProfile

The first section of the Login Script Requirements Worksheet identifies the standard drive mappings for use on the network and the login script where the mapping will be performed. Drive letters, such as F:, G:, and S1:, are assigned to the same path for all users, so they are included in all container scripts. Eric has also included a profile script named EngProfile to give users in the Mfg and Engineering containers common login script commands and messages. Notice that in addition to a common drive letter for each volume, each container login script maps an H: drive to the user's home directory. The Directory Map objects created in Chapter 3 will be used to map the L: drive to each department's work directory. The Messages section of Table 7-7 defines message needs for each group of users and the login script where the message will be placed. Notice that the EngProfile profile login script will be used to send a message to users in the Engineering and Mfg containers about the weekly meeting.

Writing Login Scripts

After identifying login requirements, the next step is to plan and write the necessary login script commands. To write the login script commands for the Engineering container, Eric developed the Container Login Script Worksheet, shown in Table 7-8.

Table 7-8   Container Login Script Worksheet

Organization: *Universal AeroSpace*   Page 1 of 3

Developed by: *Eric Kenton*   Date: _____

Container Context: *Engineering.UAS*

```
REM General Commands
REM Created by: Eric Kenton
REM Last modified: 1/15/2002
NO_DEFAULT
MAP DISPLAY OFF
CONTEXT    .Engineering.UAS
MAP ROOT G:=UASHOST_CORP:
MAP ROOT H:=%HOME_DIRECTORY
MAP L:=EngData
MAP INS S1:=UASHOST_SYS:PUBLIC
CLS
WRITE "Good %GREETING_TIME,   %LOGIN_NAME"
WRITE "Welcome to the Universal AeroSpace network system"
DISPLAY UASHOST_CORP:\Shared\Messages\%DAY_OF_WEEK.MSG
IF DAY_OF_WEEK="Monday" and HOUR24 < "09" THEN BEGIN
    WRITE "Weekly design meeting at 9:00 a.m. in conference
room"
    FIRE PHASERS 2
END
PAUSE
```

```
REM Commands for Design Workgroup
IF MEMBER OF "Design" THEN
    MAP ROOT P:=L:CAD
END
```

```
REM Commands for ISMgrs Workgroup
IF MEMBER OF "ISMgrs" THEN BEGIN
    MAP F:=UASHOST_SYS:
END
```

```
REM End of Login Script Commands
```

Table 7-8   Container Login Script Worksheet (continued)

Organization: _Universal AeroSpace_   Page 2 of 3

Developed by: _Eric Kenton_   Date: _____

Container Context: _.Mfg.UAS_

```
REM General Commands
REM Created by:Eric Kenton
REM Last modified: 1/15/2002
NO_DEFAULT
MAP DISPLAY OFF
CONTEXT .Mfg.UAS
MAP ROOT G:=UASHOST_CORP:
MAP ROOT H:=%HOME_DIRECTORY
MAP L:=MfgData
MAP INS S1:=UASHOST_SYS:PUBLIC
CLS
WRITE "Good %GREETING_TIME, %LOGIN_NAME"
WRITE "Welcome to the Universal AeroSpace network system"
DISPLAY UASHOST_CORP:\Shared\Messages\%DAY_OF_WEEK.MSG
PAUSE
```

```
REM Commands for Design Workgroup
IF MEMBER OF "Design" THEN
    MAP ROOT P:=L:CAD
END
```

```
REM Commands for ISMgrs Workgroup
IF MEMBER OF "ISMgrs" THEN BEGIN
    MAP F:=UASHOST_SYS:
END
```

```
REM End of Login Script Commands
```

7

Table 7-8 Container Login Script Worksheet (continued)

Organization: _Universal AeroSpace_   Page _3_ of _3_

Developed by: _Eric Kenton_   Date: _____

Container Context: _.Mgmt.UAS_

```
REM General Commands
REM Created by:Eric Kenton
REM Last modified: 1/15/2002
NO_DEFAULT
MAP DISPLAY OFF
CONTEXT .Mgmt.UAS
MAP ROOT G:=UASHOST_CORP:
MAP ROOT H:=%HOME_DIRECTORY
MAP L:=MgmtData
MAP INS S1:=UASHOST_SYS:PUBLIC
CLS
WRITE "Good %GREETING_TIME, %LOGIN_NAME"
WRITE "Welcome to the Universal AeroSpace network system"
DISPLAY UASHOST_CORP:\Shared\Messages\%DAY_OF_WEEK.MSG
PAUSE
```

```
REM Commands for ISMgrs Workgroup
IF MEMBER OF "ISMgrs" THEN BEGIN
    MAP F:=UASHOST_SYS:
END
```

```
REM End of Login Script Commands
```

The worksheet is divided into sections, with REM statements defining the start of each section. The REM General Commands section contains any initializing commands, such as NO_DEFAULT, MAP DISPLAY OFF, and MAP S1:=UASHOST_SYS:##UAS. In addition, this section can be used to clear the screen and display a greeting message to the user. Notice how the CLS command is used to clear the screen before displaying messages. This section also contains drive mappings and messages for all users in the container. Notice the use of the EngData Directory Map object created in Chapter 3 to map drive L: to the Engineer structure. By using the Directory Map object, the Engineer directory can be changed to another volume without modifying the login script. The REM Commands for Workgroup sections contain login script commands performed only for users who are members of the specified groups. In the Engineering container worksheet, if a user is a member of the Design workgroup, he or she gets a P: drive mapping to the Publish\Shared directory. The REM End of Login Script Commands section contains commands that all users perform before exiting the login script.

Table 7-9 shows the Profile Login Script Worksheet that Eric developed for the Engineering and Web site development users to identify the profile login script commands and the names of users assigned to the profile script. The worksheet for the EngProfile profile script uses the search drive S16: to add the search drive to the end of existing search drives mapped for that user.

Table 7-9   Profile Login Script Worksheet

Organization: _Universal AeroSpace_   Page _1_ of _2_

Developed by: _Eric Kenton_   Date: _____

Profile Script Name: _EngProfile_   Container Context: _Engineering.UAS_

Login script for: **EngProfile**   profile object

Users: _LJarka_   _TRucci_

            RPence   _PAlm_

```
REM Created by: Eric Kenton
REM Last modified: 1/15/2002
MAP S:=UASHOST_CORP:\Engineer\Shared
IF DAY_OF_WEEK="Monday" AND HOUR24 < "09" THEN
    FIRE 2
    WRITE "Remember meeting at 9:00 a.m. in conference
room 100"
    PAUSE
END
```

7

Organization: _Universal AeroSpace_   Page _2_ of _2_

Developed by: _Eric Kenton_   Date: _____

Profile Script Name: _WebProfile_   Container Context: _Engineering.UAS_

Login script for: **WebProfile**   profile object

Users: _KThiele_   _____

            KMeans   _____

            JDamrau   _____

```
REM Created by: Eric Kenton
REM Last modified: 1/15/2002
MAP ROOT W:=UASHOST_CORP:IS\Web
IF DAY_OF_WEEK="Wednesday" AND HOUR24 < "10" THEN
    FIRE 2
    WRITE "Remember meeting at 10:00 a.m. in conference
room 100"
    PAUSE
END
```

Entering Login Scripts

Defining and writing the login script commands can be the most difficult part of setting up the user environment, especially if you're not a programmer. Although the container and profile login scripts for the activities have been written for you in the projects at the end of the chapter, you'll get the opportunity to create your own login script programs for the Business office users. After the login script programs have been completed, you can begin the relatively fun part of using NetWare utilities to enter and print each of your login scripts. As a CNA, you'll need to learn how to use ConsoleOne to implement and maintain container, profile, and user login scripts. In the following activities, you use ConsoleOne to enter the login scripts shown in Tables 7-8 and 7-9. You then use NetWare's NLIST command-line utility and Notepad to print your login scripts to the classroom printer.

Activity 7-11: Entering the Container Login Scripts

Time Required: 10 minutes

Objectives: Create and enter login script commands and variables.

Description: In this activity, you use ConsoleOne to enter the container login script commands for the Engineering, Mfg, and Mgmt containers.

1. If necessary, start your computer, and log in as KThiele.

2. Start ConsoleOne, and expand **UAS_Tree** and your **##UAS** container.

3. Enter the Engineering container login script:

    a. Right-click the **Engineering** container, and then click **Properties** to open the Properties of Engineering dialog box.

    b. Click the **Login Script** tab.

    c. Enter the login script commands shown in Table 7-8 for the Engineering OU.

    d. Click **OK** to save the container login script and return to the main ConsoleOne window.

4. Repeat Step 3 to enter the Mfg container login script.

5. Repeat Step 3 to enter the Mgmt container login script.

6. If you're continuing to the next activity, minimize ConsoleOne and stay logged in. If not, exit ConsoleOne, and log out.

Activity 7-12: Printing Your Login Scripts

Time Required: 10 minutes

Objective: Print login script files.

Description: In this activity, you use the NLIST command and Notepad to print your container login scripts.

1. If necessary, log in with your KThiele user name and password, and start ConsoleOne.

2. To verify that you have an H: drive mapped to Kellie's home directory, double-click the **My Computer** icon, and check for an H: drive letter. If you do not have a drive letter mapped to the KThiele home directory, you can use the C: drive for this activity.

3. Open a command-prompt window by clicking **Start**, **Run** and entering **CMD**.

4. Save the Engineering container login script as the EngScrpt.txt file on your H: or C: drive by entering the following commands, pressing **Enter** after each one:

In the last code line below (beginning with "NLIST"), do not press Enter until you have typed "EngScrpt.txt".

```
H: (or C:)
MD LoginScripts
CD LoginScripts
CX .##UAS
NLIST "Organizational Unit"=Engineering SHOW "Login Script" >
EngScrpt.txt
```

`CX .##UAS` (Enter `CX .##UAS.CLASS` if your UAS container is located within the CLASS Organization of your classroom server.)

5. Enter the NLIST command in Step 4 to save your Mfg container login script as the MfgScrpt.txt file on your H: or C: drive. Substitute **Mfg** for Engineering and replace EngScrpt.txt with **MfgScrpt.txt**. On your student answer sheet, record the commands you use.

6. Type **EXIT**, and then press **Enter** to return to your Windows desktop.

7. Copy and paste your Mgmt container login script to Notepad:

   a. Restore ConsoleOne.

   b. Right-click your **Mgmt** container, and then click **Properties** to open the Properties of Mgmt dialog box.

   c. Click the **Login Script** tab to display the login script commands.

   d. Highlight all login script commands, and press the **Ctrl+C** key combination to copy the login script to the Clipboard.

   e. Click **Cancel** to close the Properties of Mgmt dialog box, and then start Notepad.

   f. Click in the Notepad window, and then press the **Ctrl+V** key combination to paste the login script commands into the Notepad window.

   g. Click **File**, **Print** on the Notepad menu bar to print the Mgmt container login script.

8. Print the Engineering container login script:

   a. Click **File**, **Open** on the Notepad menu bar, and then select your H: or C: drive.

   b. Navigate to your LoginScripts folder, and double-click the **EngScrpt.txt** file.

   c. Click **File**, **Print** on the Notepad menu bar to print the login script to your classroom printer.

9. Print the Mfg container login script:

   a. Click **File**, **Open** on the Notepad menu bar, and then select your H: or C: drive.

   b. If necessary, navigate to your LoginScripts folder, and double-click the **MfgScrpt.txt** file.

   c. Click **File**, **Print** on the Notepad menu bar to print the login script to your classroom printer.

10. Retrieve your output from the classroom printer, and exit Notepad without saving the file.

11. Exit ConsoleOne, and log out.

Activity 7-13: Entering the Profile Login Scripts

Time Required: 15 minutes

Objectives: Create and enter login script commands and variables.

Description: As you have learned, entering a profile login script requires that you create a profile object, enter the commands, and then assign the users of the profile script the Read Attribute right to the Login Script property. In this activity, you use ConsoleOne to create the EngProfile profile object, assign all users rights to read the Login Script property, and then enter and print the login script commands.

1. If necessary, start your computer, log in with your assigned UasAdmin user name and password, and start ConsoleOne.

2. Modify the login script commands in the existing WebProfile object to match the commands in Table 7-9. On your student answer sheet, record the commands you use.

   a. Click your **##UAS** container to display all objects in the Object frame.

   b. Right-click **WebProfile**, and then click **Properties** to open the Properties of WebProfile dialog box.

   c. Click the **Login Script** tab to display the existing login script commands.

   d. Make the necessary changes (referring to Table 7-9), and then click **Apply** and **Close** to save your changes and return to the main ConsoleOne window.

3. In Activity 7-2, you attached the WebProfile script to the KThiele user account. Now you'll attach the WebProfile object to Kari Mean's user account:

   a. If necessary, expand your **##UAS** container.

   b. Click the **Engineering** OU to display all users in the Object frame.

   c. Right-click **KMeans**, and then click **Properties** to open the Properties of KMeans dialog box.

   d. Click the **Login Script** tab to display your personal login script page.

   e. Click the **Browse** button next to the Profile text box to open the Select Object dialog box.

   f. Click the **up arrow**, double-click the **WebProfile** object, and then click **OK** to add the WebProfile object to the Profile text box.

   g. Click **OK** to save your changes and return to the main ConsoleOne window.

   h. You will add the WebProfile script to Julie Damrau's account in the end-of-chapter case projects.

4. Create the EngProfile profile object:

   a. Click the **Engineering** OU, and press **Insert** to open the New Object dialog box.

   b. Click the **Profile** object type, and then click **OK** to open the New Profile dialog box.

   c. Enter the profile name **EngProfile**, and then click the **Define additional properties** check box.

   d. Click **OK** to create the profile object and open the Properties of EngProfile dialog box.

   e. Click the **Login Script** tab.

   f. Enter the login script commands for EngProfile (referring to Table 7-9).

5. Grant all users in the Engineering and Mfg containers Read rights to all properties of the EngProfile object:

   a. Click the **NDS Rights** tab to display the trustees of the EngProfile object.

   b. Click the **Add Trustee** button to open the Select Object dialog box.

   c. Click the **Engineering** container, click the **Mfg** container while holding down the **Ctrl** key, and then click **OK** to add them to the Rights assigned to selected objects dialog box.

   d. Click the **[All Attributes Rights]** object, and verify that the selected objects have Read and Compare rights.

   e. Click **OK** to save the trustee assignments and return to the Properties of EngProfile dialog box.

   f. Click **OK** to save your changes and return to the main ConsoleOne window.

6. Attach the EngProfile script to the users indicated in the Profile Login Script Worksheet (see Table 7-9):

   a. Right-click **LJarka**, and then click **Properties** to open the Properties of Ljarka dialog box.

   b. Click the **Login Script** button.

   c. Click the **Browse** button next to the Profile text box to open the Select Object dialog box.

d. In the Browse context section, navigate to the Engineering container.

e. Double-click the **EngProfile** profile object.

f. Click **OK** to save the profile script assignment.

g. Repeat Steps 7a through 7f for the users TRucci and PAlm.

7. Use the copy-and-paste method to print the EngProfile and WebProfile login scripts.

8. Close any open windows and applications, and log out.

Testing and Debugging Login Scripts

After entering the login scripts, you should test the login script system for at least one user in each work-group by logging in with that user's name and checking that all commands run correctly. When establishing login scripts, don't be discouraged if not everything works correctly the first time. Although careful planning and design can eliminate many potential problems, small errors caused by missing or invalid login script commands, incorrect paths, or lack of user access rights can still be frustrating. In the following activity, you test the user login scripts and correct any problems.

Activity 7-14: Testing the Login Scripts

Time Required: 15 minutes

Objectives: Create and enter login script commands and variables.

Description: In this activity, you test the login scripts for Lianne Jarka, Lynn Dai, Russ Pence, and Kari Means by logging in with their user names and verifying drive mappings and printer assignments.

Depending on the classroom tree structure, you may need to add ".CLASS" to the end of distinguished user names shown in Steps 2, 6, 9, and 12.

1. If necessary, start your computer to obtain a Novell Login window.

2. Test the login script for the Engineering container by logging in as LJarka:

a. Enter **.LJarka.Engineering.##UAS** in the Username text box and Lianne's password in the Password text box.

b. Click the **Advanced** button, and then click the **Scripts** tab.

c. Click **OK** to log in.

3. Verify that the correct welcome and informational messages you set up in the login script are displayed, and note any error messages on your student answer sheet.

4. Double-click the **My Computer** icon, and record the drive mappings for LJarka on your student answer sheet.

5. Log out to display a new login window.

6. Test the login script for the Mfg container by logging in as Russ Pence:

a. Enter **.RPence.Mfg.##UAS** in the Username text box and Russ's password in the Password text box.

b. Click **OK** to log in.

7. Double-click the **My Computer** icon, and record the drive mappings for RPence on your student answer sheet.

8. Log out to display a new login window.

9. Test the Mgmt container login script by logging in as Lynn Dai:

a. Enter **.LDai.Mgmt.##UAS** in the Username text box and Lynn's password in the Password text box.

b. Click **OK** to log in.

10. Double-click the **My Computer** icon, and record the drive mappings for LDai on your student answer sheet.

11. Log out to display a new login window.

12. Test the login script for the WebProfile object by logging in as Kari Means:

    a. Enter **.KMeans.Engineering.##UAS** in the Username text box and Kari's password in the Password text box.

    b. Click **OK** to log in.

> Notice the error message you get when attempting to map a drive to the Web directory. This error can be caused by insufficient rights to the IS\Web directory or not having the Read right to the Login Script property. You'll correct this problem in the next activity.

13. Double-click the **My Computer** icon, and record the drive mappings for KMeans on your student answer sheet.

14. Close any open windows, and log out.

Activity 7-15: Debugging a Login Script

Time Required: 10 minutes

Objectives: Create and enter login script commands and variables.

Description: A frequent problem when testing login scripts is receiving invalid drive mapping messages. The most common cause of these messages is an incorrectly typed path statement in the login script or insufficient rights for the user in the specified directory path. For example, earlier you created a WebProfile login script to give users working on the Web site a drive mapping to the Web directory. Kari Means is part of this profile, but she is not a member of the WebMgrs group. In this activity, you make Kari a member of the WebMgrs group and then log in as Kari to verify her drive mappings.

1. If necessary, start your computer, and log in with your UasAdmin user name and password.

2. Start ConsoleOne, and expand **UAS_Tree** and your **##UAS** container.

3. Make Kari a member of the WebMgrs group. On your student answer sheet, record the steps you use.

4. Exit ConsoleOne, and log out.

5. Log in as KMeans, and record any error messages on your student answer sheet.

6. Double-click the **My Computer** icon, and record Kari's drive mappings on your student answer sheet.

7. Close the My Computer window, and log out.

MANAGING USER ENVIRONMENTS WITH Z.E.N.WORKS FOR DESKTOPS

You have learned how to use login scripts to help create consistent, standardized drive pointers for users each time they log in to the network. However, login scripts are only part of the solution to making the network easy to use and maintain; users also need a consistent desktop environment and access to required applications from any workstation they work on. In the past, the network administrator had to install applications and modify workstation configurations on many different computers to accommodate the varying computing needs of people who used those machines. Manually installing applications and setting up or restoring user desktops can be a labor-intensive task that takes time away from other network administration priorities. Novell's Z.E.N.works for Desktops (ZfD) package enables network administrators to centrally monitor and manage software and workstation configurations so that users have easy mobility among workstations. In the following sections, you learn what a CNA needs to know about using the Novell Z.E.N.works package to set up and manage user desktop environments.

Z.E.N.works for Desktops 3 Overview

The actual cost of hardware and software is only a small part of the total cost of owning a computer. In addition to the physical and software components, the cost of ownership, which is becoming a major concern for many organizations, includes the ongoing costs of maintaining and upgrading the computer hardware, software installation and configuration, troubleshooting, and user support and training. Although the Windows environment makes it easy for users to interact with and personalize their desktop computers, because of its complexity, it can actually increase the total cost of ownership; network administrators must spend more time configuring, managing, and supporting Windows environments. In addition, configuration time can increase when users move to different workstations, yet want to access their same desktop environment. In a large network, another concern is providing help desk support for users when they have problems or questions.

Novell's **Zero Effort Networking (Z.E.N.works) for Desktops (ZfD)** can make the network easier for users to work with and reduce the time you have to spend at each user workstation. In addition, ZfD offers a remote-control capability that gives you a secure way to take control of a client computer's display, keyboard, and mouse; in this way, you can help a user fix a problem or change a workstation's configuration without having to physically go to that workstation. The ZfD product consists of client and server components that allow network administrators to use eDirectory Services to centralize configuration information for applications, users, and workstations; this method reduces the time and repetitiveness of workstation configuration and management.

Benefits and Features

Z.E.N.works for Desktops has benefits in the following areas of network management:

- *Application management*—ZfD includes an Application Launcher, which enables you to centrally distribute, upgrade, and manage applications on any Windows-based workstation attached to your network.

- *Workstation management*—The Workstation Manager component allows you to store user and desktop configurations for Windows workstations in eDirectory. Because ZfD uses eDirectory to extend Windows features, such as policies, printers, and user profiles, these features are manageable from a centralized location by using ConsoleOne.

- *Remote control*—With ZfD, you can securely manage and interact with workstations from a remote location. This makes troubleshooting user problems and changing configurations much more convenient on large networks.

Hardware and Software Requirements

To use Z.E.N.works for Desktops, your server must be running NetWare 4.11 or higher with the latest support packs installed. Windows 95/98 workstations need to have Novell Client 3.3 or later installed, and Windows NT/2000 workstations need to have at least Novell Client 4.8 or later installed. Following are the minimum hardware requirements for workstations; keep in mind that these are *minimum* hardware requirements that might not provide adequate performance:

- Processor: Pentium 75 MHz or higher

- Memory: 16 MB for Windows 95/98 or 128 MB for Windows NT/2000

- Hard disk space: 4 MB (workstation) or 24 MB (full installation)

In addition, to configure and manage Z.E.N.works for Desktops, you need to use ConsoleOne because NetWare Administrator and iManager do not currently have ZfD management capabilities.

Installing Z.E.N.works

Before taking advantage of the Z.E.N.works features, you need to install Z.E.N.works for Desktops on your server and, if necessary, update the client on workstations. Eric installed Z.E.N.works for Desktops on the UASHOST server by going through the following process:

1. Because the Z.E.N.works for Desktops installation needs to replace certain Java utilities on the server, before starting the installation, Eric went to the server console and entered the command UNLOAD JAVA to stop Java applications on the server. If this is not done, the Z.E.N.works for Desktops installation program issues an error message.

2. Next, Eric logged in to the network from his workstation with the Admin user name and password to have Supervisor rights to the network.

3. After successfully logging in, he inserted the Z.E.N.works for Desktops CD into the workstation's CD drive. The Z.E.N.works for Desktops installation wizard automatically started and displayed the language selection window.

4. Eric clicked the English language option to display the installation options and then clicked the Install Z.E.N.works option.

5. He clicked Next in the Novell Product Installation window to display the License Agreement window.

6. After reading the agreement, he clicked Accept to display the Install Prerequisites window. After reading the prerequisites, he clicked Accept to continue.

7. To be able to select specific options, Eric clicked the Custom radio button, and then clicked Next to continue.

8. He clicked the Clear All button and selected only the following components:
   - Application Management
   - Automatic Workstation Import
   - Workstation Management

9. After selecting these components, Eric clicked Next to display the installation window.

10. He clicked Next to install Files, Schema Extensions, and NDS Objects.

11. He clicked Next to select the default UAS_TREE, and then clicked Next again to accept the UASHOST server.

12. Eric then verified that the English language was selected, and clicked Next to continue.

13. He selected None for the Import/Removal role of the UASHOST server, and then clicked Next to display the installation summary window.

14. He then clicked Finish to begin installing the displayed components.

15. When Eric saw the message asking whether to replace newer files, he clicked the Never overwrite newer file radio button, and then clicked OK.

16. After all files were copied, he read and closed the log file to complete the installation.

17. He then closed all open windows, and logged out.

18. To finish the installation, he restarted the server by entering the command RESTART SERVER at the server console.

MANAGING WORKSTATIONS

In addition to installing and configuring applications on each workstation, network administrators need to be able to maintain a consistent desktop environment and keep track of each client's hardware and software configurations. The key to managing Windows desktop environments is using policies, which are powerful Windows desktop management tools that allow user workstations to be customized for individual user needs. However, when implementing a network with many Windows computers, managing workstation and user policies with the Windows 2000 Professional local policy-editing program can be a time-consuming chore. Z.E.N.works makes Windows policies easier to manage and more powerful by adding Policy Package objects to eDirectory.

Policy Package objects allow you to manage the way users access their workstations and connect to the network. There are two types of policy packages: Workstation policies and User policies. With Workstation policies, you can configure settings such as the path to Windows setup files, file and printer sharing, workstation passwords, and run options. Run options can be used to configure which applications automatically run on a workstation regardless of which user logs in. For example, you could use a Workstation policy package to specify that workstations automatically start Novell Application Launcher (NAL.exe) instead of placing the command in a container login script. User policy packages affect users' access to workstations and their desktop restrictions, regardless of where they log in to the network. You can use User policy packages to define restrictions, such as hiding the Entire Network option in Network Neighborhood or hiding the Run or Find commands, for example. You can also define a desktop environment, including wallpaper, screen saver, sounds, and colors. When a policy package is applied to a Windows 95/98 workstation, the restrictions made to the workstation's Registry are applied to the next user, unless he or she has a policy that changes the Registry settings. As a result, if the Admin user logs in to a 95/98 workstation that has previously been used by a restricted user, the restriction is applied to the Windows environment for the Admin user. For example, if the previous user was restricted from using the Windows Start, Run option, the Admin user would also be unable to run programs from the Start, Run option. As a result, when setting up restricted User policy packages, you should create an open policy package that enables all Windows functions and then associate the open policy with your Admin user. In this way, when you log in as the Admin user from a restricted workstation, you will have access to all Windows features. In the following activities, you learn how to create User policy packages and then use them to set up open and restricted desktop environments.

Activity 7-16: Creating an Open Policy Package for the Admin User Account

Time Required: 15 minutes

Objective: Create an open access workstation environment for network administrators.

Description: Before setting up the User policy packages, Eric created a open access policy package and associated it with his Admin user account. In this activity, you create an open access policy package for Windows 2000 workstations that provides a standard desktop environment for your UasAdmin user.

1. If necessary, start your computer, and log in with your assigned UasAdmin user name and password.

2. Start ConsoleOne, and expand **UAS_Tree** and your **##UAS** container.

3. Create an open policy package for your UasAdmin user account:

   a. Click your **##UAS** container, and then click the **New Object** button on the ConsoleOne toolbar to open the Create Object dialog box.

   b. Scroll down and double-click **Policy Package** to start the Policy Package Wizard. Record the policy options on your student answer sheet.

   c. Click the **User Package** object in the Policy Package pane on the left, and then click the **Windows 2000 Group Policy** item in the Policies pane on the right.

   d. Click the **Next** button to display the Policy Package Name and Container text boxes.

   e. Enter **Admin Policy** in the Policy Package Name text box, and verify that your ##UAS container is displayed in the Container text box.

   f. Click the **Next** button to display the Summary dialog box.

   g. Click the **Define Additional Properties** check box, and then click the **Finish** button to open the Properties of Admin dialog box.

   h. Click the **down arrow** on the Policies tab, and then click the **Win95-98** option to open the Win95-98 User Policies dialog box, similar to the one in Figure 7-9.

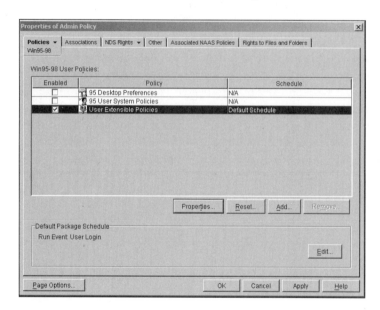

Figure 7-9   The Win95-98 User Policies dialog box

4. Configure the user policy package to reset all restrictions:

   a. Click the **User Extensible Policies** check box, and then click the **Properties** button to open the User Extensible Policies dialog box.

   b. In the ADM Files section, click the **\zen\admfiles\admin.adm** file to display the associated polices, as shown in Figure 7-10.

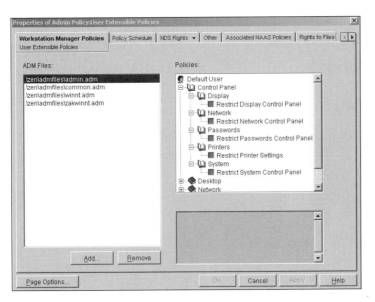

Figure 7-10   The User Extensible Policies dialog box

c. In the Policies section, double-click the **Control Panel** policy (and expand each item under that policy) to show all the options, as shown in Figure 7-11. A gray check box indicates that the policy setting will not be changed on the user workstation. A check mark in the check box indicates that the policy will be applied. A clear (white) check box indicates that the policy will be reset.

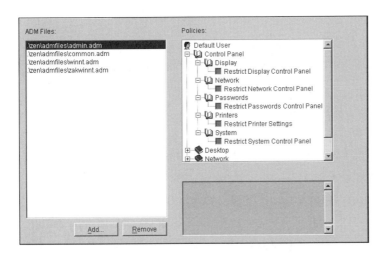

Figure 7-11   Options for the Control Panel policy

d. Double-click each check box to reset all Control Panel restrictions for the Admin user.

e. Scroll down the list in the Policies section, and double-click the **Shell** policy to view all the options.

f. Double-click each of the policies in the Restrictions policy to reset all restrictions.

g. Double-click the **System** policy to view all the options, and double-click each policy check box to reset all restrictions.

h. Click **OK** to save your changes and return to the Policies tab of the Properties of Admin dialog box.

5. Reset all restrictions on the Windows NT/2000 policies:

   a. Click the **down arrow** on the Policies tab, and then click the **WinNT-2000** option.

   b. Click the **User Extensible Policies** check box, and then click the **Properties** button to open the User Extensible Policies dialog box.

   c. Click the **\zen\admfiles\admin.adm** file to display the associated policies.

   d. Expand each policy and remove any restrictions by double-clicking the check box until it is white (clear with no check mark).

   e. Click **OK** to save the new policy settings and return to the Policies tab of the Properties of Admin dialog box.

6. Associate the Admin policy package with your UasAdmin user account:

   a. Click the **Associations** tab to open the Associations dialog box.

   b. Click the **Add** button to open the Select Object dialog box.

   c. Double-click the **UasAdmin** user to associate the policy with your Admin user name.

7. Click **OK** to save your changes to the Admin policy and return to the main ConsoleOne window.

8. If you're continuing to the next activity, leave ConsoleOne open and stay logged in. If not, exit ConsoleOne, and log out.

Activity 7-17: Creating a Standard User Desktop

Time Required: 15 minutes

Objective: Use Z.E.N.works for Desktops to configure a user environment.

Description: Universal AeroSpace management wanted to create a common desktop for all users in the Engineering department. To create a common desktop wallpaper and configure consistent restrictions for all Engineering users, Eric created a Windows 2000 policy package in the Engineering OU and then associated the policy with the Engineering container. In this activity, you create a User policy package for your Engineering users that prevents them from using the Run command on the Start menu and creates a company-standard desktop wallpaper.

1. If necessary, log in with your UasAdmin user name and password, and start ConsoleOne.

2. Copy the official UAS wallpaper to your Apps\Desktop folder:

   a. Double-click the **My Computer** icon to display all existing drive pointers.

   b. Double-click the **F:** drive pointer, and then double-click the **Software.cti** folder.

   c. Double-click the **Design** folder to display the UAS.bmp file.

   d. Right-click the **UAS.bmp** file, and then click **Copy**.

   e. Click the **up arrow** three times to return to the My Computer window.

   f. Double-click the **G:** drive letter, and navigate to your Apps directory. If necessary, create a new folder named **Desktop**.

   g. Right-click your **Desktop** folder, and click **Paste** to copy the UAS.bmp file to your Desktop folder.

   h. Close the Desktop window.

3. Create a Windows 2000 User policy package for the Engineering container:

   a. If necessary, expand **UAS_Tree** and your **##UAS** container in the ConsoleOne window.

   b. Click the **Engineering** OU to display all objects in the Object frame.

c. Click the **Create Policy Package** icon on the ConsoleOne toolbar to open the Policy Package Wizard dialog box.

d. In the Policy Package pane, click the **User Package** object, and then click the **Windows 2000 Group Policy** item in the Policy pane.

e. Click the **Next** button to display the Policy Package Name and Container text boxes.

f. Enter **Engineering Policy** in the Policy Package Name text box.

g. Verify that Engineering.##UAS is displayed in the Container text box, and then click the **Next** button to display the Summary dialog box.

h. Click the **Define Additional Properties** check box, and then click the **Finish** button to create the policy package and open the Policies tab of the Properties of Engineering dialog box.

4. Configure the user policy package to restrict the use of the Run command:

a. Click the **down arrow** on the Policies tab, and then click the **WinNT-2000** option to open the WinNT-2000 User Policies dialog box.

b. Click the **User Extensible Policies** check box, and then click the **Properties** button to open the User Extensible Policies dialog box.

c. In the ADM Files section, click the **\zen\admfiles\admin.adm** file to display the associated policies in the Policies section.

d. Scroll down the list in the Policies section, expand the **Shell** policy, and then expand the **Restrictions** policy.

e. Double-click to place a check mark in the **Remove 'Run' command** policy.

5. Configure the User policy package to use the official UAS wallpaper:

a. Expand the **Desktop** policy, and then double-click the **Wallpaper** policy to place a check mark in its check box, as shown in Figure 7-12.

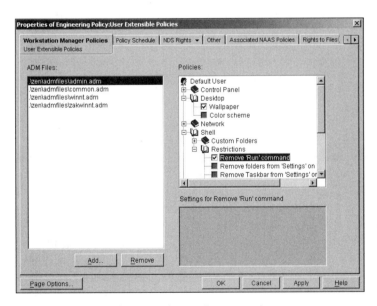

Figure 7-12   Configuring the Wallpaper policy

b. Enter the path **\\uashost\##corp\apps\desktop\uas.bmp** in the Wallpaper name text box, the **Tile Wallpaper** check box, and click to remove the check mark, if necessary.

6. Click **OK** to save your configuration and return to the Policies tab of the Properties of Engineering dialog box.

7. Associate the Engineering policy with all users in the Engineering OU:

   a. Click the **Associations** tab to open the Associations dialog box.

   b. Click the **Add** button to open the Select Object dialog box.

   c. Click the **up arrow** to display your Organizational Units.

   d. Click the **Engineering** OU, and then click **OK** to add Engineering OU to the Associations dialog box.

   e. Click **OK** to save the policy changes and return to the main ConsoleOne window.

8. Exit ConsoleOne, and log out.

9. Test the settings by logging in as an Engineering user:

   a. Enter **KMeans** in the Username text box and the password for KMeans in the Password text box.

   b. Click the **Advanced** button, and change the default context to your Engineering.##UAS container.

   c. Click **OK** to log in as KMeans.

   d. On your student answer sheet, record the wallpaper that is displayed.

   e. Click the **Start** button and verify that the Run command is removed. Record the results on your student answer sheet.

   f. Log out.

10. Log in with your UasAdmin user name and verify that the restrictions are not effective.

Now that the login scripts and policy packages are operational, all your hard work is starting to pay off; your network users are able to log in with a consistent desktop and use a standard set of drive pointers to access the network file system. Your next task in setting up your version of the UAS network will be to implement a network printing system that allows your users to easily access network printers from any networked computer.

CHAPTER SUMMARY

- Establishing a workstation environment and providing access to network files are important responsibilities of a network administrator. NetWare offers a powerful way to automate workstation setups through the use of login scripts.

- NetWare login scripts contain commands to provide the drive mappings and other workstation setup functions needed during login. Novell supplies a set of commands that can be included in login script files to map drive letters, set the DOS environment of a workstation, display messages and files, run other programs, and issue certain commands based on specified conditions.

- By using login script variables with commands, you can create general-purpose login scripts that work for multiple users. Login script variables are divided into date variables, such as DAY_OF_WEEK; time variables, such as HOUR24; user variables, such as HOME_DIRECTORY; and workstation variables, such as OS and OS_VERSION. A common example of using a login script command with a variable is mapping a drive pointer to users' home directories by including the MAP ROOT H:=%HOME_DIRECTORY command in the login script. The percent sign preceding a variable name tells NetWare to substitute the value of the variable when the login script command runs.

❐ Novell Client can run four types of NetWare login scripts: container login scripts, profile login scripts, user login scripts, and default login scripts. The container login script is a property of the container object, and its commands run first when users in that container log in. After the container login script has ended, if the login script processor identifies a profile object for a user, the login script commands in the profile object run. Last, the system checks for commands in the user's Login Script property. If no user login script exists, the login script processor runs the default login script commands stored in the client software.

❐ Whenever possible, most login script commands should be stored in the container login script. By including the NO_DEFAULT command in the container login script, you can prevent NetWare from running the default login script statements. If you place the EXIT command at the end of the container login script, the login script processing will end and no profile, user, or default login scripts will run. Creating a login script for each user prevents the default login script from being run and provides extra security.

❐ The ConsoleOne utility is used to maintain the container, profile, and user login scripts. The container login script is created and maintained by selecting a container's Login Script property. Implementing a profile login script requires creating a profile object and then granting users the Read Attribute right to the Login Script property. The user login script is created and maintained by selecting the user object and then clicking the Login Script tab in the Properties dialog box.

❐ When testing login scripts, make sure the user has access rights to the directory paths in the MAP statements.

❐ With Z.E.N.works for Desktops, network administrators can centrally manage user desktop configuration and applications through the use of User and Workstation policies.

❐ Policy Package objects are created in the eDirectory tree and then associated with the appropriator users. You should create an open policy package for the Admin user that enables all workstation functions so that user workstation restrictions aren't applied.

KEY TERMS

container login script — A login script that is a property of a container object and is run by all users in that container when they log in to the network.

date variable — A login script variable that contains date information, such as day of week, month, and year.

default login script — Commands stored in Novell Client that run when a user does not have a personal user login script.

identifier variable — A login script variable used in login script commands to represent such information as the user login name, date, time, and DOS version.

login script variable — A reserved word in the login script language with a variable value that's unique to the user logging in. For example, the HOME_DIRECTORY variable contains the path to the user's home directory.

Policy Package object — An eDirectory object used to manage the way users access their workstations and connect to the network.

profile login script — An eDirectory object that contains login commands common to multiple users.

syntax — Rules to be followed when writing login script commands.

time variable — A login script variable that contains system time information, such as hour, minute, and a.m. or p.m.

user-defined variable — A login script variable that allows users to enter parameters for their personal user login scripts.

user login script — Personalized login script commands for a single user that are stored in the Login Script property of a user's eDirectory account. A user's personal login script runs after any container or profile script commands are finished.

workstation variable — A login script variable that contains information about the workstation's environment, such as machine type, operating system, operating system version, and station node address.

Zero Effort Networking (Z.E.N.works) for Desktops (ZfD) — A Novell product that enables network administrators to centrally manage users' desktop environments.

REVIEW QUESTIONS

1. Which of the following is the main purpose of login scripts?

   a. setting the user's desktop environment

   b. mapping drive letters

   c. providing informational messages

   d. running applications

2. Which of the following login script files would most likely contain the NO_DEFAULT command?

   a. default

   b. user

   c. container

   d. profile

3. Which of the following commands is used to display the contents of an ASCII text file onscreen? (Choose all that apply.)

   a. DISPLAY

   b. WRITE

   c. MESSAGE

   d. FDISPLAY

4. Which of the following commands is used to display a brief message onscreen?

   a. DISPLAY

   b. WRITE

   c. MESSAGE

   d. FILE

5. Which of the following login scripts runs first to standardize the environment for all users in a department directory?

   a. default

   b. user

   c. container

   d. profile

6. Which of the following login scripts provides drive mappings and other setup commands that are common to users in multiple containers?

   a. default

   b. user

   c. container

   d. profile

7. The default login script runs if there is no _____ login script.

   a. default

   b. user

c. container

d. profile

8. Which of the following commands can be used in a container login script to stop the default login script from running but allow profile or user scripts to run?

a. NO_DEFAULT

b. EXIT

c. SKIP_DEFAULT

d. EXIT /NO_DEFAULT

9. In addition to the command used in Question 8, describe three other ways you can prevent the default login script commands from running.

_____

_____

_____

7

10. Suppose the first network drive on your workstation is L:. Which drive letter would the MAP *3:=DATA login script command use to access the DATA volume?

11. Write a login script command that displays a "Welcome to Universal AeroSpace" message containing today's date, including the day, month, and year.

_____

12. Write a condition that could be used to determine whether a user is logging in on the third day of the week.

_____

13. Write a MAP command that uses variables to map H: as a root drive pointer to the user's home directory.

_____

14. Which of the following login script variables can be used to change the default drive to the user's home directory on drive H:?

a. %LOGIN_NAME

b. %CONTEXT

c. %HOME_DIRECTORY

d. %PATH

15. Which of the following commands prevents the output of MAP commands from being displayed?

a. MAP OFF

b. DISPLAY OFF

c. MAP DISPLAY OFF

d. NO_OUTPUT

16. Write a command to output the login script commands from the UAS Organization to a file named Uas.txt.

_____

17. Write a login script command to display a greeting message that includes the user's login name and general time of day in the format "Good afternoon (morning, evening), EKenton."

_____

18. Write a command to display the contents of the DailyMst.txt file located in the SYS:Public directory.

_____

19. List the login scripts in the sequence they run.

_____

_____

_____

_____

20. Write a login script command that maps drive letter W: to the UASHOST_CORP:Inventry directory for all users who are members of the AcctGrp.

_____

21. The IS manager of a multicontainer organization wants you to map a standard drive letter for all users in all the company's OUs and make sure that this drive mapping overrides mappings in existing scripts. Which of the following login scripts would you use?

    a. container

    b. user

    c. profile

    d. modify the default script

22. Write a MAP command that maps a search drive to the SYS:Public directory and add that search drive to the end of the existing search drives on the workstation.

_____

23. Write a login script command that sets the context of the workstation to the Sales OU of the ACME Organization.

_____

24. One of the users in a department logs in and sees all his network drive mappings except one. What is the most likely problem?

    a. The Run scripts option isn't selected in Novell Client.

    b. There are insufficient file system rights for this user.

    c. There are insufficient eDirectory rights for this user.

    d. The MAP command contains the wrong path.

25. A user logs in and sees no network drive mappings. What is the most likely problem?

    a. The Run scripts option isn't selected in Novell Client.

    b. There are insufficient file system rights for this user.

    c. There are insufficient eDirectory rights for this user.

    d. The MAP command contains the wrong path.

26. Which of the following is not a feature of Z.E.N.works for Desktops?

    a. application management

    b. server management

    c. policy management

    d. remote-control capabilities

27. Describe the purpose of an open policy package for the Admin user account.

UNIVERSAL AEROSPACE CASE PROJECTS

Your next task is to apply what you have learned about setting up the login scripts in this chapter's activities to implementing login scripts for users in the Business office. In the following projects, you set up and test container, profile, and user login scripts for the Business office users.

Case Project 7-1: Writing the Business Container Login Script

In this project, you apply what you learned in this chapter to writing a login script for the Business container. To do this, you need to copy the Container Login Script Worksheet in Appendix D, and refer to the login script requirements in Table 7-10 to fill out this worksheet.

Be sure to include a command that will display the daily message file, as in the Engineering container script. Notice that the Business container login script needs a special workgroup section for each department to map the L: drive to the department's directory. Use the Directory Map objects you created in Chapter 3 to map drive letters to each department's directory.

7

Table 7-10   Business Office Login Script Requirements

Organization: _Universal AeroSpace Business office_   Page __1__ of __2__

Developed by: _Eric Kenton_ _____   Date: _____

Drive Mappings			
Users	**Drive**	**Path**	**Script**
All	G:	UASHOST_CORP:	All containers
All	S1:	UASHOST_SYS:Public	All containers
All	H:	%HOME_DIRECTORY	All containers
Accounting	L:	Accounting Directory Map object	Business container
Desktop Publishing	L:	Publishing Directory Map object	Business container
Marketing	L:	Marketing Directory Map object	Business container
Accounting and Marketing users	I:	UASHOST_CORP:\Inventry	InvApp profile
Accounting and Marketing users	Search drive	UASHOST_CORP:\Inventry	InvApp profile
Julie Damrau	W:	UASHOST_CORP:\IS\Web	WebProfile profile

Organization: _Universal AeroSpace Business office_   Page _2_ of _2_

Developed by: _Eric Kenton_   Date: _____

Messages		
Users	**Description**	**Script**
All	Login greeting message	Business container
All	Daily message file for Monday through Friday	Business container
Accounting	Weekly budget meeting on Monday morning at 9:00 a.m.	Business container
Inventory Planning	Monthly meeting on the first Monday of each month from 8:00 a.m. until 9:00 a.m	InvApp profile script
Marketing	Monthly meeting held at 9:00 a.m. on the first Wednesday of each month to discuss documentation and promotional needs	Business Container

Case Project 7-2: Writing the Profile Login Script

In Table 7-10, Eric identified an InvApp profile script. Copy the Profile Login Script Worksheet in Appendix D to write the necessary login script for the InvApp profile object. Before entering and testing your login scripts, have your instructor review them. Although your commands can vary slightly, your instructor will check to be sure your script includes the commands needed to perform the activities in the remainder of this book.

Case Project 7-3: Entering and Testing the Container Login Script

After your login script commands have been checked, use ConsoleOne to enter the login script commands for the Business container. Follow the procedure described in this chapter to print the contents of your Business container login script. On your student answer sheet, record the commands you use.

Case Project 7-4: Entering the Profile Script

After the container login script has been tested, your next step is implementing the InvApp profile script by following these steps:

1. Start ConsoleOne.
2. Create the InvApp object in your Business container and then enter the login script commands you defined in Case Project 7-2.
3. Grant the users in the Profile Login Script Worksheet the necessary rights to read the Path property.

4. Attach the InvApp profile to the users identified in the Profile Login Script Worksheet.

5. Attach the WebProfile object to Julie Damrau's login script.

6. Use the procedure described in this chapter to print a copy of the InvApp profile login script. On your student answer sheet, record the commands you use.

Case Project 7-5: Testing the Login Scripts

To test your login scripts, you need to log in as each of these users and check for any error messages:

❏ JDamrau

❏ TBlackwell

❏ LHiller

If you get error messages, review and, if necessary, modify the login script command. Make sure all users have the necessary rights to the directories specified in the MAP commands as well as Read rights to the Path property of any Directory Map objects. After verifying that there are no login script error messages, use My Computer to record the drive mappings and any informational messages on your student answer sheet.

Case Project 7-6: Creating a Desktop Policy for the Accounting Department

In this project, you create a desktop policy package for the Accounting department that uses the official UAS wallpaper; the policy package must also prevent users from using the Run command and My Network Places. After creating the new policy package, log in as the Terry Blackwell user, and record the results on your student answer sheet.

8

IMPLEMENTING NETWORK PRINTING

After reading this chapter and completing the exercises, you will be able to:

♦ Explain how printers are accessed on a network

♦ Describe and set up a legacy queue-based printing system, including print queues, printers, and print servers

♦ Describe the Novell Distributed Print Services components, and use NetWare Administrator and iManager to create and configure NDPS components

♦ Install printers on user workstations by using Windows Add Printer, NDPS Remote Manager, and iPrint

♦ Define and implement a network printing environment that uses iPrint to enable users to access and manage printers across networks

As described in Chapter 1, sharing printers is an important benefit of implementing a network system. Network printing offers cost savings, increased workspace for users, and multiple printer selection options. As a result, to become a NetWare CNA, Novell requires you to know how to use NetWare's new Novell Distributed Print Services (NDPS) system along with the legacy queue-based printing system to set up, customize, and maintain the printing environment on your network. NDPS's new iPrint capability included with NetWare 6 further enhances network printing by allowing administrators and users to install, access, and configure network printers through a Web browser. This chapter covers the printing concepts and skills needed to understand and implement an NDPS network printing environment that uses iPrint so that you can access and manage printers from any networked location through the power of Novell's OneNet Strategy.

NETWORK PRINTING OVERVIEW

As shown in Figure 8-1, the basic function of network printing is to take output formatted by an application running on the user's computer and then send that output to a shared printer attached to the network.

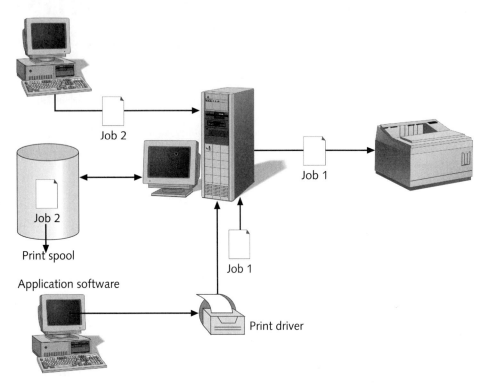

Figure 8-1   Network printing: The print server spools Job 2 to a storage area until Job 1 finishes printing

Because a physical printer can print output from only one application at a time, network printing needs to provide a way to control the flow of output from multiple user applications to a single network printer. This is usually accomplished by sending output from a user's computer to a print job on a server, where it's held until the network printer it needs is available. The process of sending output from a user's computer to a print job storage area is referred to as **spooling**. As illustrated in Figure 8-1, the **print server** software actually makes network printing happen by retrieving print jobs and sending them to the assigned network printer. When a network printer finishes printing the output for one application, the print server retrieves the next application's print job for that printer and sends it to the printer. Because of print spooling, applications can quickly send their output to a network printer and continue processing information without having to wait for the output to be physically printed.

Queue-based Printing System Components

Queue-based printing, available since NetWare 3, was designed to support simple printers and DOS-based applications. Because many NetWare networks still use queue-based printing systems, as a CNA you'll be required to know the basic components and operation of queue-based printing. Before implementing a queue-based printing environment for your network, you need to understand how the basic printing components that make up queue-based printing work together. In the following sections, you learn how these four queue-based printing objects are implemented in a NetWare printing environment:

- Print queue
- Printer
- Print server
- Client

Print Queues

A **print queue** is a network object that represents a network holding area for storing output from workstations in a form ready to send directly to a printer. As shown in Figure 8-2, a print queue allows multiple workstations on a network to use the same printer by storing the printer output from each client as a separate print job. After being stored in the print queue, print jobs are then printed one at a time as the printer becomes available.

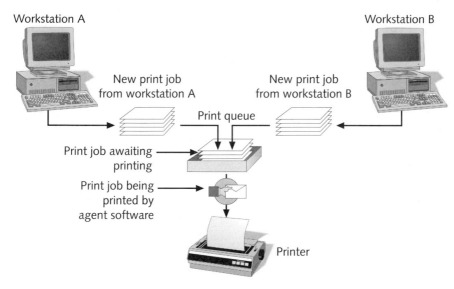

Figure 8-2   Queue-based printing

In queue-based printing, print jobs are actually files containing output formatted for a specific printer. In many ways, having a client send output to a print queue is similar to storing files on a volume. For example, when saving a file on a server, the data is transferred from the client to the server and then stored in a file located in the specified directory. Because an application's printer output is actually data being transmitted to a printer, placing a job in a print queue follows a similar process, in which the printer data from the application is stored in a file called a print job. Just as data files are stored in directories, print job files are located in special print queue directories, as illustrated in Figure 8-3.

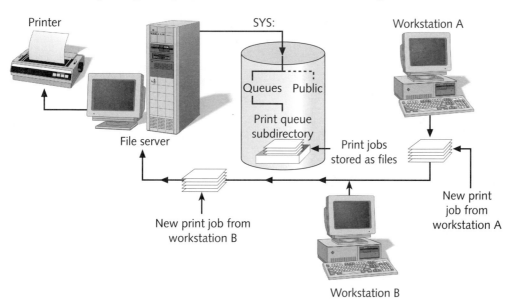

Figure 8-3   A NetWare print queue

In a NetWare queue-based printing system, network print queues are actually subdirectories of the Queues directory and can be placed on any volume. As described later in this section, print queues are created by using NetWare Administrator. When setting up a NetWare queue-based printing environment, at least one print queue is created for each networked printer. For user workstations that need to print to a specific printer, you use the Add Printer Wizard to specify that they send their output to a print queue. DOS-based applications can be directed to send their output to a print queue by using the NetWare CAPTURE command-line utility. After print jobs have been stored in the print queue, the printer assigned to the print queue prints the jobs in the order they were received. After a job has been printed, it's automatically deleted from the print queue.

One of the tasks involved in network printing is managing jobs in print queues. By default, the network administrator who created the print queue becomes the print queue operator, authorized to rearrange the sequence of print jobs, remove a print job, or place a print job on hold. NetWare also allows other users besides network administrators to be print queue operators. You might want to honor other users in your organization with the title of print queue operator to delegate the work of managing jobs on several print queues.

Printers

To successfully format and print information on a printer, the application running on the user workstation must be configured with the correct printer driver for the printer's make and model. Because of the variety of makes and models available, you should have this information for your network's printers so that you can correctly configure network printing, thus ensuring that formatted output goes to the correct printer. For example, a user's workstation might be configured to support both a Lexmark Optra Plus laser printer and a Hewlett-Packard (HP) Deskjet inkjet printer. When a user selects the Lexmark Optra Plus laser printer and prints a document, the network printing configuration must be set up to ensure that the output is sent to the laser printer for which it was formatted.

Printers can be attached to the network in one of the following three ways, as illustrated in Figure 8-4:

- Locally to the print server
- Remotely through a workstation
- Directly to the network cable

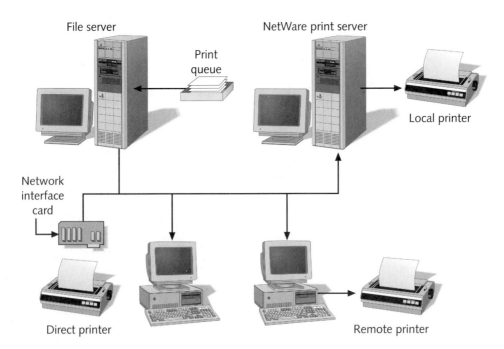

Figure 8-4 Printer attachment methods

When configuring the network printing environment, carefully consider the advantages of each attachment method to determine how it will affect the way printers are distributed on the network. Many network administrators use a combination of printer attachments, based on the type of printer and its use. The following sections describe the three printer attachment options and how they affect network printing.

Remote Attachment **Remote printers**, which are attached to other clients on the network, are also called **manual load printers** because you must manually load software on the client computer to connect the printer to the print server. After the software has been loaded on the client computer, print jobs can be sent to its remote printer, using the network cable to transmit packets of printed data from the print server to the client with the remote printer attached. NetWare includes the NPTWIN95 utility, which can be loaded on a Windows 95/98 client computer that has an attached network printer. NPTWIN95 receives the packets of printer output directed to it from the print server and then prints the output on the attached network printer without interfering with the Windows 95/98 client being used for other processing. The advantage of using remote manual load printers attached to client computers is that you can select a convenient location for the printer, making it easier for users to retrieve their printed output. The disadvantages of manual load printers include the lack of support for printers attached to Windows 2000 computers, the additional setup time to load the NPTWIN95 software on Windows 95/98 computers, the need to leave the client computer on to access network printers, and the possible decrease in printing performance for large graphical print jobs. This is caused by applications running on the client computer and the extra load on the network cable when sending printer output from the print queue to the network printer.

Local Attachment Locally attached printers are attached directly to a printer port on the server running the print server software (PSERVER.NLM). In NetWare, these printers are called **automatic load printers** because output is sent directly from the print server to the local printers through the ports on the server. Automatic load printers can be attached to the **parallel (LPTn)** or **serial (COMn)** port of the server running the print server software. Compared to manual load printers, the advantages of automatic load printers include better printing performance and less network traffic. The improved performance is a result of less software overhead because the print server does not have to communicate with a client computer running NPTWIN95. Network traffic is reduced because print jobs do not need to be sent from the print server to a printer attached to a client somewhere on the network.

Direct Attachment A popular alternative to using remote printers attached to a client computer is to attach the printer directly to the network cable with a special network card for the printer or by using a dedicated print server device, such as Hewlett-Packard's JetDirect products. Dedicated print server devices have a network port, one or more printer ports, and built-in software that enables them to receive print jobs from the network and print them on attached printers. Many high-speed laser printers have an option that includes a network card for attaching printers directly to the network cable. With the direct attachment option, the printer can become its own print server and print jobs directly from a NetWare print queue. The direct printer attachment is often used in networks that need high-speed laser printers, which don't operate efficiently when attached as remote printers.

The main disadvantage of attaching printers directly to the network is the cost and availability of the network attachment option for each printer. Another possible disadvantage of making each directly attached printer its own print server is the need to use an additional network connection for each print server device. Because your NetWare license supports a limited number of network connections, having several direct-attachment printers acting as independent print servers could potentially cause your server to reach the maximum licensing limit. If this happens, additional users will not be allowed to log in. You can usually get around the use of extra license connections by configuring the directly attached printers as remote printers controlled through a common NetWare print server, as described in the following section.

Before setting up any network printing system, you need to identify the printers in terms of printer type, location, name, and attachment method. For example, Universal AeroSpace just purchased a Lexmark Optra R+ printer that Luke McMann wants all IS users to be able to share. Because the NetWare server is located near the IS department, Eric Kenton decided to attach the printer locally to the NetWare server. Eric plans to develop a more sophisticated printing system using NDPS, but for simplicity's sake, he decided that for now he could implement queue-based printing to share the new printer. Table 8-1 contains the information Eric used to identify the new printer, including its name, make and model, and attachment method.

Table 8-1   IS Department Printer Information

Printer Name	Make/Model	Port and Interrupt	Location	Users	Print Queue Name/Volume	eDirectory Context	Operator
IS_P	Lexmark Optra R+	LPT1 Polled	Server AutoLoad	ISMgrs group	IS_Q CORP volume	.IS.UAS	ISMgrs group

Print Servers

A print server actually makes queue-based network printing happen by taking print jobs from print queues on NetWare servers and sending them to the assigned printer, as shown in Figure 8-5.

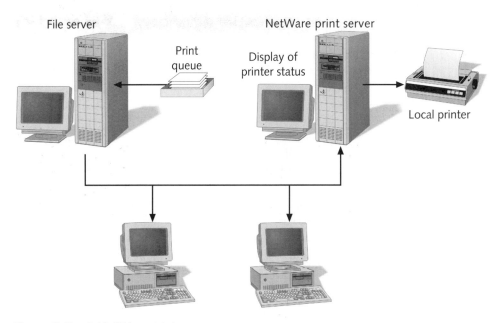

Figure 8-5   A NetWare print server

Printers can be attached directly to the print server as with local printers, attached remotely through a client running the NPTWIN95 software, or attached directly to the network through a device such as the HP JetDirect. In addition to printing, print servers are responsible for sending control commands to the printers and reporting printer status to the print server operator. In NetWare queue-based printing, each print server is defined by an eDirectory print server object that contains the print server name along with the names of up to 255 printer objects. After the print server object has been created and configured, the NetWare print server software can be loaded and run as a nondedicated print server from the file server computer by loading the Pserver.nlm program.

Setting Up Queue-based Printing

Setting up a simple queue-based network printing system involves these basic steps:

1. Define the network printers and how they will be attached.

2. Create a print queue for each printer.

3. Create an eDirectory printer object to represent each printer.

4. Define a print server object to send output from the print queues to the corresponding printer.

5. Load the print server and any remote printer software.

In the following activities, you perform each of these steps to share the printer attached to your classroom server. Because only one print server can be loaded on your classroom server at one time, you need to coordinate the final activity of loading and testing your print server with other students in the class.

Activity 8-1: Defining the Network Printer and Print Server

Time Required: 10 minutes

Objective: Implement a legacy queue-based printing system.

Description: Using Table 8-1 as a guide, on your student answer sheet, document the information you need to create your ##IS_P printer. The information should include the print queue name along with the name and context of your printer server object.

Activity 8-2: Creating a Print Queue

Time Required: 10 minutes

Objective: Implement a legacy queue-based printing system.

Description: After defining the names and eDirectory contexts for the printer, print queue, and print server, Eric used NetWare Administrator to create the queue-based printing objects. In this activity, you use NetWare Administrator to create the ##IS_Q print queue object you identified in Activity 8-1 for your version of the UAS network.

1. Start your computer, and log in to the network with your UasAdmin user name and password.

2. Start NetWare Administrator and, if necessary, open a browse window to your ##UAS container.

3. Create a print queue object named ##IS_Q in your .IS.##UAS container:

   a. If necessary, double-click your **##UAS** container to display your OUs.

   b. Click the **IS** OU, and then press **Insert** to open the New Object dialog box.

   c. Scroll down and double-click the **Print Queue** object to open the Create Print Queue dialog box, shown in Figure 8-6.

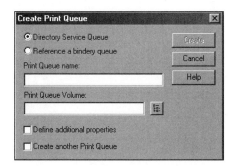

Figure 8-6 The Create Print Queue dialog box

   d. Enter **##IS_Q** (replacing ## with your assigned student number) in the Print Queue name text box.

   e. Click the **Browse** button to the right of the Print Queue Volume text box.

   f. Double-click the **UASHOST_CORP** volume object in the Available objects pane.

   g. Click the **Create** button to create the print queue and return to the NetWare Administrator browse window.

4. Add your ISMgrs group as the print queue operator:

a. Double-click your newly created print queue to open the Print Queue dialog box, shown in Figure 8-7.

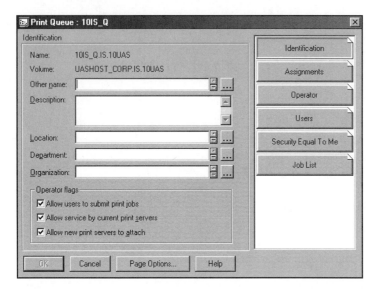

Figure 8-7   Checking print queue operators and users in the Print Queue dialog box

b. Click the **Operator** button, and record any existing print queue operators on your student answer sheet.

c. Click the **Add** button to open the Select Object dialog box.

d. Double-click your **ISMgrs** group to add it as a print queue operator.

5. To document the print queue users, click the **Users** button, and record the existing print queue users on your student answer sheet.

Notice that by default the container where the print queue is located is made a user of the print queue. Because your IS.##UAS Organization is a user, all users in the IS OU can send output to this print queue.

6. Click **OK** to save your changes and return to the NetWare Administrator browse window.

7. If you're continuing to the next activity, leave NetWare Administrator open and stay logged in. If not, exit NetWare Administrator, and log out.

Activity 8-3: Creating the Printer Object

Time Required: 10 minutes

Objective: Implement a legacy queue-based printing system.

Description: Now that you've created the print queue and defined the users and operators, the next step is to create and define the printer object, the printer attachment method, the port and interrupt to be used, and the print queue from which the printer will get its output. In this activity, you use NetWare Administrator to create and define the ##IS_P printer object you identified in Activity 8-1.

1. If necessary, start your computer, log in with your UasAdmin user name and password, and start NetWare Administrator.

2. Create a printer object named ##IS_P in your IS.##UAS container:

a. Click the **IS.##UAS** OU, and then press the **Insert** key to open the New Object dialog box.

b. Scroll down and double-click the **Printer (Non NDPS)** object to open the Create Printer dialog box.

c. Enter ##**IS_P** in the Printer name text box.

d. Click the **Define additional properties** check box.

e. Click the **Create** button to create the printer object and open the Printer (Non NDPS) dialog box, shown in Figure 8-8.

3. For your newly created printer object to receive output, you need to identify which print queue the printer will use:

a. Click the **Assignments** button, and record any print queue assignments on your student answer sheet.

b. Click the **Add** button to open the Select Object dialog box.

c. Double-click your ##**IS_Q** print queue in the Available objects section to add it to the print queue assignment.

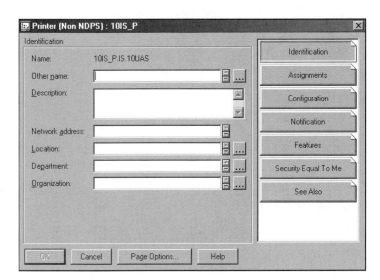

Figure 8-8 Configuring the printer object in the Printer (Non NDPS) dialog box

4. The final step in configuring the printer object is to define the attachment method along with the printer port and interrupt to be used:

a. Click the **Configuration** button to display the configuration information (see Figure 8-9). Notice that by default the printer is defined as a parallel printer with a text banner type. The service interval of 5 specifies that the print server will check the print queue every five seconds to see if there are any jobs to be printed. Be default, the printer starts with forms type 0 mounted. The "Minimize form changes within print queues" setting tells the printer to print all jobs with forms number 0 before checking for jobs with forms number 1, and so on.

b. To set the attachment method and port information, you need to click the **Communication** button to open the Parallel Communication dialog box, shown in Figure 8-10. Notice that the default port is LPT1 with the Polled interrupt setting. With the polled method, the computer checks the printer frequently to see if it is ready. Using the polled method prevents the printer from interrupting the computer processor every time it's ready to print and can provide better server performance.

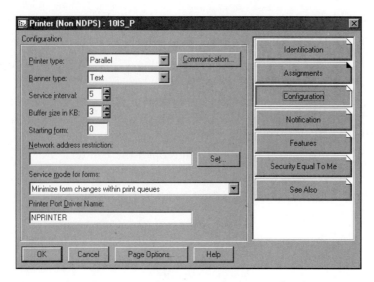

Figure 8-9   Viewing configuration information for the printer

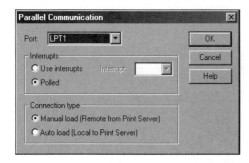

Figure 8-10   The Parallel Communication dialog box

    c. Notice that the connection type is also defined by default. Because your classroom printer will be attached directly to the server, click the **Auto load (Local to Print Server)** radio button.

    d. Click **OK** to save your changes and return to the Printer (Non NDPS) dialog box.

    e. Now that the printer configuration has been defined, click **OK** to return to the NetWare Administrator browse window.

5. If you're continuing to the next activity, leave NetWare Administrator open and stay logged in. If not, exit NetWare Administrator, and log out.

Activity 8-4: Creating the Print Server

Time Required: 10 minutes

Objective: Implement a legacy queue-based printing system.

Description: As described previously, queue-based printing requires a print server to take output from a print queue and send it to the appropriate network printer. To work, the print server software needs to know what printers it controls as well as who the print server operators and users are. The names of the printers, operators, and users are supplied to the print server software by creating and configuring an eDirectory print server object. In this activity, you create a print server for your ##UAS container and then configure it to manage your IS_P printer.

1. If necessary, start your computer, log in with your UasAdmin user name and password, and start NetWare Administrator.

2. Create a print server object named **##UAS_PS** in your **##UAS** container:

   a. Click your **##UAS** container, and press **Insert** to open the New Object dialog box.

   b. Scroll down and double-click the **Print Server (Non NDPS)** object to open the Create Print Server dialog box.

   c. Enter **##UAS_PS** in the Print Server name text box, and click the **Define additional properties** check box.

   d. Click the **Create** button to create the print server object and open the Printer (Non NDPS) dialog box.

3. Assign your printer to the new print server:

   a. Click the **Assignments** button, and then click the **Add** button to open the Select Object dialog box.

   b. Double-click your **IS** container in the Browse context section to display your printer in the Available objects section.

   c. Double-click your **IS_P** printer in the Available objects section.

4. Document the default users and operators of the new print server and make your ISMgrs group an operator of the print server:

   a. Click the **Users** button, and record the users of the print server on your student answer sheet.

   b. Click the **Operator** button, and record the name of the print queue operator on your student answer sheet.

   c. Click the **Add** button to open the Select Object dialog box, and then double-click your **IS** container in the Browse context section.

   d. Double-click your **ISMgrs** group in the Available objects section.

5. Click **OK** to save your print server configuration and return to NetWare Administrator.

6. Exit NetWare Administrator.

7. If you're continuing to the next activity, stay logged in. If not, log out.

Activity 8-5: Setting Up a Network Printer on the User Workstation

Time Required: 10 minutes

Objective: Implement a legacy queue-based printing system.

Description: There are two methods you can use to send output from your Windows client to your print queue. You can create a network printer by using the Add Printer function, or you can redirect a local printer port to the NetWare print queue. The disadvantage of the second method is that you have to be sure the network printer uses the same print driver as the local printer. If you send output to a network printer that's formatted for another type of printer, you might generate a lot of garbage output. As a result, it's usually better to create a network printer that uses the correct print driver for the queue you have selected. In this activity, you create a printer that will send output to your IS_Q print queue.

1. If necessary, start your computer, and log in with your UasAdmin user name and password.

2. Click **Start**, **Settings**, **Printers** to open the Printers window.

3. Double-click the **Add Printer** icon to start the Add Printer Wizard, and then click the **Next** button to continue.

4. Click the **Network printer** radio button, and then click the **Next** button.

5. Click the **Next** button to display the Browse for Printer dialog box.

6. Double-click the **NetWare Network** option, and then double-click the **Novell Directory Services** option.

7. Double-click your **##UAS** container to display your OUs, and then double-click your **IS** OU to display your printer and print queue objects.

8. Click your **##IS_Q** print queue object, and then click the **Next** button to display a message informing you that the server does not have the correct printer drivers installed. Click **OK** to close the window and display the Add Printer Wizard.

9. Select the manufacturer and printer identified for your classroom printer, and click **OK** to continue.

10. If you receive a message that the driver is already installed, click the **Keep existing driver (recommended)** option.

11. Respond with **Yes** to use this printer as the default, and then click the **Next** button to display the summary window.

12. Click the **Finish** button to return to the Printers window, with your new printer displayed.

13. Start WordPad, and create a simple document. Save it in the G:\Shared directory with the name ISPDemo.

14. Print the document to your IS_P printer, and exit WordPad. (This step places your output in the print queue, but no output will be printed until you load your print server in Activity 8-6.)

15. Verify that the output is in the print queue:

    a. Start NetWare Administrator.

    b. Double-click your **##IS_Q** print queue object to open the Print Queue dialog box.

    c. Click the **Job List** button to display all jobs in the print queue. Your new entry should be listed. Record the job name on your student answer sheet.

    d. Click **Cancel** to return to the NetWare Administrator browse window.

16. Exit NetWare Administrator, and log out.

Activity 8-6: Loading and Testing Your Print Server

Time Required: 10 minutes

Objective: Implement a legacy queue-based printing system.

Description: Before network printing can start, you need to run the print server software on the NetWare server. Because only one print server can run on a NetWare server at one time, you need to coordinate this activity with the other students in your class. In this activity, you load your print server on the UASHOST NetWare server and retrieve your output.

To perform this activity and test your print server, you need to have the printer model you selected in Step 9 of Activity 8-5 attached to the LPT port of the NetWare server.

1. Wait for your turn to access the server console.

2. Depending on your classroom server tree structure, enter one of the following commands replacing ## with your assigned student number:

   ```
   PSERVER    .CN=##UAS_PS.O=##UAS
   PSERVER    .CN=##UAS_PS.OU=##UAS.O=CLASS
   ```

3. Click to highlight the **Printer Status** option, and press **Enter** to display a printer list.

4. Press **Enter** to display a printer status window. Your document should now be printing on the classroom printer.

5. Press the **left arrow** key to highlight the Printer Control option, and press **Enter** to display a printer control menu.

6. Highlight the **Form Feed** option, and press **Enter** to eject a page.

7. Press the **Esc** key twice to return to the Available Options menu.

8. Perform the following steps to unload your print server:

    a. Highlight the **Print Server Information** option, and press **Enter** to display the Printer Server Information and Status window.

    b. Press **Enter** to display the Print Server Status Options menu.

    c. Click the **Unload after active print jobs** option, and press **Enter** to unload your print server and return to the console screen.

9. Retrieve your output from the classroom printer.

Troubleshooting Queue-based Printing

Despite your best efforts, with so many components having to work together, things can go wrong, resulting in network printing problems. As with any form of problem solving, approaching the problem in a systematic, logical way usually produces the best results. Typically, when you begin troubleshooting a network printing problem, you should gather information about the problem and how it occurs. Part of this process is determining whether the particular printing process worked in the past. If printing has been working, you need to look for anything that has changed, such as printer drivers, printer or print queue configurations, or physical moving of equipment. If the printing process has not been used previously, look for problems in the initial setup and configuration. For example, one of the most common problems in setting up queue-based printing is forgetting to assign the printer to a print queue. If this is the case, print jobs will be sent to the print queue but will not be printed. The most obvious sign of this problem is a lot of print jobs in the print queue. If printing has been working in the past, before spending a lot of time digging into the details, you should try these Novell-recommended quick-fix techniques:

1. If the printer status is offline or out of paper:
    - Turn the printer off and on, and then retry the output.
    - Check the printer self-test to make sure the printer functions properly.
    - Check the printer cover and paper feed.
    - Check the cable type and connections.
    - Test the cable with a working printer.

2. If printer output is garbled:
    - Check the printer software setting and language.
    - Check for the correct printer driver installed on the workstation.
    - Turn the printer off and on, and then retry the output.

3. If print jobs are not going to the print queue:
    - Check the print queue setting for the printer on the user workstation.
    - Check the language setting on the printer.

If the queue-based printing problems cannot be corrected with these quick fixes, you need to determine whether the problem occurs before or after the print queue. You can perform the following steps to determine whether the printing problem occurs before or after the print job reaches the print queue:

1. Stop print jobs from leaving the print queue by performing the following steps:
    - If necessary, log in as the network administrator or print queue operator, start NetWare Administrator, and expand the container where the print queue is located.
    - Right-click the print queue, and click Details to open the Print Queue dialog box, similar to the one shown previously in Figure 8-7.

- Click the Allow service by current print servers check box to disable this option.
- Click OK to save the setting and minimize NetWare Administrator.
- Use an application such as Notepad to send a job to the printer.
- Maximize NetWare Administrator, right-click the printer, and click Details.
- Click the Job List button to display the print jobs.

2. If the print job never arrives at the print queue or if the print job status indicates "Adding" and does not change to "Ready," the problem is probably in the workstation. Check the printer redirection for the workstation by performing these steps:

- Click Start, Settings, Printers to open the Printers window.
- Right-click the printer being checked, and then click Properties.
- Click the Ports tab, and verify that the print queue is correctly identified in the Port and Printer columns.

3. If the print job is placed in the print queue and is in the Ready status, perform the following steps to enable service by the print server and monitor the printer status:

- Use NetWare Administrator to click the Allow service by current print servers check box, as described in Step 1.
- In the Print Queue dialog box, click the Assignments button, and verify that the print queue is assigned to a printer and print server.
- Verify that the print server is loaded on the NetWare server by going to the server console and pressing Ctrl+Esc to display all modules. If necessary, load the print server as described in the previous section.

4. If the print job is printed but there's no output from the printer, check the following:

- Turn the printer off and on.
- Check the printer cable.
- Check the printer language settings.
- Check the print server configuration, and then unload and reload the print server. Reloading the print server can sometimes correct printing problems.

Printing problems can be tricky to find, requiring a lot of checking and experimenting. The more experience you have, the quicker you will recognize common problems and be able to figure out solutions. If the problem persists, try re-creating the printer objects and then adding the new printer to the workstation. For a number of reasons, printer objects have been known to become corrupted, and the only solution is to re-create them. As with all troubleshooting, change only one item at a time, and then test the system. Making multiple changes can further complicate the problem, making it harder to solve.

IMPLEMENTING NOVELL DISTRIBUTED PRINT SERVICES

Although queue-based printing works fine for small networks in which the printer can be attached to the server, setting up and maintaining queue-based printing on larger, more complex networks, with printers attached directly to the network cable, is a lot of work. The **Novell Distributed Print Services (NDPS)** system is the result of a joint effort by Novell, Hewlett-Packard, and Xerox to develop a truly distributed network printing system based on the International Standards Organization (ISO) 10175 Document Printing Application (DPA) standard. Because this standard is supported by most printer manufacturers, NDPS will support existing and future printer products. NDPS is an improvement over earlier NetWare printing solutions because it makes network printing easier to configure, use, and manage. In addition, as part of Novell's OneNet strategy, the NetWare 6 NDPS system includes support for iPrint, which is based on the new Internet Printing Protocol (IPP) standard. Because iPrint uses the IPP standard, NDPS printers can be accessed and managed across the Internet and within the corporate intranet.

NDPS is designed to simplify setting up and maintaining network printing by taking advantage of new client software and more sophisticated printers. In NDPS printing, each printer is represented by an agent that can advertise itself on the network. An NDPS printer with embedded printer agent software enables you to simply connect the printer to the network to make it available to all users. After it's connected to the network, the NDPS printer agent running on the printer communicates directly with NDPS-compatible clients on user workstations so that users can spool output directly to a print job stored on a NetWare server. The printer agent also performs the tasks of a print server by sending print jobs to the printer.

Because most printers currently on the market do not have embedded printer agents, NetWare includes NDPS Manager, which you can run on your NetWare server to manage printer agents for printers that do not have their own embedded printer agents. With NDPS Manager, any printer can be attached to the network by using the local, remote, or direct attachment methods described in the queue-based printing section earlier in this chapter. Printer agent software running on NDPS Manager transfers data from the user's workstation to the printer through a printer gateway. NetWare includes NDPS printer gateways for a variety of printer models and attachment methods. NDPS also makes installing printers on user workstations easier by automatically downloading the necessary printer driver to the user's workstation during printer installation. Users will benefit from NDPS printing by being able to quickly view printer status so that they can send jobs to printers that are not as busy. In addition, users can search the network for printers that have certain capabilities, such as color printing. In the following sections, you learn how to set up and configure a NetWare NDPS printing system to meet the needs of UAS users.

Setting Up NDPS Components

Before implementing the NDPS network printing environment for the UAS network, you need to understand the basic NDPS components and how they work together. In the following sections, you learn about these NDPS components and how they are implemented in an NDPS printing environment:

- Physical printers
- NDPS Manager
- Brokers
- NDPS printer agents
- Gateways

In subsequent activities, you apply these NDPS components to setting up a printer for the Universal AeroSpace IS department. Later in the chapter, you use the concepts and techniques you have learned to plan and implement NDPS printing for your version of the UAS network.

Physical Printers

Printers come in a wide variety of makes, models, and capabilities. To correctly format data and take advantage of a printer's capabilities, user workstations need to have the correct software driver loaded for the printer model they are using. As a result, to correctly configure network printing, network administrators need to define the make and model of each printer used on the network. Because NDPS directly supports a limited number of printer makes and models, to make configuring printers easier, Eric recommended purchasing a printer that is included in the NDPS printer list. UAS was already using Lexmark printers, so Eric recommended purchasing Lexmark Optra R+ printers for network printing.

In addition to defining the type of printer used, you need to identify how each printer will be attached to the network. As in queue-based printing, NDPS printers can be physically attached to the network in one of three ways:

- Locally to the server
- Remotely through a workstation
- Directly to the network cable

In the following activity, you define the characteristics and attachment method to be used in setting up the NDPS printer for the IS department.

Activity 8-7: Defining a Physical Printer

Time Required: 5 minutes

Objective: Identify physical printer characteristics and drivers.

Description: In this activity, you identify the characteristics of the printer you will be using for your version of the IS department's network printer.

1. Based on the network configuration supplied by your instructor, use your student answer sheet to identify the make and model of the printer you will be using to simulate the IS department's network printer.

2. Based on the configuration information supplied by your instructor, on your student answer sheet, document the attachment method to be used for your IS department's network printer.

Brokers

Printer agents need to register their printing services on the network and be able to send messages to users and operators. The NDPS **Broker** component provides these services to the printer agents running on the network and includes the following services for all printer agents:

- *Resource Management Service (RMS)*—This service stores network resources, such as software drivers, fonts, and forms, in a central location and then provides these resources to clients that make a request for them. NDPS uses RMS to download printer drivers and other setup information, such as banners, to NDPS clients.

- *Event Notification Service (ENS)*—Printer agents use this service to send printer status messages to users via popup windows, e-mail, or log files.

- *Service Registry Services (SRS)*—This service allows NDPS printers to advertise their presence so that NDPS clients can access them. SRS also maintains printer information, such as the device type, device name, and network address. SRS reduces network traffic by eliminating the need for each printer to broadcast its presence on the network by sending out Service Advertising Packets (SAPs) at frequent intervals.

Before creating and running printer agents, a Broker must be running on the local network. If it's not, or if the nearest Broker requires network traffic to go across more than three routers, you need to create and load an additional Broker on the NetWare server. As with NDPS Manager, a Broker consists of an eDirectory object and software loaded on the server. After creating and loading NDPS Manager, Eric used the iManager utility to create a Broker object and then loaded the Broker software on the UASHOST server. A second Broker object will be needed on the new server planned for the AeroDyn division because sharing services across the WAN wouldn't be feasible. In the following activity, you use iManager to create a Broker object for your version of the UAS network.

Activity 8-8: Creating an NDPS Broker

Time Required: 10 minutes

Objective: Create and configure an NDPS Broker.

Description: In this activity, you use the iManager utility to create a Broker object for your ##UAS organization. This activity is optional because to create a Broker object, you must be able to log in to the Novell network with the Supervisor right to the SYS volume.

1. If necessary, start your computer.

2. Click the **Workstation only** check box, and enter the user name and password you use to log on to the local Windows 2000 workstation.

3. Start your Web browser, and enter the URL **https://ip_address:2200**, replacing *ip_address* with the IP address of your UASHOST server.

4. Click the **UASHOST** server object under the eDirectory iManager heading to open the Login window.

5. Log in with the administrative user name and password:

   a. Enter the administrative user name in the User Name text box.

   b. Enter the administrative password in the Password text box, and the administrative context in the Context text box.

   c. Click the **Login** button to log in and open the iManager window.

   d. Expand the iPrint Management options by clicking the **+** symbol to the left of iPrint Management.

6. To create the NDPS Broker, click the **Create Broker** option to open the Create Broker window.

7. Enter the name **UAS_Broker** in the Broker name text box.

8. If your ##UAS organization is not displayed in the Container name text box, click the **Browse** button to open the eDirectory Object Selector window and follow these steps:

   a. Navigate to your ##UAS container.

   b. Click your **##UAS** container to insert it in the Container name text box.

9. Click the **Browse** button to the right of the RMS volume text box to open the eDirectory Object Selector window.

10. Click the **UASHOST_SYS** volume to place this volume in the RMS volume text box.

11. Click **OK** to create the Broker object, and then click **OK** to close the "The Create Broker Request succeeded" message and return to the iManager window.

12. Click the **Exit** button on the toolbar to return to the iManager Login window.

13. Exit your Web browser, and log off.

NDPS Manager

As described earlier, each physical printer in NDPS must be represented on the network by a printer agent. NDPS-enabled printers have printer agent software embedded in the physical printer. Non–NDPS-enabled printers don't have their own embedded printer agents; as a result, the printer agent software for these printers must run on a NetWare server. **NDPS Manager** consists of software along with an eDirectory object used to create, manage, and run printer agents for printers that do not have embedded printer agents. NDPS Manager's eDirectory object contains configuration information that tells the NDPS Manager software where to store print jobs and which users have rights to perform management tasks. After the NDPS Manager object is created, the NDPS Manager software needs to be loaded on the server to create and run printer agents. In addition to running a printer agent for each non–NDPS-enabled printer, NDPS Manager enables administrators to manage and configure the printer agents from the NetWare server console. Figure 8-11 shows the relationship between NDPS Manager, printer agents, and physical printers.

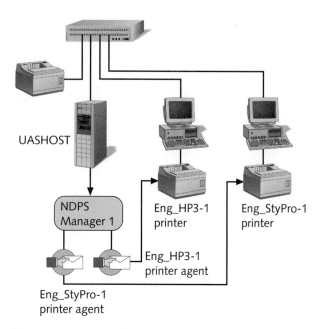

Figure 8-11   NDPS Manager

 Only one NDPS Manager at a time can be loaded on a NetWare server.

There's no limit on the number of printer agents that can be controlled from one NDPS Manager, but a large network can have multiple NDPS Managers running on separate NetWare servers to delegate administrative tasks or reduce network traffic across routers and WANs, as shown in Figure 8-12.

Because the UAS printers do not have embedded printer agent software, before creating printer agents, Eric created an NDPS Manager object named UAS_NDPSM in the UAS_Tree container. The UAS_NDPSM object contains the configuration and security information needed to load the NDPS Manager software. When configuring the UAS_NDPSM object, Eric selected the CORP volume rather than the SYS volume as the location for the print job database. Using a volume other than SYS for storing print jobs protects the SYS volume from filling up with print jobs waiting to be printed. If the SYS volume becomes full, the NetWare server will go down, with the possible loss of data and productivity.

Because of Novell's OneNet strategy, NDPS printer management tasks have been included in iManager rather than ConsoleOne; NetWare Administrator still retains the NDPS management functions from earlier NetWare versions. Although either NetWare Administrator or iManager can be used to create NDPS objects, Eric elected to use iManager to get more experience with Novell's OneNet strategy. After creating the NDPS object, Eric activated the manager by loading the NDPS Manager software on the UASHOST server and updating the startup files. In the following activity, you use the iManager utility to create an NDPS Manager for your version of the UAS network and learn how to load the NDPS Manager on the NetWare server.

Activity 8-9: Creating an NDPS Manager

Time Required: 10 minutes

Objectives: Create and configure an NDPS Manager.

Description: In this activity, you use the iManager utility to create an NDPS Manager for your ##UAS organization.

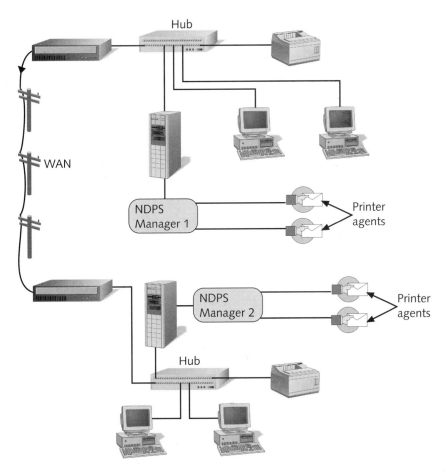

Figure 8-12   Multiple NDPS Managers

 Because the classroom server can have only one NDPS Manager loaded at a time, you must use the UAS_NDPS object set up by your instructor, rather than your own NDPS Manager object, to create your printer agents.

1. If necessary, start your computer.

2. Click the **Workstation only** check box, and enter the user name and password you use to log on to the local Windows 2000 workstation.

3. Start your Web browser software, and enter the URL **https://ip_address:2200**, replacing *ip_address* with the IP address of your UASHOST server.

4. Click the **UASHOST** server object under the eDirectory iManager heading to open the Login window.

5. Log in with your UasAdmin user name and password:

   a. Enter **UasAdmin** in the User Name text box.

   b. Enter your password in the Password text box and your **##UAS** container in the Context text box.

   c. Click the **Login** button to log in and open the iManager window.

   d. Click the **+** symbol to the left of the iPrint Management option to open a window, similar to Figure 8-13.

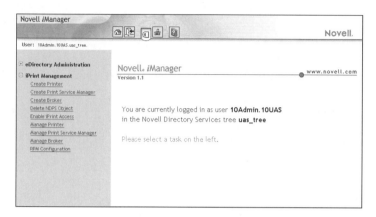

Figure 8-13   Selecting an iPrint Management option

6. To create the NDPS Manager object, click the **Create Print Service Manager** link to open the Create Manager window shown in Figure 8-14.

   a. Enter **UAS_NDPSM** in the Manager name text box.

   b. If your ##UAS organization is not displayed in the Container name text box, click the **Browse** button (the magnifying glass icon) to the right of the Container name text box to open the eDirectory Object Selector window.

   c. Navigate to your ##UAS container.

   d. Click your **##UAS** container to insert it in the Container name text box.

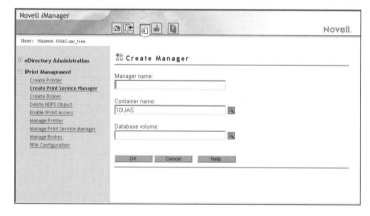

Figure 8-14   Creating an NDPS Manager

7. Click the **Browse** button to the right of the Database volume text box to open the eDirectory Object Selector window.

8. Click your **UASHOST_CORP** volume to insert it in the Database volume text box.

9. Click **OK** to create the NDPS Manager object, and then click **OK** to close the "The Create Manager Request succeeded" message box and return to the iManager window.

10. Click the **Exit** button on the toolbar to return to the iManager Login window.

11. Exit your Web browser, and log out.

Loading Broker and NDPS Manager Software

Before creating the other NDPS objects, the Broker and NDPS Manager software components need to be loaded onto the NetWare server. Eric used Remote Manager to load the UAS_BROKER and UAS_NDPS

Manager software onto the UASHOST server. You can follow along if you have access to a user account with the Supervisor right to the NetWare server:

1. First, Eric used his Web browser to enter the URL https://*ip_address*:2200 (*ip_address* represents the IP address assigned to the UASHOST server) to open the NetWare Web Manager window.

2. Next, he clicked the UASHOST object under the NetWare Remote Manager heading to open the Login window.

3. Eric entered the Admin user name and password, and then clicked OK to open the NetWare Remote Manager window, similar to the one in Figure 8-15. (The volumes displayed in your Remote Manager window will depend on the server configuration.)

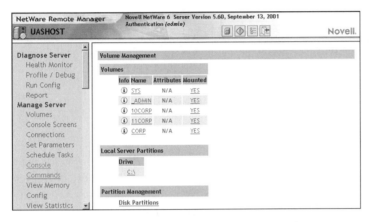

Figure 8-15   The NetWare Remote Manager window

4. Eric next clicked the Console Screens link on the left to open the Current Screens window (see Figure 8-16).

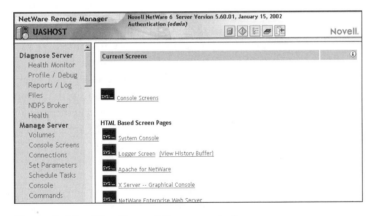

Figure 8-16   The Current Screens window

5. He then clicked the System Console link, entered the command LOAD BROKER .UAS_BROKER.UAS, and pressed Enter to load the Broker software.

6. He then entered LOAD NDPSM .UAS_NDPSM.UAS in the command window, as shown in Figure 8-17, and pressed Enter to load the NDPS Manager software.

7. After loading the Broker and NDPS Manager software, Eric closed the UASHOST – System Console window and returned to Remote Manager.

8. Eric then clicked the Exit button on the Remote Manager toolbar, and clicked Yes to end the remote management session and close his Web browser.

```
Novell NetWare 6
(C) Copyright 1983-2001 Novell Inc. All Rights Reserved. Patent Pending.
Server Version 5.60 September 13, 2001

Tuesday, January 22, 2002   6:47:16 pm CST
UASHOST:
UASHOST:

Loading Module XSETROOT.NLM                              [    OK    ]
Loading Module JNDPS.NLM                                 [    OK    ]
  Auto-Loading Module DPRPCNLM.NLM                       [    OK    ]
  Auto-Loading Module DPLSV386.NLM                       [    OK    ]
  Auto-Loading Module NIPPED.NLM                         [    OK    ]
Loading Module MLIB.NLM                                  [    OK    ]
Loading Module NAWT.NLM                                  [    OK    ]
Loading Module ICEWM.NLM                                 [    OK    ]
  Auto-Loading Module ICELIB.NLM                         [    OK    ]
Loading Module NWBG.NLM                                  [    OK    ]
Loading Module FONTMN.NLM                                [    OK    ]
Loading Module NWBGPNT.NLM                               [    OK    ]
Loading Module NWBGPNT.NLM                               [    OK    ]

Loading Module JNCPV2.NLM                                [    OK    ]
UASHOST:
```

```
LOAD NDPSM .UAS_NDPSM.UAS
```

Figure 8-17   Entering commands to load the NDPS Manager software

Printer Agents

As described previously, **printer agents** are software components that represent network printers, forming the core of the NDPS architecture; each physical printer on the network must be represented by a printer agent. To configure and manage NDPS, you need to understand and work with printer agents, which perform the following three basic functions for a networked printer:

- Receive spooled output from applications running on client computers and store the output as a print job in a database located on the NetWare server

- Act as a print server by taking print jobs from the server database and printing them on the printer

- Provide printer status and control information to network clients through the Broker

When using NDPS-embedded printers, the printer agent is contained in the printer itself. For non–NDPS-embedded printers, such as the UAS printers, the printer agent is contained in the NDPS Manager software running on the NetWare 6 server. This software acts as a liaison between the physical network printer it represents and the client computer, as shown in Figure 8-18. When a user prints to a network printer, the output first goes to the printer agent representing that printer, which spools the output to a database file on the NetWare server until the printer is ready. When the printer is available, the printer agent takes a print job from the database file and then uses its assigned gateway to transmit the print job to the network printer, along with any special configuration commands.

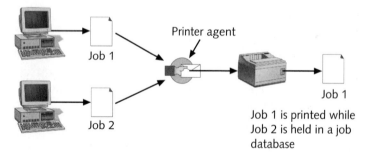

Printer agent

Job 1

Job 2

Job 1

Job 1 is printed while
Job 2 is held in a job
database

Figure 8-18   A printer agent

To spool printer output and work with other network services, a printer agent needs to be configured with basic printer information, including a name that references the physical printer, the make and model of the physical printer, and the gateway to be used by the printer attachment method. In addition, to access printers using iPrint's Internet Printing Protocol (IPP), printer agents need to be IPP enabled. When the first printer agent on an NDPS Manager is IPP enabled, NetWare automatically loads the IPPSRVR.NLM module to handle IPP-based printing functions. Printer agents that are not IPP enabled are accessible only to users who have Novell Client loaded.

Printer agents can be classified as public access or controlled access. As the name implies, **public access printers** are available to anyone with an attachment to the network. These printers are the easiest to set up because they do not require a corresponding eDirectory object. **Controlled access printers** provide more security and manageability, but for each controlled access printer, you need to create and configure an eDirectory object and then grant access to that object for the appropriate users or groups. To restrict use of the IS department printer to only IS users, Eric decided to create a controlled access printer agent named IS_OptR_1 for the IS department and place the printer agent object in the IS.UAS context.

Gateways

Before creating the printer agent, Eric needed to define a gateway for connecting the printer agent to the physical printer. As described earlier, for printer agent software running on NDPS Manager to access a physical printer, the printer agent needs to use one of the gateways shown in Figure 8-19.

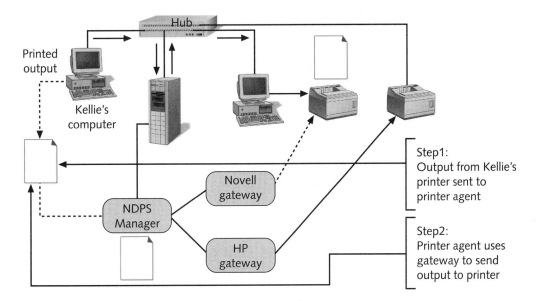

Figure 8-19   The printer agent uses a gateway to access a printer

As you can see in the diagram, **gateways** are used to connect physical printers to their associated printer agents running on NDPS Manager. Gateways ensure that printer agents can communicate with physical printers regardless of the attachment method or port connecting the printer to the network. When you create a printer agent, in addition to selecting the NDPS Manager that will host the agent, you need to identify the gateway and the physical printer's make, model, and connection information (port and address). To send output from the printer agent to the correct printer, you configure a gateway with the connection information that identifies the correct physical printer. The method for identifying the physical printer depends on the gateway type. For example, printers attached to the network through dedicated print server interfaces, such as the HP JetDirect print servers at UAS, use specialized gateways supplied by the printer manufacturers. These gateways typically require you to identify the printer by the IP address assigned to the dedicated print server interface.

NetWare 6 is currently shipping with several gateways, including the Hewlett-Packard (HP) gateway, the Xerox gateway, the EpsonNet gateway, the Lexmark IP gateway, the IPP gateway, and the Novell gateway. Using Novell's System Development Kit (SDK), other OEM (original equipment manufacturer) companies are developing gateways for their printers.

The HP and Xerox Gateways   The HP gateway software connects printer agents to printers attached to the network via an HP JetDirect print server or an HP JetDirect card. This gateway can be configured to locate all printers attached to the network via an HP JetDirect print server or JetDirect card and then automatically create printer agents for them. On a large network with many directly attached printers, this can save a lot of time over manually creating printer agents for each printer. The Xerox gateway is similar in function to the HP gateway, except that it's designed to find and configure Xerox printer products.

The Novell Gateway   The Novell gateway consists of two major components: the Print Device Subsystem (PDS) and the Port Handler (PH). The PDS translates control information, such as commands for landscape or duplex printing, to the appropriate escape code sequence for the printer. The PH is responsible for directing output to the correct physical printer using one of the following methods:

- *Local ports*—The PH enables printer agents to communicate with printers attached to the gateway computer's parallel or serial port.

- *Remote printers*—The PH provides communication between a printer agent and a remote printer. The remote printer can be attached to a client computer running remote printer software or directly attached via a dedicated print server device, such as HP's JetDirect or Intel's NetPort.

- *Print queue*—For devices that support printing only from a queue-based system, the PH can send printer output from a printer agent to a specified print queue serviced by a dedicated print server device, such as earlier versions of Intel's NetPort or HP's JetDirect products.

The HP LaserJet 5si PostScript printer that Eric purchased for the IS department did not have a built-in network card, so Eric first attached the printer to his workstation and created a printer agent using the Novell gateway. Later, when he received JetDirect print servers, he moved the printer from his workstation and created a new printer agent using the HP gateway. Although printer agents can be created with iManager, Eric used NetWare Administrator because it has more options for selecting gateways and configuring the printer attachment. In Activity 8-10, you use NetWare Administrator to create a printer agent, using the Novell gateway, for your version of the UAS network. If your classroom has a printer attached to an HP JetDirect or similar print server, you can also perform Activity 8-11 to create another printer agent based on the HP gateway.

Activity 8-10: Creating a Printer Agent Using the Novell Gateway

Time Required: 10 minutes

Objectives: Create and configure a printer agent using the Novell gateway.

Description: In this activity, you use NetWare Administrator to create a controlled access printer agent named ##IS_OptR_1, using the Novell gateway. This activity is written so that you can create the printer agent even if your workstation does not have an attached printer.

1. If necessary, start your computer, and log in with your UasAdmin user name and password.

2. Start NetWare Administrator, and open a browse window to your ##UAS container.

3. If necessary, double-click your **##UAS** container to expand it.

4. Click your **IS** OU, and press **Insert** to open the New Object dialog box.

5. Scroll down and double-click the **NDPS Printer** object to open the Create NDPS Printer dialog box (see Figure 8-20).

6. Enter **##IS_OptR_1** in the NDPS Printer Name text box (replace ## with your assigned student number) and verify that the Create a New Printer Agent radio button is selected.

7. Click the **Define Additional Properties** check box, and then click the **Create** button to open the Create Printer Agent dialog box, shown in Figure 8-21.

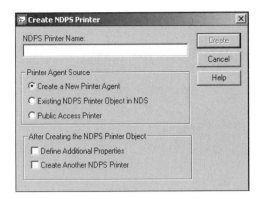

Figure 8-20   The Create NDPS Printer dialog box

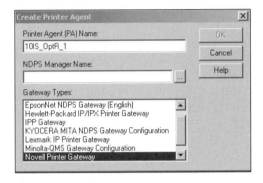

Figure 8-21   The Create Printer Agent dialog box

8. Next you need to select the NDPS Manager currently loaded on your NetWare server. In this step, you should follow the procedure to select the classroom NDPS Manager from the UAS Organization. Click the **Browse** button to the right of the NDPS Manager Name text box to open the Select Object dialog box.

Although you created an NDPS Manager option in a previous activity, you need to use the NDPS Manager installed on your classroom server.

a. In the Browse context section, navigate to the UAS container, if necessary, and then double-click the **UAS** container.

b. Double-click the **UAS_NDPSM** object in the Available objects section.

c. Verify that the Novell Printer Gateway option is selected, and then click **OK** to open the Configure Novell PDS for Printer Agent dialog box, shown in Figure 8-22.

9. Scroll down and click the **Lexmark Optra R** option in the Printer Type list box.

10. Click **OK** to open the Configure Port Handler for Printer Agent dialog box, shown in Figure 8-23.

11. In the Connection Type section, click the **Local (physical connection to server)** radio button, and in the Port Type section, click the **LPT1** radio button used to connect the printer to the NetWare server.

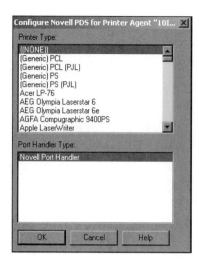

Figure 8-22   The Configure Novell PDS for Printer Agent dialog box

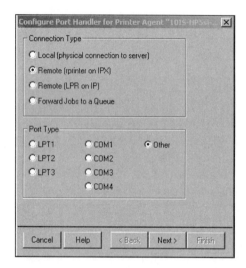

Figure 8-23   The Configure Port Handler for Printer Agent dialog box

12. Click the **Next** button to set controller type and interrupts, as shown in Figure 8-24. In this dialog box, you identify the interrupt used by the client computer to monitor the printer port you selected. Unless you're sure of the interrupt number used by your client computer's LPT port, click the **None (polled mode)** radio button.

13. Click the **Finish** button to create the printer agent for your ##IS_OptR_1 printer. You'll see a Loading Printer Agent wait message while the system creates and loads your printer agent.

14. Because a printer is not currently connected to the new printer agent, you'll see a message indicating that the printer needs attention. This problem will be corrected later by loading the remote printer software. For now, click **OK** to continue.

15. After the printer agent is created, the Select Printer Drivers dialog box opens, where you identify the printer driver for the client to use when formatting output for this printer.

16. Click the **Windows 2000 Driver** tab, and verify that Lexmark Optra R (or the driver for your printer) is selected. You can also click the Windows 95/98 and Windows NT4 Driver tabs to select printer drivers for users accessing the printer from those operating systems.

17. Click the **Continue** button to open the Information – NDPS summary window. If you're satisfied with the selections, click **OK** to continue.

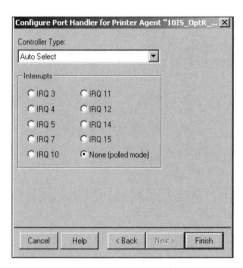

Figure 8-24   Configuring the port and interrupts

18. Because no printer is currently connected to the new printer agent, you'll see an error message informing you that printer details cannot be viewed. Click **OK** to continue and open the NetWare Printer Control dialog box for your ##IS_OptR_1 printer (see Figure 8-25).

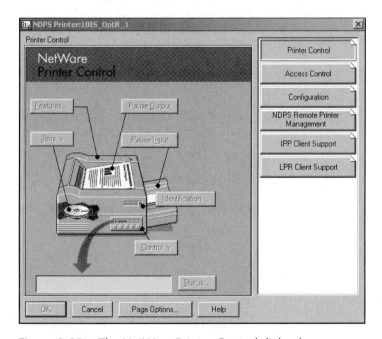

Figure 8-25   The NetWare Printer Control dialog box

19. Click the **Access Control** button to display access control information.

20. Click the **Users** icon to display the users who will be allowed to send output to the printer, and record their names on your student answer sheet.

21. Make the user name you created for yourself in Chapter 2 an operator of the printer:

   a. Click the **Operators** icon to display the current operators, and record their names on your student answer sheet.

   b. Click the **Add** button to open the Select Object dialog box.

   c. Double-click the user name you created in Chapter 2 in the Available objects section to add it to the Current Operators list box.

22. Click the **Printer Control** button to return the NetWare Printer Control dialog box.

23. Click **OK** to save your changes and return to the NetWare Administrator browse window.

24. If you're continuing to the next activity, leave NetWare Administrator open and stay logged in. If not, exit NetWare Administrator, and log out.

Activity 8-11: Creating a Printer Agent Using the HP Gateway

Time Required: 10 minutes

Objectives: Create and configure a printer agent using the HP gateway.

Description: In this optional activity, you use NetWare Administrator to create a second printer named IS_OptR_2, using the HP gateway. To perform this activity, you need to have a printer attached to your classroom network using the HP JetDirect or an equivalent interface.

1. If necessary, log in with your UasAdmin user name and password, and start NetWare Administrator.

2. Click your **IS** container, and press the **Insert** key to open the New Object dialog box.

3. Double-click the **NDPS Printer** object to open the Create NDPS Printer dialog box.

4. Enter **##IS_OptR_2** in the NDPS Printer Name text box (replace ## with your assigned student number), and verify that the Create a New Printer Agent radio button is selected.

5. Click the **Define Additional Properties** check box, and then click the **Create** button to open the Create Printer Agent dialog box.

6. Follow these steps to select the classroom NDPS Manager from the UAS Organization:

    a. Click the **Browse** button to the right of the NDPS Manager Name text box to open the Select Object dialog box.

    b. In the Browse context section, navigate to and double-click the **UAS** Organization.

    c. Double-click the **UAS_NDPSM** object in the Available objects section.

    d. Click **Hewlett-Packard IP/IPX Printer Gateway**, and then click the **OK** button to open the Configure HP Printer Gateway for PA dialog box, shown in Figure 8-26.

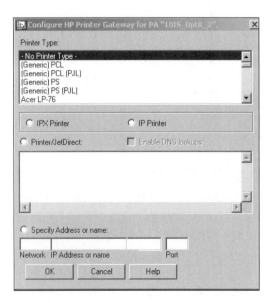

Figure 8-26   The Configure HP Printer Gateway for PA dialog box

7. Scroll down and click the correct printer type in the Printer Type list box, and then click the **IP Printer** radio button.

8. To identify the printer by IP address, click the **Specify Address or name** radio button, and then enter the IP address assigned to your JetDirect interface. If you do not know the IP address, you can click the **Printer/JetDirect** radio button to display a list of JetDirect interfaces that have been automatically detected on the network.

9. Enter the port number of the JetDirect interface used to connect the printer, and then click **OK**.

10. If a JetDirect interface is not found or the printer is not connected or turned on, you'll see a message indicating that the printer needs attention. This problem will be corrected later by connecting the JetDirect printer. For now, click **OK** to continue.

11. After the Printer Agent is created, the Select Printer Drivers dialog box opens, where you identify the printer driver that the client should use when formatting output for this printer.

12. Click the **Windows 2000 Driver** tab and verify that the Lexmark Optra R (or the driver for your printer) is selected. (*Note*: If you have a printer attached to your workstation, use the printer type identified by your instructor.) You can also click the Windows 95/98 and Windows NT4 Driver tabs to select printer drivers for users accessing the printer from those operating systems.

13. Click the **Continue** button to display the Information – NDPS summary window. If you're satisfied with the selections, click **OK** to continue.

14. If necessary, double-click your **##IS_OptR_2** printer to open the NetWare Printer Control dialog box (shown previously in Figure 8-25).

15. Click the **Access Control** button to display the access control information.

16. Click the **Users** icon to display the users who will be allowed to send output to the printer, and record their names on your student answer sheet.

17. Make your user name an operator of the printer:

    a. Click the **Operators** icon to display the current operators.

    b. Click the **Add** button to open the Select Object dialog box.

    c. Double-click your user name in the Available objects section to add it to the Current Operators list box.

18. Click the **Printer Control** button to return to the NetWare Printer Control dialog box.

19. Click **OK** to save your changes and return to the NetWare Administrator browse window.

20. Exit NetWare Administrator, and log out.

Installing NDPS Printers on User Workstations

After setting up the NDPS printing components for the IS department's printer, Eric's next task was installing the printer on user workstations. As with queue-based printing, to use an NDPS printer, a workstation must have a printer driver and client. The driver is used by applications to format the data correctly for the printer's make and model, and the printer client is responsible for sending output to the network printer agent. As with queue-based printers, you can manually install a network printer on a user's workstation with the Add Printer function in the Windows Printers dialog box. Manually adding printers to user workstations can be time-consuming for network administrators and might require extra training to instruct users on how to add their own printers. A preferred alternative is having Novell Client automatically install the NDPS printers when users log in. To automatically install printers on user workstations, you use NetWare Administrator to add the printers to the NDPS Remote Printer Management dialog box, as shown in Figure 8-27.

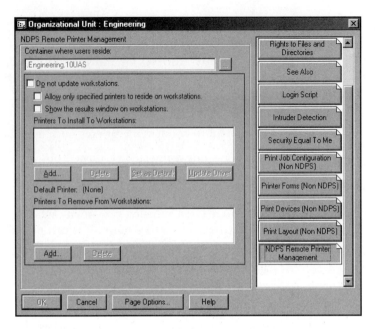

Figure 8-27   The NDPS Remote Printer Management dialog box

When you add a printer to the Printers To Install To Workstations section, it's installed upon login on the workstation of any user existing in that container. For example, if you add the ##IS_OptR_1 printer to the Printers To Install To Workstations section, when users in the IS OU, such as Luke McMann, log in, Novell Client checks to see whether the ##IS_OptR_1 printer has been installed; if not, Novell Client automatically installs the printer. In the following activity, you add your ##IS_OptR_1 printer to the Printers To Install To Workstations section for the IS OU, and then log in and verify that the printer has been installed.

Activity 8-12: Automatically Installing Printers

Time Required: 10 minutes

Objective: Install printers on user workstations.

Description: In this activity, you use NetWare Administrator to add your ##IS_OptR_1 printer to the IS container's NDPS Remote Printer Management dialog box, and then verify that the printer is automatically installed by logging in as Luke McMann.

1. If necessary, start your computer, and log in with your UasAdmin user name and password.

2. Start NetWare Administrator and, if necessary, open a browse window to your ##UAS Organization.

3. Right-click your **IS** OU, and then click **Details** to open the Organizational Unit : IS dialog box.

4. Scroll down and click the **NDPS Remote Printer Management** button to display the Printers To Install To Workstations section.

5. Click the **Add** button to display the Available Printers options.

6. Click your **##IS_OptR_1** printer, and then click **OK** to add it to the Printers To Install To Workstations section.

7. Click **OK** to save your changes and return to NetWare Administrator.

8. Exit NetWare Administrator, and log out.

9. Log in as Luke McMann by entering **LMcMann** in the Username text box and clicking the **Advanced** button to change the default context to your IS.##UAS container.

10. Verify that your ##IS_OptR_1 printer is installed:

    a. Click **Start**, **Settings**, **Printers** to open the Printers window.

    b. Verify that your ##IS_OptR_1 printer is installed. Record the printer names on your student answer sheet.

11. Close the Printers window, and log out.

Troubleshooting NDPS Printing

Many of the basics you learned about troubleshooting queue-based network printing problems apply to NDPS printing. Following are some "quick" fixes Novell recommends for solving problems that occur when setting up NDPS printing:

1. Attempt to resolve any error messages received for the server, printer agent, or client by using the following suggestions:

   - If the error message says that the client could not connect to the printer agent, verify that the NDPS Manager and Broker are both loaded and running. If they are both loaded, unload and then load the NDPS Manager.

   - Verify that the Autoexec.ncf file contains a LOAD NDPSM command and that the correct distinguished name of the NDPS Manager is specified.

   - If the client receives a message that a print job was rejected, check to see that the spooling volume for the printer agent has enough free space. If possible, use a volume other than SYS and set a limit on the spooling space.

2. If a network printing problem is limited to a single workstation, check the following:

   - Check the printer's job list to ensure that the job is getting to the spooling volume.

   - Review any changes made since the printer agent was properly working.

   - Check the printer configuration.

3. If a network printing problem affects several workstations, check the following:

   - In Novell Printer Manager, check the Printer Information dialog box for any NDPS error messages.

   - Check for printer error conditions (printer beeps or LCD panel lights) and error messages.

   - Turn the printer off and on. If the job is still in the printer agent job list, delete it.

In addition to the preceding procedures, the following tables contain tips for troubleshooting NDPS printing based on the scope of the printing problem. Table 8-2 contains suggestions on isolating specific NDPS printing problems for a single workstation that's unable to print to an NDPS printer that other user workstations are using successfully.

8

Table 8-2   Isolating Single-Workstation Printer Problems

Condition	Possible Problem	Action
The user workstation is printing to a print queue, but the printer receives no output. This could happen for non-NDPS clients, such as DOS or Macintosh computers.	The print queue is not being serviced by a printer agent or queue-based print server.	Use NetWare Administrator to verify that the print job is in the print queue. Verify that the print queue is being serviced by a print server or printer agent. If necessary, associate the print queue with the appropriate NDPS printer agent and verify that the printer agent is printing jobs for other workstations.
	The print job is being sent to the wrong print queue.	Check the printer configuration on the workstation to be sure it's associated with the correct print queue.
	The printer is using an incorrect print driver, causing the print device to disregard the print job.	Check the printer configuration on the workstation to make sure the printer is using the correct driver for the printer agent that services the corresponding print queue.
Print jobs do not appear in the printer agent's job list.	The Windows printer configuration is not correct.	Click Start, Settings, Printers, and check the printer status to see if any problems are evident. Check the driver and printer port configuration. The port should be configured to print to the correct printer agent or print queue.

Table 8-3 contains suggestions for troubleshooting problems that could prevent an NDPS printer from printing jobs for all workstations.

Table 8-3   Isolating NDPS Printer Problems

Condition	Possible Problem	Action
Printer agent problem	Printer agent is unable to connect to the print device.	Check the printer status on the server console or through NetWare Administrator.
Printer not connected	The printer agent is configured as a local printer on the Novell gateway, and the printer is not attached to the server or is turned off.	Attach or turn on the printer and retry printing.
	The printer agent is configured as a remote printer on the Novell gateway, and the NPTWIN95 remote printer software is not loaded, or the computer hosting the printer has been shut down.	Load the NPTWIN95 software on the workstation hosting the print device and connect it to the correct printer agent. Start the computer hosting the print device and retry.
I/O error	The printer agent is configured as a local printer on the Novell gateway, using the same port as a printer agent that's already loaded.	Determine which printer agent should be using that printer port on the server and then delete the incorrectly configured printer agent and re-create it, using a different gateway or printer port.
	The printer agent is configured as a directly attached printer using a printer interface, and the printer interface is not connected to the network or is turned off.	Reconnect or turn on the printer interface and try again. If necessary, wait until there's no printer activity, and then unload and load the NDPS Manager on the server.

Table 8-3   Isolating NDPS Printer Problems (continued)

Condition	Possible Problem	Action
	The printer agent is configured as a printer attached directly to the network, using a gateway such as HP JetDirect, and the printer interface is disconnected from the network or turned off.	Reconnect the printer interface and then turn it off and on. If the status does not change after a few minutes, wait until there's no printing activity and then unload and reload the NDPS Manager on the server.
Printer not bound	The printer gateway is not available, or the print device is disconnected from the gateway.	Reconnect the printer to the printer interface and retry.
Printer offline	The printer is out of paper or turned off.	Make sure the print device is on, and check for any error messages on the print device panel.
	The printer cable is defective or disconnected.	Check the printer cable to make sure it's securely attached to the print device and interface. If the printer still shows offline status, test and replace the printer cable.
Printer status is grayed out	NDPS Manager is not loaded.	Load the NDPS Manager on the server console.
	The wrong NDPS Manager is loaded.	If you have multiple NDPS Managers in your tree, verify that the correct NDPS Manager for the printer is loaded. If necessary, unload the incorrect NDPS Manager and load the correct one.
	The new printer agent encountered an error when first loading.	If a print device or interface is not attached to the network, the printer is turned off, or the remote printer software has not yet been loaded on a Windows 95/98 computer, you'll see an error message when creating the printer agent and the status will be grayed out in the Printer Control dialog box. Close the Printer Control dialog box, and then reopen it to view the printer status.
Jobs print but remain in the job list	User or operator hold is on.	Click the Configuration button in the Printer Control dialog box, and then modify the Job Hold settings of any job configurations listed in the Printer Configurations dialog box.
Jobs removed from the job list but not printed	Incorrect driver language	Verify that the correct printer driver is configured for the printer agent. Incorrect drivers can cause the printer to disregard print jobs.
	Cable problem	Faulty printer cables or broken wires can prevent data from reaching the print device. Test and replace the printer cable.
Jobs not displayed in the job list	Workstation printer configuration problem	Check the printer configuration on the workstation to make sure it's using the correct driver and is printing to the correct printer agent or print queue.
	Users do not have rights to print to the printer.	Verify that the printer agent is in the same container as the users who are printing. Verify that users who are not in the same container as the printer agent have been added to the access control list.

8

An important part of any printer troubleshooting process is tracking print jobs from the workstation to the printer agent. In the following activity, you practice the steps for tracking print jobs by walking through two sample problems.

Activity 8-13: Troubleshooting NDPS Printing

Time Required: 10 minutes

Objective: Troubleshoot NDPS printing.

Description: In this activity, you create two NDPS printing problems and then document the results.

1. If necessary, start your computer, and log in with your UasAdmin user name and password.

2. Start NetWare Administrator and, if necessary, open a browse window to your ##UAS container.

3. Pause the ##IS_OptR_1 printer output:

   a. If necessary, expand your **IS** OU.

   b. Double-click your **##IS_OptR_1** printer to open the Printer Control dialog box.

If you receive an "Error opening Xerox file" message, click OK and continue the activity.

   c. Click the option to pause printer output.

   d. Click **Cancel** to save your settings and return to NetWare Administrator.

4. Send a document to your printer:

   a. Start WordPad, and create a simple document containing your name and today's date.

   b. Print the document to your ##IS_OptR_1 printer.

   c. Exit WordPad without saving your document.

5. Check the job list of the ##IS_OptR_1 printer:

   a. Double-click your **##IS_OptR_1** printer to open the Printer Control dialog box.

   b. Click the **Jobs v** button, and then click **Job List** in the list that appears.

   c. Record the jobs on your student answer sheet, and identify which job was printed in Step 4. After recording the jobs, close the window containing the job list.

   d. Click **Cancel** to return to NetWare Administrator.

6. Repeat Step 3 to restart your ##IS_OptR_1 printer. Record your printer status, along with any messages, on your student answer sheet.

7. Wait for the instructor to unload the NDPS Manager software.

8. Repeat Step 4 to send a print job to your ##IS_OptR_1 printer.

9. Repeat Step 5 to record the status of your ##IS_OptR_1 printer on your student answer sheet.

10. Exit NetWare Administrator, and log out.

iPrint and the Internet Printing Protocol (IPP)

To use NDPS printers, a computer must have a printer driver installed and configured to send output to a printer agent. In earlier versions of NetWare, the Novell client software had to be installed on the user's workstation before NDPS printer agents could be installed and accessed. In NetWare 6, Novell has removed the requirement for the Novell client and replaced it with the iPrint system. As part of Novell's OneNet strategy, iPrint makes network printing independent from the client software and type of network connection. By using the industry-standard Internet Printing Protocol (IPP), iPrint enables users to print from anywhere to anywhere. Using iPrint, users can use a Web browser to locate printers and then automatically download and install the latest printer drivers on their workstations. The iPrint system consists of three major components:

- A print provider that consists of a set of browser plug-ins installed on a user's workstation with a Web browser

- The IPP server software installed on the NetWare 6 server during server installation (the IPP server software, which consists of the IPPSRVR.NLM module, is automatically loaded on the server when the first iPrint printer is configured).

- A set of HTML pages on the NetWare server that enables users to install the iPrint client and to set up and access network printers

In the following sections, you learn how to use NetWare Administrator and iManager to enable your IS department printer agent for IPP printing and how to use iPrint to install and access printers from your workstation.

Enabling Printers for iPrint

For an existing NDPS printer agent to be accessed from iPrint using IPP, the printer must first be IPP enabled. Enabling a printer agent identifies and connects it to the IPPSRVR software running on the NetWare 6 server. If the IPPSRVR software is not running, it's automatically loaded when the first printer agent is IPP enabled. You can use NetWare Administrator or iManager to enable an existing NDPS printer. In the following activity, you use iManager to enable your ##IS_OptR_1 printer for iPrint access.

Activity 8-14: Enabling an NDPS Printer for iPrint

Time Required: 10 minutes

Objective: Enable NDPS printers for iPrint access.

Description: In this activity, you use iManager to enable your ##IS_OptR_1 printer for iPrint access.

1. If necessary, start your computer. When the Novell Login window appears, click the **Workstation only** check box.

2. Enter your local user name and password for logging on to the Windows 2000 computer.

3. Start Internet Explorer, and enter the URL **https://ip_address:2200** (replacing *ip_address* with the IP address of your NetWare 6 server).

4. Click **OK** and then click **Yes** to display the NetWare Web Manager menu.

5. Click the **UASHOST** server under the eDirectory iManager heading to display the Login window.

6. Enter your user name, password, and context to your assigned UAS container, and then click the **Login** button.

7. Expand the **iPrint Management** heading, and then click the **Enable iPrint Access** link to display the NDPS Manager text box.

8. Click the **Browse** button to the right of the NDPS Manager text box to open the eDirectory Object Selector window.

9. Click the **up arrow** to display the UAS Organization.

10. Click the **down arrow** to the left of the UAS Organization to display the UAS_NDPSM Print Service Manager.

11. Click the **UAS_NDPSM** Print Service Manager to insert it into the NDPS Manager text box, and then click **OK** to display the Printer Agents section, similar to the one in Figure 8-28. On your student answer sheet, record the printer agents you see.

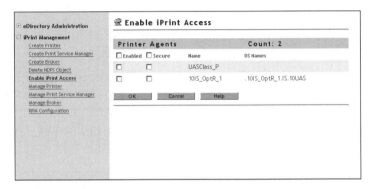

Figure 8-28   Enabling an NDPS printer for iPrint access

12. Click the check boxes in the Enabled and Secure columns to the left of your ##IS_OptR_1 printer.

13. Click **OK** to open the Results section, and then click **OK** to return to the iManager menu.

14. Click the **Exit** button on the iManager toolbar to return to the Login window.

15. Close your browser.

Installing the iPrint Client and IPP Printers

With Novell's iPrint system, you can install the printer driver and client on a user workstation from your Web browser. Using iPrint simplifies the task of setting up a network printer and enables computers to print to NDPS printers without using Novell Client. This feature will be important for the UAS Shipping and Receiving computers, which do not use Novell Client. As described earlier, iPrint uses the IPP standard to enable users to install, access, and manage printers across the Internet using their Web browsers. On the NetWare server, iPrint works through the IPPSRVR.NLM software and a set of HTML pages available from the NetWare Web server. Installing a printer on the user workstation involves three steps:

1. Access the iPrint Web site from the workstation browser by entering the URL for the NetWare Web server and a port number. Port number 631 is used for public access printers that do not require a user name, and port number 443 is used for controlled access printer agents that require a valid user name.

2. Download the IPP client software from the NetWare Web server to the user workstation. This process is performed automatically the first time an IPP printer is installed on the workstation.

3. Install a printer for the IPP-enabled printer agent. The printer consists of an IPP connection to the printer agent along with the correct driver software for formatting the printer output at the workstation.

In the following activities, you use these steps to install the IS_OptR_1 printer on Kellie's workstation, and then use iManager to verify that print jobs are being sent to the printer.

Activity 8-15: Using iPrint to Install the IS Department Printer

Time Required: 10 minutes

Objective: Use iPrint to install a printer on a workstation.

Description: In this activity, you install the iPrint client on your workstation, and then use iPrint to install and send output to your IS department printer.

1. If necessary, start your computer.

2. Log in to the Novell network with your UasAdmin user name and password.

3. Remove any existing copies of the ##IS_OptR_1 printer:

   a. Click **Start**, **Settings**, **Printers** to open the Printers window.

   b. If an ##IS_OptR_1 printer is installed, click the printer, press **Delete**, and then click **Yes** to delete the existing ##IS_OptR_1 printer.

   c. Close the Printers window.

4. Start your Web browser, enter the URL **https://*ip_address*:443/ipp** (replacing *ip_address* with the IP address of your NetWare 6 server), and press **Enter**. If necessary, click **OK** or **Yes** to close any security message boxes.

5. When you see the client installation message box, shown in Figure 8-29, click **OK**, and then follow these steps to install the iPrint client on your workstation:

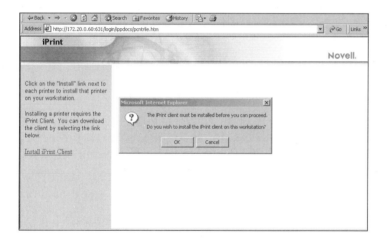

Figure 8-29   Installing the iPrint client

   a. When you see the File Download dialog box, click the **Run this program from its current location** radio button, and then click **OK** to extract the files.

   b. If you see a Security Warning message box informing you that the Authenticode signature cannot be found, click **Yes** to continue and run the Nipp.exe program from your server's IP address.

   c. Click **OK** to select English as your language and start the iPrint Installation Wizard.

   d. When you see the Welcome window, click the **Next** button to display the license agreement window.

   e. Read the agreement, and then click **Yes** to accept the license agreement and display the Select Program Folder dialog box.

   f. Click the **Next** button to accept the default folder location and begin file copying.

8

g. If you see any ReadOnly File Detected message boxes, respond by clicking **Yes** to overwrite the indicated files. Record any overwritten filenames on your student answer sheet.

h. After the installation is finished, verify that the Yes, I want to restart my computer now radio button is selected, and then click the **Finish** button to restart your computer.

6. After your computer restarts, click the **Workstation only** check box and log on to your local Windows 2000 computer with the Administrator user name and password.

7. Start your Web browser and enter the iPrint URL shown in Step 4.

8. A list of IPP-enabled printers should be displayed, similar to the example shown in Figure 8-30.

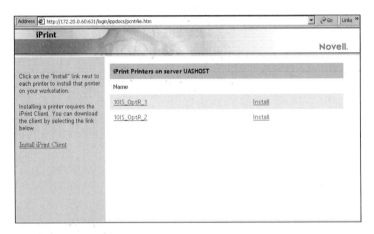

Figure 8-30   Viewing the list of IPP-enabled printers in iPrint

9. Click your **##IS_OptR_1** printer, and then click **OK** to open the Novell iPrint – Printer authentication dialog box. The authentication dialog box is necessary to determine whether you have rights to install the controlled access printer.

10. Enter your **UasAdmin** user name and password, and then click **OK** to install the printer and open the Printer Operations window, where you can check the jobs waiting to be printed and view printer information and status. After checking the printer status and information, click the Web browser's **Back** button to return to the list of iPrint-enabled printers.

11. If you created a second printer using the HP gateway in Activity 8-11, repeat Steps 9 and 10 to install that printer.

12. Close your Web browser.

13. After the installation is finished, perform the following steps to verify that the printer has been added to your workstation.

a. Click **Start**, **Settings**, **Printers**.

b. Verify that your IS_OptR_1 printer is available.

c. Close the Printers window.

14. Log out.

Activity 8-16: Testing the IS Department Printer

Time Required: 10 minutes

Objective: Use iManager to verify the status of print jobs.

Description: In this activity, you send output to the IS department printer you installed on your workstation, and then use the iManager utility to verify that print jobs have been sent to the printer.

1. Log in to the network as KThiele:

   a. Enter **KThiele** in the Username text box.

   b. Click the **Advanced** button, and then click the **Contexts** browse button to navigate to your IS.##UAS container.

   c. Click **OK** to log in, and enter the password you gave to your KThiele account in the Password text box.

   d. If necessary, log on to your local Windows 2000 computer.

2. Start WordPad by clicking **Start**, **Programs**, **Accessories**, **WordPad**.

3. Type the following text: **This is a test of the IS printer by <Enter your name here>.** Then click **File**, **Print** on the WordPad menu bar to display a list of available printers.

4. Click your **##IS_OptR_1** printer icon, and then click the **Print** button.

5. If you created a second ##IS_OptR_2 printer in Activity 8-11, perform the following steps to print a copy of your test to that printer:

   a. Click **File**, **Print** on the WordPad menu bar to display the available printers.

   b. Click your **##IS_OptR_2** printer icon, and then click the **Print** button.

   c. If you have a printer attached to the HP JetDirect interface, your print job should be printed.

6. Click **File**, **Exit** on the WordPad menu bar, and then click **No** when asked to save the document.

7. Start your Web browser and load the iManager utility:

   a. Start the Web browser and enter the URL **https://*ip_address*:2200** (replacing *ip_address* with the IP address of your NetWare 6 server).

   b. If necessary, click **OK** and then click **Yes** to close the Security Alert message boxes.

   c. Click the **UASHOST** icon under the eDirectory iManager heading to open the Login window.

   d. Enter **UasAdmin** in the User Name text box and your password in the Password text box.

   e. Enter **UAS** in the Context text box.

   f. Verify that UAS_Tree is entered in the Tree text box, and then click the **Login** button to display the iManager home page.

   g. Click the **+** symbol to the right of the iPrint Management option.

8. View the jobs for your IS_OptR_1 printer:

   a. Click the **Manage Printer** link to display the Manage Printer window.

   b. Click the **Browse** button next to the NDPS Printer text box, and navigate to your IS.##UAS container.

   c. Click your **##IS_OptR_1** printer icon to place this printer into the NDPS Printer text box.

   d. Click **OK** and, if necessary, click **Yes** to any security message boxes to display the Manage Printer: ##IS_OptR_1.IS.##UAS window, shown in Figure 8-31. (The options in the left-hand frame might vary based on the rights given to your user name.)

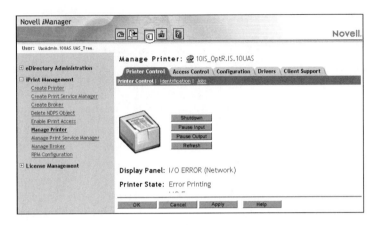

Figure 8-31   Viewing print jobs in iManager

    e. Click the **Printer Control** tab, if necessary, and then click the **Jobs** link. Record the print job information on your student answer sheet.

    f. Click the other tabs to view access control, configuration, drive, and client support information about your printer.

  9. If you created another printer in Activity 8-11, repeat Step 8 to view the jobs for your IS_OptR_2 printer.

10. Click the **Exit** button on the iManager toolbar to return to the Login window.

11. Close your Web browser, and log out.

Defining a Printing Environment

Now that you have had a chance to become more familiar with setting up NDPS printing components, it's time to apply this new knowledge to implementing the network printers for your version of the UAS network. Eric's first task in establishing the network printing environment was to define the printing needs to be supported on the network, which involved these steps:

1. Define the printing requirements of each user's applications.

2. Determine printer types, locations, and attachment methods.

3. Define names for all printers and identify any required print queues.

4. Plan the eDirectory context for each printer object.

In the following sections, you learn how to apply these steps to defining a network printing environment for your UAS organization using the NDPS Definition Form that Eric developed.

Step 1: Defining Printer Requirements

The first step in defining a printing environment is to identify the number and types of network printers that the organization will need. To do this, you need to analyze the requirements of each user's application software and his or her printing needs. Table 8-4 summarizes the printing needs for Engineering, Mgmt, and Mfg users in the UAS network.

After identifying the printing needs, the next step is to identify each network printer agent and the gateway for attaching it to the NDPS Manager. In a multiserver environment, you should also consider how many NDPS Managers will be needed to reduce network traffic across routers. Eric used the NDPS Definition Form, shown in Figure 8-32, to identify the printer agents, gateways, and NDPS Managers in the UAS network.

Table 8-4   UAS Printing Requirements

All Users	All users should have access to a color inkjet printer.
Engineering	The department's Lexmark Optra laser printer will be connected directly to the network and be available to all Engineering users to print correspondence and instruction manuals.
Mgmt	The department's Lexmark Optra laser printer will be connected directly to the network and available to the Mgmt users.
Mfg	Until they are attached directly to the network by using a JetDirect print server, the two Lexmark Optra laser printers in the Mfg department will be attached to the Receiving1 and Shipping1 computers. Russ Pence will manage the printers.

NDPS Definition Form

NDPS Manager: _UAS_NDPSM_   eDirectory Context: _UAS_
Server: _UASHOST_   Database Volume: _CORP_
Managers: _UasADMIN_

Printer Name	Make/Model	NDPS Printer Classification	eDirectory Context	Attachment Method	Gateway Type	Port Interrupt	Associated Print Queue	Users	Operators
IS_OptR_1	Lexmark Optra R	Controlled access	.IS.UAS	File server	Novell	LPT1 Polled	IS_OptR1_Q	IS OU	ISMgrs group
IS_OptR_2	Lexmark Optra R	Controlled access	.IS.UAS	Direct using JetDirect box	HP			IS and Engineering OUs	ISMgrs group
UAS_Color	HP Color LaserJet 5	Public access		Direct using JetDirect box	HP			All users	ISMgrs group
Eng_OptR_1	Lexmark Optra R	Controlled access	.Engineering.UAS	Direct using JetDirect box	HP			Engineering and Mgmt OUs	EngMgr role org
Mgmt_OptR_1	Lexmark Optra R	Controlled access	.Mgmt.UAS	Direct using JetDirect box	HP			Mgmt OU	AdmAsst org role
Rec_OptR_1	Lexmark Optra R	Controlled access	.Mfg.UAS	Remote to Receiving workstation	Novell	LPT1 Polled	Rec_OptR1_Q	Production group	MfgMgr role org
Shp_OptR_1	Lexmark Optra R	Controlled access	.Mfg.UAS	Remote to Shipping workstation	Novell	LPT1 Polled	Shp_OptR1_Q	Production group	MfgMgr role org

Figure 8-32   Use this form to identify printer agents, gateways, and NDPS Managers in the UAS network

The top part of the NDPS Definition Form identifies the NDPS Manager object and the NetWare server that will run the NDPS Manager software. Because an NDPS Manager can support an unlimited number of printer agents, one server running the NDPS Manager software is usually enough for most organizations, except when the organization's network is connected over a WAN. For example, because the AeroDyn division is connected across a T1 line, Eric is planning to use a separate NDPS Definition Form for the AeroDyn division. The NDPS Definition Form also includes columns for identifying the printer model, along with users and applications, for each network printer attached to a print server. To keep the printing system as simple as possible, Eric standardized the make and model of the printers to be used on the network when purchasing new equipment.

After analyzing UAS users' needs, Eric installed one laser printer for generating word-processing documents and reports in each department. In addition, he installed a color laser printer available to all users for printing graphs and presentation material. Because the output going to the Shipping and Receiving printers will initially come only from the computers in those departments, Eric decided to attach these printers to the LPT ports of the Shipping and Receiving workstations so that they can print directly to the local printer, thus reducing network traffic. By creating NDPS printer agents for these printers, they will be available on the network. In addition, all networked computers should have access to the color laser printer attached directly to the network. To simplify setup and maintenance, Eric defined the color laser printer as a public access printer.

Step 2: Determining Printer Location and Attachment Method

After identifying the printers that will meet the projected printing requirements of users, the next consideration is the physical location of the printers, including how they will be attached to the network. There are several rules Eric considered when planning locations for the printers and how they would be attached to the network:

- Attempt to place the printer close to the user who is most responsible for it.

- Determine whether the printer will be attached locally to the server, remotely to a client, or directly to the network.

- Identify the printer port and interrupt each printer is going to use.

- Avoid attaching remote printers to clients that are not running 32-bit operating systems, such as Windows 95, 98, or 2000/NT.

- Use a direct attachment option for printers that are commonly accessed by multiple users.

The NDPS Definition Form shows how Eric has identified the attachment method and location information for each printer in the UAS network. Notice that the form shows the gateway to be used and the printer port/interrupt used with Novell gateways to connect the printer to the network.

Step 3: Defining Printer Names

To keep your printing system as simple as possible, select printer and print queue names that will enable you to quickly identify the printer when working with the printing environment. One method is defining one- to six-character codes that identify the printer's location, model, and number so that each printer name consists of the codes for location, model, and number, separated by hyphens or underscores. For example, Eric used Eng_OptR_1 to identify the first Lexmark Optra R laser printer installed in the Engineering department.

 When naming your printers, you need to precede the printer name with your assigned student number for all students to share the same NDPS Manager program.

If additional Optra laser printers are installed in the Engineering department, their names would be Eng_OptR_2 and Eng_OptR_3. Notice that the NDPS Definition Form also contains a column for print queue names. If a printer agent is required to support non-NDPS clients, a print queue must be created. In this case, the print queue name should be the same as the printer agent name, followed by an underscore and the letter Q. As described earlier, each print queue consists of a subdirectory within the Queues directory. Because any NetWare volume can be used to store print queues, when defining print queues, you need to assign each one to the NetWare volume where its Queues directory is located.

 To prevent print queues that contain many large print jobs from filling up the SYS volume, Novell recommends that you place large print queues on a volume other than SYS.

In addition to using printer names when creating printer agents and queues, it's a good idea to physically label each printer in the office with its assigned name. This makes it easier for the network administrator and users to identify printers when working with the printing system.

Step 4: Planning the eDirectory Context

As with all network objects, you need to define printers, print queues, and print servers in the eDirectory tree. Before you can implement network printing, you need to plan where you'll place printing objects in the tree structure. Placing printers and print queues in the same container as users gives you convenient access because you can select the printer by its name instead of specifying its context. For example, if the Eng_OptR_1 laser printer object is placed in the Engineering container, all users in the Engineering department could send output to the printer. Users whose current eDirectory contexts are located in another department's container would have to browse to the printer or use a distinguished name for the printer. Another reason for placing printer agents in the container where they are most frequently accessed is that the container storing the printer agent by default becomes a user of that printer agent. If necessary, you can make other users, groups, or containers users of a printer agent object through NetWare

Administrator, as described in the following section. Notice in the NDPS Definition Form that Eric has located printers in the Engineering or Mfg departments and given the Mgmt container rights to the Engineering laser printer so that Mgmt users can access this printer if their printer is down. In addition, Eric has granted Engineering users rights to use the IS printer in case their printer is out of action.

By default, only the users in the container where the printer agent is created are users of the printer. To allow users from other containers to use a printer agent, their user names or groups they belong to need to be added to the printer agent's access control list.

The NDPS Manager object is accessed from the NetWare server and can service printers and users in any container. As shown in the top line of the NDPS Definition Form, Eric has placed the NDPS Manager object in the UAS Organization container, along with the NetWare server object.

SETTING UP THE PRINTING ENVIRONMENT

8

After defining the printing components and their location in eDirectory, you can continue implementing the network printing environment by using NetWare Administrator or iManager to create and configure eDirectory objects for print queues, printers, and the print server by following these steps:

1. Create and configure printer agents.

2. Create print queues for non-NDPS clients.

3. Load the necessary remote printer software.

4. Configure printers on client computers.

To become a NetWare CNA, you need to know how to use NetWare Administrator and iManager to set up an NDPS printing environment. In the following sections, you learn how to use both utilities to set up the printing environment Eric identified for the Engineering and Mfg departments.

Creating and Configuring Printer Agents

After the NDPS Manager has been loaded onto your network, you can create the printer agents for the Engineering, Mgmt, and Mfg departments identified on the NDPS Definition Form. In the following activities, you use both NetWare Administrator and iManager to create printer agents.

Because it's probably not practical for you to load the NDPS Manager you created in the previous activity, you need to use the classroom UAS_NDPS Manager when you create your printer agents.

Activity 8-17: Creating a Public Access Printer

Time Required: 10 minutes

Objective: Use NetWare Administrator to create printer agents.

Description: In this activity, you use NetWare Administrator to create and configure a printer agent for your version of the public access UAS_Color color laser printer. To have this printer send output to the classroom printer, in this activity you configure the printer agent you created using the Novell gateway and send output to the classroom print queue. To make your printer agent name unique, precede it with your assigned student number.

1. If necessary, start your computer, and log in with your UasAdmin user name and password.

2. Start NetWare Administrator and, if necessary, open a browse window for the classroom UAS_Tree.

3. To create a printer agent that sends output to a print queue, you need to specify a user name that has rights to use the print queue. To satisfy this requirement, Eric created a user named Guest with no password. He then granted the Guest user the right to use the print queue. In this step, you create a user named Guest with no password in your ##UAS Organization. Because all users have been given rights to Class_Q during the classroom server setup, you will not need to add your Guest account as a user of the print queue.

   a. Click your **##UAS** container to highlight it.

   b. Click the **Create User Object** button to open the Create User dialog box.

   c. Enter **Guest** in the Login name text box.

   d. Enter **Print queue user** in the Last name text box.

   e. Click the **Create** button to create the Guest user account and return to the main NetWare Administrator window.

4. Double-click the classroom **UAS** Organization and, if necessary, scroll down until you can see the classroom UAS_NDPSM object.

5. Double-click the **UAS_NDPSM** object to open the NDPS Manager:UAS_NDPSM dialog box, and then click the **Printer Agent List** button to display the Printer Agent List section, shown in Figure 8-33.

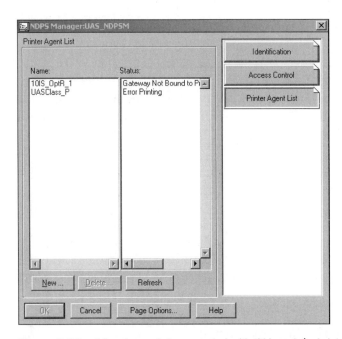

Figure 8-33   Viewing printer agents in NetWare Administrator

6. Click the **New** button, and then enter **##UAS_Color** in the NDPS Printer Agent Name text box. (Replace ## with your assigned student number.)

7. Verify that the UAS_NDPSM.UAS Manager and Novell Printer Gateway are selected, and then click **OK** to create the printer agent and open the Configure Novell PDS for Printer Agent dialog box.

8. Select your classroom printer type, and then click **OK** to open the Configure Port Handler for Printer Agent dialog box.

9. To have your public access printer send print jobs to the classroom network printer, click the **Forward Jobs to a Queue** radio button, and then click the **Next** button.

10. Click the **Browse** button to the right of the Queue Name text box (see Figure 8-34) to open the Select Object dialog box.

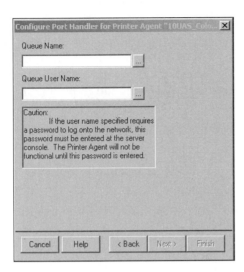

Figure 8-34   Forwarding output to a print queue

11. Double-click the **Class_Q** print queue in the Available objects section.

12. Click the **Browse** button to the right of the Queue User Name text box to open the Select Object dialog box.

13. In the Browse context section, navigate to your ##UAS Organization. Double-click the **Guest** account, and record the caution message on your student answer sheet.

14. Click the **Finish** button to load the printer agent and open the Select Printer Drivers dialog box. If you see a "Printer needs attention" warning message box, click **OK** to continue.

15. Click the **Windows 2000 Driver** tab, and select the driver for your classroom printer. If the printer is not listed, click the **[None]** option, and if necessary, add the driver later in Windows Control Panel.

16. Click the **Continue** button to open a summary window showing your driver selections.

17. Click **OK** to close the window and return to the NDPS Manager:UAS_NDPSM dialog box.

18. Verify that your printer is listed, and click **Cancel** to return to NetWare Administrator.

19. If you're continuing to the next activity, stay logged in and leave NetWare Administrator open. If not, exit NetWare Administrator, and log out.

Activity 8-18: Creating the Controlled Access Printers

Time Required: 15 minutes

Objective: Use NetWare Administrator to create printer agents.

Description: In this activity, follow the procedure in Activity 8-17 and use NetWare Administrator to create and configure the printer agents you defined for the Engineering and Mgmt departments. To make your printer agent names unique, you need to precede them with your assigned student number. After completing this activity, exit NetWare Administrator and stay logged in for the next activity.

Activity 8-19: Creating Printers Using iManager

Time Required: 10 minutes

Objective: Use iManager to create and configure printer agents.

Description: In this activity, you use the iManager utility to create and configure the printer agents for your version of the Receiving and Shipping printers. This is a multistep process in which you create the printer agents and then IPP-enable them. Again, to make your printer agent names unique, you need to precede them with your assigned student number.

1. If necessary, start your computer, and log in with your UasAdmin user name and password.

2. Load the iManager home page:

   a. Start your Web browser, and enter the URL **https://ip_address:2200** (replacing *ip_address* with the IP address of your NetWare server).

   b. If necessary, click **OK** and then click **Yes** to close the Security Alert message boxes and open the NetWare Web Manager home page.

   c. Click the **UASHOST** server under the eDirectory iManager heading to open the Login window.

   d. Enter your UasAdmin user name, password, and context, and then click the **Login** button to open the iManager home page.

3. Expand the **iPrint Management** options.

4. Create a printer agent for your version of the Receiving department printer:

   a. Click the **Create Printer** link to open the Create Printer window, shown in Figure 8-35.

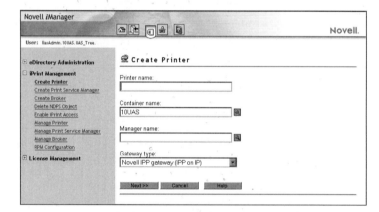

Figure 8-35 The iManager Create Printer window

   b. Enter the name of your Receiving department printer, shown previously in Figure 8-32 (preceded by your student number), in the Printer name text box.

   c. Click the **Browse** button next to the Container name text box, and click the **Mfg** OU.

   d. Click the **Browse** button next to the Manager name text box and then navigate to the UAS Organization. Click the **UAS_NDPSM** printer manager object to place it in the Manager name text box. (Do not select the NDPS Manager object in your ##UAS container unless it's loaded on the NetWare server.)

   e. Verify that the Novell IPP gateway is selected, and click the **Next** button to display the Printer URL text box.

   f. Enter the URL **ipp://ip_address/ipp/##Rec_OptR_1** (replacing *ip_address* with the IP address of your NetWare server). Be sure to use the correct capitalization.

   g. Click the **Next** button, and if necessary, click **Yes** in any Security Alert message boxes to load the printer agent and display the Driver Select window.

h. Scroll down the Windows 2000 list box, and click the **Lexmark Optra R** (or a driver that matches your network printer).

i. After selecting the drivers, click the **Next** button to create the printer agent.

j. When you see the Create Printer request succeeded message, click **OK** to return to the iManager home page.

5. Repeat Step 4 to create a printer for your version of the Shipping department printer.

6. Enable the printer for iPrint access:

a. Click the **Enable iPrint Access** link to open the Enable iPrint Access window.

b. Click the **Browse** button next to the Manager name text box and navigate to the UAS Organization.

c. Click the **UAS_NDPSM** object.

d. Verify that the UAS_NDPSM.UAS object is selected in the Manager name text box, and then click **OK** to open the Enable iPrint Access window (see Figure 8-36 for a list of printers that Eric enabled), which lists existing printers. (Figure 8-36 is an example; the printers in your Enable iPrint Access window will vary, depending on your server's setup.)

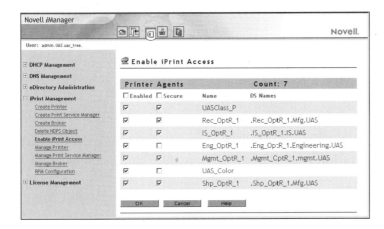

Figure 8-36   Viewing existing printers in the Enable iPrint Access window

e. Click the check boxes in the Enabled and Secure columns for all your printers except the public access ##UAS_Color printer. Because this printer is public, Eric didn't enable secure printing on it, as shown in Figure 8-36.

f. Click **OK** to display the results window, and then click **OK** to return to the iManager home page.

7. Click the **Exit** button on the iManager toolbar to end your iManager session and return to the Login window.

8. Close the Web browser.

Activity 8-20: Creating Print Queues for Non-NDPS Clients

Time Required: 10 minutes

Objective: Use NetWare Administrator to create and configure print queues.

Description: Currently, an older DOS computer in the Receiving department runs a simple word-processing program to print work orders. Because this computer will not be updated with the NDPS client software, you need to create a print queue and associate it with your laser printer. In this activity, you create print queues for your version of the Receiving department printer and then associate it with the corresponding printer agent.

1. If necessary, start your computer, and log in with your UasAdmin user name and password.

2. Start NetWare Administrator, and open a browse window for your ##UAS organization.

3. Create a print queue named ##Rec_OptR1_Q in your Mfg.##UAS container:

   a. If necessary, open a browse window to your Mfg.##UAS container.

   b. Click your **Mfg.##UAS** container to highlight it.

   c. Click the **Create Print Queue object** icon on the toolbar to open the Create Print Queue dialog box.

   d. Enter **##Rec_OptR1_Q** in the Print Queue Name text box.

   e. Click the **Browse** button next to the Print Queue Volume text box to open the Select Object dialog box. Navigate to and double-click **UASHOST_CORP** in the Available objects section.

   f. Click the **Create** button to create the ##Rec_OptR1_Q print queue.

4. Configure the ##Rec_OptR_1 printer to look for jobs in the ##Rec_OptR1_Q print queue:

   a. Double-click your **##Rec_OptR_1** printer to open the NetWare Printer Control dialog box.

 If you see an error message stating that the Xerox index file was not found, click OK until the NetWare Printer Control dialog box is displayed.

   b. Click the **Jobs v** button to display a popup menu.

   c. Click **Spooling Configuration** on the Jobs v menu to open the Spooling Configuration dialog box.

   d. Click **Add** to open the Select Object dialog box.

   e. Double-click **##Rec_OptR1_Q** in the Available objects section.

   f. Click **OK** to save the change to the Spooling Configuration dialog box.

   g. Click **Cancel** to return to the NetWare Administrator browse window.

5. Exit NetWare Administrator, and log out.

Configuring Printers on Client Computers

As you have learned, for users to access NDPS printers, they need to have the IPP or NDPS client software installed on their workstations along with the necessary printer drivers. In Activity 8-15, you learned how to use iPrint to select and install the IS department printer on your workstation. In addition to selecting printers by name, with NDPS you can have printers automatically installed on user workstations or selected from a map of the facility. In the following sections, you learn how to perform both these tasks.

Automatically Installing Printers on User Workstations

You have learned how to use the Novell iPrint utility to select and install a printer to which you have access. However, installing NDPS printers in this manner can be time-consuming and might require special training for users to install their own printers. To speed up and simplify the task of installing NDPS printers on user workstations, Novell has provided NDPS with the ability to automatically install printers on user workstations when users log in. When users log in, Novell Client checks the context of their containers to see if any printers are associated with the users. If you associate an NDPS printer agent with an

Organization or OU container, when a user logs in from that context, the client automatically updates the printer configuration to include the printer agents associated with the user's home container. For example, to save the time it takes to manually select each printer for Engineering and Mgmt users, Eric configured the printers to be automatically installed when users log in. In the following activity, you use NetWare Administrator to configure your Engineering and Mgmt containers for automatic installation.

Activity 8-21: Configuring Automatic Installation of Printers

Time Required: 10 minutes

Objective: Use NetWare Administrator to configure automatic installation of printers.

Description: Manually installing and configuring a standard set of printers on users' computers can be time-consuming, even when using iPrint. As a result, Eric configured NDPS to automatically install the department printers on user workstations attached to the network. In this activity, you configure a standard set of printers to be installed on your version of the UAS network.

1. If necessary, start your computer, and log in with your UasAdmin user name and password.

2. Start NetWare Administrator and, if necessary, open a browse window to your ##UAS container.

3. Set up automatic printer installation for your Engineering OU:

   a. Right-click your **Engineering** OU, and then click **Details** to open the Organizational Unit : Engineering dialog box.

   b. Scroll down and click the **NDPS Remote Printer Management** button to display the Printers To Install To Workstations section, shown previously in Figure 8-27.

   c. Click the **Add** button under the Printers To Install To Workstations section to display the Available Printers options.

   d. Click your **##UAS_Color** printer and hold down the **Ctrl** key while you click your **##Eng_OptR_1** printer.

   e. Click **OK** to add both printers to the Printers To Install To Workstations section.

   f. Click **OK** to save the changes and return to NetWare Administrator.

4. Repeat Step 3 to set up automatic printer installation for your Mgmt OU.

5. Repeat Step 3 to set up automatic printer installation for your Mfg OU.

6. Exit NetWare Administrator, and log out.

Using the iPrint Map Utility

For users to access NDPS printers, they need to have either iPrint or Novell Client, along with the printer drivers they will access, installed on their workstations. However, occasionally users need to send output to printers in other locations that are not included in the automatic printer setup. Although Eric plans to train users on how to use iPrint to select and install printers, this process can lead to confusion when users don't know the name of the printer they want to use. To make selecting a printer easier, Novell has included the Map utility with iPrint, which enables network administrators to place printer icons on a map of the facility. The map can then be displayed in a browser window, and users can select and install a printer by simply clicking on the location of the printer they want to send output to. In this section, you learn how to use the iPrint Map utility to construct a map of your UAS printers, and then use it to install printers on user workstations. Using this utility involves the following steps:

1. *Scan in a map of the facility and save it as a JPG file.* Eric scanned in a copy of the UAS facility plan and saved it as a JPG file in the SYS:Login\Ippdocs\ Images\Maps folder. Storing the image in this folder is important so that the default iPrint Web server configuration can access it.

2. *Use the Novell iPrint Map utility to add existing printers to the facility map.* After saving the scanned image, Eric used the latest version of Internet Explorer (IE version 5.5 is required to use the Map utility) to run the Maptool.htm file on the NetWare 6 server. This file is used to place icons representing printers on a scanned image. Each icon has the IPP address of the associated printers, along with a description and title. Eric used the UAS floor plan and the iPrint Map utility to place each printer on the floor plan.

3. *Save the facility map in a folder accessible to users.* After adding all printers, Eric saved the floor plan map in the Ippdocs subdirectory of the Login directory as an HTML file. By placing the printer map in the Login directory, all users can access it to select and install printers on their computers, even if they are using a computer in another part of the country.

In the following activity, you use the facility map Eric saved in the Utility directory to create a printer map for your version of the UAS network.

Activity 8-22: Creating a Facility Printer Map

Time Required: 10 minutes

Objective: Use the iPrint Map utility to create a map of printers in a facility.

Description: In this activity, you use the same procedure that Eric did to create a facility map for users to find and install printers. To perform this activity, you need Internet Explorer 5.5 or later. If necessary, upgrade your workstation to the latest browser version.

1. If necessary, start your computer, and log in to the Novell network with your UasAdmin user name and password.

2. Use the iPrint Map utility to open a facility printer map:

   a. Start Internet Explorer (version 5.5 or higher).

   b. Open the Map tool, shown in Figure 8-37, by clicking **File**, **Open** on the menu bar, entering **F:\Login\ippdocs\maptool.htm**, and pressing **Enter**.

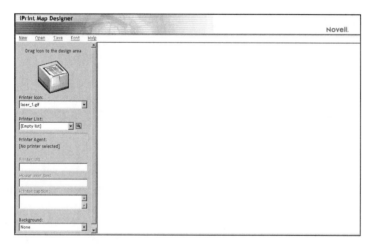

Figure 8-37   The iPrint Map utility

3. Click the **Printer icon** list arrow, and then click **laser_5.gif** in the list to display a laser printer icon, as shown in Figure 8-37. Notice the various icons you can use to represent different types of printers. (The number after the name indicates the icon size, smaller numbers are larger icons.)

4. To select printers, you need to identify the IP address of your NDSP Manager:

   a. Click the **Browse** button next to the Printer List text box to open the Change printer list — Web Page Dialog dialog box.

b. Enter the IP Address of your UASHOST classroom server in the NDPS Manager Address text box, and click **OK**.

c. If asked to log in, enter your UasAdmin user name and password.

5. The next step in building a printer map is to select a graphic file for your background floor plan. When the Map tool loads, it automatically scans the Login\ippdocs\images\maps directory for any graphics files. In this step, you select the UasFloor.jpg file Eric previously scanned and saved in the Maps directory:

a. In the frame on the left, scroll down and click the **Background** list arrow to display all the graphic files in the Maps directory.

b. Click the **UASfloor.gif** file to display the UAS layout in the graphics frame on the right.

6. Place your ##Eng_OptR_1 printer on the floor plan:

a. Click the **Printer List** list arrow to display all the printers managed by the NDPS Manager you selected in Step 4.

b. Click your **##Eng_OptR_1** printer.

c. Drag and drop the printer icon in the Engineering department next to Kari Means.

d. In the Printer URL text box, enter **http://*ip_address*/ipps/##Eng_OptR_1.** (Replace *ip_address* with the IP address of your UASHOST server and replace ## with your assigned student number.)

7. Repeat Step 6 to place your ##Mgmt_OptR_1 printer next to Lynn Dai's desk. Enter **http://*ip_address*/ipps/##Mgmt_OptR_1** in the Printer URL text box.

8. Repeat Step 6 to place your ##IS_OptR_1 printer across from Kellie's office. Enter **http://*ip_address*/ipps/##IS_OptR_1** in the Printer URL text box.

9. Save your facility printer map in the ippdocs folder:

a. Click the **Save** link to open the Save dialog box.

b. Click your **F:** drive and navigate to the Login\ippdocs folder.

c. Enter **##UASPrinters** in the File name text box, and click the **Save** button.

10. Close your Web browser.

11. Test your printer map by starting your Web browser and entering the URL **http://*ip_address*:631/Login/ippdocs/##UASPrinters.htm**. (Replace ## with your assigned student number and *ip_address* with the IP address of your NetWare server.)

12. Your UAS floor plan will be displayed, showing the printers in the locations where you placed them. Place your cursor over each printer icon on the map, and verify its description.

13. Click your **Mgmt** department laser printer, and use IPP to install it on your workstation.

14. Close your Web browser.

15. Click **Start**, **Settings**, **Printers** to open the Printers window, and record the network printers on your student answer sheet.

16. Close the Printers window. If you're continuing to the next activity, stay logged in; if not, log out.

Activity 8-23: Testing and Troubleshooting Printer Configurations

Time Required: 10 minutes

Objective: Test and verify network printing operation.

Description: Before advertising that you have set up the network printing environment for the Engineering users, you should test each printer along with your client installation to be sure it works as expected. In this activity, you test your NDPS setup by logging in as a user from each department and sending output to the department printer. You then use iManager to verify that the print jobs are sent to the correct printer agents.

1. If necessary, start your computer, and log in as LJarka.

2. Verify that the ##Eng_OptR_1 printer was automatically installed on your workstation.

3. Verify that the ##UAS_Color printer was automatically installed on your workstation.

4. Send output to your ##Eng_OptR_1 printer.

5. Send output to your ##UAS_Color printer.

6. Log out, and then log in as LDai.

7. Send output to your ##Mgmt_OptR_1 printer.

8. Log out, and then log in as RPence.

9. Verify that the ##Rec_OptR_1 printer is automatically installed on your workstation.

10. Send output to the ##Rec_OptR_1 printer, and then send output to the ##UAS_Color printer.

11. Log out, and then log in with your UasAdmin user name and password.

12. Start your Web browser, and open the iManager home page.

13. View and record the print jobs in your ##UAS_Color printer agent.

14. View and record the print jobs in your ##Eng_OptR_1 printer agent.

15. View and record the print jobs in your ##Mgmt_OptR_1 printer agent.

16. Log out.

It's been a lot of work, but the printers for the Engineering, Mgmt, and Mfg departments are installed and ready for their users. Tomorrow you plan to help Eric train users on how to use iPrint to install and access the network printers. What you've learned in setting up printing for these departments should make the Business office's printing setup go more easily.

CHAPTER SUMMARY

❑ In cooperation with Hewlett-Packard and Xerox, Novell has developed a new network printing environment called Novell Distributed Printing Services (NDPS). As a CNA, you'll need to know the printing components and utilities that make up NDPS and be able to competently set up and maintain a NetWare printing environment consisting of an NDPS Manager, printer agents, gateways, Brokers, print queues, and client workstations.

❑ Printer agents are software that make up the core of NDPS. Client computers send formatted printer output to printer agents, which then control the physical printer. When setting up NDPS, you need to create and configure one printer agent for each physical printer.

❑ As part of the Novell OneNet strategy, iPrint uses the Internet Printing Protocol (IPP) to enable printers to be installed, accessed, and managed anywhere from a Web browser. iPrint consists of three components: the IPPSRVR module on the NetWare server, a Web browser client, and NDPS printers that are enabled for IPP access.

❑ The component used to create and run printer agents is called the NDPS Manager. By using specialized gateways, NDPS printers can be remotely attached to client computers, locally attached to the server, or directly attached to the network.

❐ Because not all clients are immediately compatible with NDPS, Novell offers backward-compatibility with older clients through the use of print queues, which consist of a directory on the file system for holding print jobs until the printer is ready to use them.

❐ The first task in establishing the printer environment is to define the printing requirements for each user's applications, determining the types and number of printers required, their location on the network, and their attachment method.

❐ After defining the printing environment, the next step is to install the printing system. NetWare Administrator is used for most of the work involved in setting up and maintaining the NetWare printing system. To install the printing system, you need to create the NDPS Manager followed by the printer agents. The printer configuration can also include a notification list consisting of user names to receive printer messages.

KEY TERMS

automatic load printer — A printer that is attached directly to the server's printer port or to a port on the workstation.

Broker — An NDPS component responsible for sending printer messages and notifications, using the Event Notification System (ENS), Resource Management Service (RMS), and Service Registry Services (SRS).

controlled access printer — An NDPS printer that exists as an object in the eDirectory tree. By default, only users in the same container as the controlled access printer can send output to it.

gateway — The NDPS component that works with the printer agent to send output from the printer agent to the network print device.

manual load printer — A remote printer attached to a port on a networked workstation and controlled by the print server.

NDPS Manager — The NDPS component that manages the printer agent for printers that do not have an embedded printer agent.

Novell Distributed Print Services (NDPS) — A new printing system developed by Hewlett-Packard and Novell to make network printer configuration and access more convenient.

parallel port (LPTn) — A common printer port used on personal computers. Parallel ports require thicker cables to transmit several bits of information at one time.

print queue — A network object representing a holding area where print jobs are kept until the printer is available. In NetWare, a print queue is a subdirectory of the Queues directory, located in the volume specified during print queue creation.

print server — A component of queue-based printing that manages network printers by taking jobs from print queues and sending them to the appropriate network printer.

printer agent — The software component of NDPS that transfers output from the client and controls the physical printer.

public access printer — An NDPS printer that is attached to the network but does not have an eDirectory object in the tree. Any user attached to the network can send output to a public access printer without having to log in to the network.

queue-based printing — A printing system implemented in NetWare 3 that's designed to support simple printers and DOS-based applications.

remote printer — A printer attached to the port of a networked workstation and controlled by the print server.

serial port (COMn) — A printer port often used to connect communication devices, such as modems and printers, to send signals over long cables. Serial ports send only one bit of data at a time, so serial cables can consist of only a few wires.

spooling — The process of sending output from a user's computer to a print job storage area.

REVIEW QUESTIONS

1. Which of the following is the network printing component that provides backward-compatibility by holding printed output until the printer is ready to print?

   a. print server

   b. print queue

   c. gateway

   d. printer agent

2. Which of the following is the queue-based printing component that controls print jobs on the physical printer?

   a. print server

   b. print queue

   c. gateway

   d. printer agent

3. Which of the following utilities can be used to create print queues?

   a. NetWare Administrator

   b. ConsoleOne

   c. iManager

   d. Remote Manager

4. In the queue-based printing system, user workstations send their output to which of the following?

   a. print server

   b. print queue

   c. gateway

   d. printer agent

5. Which of the following is the NDPS printing component that manages each physical printer?

   a. print server

   b. print queue

   c. gateway

   d. printer agent

6. Which of the following must be running before you can create printer agents? (Choose all that apply.)

   a. NDPS Manager

   b. IPPSRVR

   c. Broker

   d. print server

7. A network printer attached to a client is called a _____ printer.

   a. locally attached

   b. directly attached

   c. system

   d. remotely attached

8. Which of the following is the first step in setting up a network printing environment?

   a. Create printer agents.

   b. Create and load the NDPS Broker.

   c. Create and load the NDPS Manager.

   d. Install IPP on your administrative workstation.

9. Which of the following utilities can be used to create printer agents?

   a. iManager

   b. Remote Manager

   c. ConsoleOne

   d. NetWare Administrator

10. A printer attached to a server is referred to as which of the following?

   a. manual load printer

   b. local printer

   c. directly attached printer

   d. system printer

11. Automatic load printers is the term Novell uses for _____ attached printers.

   a. locally

   b. remotely

   c. directly

   d. IPP

12. Printer agents that can be accessed without logging in are referred to as which of the following?

   a. automatic load printers

   b. controlled access printers

   c. public access printers

   d. global printers

13. The _____ URL is used to access the iManager utility.

14. Which of the following NDPS components helps clients find network printer agents?

   a. NDPS Manager

   b. printer agent

   c. Broker

   d. print queue

15. Novell's iPrint is based on which of the following industry standards?

   a. IPP

   b. 802.3

   c. IEEE

   d. X.500

16. True or false: Most printers today have embedded printer agents.

17. List two steps for using iManager to create an IPP-enabled printer agent.

_____

_____

18. The _____ URL is used to access the iPrint installation utility.

19. Remote printers are also called which of the following?

    a. automatic load printers

    b. controlled access printers

    c. manual load printers

    d. global printers

20. List the two steps for implementing an NDPS Manager on a NetWare server.

    _____

    _____

21. Which of the following is not a step in implementing network printing?

    a. defining printer names

    b. defining the context for NDPS objects

    c. creating a Printers container

    d. creating and loading NDPS Manager

22. The _____ directory contains the URL for the iPrint Map utility.

UNIVERSAL AEROSPACE CASE PROJECTS

In this chapter, you have been following the steps Eric used to define and implement network printing for the Engineering, Mgmt, and Mfg departments. In the following projects, you set up and test network printing for the users in the Business office.

Case Project 8-1: Defining Business Office Printing Needs

Copy the NDPS Definition Form from Appendix D and use it to define each printer and print queue, along with operators and users, to meet the printing needs for the Business office and the Marketing department, as defined in Table 8-5. If your lab has a laser printer attached to the network, use it instead of the Lexmark Optra R mentioned in the table for the Business office.

After completing your NDPS Definition Form, have your instructor verify it against the answer key. Make any necessary changes to include all the printer information in the master NDPS Definition Form so that you'll be able to do the projects in later chapters.

Table 8-5 Business/Marketing Network Printing Needs

Department	Network Printing Needs
Accounting	All Accounting users should have access to the Lexmark Optra R printer attached to Amy Pan's computer.
Marketing	The Marketing department will share a Lexmark Optra R printer attached to the network by using the HP JetDirect dedicated print server.
Desktop Publishing	A high-resolution PostScript laser printer will be attached directly to the network and shared by Desktop Publishing users to print manuals and sales fliers. Kari Means and Lynn Dai also need to be able to send output to the PostScript laser printer.

Case Project 8-2: Setting Up Network Printing

In this project, you apply what you learned in this chapter to using NetWare Administrator to create eDirectory objects in the Business container for the printer agents and print queues defined on your NDPS Definition Form.

Case Project 8-3: Testing Your Printing Setup

In this project, you test each of your Business office printers. You then send output to the printer and use iManager to verify that the results have been sent to the correct printer.

Case Project 8-4: Performing a Print Services Quick Setup for the Business Office

Follow these steps to perform a quick setup for the Business office's print services:

1. If necessary, start your computer, and log in with your UasAdmin user name and password.
2. Start NetWare Administrator, and open a browse window to your ##UAS organization.
3. Click your **Business** OU.
4. Click **Tools**, **Print Services Quick Setup (Non-NDPS)** on the menu bar.
5. Record the following information on your student answer sheet:
    - ❑ Print server name
    - ❑ Printer name
    - ❑ Printer type
    - ❑ Print queue name and volume
6. Change the printer name to **Bus_P**.
7. Click the **Create** button to create the queue-based printing system.
8. Document your results.
9. Add the Bus_P printer to your desktop.

Case Project 8-5: Troubleshooting Network Printing

In this project, your instructor will create one of the "bugs" described in the "Troubleshooting NDPS Printers" section in your Business printing system. Your job is to use the techniques and fixes described in this chapter to find, document, and correct the problem. Record your findings on your student answer sheet.

8

ACCESSING AND MANAGING THE NETWORK WITH NOVELL'S ONENET UTILITIES

After reading this chapter and completing the exercises, you will be able to:

♦ Implement and use iFolder to access files and directories

♦ Set up and use NetStorage to access network files

♦ Use NetWare 6 remote management tools, including Remote Manager, RConsoleJ, and iMonitor, to access and manage the NetWare 6 server from your workstation

♦ Explain NetWare 6 licensing and view and install NetWare license information using iManager

---

After Eric Kenton finished setting up the network printing system for Universal AeroSpace, he installed the necessary application software on user workstations and then began training users on the new network system. An important consideration for Marketing and Management users is being able to use NetWare 6 to access their documents and data files when they are away from the office. For example, David Heise, the president of UAS, spends time away from the office visiting other facilities and customer sites. In addition, Marketing staff members need to be able to access the customer database and other documents from laptop computers that aren't always attached to the network. As part of the OneNet strategy, Novell has solved many of these access problems by including new utilities with NetWare 6. These utilities enable users to access network data from any remote computer by using iFolder and NetStorage. In this chapter, you learn how Eric used these utilities to give users access to their documents and data files from any location. In addition, you learn how to use Novell's OneNet utilities to remotely monitor and manage the NetWare 6 server and maintain server licenses from your Web browser.

WORKING WITH IFOLDER

Login scripts provide drive mappings for users to access network data, but they aren't effective unless the user's computer is attached to the network. Users with laptop computers often need to access data and files when they're away from the office or not attached to the network. In addition, traveling users might want to access files from computers located outside the organization. One of the goals of Novell's OneNet strategy is to ensure that users have access to their network data and resources independent of the network connection. As illustrated in Figure 9-1, **iFolder** is an important part of the OneNet strategy because it enables files to be kept on a local computer or laptop and synchronized with the network—either across the Internet or when the user's computer is reattached to the local network.

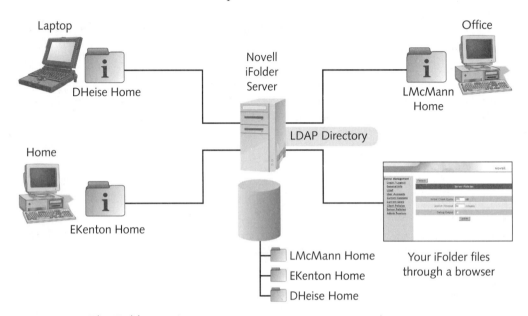

Figure 9-1 The iFolder service

With iFolder, users can have automatic, secure, and transparent synchronization of files between their hard drives and the iFolder server. Before Eric installed iFolder, Universal AeroSpace users either copied the files they needed to their laptops or attached the files to e-mail messages so that they could access the files from remote locations. After iFolder is installed and configured, users can access the latest version of their data from the computers they regularly use or, by using a Java-enabled browser, any computer attached to the Internet. Being able to access their files from any computer, from any location, has helped eliminate the file-overwriting errors and time-consuming tasks often associated with manually copying files between local computers and the network. Novell lists the following benefits of implementing iFolder:

- A simple and secure way to access, organize, and manage files from any computer

- Automatic synchronization of data across multiple workstations, enabling users to access their files from any workstation by using the iFolder client or a Web browser

- Secure access to files using a Web browser, allowing users to access their files from computers at other locations

- Encryption of sensitive files stored on the server, protecting them from unauthorized access

- The ability to work on files offline and have them automatically synchronized to the server the next time the computer is logged in to the network

In the following sections, you learn about iFolder's components and how to set up and configure iFolder so that you can access and synchronize files between computers.

iFolder Components and Installation

The iFolder software consists of a server component, a Novell Client component, and a Java applet component. These three components work together to give users access to their iFolder files from anywhere in the world, even if their computers are temporarily offline from the network. In addition to helping traveling users with mobile computers access their files while offline, iFolder is helpful when users need to access their files but the server is unavailable because of network connection problems or other hardware failures. Because changes are made to the local files and then synchronized to the server, users can continue to work on their documents until the server is back online. In the following sections, you learn about iFolder's components and how Eric implemented them on the UAS network.

The iFolder Server Component

The iFolder server component, the central piece of the iFolder system, is required to synchronize files between workstations and allow access to files over the Internet. The server component also supplies a Server Management console and an iFolder Web site. Network administrators can use the Server Management console to perform administrative tasks for all iFolder user accounts. The iFolder Web site, where the iFolder client software can be downloaded, makes it possible for users to view and download iFolder files through the Java applet running on their Web browsers. Novell has designed the iFolder server component so that in the future it can be installed and run from other server platforms, such as Windows NT or Windows 2000. The iFolder server component can be installed on the NetWare 6 server either during or after the server installation, and server must meet the following minimum requirements:

- There must be 10 MB of free space on the SYS volume.

- The iFolder server must have the Root Certificate to issue the public keys for securely encrypting data transmissions through public key cryptography (described in Chapter 10). If necessary, copy the Root Certificate from the Certificate Authority to the server that will host the iFolder service.

- If using DNS names for your iFolder server, verify that the DNS name and corresponding IP address of the iFolder server are in the SYS:Etc\Hosts file of the server hosting the iFolder service.

To keep the initial installation of the NetWare 6 server simple and straightforward, Eric chose to install iFolder separately after installing NetWare 6. He used the following steps to install iFolder:

1. First, Eric inserted the NetWare 6 CD into the UASHOST server.

2. He pressed Ctrl+Esc to select the server console screen (described in Chapter 12).

3. He entered the command CDROM, and then pressed Enter to mount the CD as a volume on the server.

4. After mounting the NetWare 6 Installation volume, he again pressed Ctrl+Esc to select the X Server - Graphical Console.

5. At the graphical console, Eric clicked Novell and then Install to display the Installed Products window.

6. He clicked Add to display the Source Path window. After clicking the Browse button to select the NetWare 6 volume, he clicked OK. The installation files were then copied to the server, and he clicked OK again to display the Components window.

7. The Components window displayed check marks to indicate the default installed components. Eric clicked Clear All to prevent reinstalling existing components. Next, he clicked the Novell iFolder Storage Services check box, and then clicked Next to display the Login window.

8. Eric entered his Admin user name, password, and context in the appropriate fields, and clicked OK to log in.

9. After he successfully logged in, the Configure IP-based Services window was displayed, showing the IP address assigned to the iFolder service. To access the iFolder service without specifying a port number, Eric chose to give the iFolder service its own IP address. For example, because the UASHOST server and iPrint services were using the IP address 172.20.0.60, and the

Apache-based services were using 172.20.0.61, Eric verified that the Multiple IP addresses radio button was selected, and then entered an address of 172.20.0.62 for the iFolder service. Using a separate IP address for the iFolder service makes it easier for users to access it and offers more flexibility if the service needs to be moved to another server in the future.

10. Eric then clicked Next to display the LDAP Configuration window.

 The iFolder service uses the X.500 LDAP service to process user login requests. By default, the LDAP service uses port number 389 for clear text packets and port number 636 for SSL-encrypted packets. Port 636 is a good choice if the iFolder service and the LDAP server are running on different servers to encrypt communication and data that's transferred across the wire between the LDAP server and the iFolder server.

11. Because the iFolder service and LDAP are running on the UASHOST server, Eric left the Clear Text port at the default setting of 389 and the SSL port at the default setting of 636.

12. In addition to the selection of a port number, the LDAP Configuration window contains an option to allow clear text passwords. By checking the iFolder installation documentation, Eric learned that if using port 389, the LDAP Group object must be marked to allow clear text passwords. Eric clicked the Allow Clear Text Passwords check box, and then clicked Next to save the LDAP configuration options and display the iFolder Server Options window.

13. The iFolder Server Options window contains fields for the location of user data, the network domain, and the administrator's name and e-mail address. By default, the installation program places users' iFolder data in the iFolder directory on the SYS volume. To prevent the SYS volume from filling up with user files, Eric entered CORP:\iFolder in the User Data text box to place the users' iFolder files on the CORP volume.

14. Eric then clicked Next to accept the default settings of "uas.com" for the network domain, "admin" for the administrator's user name, and "admin@uashost.uas.com" for the e-mail address. (If no DNS name is given to the SERVER during installation, the Network Domain text box will be blank.)

15. When the summary window was displayed, Eric clicked the Customize button and performed the following steps to customize the LDAP service so that it could find users in all OUs of the UAS Organization:

    a. In the Product Customization window, Eric expanded the NetWare 6 Services option, and then clicked the Novell iFolder Storage Services item.

    b. He clicked the Configure button to display the Advanced settings window.

    c. He clicked the iFolder Primary LDAP Settings tab and verified the following: (To have iFolder look for users in other contacts, you can add contacts to the LDAP Login Dn Context text box by separating them with semicolons.)

        - The DNS name of the server (uashost.uas.com) was entered in the LDAP Host text box (if DNS is not installed, this entry should be changed to the IP address of the iFolder server).

        - The UAS Organization was entered in the LDAP Login Dn Context text box. (To have iFolder look for users in other contexts, you can add contexts to the LDAP Login Dn Context text box by separating them with semicolons.)

        - The LDAP Port was set to 389 (clear text).

    d. To have the iFolder server search for user accounts in the OUs, Eric clicked the Subcontainer Search check box to select this option. Although selecting this option enables the iFolder server to find user accounts in the department OUs, it requires some additional post-installation steps for iFolder to perform subcontainer searches.

    e. He clicked OK to save the changes and display the iFolder Primary LDAP Settings message box. After reading the information message, Eric clicked OK again to close the message box and return to the Product Customization window.

    f. Next, he clicked OK to return to the summary window.

16. Eric then verified the contents of the summary window and clicked Finish to complete the installation of the iFolder service. When Eric saw the Product Conflict message box telling him that he had a newer or identical copy of LDAP Services on the server, he clicked No to prevent replacing the existing LDAP services.

17. After all files were copied to the server, Eric read the Installation Complete message box, and then clicked Close to return to the graphical console.

After finishing the iFolder installation, Eric needed to give the iFolder service the rights necessary to search subcontainers for user names. To do this, Eric could assign the [Public] object Browse and Read rights to the CN property or the UAS tree, or he could create an LDAP proxy user account with Browse and Read rights to the tree CN object and then add the proxy user to the LDAP group. Because the UASHOST server will host Internet services, Eric decided to create a proxy user, as described in the following steps, to keep the iFolder installation simple:

1. Eric started his administrative workstation, logged in with the Admin user name and password, and then started ConsoleOne.

2. After expanding the UAS_Tree and UAS Organization, he used ConsoleOne to create a user named ProxyUser with no password in the UAS Organization.

3. He then added the new user account as a trustee of the UAS_Tree with Read and Browse rights by following these steps:

   a. He right-clicked the UAS_Tree object, and then clicked Properties.

   b. He clicked the Add Trustee button, navigated to the UAS Organization, and double-clicked the ProxyUser account he created in Step 2.

   c. In the Rights assigned to selected objects dialog box, he clicked OK to add ProxyUser to the Trustee list box with the default Browse Entry right as well as Read and Compare Attribute rights.

   d. He then clicked Apply and Close to save the changes and return to ConsoleOne.

4. To complete the setup, Eric added the ProxyUser account to the LDAP Group object by performing these steps:

   a. He clicked the UAS Organization to display all objects, right-clicked the LDAP Group object in the Object frame, and then clicked Properties.

   b. He clicked the Browse button next to the Proxy Username text box to locate the ProxyUser account he created in Step 2.

   c. He double-clicked the ProxyUser account to insert it into the Proxy Username text box.

   d. Finally, he clicked Apply and Close to save the changes and return to ConsoleOne.

5. After completing the configuration changes, Eric exited ConsoleOne and logged out.

The iFolder Client Component

Two iFolder client components are available: the iFolder client and the iFolder Java applet. The iFolder client must be installed on a computer running Novell Client, but the Java applet can be installed on any computer with a Java-enabled Web browser, such as Netscape or Internet Explorer. Either the iFolder client or Java applet must be installed on any workstation used to access iFolder files. The iFolder clients are installed from the Web site located on the NetWare 6 server. The iFolder client component can be installed on Windows 9x/Me, Windows NT, or Windows 2000 to perform the following tasks:

- Update data across multiple workstations

- Allow access to synchronized files through the workstation's My Documents\iFolder directory

- Minimize bandwidth usage by using delta block synchronization to update only the data blocks that change in a file

- Use a restore bin to contain files that have been deleted from other computers

- Allow access to files from a computer that's disconnected from the network

- Allow encryption of files stored on the server

- Encrypt files on the client so that confidential files can be securely transmitted to a server and stored in an encrypted state

After installing the iFolder client, an icon is placed on the user's computer desktop that points to the user's iFolder home directory, located in My Documents\iFolder\userid\Home. The iFolder directory acts like any other directory on the user's hard drive, so users can place data in the iFolder directory by simply dragging and dropping files or folders or by saving files directly to My Documents\iFolder\userid\Home. Users can open and edit files in the iFolder directory just as they would with any other files on the computer. Applications associated with a file in the iFolder directory must be installed on the local workstation. For example, if you have a Word document in your iFolder directory, you need to have Microsoft Word installed on your local workstation to access the document files. When a user places a new file or folder in the iFolder directory, it's automatically synchronized to the iFolder server, and the user can view and access it from any workstation with the iFolder or Web browser client. Any changes made to files in the iFolder directory, from any workstation, are automatically synchronized to the iFolder server, ensuring that users are always working with the latest copy of a file or folder. The user or network administrator can determine the frequency of synchronizing iFolder directories by right-clicking the iFolder icon and selecting iFolder Preferences.

The iFolder Java Applet Component

The iFolder Java applet allows users to access files and perform normal file operations—such as copy, delete, rename, download, and upload—from any Java-enabled browser. An advantage of the iFolder Java applet is that by using a Web browser, users can access their iFolder files from a computer that does not have the iFolder client installed. With the iFolder Java applet, users no longer have to bring a laptop with them everywhere they go because they can use any computer with Internet access to download and work on their files. The iFolder applet client works well in organizations where users often travel between different facilities. For example, when Marketing users travel from the UAS home office to the AeroDyn facility, they can simply use the computers and software at AeroDyn to access their iFolder files. In the following activity, you learn how to install the iFolder client component.

Activity 9-1: Installing the iFolder Client Component

Time Required: 10 minutes

Objective: Install the iFolder client on a workstation.

Description: After hearing about the capabilities of iFolder, David Heise and Luke McMann were anxious to begin using iFolder so that they could access their files when traveling to the AeroDyn facility. In this activity, you perform the steps Eric used to install the iFolder client on David's computer. Before performing this activity, you need to obtain the IP address of your iFolder server.

1. Obtain the IP address of your iFolder server, and record it on your student answer sheet. You can get the IP address from your instructor, or by pressing Ctrl+Esc while at the server console and selecting the Apache for NetWare option.

2. If necessary, start your computer, and log in with your UasAdmin user name and password.

3. Start your Web browser software, and enter the URL **https://*ip_address*** (replacing *ip_address* with the IP address of your iFolder server) to display the iFolder Welcome window, shown in Figure 9-2.

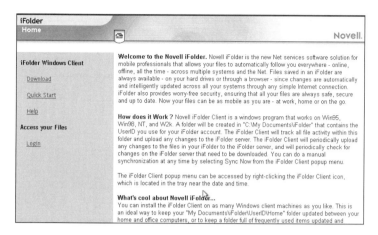

Figure 9-2 The iFolder Welcome window

4. Click the **Download** link to open the File Download dialog box.

5. Depending on your browser, either click the **Run this program from its current location** radio button, and then click **OK** to extract the files, or click the **Open** button to extract the files.

6. If you see the Security Warning message, click **Yes** to run the iFolderClient.exe program and display the Novell iFolder Setup window.

7. Click **Next** to display the Language selection window.

8. Click **Next** to accept the default English language and display the license agreement window.

9. Read the license agreement, and then click **File**, **Close** on the menu bar to close the license agreement window.

10. Click **Yes** to accept the license agreement and display the destination location window.

11. Click the **Next** button to copy files into the default C:\ProgramFiles\Novell\iFolder location and display the completion window.

12. Click the **Finish** button to end the installation and display the Readme text file.

13. Close the Readme file window, and then click the **Finish** button to restart your computer.

Activity 9-2: Creating an iFolder User Account

Time Required: 10 minutes

Objective: Create iFolder user accounts.

Description: After installing the iFolder client, Eric tested the system by creating an iFolder user account for his EKenton user name. In this activity, you create an iFolder user account for the user name you created for yourself.

1. Log in to the Novell network with the user name and password you created for yourself.

2. After you log in, the Novell iFolder Setup Complete message box is displayed. Read the message and use it to answer the questions on your student answer sheet.

3. Click the **Continue** button to close the window and display the iFolder Login window.

4. Log in to iFolder with the user name you created for yourself in the IS Organizational Unit:

   a. Enter your user name in the UserID text box and your password in the Password text box. Verify that the Place a shortcut to iFolder on the desktop check box is selected, and then click the **Login** button to log in and open the Novell iFolder New Internet Folder Setup dialog box.

9

    b. Verify that the Enable automatic login at startup check box is not selected and that the Encrypt files check box is selected, and then click **OK** to open the Get Pass Phrase dialog box.

    c. Enter a short phrase used to encrypt the files in both the Enter pass phrase and Confirm pass phrase text boxes, and then click the **Remember pass phrase** check box.

    d. Click **OK** to create a folder for your user name and place an iFolder icon on the desktop.

5. Log out.

Managing iFolder

After installing the iFolder software on the NetWare 6 server and clients, Eric's next task was to customize the iFolder server and clients by performing the following tasks:

- Customize the iFolder Web site.
- Use the Server Management console to manage iFolder user accounts and perform common iFolder administrative tasks.
- Optimize the iFolder server.

In the following sections, you learn what a CNA needs to know about performing these tasks with the iFolder Server Management console.

Customizing the iFolder Web Site

The iFolder Web site contains the iFolder Client Quick Start Guide and other important information about using the Novell iFolder system. In addition, the iFolder Web site is where users download the iFolder client and access their iFolder files by using a Java-enabled browser. Because the iFolder Web site is accessed by users in the organization, you might want to customize the iFolder Web page to fit your organization's internal needs. To access the default iFolder Web site, users simply need to enter the iFolder server's IP address or DNS name in their browsers.

Using the iFolder Server Management Console

The **Server Management console** lets the network administrator perform administrative tasks, such as managing iFolder user accounts and customizing the activity between the iFolder server and clients. Eric accessed the Server Management console from his Web browser by entering *https://172.20.0.62/ iFolderServer/Admin* (172.20.0.62 is the IP address Eric assigned to his iFolder service during installation) to display the Server Management console, shown in Figure 9-3.

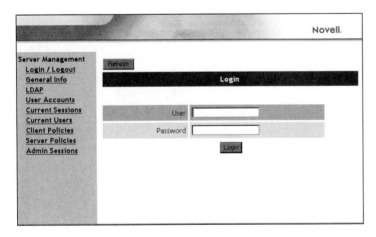

Figure 9-3   The Login window of the Server Management console

To manage iFolder user account information, Eric logged in with his administrator user name and password. After logging in, administrators can view and modify iFolder user accounts and perform the following administrative tasks:

- Set specific policies for iFolder clients and servers.

- View general server information.

- View and change LDAP settings.

- View and manage user account information. Administrators can use the Server Management console to remove user accounts, change disk storage quotas for users on the iFolder server, and set specific policies for individual users.

- View client connections to see which users are currently accessing the iFolder service.

- Configure client policies that are applied by default to iFolder clients, such as hiding iFolder client options or remembering passwords and pass phrases so that iFolder users cannot change them. For example, you could increase security by hiding the option that requests users to select encryption of the iFolder data, so the data is always encrypted without users being aware of it.

- Remove an iFolder user account.

- Restore a user's iFolder data to another iFolder server.

Before letting users access iFolder, Eric wanted to set storage quotas and increase security by hiding the option to encrypt files. In the following activity, you use the Server Management console to view and document your iFolder server's configuration settings.

Activity 9-3: Viewing iFolder Configuration Settings

Time Required: 10 minutes

Objective: Use the iFolder Server Management console to access configuration information.

Description: Eric used the iFolder Server Management console to set up user disk quota policies and server configuration settings. In this activity, you use the iFolder Server Management console to document the user disk quota and configuration settings on your iFolder server. To perform this activity, you need access to an administrator user name and password with rights to run the Server Management console. If you do not have access to the Novell Admin user name and password, read the steps in this activity, and use the screenshots to answer the questions on your student answer sheet.

1. If necessary, start your computer, and log in to your local workstation by clicking the **Workstation only** check box and entering your administrator user name and password.

2. Click **Cancel** when you see the Novell iFolder Login window.

3. Start your Web browser software, and enter the URL **https://*ip_address*/iFolderServer/Admin** in the Address text box (replacing *ip_address* with the IP address assigned to your classroom iFolder service).

4. If necessary, respond to the Security Alert message window(s) by clicking **OK** or **Yes**.

5. If necessary, click the **Login/Logout** link under the Server Management heading to display the Login window.

6. Enter the Admin user name and password, and then click the **Login** button to log in to the iFolder server and display the General Information window (see Figure 9-4). If you get a message saying the login failed, log out and restart the NetWare 6 server to Reload iFolder.

To provide additional security, the connection between your browser and the iFolder server is terminated after a few minutes of inactivity.

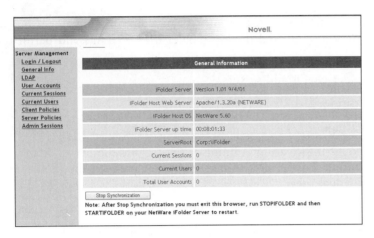

Figure 9-4   The General Information window

7. Record the information requested on your student answer sheet.

8. Click the **LDAP** link to display the LDAP window (see Figure 9-5). Record the information requested on your student answer sheet.

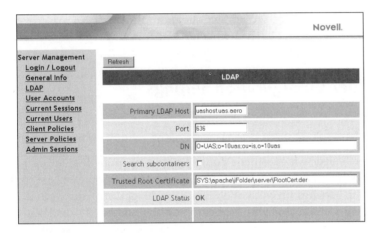

Figure 9-5   The LDAP window

9. Click the **User Accounts** link to display the User Account window (see Figure 9-6). Record your iFolder user name information on your student answer sheet.

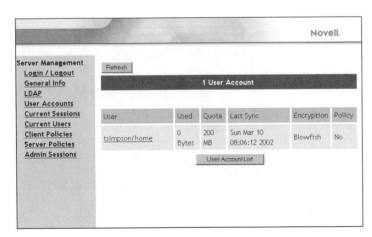

Figure 9-6   The User Account window

10. Click the **Client Policies** link to display the window shown in Figure 9-7. Record your client policy information on your student answer sheet.

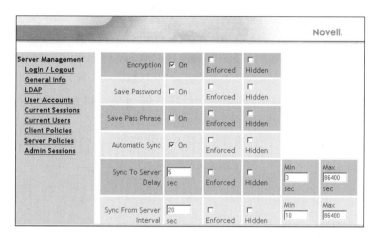

Figure 9-7   Viewing client policy information in the Server Management console

11. Click the **Server Policies** link to display the Server Policies window (see Figure 9-8). Record your server policy information on your student answer sheet.

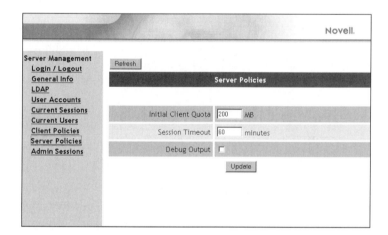

Figure 9-8   Viewing server policy information in the Server Management console

12. Click the **Login/Logout** link, and then click the **Log out** button to log out.

13. Exit your Web browser.

14. Log off the local workstation.

Optimizing the iFolder Server

Eric did not encounter any problems with the default performance of the iFolder server because the UAS network has a limited number of iFolder users. However, as the number of users increases, and the amount of storage space managed by iFolder grows, network administrators need to consider improving the performance of the iFolder server in the following ways:

- Add more RAM to the server to provide more memory for caching iFolder data. Because memory cache is many times faster than disk access, increasing RAM can significantly improve speed when synchronizing data to the iFolder clients.

- Add an additional server to split the processing load. Although the iFolder service could be moved to another server, moving other files and applications from the iFolder server to a new server might be easier. UAS, for example, is planning to install a new server in the Engineering department to handle processing for CAD applications and data.

- Increase the number of threads available to the NetWare 6 Apache Web server. **Threads** are processes that the CPU is working on, and a multi-CPU server can work on multiple threads at the same time. Increasing the number of threads makes more CPU processing available for iFolder requests instead of other Web server work. Although Novell recommends that one thread should be allocated for each iFolder client, iFolder has been tested with up to 25 clients per thread.

- Set quotas limiting the amount of disk space allocated to each user. Allocating large amounts of disk space to users can decrease the iFolder server's performance.

- Change the default synchronization delay parameters when you have many users and need to improve iFolder performance.

Using iFolder

After iFolder has been installed on the NetWare server, users can begin using it to access their files from any computer. Except for installing the iFolder server and optionally changing the default configuration parameters, the administrator doesn't need to perform any setup for users. Users can install and use the iFolder client, or they can access iFolder from their Web browsers using the iFolder Java applet. In the following sections, you learn how to access iFolder using both the iFolder client and the Java applet.

Installing and Using the iFolder Client

With minimum training, users can easily install the iFolder client on their workstations and then log in. The iFolder service then automatically creates accounts for users the first time they log in after installing the iFolder client. In the following activities, you learn how to install and configure the iFolder client and then access iFolder files from multiple computers.

Activity 9-4: Configuring the iFolder Client

Time Required: 10 minutes

Objective: Configure the iFolder client.

Description: After installing the iFolder client on his workstation and configuring the server, Eric wanted to test the iFolder service by configuring his iFolder client and then putting data into iFolder. In this activity, you learn how to configure the iFolder client on your computer and record default configuration settings.

1. If necessary, start your computer, and log in to the Novell network with the user name and password you created for yourself:

    a. Enter your user name and password.

    b. Click the **Advanced** button.

    c. Enter the context to your IS organizational unit in the Context text box.

    d. Click the **Windows NT/2000** tab, and, if necessary, enter your user name.

    e. Click **OK** to log in.

2. Log in to the iFolder service with your user name and password.

3. Right-click the **iFolder** icon in the taskbar, and on your student answer sheet, list the available options.

4. Click each option, and briefly describe its contents on your student answer sheet.

5. If you're continuing to the next activity, stay logged in; if not, close any open windows and log out.

Activity 9-5: Accessing iFolder from the Desktop

Time Required: 10 minutes

Objective: Access files using the iFolder client.

Description: To test iFolder, Eric copied some files into his iFolder directory and then went to another workstation and accessed the files using a Web browser. In this activity, you move files into your iFolder directory and then work with another student to install iFolder and maintain the files from your partner's computer.

1. If necessary, start your computer, and log in to the Novell network with the user name and password you created for yourself.

2. If necessary, log in to iFolder with your user name and password.

3. Copy the StaffDev.frm file from the F:Software.cti\WP to your iFolder drive:

   a. Double-click the **My Computer** icon, and then double-click your **SYS on Uashost (F:)** drive to open a window displaying all directories in your SYS volume.

   b. Double-click the **Software.cti** directory to open it, and then double-click the **WP** subdirectory.

   c. Right-click the **StaffDev.frm** file, and then click **Copy**.

   d. Close the Forms directory window.

   e. Right-click the **iFolder** home directory icon on your desktop, and then click **Paste**.

   f. Double-click your **iFolder** home directory, and verify that the StaffDev.frm file has been added.

   g. Right-click your **StaffDev.frm** file, and then click **Rename**.

   h. Change the StaffDev.frm extension to **txt**, and then press **Enter**.

   i. Close your iFolder home directory window.

4. Create a file and save it in your iFolder directory with the name Expense.txt:

   a. Start WordPad by clicking **Start**, **Programs**, **Accessories**, **WordPad**.

   b. Enter your name on the first line, leave a blank line, and type the words **Expense Report** on the third line.

   c. Click **File**, **Save as** on the menu bar to open the Save As dialog box.

   d. Double-click **iFolder** in the My Documents window, double-click your user name, and then double-click **Home**.

   e. Enter **Expense** in the File name text box, verify that Rich Text Format (RTF) is selected in the Save as type text box, and then click the **Save** button to save your WordPad document.

   f. Exit WordPad.

5. Verify that the Expense.rtf file is in your iFolder window.

6. To force synchronization with the iFolder server, right-click the **iFolder** icon in the taskbar, and then click the **Sync Now** option.

7. Close any open windows, and log out.

8. Wait for your lab partner to complete Step 7, and then exchange computers.

9. Log in from your lab partner's computer with your user name and password.

10. Log in to iFolder with the same user name and password you used on your computer.

11. Enter your pass phrase, and then click **OK** to create an iFolder home icon for your user name on your lab partner's computer.

12. Double-click your **iFolder** icon to display all files in your iFolder home directory. If you do not see any files, the iFolder service hasn't yet synchronized with the local computer. To force synchronization, right-click the **iFolder** icon on the taskbar, and then click **Sync Now**.

13. Open the Expense.rtf file, add an expense line that reads **mm/dd/yy Meals 25.50**, and then save the Expense document.

14. Exit WordPad.

15. Right-click the **iFolder** icon in the taskbar, and then click the **Sync Now** option.

16. Log out.

17. Wait for your lab partner to complete Step 16, and then return to your computer.

18. Log in with your user name, and open your iFolder directory.

19. Use WordPad to open the Expense.rtf file. On your student answer sheet, record the contents and your observations.

20. Exit WordPad, close your iFolder window, and log out.

Using the iFolder Java Applet

As you learned in the previous activity, the iFolder client can be useful when users need to maintain access to their files on multiple computers or access their files from a laptop that's offline. However, often it's not practical to install the iFolder client and place the iFolder directory on remote computers that users don't access frequently. For example, David Heise needs to access certain documents when visiting customer locations and does not want to install the iFolder client and iFolder home directory icon on these computers because he might not use the same computer next time he visits the location. As a result, Eric trained Universal AeroSpace users on how to use the Java applet to access their iFolder files from a Web browser.

Activity 9-6: Accessing iFolder from a Web Browser

Time Required: 10 minutes

Objective: Access iFolder files from a Web browser.

Description: Before training UAS users, Eric tested access to his iFolder files using a Web browser from a computer that didn't have iFolder or Novell Client installed. In this activity, you learn how to use your Web browser to download and upload your iFolder files, using only the iFolder Java applet.

1. If necessary, start your computer to obtain the Novell Login window.

2. To simulate accessing iFolder files from a computer that does not have Novell Client installed, log in with your local user name by clicking the **Workstation only** check box, and then entering your local user name and password.

3. Click the **Cancel** button to close the iFolder login window.

4. Start your Web browser software, enter the URL **https://ip_address http://ip_address** (replacing *ip_address* with the IP address assigned to your iFolder server), and then press **Enter**. (Using "https" encrypts data transmissions by using a secure port, thus increasing security.)

5. Click the **Login** option under the Access your Files heading, and then click **Yes** to proceed with the security certificate.

6. If this is the first time you have accessed iFolder from a Web browser, you'll see a security warning asking if you want to install and run the JVM6.tmp script. Click **Yes** to install the script and display the Login window.

7. Enter your user name, password, and pass phrase.

8. Click the **Connect** button to log in and display your iFolder home directory.

9. Double-click your home directory to expand it, and record the filenames on your student answer sheet.

10. On your student answer sheet, record the options that are available when the home directory is highlighted.

11. Click the **Expense.rtf** file, and record the available options on your student answer sheet.

12. Click the **Download** option, and download the file to your desktop.

13. Minimize your Web browser.

14. Start WordPad, and open the **Expense.rtf** file on your desktop. Use WordPad to add the following line:

    mm/dd/yy   Room   129.00

15. Save the Expense.rtf file, and exit WordPad.

16. Upload the updated file:

    a. Maximize your Web browser.

    b. Click your home directory, and then click the **Upload** button to open the Novell iFolder Upload dialog box.

    c. Click the **Expense.rtf** file in the Desktop list, and click the **Open** button.

    d. Click **Yes** to respond to the upload warning message and continue with the upload process.

17. Click the **Logout** option to exit your session.

18. Close your Web browser.

19. Delete the Expense.rtf file from the desktop, and log out.

20. Log in with your user name and password.

21. Log in to iFolder with your user name and password.

22. Double-click your iFolder home directory, and open the **Expense.rtf** file.

23. On your student answer sheet, record your observations about the change you made.

24. Log out.

9

INSTALLING AND USING NETSTORAGE

Although iFolder can give users access to their data from any networked computer or even from computers (such as laptops) not attached to the network, it requires installing the iFolder client or Java applet on users' computers as well as placing files in the iFolder directory. Because some users need to be able to access files that are in shared directories on the server, placing these files in the iFolder client is not practical. In addition, when visiting other sites and using other people's computers, installing the iFolder client or even the Java applet on their computers isn't always feasible.

Novell NetStorage solves some of these problems by giving users secure access to files on the NetWare server from any Internet location; it does this by using an existing Web browser or Microsoft Web Folder, with no additional client or applet to download or install on the user's workstation. With NetStorage, users can securely copy, move, rename, delete, read, and write files between any Internet-enabled machine and the Novell network. NetStorage supports Internet standards such as HTTP, HTTPS, HTML, XML, and WebDAV, making it compatible with most client computer systems, including Windows, Macintosh, and Linux. In addition, NetStorage includes a gadget for NetWare WebAccess so that users can access network files and folders through the NetWare WebAccess page. In the following sections, you learn how to set up and use Novell NetStorage so that users in your UAS organization can access and manage network files.

Installing NetStorage

Like iFolder, Novell NetStorage can be installed either during NetWare 6 installation or after. As with iFolder, Eric preferred to install NetStorage after the NetWare 6 installation to keep the initial installation as simple as possible. To install and use NetStorage, there must be at least one NetWare 6 server in the eDirectory tree where NetStorage will be installed and workstations must have a minimum of Netscape 4.7 or Internet Explorer 5.0 installed. Because NetStorage is configured during installation, any changes you need to make to the initial configuration can be made only by removing and reinstalling NetStorage. To avoid reinstalling, make sure the following information is available before starting the NetStorage installation:

- Identify the IP address or DNS name of the primary NetWare 6 server. The primary server must have a Master or Read/Write replica of the eDirectory tree. NetStorage does not need to be installed on the primary server, but you need to identify this server in the NetStorage Install window. The primary server comes into play when a user attempts to log in to NetStorage. During login, NetStorage searches the eDirectory database on the primary server to locate the user name and password. When NetStorage finds the user in the eDirectory database, it authenticates the user to eDirectory.

- Identify the eDirectory context of users who will use NetStorage. NetStorage searches for user accounts in the contexts you specify in the NetStorage Install window. The context is indicated by inserting a colon after the primary server's IP address or DNS name and then entering the container's distinguished name. For example, to search for users in the UASHOST server, Eric entered "172.20.0.60:UAS."

- In addition to the primary context, the NetStorage Install window contains two more fields where you can specify the primary servers and eDirectory contexts from additional eDirectory trees that the NetStorage service will support.

- The final field in the NetStorage Install window is where you specify the IP address or DNS name of your iFolder server. For users to be able access their iFolder files through NetStorage, you must specify the iFolder server.

After identifying the UASHOST server as the primary NetStorage server and obtaining its IP address and DNS name, Eric installed NetStorage by performing these steps:

1. Because installing NetStorage requires shutting down the server and restarting, Eric picked a time to perform the installation during the weekend when the server was not needed.

2. To start the installation, Eric inserted the NetWare 6 CD into the UASHOST server, and then pressed Ctrl+Esc to select the server console screen.

3. He entered the command CDROM, and then pressed Enter to mount the CD as a volume on the server.

4. Next, he pressed Ctrl+Esc to select the X Server - Graphical Console.

5. At the graphical console, Eric clicked Novell and then Install to display the Installed Products window.

6. He clicked Add to display the Source Path window, clicked the Browse button to select the NetWare 6 CD volume, and then clicked OK. The installation files were then copied to the server.

7. Eric clicked OK again, and the Components window was displayed with check marks indicating the default installed components. He clicked Clear All to prevent reinstalling existing components, clicked the Novell Storage check box, and then clicked Next to display the login window.

8. After Eric logged in to the network with his Admin user name and password, the LDAP Configuration window was displayed.

9. Eric verified that 389 was entered in the Clear Text Port text box and 636 was entered in the SSL Port text box.

10. He clicked the Allow Clear Text Passwords check box to enable this option, and then clicked Next to display the NetStorage Install window.

11. In the NetStorage Install window, Eric verified that the IP address and context of the UASHOST server (172.20.0.60:UAS) was entered in the Primary Server text box and that the IP address of the iFolder service (172.20.0.62) along with port 80 was entered in the iFolder Server and iFolder Port text boxes. He then clicked Next to display the installation summary window.

12. After verifying that Novell NetStorage and NetWare Port Resolver were listed in the summary window, Eric clicked Finish to copy the NetStorage files and complete the installation.

13. When the Installation complete message box was displayed, Eric clicked Close to return to the graphical console.

14. Finally, Eric restarted the server by entering RESTART SERVER at the console command prompt.

Using NetStorage

Starting NetStorage on the server side happens automatically when the server restarts. To use NetStorage from the client side, the date and time on the server *must* match very closely with the date and time on user workstations. If the time on the workstation differs too much from that on the server, file updates might not be properly synchronized with the changes made from the local network. If workstations are logging in using Novell Client, the client software automatically sets the workstation date and time to match the server. If users are logging in to local workstations that don't have Novell Client installed, the workstation time must be set close to the server's time for NetStorage to properly synchronize changes made to network data. After the date and time conditions are met, users can use Microsoft Web Folder or a Web browser to access NetStorage services. To access NetStorage services from a Web browser, enter the URL *http://ip_address/oneNet/NetStorage* (replacing *ip_address* with the IP address or DNS name of the NetWare server running NetStorage services). The NetStorage service then prompts users to enter their eDirectory user name and password. After logging in, NetStorage reads user login scripts, drive mappings, and user object properties to determine the location of home directories. The NetStorage Web page then displays the network files and folders currently accessible to the user. After a user has logged in to NetStorage, he or she will see folders and files that can be manipulated in much the same way as in Windows Explorer. The same conventions are used to expand and close directories and to open, move, delete, copy, and rename files. Unlike Windows Explorer, local files and folders are not accessible from the NetStorage window. In addition, users cannot map drives or change login scripts from the NetStorage Web page. In the following activity, you use NetStorage to access files available to your user name.

Activity 9-7: Using NetStorage to Access Files

Time Required: 10 minutes

Objective: Access files using NetStorage.

Description: After installing NetStorage on the UASHOST server, Eric tested the system by logging in to the NetStorage server with his EKenton user name and then verified access to his files and folders. In this activity, you log in to the NetStorage server and practice accessing your files and folders.

1. If necessary, start your computer, and log in to Novell Client with your user name and password. When the Novell iFolder Login window is displayed, click **Cancel** to bypass the iFolder login.

2. Copy files to your home directory:

   a. Use My Computer to open a window to the G:\Forms directory.

   b. Right-click the **Memo.frm** file, and then click **Copy**.

   c. Close the Forms directory window.

   d. Use My Computer to open a window to your home directory on drive L:.

e. Click **Edit**, **Paste** on the menu bar to paste the file into your home directory.

f. Close your home directory window, and log out.

3. Log on to your local Windows 2000 workstation by clicking the **Workstation only** check box and then entering your local user name and password.

4. Start your Web browser, enter the URL **http://ip_address/oneNet/NetStorage**, and press **Enter**. (Replace *ip_address* with the IP address assigned to your NetWare 6 server.) Be careful when you enter the URL because it is case-sensitive.

5. When the Login window is displayed, enter your user name and password to log in and display the NetStorage home page for your user name.

6. On your student answer sheet, record the folders in the navigation pane.

7. Click your home directory, and on your student answer sheet, record the files it contains.

8. Open the **Memo.frm** file using WordPad, and change the contents. Record the results on your student answer sheet.

9. Close your Web browser, and log out.

USING NETWARE 6 REMOTE MANAGEMENT UTILITIES

An important part of Novell's OneNet strategy is to enable network administrators to manage the network and server from any networked computer. As part of this OneNet strategy, Novell has included the iManager, Remote Manager, iMonitor, and RConsoleJ remote management utilities with the NetWare 6 operating system. In Chapters 4 and 8, you learned how to use iManager to create users, groups, and printers from a Web browser. You have also been introduced to the Remote Manager utility to perform certain administrative tasks, such as creating volumes and accessing the server console. As its name implies, the iMonitor utility provides network monitoring and diagnostic capabilities to help you identify and isolate network and server performance problems. In the following sections, you learn more about using the Remote Manager and iMonitor utilities to manage and monitor your server and network performance.

The Remote Manager Utility

Remote Manager, perhaps the most powerful of NetWare 6's remote management utilities, enables you to monitor your server's health, change configuration parameters, and perform diagnostic and debugging tasks. To use Remote Manager, the server and workstation must meet the software requirements shown in Table 9-1.

Table 9-1   Remote Manager Software Requirements

Software	Requirement
NetWare operating system	NetWare 5.1 or later
Browser	One of the following: ■ Netscape 4.5 or later ■ Internet Explorer 5 or later ■ NetWare server browser
NetWare NLMs loaded on the server	PORTAL.NLM and HTTPSTK.NLM

To access the Remote Manager utility, start your Web browser and enter the URL *https://server_ip_address:8009* or *http://server_ip_address:8008* to go directly to the Remote Manager page. You can also enter *https://server_ip_address:2200* to display the NetWare Web Manager window, shown in Figure 9-9, and then select your server under the NetWare Remote Manager heading.

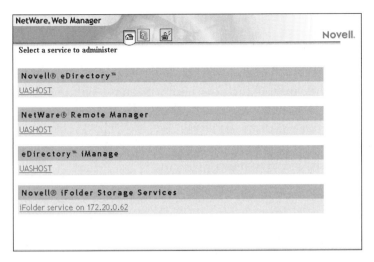

Figure 9-9   Selecting a service in NetWare Web Manager
When using NetWare 6.5, you will see the NetWare 6.5 Welcome as shown in Figure D-17.

The Remote Manager's opening page is divided into several sections, as shown in Figure 9-10.

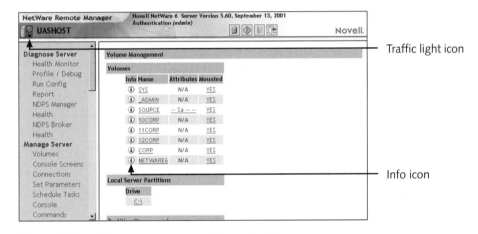

Figure 9-10   The opening page of Remote Manager

The overall health indicator in the upper-left corner of the page (in Figure 9-10, it's the traffic light icon) gives you a quick look at your overall server health. The header frame at the top center of the page contains general information about the server and icons used to exit Remote Manager and to view volumes, the health monitor, and configuration information. The navigation frame at the left side of the window lists general tasks you can perform in Remote Manager and supplies links to specific pages for performing these tasks. The main content frame in the middle of the window changes depending on which link you click in the header or navigation frame. The online help frame displays help information for the content being viewed in the main content frame. In the activities in the following sections, you learn how to use these frames to diagnose your server's health, manage NetWare servers and volumes, check server application usage, view server hardware configurations, access Novell eDirectory information, and monitor license usage.

Monitoring Server Health and Performance

The overall health indicator in the upper-left corner of Remote Manager's opening page gives a quick indication of the overall server status by displaying one of the following colors:

- *Green*—Represents a server in good health.

- *Yellow*—Provides a warning of possible problems with the server's health or performance.

- *Red*—Represents a server in bad health, which requires the administrator's response.

- *Black*—Indicates that communication with the server has been lost (the server might be down).

If the overall health indicator is not green, you can click the Health Monitor link under the Diagnose Server heading to view the status of individual indicators (see Figure 9-11).

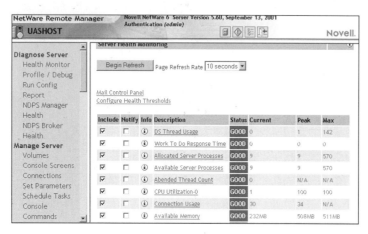

Figure 9-11   Viewing the status of health monitor indicators

If any of the indicators are yellow or red, they need attention. For example, if the Available Memory indicator is yellow or red, it indicates that the system is running short of memory. You can view more detailed information about the indicator by clicking on it to see a graph of the usage, as shown in Figure 9-12.

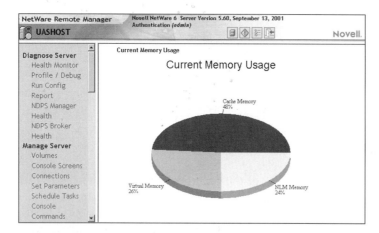

Figure 9-12   The Current Memory Usage graph

In this example, the memory usage is in good shape, with almost half the memory reserved for caching files. If the cache memory drops below 30% of the total memory, it might indicate that RAM should be added to the server. If NLM memory usage is more than the cache memory, you might be able to correct the problem by unloading some unneeded modules. For example, exiting the X Server graphical console can free up quite a bit of memory. To determine which NLMs are currently loaded, click the Run Config Report link to view server configuration settings and a list of currently loaded modules, as shown in Figure 9-13.

You can click the NDPS Manager Health and NDPS Broker Health links to view the status of printer agents, the NDPS Manager, and the Broker. These options can be helpful when debugging printer problems, as described in Chapter 8.

When viewing the Health Monitor page, you click the Configure Health Thresholds link to view or set suspect and critical values for a variety of indicators, as shown in Figure 9-14.

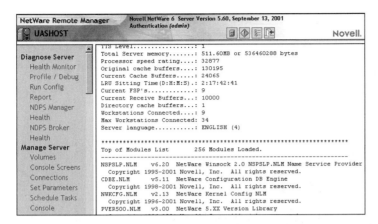

Figure 9-13   Viewing currently loaded NLMs in the Run Config Report

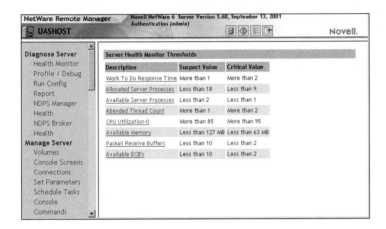

Figure 9-14   Setting suspect and critical values for indicators

The Suspect Value column identifies the criteria for displaying a yellow indicator, and the Critical Value column identifies the criteria for displaying a red indicator. To change the criteria, click the indicator, enter the new suspect or critical value, and then click OK. In the following activity, you use the Health Monitor to view the performance indicators on your server.

Activity 9-8: Monitoring Server Health

Time Required: 10 minutes

Objective: Use Remote Manager to check server health and performance.

Description: Eric noticed that the server was not responding as fast as he felt it should. To help identify any problems, he used Remote Manager to check the individual server indicators. Periodically, he noticed that the overall health indicator was yellow, so he used the Health Monitor to view the status of individual indicators. In this activity, you use Remote Manager to document several performance indicators on your student answer sheet. To perform this activity, you need access to a user with the Supervisor right to your server. If you do not have access to a user name with this right, examine the following steps and use the screenshots to fill in your student answer sheet.

1. If necessary, start your computer, and log in to Novell Client with your UasAdmin user name and password. If necessary, click **Cancel** to bypass the iFolder login.

2. Start your Web browser, and enter the URL **https://ip_address:8009** (replacing *ip_address* with the IP address of your server) to open the Enter Network Password dialog box.

3. Enter the user name and password of the user who has the Supervisor right to your server, and then click **OK** to display the Remote Manager main window.

4. Click the **traffic light** icon to display the Server Health Monitoring window.

5. Scroll through your server's health monitors and check their status. On your student answer sheet, record any indicators that display a yellow or red status.

6. Click the **Info** icon (an *i* in a circle) next to the Available Memory indicator to display the Available Memory information window (see Figure 9-15).

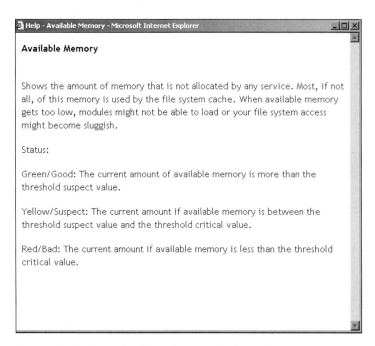

Figure 9-15   The Available Memory information window

7. Record the criteria for the green, yellow, and red indicators on your student answer sheet.

8. Close the Available Memory information window.

9. Click the **Configure Health Thresholds** link, and record the values in the Suspect and Critical columns on your student answer sheet.

10. Click the **Exit** button, click **Yes** to exit NetWare Remote Manager, and then log out.

Managing the Server

Server management includes managing volumes and user connections, viewing and setting parameters, viewing system statistics, managing memory, and accessing current console screens. Being able to access the server console screens remotely is a powerful management feature when troubleshooting or repairing NetWare server problems. In the following activity, you use the Manage Server options in Remote Manager to view and record information about your server's volume and memory usage.

Activity 9-9: Performing Server Management Tasks

Time Required: 10 minutes

Objective: Use Remote Manager to view server volume and memory usage.

Description: Being able to manage the UASHOST server from remote locations has been convenient for Eric when he's away from the office. In this activity, you use various server management options to learn how Eric was able to manage the server on the road.

1. If necessary, start your computer, and log in to Novell Client with your UasAdmin user name and password. If necessary, click **Cancel** to bypass the iFolder login.

2. Start your Web browser, and enter the URL **https://*ip_address*:8009** (replacing *ip_address* with the IP address of your server) to open the Enter Network Password dialog box.

3. Enter the user name and password of the user who has the Supervisor right to your server, and then click **OK** to display the Remote Manager main window.

4. In the main window, click the **Volumes** link to display the Volume Management window showing the status of all volumes (see Figure 9-16).

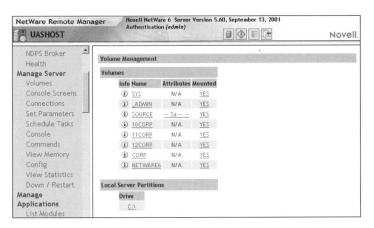

Figure 9-16   The Volume Management window

5. On your student answer sheet, record the names and attributes of the first four volumes.

6. Click the **Console Commands** link to display a list of all console commands.

7. Click the **Info** icon to the right of these commands: CONFIG, CLEAR STATION, and CLS. On your student answer sheet, record the description of each command along with the sample command provided in the Info window.

8. Click the **View Memory Config** link to display the System Memory Information window.

9. On your student answer sheet, record the total system memory size and current cache memory.

10. You can stay logged in and leave your Remote Manager window open for the next activity. If you're not continuing to the next activity, click the **Exit** button, click **Yes** to exit NetWare Remote Manager, and log out.

Activity 9-10: Managing Volumes

Time Required: 10 minutes

Objective: Use Remote Manager to access data.

Description: In addition to being able to view and change system configurations in Remote Manager, you can view volume information, mount or dismount volumes, and perform many file management tasks, such as uploading, downloading, renaming, and deleting files. Eric used Remote Manager while at Comdex in Las Vegas to replace a .dll file for one of the engineering applications. In this activity, you use NetWare Remote Manager to simulate accessing volume information and then uploading and renaming a file.

1. If necessary, start your computer, and log in to Novell Client with your UasAdmin user name and password. Click **Cancel** to bypass the iFolder login, if necessary. Follow these steps to start Remote Manager:

   a. Start your Web browser, and enter the URL **https://*ip_address*:8009** (replacing *ip_address* with the IP address of your server) to open the Enter Network Password dialog box.

   b. Enter the user name and password of the user who has the Supervisor right to your server, and then click **OK** to display the Remote Manager main window.

2. Under the Manage Server heading in the main window, click the **Volumes** link.

3. Click the **Info** icon next to your ##CORP volume, and record the volume statistics requested on your student answer sheet.

4. Click the **Volumes** link to return to the Volume Management window, and then click your **##CORP** volume object.

5. Navigate to your NASA folder.

6. Click the **Upload** button.

7. Click the **Browse** button to navigate to the WINNT\System32 directory on your local workstation.

8. Double-click any file with a .dll extension.

9. Click the **Upload** button. The file will be copied to your NASA folder.

10. You can stay logged in and leave your Remote Manager window open for the next activity. If you're not continuing to the next activity, click the **Exit** button, click **Yes** to exit NetWare Remote Manager, and then log out.

Activity 9-11: Accessing eDirectory

Time Required: 10 minutes

Objective: Use Remote Manager to access eDirectory objects.

Description: When working with a remote server, sometimes you need to find and view objects. Although the iManager utility is used for most eDirectory maintenance and management functions, Remote Manager enables administrators to browse the eDirectory tree and view or delete objects. In this activity, you use Remote Manager to browse the UAS_Tree and view your eDirectory objects.

1. If necessary, start your computer, and log in to Novell Client with your UasAdmin user name and password. Click **Cancel** to bypass the iFolder login, if necessary. Follow these steps to start Remote Manager:

   a. Start your Web browser, and enter the URL **https://*ip_address*:8009** (replacing *ip_address* with the IP address of your server) to open the Enter Network Password dialog box.

   b. Enter the user name and password of the user who has the Supervisor right to your server, and then click **OK** to display the Remote Manager main window.

2. Click the **Access Tree Walker** link under the Manage eDirectory heading.

3. Expand your **##UAS** container, and view the details on each user. Notice that the only eDirectory function you can perform is to delete an eDirectory object, so be careful.

4. Expand your **Engineering** container, and click your **TRucci** user.

5. On your student answer sheet, record the following information for your TRucci user: CN data, group membership, and home directory.

6. Click the **View eDirectory Partitions** link to display a window similar to the one in Figure 9-17.

7. On your student answer sheet, record any partitions in your ##UAS structure.

8. You can stay logged in and leave your Remote Manager window open for the next activity. If you're not continuing to the next activity, click the **Exit** button, click **Yes** to exit NetWare Remote Manager, and log out.

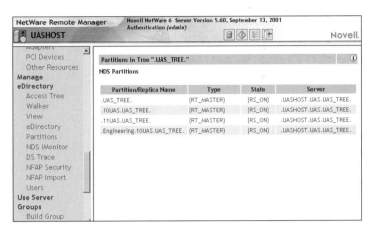

Figure 9-17   Viewing information on eDirectory partitions

Activity 9-12: Viewing the Server Hardware Environment

Time Required: 10 minutes

Objective: Use Remote Manager to view hardware information.

Description: Using Remote Manager, you can view your server's current hardware configuration settings, which is useful when diagnosing problems or planning for new equipment. For example, at Comdex Eric found a 1 GB network card that he wanted to install in the UASHOST server. He used Remote Manager to view the server's hardware configuration so that he could check the slots and interrupts to determine the feasibility of installing the new network card. In this activity, you use the options under the Manage Hardware heading to document your server's available ports and interrupts.

1. If necessary, start your computer, and log in to Novell Client with your UasAdmin user name and password. Click **Cancel** to bypass the iFolder login, if necessary. Follow these steps to start Remote Manager:

   a. Start your Web browser, and enter the URL **https://*ip_address*:8009** (replacing *ip_address* with the IP address of your server) to open the Enter Network Password dialog box.

   b. Enter the user name and password of the user who has the Supervisor right to your server, and then click **OK** to display the Remote Manager main window.

2. Scroll down the navigation frame to the Manage Hardware heading, and on your student answer sheet, record the options under it.

3. Click the **Processors** link to display the Processor Information window (see Figure 9-18).

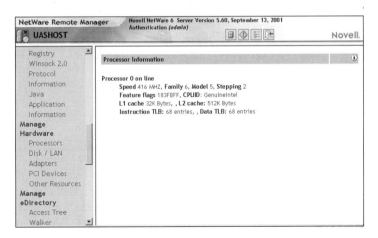

Figure 9-18   The Processor Information window

4. Record the processor information on your student answer sheet.

5. Under the Manage Hardware heading, click the **Disk/LAN Adapters** link.

6. Click the **Info** icon next to Network Adapter to display a window similar to the one in Figure 9-19.

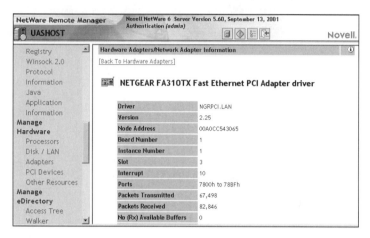

Figure 9-19   Viewing information on network adapters

7. On your student answer sheet, record the interrupt, slot, and ports used by your network adapter.

8. Under the Manage Hardware heading, click the **Other Resources** link to display the Hardware Resources window.

9. Click the **Interrupts** option to display the Interrupts window (see Figure 9-20).

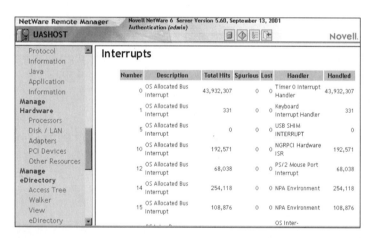

Figure 9-20   The Interrupts window

10. On your student answer sheet, list the interrupts in use and any available or unused interrupts.

11. Click the **Exit** button, and, if necessary, click **Yes** to close the NetWare Manager window.

The iMonitor Utility

Like Remote Manager, the iMonitor utility provides monitoring and diagnostic capabilities for all servers in the eDirectory tree. Remote Manager provides only minimum information on the eDirectory tree, but the iMonitor utility is designed to be a major troubleshooting tool for monitoring and repairing eDirectory tree problems. Monitoring and diagnosing the eDirectory tree requires the administrator to be able to look at partitions and replicas on a server basis. iMonitor can be run on any platform that supports eDirectory 8.6, including NetWare, Windows NT/2000, Linux, and Solaris. On NetWare servers, iMonitor listens on the default HTTP port 8008. Upon login, the user's port is redirected to 8009. To run iMonitor, your server and workstation must meet the requirements shown in Table 9-2.

Table 9-2   iMonitor Software Requirements

Software	Requirement
Browser	Internet Explorer 4 or later
	Netscape 4.06 or later
	NetWare server console browser
Platform	NetWare 5 support pack 5 or later
	Windows NT/2000
	Linux
	Solaris
	Tru64 Unix
eDirectory	Version 8.6 or higher

In the following activity, you learn how to use iMonitor to access and monitor your eDirectory tree information.

Activity 9-13: Using iMonitor

Time Required: 10 minutes

Objective: Use iMonitor to access server and eDirectory information.

Description: Although the eDirectory tree is an extremely stable and reliable platform, occasionally problems can occur as a result of replication errors caused by communication media failure or server hardware problems. In this activity, you use iMonitor to check the status of your eDirectory tree. As with the Remote Manager activities, you need access to a user name and password that has the Supervisor right to the NetWare 6 server to perform the steps in this activity.

1. If necessary, start your computer, and log on to your Windows 2000 computer with your local user name and password.

2. Start your Web browser software, and enter the URL **https://ip_address:2200** (replacing *ip_address* with the IP address of your server).

3. In the Security Alert message box, click **Yes** to display the NetWare Web Manager window.

4. Click your server name under the Remote Manager heading to open the Enter Network Password dialog box.

5. Enter your Admin user name and password to display the NetWare Remote Manager window.

6. Scroll down to the Manage eDirectory heading, and click the **NDS iMonitor** link to display the Agent Summary window (see Figure 9-21).

7. A useful eDirectory troubleshooting technique is performing a DSTRACE on the eDirectory tree transactions to look for error conditions or messages that can be used to identify and correct a problem. In this step, you perform a DSTRACE and record your observations on your student answer sheet:

   a. Click the **Trace Configuration** link, and then, if necessary, click **Yes** in the Security Alert message box to display the Trace Configuration window, shown in Figure 9-22.

   b. In the DS Trace Options section, verify that the following options are selected: Inbound Synchronization, Initialization, Outbound Synchronization, and DS Agent. Click the **NCP client** and **Streams** check boxes to select these options.

9

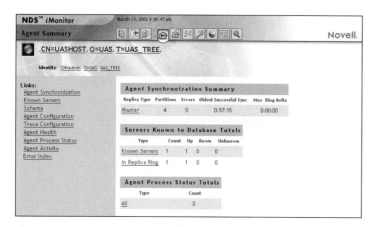

Figure 9-21   The Agent Summary window in iMonitor

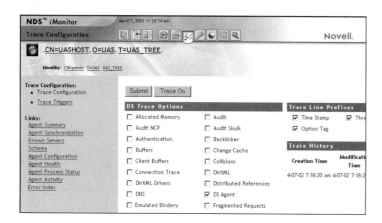

Figure 9-22   The Trace Configuration window

    c. At the top of the Trace Configuration window, click the **Submit** button to start the trace.

    d. In the Trace History section, click the **View** icon (magnifying glass).

    e. Scan the output, and record any observations on your student answer sheet.

8. Another important eDirectory troubleshooting aid is checking to make sure eDirectory replicas are synchronized on the servers. Follow these steps to view your replica synchronization status in iMonitor:

    a. Click the **Agent Synchronization** link under the Links heading to display the Agent Synchronization summary window.

    b. The Partition Synchronization Status heading contains information on each partition. Scroll down the list and locate your ##UAS partition information. On your student answer sheet, record the Error count and Last Successful Sync information for your partition.

    c. Click your **##UAS** partition and scroll down to view the information. On your student answer sheet, record the date and time your ##UAS partition was created.

    d. Click the **Home NetWare Manager** button (a server with a bull's-eye target next to it) at the top of the iMonitor window to return to Remote Manager.

9. The DSREPAIR utility plays a major role in identifying and fixing inconsistencies in the eDirectory partition replicas. Follow these steps to run DSREPAIR and then view the DSRE-PAIR log for any possible problems:

    a. Scroll down and click the **NDS iMonitor** link under the Manage eDirectory heading to return to the iMonitor window.

    b. Click the **Repair** button (a wrench icon) to display the NDS Repair Switches window.

    c. On your student answer sheet, record the repair option settings. Do not start the repair at this time unless told to do so by your instructor.

10. Exit iMonitor by clicking the **Logout** button, and log out.

The RConsoleJ Utility

Although you can use Remote Manager to perform the same server operations, if you are currently using ConsoleOne and are logged in as the Admin user, with RConsoleJ you don't need to start a Web browser and log in to the server again to access the server console from ConsoleOne. To use RConsoleJ, RCONAG6.NLM must be loaded at the server you want to access. This module sets the password, TCP port, and IPX/SPX port that will be used to gain access to the target server. To run RConsoleJ at the workstation, you need to be logged in as the Admin user and running ConsoleOne at the workstation. In the following activity, you verify that RCONAG6.NLM is running and then use RConsoleJ from ConsoleOne to gain access to your NetWare server.

Activity 9-14: Using RConsoleJ

Time Required: 10 minutes

Objective: Use RConsoleJ to access the NetWare 6 server console.

Description: When using ConsoleOne, Eric often finds it more convenient to use the RConsoleJ utility than to start Internet Explorer and log in to the Novell network to use Remote Manager. In this activity, you learn how to use RConsoleJ from ConsoleOne to access and manage your server. (To perform this activity, you need access to the NetWare server, or you need to get the password assigned to RConsoleJ from your instructor.)

1. (Optional) If you have access to the NetWare server console in this step, load RConsoleJ on the NetWare server and assign a password:

    If you do not have access to the server console, your instructor can demonstrate loading RCONAG6 on your classroom server.

    a. Press **Ctrl+Esc** to display the Current Screens list.

    b. Enter **1**, and then press **Enter** to display the System Console screen.

    c. Enter **RCONAG6**, and then press **Enter** to display the Enter a password prompt.

    d. Enter a password, and then press **Enter**. Record the password on your student answer sheet.

    e. Press **Enter** to use the default TCP port number 2034.

    f. Press **Enter** to use the SPX port number 16800.

    g. Press **Enter** to use the default port number 2036 for a secured connection. The RConsoleJ module should now be loaded, and you'll be returned to the system console.

2. If necessary, start your computer, and log in to Novell Client with your UasAdmin user name and password.

3. If you have access to a user name with the Supervisor right to the UASHOST server, click Remote Manager's **Run Config Report** link to verify that the RCONAG6.NLM module is loaded on the server:

   a. Start your Web browser and enter the URL **https://*ip_address*:8009**.

   b. Log in with a user name that has the Supervisor right to the classroom NetWare 6 server.

   c. Click the **Run Config Report** link under the Diagnose Server heading.

   d. Click the **View Report** link to display a configuration report.

   e. Scroll down the report until you see the Top of Modules List heading. On your student answer sheet, record the number of modules loaded.

   f. Scroll down to the end of the list and verify that RCONAG6.NLM is the last module listed.

   g. Exit Remote Manager by clicking the **Exit** button and then clicking **Yes** to close the browser window.

4. Start ConsoleOne, expand the classroom **UAS** Organization, and click the **UASHOST** server object.

5. Start RConsoleJ by clicking **Tools**, **Remote Console** on the menu bar to open the Novell RConsoleJ dialog box, shown in Figure 9-23.

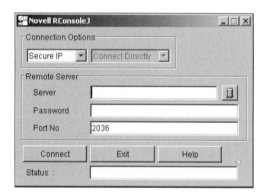

Figure 9-23   The Novell RConsoleJ dialog box

6. Click the **Browse** button next to the Server text box to display a list of remote servers running the RCONAG6 module.

7. Click your **UASHOST** server, and then click **OK** to return to the Novell RConsoleJ dialog box.

8. Enter the password assigned to the RConsoleJ module, and click the **Connect** button to log in. (Use the password you entered in Step 1 or the password supplied by your instructor.)

9. Click **OK** to accept the certificate and display the console screen.

10. To display a list of screens you can access, click the **down arrow** next to the Server Screens text box, as shown in Figure 9-24.

11. Click the **Disconnect** button to the right of the Activate button to exit the RConsoleJ session.

You'll learn more about using NetWare console commands in Chapter 12.

12. Close the RConsoleJ dialog box to return to ConsoleOne.

13. Exit ConsoleOne, and log out.

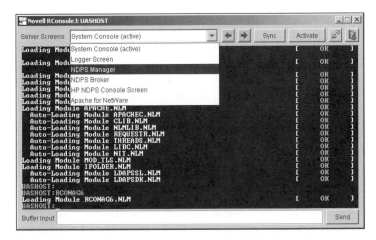

Figure 9-24   Viewing the list of available screens

9

MANAGING NOVELL LICENSING SERVICES

In previous versions of NetWare, clients have access to NetWare servers through a licensed connection system known as **Server Connection Licensing (SCL)**. In SCL, each pre–NetWare 6 server is assigned a number of connections based on the installed license certificates. When a user connects to a pre–NetWare 6 server, one of the license connections is allocated to that client for the duration of the user's session. When the user logs out and turns off the workstation, the licensed connection is made available for another client to attach to that server. In the SCL system, organizations need to purchase licenses for the total number of concurrent users on each NetWare server. For example, if Universal AeroSpace had 50 employees who connected to two servers, Luke would need to purchase 100 connection licenses.

The Novell Licensing Services that ship with NetWare 6 support a new type of licensing system: **User Access Licensing (UAL)**. With the UAL system, users gain access to network services by connecting to the network rather than an individual server. When they first log in to the server, user objects receive a permanent license unit, so they can access network services on any network server in the tree at any time from any computer. That means a user needs only one license, regardless of the number of servers he or she needs to log in to. In the new UAL model, an organization purchases licenses for the total number of user objects in the tree, instead of purchasing licenses for each server. When users log in to the network, they obtain a license unit reserved for a minimum of 90 days. If a user does not log in within the 90-day time period, the license is released and made available to the next user who needs it. The 90-day limit begins each time a user logs in to the network. Unlike the SCL model, in which print servers and other network resources required licensed connections, in the UAL model, non-user objects, such as printers and Z.E.N.works, do not use user licenses. The major disadvantage of the UAL model is in networks that have public access—such as those at schools, libraries, or other facilities—requiring many user accounts that often aren't logged in at the same time. For example, a school with accounts for several hundred students might have only 50 who log in at one time because of a limited number of workstations. In this type of environment, it would be prohibitively expensive to purchase licenses for each possible user. As a result, because NetWare 6 does not support the SCL model, the best alternative in environments that support many unlicensed users is creating a few generic user accounts for all nonlicensed users.

Because managing network usage in the UAL model is a priority, network administrators can use the new NetWare Usage tool in Remote Manager to view the total number of licenses and to generate reports showing user access information. In addition, you can use the iManager utility to view license certificates and install additional licenses. Because the server installation software installs the Novell Licensing Services but not the license certificates, network administrators need to know how to use iManager to install UAL license certificates separately. In the following sections, you learn how Eric used iManager to install his license certificates and see how to use Remote Manager's NetWare Usage tool to monitor license usage data.

Using iManager to Install and View License Certificates

There are two types of NetWare license certificates: NetWare 6 Server certificates and NetWare 6 User certificates. The **NetWare 6 Server certificate**, installed during the NetWare 6 server installation, is necessary for the server to run. The **NetWare 6 User certificate** is a UAL license certificate that supports user connections to the network. NetWare 6 User certificates are not installed during server installation, but need to be added by using iManager after the server is up and running. Eric performed these steps to install his NetWare 6 User certificates:

1. First, he started his administrative workstation and logged in to the network with the Admin user name and password.

2. Next, he started his Web browser and entered the URL *https://172.20.0.60:2200* to open the NetWare Web Manager portal.

3. He clicked the UASHOST server under the iManager heading to display the Login window.

4. He entered Admin in the User Name text box and his password in the Password text box.

5. After verifying that the context was set to UAS and the Tree text box contained UAS_Tree, Eric clicked the Login button to log in and display the Novell iManager window.

6. He expanded the License Management option, and then clicked the Install a License link to display the Install a License window, similar to the one in Figure 9-25.

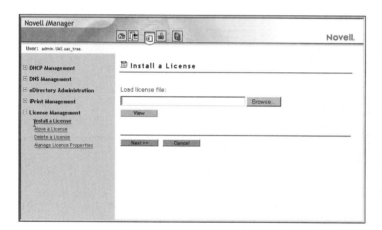

Figure 9-25   The Install a License window

7. He then inserted the license certificate disk into the floppy disk drive, and clicked the Browse button next to the Load license file text box to display the Choose file window.

8. He then navigated to the floppy disk and double-clicked the license file named 403748762.nlf to insert it into the Load license file text box. (Each license file is uniquely named with a serial number and the extension .nlf, which stands for "Novell license file.")

9. He clicked the View button to verify the license file in the NetWare 6 User certificate, as shown in Figure 9-26.

10. He clicked the Close button to return to the Install a License window, and then clicked the Next button to display the certificates listed in the license file.

11. He clicked the check box next to the NetWare 6 User License (see Figure 9-27), and then clicked the Next button to display the window for specifying where to install the certificate.

12. Eric clicked the Browse button next to the Location text box to navigate to the root of the UAS_Tree, and clicked the UAS Organization to place the certificate in the same context as the UASHOST server.

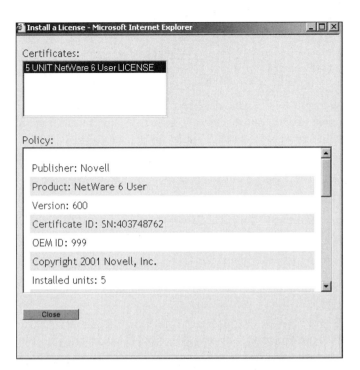

Figure 9-26   Verifying license file information

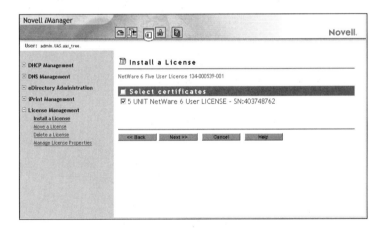

Figure 9-27   Selecting a certificate to install

13. Next, Eric clicked Install to install the NetWare 6 license certificate. After the installation was completed, the system displayed a "Successfully installed the following licenses" message box.

14. Eric noted that the license was correctly installed and then clicked the Done button to return to the Novell iManager window.

15. He clicked the Exit button to exit iManager and return to the Login window.

16. Eric then exited his browser to end the remote session and logged off.

If you have access to a user name and password with the Supervisor right to the UASHOST classroom server, you can perform the following activity to view license information.

Activity 9-15: Using iManager to View License Information

Time Required: 10 minutes

Objective: Use iManager to access NetWare 6 license information.

Description: After installing the NetWare 6 User certificate, Eric used iManager to document information on his existing licenses. In this activity, you follow Eric's steps to document information on your server's license certificates. To perform this activity, you need access to a user name with the Supervisor right to the classroom UAS_Tree.

1. Start your computer, and log in to the Novell network with your UasAdmin user name and password.

2. Start your Web browser software, and enter the URL **https://*ip_address*:2200** (replacing *ip_address* with the IP address of your UASHOST server).

3. If necessary, click **OK** and **Yes** to bypass the security message boxes.

4. Click your **UASHOST** server under the eDirectory iManager heading to display the Login window.

5. Enter the user name, password, and context of a user account with the Supervisor right to the UAS_Tree, and then click the **Login** button to display the Novell iManager window.

6. Expand the **License Management** option.

7. Click the **Manage License Properties** link to display the Manage License Properties window.

8. Click the **Browse** button next to the Object name text box, and navigate to the classroom UAS Organization. On your student answer sheet, record the Novell license certificate objects located in the UAS Organization.

9. Click one of the objects to insert it into the Object name text box, and then click **OK** to display information about that object. Record the information on your student answer sheet.

10. Click **OK** to return to the Novell iManager window.

11. Repeat Steps 7–10 to record information about another license object on your student answer sheet.

12. Click the **Exit** button to exit Novell iManager and return to the Login window.

13. Exit your Web browser, and log out.

Using Remote Manager to View License Information

Monitoring license usage is an important task for network administrators to keep track of license usage and prevent problems caused by a lack of licenses. The Remote Manager utility has a license usage information option so that administrators can view or print license usage reports. If you have access to a user name and password with the Supervisor right to the UASHOST server, you can follow along with Eric as he checks license usage information on the UAS network.

1. Eric started his workstation and logged in with the Admin user name and password.

2. Next, he started his Web browser software and entered the URL *https://172.20.0.60:8009* to display the Login window.

3. He logged in to NetWare Remote Manager with the Admin user name and password.

4. After the NetWare Remote Manager window was displayed, he scrolled down to the NetWare Usage heading and clicked the Usage Information link to display the NetWare Usage Information window, shown in Figure 9-28.

5. He then clicked the Go! button to display a usage report, similar to the one in Figure 9-29.

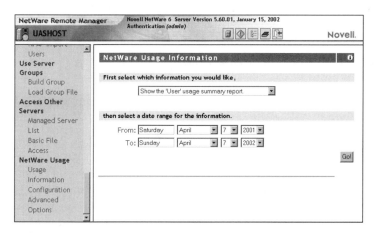

Figure 9-28   The NetWare Usage Information window

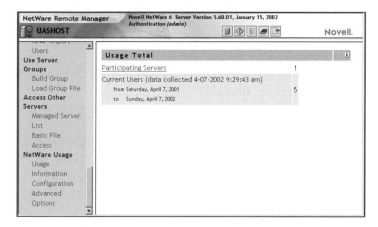

Figure 9-29   Viewing the usage report in Remote Manager

6. After viewing the usage report, Eric clicked the Exit button to exit NetWare Remote Manager and then clicked Yes to close the Web browser window.

Congratulations—you're now part of the Novell OneNet world. Knowing how to access and manage data and network configurations from anywhere, anytime, will give you some valuable skills for your network management career. Eric predicts that Novell is going to be advancing this technology rapidly in future releases.

Chapter Summary

- ❏ By storing files on the local computer and synchronizing them with the network, the iFolder service enables users to access their files from multiple workstations without having to be logged in to the network.

- ❏ To use iFolder, you must first install the iFolder service on a server and then install the iFolder client or a Java applet on the user workstation.

- ❏ The iFolder Java applet enables users to access their files from a Web browser without having to install the iFolder client on the workstation.

- ❏ The NetStorage service provides access to user files and folders from a Web browser without the need to install any component on the user workstation.

- ❏ Remote Manager enables the administrator to perform a number of administrative tasks on the server from anywhere by using a Web browser.

❑ Remote Manager makes it possible to access server volumes, configuration parameters, the eDirectory tree, and hardware information from any computer.

❑ iMonitor offers many of the capabilities of Remote Manger, along with the flexibility to be used from multiple platforms, including Windows NT/2000, Linux, and Sun Solaris.

❑ The RConsoleJ utility provides remote access to server consoles from ConsoleOne and can be used to access and manage your servers without using the server console or starting a Web browser.

❑ NetWare 6 uses a new license system called User Access Licensing (UAL). It differs from previous license systems in that it assigns a license to a user account that can access all NetWare servers in the tree. Previous versions of NetWare used the Service Connection Licensing (SCL) model, which required each server to have licenses for as many users as could be logged in. Although the UAL system is an advantage for organizations with multiple servers, it can create problems for organizations that have many users who infrequently log in.

❑ Licenses can be added and managed by using the Novell iManager utility. License usage information can be viewed from Remote Manager with the Usage Information option.

KEY TERMS

iFolder — A NetWare service that enables files to be kept on a local computer (or one that's not attached to the network) and synchronized with the network.

NetWare 6 Server certificate — A license certificate installed during the NetWare 6 server installation; this certificate is necessary for the server to run.

NetWare 6 User certificate — A UAL license certificate that supports user connections to the network. This certificate is not installed during the NetWare 6 server installation; it's installed later by using iManager.

Novell NetStorage — A NetWare service that gives users secure access to files on the NetWare server from any Internet location.

Server Connection Licensing (SCL) — The license model used by pre–NetWare 6 servers that requires each server to have a license for each connection, including connections made by printers and other non-user resources.

Server Management console — The iFolder component that enables network administrators to perform administrative tasks, such as managing iFolder user accounts.

thread — A process that's currently being worked on by the CPU.

User Access Licensing (UAL) — The NetWare 6 licensing system, in which each user account is provided with a fixed license to access any server in the tree the first time the user logs in.

REVIEW QUESTIONS

1. Which of the following OneNet utilities allows access to network data from a Web browser without adding a client to the user workstation?

   a. iFolder

   b. NetStorage

   c. RConsoleJ

   d. iManager

2. Which of the following OneNet utilities allows access to server console screens from a Web browser?

   a. Remote Manager

   b. RConsoleJ

   c. iManager

   d. iMonitor

3. Which of the following OneNet utilities provides secure and transparent synchronization of files between the local hard disk and the server?

   a. iFolder

   b. NetStorage

   c. WebDAV

   d. Remote Manager

4. Which of the following utilities can be used to access the server console from ConsoleOne?

   a. iMonitor

   b. RConsoleJ

   c. RConsole

   d. Remote Manager

5. Which of the following is *not* a benefit of iFolder?

   a. secure access to network files from any computer using only a Web browser or Microsoft Web Folder

   b. automatic synchronizing of data across multiple workstations

   c. encryption of sensitive files to protect them from unauthorized access

   d. the ability to work on files offline

6. True or false: The iFolder server component cannot be installed during NetWare 6 installation.

7. The iFolder client can be installed on which of the following platforms? (Choose all that apply.)

   a. Linux

   b. Windows NT

   c. Windows 2000

   d. Windows 9x

   e. Windows 3.1

   f. Windows Me

8. Accessing iFolder files from a Web browser requires which of the following?

   a. the iFolder client on the workstation

   b. a Java applet installed in the Web browser

   c. no additional software

   d. Internet Explorer 5.5 or later installed on the workstation

9. Client iFolder policies can be used to do which of the following? (Choose all that apply.)

   a. enforce encryption

   b. set user quota limits

   c. save passwords and phrases

   d. force password changes after the specified number of days

   e. set session timeout values

10. Server iFolder policies can be used to do which of the following? (Choose all that apply.)

   a. set initial disk quotas

   b. set session timeout values

   c. enforce encryption

   d. save passwords and phrases

   e. force password changes after the specified number of days

11. If you have multiple CPUs on your server and many iFolder user accounts, you could help increase iFolder Apache server performance by doing which of the following?

    a. increasing the disk quota limits

    b. adding additional iFolder servers

    c. increasing the number of threads

    d. reducing the default synchronization interval

12. Which of the following options can be performed by right-clicking the iFolder icon in the taskbar? (Choose all that apply.)

    a. logging in or out

    b. changing passwords

    c. viewing disk quotas

    d. setting synchronization intervals

13. True or false: To access iFolder files using a Web browser, you first need to download the file to your local disk.

14. True or false: To access NetStorage files using a Web browser, you first need to download the file to your local disk.

15. Which of the following requirements must be met to use NetStorage on a client? (Choose all that apply.)

    a. The NetStorge client software must be downloaded and installed on the client.

    b. The date and time settings must be close to the server's date and time.

    c. NetStorage must be installed on the server.

    d. The context(s) for the user accounts must be specified during NetStorage installation.

16. True or false: To change the configuration of NetStorage, you need to reinstall it.

17. When using Remote Manager, a black light in the overall health indicator indicates which of the following conditions?

    a. Server is in good health.

    b. Server is in suspect health.

    c. Server requires administrator response.

    d. Server is not responding.

18. Which of the following utilities can be used to view printer agent error messages?

    a. iMonitor

    b. iManager

    c. Remote Manager

    d. RConsoleJ

19. You can use the Configure Health Thresholds link in the Health Monitor window to do which of the following?

    a. view the criteria for green, yellow, and red indicator lights

    b. set the suspect and critical values

    c. view interrupt usage

    d. view memory usage

20. Which of the following utilities is used to help troubleshoot eDirectory problems?

    a. iManager

    b. RConsoleJ

    c. iMonitor

    d. NDS Manager

21. Which of the following license methods assigns a license to each user account for at least 90 days?

    a. SCL

    b. UAL

    c. SASS

    d. ULA

22. Pre–NetWare 6 servers use which of the following license methods?

    a. SCL

    b. UAL

    c. SASS

    d. ULA

23. Which of the following license methods have the advantage of not requiring licenses for printers and print servers?

    a. SCL

    b. UAL

    c. SASS

    d. ULA

24. Public organizations with a single server would benefit from which of the following license methods?

    a. SCL

    b. UAL

    c. SASS

    d. ULA

25. True or false: A NetWare 6 User certificate is usually installed during the server installation.

UNIVERSAL AEROSPACE CASE PROJECTS

Eric's test of the iFolder and NetStorage services paved the way for their use in the UAS organization. In the following projects, you continue to work with iFolder, NetStorage, and Remote Manager to simulate scenarios in Universal AeroSpace's operations.

Case Project 9-1: Using NetStorage

A real test of the NetStorage service came when David Heise went on a trip to a NASA contractor and wanted to download some CAD drawings for their engineers to analyze. To make the files available to David, Lynn Dai copied the files into David's home directory so that he could download them using NetStorage. In this project, you simulate this situation by performing the following steps:

1. Log in with your UasAdmin user name and password and, if necessary, grant the user Lynn Dai the Create right to David's home directory.

2. Log out.

3. Log in to the Mgmt context with Lynn Dai's user name and password.

4. Copy the Vehicle.bmp file from the SYS: Software.cti\Design directory to David's home directory.

5. Log out.

6. Simulate David working from a remote computer by clicking the Workstation only check box to log on to your Windows 2000 computer.

7. Start your Web browser software, and access NetStorage by logging in with David's user name and password.

8. Access the Vehicle.bmp file using the local workstation's paint software.

9. Save the file on your local hard drive, and record the results on your student answer sheet.

Case Project 9-2: Using iFolder

The UAS Corporation's first real test of the iFolder service came when Julie Damrau wanted to work on her year-end spreadsheet while traveling. To do this, she installed the iFolder client on her laptop and then copied the files to her iFolder directory. In this project, you simulate this task by performing the following steps:

1. Log in with Julie Damrau's user name and password.

2. If necessary, install the iFolder client as described in Activity 9-1.

3. Log in to iFolder with Julie Damrau's user name and password.

4. Copy the BegYear and EndYear worksheet files to Julie's iFolder directory:

   a. Use My Network Places to navigate to the UASHOST server.

   b. Double-click the SYS volume, and navigate to the Software.cti\SP folder.

   c. Copy the BegYear.wk1 and EndYear.wk1 files, and paste them into the iFolder directory.

5. Log out.

6. Simulate being offline by clicking the Workstation only check box to log on to your local Windows 2000 computer.

7. Open the EndYear.wk1 file and make some changes.

8. Save the file, and close iFolder.

9. Log out.

10. Simulate being back in the office by logging in to Novell Client with Julie's user name and password.

11. Use the iFolder Sync Now option to update your changes.

12. Verify that your changes have been synchronized with the server and have your instructor initial your student answer sheet.

13. Log out.

Case Project 9-3: Using Remote Manager

While attending a computer conference in Orlando, Florida, Eric wanted to upload some software he purchased to a new folder in the Apps directory of the UASHOST server. In this project, you perform the following steps to create a subfolder in the Apps directory and then copy files from your local workstation to the folder:

1. Start your computer, and to simulate being at a remote computer, click the Workstation only check box to log on to your Windows 2000 computer.

2. Start your Web browser software, and log in to Remote Manager by entering .UasAdmin.##UAS in the User Name text box and your password in the Password text box.

3. Click your ##CORP volume, and then click your Apps folder to expand it.

4. Find the "." entry located at the top of the Name column; this entry is used to work with the current folder. To create a subfolder within the currently selected Apps folder, click the Info icon to the left of the "." to display information about your Apps folder.

5. Scroll down and enter LanMan in the New name text box to the right of the Create Subdirectory button.

6. Click the Create Subdirectory button to display the newly created LanMan folder in the Apps directory listing.

7. Click the LanMan folder, and then click the Upload button to upload the Freecell.exe program to your LanMan folder.

8. Exit Remote Manager, and log out.

9. Log in to Novell Client as KThiele, and verify that the Freecell.exe program can be run.

10. Have your instructor initial your student answer sheet.

9

10

IMPLEMENTING INTERNET SERVICES

After reading this chapter and completing the exercises, you will be able to:

♦ Describe NetWare 6 Internet/intranet services, including Net Services and Web Services components

♦ Install and configure Novell Web Services components

♦ Describe public key cryptography and use the Novell Certificate Authority service to export public and private keys

♦ Describe external security policies and strategies, including firewalls, virus protection, and defense against denial-of-service attacks

As you have learned in previous chapters, Novell's OneNet strategy uses the Internet to make network services and information available from anywhere at any time. To support the OneNet features of NetWare 6, network administrators need to understand the components that make Internet services available on a NetWare 6 server; they also need to know how to implement these services and secure them from unauthorized access and attacks. In addition to Internet services, NetWare 6 includes Web and FTP services that can be installed and configured to deliver information to the Internet. In this chapter, you learn about the Internet service components available with NetWare 6 and how Universal AeroSpace used them to implement a Web site and secure its network against unwanted access.

NetWare 6 Internet Service Components

Novell is a leader in Internet/intranet services that help simplify the implementation of business networks by providing a common set of services for accessing data and resources with a variety of workstation and server operating systems. The NetWare 6 Internet service components can be divided into Net Services and Web Services components, as shown in Figure 10-1.

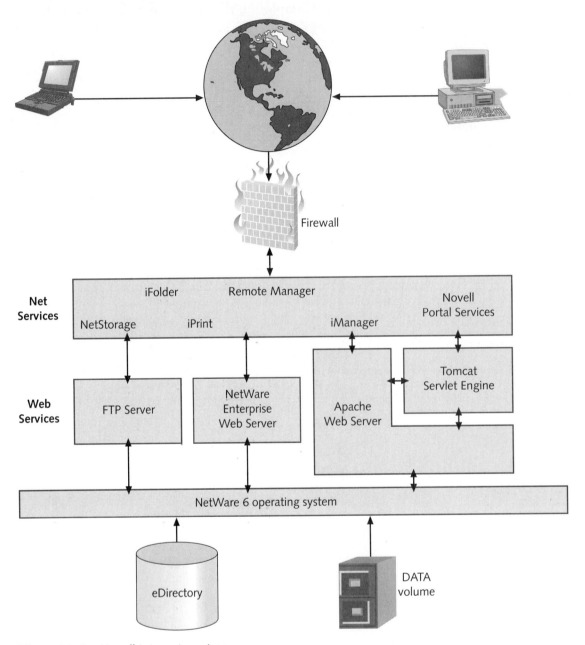

Figure 10-1   Novell Internet services

Web Services are TCP/IP-based applications that make network data and services available to users, such as Web sites and FTP servers. To access a Web service, users need to have the correct client software running on their computers. For example, to access a Web site, you need to run a Web browser, such as Internet Explorer or Netscape.

Net Services components extend the capabilities of standard Web services and include many of the services you have worked with already, such as iFolder, NetStorage, iPrint, iManager, and Remote Manager. As illustrated in Figure 10-1, a network can be configured so that requests for Net Services originating at user workstations or laptops are sent via the Internet to a firewall running on a server or router. After being checked through the firewall, the request is routed to the appropriate services based on its IP address and port number. Although IP addresses are used to direct a packet to the correct computer, port numbers are used to transfer the information in the packet to the appropriate application. When an application starts, it registers a port number with TCP/IP. When a packet is received at the workstation, the TCP/IP protocol stack uses the port number to determine which application running on the computer should get the packet's information. Table 10-1 contains a list of commonly used applications and their default port numbers.

Table 10-1   Commonly Used Port Numbers

Port Number	Application
21	FTP
23	Telnet
25	SMTP e-mail protocol
80	Web server
110	Post Office Protocol (POP3)

10

To gain access to NetWare files and resources, Novell Net Services run as applications on Web Services components, such as Apache Web Server. Novell chose Apache Web Server to host the Net Services components because it's an open-source Web server that's public-domain software, meaning it's freely available and can be modified to run on other operating system platforms. By running through Apache Web Server, Novell Net Services can be implemented on any network operating system platform that supports Apache Web Server, including Unix, Linux, and Windows 2000. For example, because the iFolder service uses Apache Web Server to synchronize files with the server, it can be installed on NetWare 6, Linux, or Windows 2000 servers. In addition to processing requests for Net Services, NetWare Web Services components can make data available through a new feature called Novell Portal Services. In the following sections, you learn about Novell's Web Services components as well as how Novell Portal Services can be used to customize Web access.

Apache Web Server for NetWare

Apache Web Server is open-source Web server software originally developed by the Apache Group, a non-profit organization. Being public-domain software, Apache Web Server is free to any organization or individual who wants to use it to implement Web-based services. Currently, over 60% of all Web-hosting organizations are using Apache Web Server; because it is such a common platform for implementing Web-based services, Novell made Apache Web Server an integral part of NetWare 6's Internet services, and it's installed by default during the NetWare 6 installation. Because of its tight integration with Novell's Net Services, it requires no special configuration by the network administrator. Apache Web Server is used by these NetWare 6 Web-based services:

- NetWare Web Manager
- NetWare Web Search Server
- NetWare WebAccess
- iFolder
- iManager

Tomcat Servlet Engine for NetWare

The Tomcat Servlet Engine, also developed by the Apache Group, is used to run Java-based Web applications. It is used by several NetWare 6 components, including Novell Portal Services and NetWare Web Search Server. Although network administrators rarely need to configure or manage the Tomcat Servlet Engine, programmers developing Web-based applications often work with Tomcat because it runs on a wide variety of operating systems.

Novell Portal Services

Novell Portal Services (NPS) is the leading portal strategy for delivering the right information to the people who are authorized to use it. Using NPS, personalized Web pages can be delivered to users regardless of operating system platform or network structure. With NPS, network administrators can protect and control access to network resources, delivering personalized data to people based on their company roles, locations, and group associations. NPS consists of a number of Java applications, called **Java servlets**, that run on Apache Web Server, as shown in Figure 10-2. NPS enables users to easily gain access to the Web sites and applications they are authorized to use by building customized Web pages based on users' needs and access rights.

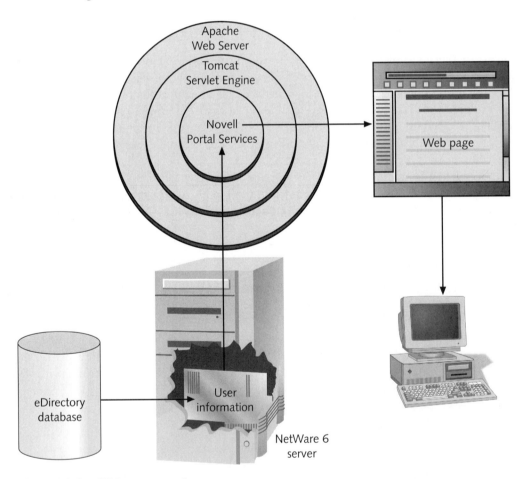

Figure 10-2   NPS components

The Tomcat Servlet Engine shown in Figure 10-2 is a Web server application that runs Java servlets. To run NPS, the servlet engine must support the Sun Microsystems Java 2.2 Servlet specification, which enables NPS to be installed and run on a variety of Web server platforms, as long as they support a Java 2.2–compliant Web application server. NetWare 6 ships with a Java 2.2–compliant servlet engine called Tomcat that runs on Apache Web Server. When users access the portal service URL on the NetWare 6 server, Apache Web Server, which is hosting the portal service, sends users an authentication page consisting of an HTML form that allows them to log in. Users then submit their user names and passwords to the Apache Web server, which passes the information to the NPS Java servlet running on the Tomcat Servlet Engine. The NPS Java servlet then accesses the directory to authenticate users and build a Web page of data that's customized in its content and the way it's displayed. The data's display is based on the user's access rights and the layout format, which can be defined with eXtensible Stylesheet Language (XSL). During installation, NetWare 6 automatically creates directory objects to support NPS's additional capabilities and features. NPS configuration is managed through the Portal Admin browser-based utility, so you can use Netscape Navigator 6.0 or later or Internet Explorer 5.0 or later to access this utility.

Novell Web Manager is an example of an NPS application that customizes the content of browser-based management utilities, such as iManager and Remote Manager, based on the user's access rights. When you access Novell Web Manager from a browser with the URL *https://ip_address:2200* (*ip_address* is the IP address of your NetWare 6 server), you get a customized Web page containing the management utilities available on your server. After you select a utility, NPS displays a login page for authenticating your user name and password and customizes the options available on the management utility's main page based on your access rights. For example, if you log in as the network Admin user when accessing Remote Manager, you see all the program options, as shown in Figure 10-3.

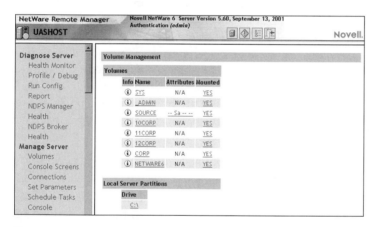

Figure 10-3   Remote Manager from the Admin portal

However, when you log in as a user who does not have the Supervisor right to the NetWare 6 server, you see only the options shown in Figure 10-4. Notice in this figure that when accessing Remote Manager, you see only the volume options. The other options shown in Figure 10-3, such as Diagnose Server and Manage Server, are not included because they require the Supervisor right to the NetWare server.

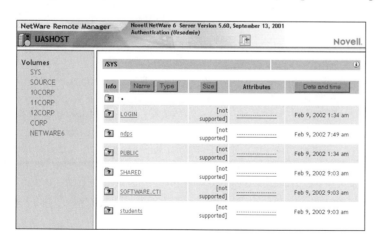

Figure 10-4   Remote Manager from a student account portal

Universal AeroSpace is planning to use NPS to automatically display customized pages to users so that they can access the data and services they need quickly and easily, without having to go to multiple Web pages. For example, Lynn Dai currently maintains separate databases of employee information for each department, which makes it difficult for her to quickly access information such as performance reviews and contract agreements when needed. In addition, when an employee calls with a question about retirement benefits, Lynn must access the department's database where that employee's information is stored. Because the databases contain sensitive information that must be kept secure, every time Lynn accesses one of them she must log in and be authenticated with a password. This procedure has been time-consuming, so Lynn needs a solution that makes all the databases available through a single login and can correlate the information from all databases into a single report. In addition, she would like to have certain employee information, such as retirement and benefit data, available for employees to access directly.

After analyzing the requirements, Luke McMann is planning to use NPS to help build a system that will meet Lynn's needs. Because UAS is using Lotus PeopleSoft to gather, store, and manage information in an Oracle database, the first step will be to synchronize the Oracle database information with eDirectory by using Novell's DirXML product. DirXML is rapidly becoming the industry standard for directory-to-directory communication. With DirXML, UAS can maintain the Oracle database for the PeopleSoft application and connect it to the eDirectory database to provide portal access to the Oracle database from NPS. The second step will be to create a template portal for each role in the company. Each department director will be given a portal for accessing information about the employees in his or her department. As David Heise's administrative assistant, Lynn also handles human resource tasks and will have a portal that accesses the entire company's personnel database. Through her customized portal, she will be able to securely access employee information immediately without having to log in and be authenticated each time she opens a different database. In addition, each employee's portal will be customized so that he or she can access personal benefit and retirement information. Using their portals, employees can look up their own financial information and calculate their retirement and benefit information instead of calling Lynn whenever they have questions.

NetWare Web Search Server

NetWare Web Search Server can make data on your network or the Internet searchable in minutes. It bridges all types of networks—from file servers to intranets and the Internet—delivering requested information in a minimum amount of time. Installed by default during the NetWare 6 installation, NetWare Web Search Server is ready to run simply by pointing it at the Web or file servers you want included in the search index. It then generates keyword indexes from the information found in the selected locations and returns time-saving keyword searches for users to find data quickly. Using a powerful yet simple template-based architecture, network administrators can customize search forms and search results pages to get the information users need. By using the included parameters, variables, and basic HTML, Web Search Server enables administrators to build their own templates for creating customized searches that users can access easily.

NetWare Enterprise Web Server

Apache Web Server is automatically installed during the NetWare 6 installation, but its primary purpose is to provide support for NPS and Net Services, such as iFolder and NetStorage. To host a company's Web or FTP site, you need to install and configure NetWare Enterprise Web Server, which is an HTTP-based service for sending Web pages to browsers on the Internet or within the company intranet. Enterprise Web Server is optimized to run in the NetWare environment and is a critical component in building a company's Internet or intranet information system. In addition to providing a public Web site on the Internet, Enterprise Web Server can be used to create intranet Web sites to enhance interdepartment communication or provide information to the entire company. Following are traditional categories of Webs, each playing a unique role in sharing information:

- The most popular of all Webs is the World Wide Web (WWW) available through the Internet. Hosting a Web server with Internet access requires a persistent Internet connection accessible to anyone running a Web browser. When using the Internet to provide access to Net Services, a firewall is required to provide security for Web servers. As described in the "Firewall Security" section later in this chapter, firewalls prevent Internet users from accessing the company's network-based resources.

- Another important use of NetWare Enterprise Web Server is hosting a private intranet Web site to enhance communication and distribution of information within a company. UAS is planning to host both Internet and intranet Web sites. The intranet's target audience will be the employees at the UAS and AeroDyn facilities, and the Internet Web site's target audience will be outside companies and the public. Although employees inside the company will be able to access both Web sites, the firewall will prevent people outside the company from accessing the intranet Web site.

- NetWare Enterprise Web Server is also a necessary component in developing an extranet. An **extranet** is a combination of public and private Web sites, usually created to expedite communication and cooperation among companies that work closely together. For example, UAS is planning to implement an extranet with NASA so that space agency officials can directly enter orders and specifications for special parts and materials.

FTP Server

Before the advent of HTTP and World Wide Web servers, File Transfer Protocol (FTP) servers provided a means of transferring files from one Internet host to another. FTP servers are designed as a highly efficient and secure method of transferring files to and from Internet sites. Web servers can transfer files using HTTP, but FTP servers generally offer more efficient and reliable delivery through their specialized transfer protocol. They are also commonly used to upload content to Web sites. NetWare 6 includes an FTP server for transferring files to and from NetWare volumes, posting new content to Web sites, and downloading large documents and software. UAS is planning to use the NetWare FTP server to transfer large engineering files to customers, and David wants customers to be able to use the FTP server to download software updates that AeroDyn programmers have developed.

NetWare Web Manager

NetWare Web Manager is the portal service used to configure and manage NetWare Web Services and access other Web-based management tools. Because NetWare Web Manager is a Java-based browser utility, you can use it to manage Web Services from any location on the Internet. In the following section, you learn how to use NetWare Web Manager to access and configure NetWare Enterprise Web Server and FTP Server.

INSTALLING AND CONFIGURING WEB SERVICES

As described previously, Web Services are TCP/IP applications that deliver information to clients running on user workstations. Web servers operate in a client-server relationship, in which the Web service running on the NetWare server processes requests from clients running on user workstations. A Web browser, such as Netscape Navigator or Internet Explorer, acts as a client requesting information from the Web server. A Web server uses a specified directory in the file system, referred to as the "content directory," to store all files it makes available to clients. All files in the content directory and its subdirectories are available to the browser clients. NetWare Enterprise Web Server, based on Netscape Web Server, is included on the NetWare 6 operating system CD. In addition, other commonly used Web servers are available for hosting Web sites, including Apache, iPlanet, and Microsoft Internet Information Server.

As you have learned, Apache Web Server offers a solid, secure platform for hosting Web sites. Because it has open-source code, third-party companies can offer tools and enhancements to make it even more powerful and flexible.

The iPlanet Web server is an LDAP-only server designed for user authentication and management, electronic commerce (e-commerce), extranet, and Internet applications and is the foundation for a suite of e-commerce–delivered products from the Sun-Netscape alliance. Because the same team that built the Standalone LDAP (SLDAP) server also created the iPlanet Web server, it has a fully LDAP-compliant directory capability, making it compatible with several other LDAP-compliant directory services, such as eDirectory and Microsoft Active Directory. The iPlanet Web server was designed for use on servers operating outside a corporate firewall, so it makes a good choice for an Internet-based Web server that can securely deliver data to Internet users, without risking unauthorized access to data stored on servers that operate behind the corporate firewall.

Microsoft offers two levels of its Web server product: Microsoft Personal Web Server (PWS) and Internet Information Server (IIS). To deliver Web site content for personal intranet applications, Microsoft designed PWS for use on Windows 95/98 and NT workstations and includes a limited version of IIS for Windows 2000 Professional computers. Although it offers all basic Web server functions, PWS and the Windows 2000 Professional version of IIS do not have all the security options and capabilities needed to deliver and secure company Web sites on the Internet. IIS version 5, installed automatically with Windows 2000 Server, is an integral part of the Windows 2000 Internet capabilities, much as Novell uses Apache Web Server to host its Net Services. In addition to hosting the Microsoft Internet services, IIS can be configured to host corporate Web sites in much the same way as NetWare Enterprise Web Server. The main disadvantage of the IIS 5 Web server is that it's a proprietary Web server that runs only on Windows 2000 servers. This tight integration can be an advantage when you're using all Microsoft-based services, but it is not open for other developers, thereby limiting your Internet service options.

In the following sections, you see how Eric Kenton installed NetWare Enterprise Web Server and used Web Manager to view and configure the Web server so that you can host your version of the UAS Web site.

Working with NetWare Enterprise Web Server

NetWare Enterprise Web Server can be installed during or after the NetWare 6 server installation. As described in Chapter 12, Eric chose to install most optional components after the initial server installation to keep installation as simple and focused as possible. If you have sole access to a NetWare 6 server with the Supervisor right, you can follow the steps Eric used to install NetWare Enterprise Web Server on your NetWare 6 server:

1. First, Eric inserted the NetWare 6 CD into the UASHOST server, and pressed Ctrl+Esc to select the system console screen, as described in Chapter 12.

2. He entered the command CDROM and pressed Enter to mount the CD as a volume on the server.

3. After mounting the NetWare 6 Installation volume, he pressed Ctrl+Esc to select the X Server - Graphical Console.

4. At the graphical console, Eric clicked Novell and then Install to display the Installed Products window.

5. He clicked Add to display the Source Path window, clicked the browse button to select the NetWare 6 volume, and clicked OK. He clicked OK again in the Source Path window to copy the installation files to the server, and the Components window was displayed with check marks indicating the default installed components.

6. Eric clicked Clear All to prevent reinstalling existing components, clicked the NetWare Enterprise Web Server check box, and clicked Next to display the login window.

7. Eric entered his Admin user name, password, and context in the appropriate fields and then clicked OK to log in. Next, the Configure IP-based Services window was displayed, showing the IP address assigned to the existing Net Services.

8. Eric assigned a unique IP address to Enterprise Web Server, using the same network address range as the NetWare 6 server. For example, because the UASHOST server's IP address is 172.20.0.60, he assigned Enterprise Web Server the IP address 172.20.0.61. He will then program the firewall to send incoming packets that request port 80 to this IP address.

9. After verifying the IP address, Eric clicked Next to display the LDAP Configuration window.

10. By default, Enterprise Web Server uses port number 389 for clear text transmissions and port number 636 for SSL-encrypted transmissions. To allow users to log in to the network through the unencrypted port 389, Eric also clicked the Allow Clear Text Passwords check box. After verifying and recording the contents of the LDAP Configuration window, Eric clicked Next to display the Installation Summary window.

11. After verifying that NetWare Enterprise Web Server and NetWare Port Resolver were listed, Eric clicked Finish to copy the necessary files and complete the installation of NetWare Enterprise Web Server.

12. After the installation was finished, Eric clicked Close to close the Installation complete message box and return to the X Server - Graphical Console. Enterprise Web Server was then ready to configure and use.

10

Operating and Configuring Enterprise Web Server

Before using Enterprise Web Server, you must use Web Manager to start the Web server and make any necessary configuration changes. In this section, you learn how Eric used a Web browser from his administrative workstation to start Enterprise Web Server, access and change basic configuration settings, and establish a virtual Web site for the Engineering department.

After Enterprise Web Server was installed, Novell Portal Services displayed the NetWare Enterprise Web Servers option in the Web Manager window (see Figure 10-5) when Eric entered the URL 172.20.1.60:2200 in his browser's Address field.

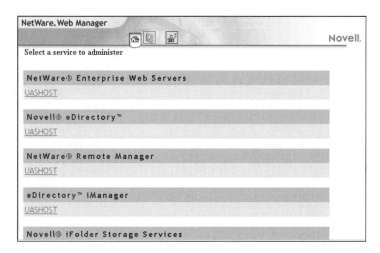

Figure 10-5   Selecting a service to administer in Web Manager
When using NetWare 6.5, you will see the NetWare 6.5 Welcome as shown in Figure D-17.

After selecting the NetWare Enterprise Web Servers option, the Enter Network Password dialog box opened, requesting Eric's user name and password. To manage Enterprise Web Server, Eric logged in using a user name and password with the Supervisor right to the UASHOST server running the Web server application. After he successfully logged in, NetWare Web Manager displayed the Server Preferences window, shown in Figure 10-6.

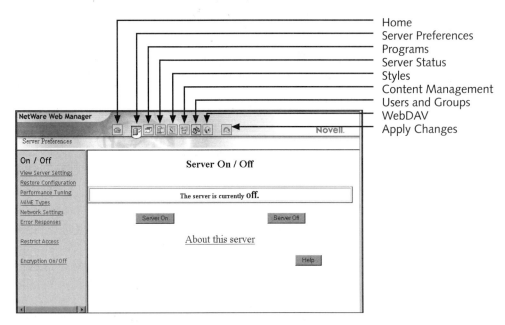

Figure 10-6   The Server Preferences window
NetWare 6.5 uses Apache Manager as described in Appendix F.

The buttons, described in Table 10-2, across the top of the menu bar represent different configuration windows.

Table 10-2   Enterprise Web Server Configuration Buttons

Button Name	Description
Server Preferences	Use this option to start and stop the Web server and perform the following configuration options (refer to Figure 10-6): • View Server Settings • Restore Configuration • Performance Tuning (such as enabling DNS and caching) • MIME Types • Network Settings (such as server name, port number, and IP address) • Error Responses • Restrict Access • Encryption On/Off
Programs	Use this option to set the CGI directory and file types and activate server-side Java script processing.
Server Status	Use this option to monitor current Web server activity and view error, archive, and access logs.
Styles	Use this option to set and change style sheets for Web Services.
Content Management	Use this option to set the current content directory path and user document directories and to create and manage virtual Web sites.
Users and Groups	Use this option to configure the directory service the Web server will use when authenticating users. Options include using a local database, the LDAP server, or eDirectory.
WebDAV	Use this option to check the status of the WebDAV service and turn WebDAV services on or off.
Apply Changes	Use this option to apply the changes you have made to the currently running Web service. If this button is not clicked, the changes are not made until after the system is restarted.

There are many configuration options and settings, but the most common tasks for network administrators are starting and stopping Web Services, changing the default path to the content directory, creating virtual Web sites, configuring document preferences, and setting up public and restricted access sites. In the following sections, you learn how Eric used the Web Manager utility to perform these tasks for the UAS Web site. When changing the Web server's configuration parameters, remember to always save and apply the changes. To submit changes made to a form, click the Save button and then the Save and Apply button to save and apply the changes, or click the Cancel button to reject your changes.

Starting and Stopping Web Services

After selecting the NetWare Enterprise Web Servers option and logging in, the Server Preferences window is displayed, with options on the left side of the window to open different configuration windows. For example, in Figure 10-6, the Server Preferences window is displaying the Server On/Off window. Notice that initially the Enterprise Web server is set to "off." To start Enterprise Web Server, Eric simply clicked the Server On button and then clicked OK when the browser displayed the Success message box. Sometimes you need to stop the Web server before making configuration changes; to do this, you click the Server Off button or enter NSWEBDN at the NetWare 6 server console screen. To restart the server, you can click the Server On button in the Web Manager window or enter the NSWEB command at the NetWare 6 server console screen.

Changing the Path of the Default Web Content

After verifying that the server was operating properly, Eric wanted to move the Web site's contents from the default location to the IS\Web directory in the CORP volume. By default, the Web content directory is located on the SYS volume, in the SYS:Novonyx\SuiteSpot\Docs directory. Because the Web site is expected to grow quite large, Eric wanted to move the content directory to the CORP volume to avoid the risk of accidentally bringing down the NetWare 6 server by filling up the SYS volume. To move the content directory in Web Manager, Eric followed these steps:

1. First, he clicked the Content Management button on the NetWare Web Manager toolbar to display the Primary Document Directory window, shown in Figure 10-7.

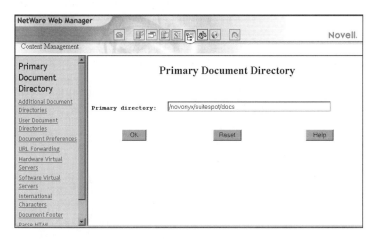

Figure 10-7   The Primary Document Directory window
NetWare 6.5 uses Apache Manager as described in Appendix F.

2. Next, he entered the path CORP:\IS\Web in the Primary directory text box and clicked OK to display the change window.

3. He then clicked the Save and Apply button to save the new content directory path and apply the path to the Web server.

Creating a Virtual Document Directory

Because the Engineering department will be running its own Web site, Eric needed to create a virtual document site so that the Engineering department could keep its own specialized content in a separate subdirectory of the main IS\Web content directory. Internet users could then access the Engineering Web site with the URL *www.uas.com/engineering*. To configure NetWare Enterprise Web Server to use a virtual directory named Engineering, Eric performed the following steps:

1. In the Content Management window, shown previously in Figure 10-7, Eric clicked the Additional Document Directories link to display the Additional Document Directories window, shown in Figure 10-8.

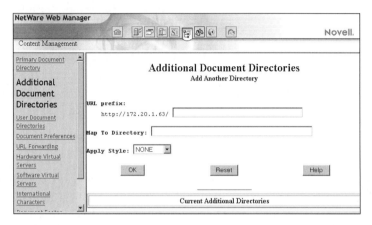

Figure 10-8   The Additional Document Directories window
NetWare 6.5 uses Apache Manager as described in Appendix F.

2. He entered Engineering in the URL prefix text box and entered the path to the Engineering directory in the Map To Directory text box.

3. After verifying that the entries were correct, Eric clicked the OK button and then clicked the Save and Apply button to apply the changes to the currently running Web server and return to the Web Manager window.

Configuring Document Preferences

When NetWare Enterprise Web Server receives a request from a browser that does not specify the name of a page file, it uses a default index filename specified in the Document Preferences window (see Figure 10-9).

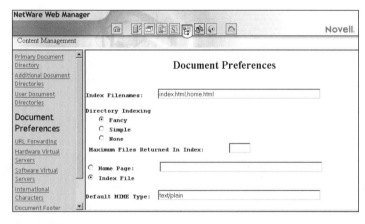

Figure 10-9   The Document Preferences window
NetWare 6.5 uses Apache Manager as described in Appendix F.

For example, given the configuration shown in Figure 10-9, if users enter the URL *http://uas.com* in their Web browsers, Enterprise Web Server sends back the contents of the Index.html file. You can specify multiple index filenames by separating the filenames with commas. With multiple filenames, Enterprise Web Server searches for the filenames in the order specified and then uses the first filename it finds as the home page.

If no default index file is specified or none of the specified index filenames is found in the content directory, Enterprise Web Server can be configured to generate a page listing all files found in the root of the document content directory and then send that listing to the Web browser. This option can be useful if you're preparing a Web site that allows users to select from multiple files. The following three directory indexing options are available:

- *Fancy*—Generates a graphical icon that represents the type of file and includes the file size and date it was last modified. The disadvantage of using the Fancy directory indexing option is that it takes longer to prepare.

- *Simple*—Generates a simple list of filenames and returns it to the browser.

- *None*—No directory indexing will be performed. If the index filename is not found, Enterprise Web Server returns an error message.

Eric performed the following steps to configure the UASHOST Enterprise Web server to use the default index file UASWeb.html and prevent document indexing:

1. After using NetWare Web Manager to select the Enterprise Web Server option, Eric clicked the Document Preferences link in the Content Management window to display the Document Preferences window, shown previously in Figure 10-9.

2. Eric entered UASWeb.html, followed by a comma before the existing filenames, in the Index Filenames text box.

3. To prevent document indexing, he clicked the None radio button under the Directory Indexing heading. After verifying the entries, Eric clicked OK to display the Save and Apply window.

4. He clicked the Save and Apply button to save the configuration change, apply it to the currently running Web service, and return to the Content Management window.

5. Eric clicked the Home button to return to the NetWare Web Manager window.

Setting Up Public and Restricted Access

After Enterprise Web Server is installed, anyone accessing the server from a Web browser can open document files in the SYS:Novonyx\SuiteSpot\Docs directory or any of its subdirectories. If you change the primary document directory, create additional document directories, or want to restrict access to documents, you need to click the Restrict Access link under Server Preferences, and then scroll down to the Public Directory Designations list box (see Figure 10-10).

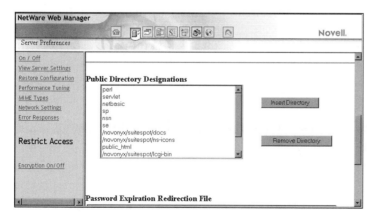

Figure 10-10 Viewing the Public Directory Designations list box
NetWare 6.5 uses Apache Manager as described in Appendix F.

All users are given access to any directory in the Public Directory Designations list box. If the directory or filename being accessed exists but is not included in this list box, Enterprise Web Server displays a dialog box asking the user to enter a user name and password for logging in. If the user account has at least Read and File Scan rights to the specified file, the Web server sends the file to the user's Web browser. When Eric changed the default path for the Web server content directory to the CORP volume and created the virtual document site for the Engineering department, he performed the following steps to add the path to Public Directory Designations:

1. In the NetWare Web Manager window, Eric clicked the UASHOST server link under the NetWare Enterprise Web Servers heading to open the Server Preferences window.

2. He clicked the Restrict Access link to display the Public Directory Designations list box, similar to the one shown previously in Figure 10-10.

3. Enterprise Web Server allows access to the directory paths in the Public Directory Designations list box without requiring users to log in with a valid user name and password. To add the new primary document directory path to the Public Directory Designations list box, Eric clicked the Insert Directory button, entered the path CORP:IS\Web in the New Public Directory text box, and then clicked OK to return to the Restrict Access window.

4. He then clicked the Save Changes button. When he received the Success message box, he clicked OK to return to the Restrict Access window.

5. To finish configuring Enterprise Web Server, Eric clicked the Apply Changes button (looks like a curved arrow) on the Web Manager toolbar to display the Apply Changes window.

6. To apply the changes, he clicked the Apply Changes button and then clicked OK in the Success message box.

7. He then clicked the Home button to return to Web Manager's main window.

8. To close Web Manager and log out, he exited the Web browser.

In the following activity, you use Web Manager to administer Enterprise Web Server to create a virtual document site for your UAS Engineering department.

Activity 10-1: Creating a Virtual Document Site

Time Required: 15 minutes

Objective: Use Web Manager to configure NetWare Enterprise Web Server.

Description: After NetWare Enterprise Web Server was installed and configured, Julie Damrau began developing and testing the main UAS Web site using the default content directory path Eric specified. Kari Means, in the Engineering department, was also anxious to start testing the department's Web site using the content in the IS\Web\Engineer directory. To allow Kari to begin testing the Web site content, Eric created a virtual Web site for the Engineering department. In this activity, you use Web Manager to check and configure the Web server for your virtual Web site. To perform this activity, you need access to a user name and password that has rights to administer NetWare Enterprise Web Server. If you do not have access to an administrative user name and password, your instructor can demonstrate this activity.

1. If necessary, start your computer, and log in to the Novell network with your assigned UasAdmin user name and password.

2. Start your Web browser and enter the URL **https://*ip_address*:2200** (replacing *ip_address* with the IP address of your UASHOST server).

3. If necessary, click **OK** and **Yes** to respond to the Security alert message boxes and display the NetWare Web Manager window.

4. Click the **UASHOST** server link under the NetWare Enterprise Web Servers heading to display the Login window.

5. Log in with your administrative user name and password to display the Server Preferences window.

6. Click the **Content Management** button to display the Primary Document Directory window.

7. Click the **Additional Document Directories** link to display the Add Another Directory pane.

8. In the URL prefix text box, enter **##Engineering** (replacing ## with your assigned student number).

9. In the Map To Directory text box, enter **uashost\##corp:is\web** as the path to your Web directory.

10. Click **OK** to display the Save and Apply Changes window.

11. If necessary, scroll down and click the **Save and Apply** button to save your entry and apply the change to the server.

12. When you see the Success message box, click **OK** to return to the Additional Document Directories window.

13. Click the **Home** button to return to the NetWare Web Manager window.

14. End your session by closing your Web browser.

15. Close any open windows, and log out.

Working with NetWare FTP Server

NetWare FTP Server is a Web Services application that allows users to transfer files to and from the NetWare volumes that have been configured as part of the FTP content. After logging in to NetWare FTP Server, users can also navigate to other NetWare servers and volumes where they have access rights, even though the other servers are not running the FTP Server software. As with other Web-based services, FTP services require server and client components. FTP clients send requests for services to an FTP server, which then processes the request and returns results to the client. Clients connect to an FTP server by using an anonymous user name or by logging in with an authorized user name and password. Authorized users can be given access to resources that are not available to anonymous users. Typically, anonymous users are limited to downloading files and software from specific directories, whereas authorized users can upload files and access other restricted directories not available to anonymous users.

To access files on an FTP site, computers must have FTP client software. Most Web browsers have a built-in FTP client for accessing FTP servers with the URL *ftp://ip_address/dns_name*. In addition to the built-in FTP clients, there are a number of dedicated FTP clients designed to work directly with FTP servers from various operating system and application environments. Many dedicated FTP clients enable the operator to enter commands directly from the FTP command prompt; other clients use a graphical environment to access the FTP server's files and directories. For example, FTP Explorer and CuteFTP are free for home and educational use. Table 10-3 compares the features and limitations of some commonly used FTP clients.

Table 10-3 FTP Clients

FTP Client	Features	Limitations
CuteFTP from Globalscope.com	Easy to use and very reliable Graphical user interface Available in shareware and full versions	Limited options Does not use command prompts
Windows FTP command	Available from Windows Start, Run Uses command prompts	Does not have a graphical user interface More difficult to use
Internet Explorer	Easy access to FTP sites from the IE Web browser	Limited commands

10

Setting up NetWare FTP Server requires installing the FTP software on the NetWare 6 server and then configuring the software to provide access to the content directories. In the following sections, you learn how Eric installed the FTP software on the UASHOST server and then configured it for user access. You then use NetWare FTP Server to access files and upload content to your Web site.

Installing NetWare FTP Server

Eric performed the following steps to install the NetWare FTP Server software on the UASHOST server. If you have access to a server that you can use to install the FTP software, you can follow these steps to set up an FTP server on your computer:

1. First, Eric inserted the NetWare 6 CD into the UASHOST server, and pressed Ctrl+Esc to select the system console screen, as described in Chapter 12.

2. He entered the command CDROM and pressed Enter to mount the CD as a volume on the server.

3. After mounting the NetWare 6 Installation volume, he pressed Ctrl+Esc to select the X Server - Graphical Console.

4. At the graphical console, Eric clicked Novell and then Install to display the Installed Products window.

5. He clicked Add to display the Source Path window, clicked the browse button to select the NetWare 6 volume, and then clicked OK. He clicked OK again in the Source Path window to copy installation files to the server, and the Components window was displayed with check marks indicating the default installed components.

6. Eric clicked Clear All to prevent reinstalling existing components, clicked the NetWare FTP Server check box, and clicked Next to display the login window.

7. He entered his Admin user name, password, and .UAS context in the appropriate fields, and then clicked OK to display the LDAP Configuration window.

8. In the LDAP Configuration window, Eric verified that the default values of 389 for the Clear Text port and 636 for the SSL port were set. He clicked the Allow Clear Text Passwords check box, and then clicked Next to display the Summary window.

9. After verifying that the NetWare FTP Server and NetWare Port Resolver components were listed, Eric clicked Finish.

10. Eric received a Product Conflict message box informing him that LDAP Services version 3.2.0 was already installed and asking whether he wanted to replace the current version with the version being installed. Because the version numbers of the LDAP service being installed are the same or older than the version currently on his system, Eric clicked No when asked if he wanted to replace the existing version.

11. After file copying was finished, the Installation complete window displayed the option to view the Readme file. Eric clicked Close to exit the FTP Server installation program and return to the X Server - Graphical Console.

Configuring the FTP Server

As with Enterprise Web Server, NetWare FTP Server is configured by using the Web Manager portal. You can use Web Manager's FTP option to turn the FTP server on and off, set the default home directory path, and configure user access. The default home directory is set to the SYS:Public directory of the server hosting the FTP services. Universal AeroSpace wants all users to be able to use the FTP server to get software updates from the AeroDyn directory structure but wants only IS users to upload files to the Update directory. Eric performed the following steps to create a directory for software updates and then changed the default path from SYS:Public to CORP:Shared\Download:

1. After logging in with his Admin user name and password, Eric used ConsoleOne to create the Download subdirectory within the CORP:Shared directory.

2. Next, he used ConsoleOne to add [Public] as a trustee of the Download directory with Read and File Scan rights. To allow the IS department to manage the Download directory, Eric then added the IS OU as a trustee of the Shared\Download directory with all rights except Supervisor and Access Control.

3. To give all users access to the FTP site without having unique user names, Eric created a user named Anonymous with no password in the UAS Organization. Eric then exited ConsoleOne, started his Web browser, and started Web Manager by entering *https://172.20.1.60:2200* as the URL.

4. After the NetWare Web Manager window was displayed, he clicked the UASHOST server link under the NetWare FTP Server heading. He then logged in with the Admin user name and password to display the FTP Server On/Off window.

5. After starting FTP Server, he clicked the Server Settings link to display the FTP Server General Settings window, similar to the one in Figure 10-11.

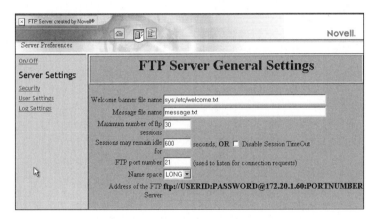

Figure 10-11   The FTP Server General Settings window

6. To change the default path of the FTP home directory, Eric clicked the User Settings link and replaced the existing path of SYS:Public with the new path of CORP:Shared\Download in the Default home directory text box, as shown in Figure 10-12.

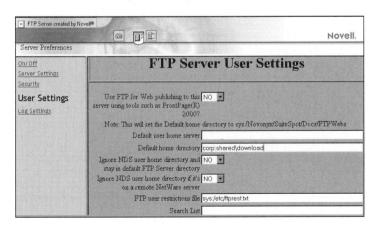

Figure 10-12   Changing the default home directory path in the FTP Server User Settings window

7. To have all users access the default home directory rather than their home directories, Eric changed the settings for the Ignore NDS user home directory and stay in default FTP Server directory option and the Ignore NDS user home directory if it's on a remote NetWare server option to Yes.

8. To allow the public to download files from the Shared\Download folder, Eric needed to enable anonymous access to the FTP server. NetWare FTP Server supports an anonymous user account to give users without user names on the system access to files intended for public use. When enabling anonymous user access, the network administrator needs to specify the path to the anonymous user home directory and indicate whether an e-mail address is required for the password. The e-mail address does not cause any access restriction, but gives network administrators a way to track access to the FTP site and send messages to users. To enable anonymous access to the Shared\Download directory, Eric scrolled down to the FTP Server Anonymous Users window, shown in Figure 10-13.

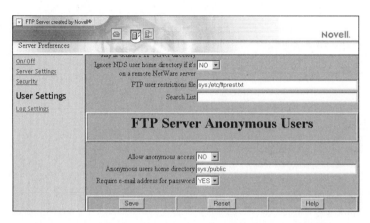

Figure 10-13   The FTP Server Anonymous Users window

9. He clicked the Allow anonymous access list arrow and selected Yes, and then entered the path to the CORP:Shared\Download directory in the Anonymous users home directory text box.

10. After making these changes, Eric clicked the Save button and then clicked OK in the Success message box to return to the FTP Server User Settings window.

11. Eric left the FTP Server window open while he continued with the FTP Server configuration.

After updating the default directory path, Eric's next job was to grant all users access to read files from the FTP server but allow only the users in the IS OU to upload files. The FTP service enables administrators to set access restrictions for containers and users in the SYS:\Etc\Ftprest.txt file. Restriction lines in the Ftprest.txt file contain the name of the entity and one of the following access restrictions:

■ *DENY*—Denies access to the FTP server for the specified user or container.

■ *READONLY*—Gives read access rights to the specified client.

■ *NOREMOTE*—Restricts access to allow only local access to the client.

■ *GUEST*—Allows the specified client to have only the permissions given to the Guest user account.

■ *ALLOW*—Gives the specified client read and write access to the FTP server directory.

When modifying the FTP server restrictions file, Novell recommends the following:

■ Each line can have only one entity and its corresponding access rights. For example, the following line would give all users in the .UAS container Read Only rights to the FTP server:

```
*.UAS READONLY
```

- The entities are assigned rights in the order they appear in the restriction file. If different rights apply to the same entity, those that appear last in the restriction file apply.

- If the restriction file is empty or does not exist, access is given to all users.

To enable users in the IS OU to use the FTP server to upload files but restrict other users to Read Only access, Eric used Notepad to edit the Ftprest.txt file in the SYS:\ETC directory, as shown in Figure 10-14. After making all the necessary changes to this file, Eric saved the file and exited Notepad.

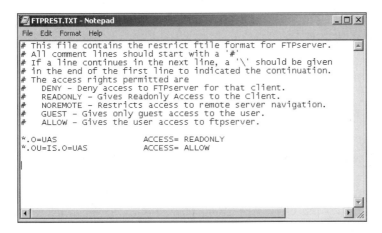

Figure 10-14   Editing the FTP restrictions file

The final step of completing the FTP Server configuration is to stop and then restart the FTP service. After making his configuration changes, Eric performed the following steps to restart the FTP service:

1. First, he clicked the On/Off link in the Server Preferences window to display the current FTP server status.

2. Next, he clicked the Server Off button to halt the FTP server.

3. To restart the service, he clicked the Server On button.

4. He exited the FTP Server On/Off window by clicking the Home button to return to Web Manager's main window.

5. He then logged out by exiting the Web browser.

Accessing FTP Folders and Files

After FTP Server is up and running, you can use any FTP client to log in to the FTP server and transfer files. In the following activity, you use an FTP client to access the classroom FTP server and perform several commands.

Activity 10-2: Working with FTP Services

Time Required: 10 minutes

Objective: Use Web Manager to configure NetWare FTP Server.

Description: After configuring the Web server, Eric informed Kellie Thiele that the site was ready to use. Kellie then logged in to the FTP server and transferred some files to the Download directory. In this activity, you use an FTP client to log in to the classroom FTP server using the KThiele account and perform some FTP activities, including creating a directory and transferring files. You then log in as an anonymous user and download a file.

1. If necessary, start your computer, and log in to the Novell network with your UasAdmin user name and password.

10

2. Use Notepad to create a new text file named ##Readme.txt (replace ## with your assigned student number) in the root of your C: drive that contains the following message:

```
Date: (today's date)
Created by: (your name)
This file contains instructions on installing the latest updates to our
station thruster control software.
```

3. Exit Notepad and save your file.

4. To open an FTP client window, click **Start**, **Run** and enter **FTP** *ip_address* (replacing *ip_address* with the IP address of your UASHOST server). Then press **Enter** to display a "User <*ip_address*:(none)>" login prompt.

5. Enter the distinguished name for your KThiele user and press **Enter** to display the Password prompt.

6. Enter **password**, and press **Enter** to display the User kthiele Logged in Successfully message.

7. Enter **?**, and press **Enter** to display a list of FTP commands.

8. Enter the command **Put C:\##readme.txt**, and press **Enter** to send your file to the FTP server.

9. Enter **Bye** to exit the FTP client and return to your Windows desktop.

10. Start your Web browser and enter the URL **ftp://***ip_address* (replacing *ip_address* with the IP address of your UASHOST server) to display the Login As dialog box.

11. Click the **Login Anonymously** check box, and then click the **Login** button to display a window showing all files in the FTP site. (If you cannot log in anonymously, log in with your .uasadmin.##uas user name.)

12. Open another student's file by double-clicking it.

13. Read the file and close the window.

14. If necessary, use My Computer to create a folder named **Downloads** at the root of your C: drive.

15. Download a file to your computer.

    a. Right-click a filename, and then click **Copy to folder** to open the Browse for Folder dialog box.

    b. Navigate to your C: drive, and select your Downloads folder.

    c. Click **OK** to download the file.

16. Log out by exiting the Web browser.

17. Verify that the file has been downloaded by using My Computer to navigate to your Downloads folder, and double-click the new file.

18. Close all windows, and log out.

WORKING WITH CERTIFICATE SERVICES

A critical part of implementing services across a public network, such as the Internet, is providing security. In previous chapters, you have learned how file system and eDirectory security use trustee assignments to grant users the rights they need to access data and manage network objects, but still prevent unauthorized access. **Public key cryptography** is a security system that authenticates users and organizations to ensure that they are who they claim to be and encrypts data transmissions to prevent information from being intercepted by unauthorized people. Table 10-4 shows how public key cryptography relates to file system and eDirectory security.

Table 10-4 Network Security Systems

Security System	Description
eDirectory security	Uses a system of granting and withholding rights to containers and objects in the eDirectory tree
File system security	Uses a system of granting and withholding rights to directories and files in the file system to control access to data
Role-based security	Assigns users to roles that have a predefined set of operations that can be performed within a specified context
Public key cryptography	Uses authentication and encryption to secure communication and transmissions between senders and receivers

Public key cryptography provides both authentication and encryption security through the use of mathematically related sets of digital codes called key pairs. A key pair consists of a public and private key that is unique to an individual, application, or organization. The **private key** is kept solely by the owner of the key pair and used to create digital signatures and encrypt and decrypt data. The **public key** is made available to all network users and used by outside entities to encrypt data sent to the key pair owner. The received data can be decrypted and read only by using the owner's corresponding private key. In addition to decrypting data packets, the owner of a key pair also uses the private key to create digital signatures. Just as a personal signature on a paper document authenticates it, a digital signature is used to authenticate an electronic document as being from a specific user or an organization. To create a digital signature, the cryptography software that creates the signature mathematically links the data being signed with the sender's private key. The receiver of the data can then use the sender's public key to verify the digital signature, as illustrated in Figure 10-15.

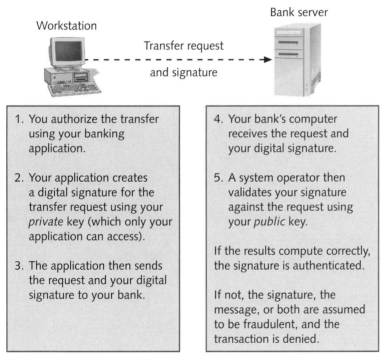

Figure 10-15 Digital signature authentication

An important part of public key cryptography is verifying that the public key used to encrypt data and check digital signatures is actually from the individual or organization that it claims to be. One method of providing reliable public keys is to actually meet with the individual or organizational representative and then exchange public keys using a physical medium, such as a floppy diskette. However, exchanging public keys on diskettes is not feasible for e-mailing a large number of people or conducting e-commerce with other organizations, so a more efficient, practical method of distributing reliable public keys was developed. Public key cryptography uses the Certificate Authority (CA) service to mediate the exchange of public keys. The public key cryptography software running on an entity creates a public and private key pair. To get the public key authorized, an entity needs to send its public key along with other identification information to a CA. The CA validates an owner's key pair by creating a certificate containing the owner's public key along with the CA's digital signature. As illustrated in Figure 10-16, the CA is responsible for verifying that the requesting entity's identity is established before validating the requester's public key certificate.

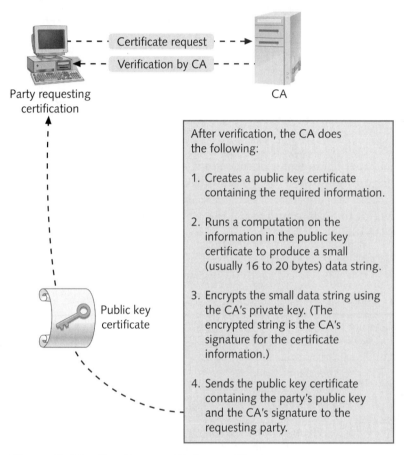

Figure 10-16   Creating a public key certificate

Public key certificates contain, at a minimum, the entity's public key, a subject name, and a CA-generated digital signature. Public key certificates generated by most commercial CAs use the X.509v3 format and contain the following information:

- The name of the user or organization (subject name)
- The public key of the user or organization
- The length of time the public key certificate is valid
- The name of the CA that signed the public key certificate (issuer)
- The digital signature created by the CA

Before using an entity's public key to encrypt data or verify a digital signature, the cryptography service running on the user's workstation checks the digital signature on the public key certificate against a list of known CAs. If the digital signature is not recognized as coming from a known CA, the cryptography service either discards the data or asks the user if he or she wants to trust the entity issuing the public key.

When planning cryptography services, you need to be able to determine the type of CA service your applications and users will require. There are two basic types of CA services: external and internal. When using an external CA service, you need to submit requests for public key certificates to recognized organizations, which verify your identity and provide a public key certificate that can be imported into applications and clients. Using recognized external CAs is important for Web servers and other Internet services that deliver information and services to the public sector. By using public key certificates signed by recognized external CAs, your public keys will be trusted by any Web browser, thus making e-commerce transactions easier and less risky for users. On the other hand, obtaining signed public key certificates from external CAs can be expensive and time consuming when implementing internal applications and services. Internal CA services run on a local server and can be used to automatically issue and sign public key certificates for applications and services available to authorized users of the network. For example, transactions between Novell OneNet utilities and Web Services running on a NetWare 6 server take place using public key certificates issued and signed by the internal Novell Certificate Server running on the NetWare 6 server. In the next section, you learn about Novell Certificate Server and its functions.

Novell Certificate Server

Novell Certificate Server, included with NetWare 6, integrates public key cryptography services into eDirectory and enables administrators to create, issue, and manage user and server certificates. It helps network administrators meet the challenges of public key cryptography with the following functions:

- Creating an Organizational CA in the eDirectory tree that allows your CA server to internally issue user and server certificates without going to an external CA, thereby reducing costs and the time needed to implement Net Services for your organization

- Storing key pairs in the eDirectory tree to provide security against unauthorized access and tampering yet make public keys available to all network entities

- Allowing centralized management of public key certificates by using ConsoleOne snap-ins

- Supporting commonly used e-mail clients and Web browsers

Novell Certificate Server consists of PKI.NLM and a snap-in module for ConsoleOne that administrators use to request, manage, and store public key certificates and their associated key pairs in the eDirectory tree. Using Novell Certificate Server, administrators can establish an Organizational CA that is specific to their organization's eDirectory tree. Because Novell International Cryptography Infrastructure (NICI) is used to support all cryptography and signature functions, a single version of Novell Certificate Server can be used throughout an organization's entire intranet. NICI must be installed on both the Novell server and client to provide secure, two-way communication between applications using public key cryptography.

Novell Certificate Server is installed by default on the first NetWare 6 server installed in a tree. If an eDirectory tree already contains an older version of the Novell CA, you need to upgrade the existing certificate server to the latest NetWare 6 CA version before installing the new NetWare 6 server, as described in Chapter 12. After installing Novell Certificate Server and creating an Organizational CA for the UAS_Tree during the NetWare installation, Eric used ConsoleOne to perform the following CA management tasks:

- Create a Server Certificate object for the UASHOST server

- Request a public key certificate from an external CA

- Create a user certificate

- Create trusted root containers and objects

Securing Net Services

Making Net Services and information available on the Internet exposes the NetWare server and user workstations to potential attacks on an organization's information system. Although public key cryptography secures data through encryption and identifies entities with digital signatures, it does not prevent outside hackers from attacking your system and gaining unauthorized access to network services and data. As network and data communications have become more complex, so has the level of attacks against their operations. The most common types of hacker attacks on information systems can be divided into these five general categories:

- *Intrusion*—The most common type of attack, **intrusion** involves an unauthorized person gaining access to the system through the illegal use of another user's account, usually accomplished by learning or guessing user names and passwords. Often, intrusion involves getting access to user names and passwords from knowledge gained from insiders, through guesswork, or with software that can break down passwords using mathematical or random processes. If potential intruders can gain access to the server console, they might be able to change the administrator's password or download a file containing user names and encrypted passwords. This file can later be entered into a program that attempts to decrypt passwords with a variety of techniques. Intrusion can best be prevented by physically securing the servers and ensuring that users have passwords of at least eight characters that combine both letters and numbers.

- *Spoofing*—Using underhanded or illegal means to gain access to a computer or network by masquerading as an authorized user or entity, **spoofing** often involves sending packets that have been modified to a server to make it seem as though they originated from an authorized entity. Public key encryption helps prevent spoofed packets by requiring a digital signature that can be authenticated only by using the public key supplied by the actual entity. Because the intruder does not have the actual entity's private key, digital signatures cannot be spoofed.

- *Virus attacks*—**Viruses** are programs or macros embedded in other software or e-mail attachments in such a way that when the program or e-mail is opened, the virus code runs. Like viruses in the real world, computer viruses can spread to other computers on the network by embedding themselves in network software or sending e-mail messages to users in the infected computer's address list. Viruses can simply be nuisances that slow down a computer, or they can be more serious, attacking the local computer's software and causing data loss and system crashes. In this section, you learn more about the types of computer viruses and the measures Eric took to prevent or reduce the spread of viruses on the UAS network.

- *Denial-of-service attacks*—Although less common than intrusion or virus attacks, **denial-of-service** attacks can prevent users from accessing network services. These attacks are usually caused by a bombardment of packets sent to a server from someone without authorized access. The packet bombardment overloads memory or CPU time, causing legitimate users' connection requests to be denied. In this section, you learn about some of the common denial-of-service attack methods and how Eric helped secure the UAS network against them.

- *Information theft*—This type of attack involves illegally intercepting and reading information transmitted between computers through the use of wire taps and sniffer software. The best defenses against **information theft** are implementing public key cryptography and keeping sensitive data on isolated or private networks.

David asked the IS department to develop an Internet security plan for protecting the UAS network against known security threats and to include a proposal for any additional software needed. After meeting with the other members of the IS department, Luke decided that the proposal should cover internal security against hacking, firewall security to control access from untrusted networks, a virus protection plan, and a defense against common denial-of-service attacks. Figure 10-17 is the diagram he created to illustrate the multiple-level security system he's proposing to management.

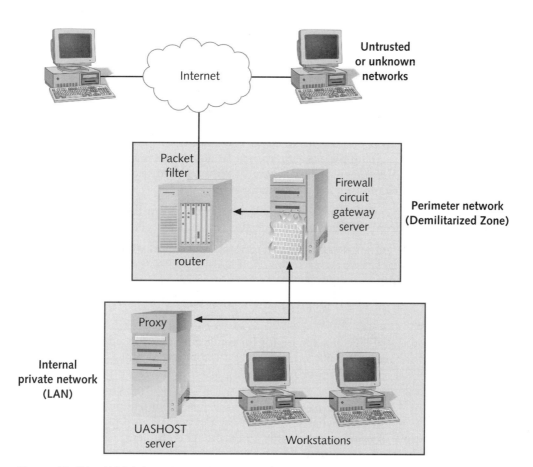

Figure 10-17 UAS Internet security proposal

The security plan consists of two major layers. The outer perimeter, also referred to as the Demilitarized Zone (DMZ), is where packets from the outside world first enter the UAS network. The inner layer consists of the local area network, which is secured with file system and eDirectory security, as described in previous chapters. The DMZ, the area most vulnerable to attacks, is where the Internet router and firewall software are located. If the firewall server finds no anomalies in a packet, the packet is passed to the internal router and then relayed to the appropriate service. Rather than expose the UASHOST server to attacks in the DMZ, Luke recommended installing another NetWare server for running the firewall software. Luke suggested Novell's Border Manager because it includes firewall, packet filter, and proxy server components. In the following sections, you learn about these security measures, and see how Luke and Eric plan to implement them in their security plan for the UAS network.

Internal Security

Luke decided that the first step in the UAS security plan was ensuring that essential internal network components and data were protected from unauthorized access and hacking. Internal security involves placing the NetWare servers in secure locations and making sure all users have adequate passwords of at least eight characters that are changed periodically, as described in Chapter 4. Internal security also involves making proper file system and eDirectory trustee assignments, as described in Chapters 5 and 6. After reviewing the existing internal security measures, Luke recommended increasing security by having Eric take the following precautions:

- Ensure that server rooms are kept locked during off-hours. If unauthorized people have physical access to the server, they could load software from a diskette, switch the server into debug mode to modify system settings, change the server time, or shut down the server. Luke recalled an incident in which a server was actually stolen from an unlocked server room and never found; the network administrator discovered the problem when users started calling in because they received "Server not found" messages when they attempted to log in. In some organizations, the server can be further secured by removing input devices, such as the keyboard and mouse, and even removing the monitor. The server is then remotely managed with Netware Remote Manager.

- Provide extra security by using the console screen saver and Secure Console commands. The console screen saver can be activated by entering the command SCRSAVER on the system console and then supplying a password. To access the server console and enter commands, you provide the screen saver password or the Admin user password. The SECURE CONSOLE command provides the following security:

  - Requires that all NetWare Loadable Modules be loaded from the SYS:System directory to prevent someone from loading software on the server from a floppy diskette

  - Prevents keyboard entry into the operating system debugger, which enables knowledgeable operators to change operating system configurations, thus potentially gaining access to data or shutting down the server

  - Prevents the server date and time from being changed

- Change user password restrictions to require a password of at least eight characters that's changed every 60 days. The availability of software for breaking down encrypted passwords has alerted Luke to the need for increasing password security. If potential intruders have access to the server, they could download or use a network sniffer program to retrieve a list of user names and encrypted passwords. These programs use mathematical or random techniques to break the encryption code and discover the passwords. The best protection is longer passwords that consist of both alphabetic and numeric characters. With each extra password character, the number of possible combinations goes up exponentially. With an eight-character password, the time needed to break it down becomes too long to be practical. Luke asked Eric to change the password restriction policy on all users to specify longer passwords and ensure that intruder detection is set for all OUs. Users should also be trained to use random passwords of both alphabetic and numeric characters rather than common names, which are much easier for password-breaking programs to discover.

- Review the file system and eDirectory security to ensure that users have only the rights they need to perform their assigned tasks. Eric found that good documentation is the best way to check these security areas. He used the Directory Trustee and eDirectory Security Worksheets (created in Chapters 5 and 6) with ConsoleOne to confirm the trustee assignments made to each directory and container.

Common Internal Security Violations

Despite a good security plan and documentation, it's possible for users to gain excessive rights to your system and compromise network security, through an error in trustee assignments or by unauthorized access. Following are some ways in which users could gain unauthorized access rights to your network system:

- As described in Chapter 4, password security is your front-line defense against internal security violations. If intruders learn the password for the Admin or another user account, they could gain unauthorized access to the network. Even though Novell passwords are encrypted, potential intruders can use sniffer software to read packets from the network cable and build a list of user names and encrypted passwords; to break the encryption code to get the actual password, they can use password-breaking programs. The best defense against password-breaking programs is using longer passwords that contain both alphabetic and numeric characters. Eric also implemented Novell's intruder detection option to prevent guessing at passwords and placed time and station restrictions on security-sensitive user accounts to prevent intruders from logging in during off-hours or from remote workstations.

- Despite your best planning and documentation, user accounts might be assigned unauthorized rights to the eDirectory tree or file system. Although administrators could inadvertently make errors in trustee assignments, incorrect rights assignments can also happen if intruders have access to the server or an administrative workstation that has been left logged in. The best protection against this type of attack is to physically secure the server and always log out or lock your administrative workstation when away from your desk. In addition, you should periodically check trustee assignments and use one of the following tools to track internal security compromises:

  - Novell Advanced Audit Service, included with NetWare 6, can help you track unauthorized or unusual actions by configuring policies in eDirectory containers that record certain user actions. For example, you can configure auditing to record such events as logging in with certain user accounts (such as Admin), creating objects, changing passwords or other user properties, and opening, deleting, and modifying files.

  - BindView Solutions for Novell from the BindView Corporation (*http://www.bindview.com*) can help automate the search for user objects with too many rights and rogue Admin user accounts. The bv-Control product features the BindView RMS Console used for reporting on and administering almost all aspects of network servers. Using bv-Control for eDirectory, Eric can perform security checks across the eDirectory tree for possible security or configuration vulnerabilities, and use the bv-Control ActiveAdmin technology to resolve any security problems. With BindView tools, Eric can get effective rights information and reports in minutes, generate policy compliance reports for UAS management staff, and check server configuration settings to alert him of potential problems.

- Another possible security compromise involves creating a rogue Admin account that has the Supervisor right to the eDirectory tree. Typically, these accounts are created by an intruder running a program on the server console or from an administrative workstation left logged in and unlocked. One method used to create rogue Admin accounts is through the old NetWare bindery database. NetWare 3 used a bindery database rather than eDirectory to store user accounts and access rights. To maintain compatibility with earlier NetWare servers, NetWare 6 still maintains a bindery database. If a Supervisor user is created in the bindery database, that account can gain the same rights to the tree as the Admin user. For example, there's a NetWare Loadable Module called BURGLER.NLM that can create a hidden Supervisor account in the bindery with the same rights as the eDirectory tree Admin user. Because BURGLER.NLM must be run from the server console, the best prevention is to physically secure the server and use the SECURE CONSOLE and SCRSAVER commands to limit access to the server console prompt.

When an internal security problem is identified, it is important to know how to identify and correct it. When tracing internal security violations involving excessive rights, you should follow these steps to track the problem to the source:

1. Identify the user account with excessive rights and the directory or container where the rights are being used.

2. Identify the effective rights of the user in the directory or container.

3. Identify any groups the user is associated with.

4. Use the following procedure to check trustee assignments to the container or directory where the user has excessive rights:

   a. Use ConsoleOne to display the trustee assignments in the directory or container.

   b. Check whether the user is a trustee of the directory or container and, if necessary, remove or change the user's trustee assignment.

   c. Verify that the user is not security equivalent to any other users in the trustee list for the directory or container being checked.

d. Identify any groups that are trustees of the directory or container being checked. If the user is a member of a group that's granting excessive rights, remove the user from that group and then make sure he or she has only the rights needed to perform the task.

e. Check for any trustee assignments being granted to Organizational Role objects. If an Organizational Role object is a trustee, determine whether the user in question is an occupant of that organizational role and, if necessary, remove the user from any roles granting excessive rights.

5. Move up one directory or container level and repeat Step 4.

6. Continue the process of working up the directory structure or eDirectory tree until you reach the root of the volume or tree.

7. If working with the file system, and the user has the Supervisor right at the root of the volume, check the user's effective rights to the server object in the eDirectory tree. If the user has the Write Attribute right to the server object's ACL property, he or she will inherit the Supervisor right to all volumes on that server.

In the following activity, you use ConsoleOne to practice the steps for finding an internal security violation.

Activity 10-3: Troubleshooting Effective Rights

Time Required: 10 minutes

Objective: Use ConsoleOne to troubleshoot excessive user rights.

Description: Not long after completing the initial system setup, Kellie reported that Lynn Dai had the Supervisor right to Kellie's home directory, and asked Eric to check whether this rights assignment was correct. In this activity, you use ConsoleOne to determine how Lynn gained the Supervisor right to Kellie's home directory.

1. If necessary, start your computer, and log in to the Novell network with your UasAdmin user name and password.

2. Start ConsoleOne, and expand **UAS_Tree** and your **##UAS** container.

3. Expand the **UASHOST_CORP** volume and **IS** directory.

4. Check the trustees of Kellie's home directory:

a. Right-click the **KThiele** home directory, and then click **Properties** to open the Properties of KThiele dialog box.

b. Click the **Trustees** tab to display the Trustees list box.

c. Click the **Effective Rights** button to open the Effective Rights dialog box.

d. Click the **Browse** button to navigate to the Mgmt container, click the **LDai** user, and then click **OK** to display Lynn's effective rights. Record the effective rights on your student answer sheet, and then click **Close** to return to the Trustees list box.

e. Record the existing trustees of Kellie's home directory on your student answer sheet.

f. Click **Cancel** to return to the main ConsoleOne window.

5. Check whether Lynn is security equivalent to any of the trustees of Kellie's home directory:

a. If necessary, click the OU containing the user account you're checking. Right-click the user name, and then click **Properties** to open the Properties dialog box.

b. Scroll to the right and click the **Security Equal to Me** tab. On your student answer sheet, record the results for each trustee.

c. Click **Cancel** to return to the main ConsoleOne window.

d. If necessary, repeat Steps a–c for each account you're checking.

6. Repeat Step 4 to check the trustees of the IS directory, and record the results on your student answer sheet.

7. Repeat Step 5 to determine whether Lynn is security equivalent to any of the trustees of the IS directory.

8. Repeat Step 4 to check the trustees of the UASHOST_CORP volume, and record the results on your student answer sheet.

9. Repeat Step 5 to determine whether Lynn is security equivalent to any of the trustees of the UASHOST_CORP volume.

10. Check Lynn's effective rights to the UASHOST server:

   a. Right-click the **UASHOST** server object, and then click **Properties** to open the Properties of UASHOST dialog box.

   b. Click the **down arrow** on the NDS Rights tab, and click **Effective Rights** to open the Effective Rights to UASHOST.##UAS dialog box.

   c. Click the **Browse** button to navigate to the Mgmt OU, click **LDai**, and then click **OK** to display Lynn's effective rights. On your student answer sheet, record these rights, and identify any rights that would affect her rights in the file system.

11. Determine the trustees of the UASHOST server:

   a. Click the **down arrow** on the NDS Rights tab, and click **Trustees of this Object** to display the trustees of the UASHOST server. On your student answer sheet, record the trustees, and identify any trustee assignments that would give Lynn rights to the server.

   b. Click **Cancel** to return to the main ConsoleOne window.

12. Determine the trustees of the UAS Organization:

   a. Right-click your **##UAS** Organization, and then click **Properties** to open the Properties of ##UAS dialog box.

   b. Click the **NDS Rights** tab to display the existing trustee assignments. On your student answer sheet, identify any trustee assignments that could give Lynn excessive rights to the Organization.

   c. Click **Cancel** to return to the main ConsoleOne window.

13. Propose a solution to the problem.

14. Exit ConsoleOne, and log out.

Firewall Security

Outside the network environment, firewalls are often used to separate people and equipment from possible dangers. For example, in your automobile, a firewall separates the car's potentially explosive engine from the driver. In computing environments, firewalls are used in a similar way to protect your computer and data from the potential hazards of the Internet environment. Computer firewalls control access between the company's private network and an untrusted external entity on the Internet. **Firewalls** consist of software that runs on a server or specialized hardware, such as a network router, and can be configured to provide protection from external threats in the following ways:

- Enforce corporate security and access control policies by controlling the type of traffic permitted between the internal private network and the Internet.

- Keep log files of information about external traffic to better monitor the source and frequency of unauthorized access attempts.

- Provide a central point that all network traffic must pass through before reaching the internal private network. Having a single point of access eliminates the possibility of the UAS network being open to external Internet users and allows Eric to redefine access policies in the event of any security breaches.

- Act as a traffic cop by permitting only selected services, such as FTP or WWW, to access the network.

- Create firewall partitions that limit security breaches or prevent intruder attacks from spreading across the company intranet.

A firewall's primary objective is to prevent entities on untrusted or unknown networks from accessing services and computers on the trusted or internal network. When configuring Internet security, the IS department needed to identify the network address of each trusted and untrusted network. A **trusted network** consists of your organization's private network along with the firewall server and networks it covers; it can exist within the company intranet and include the network addresses of other computers and networks on the Internet that you regularly communicate and do business with. To avoid explicitly identifying trusted network addresses for users who need to get through the firewall to access services and resources on your internal network, you can implement a **virtual private network (VPN)**, which is a trusted network that sends packets over an untrusted network. An **untrusted network**, such as the Internet, is an external network whose administration and security policies are either unknown or out of your control. When you configure a firewall server, you can identify any untrusted networks that will interface with the firewall. An **unknown network** is neither trusted nor untrusted and, by default, is treated the same as an untrusted network. You can use firewall software to enable the following security measures on all untrusted and unknown networks:

- *Packet filtering*—A screening router often performs this process before allowing packets into the firewall server. **Packet filtering** looks at the destination and source IP addresses to determine whether the packet is from a trusted, untrusted, or unknown network. Packets from trusted networks are allowed into the internal network, but packets from other network addresses are routed through the firewall server. Packet filtering routers also record the interface from which the packet arrives or leaves. Although packet filtering can permit or deny a service, it cannot protect unsecured services from unauthorized access.

- *Virtual private networks (VPNs)*—VPNs enable two or more hosts to communicate over a public network using a secure channel. To maintain a secure channel, VPNs encrypt the data packets sent between hosts and provide for access controls. There are two basic types of VPNs: client and site. Client VPNs connect to the firewall using dial-in connections or through an ISP over the Internet. Site VPNs, which are usually for departments or external organizations, typically use dedicated network connections. Departments might use a VPN to create a secure connection across the company's private network or the Internet. For example, a college might want a VPN connection between departments across the campus network to prevent students who share the campus network from accessing confidential information, such as grades. Both intranet and Internet site VPNs can be implemented with the VPN server in the DMZ zone between the Internet and your private network *or* with the VPN server located on your private network behind the DMZ. VPN servers operating in the DMZ are easier to configure and require less overhead than setting up a VPN server behind the firewall. However, VPN servers in the DMZ are more difficult to secure and are at more risk from attacks than VPN servers on the private network.

- *Network Address Translation (NAT)*—This firewall technique translates private IP addresses used on the internal network to one or more registered IP addresses. NAT enables clients on the private internal network to access the Internet without having a "live" (registered) IP address. Not having an assigned IP address hides the client from outside entities, essentially hiding ports and services on the client from packets that originate on the Internet. NAT does not require any special software on users' computers. The computers are simply configured to use the NAT server as their default gateway, causing all packets sent to Internet sites to be routed through the NAT server. (See Appendix B for more information on NAT and IP gateway configuration.)

- *IPX/IP gateways*—These gateways perform the same basic function as NAT, with the addition of converting IPX protocol packets to IP. Using an IPX/IP gateway requires software on the client to place TCP/IP service requests inside IPX packets. The IPX packet is then sent to the gateway software, where the IP request is removed from the IPX packet and sent to the Internet. When a response is received, the IPX/IP gateway places the TCP/IP information in an IPX packet and returns it to the client. IPX/IP gateways allow the private internal network to use only the IPX protocol, thus totally isolating the internal network from the Internet.

- *Circuit-level gateways*—**Circuit-level gateways** usually run on a firewall server and inspect additional packet heading information, including type of service, port number, user name, and DNS name. Using service packet types enables these gateways to permit or deny connections to services based on the destination port number. For example, UAS wants to allow entities from untrusted networks to send requests to the Web server running on port 80 and the FTP service running on port 21. Because other port numbers are used by secured services, such as iPrint, iManager, or Remote Manager, any packets from an untrusted or unknown network to these ports will be rejected. Many hacker attacks are based on sending packets to open ports running on servers and workstations. Using a circuit-level gateway provides a means of stopping these packets from entering the private network. Because they operate at the session layer of the OSI model, circuit-level gateways have access to user information, so they can accept or reject packets based on the user name or group membership. Circuit-level gateways offer increased firewall security, but they might need special client software and are often slower than other firewall systems, such as NAT.

- *Proxy services*—By receiving and monitoring all network traffic, **proxy services** help prevent denial-of-service attacks and information theft and enable administrators to control most of the network traffic flowing through the firewall. Because proxy services are applications that operate by inspecting network packets at the application level, they are also referred to as "application-level gateways." A proxy service requires two components: the proxy server and a proxy client. The proxy server acts as the end server for service requests from the private network. The proxy clients run on user workstations and communicate with the proxy service rather than with untrusted or unknown networks. Clients from unknown or untrusted networks communicate through the proxy server to request access to FTP or Web Services. The proxy server checks the incoming packets and allows or disallows the packets based on the organization's security policy and procedures. Outgoing traffic is also routed through the proxy server. The proxy service determines the validity of the client's request based on the established security rules. If the security policy permits the client to contact the outside server, the proxy contacts the outside host on behalf of the client. If the policy prohibits contacting the outside server, the proxy rejects the request and informs the client of the policy violation. UAS is planning to use Border Manager's proxy service to help control access to outside sites and prevent denial-of-service and information theft attacks.

Protection Against Virus Attacks

Viruses are often embedded in other programs or e-mail attachments. After a virus is activated by running the program or opening the e-mail attachment, it can copy itself to other programs or disk storage areas. Each virus has a different signature, which is a bit pattern made by the virus when it's embedded in a program or an e-mail attachment. Although viruses do not directly attack the NetWare operating system and services, they can use the server and network services, such as e-mail, to rapidly spread to other computers on the network. Firewalls offer security measures to help protect a network from information theft and attacks, but they are not designed to detect and prevent viruses from entering the network. When it comes

10

to virus attacks, the best possible defense is knowing the types of virus software and how viruses enter a computer network. Viruses are classified based on how they infect computer systems:

- Boot sector viruses attack the boot record, master boot record, or file allocation table (FAT) of a hard or floppy disk. When the computer is booted from the infected disk, the virus is loaded into memory and from there copies itself to other programs, including those stored in shared directories on the server, or damages information on the local computer. Joshi and Michelangelo are examples of boot sector viruses.

- File viruses, also called Trojan horses, attack executable program files—files ending with .exe, .com, .sys, .drv, .dll, and .bin—by attaching themselves to the code in the program. The virus code waits in memory for the user to run another application and uses that event as a trigger to perform an action such as replicating itself or attacking the local computer. A Trojan horse is a destructive program often concealed as part of other software, such as a game or graphics application. Trojan horses can also contain software used for embezzlement, for example, and self-destruct after they have finished their operation.

- Macro viruses attack programs that run macros, such as spreadsheet and word-processing applications. These malicious macros start when the infected document or template is opened. The macro can erase or damage data and copy itself to other documents. A well-known example is the Melissa macro virus.

- Stealth viruses (the Tequila virus, for example) are able to disguise themselves to make it difficult for antivirus software to detect them. Passive stealth viruses can increase the size of files while still evading detection by presenting the file's original size. Certain types of stealth viruses called encrypted viruses—Cascade, for instance—mask their code or virus signatures to make it difficult for antivirus software to detect them.

- Polymorphic viruses are a rapidly growing type of stealth virus with built-in code to create random changes or mutations to their virus signatures, making reliable detection very difficult. SMEG is an example of a polymorphic virus.

- Worms are independent programs that do not replicate; instead, they copy themselves to other computers over a network. Worms can infiltrate legitimate programs to alter or destroy data and degrade system performance. For example, a worm program could infect a bank's computer and initiate fund transfers to another account. Worm attacks are usually easier to identify and recover from than other types of viruses because there's only one copy of the program to search for and remove.

Virus Prevention Techniques

Virus prevention on a network involves installing a virus protection system, making regular backups, and training users on how to reduce the risk of virus attacks. Virus protection systems scan programs on the server and user workstations and monitor program files as they are loaded to detect known virus signatures. In addition to scanning, most antivirus software warns the user of any activity that could be caused by a computer virus, such as modifying the disk boot sector or system settings.

In addition to installing antivirus software, you must also make sure that users know how their workstations might be affected by virus infections. Recognizing virus symptoms can help identify and remove new viruses before they propagate to other computers or cause more data loss. After installing and configuring the antivirus software on the UASHOST server, Eric trained the UAS users to be aware of the following common virus infection symptoms:

- A computer that fails to start normally
- Programs that do not start or fail when using common commands
- Changes in filenames or files that become unaccessible
- Unusual words or graphics appearing on the monitor

- Hard or floppy disks being unexpectedly formatted

- Slow computer performance when loading or running software

To help protect the UAS network against virus attacks, David wanted Luke to submit a virus protection plan as part of the UAS security plan. Luke's plan includes the following recommendations for configuring antivirus software and policies on the UAS network:

- Install NetWare-compatible antivirus software from one of the following vendors:
    - NetShield from Network Associates (*http://www.mcafeeb2b.com*)
    - Server Protect from Trend Micro (*http://www.antivirus.com*)
    - Norton Antivirus Corporate Edition from Symantec (*http://www.symantec.com/nav*)
    - Command Antivirus from Command Software Systems (*http://commandcom.com/products/netware.html*)

- Use the antivirus software vendor's Web site to keep the virus signature files up to date on servers and workstations.

- Configure the antivirus software to immediately send virus notifications to Eric as well as the workstation user.

- Enable the virus expiration warning to alert Eric when the signature files are out of date.

- Configure the server's virus-scanning software to scan both incoming and outgoing files of all types, including .exe, .dll, and .zip files.

- Install an antivirus software package that quarantines files to protect users from accessing a potentially infected file and spreading the virus.

- Train users on the importance of virus scans and, if possible, disable the option of canceling a virus check.

- Train users on common types of viruses and explain how they usually spread by running infected programs, opening e-mail attachments, booting from infected floppy disks, or downloading infected files from bulletin boards.

- Use Novell's Z.E.N.works for Desktops to distribute the latest virus signature updates to all workstations.

- Create write-protected emergency boot floppy disks to be used if a workstation becomes infected or damaged by a virus. Keep the emergency boot floppy disks updated with the latest virus signature updates.

- Scan all incoming and outgoing e-mail messages and attachments.

- Develop a company policy to avoid downloading e-mail attachments and software that aren't work related.

- Configure the GroupWise server to filter and eliminate unsolicited "junk" e-mail that could contain a virus or malicious program.

- Train users on antivirus software operation and encourage them to install an antivirus software package on their home computers.

Virus Removal Planning

Despite security measures and antivirus software, with all the new viruses popping up almost daily, there's always the possibility that one could slip by your antivirus software and infect your network's computers. After a virus was detected recently on the UAS network, Eric used the following procedure to isolate and remove the virus from all networked computers:

1. First, Eric isolated all systems and floppy disks that were known to be, or suspected of being, infected with the virus.

2. He then checked the support site for the antivirus software to help determine the type of virus and find any suggested clean-up procedures.

3. Eric located the clean floppy disk formatted with a boot system that he had created earlier with his antivirus software. The clean boot floppy disk also contained a copy of the virus-scanning software.

4. He used the clean floppy disk to start all infected or suspect computers. Starting from a clean floppy disk ensures that no virus code is loaded into the computer memory.

5. He used the virus-scanning software on the clean boot floppy disk to scan all physical and logical hard disks on each infected or suspect computer. He also scanned any floppy disks used with the suspect computers. During the scanning process, he removed any viruses from the files and programs of infected computers.

6. After scanning and removing any virus code, Eric restarted the system and created a system backup that excluded any infected files on the workstations or server.

7. Viruses that infect program files can create problems because the virus might have replaced instructions in the program, so it often doesn't run correctly or might "hang" when the program is loaded. To handle this problem, Eric deleted all infected programs and reloaded the software from the original CD-ROM. In one case, system files were damaged, and Eric needed to reformat the hard drive, reinstall the entire workstation, and restore the backups.

8. Finally, Eric scanned all the network drives and reloaded copies of the executable programs from backup tapes.

The server's boot sector and operating system files cannot be infected unless the server is started from an infected floppy disk. As a result, Eric has developed the habit of scanning all floppy disks before inserting them in the server and has modified the server's CMOS to prevent it from starting from a floppy disk that might have been inadvertently left in the drive.

Defense Against Denial-of-Service Attacks

Although denial-of-service attacks don't usually directly damage or steal a company's data, they can cost a company a lot of money by bogging down the organization's Web services, causing lost customer sales and reducing user productivity. Denial-of-service attacks are usually caused by flooding the server with packets or sending oversized packets to a service, causing it to crash. A properly configured firewall along with software designed for Net Services security are the best defenses against denial-of-service attacks. Table 10-5 lists several known denial-of-service attacks that Luke identified in his UAS security proposal.

Table 10-5   Common Denial-of-Service Attacks

Type of Attack	Description
Ping of death	The PING command is modified to send Internet Control Message Protocol (ICMP) ECHO packets longer than the 64 KB maximum defined in the TCP/IP RFC 791 standard. The extra bytes in the packet can cause unprotected TCP/IP software to overflow the buffer space, resulting in computer hang-ups or crashes.
Teardrop attack	The teardrop attack intentionally overlaps packet fragments, causing errors in fragment reassembly that can result in packets being resent repeatedly and flooding the server.
Land attack	The land attack sends packets with the same source and destination IP addresses, thereby flooding the service with an endless loop of packets being sent to the server.

Table 10-5   Common Denial-of-Service Attacks (continued)

Type of Attack	Description
SYN packet flooding	TCP connections require the following three-way handshake between the server and the client: 1. The client sends a packet in which the SYN flag is set in the TCP header. 2. The server sends a SYN/ACK (acknowledgment) packet back to the client. 3. The client sends an ACK packet so that data transmission can begin. A TCP SYN denial-of-service condition is caused when the client fails to send the last ACK packet and intentionally sends successive TCP connection requests to the server, filling up the server's buffer. After the server's buffer is full, other client requests are rejected, resulting in a denial-of-service condition.
Oversized UPD packets	Like the ping of death, sending oversized UDP packets can result in buffer overflows that cause the server to hang or crash.
Smurf	Smurf attacks use the ICMP ECHO in response to PING broadcasts to flood the server.

The ping of death is perhaps one of the best-known denial-of-service attacks. Normally, the PING (Packet Internet Groper) application is used as a diagnostic utility on TCP/IP networks to send ECHO packets to selected hosts and receive responses if the network and host are operational. By default, ECHO packets contain only 64 bytes of data, but the RFC standard allows up to 64 KB in a PING ECHO packet. The ping of death occurs when a PING command is sent to an IP host with more than 64 KB of data. Some older software cannot handle these large ECHO packets, which can cause the TCP/IP stack to overflow, thereby slowing down or crashing the server. It is the vendor's responsibility to ensure that its TCP/IP implementation can handle oversized ECHO packets. By going to Novell's Technical Information Web site at *http://support.novell.com*, Luke verified that all of Novell's current TCP/IP products since NetWare 3.11 are designed to discard oversized packets without hanging or crashing. In addition, Luke learned that earlier 16-bit versions of the Novell client might pause for up to 15 seconds when receiving oversized PING packets. At the Novell site, Luke also discovered that although the Novell TCP/IP stack is not affected by the teardrop attack, it might be affected by the land attack when the transport protocol is using UDP. In this case, the land attack could cause the server to hit 100% utilization. Novell currently has a TCP/IP stack fix that corrects this problem by dropping packets if the software determines that the source and destination IP addresses are the same and the IP address is not the loopback address (127.0.0.1). The fix to the Ftcpsv01.exe file can be downloaded from the Novell site. Although this fix will not be necessary for the new NetWare 6 server, Luke plans to make sure it's implemented on the older servers at the AeroDyn facility.

10

After ensuring that the system software has been updated to fix any known problems, the next part of the UAS Internet security plan to prevent denial-of-service attacks is to configure the Border Manager firewall to send security alerts for the following conditions:

- Security-sensitive NLMs being loaded or unloaded
- Oversized PING packets
- SYN packet flooding
- Oversized UDP packets

Border Manager alerts can detect many other types of denial-of-service attacks (smurf, teardrop, or land) because these attacks all share common techniques, such as using ICMP ECHO packets, overlapping fragments, and packets with the same source and destination IP addresses to create server overloads.

After completing the basic Internet security plan, Luke recommended purchasing another computer and Novell's Border Manager to act as a firewall. He plans to send Eric to a Border Manager training class to learn how to configure settings for the security measures he identified. After reviewing the security plan, David approved the expenditures and is anxious to set up the security measures before implementing UAS's Net Services.

Chapter Summary

❑ An essential part of Novell's strategy for the future is to provide Internet services that enable clients and servers using diverse operating systems to be managed and accessed as one network. To do this, Novell has developed Net Services, which includes iFolder, NetStorage, iManager, Remote Manager, iPrint, and iMonitor. Because Net Services is written to run on top of the open-source Apache Web Server, the services can be implemented on other network operating systems, such as Windows 2000, Windows NT, and Linux.

❑ NetWare Web Services includes Enterprise Web Server and FTP Server, which can be installed and customized to supply information and Web pages to the Internet and local intranet. The NetWare Web Manager portal is used to configure and manage both Enterprise Web Server and FTP Server. Typical Web server management tasks include specifying the primary document directory, creating virtual Web sites, setting document preferences, and specifying public and restricted access to Web content. FTP configuration tasks include setting the default FTP directory, providing anonymous access, and restricting user access to the FTP server.

❑ Using public key cryptography to encrypt data transmission and provide authentication with digital signatures is a vital component of securing information transmission on the Internet. Public key cryptography uses public and private keys to create digital signatures and encrypt and decrypt data transmissions. Clients use the public key to encrypt data, which can be decrypted only by the public key owner's private key.

❑ Certificate Authorities issue public key certificates for verifying that the public key belongs to the entity distributing it. Clients receiving the public key certificate can then verify the owner's identity by trusting the CA's digital signature.

❑ Internet security involves protecting Web and Net Services from threats such as data theft, hacking, and computer viruses. An Internet security plan should include a firewall to isolate the internal network from the outside Internet and implement a virus protection and data recovery plan. Firewalls should be configured to detect denial-of-service attacks, such as the ping of death, SYN packet flooding, oversized UDP packets, teardrop attacks, and land attacks.

Key Terms

circuit-level gateway — A firewall gateway that inspects packet heading information, including type of service, port number, user name, and DNS name.

denial-of-service — A form of network attack that loads the server with packets to shut down network services.

extranet — A network system that uses the Internet to connect different organizations for business transactions.

firewall — A point of access between an organization's internal private network and the Internet, used to filter packets and reduce the risk of unauthorized access to or malicious attacks on the organization's private network system and services.

information theft — A form of network attack that uses wire taps and sniffer software to illegally intercept data.

intrusion — A form of network attack that involves gaining unauthorized and illegal access to an organization's information, usually through obtaining a user's account and password.

Java servlet — An application written in the Java programming language to run on a Web server.

Net Services — A set of hardware and software components that work together to provide access to information services across the Internet or company intranet.

Novell Portal Services (NPS) — A Net Services component running on a NetWare server that provides customized pages or portals for users based on users' rights and personal style specifications.

packet filtering — A process performed by a screening router to determine whether a packet is from a trusted, untrusted, or unknown network.

private key — The digital key code used in public key cryptography that is kept solely by the owner and used to decode data and create digital signatures.

proxy service — A high-level firewall service that works at the application level to give clients on an organization's network both incoming and outgoing access to Internet services.

public key — The digital key code used in public key cryptography for clients to encrypt data being sent to a host and to verify a host's digital signature.

public key cryptography — An Internet security system that uses public and private keys to encrypt and decrypt data and create digital signatures for authenticating users.

spoofing — A method of illegally accessing network resources or attacking a network service by creating falsified packets that appear to come from an authorized entity.

trusted network — A network with an IP address range that's known to be safe or can be controlled and monitored by your organization.

unknown network — A network that is not specified as a trusted or untrusted network in a firewall. Firewalls treat unknown networks as untrusted networks.

untrusted network — An IP address range that might contain hackers or other malicious entities. Packets from networks listed as untrusted are inspected by the network firewall.

virtual private network — A trusted network that sends packets over an untrusted network, such as the Internet.

virus — A self-replicating program that can be embedded in software to propagate between computers and eventually can be triggered to affect computer performance or destroy data.

Web Services — A set of hardware and software components that provide WWW and FTP information services to clients located on the Internet or company intranet.

10

REVIEW QUESTIONS

1. Which of the following OneNet utilities allows access to network data from a Web browser without adding a client to the user workstation?

   a. iPrint

   b. iManager

   c. NetStorage

   d. iFolder

2. Which of the following is an example of a Web Services component?

   a. FTP server

   b. portal services

   c. iFolder

   d. NetStorage

3. Tomcat is an example of which of the following?

   a. Web server

   b. Java servlet

   c. servlet engine

   d. FTP server

4. Which of the following Web servers does NetWare 6 use to provide Net Services? (Choose all that apply.)

   a. Enterprise Web Server

   b. Apache Web Server

   c. Tomcat

   d. Web Manager

5. Which of the following provides customized Web pages to users based on their access rights and privileges?

   a. Web servers

   b. Novell Portal Services

   c. iManager

   d. Remote Manager

6. Java servlets require which of the following to run?

   a. Enterprise Web Server

   b. NetWare FTP Server

   c. NetWare Web Manager

   d. Tomcat

7. Which of the following is an example of a Java servlet?

   a. Tomcat

   b. Enterprise Web Server

   c. Novell Portal Services

   d. iFolder

8. The _____ button in the NetWare Enterprise Web Server management window is used to set access restrictions.

9. The _____ button in the NetWare Enterprise Web Server management window is used to identify a virtual Web document.

10. The _____ button in the FTP Server management window is used to configure anonymous user access.

11. In public key cryptography, which of the following keys is used to create digital signatures?

    a. public

    b. private

    c. digital

    d. certificate

12. In public key cryptography, which of the following keys is used to decrypt data packets?

    a. public

    b. private

    c. digital

    d. certificate

13. In public key cryptography, the CA is responsible for which of the following? (Choose all that apply.)

    a. creating public and private keys

    b. encrypting data

    c. validating that users are who they claim to be

    d. signing and issuing public key certificates

14. Which of the following attacks involves sending very large ECHO packets?

    a. ping of death

    b. SYN packet flooding

    c. teardrop

    d. land

15. Which of the following attacks involves failure to send ACK packets?

    a. ping of death

    b. SYN packet flooding

    c. teardrop

    d. land

16. Which of the following is a form of firewall packet filtering that uses port number and service types?

    a. proxy filtering

    b. circuit-level gateway

    c. packet filtering

    d. ECHO filtering

17. Which of the following is a form of firewall security that checks only packet source IP addresses?

    a. proxy filtering

    b. circuit-level gateway

    c. packet filtering

    d. ECHO filtering

18. Which of the following is software that embeds into existing programs and e-mail messages?

    a. trojans

    b. viruses

    c. ICMP

    d. hacker

19. Firewalls can be used to screen all of the following except _____.

    a. land attacks

    b. oversized packets

    c. computer viruses

    d. SYN packet flooding

20. Which of the following is a firewall application that enables administrators to control most of the network traffic flowing in and out of the network?

    a. packet filtering

    b. circuit-level gateway

    c. proxy service

    d. VPN

21. Which of the following firewall technologies would be the best choice for Universal AeroSpace to control the type of information sent between the network and clients?

    a. proxy service

    b. circuit-level gateway

    c. NAT

    d. VPN

22. Eric is concerned about maintaining a secure channel when using the Internet to connect to servers in the AeroDyn facility. Which of the following firewall technologies should he implement?

    a. NAT

    b. circuit-level gateway

    c. packet filtering

    d. VPN

23. Which of the following firewall technologies can hide client IP addresses on a private network from the Internet?

   a. packet filtering

   b. circuit-level gateway

   c. NAT

   d. VPN

24. Which of the following are the three basic components of public key cryptography? (Choose all that apply.)

   a. VPN

   b. CA

   c. public and private keys

   d. certificate signing request

25. Which of the following is *not* a firewall technology?

   a. packet filtering

   b. NAT

   c. VPN

   d. virus scanning

UNIVERSAL AEROSPACE CASE PROJECTS

In the following projects, you apply concepts and techniques from this chapter to implement Net and Web Services for your UAS network.

Case Project 10-1: Identifying Net and Web Services

In Table 10-6, identify each type of server as being a Web Services or a Net Services component and supply a brief explanation of what makes it that type of service.

Table 10-6   Service Identification Table

Service	Type of Service	Explanation
iFolder		
Enterprise Web Server		
NetWare FTP Server		
Web Manager		
Novell Portal Services		

Case Project 10-2: Creating a Web Site

Eric would like you to create a demonstration Web site for the Engineering department. He plans to use it at the next management meeting to show managers how to use the Web server to access other Web pages by supplying the Web site's name after the Universal AeroSpace URL. The Web site should simply consist of a heading along with the UAS world graphic in the Apps\Desktop folder. To perform this activity, you should follow these steps:

1. Ask your instructor for the path to your virtual document directory. Each student should be given a virtual document directory path that points to his or her ##CORP:IS\Web folder using the name ##Engineering. If you have access to an account with the Supervisor right to the Enterprise Web Server, you can create a virtual document directory by following these steps:

    a. Start your Web browser, and open the page *https://ip_address:2200* (replacing *ip_address* with the IP address of your UASHOST server).

    b. Click the Enterprise Web Servers link, and log in with your administrator user name and password.

    c. Click the Content Management button, and then click Additional Document Directories.

    d. Enter ##Engineering in the URL prefix text box.

    e. Enter the path to your ##CORP:IS\Web\Engineer directory in the Map To Directory text box.

    f. Click OK, and then click the Save and Apply button to save your changes.

2. Copy the UAS.bmp file from the SYS:Software.cti\Design folder to your ##CORP:IS\Web\Engineer directory.

3. Create a simple HTML document that displays the UAS.bmp file with a heading.

4. Save the document as Index.html in your ##CORP:IS\Web\Engineer directory.

5. Test your Web site by starting your Web browser and then entering the URL *http://ip_address/##Engineering* (replacing *ip_address* with the IP address of your UASHOST server and ## with your student number).

6. After your test document is displayed, have your instructor initial your student answer sheet.

10

Case Project 10-3: Developing a Security Plan for AeroDyn

The AeroDyn facility is planning to implement FTP Server so that users can download software files. In this project, you develop a plan to secure the AeroDyn facility from outside attacks. Your plan should include a diagram of the following network components and a brief description of what type of attacks you plan to prevent:

❑ Router

❑ Firewall

❑ AeroDyn internal private network

Case Project 10-4: Developing a Virus Protection Plan

In addition to the security measures in your plan from Case Project 10-3, Luke would like you to research the antivirus software listed in this chapter, using the supplied URLs, and then make a recommendation that includes the vendor, product, and price for a 30-station network. Your recommendation should include two antivirus software packages and state why you think this antivirus software would make a good choice for the AeroDyn network.

IMPLEMENTING MESSAGING SERVICES

**After reading this chapter and completing the exercises,
you will be able to:**

♦ Identify e-mail components, protocols, clients, and servers, and install and set up the GroupWise client to send and receive e-mail

♦ Configure and manage the GroupWise system so that you can create post office users and establish mailbox security

♦ Monitor the GroupWise system and troubleshoot common GroupWise problems

Electronic messaging and workgroup applications, such as scheduling and calendaring, are essential components of today's networked offices. Novell's GroupWise software is a highly reliable and efficient electronic messaging and workgroup application system that is integrated with eDirectory to enhance network security and provide centralized management. In this chapter, you learn about GroupWise features and components by seeing how Eric Kenton used Novell GroupWise to implement and manage an electronic messaging system for the Universal AeroSpace network.

IMPLEMENTING AN E-MAIL SYSTEM

After the basic network services and security measures were in place, the next step in setting up the UAS network was to implement an office e-mail system to improve employee productivity and communications. David Heise would also like UAS users to implement the following collaborative applications:

- *Scheduling*—For setting meeting dates, inviting people to events, and reserving resources, such as conference rooms and audiovisual equipment

- *Task Lists*—For creating prioritized to-do lists for themselves and others

- *Reminders*—For creating notes to be displayed on specific dates

E-mail Components

Like other network software, such as iFolder, FTP Server, and Enterprise Web Server, e-mail systems require both server and client components. As shown in Figure 11-1, the client component (referred to as the **front-end process**) runs on the user's workstation and provides an interface for communicating with the server component (referred to as the **back-end process**) to send or receive messages and attachments. In addition to e-mail messaging, the server and client software work together to provide collaborative office applications, such as scheduling meetings and resources, creating reminder notes, and managing to-do lists.

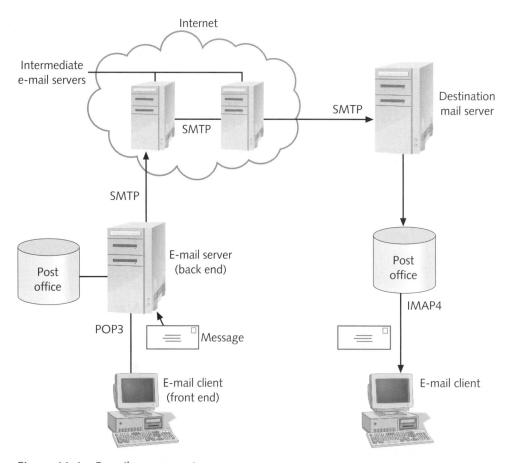

Figure 11-1 E-mail components

The post office application running on the server handles the actual delivery of e-mail messages. As illustrated in Figure 11-1, when a client sends a message, the data is first sent to the e-mail server, where the post office application interprets the recipient's address and then sends the message to the destination post office. Based on the route determined by the originating post office, the message data is sent directly to the destination server or to an intermediate server, which forwards the message to the final destination. The destination post office looks up the name of the recipient in the user list and then forwards the e-mail address to that user's mailbox. If a user name is not in the list of users on the destination server, the e-mail message is returned to the sender.

E-mail servers use software components, called agents, to assist in transferring e-mail messages. The **Message Transfer Agent (MTA)** assists the core post office software in transferring e-mail between user mailboxes and maintaining message integrity. To transfer messages, the MTA uses an algorithm for interpreting the e-mail address and finding the best route to the destination post office. You can configure the MTA to transfer mail at predetermined intervals and set criteria for selecting the best route to destination servers. The **Post Office Agent (POA)** is responsible for delivering messages from the client to the correct mailbox on the server. If the destination mailbox is located on a different server, the MTA finds the best route to the destination post office and transfers the message. The POA at the receiving server's post office then delivers the message to the correct mailbox.

E-mail Protocols

As you learned in Chapter 1, protocols are the rules used to transfer data and information between computer systems. In addition to using TCP/IP to transfer packets between computers, e-mail systems use specialized protocols to transmit messages from the client to the post office server and between post office servers. **Simple Mail Transfer Protocol (SMTP)** is a TCP/IP-based mail transfer protocol for transferring messages between servers. As part of the TCP/IP suite (see Appendix B for more information on TCP/IP), SMTP provides reliable delivery of e-mail messages by using TCP/IP to transfer data between servers. As illustrated in Figure 11-1, mail transfers between post offices often involve sending messages to intermediate servers. In this case, SMTP dynamically determines the route from the source server to the destination server. Because it's a mail transfer protocol, SMTP has limited capacity to store messages at the receiving end. As a result, it is always used with other protocols, such as POP and IMAP, that provide the capability of receiving and storing messages.

Internet Message Access Protocol (IMAP) is a standard protocol for accessing and storing e-mail messages from the post office server. To help users organize messages, IMAP has features for creating mail folders on the server for cataloging sent and received messages. The latest version of IMAP, IMAP4, has advanced features that support downloading only the e-mail address and subject, so users can decide whether they want to download the entire message or just the subject header to save download time. In addition, IMAP4 offers a powerful search feature for finding messages that contain specific text embedded in the message. For example, before reporting to management about the current status of the GroupWise system, Eric used the search feature to find all e-mail messages containing the word "GroupWise" and moved these messages into a separate folder so that he could reference them in the report.

The advanced IMAP features can be implemented only when using the actual client for e-mail access. When users access their e-mail accounts via the Web, they won't be able to download sender information and subject headers, for example.

Post Office Protocol (POP) is a standard client-server protocol for transferring e-mail messages between the client and e-mail server. POP3, the latest version of POP, contains enhancements for downloading messages to the client. Although POP and IMAP have many of the same functions, POP is referred to as a store-and-forward messaging protocol that transfers the complete message from the server to the client; IMAP4, on the other hand, enables you to select transmission options.

Common E-mail Clients

To work with e-mail systems, user workstations need to have e-mail client software installed and configured. Because most e-mail systems, such as GroupWise, use the standard POP, IMAP, and SMTP messaging protocols, they are compatible with many e-mail and workgroup clients. When researching e-mail systems, Eric wanted to find one that was compatible with the most commonly used e-mail clients. From his investigations, he determined that the most common e-mail clients include Eudora v5.1, GroupWise, Outlook Express, Outlook 2002, Netscape Messenger, and Lotus Notes. In the following sections, you learn what Eric discovered about some of these common e-mail clients and their features.

Eudora v5.1 Client

Eudora v5.1 is a standalone e-mail client created by Qualcomm to support all common e-mail protocols and servers. As a standalone e-mail client, Eudora has the advantage of being used on many different e-mail systems and being more resistant to e-mail viruses designed to attack more integrated systems, such as Outlook or GroupWise. After being installed on the user workstation, the Eudora client asks for the following e-mail server information the first time a user logs in:

- The user name and password for authenticating to the post office server
- The IP address or DNS name of the post office server
- The protocols the client application will use to connect to the post office server
- The ports used to communicate to the MTA and POA

In addition to the basic functions of sending and receiving e-mail, the Eudora client offers the following features that make it unique:

- *Eudora Shell Extensions*—This feature can be used to warn users about the potential for virus infection when running an e-mail attachment stored in the Attach directory.
- *Moodwatch*—This feature identifies potentially offensive phrases (based on user settings) and flags them with one to three chili pepper icons to denote one of the following levels:
  - One chili pepper: Message might be offensive.
  - Two chili peppers: Message is probably offensive.
  - Three chili peppers: Message is "on fire."
- *Strikeout style*—This feature, used to cross out selected text with a horizontal line, can be helpful when reviewing e-mail messages or checking off tasks in a to-do list.
- *Drag and drop*—This feature enables users to simply drag and drop attachments to e-mail messages.
- *Qualcomm PureVoice*—This add-on enables users to send messages with attached voice recordings.

Outlook Express and Outlook 2002

Outlook Express and Outlook 2002 are the two Microsoft e-mail clients. Outlook Express, which comes bundled with Internet Explorer and is designed for personal users, is an Internet-enabled e-mail client with support for the standard e-mail protocols as well as Network News Transfer Protocol (NNTP) for newsgroup access. Because it's bundled with Internet Explorer and offers many support features, many home and small-business users choose Outlook Express as their e-mail client. The full Outlook 2002 client is sold as part of the Microsoft Office suite and is intended for use in office environments that include Microsoft Exchange Server. Outlook 2002 offers all the features of Outlook Express and can also work with the Exchange server to perform scheduling, calendaring, and other collaborative functions. It includes the following features:

- Automatic completion of address information
- E-mail account selection to allow users with multiple e-mail accounts to select which one to use when they start the Outlook 2002 program
- Support for using external text editors so that users can switch between different formats, such as text, HTML, or rich text, when creating e-mail messages
- The Find feature, which offers rapid searches of folders and e-mail messages
- A mailbox cleanup feature that enables users to archive e-mail and search for messages by date, size, and other attributes to make it easier to remove items and better manage mailbox space

Lotus Notes Client

Lotus Notes is a powerful workgroup client that includes e-mail, calendaring, scheduling, and other collaborative functions for both Windows and Macintosh computers. Lotus Notes also has a complete Web browser capability, so users can access their e-mail and other features across the Internet or intranet. Some important features of the Notes client include the following:

- Support of multiple protocols, including NNTP for newsgroup access
- Automatic name-to-address resolution
- Customized views of calendars and to-do lists
- A Notes editor for creating and printing e-mail preview documents
- Animated GIFs as a visually appealing way to access other Web sites

GroupWise 6 Client

GroupWise 6 is a complete and integrated messaging system from Novell that includes both client and server components. In addition to the basic client features, the GroupWise 6 client offers the following advanced features to help increase user productivity:

- Supports multiple protocols, including NNTP for sending and receiving newsgroup postings.
- Facilitates migration from other clients by making it possible for users to import addresses and user account information from other e-mail clients, including Outlook and Netscape.
- Offers secure access to e-mail and user accounts through servers that support Secure Socket Layer (SSL) transmissions.
- Includes the ability to have multiple account signatures, making it possible to configure GroupWise clients to send data and messages to other applications, such as banking systems, that require public key encryption for authentication (see Chapter 10 for more information on using public key cryptography).
- Provides a new **caching mode** feature that automatically stores all messages and attachments on the local hard disk, thus allowing access to e-mail without being continuously connected to the network.
- Offers mailbox **mode switching** so that users can change their mailbox modes between online, caching, and remote. In online mode, messages are stored on the e-mail server. In caching mode, e-mail is automatically downloaded to the client's local hard disk. In remote mode, users can dial into a network, access e-mail messages, and selectively download messages for offline access. Also in remote mode, the client automatically dials in and initiates a connection with the server when required to send and receive e-mail.
- Includes the **AutoComplete addressing** feature, which automatically searches the address book for matching names when a user starts typing in an e-mail address and then completes the address entry for the user.
- Offers the **document management** feature for sharing documents with a group of users and maintaining multiple versions of documents.
- Uses security certificates for securing e-mail through mail authentication.

Common E-mail Back-End Servers

For e-mail clients to provide messaging and other collaborative services, such as calendaring and scheduling, they need to be connected to an e-mail server. E-mail servers provide post office and other services requested by clients. Simple clients, such as Eudora, are designed primarily to send and receive e-mail messages, so they can work with a variety of e-mail servers using standard protocols (POP3 and IMAP4). Performing more complex functions, such as calendaring and scheduling, requires tight integration between

11

the e-mail client and the server. Although many back-end servers can provide basic post office functions to clients for basic e-mail, three major back-end server products offer complete collaborative office messaging solutions for scheduling, calendaring, and task-list management: GroupWise 6 Mail Server, Microsoft Exchange 2000 Server, and Lotus Domino Mail Server. Before selecting the GroupWise system, Eric researched several back-end e-mail systems to decide which one would best meet the needs of the UAS network. The following sections describe the basic features of the major back-end messaging servers.

Microsoft Exchange 2000 Server

Microsoft Exchange 2000 Server is a sophisticated system that provides e-mail and many collaborative services, such as calendaring, scheduling, and document management, to integrated Outlook clients. To reduce the administrative costs of maintaining the messaging and collaborative services, Exchange 2000 Server is designed to be a highly reliable and scalable platform with easy-to-use administrative features. Exchange also includes built-in statistical analysis tools for proactively managing the messaging environment, monitoring server performance, and troubleshooting connectivity problems. Like the GroupWise system, Exchange is designed to support collaborative services across the Internet to give users "anytime, anywhere" access. Versions of Exchange are available for Windows NT and Windows 2000 servers. Although Exchange would provide the e-mail and collaborative services that UAS needs, it would require installing and managing a separate Windows NT or Windows 2000 server.

Lotus Domino Mail Server

Lotus Domino Mail Server is a powerful collaborative and messaging server for corporate intranets and the Internet. In addition to native support for all major Internet standards, Domino Server supports the latest in Internet messaging. Because of its easy installation and configuration, you can use the default settings to get a basic Domino mail server up and running in just a few minutes. Domino Server enables administrators to track messages across multiple domains to help determine path selection and troubleshoot delivery problems. In addition, it allows users to check the status of sent messages to determine delivery time and other tracking information. Like Exchange 2000 Server, Domino Server includes built-in statistical analysis tools for proactively managing the messaging environment, monitoring server performance, and troubleshooting connectivity problems. With Domino Server, users can integrate calendar and group scheduling features, share online work areas, and access the Web, newsgroups, and bulletin boards from any standards-based e-mail client, such as Eudora or Netscape Messenger.

GroupWise 6 Mail Server

Because the GroupWise system has been around since the early days of microcomputer networking (it was originally part of the WordPerfect office suite in the 1980s), Eric found it to be the most mature workgroup collaborative office system. Realizing the vital role that e-mail, calendaring, and document management play in an organization's operations, Novell has continued to upgrade and improve the GroupWise product through its various releases (GroupWise 4.1, 5.0, 5.2, 5.5, and now 6). With its most recent release, Novell has emphasized taking advantage of the Internet to deliver integrated collaborative services to users at any location, whether at the office, at home, or on the road.

Although GroupWise 6 offers many up-to-date features and management tools, it continues to provide backward-compatibility with earlier WordPerfect versions by retaining some WordPerfect naming conventions, such as "wp" (WordPerfect) and "of" (Office) in the file prefix or extension. GroupWise functions include e-mail messaging, calendaring, scheduling, document management, task-list management, workflow organization, and support for wireless communications.

To enable users to check e-mail and use other applications while traveling, David is planning to supply personal digital assistants (PDAs) for employees in the future. Eric liked GroupWise's support for Wireless Access Protocol (WAP)-enabled devices because users with PDAs could easily check e-mail and use other applications while on the move. After investigating the major back-end server alternatives, Eric found that GroupWise 6 equaled or exceeded the alternatives in offering all the collaborative services UAS needs. In addition, one of the biggest advantages of implementing GroupWise 6 is its tight integration with eDirectory and other Novell services, which makes configuring and managing the GroupWise 6 server easier. In the following sections, you learn how Eric installed and tested the GroupWise 6 system on the UAS network.

Installing GroupWise 6

After Eric submitted his recommendation to management, it didn't take long for David to approve the purchase of GroupWise 6. After getting the go-ahead from management, Luke sent Eric to a training class to learn the basics of setting up and configuring the GroupWise system. After completing the class, Eric performed the following steps to install GroupWise 6 on the UASHOST server. Your instructor might decide to perform this installation as a classroom demonstration. During the demonstration, you will be given the information to fill in Table 11-1.

 It's best to keep the names for the directories holding the domain directory and post office directory at eight or fewer characters. Although NetWare supports long directory names and filenames, GroupWise has problems finding directory names longer than eight characters.

Table 11-1 GroupWise Documentation Worksheet

GroupWise Directory Structure	
GroupWise System Name	
GroupWise Domain Name	
GroupWise Domain Directory Path	
GroupWise Post Office Name	
GroupWise Post Office Directory Path	
Post Office Context	
POA Network Address and Port	IP address: Client-server port: Message transfer port: HTTP port:
MTA Network Address and Port	IP address: Message transfer port: HTTP port:
Web Console Information	User name: Password:

1. Network and Server Preparation

   a. Eric started his computer and logged in with the Admin user name and password.

   b. Before installing GroupWise, you must create directories for the many GroupWise files that need to be copied to your server. Eric created a directory named Gwise6 off the root of his CORP volume.

   c. Next, Eric created the following required GroupWise directories as subdirectories within the existing CORP:\Gwise6 directory structure:

      - Mail
      - Postoff
      - Grpwise
      - Grpwise\Software

   d. Before starting the GroupWise installation, Eric verified that drive letter G: was mapped to the CORP volume.

2. Install Software

   a. Eric inserted the GroupWise CD. The GroupWise installation program automatically started and displayed the GroupWise installation options.

   b. Eric clicked the Create or update a GroupWise system option to display the Software License Agreement window showing the language selection options and license agreement.

   c. He clicked Yes to accept the license agreement and the default English language and display the Welcome to GroupWise Install window.

   d. After reading the installation overview steps, he clicked Next to display the Plan Your System window. Eric clicked the Installation Guide button to open an Adobe Acrobat document containing installation and update instructions. After reviewing the document, he exited Acrobat Reader and returned to the Plan Your System window.

   e. He then clicked Next to continue the installation and display the Administration Options window.

   f. He verified that the Create a new system or update an existing system option was selected, and then clicked Next.

   g. He selected UAS_Tree and clicked Next.

   h. He clicked Next to extend the NDS schema, and then clicked Next to display the language options.

   i. He verified that English was selected, and then clicked Next to enter the path to the ConsoleOne directory.

   j. He verified that the path was C:\Novell\ConsoleOne\1.2, and then clicked Next.

   k. He then entered \\uashost\corp\gwise6\grpwise\software as the path to the software directory, and then clicked Next to display the Select Software window, shown in Figure 11-2.

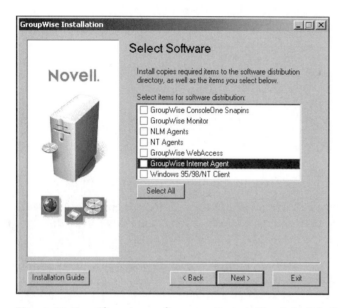

Figure 11-2   Choosing software options in the Select Software window

   l. In the Select Software window, Eric clicked the Select All button and then clicked Next. The Checking Files window was displayed while the installation software examined the files in the existing system. After the files were checked, the Ready to Install window was displayed.

   m. Eric clicked the Install button in the Ready to Install window to begin the installation.

n. After files were copied to the server, the GroupWise Partner Page window was displayed. In this window, you can click the Go to GroupWise Partner Page button to view the information on the Internet.

o. Eric clicked the Next button in the GroupWise Partner Page window to display the Determine Next Step window (see Figure 11-3).

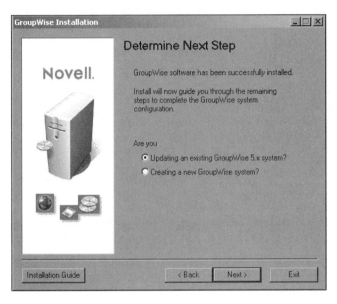

Figure 11-3   The Determine Next Step window

p. In the Determine Next Step window, Eric clicked the Creating a new GroupWise system radio button, and then clicked Next to display the Run ConsoleOne window.

q. In the Run ConsoleOne window, Eric clicked the Run button to start ConsoleOne and open the GroupWise System Setup Wizard (shown in Figure 11-4) after ConsoleOne loaded. Eric performed each of the tasks listed in the GroupWise Setup Progress window, as described in the following steps.

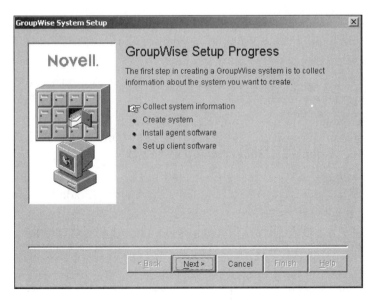

Figure 11-4   The GroupWise Setup Progress window

3. Collect System Information

   a. Eric verified that the Collect system information option was selected in the GroupWise Setup Progress window, and then clicked Next to display the Software Distribution Directory window.

   b. He verified that \\UASHOST\CORP\Gwise6\Grpwise\Software was entered as the path to the GroupWise software distribution directory, and clicked Next again to display the NDS Tree window.

   c. He verified that UAS_Tree was listed as the Current tree, and clicked Next to open the System Name dialog box asking for the name of the GroupWise system. Eric entered Universal AeroSpace, and then clicked Next to open the Primary Domain dialog box.

   d. Eric entered UASWorld as the domain name, and then clicked Next to display the Domain Directory dialog box.

   e. Filling in the GroupWise Domain Directory text box is important because it specifies the path to the GroupWise mail database, which is needed when configuring ConsoleOne. Eric entered the path \\UASHOST\CORP\Gwise6\Mail\UasWorld, and then clicked Next to create the directory and display the Domain Context window.

   f. Eric clicked the Browse button, clicked UAS Organization, and clicked OK to insert UAS into the Domain context text box. He then clicked Next to display the Domain Language window.

   g. Eric clicked Next to select the default English language and display the Domain Time Zone dialog box. He used the scroll button to select his time zone, and then clicked Next to display the Post Office Name dialog box.

   h. Eric entered UASPO in the Post office name text box, and then clicked Next to display the Post Office Directory dialog box.

   i. He entered the path to the GroupWise post office directory as \\UASHOST\CORP\Gwise6\Postoff\UASPO, recorded the path on his documentation worksheet for later reference, and then clicked Next to create the directory and display the Post Office Context dialog box.

   j. When prompted to provide the Post Office context, Eric verified that UAS was entered in the Post office context text box, and then clicked Next to display the Post Office Language dialog box.

   k. He again selected his language and time zone information, clicking Next after each entry. Next, the Post Office Link window was displayed, containing options for a Direct link or a TCP/IP link.

   l. Eric selected the TCP/IP link radio button, and then clicked Next to display the POA Network Address window, shown in Figure 11-5.

   m. To be able to use port numbers to access GroupWise from a Web browser, Eric recorded the default port numbers for the client-server port (1677), message transfer port (7101), and HTTP port (7181) on the GroupWise Documentation Worksheet.

   n. He verified that the IP Address radio button was selected and entered the IP address of the UASHOST server in the IP Address text box. He then recorded the IP address information on his GroupWise Documentation Worksheet.

   o. He clicked Next to display the MTA Network Address window, shown in Figure 11-6.

   p. Again, he verified that the IP Address radio button was selected. He then entered the IP address of the UASHOST server and recorded the IP address and port information on his GroupWise Documentation Worksheet.

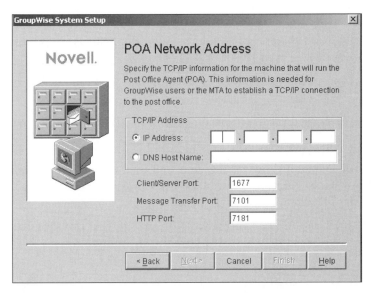

Figure 11-5 The POA Network Address window

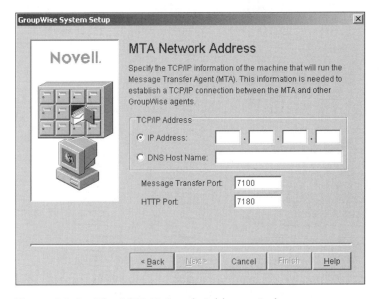

Figure 11-6 The MTA Network Address window

q. Eric then clicked Next to display the Post Office Users window. He clicked the Add button to display the Select Object dialog box, navigated to the IS Organizational Unit, and high-lighted all users in that container.

r. Next, he clicked OK to assign mailboxes for all IS users, and then repeated this process to create mail accounts for users in the other OUs.

 Note that all users in the same post office must have unique names. Users with the same name cannot be added to the post office, even though their names are located in different contexts.

s. After all user accounts were added to the Post Office Users window, Eric clicked Next to return to the GroupWise Setup Progress window.

4. Create the System

   a. Eric verified that the Create system option was selected, and then clicked Next to display the Summary window.

   b. He reviewed the information in the GroupWise installation window and clicked Next to continue the setup.

   c. After creating the system, he clicked Next to return to the GroupWise Setup Progress window.

5. Install Agent Software

   a. He verified that the Install agent software was selected, and then clicked Next to display the Select Platform dialog box. He verified that the NetWare platform was selected, and then clicked Next to display the Installation Path dialog box.

   b. He entered \\UASHOST\SYS\SYSTEM in the Installation path text box, and then clicked Next to display the Web Console Information window shown in Figure 11-7.

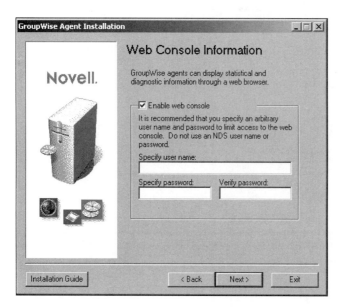

Figure 11-7 The Web Console Information window

   c. He entered Webagent in the Specify user name text box and novell in the Specify password text box, recorded the information on his GroupWise Documentation Worksheet, and then clicked Next to display the Language selection window.

   d. He verified that English was selected and clicked Next to display the Summary window.

   e. After verifying that the entries were correct, Eric clicked the Install button to begin the file-copying process.

   f. During the file-copying process, Eric received the "Read-Only File" message box for the ldapskk.nlm file. Eric clicked No when asked if he wanted to replace this file. When presented with additional "Read-Only File" message boxes, Eric continued to click No to prevent overwriting the existing LDAP files.

   g. When the Installation Complete dialog box was displayed, Eric verified that the Update AUTOEXEC File and Launch Groupwise Agents Now options were selected, and then clicked Finish to complete the agent software installation and return to the GroupWise Setup Progress window, where the Set up client software option was selected.

6. Because Eric is planning to install the client software separately, he clicked Cancel and then clicked Yes to exit the GroupWise installation program and return to the main ConsoleOne window.

7. To give IS staff and student interns the rights to access and manage the user post office data-base, Eric used ConsoleOne to assign the ISMgrs and Student groups all rights except Supervisor and Access Control to the GWise6 directory.

8. To provide a path to the GroupWise software, Eric used ConsoleOne to add the following MAP command to the end of the map commands in each OU's login script:

```
MAP ROOT M:=CORP:GWISE6
```

9. After completing the login script entries, Eric exited ConsoleOne and logged out.

10. View MTA and POA Screens

   a. After completing the installation, Eric moved to the UASHOST server console and pressed Ctrl+Esc to display the Current Screens window.

   b. He entered the number to the left of the GroupWise MTA - UASWorld option to display the GroupWise MTA information window, shown in Figure 11-8.

   c. After verifying that the MTA was running, Eric again pressed Ctrl+Esc to display the Current Screens window.

   d. He entered the number to the left of the GroupWise POA - UASPO.UASWorld option to display the GroupWise POA information window, similar to the one in Figure 11-9.

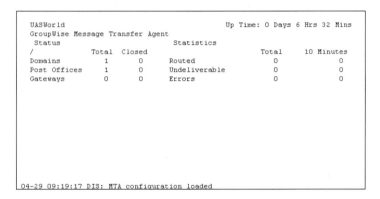

Figure 11-8 The MTA information window

```
UASPO.UASWORLD                          Up Time: 0 Days 6 Hrs 34 Mins
GroupWise Post Office Agent
 Status                      Statistics
Processing      Busy 0: 0   C/S Requests:      0   Message Files:     0
User Connections:        0   Requests Pending   0   Undeliverable:     0
File Queues:             0   Users Timed Out:   0   Problem Messages   0


09:19:19 1E4
09:19:19 29A Initializing dispatcher
09:19:19 29C Initializing dispatcher
09:19:19 2A0 Initializing worker
09:19:19 2A2 Initializing worker
09:19:19 2A4 Initializing worker
09:19:19 2A6 Initializing worker
09:19:19 2A8 Initializing worker
09:19:19 2AA Initializing worker
09:19:19 296 MTP: Listening for inbound connections
09:19:22 280 Guardian database: OK
```

Figure 11-9 The POA information window

   e. After verifying that the MTA and POA were running successfully, Eric returned to his administrative workstation. The GroupWise system was then ready for Eric to begin the client installation and configuration.

Setting Up GroupWise Client Computers

After installing GroupWise on the UASHOST server, Eric's next task was to prepare and configure the user workstations by providing a drive mapping to the GroupWise software and installing the GroupWise client. Having a common drive mapping to the GroupWise software directory is necessary to access and manage the GroupWise system. Eric decided to assign drive letter M: (for "mail") to the Gwise6 directory by modifying the container login scripts. The GroupWise client installation requires a three-phase setup. In the first phase, you run the setup program and identify the installation language and directory. The setup program then copies files to your local hard drive and restarts your computer. After the computer is restarted, in the second phase, you identify your installation options and program folder. When this phase is finished, you can view the Readme file and start GroupWise. The last phase of the client installation requires entering your user name and the post office server's IP address and port number. In the following activities, you modify your container login scripts, install the GroupWise client on your computer, and practice sending and receiving e-mail.

Activity 11-1: Modifying Login Scripts

Time Required: 10 minutes

Objective: Modify login scripts to provide a drive mapping to the GroupWise software.

Description: Before testing the GroupWise installation, Eric needed to modify the login scripts to map drive letter M: to the GroupWise software directory. In this activity, you use ConsoleOne to modify your login scripts to map drive letter M: to the GroupWise software directory on your classroom server.

1. If necessary, start your computer, and log in with your UasAdmin user name and password.

2. Start ConsoleOne, and expand **UAS_Tree** and your **##UAS** container.

3. Modify your IS OU login script to include a command to map drive letter M: to the Gwise6 directory:

   a. Right-click your **IS** OU, and then click **Properties** to open the Properties of IS dialog box.

   b. Click the **Login Script** tab to display the existing container login script commands.

   c. Add the following command to the end of your existing MAP commands:

      ```
      MAP ROOT M:=CORP:GWISE6
      ```

   d. Click the **Apply** button, and then click **Close** to return to the main ConsoleOne window.

4. Repeat Step 3 to add the MAP ROOT M:=CORP:GWISE6 command to your Engineering OU.

5. Repeat Step 3 to add the MAP ROOT M:=CORP:GWISE6 command to your Mfg OU.

6. Repeat Step 3 to add the MAP ROOT M:=CORP:GWISE6 command to your Mgmt OU.

7. Repeat Step 3 to add the MAP ROOT M:=CORP:GWISE6 command to the login script for your ##UAS Organization.

8. Exit ConsoleOne, and log out.

Activity 11-2: Installing the GroupWise Client

Time Required: 15 minutes

Objective: Install the GroupWise client on a user workstation.

Description: After adding the MAP commands to each container login script, Eric installed the GroupWise client on Kellie's computer before testing the system. In this activity, you simulate this process by being assigned a user name in the UAS network and then installing the GroupWise client on your workstation.

If possible, each student should use a different UAS user name.

1. Record your assigned user name on your student answer sheet. Possible user names are shown in Table 11-2.

2. If necessary, start your computer and log in with your assigned user name and password:

   a. Enter your assigned user name from Table 11-2 in the Username text box.

   b. Click the **Advanced** button to display the NDS tab information.

   c. Click the **Contexts** button, browse to your assigned container, and click **OK**.

   d. Enter a password for your assigned user in the Password text box, and click **OK** to log in.

3. Double-click the **My Computer** icon, and then double-click your **(M:)** drive to display the GroupWise directories.

4. Navigate to the Grpwise\Software\Client\Win32 folder by double-clicking the **GrpWise**, **Software**, **Client**, and **Win32** directories.

Table 11-2   UAS User Names for GroupWise

User name	Context	Password
JDamrau	.Business.UAS	password
BDahl	.Engineering.UAS	password
KMeans	.Engineering.UAS	password
LJarka	.Engineering.UAS	password
PAlm	.Engineering.UAS	password
TRucci	.Engineering.UAS	password
EKenton	.IS.UAS	password
BMuelner	.IS.UAS	password
CKent	.IS.UAS	password
LMcMann	.IS.UAS	password
RPence	.Mfg.UAS	password
DHeise	.Mgmt.UAS	password
LDai	.Mgmt.UAS	password
MFrias	.Mgmt.UAS	password

5. Scroll down and double-click the **Setup.exe** program to start the first phase of the installation process, which displays the Choose Setup Language dialog box.

6. Click **OK** to select the default English language and start the setup wizard.

7. If you receive a message informing you that the messaging system is not found on your computer, click **Next** to begin copying files to your computer, and then follow these steps to install the messaging software:

   a. After all messaging software files are copied, the Restart Windows dialog box opens. Verify that the **Yes** radio button is selected, and then click **OK** to close the window and restart your computer.

   b. After the computer restarts, log in with the user name you have been assigned from Table 11-2.

c. The GroupWise client installation continues with the second phase by asking you to again select the installation language.

d. Click **OK** after selecting the language to display the GroupWise Welcome window.

8. Click **Next** to display the Setup Options dialog box.

9. Verify that Standard Install is selected, and then click **Next** to display the Destination Directory dialog box.

If you are unable to perform a standard install because of insufficient disk space (for example, the installation "freezes" or fails to proceed), select the Workstation Install option to run the software from the server.

10. Click **Next** to accept the default Destination Folder path and display the Select Optional Components dialog box.

11. Record the optional components on your student answer sheet.

12. Click **Next** to select the default components and display the Select Program Folder dialog box.

13. Click **Next** to place the programs in the GroupWise folder and display the Select StartUp Folder Software dialog box.

14. Deselect any applications for the startup folder by clicking the **Clear All** button, and then click **Next** to display the Language Selection dialog box.

15. Verify that the English language is selected, and click **Next** to display the Start Copying Files summary window.

16. Verify with your instructor that the correct options are selected, and then click **Next** to start the file-copying process.

17. After all files are copied, the Setup Complete dialog box opens. Click the **Yes, I want to launch GroupWise** check box to remove the check mark, and then click the **Finish** button to open Notepad and display the Readme file.

18. Record the two GroupWise installation options on your student answer sheet, and then close Notepad.

19. The final phase of the client installation involves configuring the IP address and port for the post office server. To perform this phase, start GroupWise by double-clicking the **GroupWise** icon on your desktop. If you see the Novell GroupWise Startup dialog box (similar to the one in Figure 11-10), enter your assigned user name from Table 11-2 in the User ID (Required) text box and the password in the Password text box. Verify that the Online radio button is selected, and then enter the IP address for your GroupWise server in the Address text box and **1677** in the Port text box. Click **OK** to display an informational tip-of-the-day message.

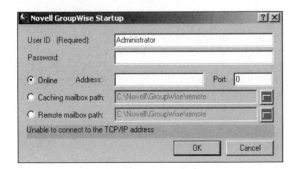

Figure 11-10   The Novell GroupWise Startup dialog box

20. Click **Close** to close the tip box and view the Novell GroupWise – Mailbox window, similar to the one in Figure 11-11.

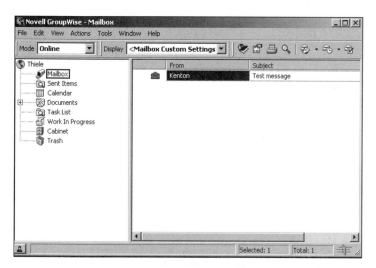

Figure 11-11   The Novell GroupWise - Mailbox window

21. Close the Novell GroupWise – Mailbox window, and log out.

Activity 11-3: Sending and Receiving E-mail

Time Required: 10 minutes

Objective: Use GroupWise to send and receive e-mail.

Description: After installing the GroupWise client on his and Kellie's computers, Eric tested the GroupWise system by logging in to his workstation with his EKenton user name and sending a message to Kellie. In this activity, you log in with the user name you were assigned in Activity 11-2 and send a message to the user name following yours in Table 11-2. The last assigned user name should send a message to the first user name. You then retrieve your mail and respond to the message.

1. When your computer restarts, log in with the user name and password you were assigned in Activity 11-2.

2. Start GroupWise by double-clicking the **GroupWise** icon on your desktop.

3. Read the GroupWise 6 tip of the day, and click **Close**.

4. Place your cursor over each GroupWise button icon and record the button description on your student answer sheet.

5. Click the **Create New Mail** button to open the Mail To dialog box.

6. Click the **Address** icon, and then click the **Novell GroupWise Address Book** tab (see Figure 11-12), which lists users in the UASPO post office.

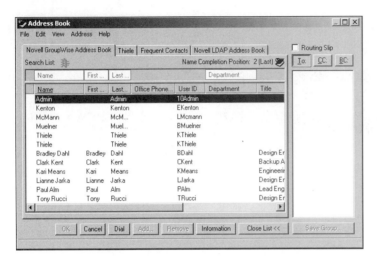

Figure 11-12   Viewing users in the GroupWise Address Book

7. Double-click the name of the user following your assigned user name in Table 11-2 (if you are the last user in the table, send mail to the first user name), and then click **OK** to insert the user name into the To field.

8. Enter **GroupWise Test** in the Subject field.

9. Enter **This is a test of the GroupWise e-mail system. Please respond when you receive this message.** in the Message text box.

10. Click the **Send** button to send the message.

11. Wait for a message to appear in the right-hand pane of the Novell GroupWise - Mailbox window. Double-click the message to read it.

12. Click the **Reply** button, and then click **OK** to accept the default Reply to sender option.

13. Enter a short reply in the Message text box, and then click the **Send** button.

14. Wait for a reply to come back from your original message, and then read and delete the reply.

15. Close the GroupWise client, and log out.

CONFIGURING AND MANAGING THE GROUPWISE SYSTEM

After the basic e-mail system was operational, Kellie took on some of the ongoing tasks of creating user accounts and distribution lists, automating e-mail functions with rules, making resources available for checkout, and monitoring GroupWise activity. To configure and manage GroupWise, ConsoleOne needs to be updated with the new GroupWise snap-ins that provide the software functions needed to work with GroupWise objects. In the following sections, you learn how to update ConsoleOne to include the new snap-ins and how to use ConsoleOne to perform basic GroupWise management and configuration tasks.

Adding GroupWise Snap-ins to ConsoleOne

Before using ConsoleOne to configure and work with GroupWise objects, it is necessary to install the GroupWise snap-ins. When Eric installed the GroupWise server, the ConsoleOne snap-ins were automatically installed on his computer to complete the initial GroupWise installation. Other workstations used to access and configure the GroupWise objects also need to have the ConsoleOne snap-ins installed. In the following activity, you install the GroupWise snap-ins on your workstation.

Activity 11-4: Installing the GroupWise ConsoleOne Snap-ins

Time Required: 10 minutes

Objective: Update ConsoleOne to access GroupWise objects.

Description: Because Kellie will be responsible for managing GroupWise in the future, Eric installed the GroupWise snap-ins on her workstation. In this activity, you use a similar procedure to install the GroupWise snap-ins to the ConsoleOne software on your workstation.

1. If necessary, start your computer, and log in with your UasAdmin user name and password.

2. In this step, you start ConsoleOne and observe the GroupWise objects before adding the snap-ins:

   a. Start ConsoleOne, and expand **UAS_Tree**.

   b. If necessary, scroll down and expand the **GroupWise System** object.

   c. Expand the **UASWorld** object.

   d. On your student answer sheet, describe the icons next to the UASPO and UASWorld GroupWise objects.

   e. Right-click the **UASPO** post office object, and click **Properties** to open the Properties of UASPO dialog box. Record the available tabs on your student answer sheet.

   f. Click **Cancel** to close the Properties of UASPO dialog box and return to the main ConsoleOne window.

   g. Exit ConsoleOne.

3. Use My Network Places to navigate to the \\UASHOST\CORP\Gwise6\Grpwise\Software\ Admin\C1Admin\Snapins directory:

   a. Double-click **My Network Places**, and then double-click **Novell Connections** to display your UASHOST server.

   b. Double-click the **UASHOST** server icon to display all volumes.

   c. Double-click the **CORP** volume object to display all directories.

   d. Double-click the **Gwise6**, **Grpwise**, **Software**, **Admin**, and **C1Admin** directories to display the Groupwise ConsoleOne directories.

4. Click **Edit**, **Select All** on the My Network Places menu bar to select all GroupWise ConsoleOne subdirectories.

5. Click **Edit**, **Copy** on the menu bar, and then close the C1Admin directory window.

6. Use My Computer to navigate to your C:\Novell\ConsoleOne\1.2 directory:

   a. Double-click the **My Computer** icon, and then double-click your **Local Disk (C:)** icon to display all directories on your C: drive.

   b. Double-click the **Novell**, **ConsoleOne**, and **1.2** directories to display the existing ConsoleOne subdirectories.

7. Click **Edit**, **Paste** on the My Computer menu bar, and then click **Yes to All** to copy the new ConsoleOne GroupWise software into your ConsoleOne\1.2 subdirectory.

8. Close the 1.2 directory window.

9. Start ConsoleOne. If this is the first time ConsoleOne has been started with the GroupWise snap-ins, the GroupWise Administrator dialog box opens, asking for the domain path to the GroupWise domain database:

   a. Click the **Browse** button to select your M: drive, navigate to the **Mail\UASWorld** directory, and then click the **wpdomain.db** database filename.

   b. Click the **Open** button to insert the path to the wpdomain.db database into the Domain Path text box, and then click **OK** to start ConsoleOne.

10. In this step, you start ConsoleOne and observe the GroupWise objects after adding the snap-ins:

    a. If necessary, expand the **GroupWise System** and **UASWorld** objects.

11

b. Right-click the **UASPO** post office object, and click **Properties** to open the Properties of UASPO dialog box. Record the available tabs on your student answer sheet.

c. Click **Cancel** to close the Properties of UASPO dialog box and return to the main ConsoleOne window.

11. Exit ConsoleOne, and log out.

Creating GroupWise Post Office Users

After installing and configuring the GroupWise software, an ongoing task is assigning new users to mailboxes and creating additional GroupWise post office objects, such as rules, nicknames, and distribution lists. As in the U.S. postal system, users need to be assigned to post offices to send and receive e-mail. During the GroupWise configuration, Eric was able to assign all users in the UAS Organization to the GroupWise 6 post office. To allow new users as well as users in other organizations to send and receive messages, Eric needed to assign them to the post office. In GroupWise, you can assign users to post offices in the following ways:

- Assign existing eDirectory users to a post office

- Assign an existing GroupWise account to a different eDirectory user

- Assign a new user to a post office when creating the user account

- Create a GroupWise external entity

In the following sections, you learn how Eric used ConsoleOne to perform these methods for assigning users to post offices. If you have access to a user name and password with the Supervisor right to your UAS_Tree, you can use ConsoleOne on your workstation to perform the following activities.

Assigning eDirectory Users to a Post Office

The best way to assign several users to a post office is to use ConsoleOne to select the GroupWise post office object and then use the Membership tab to add the user accounts. In the following activity, you use ConsoleOne to assign some of your users to the UASPO post office.

Activity 11-5: Assigning Existing Users to a Post Office

Time Required: 15 minutes

Objective: Use ConsoleOne to assign existing users to a post office.

Description: In this activity, you use ConsoleOne to add users to the membership list of the UASPO post office. To perform this activity, your user name should have been assigned the Supervisor right to the UASWorld GroupWise object and all rights except Supervisor and Access Control to the Gwise6 directory structure. All users in a post office must have unique names. Because you are sharing the post office with other students, before adding your users to the UASPO post office, you will need to rename the user objects in your Mgmt container so that their names are different from users in other student Mgmt containers. In Step 3 of this activity, you'll rename your Mgmt users so that their user names are preceded by your student number.

1. If necessary, start your computer, and log in with your UasAdmin user name and password.

2. Start ConsoleOne, and expand **UAS_Tree** and your **##UAS** container.

3. Rename the users in your Mgmt OU so that your student number precedes each user's name:

a. Click your **Mgmt** OU to display all user names in the Object frame.

b. Right-click a user name, and then click the **Rename** option.

c. Enter your assigned student number before the user name, and click **OK** to save the new name.

d. Repeat Steps 3b and 3c for each user.

4. If necessary, scroll down and expand the **GroupWise System** object, and then expand the **UASWorld** object.

5. Right-click the **UASPO** office, and then click **Properties** to open the Properties of UASPO dialog box (see Figure 11-13).

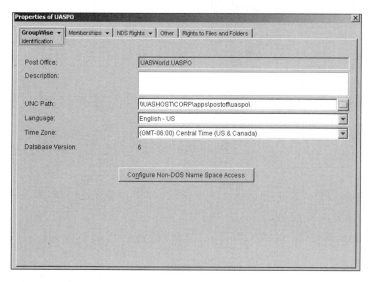

Figure 11-13   The Properties of UASPO dialog box

6. Click the **down arrow** on the GroupWise tab, and on your student answer sheet, record the available options.

7. Click the **Membership** option to display the Users text box.

8. Click the **Add** button to open the Select Object dialog box.

9. Navigate to your Mgmt.##UAS OU, and select all users by holding down the **Ctrl** key as you click on each user name.

10. Click the **OK** button to add your users to the Users text box.

11. Click **Apply** and then **Close** to update the mailbox assignments and return to the ConsoleOne window.

12. Users can also be added one at a time by using their Properties dialog boxes. In this step, you rename your RPence user in the Mfg OU and then add him to the UASPO post office:

   a. If necessary, expand **UAS_Tree** and your **##UAS** Organization.

   b. Click your **Mfg** OU to display all users in the Object frame.

   c. Right-click your **RPence** user, and click **Rename**.

   d. Enter your assigned student number before RPence's name, and click **OK** to change the user name.

   e. Right-click your **##RPence** user name, and then click **Properties** to open the Properties of ##RPence dialog box.

   f. Click the **GroupWise** tab to display a GroupWise account information window, similar to the one shown in Figure 11-14.

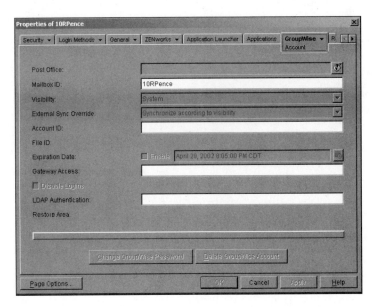

Figure 11-14 Viewing information on a GroupWise user account

g. Click the **Browse** button next to the Post Office text box to open the Select Object dialog box.

h. Double-click the **UASWorld** object to display the UASPO post office object.

i. Click the **UASPO** post office object, and then click **OK** to insert it into the Post Office text box.

j. Click the **Apply** button to assign Russ to the UASPO post office.

k. Click **Close** to return to the main ConsoleOne window.

13. If you're continuing to the next activity, leave ConsoleOne open and stay logged in; if not, exit ConsoleOne, and log out.

Activity 11-6: Assigning New Users to a Post Office

Time Required: 10 minutes

Objective: Use ConsoleOne to assign new users to a post office.

Description: Eric assigned all new users in the AeroDyn division to the post office when he created the new user accounts. In this activity, you create a new account in your AeroDyn container and then select the option to assign the new user to the post office.

1. If necessary, start your computer, and log in with your UasAdmin user name and password.

2. If necessary, start ConsoleOne, and expand **UAS_Tree** and your **##UAS** container.

3. Expand your **Mfg** container, and then click the **AeroDyn** OU.

4. Brenda Bohle has recently been hired at the AeroDyn division to implement some new Windows 2000 application servers. Create a new user named BBohle in the AeroDyn container by following these steps:

a. Click the **New User** button to open the New User dialog box.

b. Enter **##BBohle** in the Name text box (replace ## with your assigned student number).

c. Enter **Bohle** in the Surname text box.

d. Click the **Define additional properties** check box, and then click **OK** to create the new user account and open the Set Password dialog box.

e. Assign Brenda a password you can remember, and then click the **Set Password** button to open the Properties of ##BBohle dialog box.

5. Click the **GroupWise** tab, and then repeat Step 12 of Activity 11-5 to assign Brenda to the UASPO post office.

6. Click **Apply** and then click **Close** to save your changes and return to the main ConsoleOne window.

7. Exit ConsoleOne, and log out.

Creating a GroupWise External Entity

External entities are typically used to allow non-eDirectory users to have an account in a GroupWise post office. An external entity appears in the GroupWise address book for e-mail address purposes and in the eDirectory tree for administrative purposes. For example, there are user e-mail accounts for each of UAS's major customers, such as NASA administrators. To make it easier to send e-mail to these customers, Eric created external entities for the commonly used e-mail addresses. In the following activity, you use ConsoleOne to create an external entity in the UASPO post office.

Activity 11-7: Creating an External Entity

Time Required: 10 minutes

Objective: Use ConsoleOne to assign an external entity to a post office.

Description: Because UAS works with several NASA personnel and has a main contact at each supplier and subcontractor site, David would like the IS department to create external entities for these users. In this activity, you use ConsoleOne to create an external entity for a NASA contact.

1. If necessary, start your computer, and log in with your UasAdmin user name and password.

2. Start ConsoleOne, and expand the **GroupWise System** and **UASWorld** objects.

3. Right-click the **UASPO** object, and point to **New** to display the GroupWise object types that can be created. Record the available types on your student answer sheet.

4. Click the **External Entity** object type to open the Create GroupWise External Entity dialog box, shown in Figure 11-15.

5. Enter **Jerry** in the GroupWise Object ID text box.

6. Enter **Tayler** in the Last Name text box.

7. Click the **Browse** button next to the Container text box to navigate to your Mgmt container, and click **OK** to add .Mgmt.##UAS to the Container text box.

8. In the External Network ID text box, type **JerryT@nasa.gov**.

9. Click the **Define additional properties** check box, and click **OK** to create the external entity and open the Properties of Jerry dialog box.

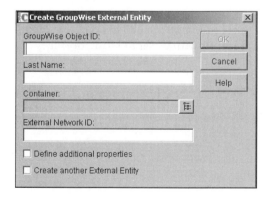

Figure 11-15   The Create GroupWise External Entity dialog box

10. Enter **IIS Medical Facility Manager** in the Title text box, and then click **OK** to save your changes and return to the main ConsoleOne window.

11. Exit ConsoleOne, and log out.

Creating Additional GroupWise Post Office Objects

ConsoleOne can also be used to create a variety of other post office objects, including GroupWise rules, nicknames, distribution lists, and resources. GroupWise **rules** contain actions that are applied to any incoming message that meets the specified conditions. For example, Eric created an out-of-the-office rule to use when he's away from the office; the rule sets up a response to e-mails with a message telling the sender when he will return. Eric's out-of-the-office rule returns the message "I will not be back in the office until Monday, April 15. In case of any urgent communication, please contact Luke McMann at LMcMann@uas.com." Rules can also be used to move incoming messages to predetermined folders based on the sender's e-mail address, subject, or character string in the message text. Eric uses this rule to help screen "junk" messages into a special folder so that he can quickly review and delete them.

A GroupWise **nickname** allows you to assign an additional e-mail name to a user and can be used to identify a role or job position, such as Payroll or Billing. By using nicknames, people can send messages to the role name if they don't know the name of the user currently assigned to that role. If another user takes on the responsibility of the role, the nickname can simply be removed from one user and applied to the new user. Eric set up nicknames for Accounting, Engineering, and Support.

A GroupWise **distribution list** is a set of users and resources that can be addressed as a group by using a unique name. Eric uses distribution lists to create e-mail groups for each department and for the entire organization. If management personnel want to send an announcement to all users in the organization, for example, they can simply select the name of the company distribution list in the To field.

GroupWise **resources** are physical assets that can be checked out or scheduled. For example, Eric created resource objects for the conference room, company vehicle, and audiovisual equipment. Because resource objects are assigned to an owner who makes decisions on scheduling and allocating the assigned resources, they must be created in the same post office as the user account assigned to them. In the following activity, you use ConsoleOne to create these additional GroupWise objects.

Activity 11-8: Creating Additional GroupWise Objects

Time Required: 10 minutes

Objective: Use ConsoleOne to create GroupWise objects.

Description: After the user mailbox accounts were set up, Eric made the GroupWise system more efficient by creating nicknames, distribution lists, and resources. In addition, he held a brief training session to show users basic GroupWise operations, including how to create rules to help manage their incoming messages. In this activity, you perform some of the same tasks by creating a distribution list for your organization, assigning resources for the conference room and the company vehicle, and setting up a computer support nickname.

1. If necessary, start your computer, and log in with your UasAdmin user name and password.

2. Start ConsoleOne, and expand **UAS_Tree** and the **GroupWise System** object.

3. Create a distribution list for the IS department:

   a. Right-click the **UASPO** object, point to **New**, and click **Distribution List** to open the Create GroupWise Distribution List dialog box.

   b. Enter **IS Department** in the Distribution List Name text box.

   c. Click the **Browse** button next to the Container text box to navigate to and select your IS.##UAS OU.

   d. Click **OK** to create the distribution list.

4. Create a resource object:

    a. Right-click the **UASPO** object, point to **New**, and click **Resource** to open the Create GroupWise Resource dialog box.

    b. Enter **Conference##** in the Resource Name text box.

    c. Click the **Browse** button next to the Container text box to navigate to and select your ##UAS Organization.

    d. Click the **Browse** button next to the Owner text box to open the Select Object dialog box.

    e. Click your **##DHeise** user, and click **OK**.

    f. Click **OK** to create the resource object and return to the main ConsoleOne window.

5. Repeat Step 4 to create a resource named ##CompanyVehicle in your ##UAS Organization owned by your ##LDai user.

6. Assign a nickname of Support to your ##BBohle user:

    a. If necessary, expand your **GroupWise System** object.

    b. Click the **UASPO** object to display all e-mail users.

    c. Right-click your **##BBohle** user, and click **Properties** to open the Properties of ##BBohle dialog box.

    d. Click the **down arrow** on the GroupWise tab, and then click the **Nicknames** option.

    e. Click **Add** to open the Create Nickname dialog box.

    f. Click the **Browse** button next to the Domain PO text box to select your UASPO object.

    g. Enter **Support** in the Object ID text box.

    h. Enter **A+ Computer Support Technician** in the Given Name text box.

    i. Click **OK** to add the nickname to the GroupWise Nicknames text box.

    j. Click **OK** to save your changes and return to the main ConsoleOne window.

7. Exit ConsoleOne, and log out.

Deleting and Renaming Post Office Objects

When users leave the organization or change their names, or when you need to make modifications such as changing nicknames, removing resources that are no longer available, or deleting obsolete distribution lists, you must be able to remove and rename post office objects. User objects can be deleted from the entire eDirectory system or from just the GroupWise post office. When you use ConsoleOne to delete a user object from an eDirectory container, you are prompted to specify which attributes to delete, as shown in Figure 11-16.

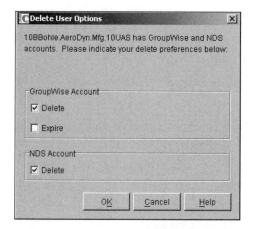

Figure 11-16   The Delete User Options dialog box

You might need to change GroupWise mailbox names if a user's name changes, if you need to implement a new naming convention for your organization, or if there are duplicate names. When you change a user mailbox name with ConsoleOne, the following changes take place throughout the entire GroupWise system:

- The user's mailbox is renamed and the address book is updated. The contents of the old mailbox are maintained with the new name.

- Distribution lists are updated with the new mailbox name.

- Any resources owned by the user are reassigned to the new user mailbox name.

- Any personal groups that contain the user name are updated as part of the nightly maintenance the POA performs.

When you rename a user mailbox, the post office database information for the user's mailbox is changed and the user database is updated. The information in the user mailbox is updated through the following process:

1. The administrator uses ConsoleOne to rename the user mailbox.

2. ConsoleOne writes the information to eDirectory, updates the domain database (Wpdomain.db), and creates an administrative message in the MTA input queue to replicate the update to other GroupWise servers.

3. The MTA transfers the administrative message to the MTA "in progress" queue and communicates the administrative message to the POA.

4. The POA creates a copy of the administrative message in the post office priority queue.

5. The POA updates the Wphost.db file for the post office to reflect the modification and deletes the administrative message from its administrative queue.

6. The POA updates the user's database with the user's new name.

In the following activity, you practice removing a user from the post office, renaming a user account, and deleting nicknames and resources.

Activity 11-9: Deleting and Renaming Post Office Objects

Time Required: 10 minutes

Objective: Use ConsoleOne to delete and rename GroupWise objects.

Description: Maintaining the GroupWise system is an ongoing task that often requires creating, renaming, and removing objects. In this activity, you rename and remove some of the post office objects you created in previous activities.

1. If necessary, start your computer, and log in with your UasAdmin user name and password.

2. Start ConsoleOne, and expand **UAS_Tree** and your **##UAS** container.

3. Use the ConsoleOne eDirectory view to rename your ##BBohle account to ##BrendaB:

   a. Expand the **Mfg** OU.

   b. Click the **AeroDyn** OU to display all users in the Object frame.

   c. Right-click your **##BBohle** user, and then click **Properties** to open the Properties of ##BBohle dialog box.

   d. Click the **GroupWise** tab to display a GroupWise account information window.

   e. In the MailboxID text box, change the name to **##BrendaB**.

   f. Click **Apply** and then click **Close** to change the mailbox ID and return to the main ConsoleOne window.

4. Use the GroupWise view method to change the ##BrendaB mailbox ID to ##Brenda:

   a. Expand the **GroupWise System** object and the **UASWorld** object.

b. Click the **UASPO** object to display all post office users in the Object frame.

c. Right-click your **##BrendaB** user, and then click **Rename** to open the GroupWise Rename ##BrendaB dialog box.

d. Enter **##Brenda** in the New GroupWise name text box.

e. Click **OK** to make your change and return to the GroupWise view.

5. Delete the Company Vehicle resource you created in Activity 11-8:

a. Click your **##UAS** Organization to display all objects in the Object frame.

b. Right-click your **##CompanyVehicle** resource, and then click **Delete NDS Object** to display the Delete message box.

c. Click **Yes** to delete the object.

6. Exit ConsoleOne, and log out.

Establishing Mailbox Security

Mailbox security can be set by the administrator or by users. Users can assign passwords to their mailboxes to prevent unauthorized access and must assign a separate password as a security measure when running the client in remote or cached mode (the user's messages are stored on the local hard drive). In addition to changing and setting passwords, administrators can set post office security levels that apply to users who do not have passwords set on their mailboxes; they can be set to low security or high security. If low security is selected, user mailboxes without passwords are left unprotected. With the high security setting, users need to have a password for their GroupWise mailbox or log in to the Novell network before accessing their mailbox. Eric used ConsoleOne to set the high security level on the UAS GroupWise system by following these steps:

1. In the ConsoleOne window, he expanded the GroupWise System object and then the UASWorld object.

2. He right-clicked the UASPO post office object and clicked Properties to open the Properties of UASPO dialog box.

3. He then clicked the down arrow on the GroupWise tab and clicked the Security option.

4. In the Security Level section, he clicked the High radio button, and then clicked the NDS Authentication check box, as shown in Figure 11-17.

5. Eric clicked Apply and then Close to save his changes and return to the main ConsoleOne window.

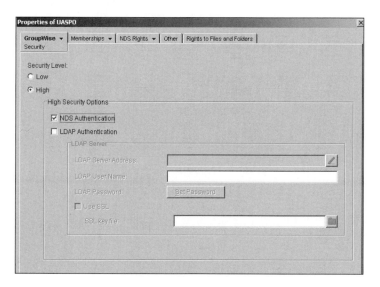

Figure 11-17   Setting security levels in GroupWise

MONITORING AND TROUBLESHOOTING A GROUPWISE SYSTEM

As with other computerized systems, monitoring performance and troubleshooting problems are ongoing tasks of system administration. In the following sections, you learn how to use the Web Console utility from your Web browser to view information on the performance of your GroupWise system. In addition, you learn how to identify and troubleshoot some common GroupWise implementation problems.

Monitoring GroupWise Agents

The two major agents for monitoring and managing the GroupWise system are the Message Transfer Agent (MTA) and Post Office Agent (POA). As described previously, the MTA is responsible for transferring messages between user mailboxes located on the same or different post office servers. The POA is responsible for communication between the client and the post office server. The POA transfers messages from the client to the server and enables the client to read any new messages in the user mailbox. Both the MTA and POA are objects in the eDirectory tree that are initially created and configured during GroupWise installation. Like other eDirectory objects, the MTA and POA objects can be viewed or modified by using ConsoleOne. The MTA and POA also have startup files in the SYS:System\Agents directory that contain agent startup and configuration information. For example, the user name, password, and port number for the agent are stored in both the agent startup file and the eDirectory object. The MTA user name and password for the UAS GroupWise system are stored in the startup file, as shown in Figure 11-18. Notice that GroupWise has shortened the name of the startup file from UASWorld to UASWorl.MTA to meet internal GroupWise requirements.

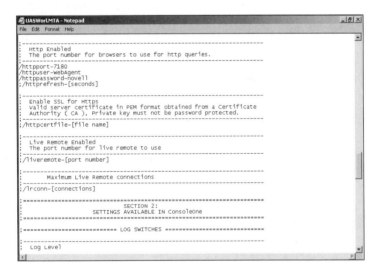

Figure 11-18 The MTA startup file

The UAS POA user name and password are stored in the UASPO.POA file (see Figure 11-19).

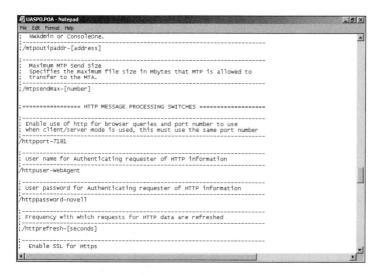

Figure 11-19   The POA startup file

To make the system more secure, Eric used ConsoleOne to place the user name and password in the eDirectory tree and then modified the startup files to remove the user name and password entries. In the following activity, you use ConsoleOne to view information about the MTA and POA objects in your GroupWise system.

Activity 11-10: Viewing Agent Configurations with ConsoleOne

Time Required: 10 minutes

Objective: Use ConsoleOne to view MTA and POA object configurations.

Description: Eric used ConsoleOne to enter a user name and password for the MTA and POA objects. In this activity, you use ConsoleOne to view your MTA and POA object configurations.

1. If necessary, start your computer, and log in with your UasAdmin user name and password.

2. Start ConsoleOne, and expand **UAS_Tree** and **the classroom ##UAS** container.

3. Click the **UASWorld** object under the UAS Organization to see the MTA in the Object frame.

4. Right-click the **MTA** object, and then click **Properties** to open the Properties of MTA dialog box. Record the TCP/IP address and port number on your student answer sheet.

5. Click the **down arrow** on the GroupWise tab, and record the available options on your student answer sheet.

6. Click the **Agent Settings** option to display the Agent Settings dialog box, similar to the one in Figure 11-20. Record any HTTP settings on your student answer sheet.

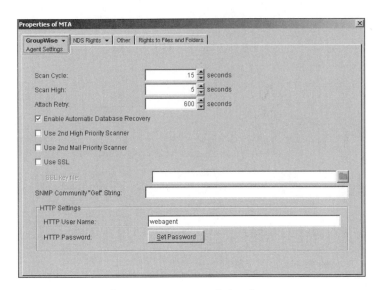

Figure 11-20   The Agent Settings dialog box

7. Click the **Cancel** button to close the Properties of MTA dialog box and return to the main ConsoleOne window.

8. Click the **UASPO** object to display the POA in the Object frame.

9. Right-click the **POA** object, and then click **Properties** to open the Properties of POA dialog box. Record the TCP/IP address and port number on your student answer sheet.

10. Click the **down arrow** on the GroupWise tab, and then click the **Agent Settings** option.

11. Record the CPU Utilization and Disk Check Delay figures on your student answer sheet. Scroll down and record any HTTP information on your student answer sheet.

12. Click **Cancel** to return to the main ConsoleOne window.

13. Exit ConsoleOne, and log out.

Using the Novell Web Console Utility

The Novell Web Console utility enables administrators to view statistics and other configuration information about the MTA and POA running on the GroupWise server. To use Web Console to access agent information, you need to provide your Web browser with the IP address and port number of the agent you want to access. After entering this information, you enter the user name and password identified during agent installation and configuration. In the following activities, you use Web Console to view statistics about your GroupWise system by accessing the POA and MTA.

Activity 11-11: Viewing MTA Statistics

Time Required: 15 minutes

Objective: Use Web Console to view MTA operations.

Description: Eric uses the Web Console utility to periodically document agent statistics on the MTA and POA. In this activity, you use Web Console to log in to the MTA and record statistics on your student answer sheet.

1. If necessary, start your computer, and log in with your UasAdmin user name and password.

2. Start your Web browser and enter the URL **http://ip_address:7100** (replacing *ip_address* with the IP address of your GroupWise server).

3. Log in with the user name Webagent and the password of novell to display the Web Console window, similar to the one in Figure 11-21. (If necessary, your instructor will supply a user name and password for your system.)

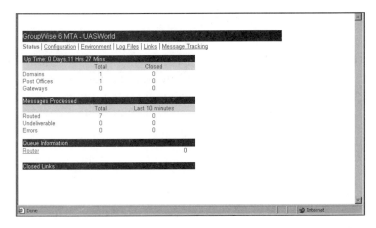

Figure 11-21   Viewing MTA information in the Web Console utility

    4. Use Web Console to answer the questions on your student answer sheet.

    5. Exit your Web browser.

    6. If you're continuing to the next activity, stay logged in; if not, log out.

Activity 11-12: Viewing POA Statistics

Time Required: 15 minutes

Objective: Use Web Console to view POA operations.

Description: Eric uses the Web Console utility to periodically document agent statistics on the MTA and POA. In this activity, you use Web Console to log in to the POA and record statistics on your student answer sheet.

    1. If necessary, start your computer, and log in with your UasAdmin user name and password.

    2. Start your Web browser and enter the URL **http://*ip_address*:1677** (replacing *ip_address* with the IP address of your GroupWise server).

    3. If necessary, log in with the user name Webagent and the password of novell to display the GroupWise 6 POA Web Console window, similar to the one in Figure 11-22. (If necessary, your instructor will supply a user name and password for your system.)

    4. Use Web Console to answer the questions on your student answer sheet.

    5. Exit your Web browser, and log out.

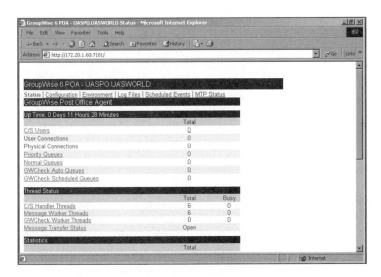

Figure 11-22   Viewing POA information in the Web Console utility

11

Identifying and Troubleshooting E-mail Problems

Problems in GroupWise e-mail systems can occur for both internal and external reasons. Internal problems are usually caused by configuration or operational problems with the client or server. Common internal problems are incorrect IP addresses, insufficient disk space for mail storage and forwarding, and incorrect routes specified for transfers between e-mail servers. External problems are often the result of problems in the connectivity channel used to transfer information between e-mail components. Common problems associated with the GroupWise system include the following:

- A corrupt mailbox database
- Shortage of mailbox space
- Queue overloads
- Connectivity problems
- E-mail virus problems

In the following sections, you learn the steps Eric took to prevent these possible problems.

Corrupt Mailbox Database

E-mail databases require periodic maintenance to clean up old user names, remove incorrect addresses, and check the relationship between addresses and their related mailboxes. In his GroupWise training, Eric learned that periodically performing the following mailbox maintenance tasks is the best way to protect the GroupWise system from mailbox corruption:

- Validating post office databases
- Recovering databases
- Rebuilding databases and their indexes

Eric learned that the frequency of performing these maintenance tasks depends on the reliability of your network and your own experience and knowledge of how often problems are likely to occur.

Mailbox Space Problems

Not maintaining the space used by mailboxes can result in a database that consumes more space than is allocated, causing the e-mail system to run out of disk space and possibly crash. One solution is to limit the size of the mailbox database and have users download and archive e-mail to their local computers. Although this approach saves space on the server, it requires users to be at their local computers to access downloaded or archived e-mail messages and attachments. The following tasks can help manage disk space use in the post office:

- Obtaining mailbox statistics from the Web Console utility
- Reducing the size of user and message databases
- Reclaiming disk space from post office databases
- Reducing the size of library and document storage areas

Queue Overloads

Excessive e-mail on a server, known as queue overload, can shut down the GroupWise e-mail server. The **queue** is a space in the e-mail database where the server temporarily stores outgoing messages while waiting to contact the destination server at a predefined interval. Using predefined intervals helps ensure maximum use of network bandwidth. The most common cause of queue overload is a heavy message load on an old e-mail server with slow performance. The slower hardware cannot clear the data in the queue as fast as new e-mail comes in, causing the backlog of e-mail in the queue to grow until the queue is overloaded, thus shutting down the server. Queue overloads can also be caused by slow bandwidths that prevent moving messages from the queue as fast as they are being generated or e-mail viruses that propagate by sending e-mail to all users in an address list. The attachment containing the virus code can infect other clients as it's distributed via e-mail; this type of virus attack can rapidly escalate, causing a queue overload problem.

Connectivity Problems

Connectivity problems are often caused by faulty hardware or incorrect driver software. If a router or switch on the network is faulty, it can cause delays in transferring data from the server, causing e-mail server problems such as queue overloads. Connectivity problems can also be caused by faulty network configurations and cable layouts that cause data collisions, slowing data flow. Network board problems on the server are fairly easy to identify because they prevent clients from connecting to the server. To help identify possible connectivity problems, Eric obtained network monitor software to view network activity, including collisions, bad network connections, and defective cards. Network monitoring software, such as LANalyzer, ManageWise, and Z.E.N.works for Servers, is available from Novell. Other organizations, such as Computer Associates and Hewlett-Packard, also provide good network monitoring tools.

Virus Problems

E-mail systems automate many tasks to assist users when forwarding messages or opening attachments. Many e-mail virus programs, called worms, are executable programs that replicate themselves by using the resources in e-mail programs or by taking advantage of known security weaknesses in the e-mail client software. To help protect the GroupWise system against viruses, Eric took the following precautions:

- He installed antivirus software on the e-mail server and clients.

- He established a system of regular updates to the antivirus software.

- He trained users to use discretion when opening e-mail messages that have executable attachments. Eric informed users that they should not open e-mail with attachments from unknown users. E-mail messages with "suspicious" attachments, such as .exe., .scr, or .com files, should also be avoided. Eric also informed users that they should not ignore any warning messages from the antivirus software or system administrator.

11

CHAPTER SUMMARY

- ❑ E-mail systems combined with other collaborative applications, such as calendaring, scheduling, and document management, play an important role in a network office environment.

- ❑ E-mail systems consist of client and server components that work together through special programs called agents. The Message Transfer Agent (MTA) is responsible for transferring messages between e-mail servers, while the Post Office Agent (POA) transfers messages between the client and the post office server.

- ❑ Standardized protocols for communicating between e-mail components include POP, IMAP, and SMTP. SMTP is used to transfer messages between the source and destination servers, and POP and IMAP are used to communicate between server and client.

- ❑ Common clients, also referred to as front ends, include Eudora v5.1, GroupWise, Outlook 2002, Outlook Express, and Lotus Notes. All clients support the standard POP3 and IMAP protocols and have specialized capabilities for e-mail and collaborative functions.

- ❑ Common e-mail back-end server products with both e-mail and collaborative applications include Microsoft Exchange 2000 Server, Lotus Domino Mail Server, and GroupWise.

- ❑ GroupWise is installed from an administrative workstation and involves creating directories for GroupWise software and database files, copying files to the GroupWise directories, and configuring agents using an upgraded version of ConsoleOne.

- ❑ Using the GroupWise system for e-mail and collaborative applications involves installing the GroupWise client on the workstation and then logging in and starting the GroupWise client from the workstation desktop.

❐ GroupWise maintenance tasks include assigning users to post offices and creating additional objects, such as distribution lists, rules, and nicknames, to enhance user access and management of messaging.

❐ With the Web Console utility, you can monitor agent statistics from a Web browser for the MTA and POA to assess system performance. Using Web Console requires logging in with a user name and password supplied in the agent startup files or through eDirectory.

❐ Common GroupWise problems, such as corrupted mailboxes, queue overloads, and shortage of disk space, can often by prevented through periodic maintenance tasks, such as validating the post office database information, rebuilding post office database and index files, and installing virus prevention software.

KEY TERMS

AutoComplete addressing — An e-mail client feature used to search the address book for matching names when a user enters an e-mail address.

back-end process — Software such as an e-mail server that processes the data or messages received from the front-end process running on a client.

caching mode — An e-mail client feature that automatically stores all messages and attachments on the local hard disk of the user workstation.

distribution list — A GroupWise object consisting of a set of users who can be addressed as a group by using a unique name.

document management — An e-mail client feature that enables you to share documents with a group of users.

external entity — An object type created to give users outside the organization an account in a GroupWise post office.

front-end process — Software such as an e-mail client that runs on a user's workstation and provides an interface that allows users to communicate with services running on a server.

Internet Message Access Protocol (IMAP) — A standardized protocol used to access and store messages from the post office server.

Message Transfer Agent (MTA) — A software component that assists the core post office software in transferring messages between mailboxes.

mode switching — An e-mail client feature that allows users to change their mailbox modes between online, caching, and remote.

nickname — A GroupWise object that assigns an account name to a role or position in the company.

Post Office Agent (POA) — An e-mail software component that is responsible for transferring messages from the client to the correct mailbox on the e-mail server.

Post Office Protocol (POP) — A standardized client/server protocol used for sending and receiving e-mail messages between the client and the e-mail server.

queue — A space in the e-mail database where the server temporarily stores outgoing messages while waiting to contact the destination server at a predefined interval.

resource — A GroupWise object representing a physical asset that can be checked out or scheduled, such as a conference room or a company vehicle.

rule — A GroupWise object containing actions that are applied to incoming messages that meet certain conditions.

Simple Mail Transfer Protocol (SMTP) — A TCP/IP-based e-mail protocol used to transfer messages between e-mail servers.

REVIEW QUESTIONS

1. Which of the following is *not* an example of a collaborative application?

   a. scheduling

   b. calendaring

   c. FTP

   d. task management

   e. reminders

2. Which of the following is an example of a front-end process?

   a. Domino Server

   b. Web Server

   c. Eudora

   d. Exchange 2002

3. Which of the following assists in transferring messages between the client and the post office server?

   a. MTA

   b. POA

   c. SMTP

   d. SNMP

4. Which of the following protocols is used to transfer messages between e-mail severs?

   a. MTA

   b. POA

   c. SMTP

   d. SNMP

5. Which of the following protocols has features for transferring only address and subject information to the e-mail client?

   a. SNMP

   b. SMTP

   c. IMAP

   d. POP

   e. IMAP4

   f. POP3

6. Moodwatch is a feature of which of the following e-mail clients?

   a. Eudora v5.1

   b. GroupWise

   c. Outlook 2002

   d. Lotus Notes

7. Mode switching is a feature of which of the following e-mail clients?

   a. Eudora v5.1

   b. GroupWise

   c. Outlook 2002

   d. Lotus Notes

11

8. Which of the following GroupWise objects can be used to send e-mail to a role or job position?

    a. distribution list

    b. nickname

    c. resource

    d. rule

9. Which of the following protocols transfers messages between e-mail servers?

    a. POP3

    b. SNMP

    c. SMTP

    d. IMAP4

10. Which of the following is *not* an e-mail protocol?

    a. POP3

    b. SNMP

    c. SMTP

    d. IMAP4

11. Which of the following is *not* a method used to assign a user to a post office?

    a. using ConsoleOne to access the properties of the user object

    b. using ConsoleOne to access the Membership tab from the properties of the post office object

    c. using Web Console to add users to the post office

    d. selecting the post office from the User Properties page while creating the user object

12. Which of the following allows non-eDirectory users to have an account in a GroupWise post office?

    a. nicknames

    b. external entities

    c. alias entities

    d. resources

    e. rules

13. Which of the following is used to represent physical assets?

    a. nickname

    b. external entity

    c. alias entity

    d. rule

    e. resource

14. During installation, user names and passwords for agents are _____.

    a. stored in eDirectory

    b. stored in the Autoexec.ncf startup file

    c. stored in the agent startup file

    d. not assigned

15. The MTA object is stored in which of the following containers?

    a. GroupWise System object

    b. Post Office object

    c. UASWorld domain object

    d. UAS Organization

16. You need to use which of the following to change the configuration of an agent object?

    a. ConsoleOne

    b. Web Console

    c. Remote Manager

    d. NetWare Administrator

17. Which of the following can be used to view statistical information about the performance of the MTA?

    a. ConsoleOne

    b. Web Console

    c. Remote Manager

    d. a text editor, such as Notepad

18. Which of the following are examples of common GroupWise e-mail problems? (Choose all that apply.)

    a. incorrect IP port number assignment

    b. connectivity problems

    c. corrupt mailboxes

    d. mailbox database running out of disk space

19. Which of the following are tasks you can perform to help prevent mailbox corruption? (Choose all that apply.)

    a. limiting the size of user mailboxes

    b. periodically validating mailboxes

    c. periodically rebuilding mailbox indexes

    d. installing antivirus software

20. True or false: Not providing enough memory during GroupWise installation is a common cause of queue overload problems.

UNIVERSAL AEROSPACE CASE PROJECTS

In the following projects, you apply concepts and techniques from this chapter to implementing e-mail services for your Business office users.

Case Project 11-1: Setting Up E-mail Accounts for Business Office Users

In this project, you apply what you have learned about assigning users to the GroupWise post office to assigning all users in your Business container to the UASPO post office.

1. Before performing this task, you need to rename all user accounts in your Business container to include your student number before the user login name.

2. Follow the procedure in Activity 11-5 to assign all users in your Business container to the UASPO post office.

Case Project 11-2: Testing Your E-mail System

In this project, you test your e-mail system by sending messages between users in the Business office and Marketing department.

1. Log in as one of your Marketing department users.

2. Start the GroupWise client.

3. Use the GroupWise Address Book to address a message to your David Heise user. (An e-mail account should have been assigned to David in Activity 11-5.)

4. Enter a message asking David to reply to the status of the NASA contract.

5. Log out.

6. Log in as your David Heise user.

7. Start the GroupWise client and read your e-mail.

8. Send a reply telling the sender that the latest contract for the EVA adapter is expected in the next week.

9. Log out.

10. Log in as the user you used in Step 1.

11. Start the GroupWise client and read David's reply.

12. Try sending e-mail to another student's Marketing user.

13. Document the results of your e-mail tests on your student answer sheet.

Case Project 11-3: Creating Additional GroupWise Objects

In this project, you create a rule that will place all incoming mail containing the word "Rover" in the Subject field into the Rover folder.

1. Log in as one of your Marketing users.

2. Start GroupWise.

3. Create a new mailbox folder named Rover.

4. Use ConsoleOne to create a new rule that places all incoming messages with the word "Rover" in the Rover folder.

5. Log out.

6. Log in as a different user and send a message to the Marketing user you used in Step 1 that contains the word "Rover" in the Subject field.

7. Log out.

8. Log in as the Marketing user from Step 1 and start the GroupWise client.

9. Verify that the message has been placed in the new Rover folder.

10. Log out.

11. Record the results on your student answer sheet.

Case Project 11-4: Creating Distribution Lists

In this project, you create distribution lists for the Marketing and Accounting departments. The Marketing distribution list should include Laura Hiller, Michael Horowitz, and Darrell Minick. The Accounting distribution list should include Terry Blackwell, George Perez, and Amy Pan. Test your distribution list by performing the following steps:

1. Log in using your user name and password.

2. Start the GroupWise client.

3. Send an e-mail to your Marketing distribution list.

4. Log out.

5. Log in as Laura Hiller and start the GroupWise client.

6. Read the message from Step 3 and record your results on your student answer sheet.

12

INSTALLING NETWARE 6

After reading this chapter and completing the exercises, you will be able to:

♦ Describe the components of the X.500 directory service model and identify commonly used directory services, including eDirectory, Active Directory, and Netscape

♦ Identify the installation requirements for NetWare 6 and plan a NetWare 6 installation

♦ Identify and use common console commands and NetWare Loadable Modules (NLMs)

♦ Identify the steps for installing NetWare 6 into an existing network

Although your primary responsibility as a network administrator will be setting up and maintaining the network environment after NetWare has been installed on the server, as a CNA you'll also need to know how to plan for and perform a basic NetWare 6 installation on a new server and upgrade earlier versions of NetWare to NetWare 6. In addition to learning how to install NetWare 6, in this chapter you learn the benefits of upgrading to NetWare 6 and the role that directory services play in network implementation.

DIRECTORY SERVICES

In Chapter 1, you learned that a directory service provides a central means of storing, managing, and accessing information about network objects. Throughout this book, you have applied Novell's eDirectory service to set up, manage, and access network objects, such as users, groups, data volumes, and printers. In addition to providing a way to organize and store network object information, directory services play an important role in integrating different network operating systems into one network system that can be centrally administered and accessed. Having resources from many different operating systems, such as Windows 2000, NetWare, and Unix, work together as one network makes it convenient for users to access information any time, from any computer, without needing to understand how to interact with a different system environment. Novell defines a directory service as a combination of a database and services that provide the following network capabilities:

- Integrate diverse systems to provide centralized organization and management

- Provide users with access to data and resources they need to perform their job duties

- Help provide connectivity between users, both within the organization and across the Internet

- Coordinate organization and network information and resources

 Although Novell uses "Directory" (uppercase) to refer to the directory service technology and "directory" (lowercase) to refer to the folder structure when discussing file storage, in this book the term "directory service" refers to the technology, and the term "directory database" is used for the database of network objects.

The **directory database** is made up of **entries** that store information about network objects. As you learned from working with eDirectory, a directory database stores entries in containers that are organized into a hierarchical tree structure. **Directory services** provide the discovery, security, storage, and relationship management functions that make the information in the database valuable. Currently, several directory services are available from different vendors. A common element of these services is their roots in the X.500 directory standard originally developed by the International Organization for Standardization (ISO) and International Telecommunication Union (ITU) committees in 1988. As a CNA, you'll be required to know the basics of the X.500 standard and be able to identify examples of the following common directory services:

- Novell eDirectory

- Microsoft Active Directory

- Netscape Directory Server 4

In the following sections, you learn the basics of the X.500 standard and review examples of using Active Directory and Netscape Directory Server.

X.500 Directory Standard

The ITU and ISO originally developed the Open Systems Interconnection (OSI) Reference Model to standardize the functional layers that make network communications work between different operating systems and hardware environments. Using the OSI model as a foundation, the ITU later created specifications for a series of recommendations known as **X.500** that define directory services. The first X.500 specification—the Directory Information Model, released in 1988—was a basic model showing how the directory service information should be displayed to the user. With the release of the 1993 X.500 specification, the ITU provided additional models to describe directory services, as shown in Table 12-1.

Table 12-1   X.500 directory service models

Model	Description
User Information Model	Describes how the data from the directory should be displayed to and accessed by the user
Directory Functional Model	Describes the overall operation of the directory service components
Operational and Administrative Information Model	Describes directory service administrative functions
DSA Information Model	Explains how Directory System Agents (DSAs) work together to provide directory access
Directory Distribution Model	Describes how DSAs distribute information between themselves
Directory Administrative Authority Model	Describes how the directory is administered
Security Model	Describes authentication and access control

Generally, the X.500 directory model describes a directory service as a collection of systems that work together to represent information about network objects in the real world. The X.500 directory model contains many components, but the following are the most vital to the operation of a basic directory service:

- Directory Information Base (DIB)

- Directory Information Tree (DIT)

- Directory User Agent (DUA)

- Directory System Agent (DSA)

- Directory Access Protocol (DAP)

- Directory Service Protocol (DSP)

- Directory Information Shadowing Protocol (DISP)

Figure 12-1 illustrates the interrelationship between these directory components. In the following sections, you learn how these basic components work together to create a complete directory service.

Directory Information Base (DIB)

As described earlier, the directory database is made up of objects called entries that contain information about objects in the real world, such as users, printers, computers, and data volumes. These objects are collectively known as the **Directory Information Base (DIB)**. Within the DIB, each entry is made up of a collection of information fields called attributes. As shown in Figure 12-2, each entry is made up of several attributes; each contains one or more values that define information about the network object.

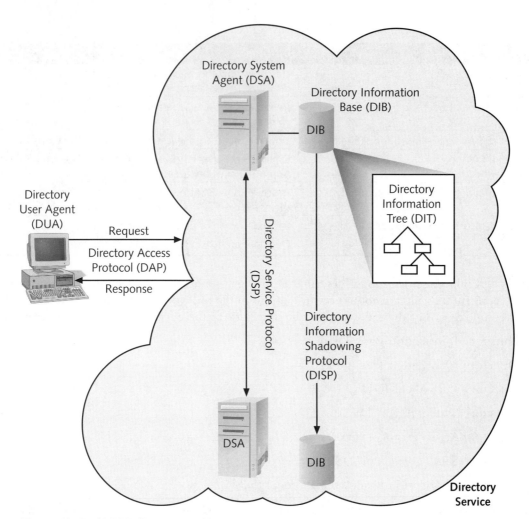

Figure 12-1 X.500 directory service components

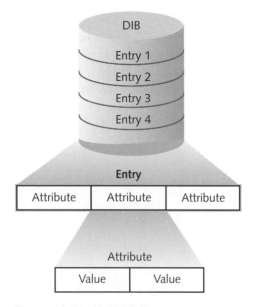

Figure 12-2 X.500 DIB components

Directory Information Tree (DIT)

As you have learned from working with eDirectory, entries in the DIB are stored in one or more containers that act like folders in the file system. Just as subfolders are arranged within folders in the file system, the hierarchical relationship between the containers in the DIB enables them to be arranged into a tree structure called the **Directory Information Tree (DIT)**, shown in Figure 12-3.

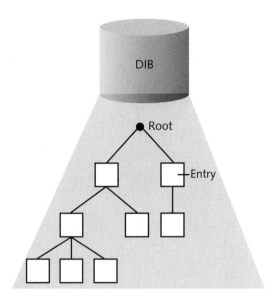

Figure 12-3   Structure of the X.500 DIT

To keep the directory organized, a set of rules known as the **Directory Schema** is enforced to ensure that the information in the DIB is not damaged or lost as modifications are made to it. The Directory Schema defines a set of attributes and valid object classes. An object class defines a type of network object, such as a user or printer, and includes all attributes that make up that object class. The Directory Schema prevents entries from having incorrect attribute types and forces all entries to be a member of a defined object class.

Directory User and Service Agents

The X.500 specification takes a client-server approach in communicating information to the directory. Processing a request for information from the directory service consists of four steps, as illustrated in Figure 12-4. In the first step, the **Directory User Agent (DUA)**, usually running on a user workstation, acts as the client to send requests from the user to the **Directory System Agent (DSA)** running on a server. Next, the DSA uses a collection of services and protocols that manage specific portions of the DIB to search and find the requested information. Third, the information is retrieved from the DIB and sent back to the DSA. The last step is sending the retrieved information from the DSA back to the DUA, where it's presented to the user.

Directory Service Protocols

Directory service protocols handle formatting and communicating requests and responses between DUAs and DSAs. As shown in Figure 12-5, the **Directory Access Protocol (DAP)** handles formatting and transmitting data between the DUA and the DSA.

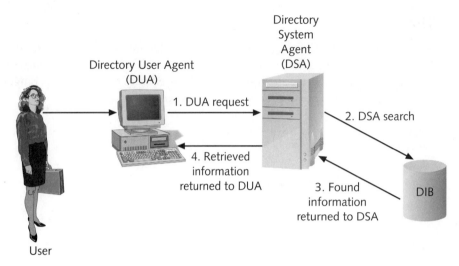

Figure 12-4   Directory agents

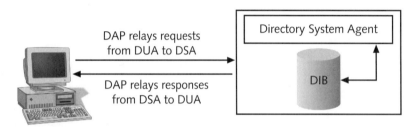

Figure 12-5   The Directory Access Protocol

If a DSA cannot fulfill the request of a DUA, it passes the request to another DSA. Communication between DSAs is accomplished with the **Directory Service Protocol (DSP)**, as illustrated in Figure 12-6.

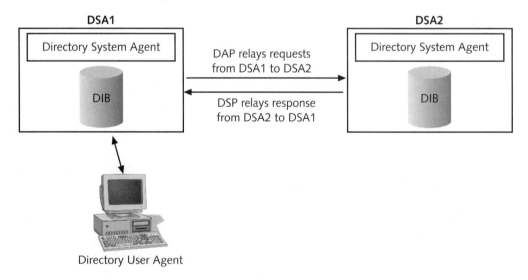

Figure 12-6   The Directory Service Protocol

The **Directory Information Shadowing Protocol (DISP)** is a special DSP that's responsible for keeping multiple copies of the DIB synchronized, as shown in Figure 12-7.

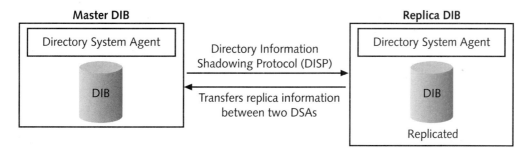

Figure 12-7   The Directory Information Shadowing Protocol

In Chapter 2, you learned that replicating is the process of synchronizing multiple eDirectory databases between NetWare servers. In X.500 terminology, the process of distributing and synchronizing the DIB among multiple locations is called **shadowing**. The Lightweight Directory Access Protocol (LDAP), used in Chapter 4 to import user objects from a Lightweight Directory Interchange Format (LDIF) file, is another important protocol based on the X.500 model. LDAP includes a standardized set of rules for formatting requests for directory services and a naming convention that separates object types by commas. An LDAP-compatible DUA formats a request independent of the network operating system and then sends that request to an LDAP-compatible DSA running on a server computer. The DSA then processes the LDAP request based on the standard set of services and returns the result to the DUA. In this way, any vendor's directory can be made compatible with LDAP by including the ability to process LDAP requests based on the structure of that directory service. Netscape Directory Server, Microsoft Active Directory, and Novell eDirectory are all compliant to varying degrees with LDAP standards, making it possible to transfer and share information between the directory services. Installing a directory service has become an essential part of setting up a network system. Some directory services, such as Netscape Directory Server and Novell eDirectory, can run on multiple types of operating systems, making it possible to integrate various platforms into one directory system. Other vendors' directory services, such as Microsoft Active Directory, are specialized to use the features of that vendor's operating system and cannot be installed on different platforms. However, by providing LDAP compatibility, Microsoft Active Directory information can be accessed and managed from other client environments, such as Linux and Macintosh. In the following section, you learn how to plan ahead for installing eDirectory on a NetWare server.

Activity 12-1: Identifying Directory Service Components

Time Required: 15 minutes

Objective: Identify the X.500 directory service components.

Description: In this activity, use Figure 12-1 to create and label a diagram that includes the following X.500 directory service components:

- Directory System Agent (DSA)
- Directory User Agent (DUA)
- Directory Access Protocol (DAP)
- Directory Service Protocol (DSP)
- Directory Information Base (DIB)
- Directory Information Tree (DIT)

After you have created your diagram of the X.500 components, refer to Chapter 2 to identify and label the following eDirectory components in your diagram:

- NetWare server
- NetWare client
- Master replica

- Read/Write replica
- UAS Organization
- Engineering OU

eDirectory Architecture

Originally known as Novell Directory Services (NDS), the NetWare 6 directory service, eDirectory, is based on X.500 standards and offers several additional features:

- ConsoleOne management of objects, partitions, replicas, and the directory schema
- Client libraries and LDAP tools for Linux, Solaris, and Tru64 Unix
- An import/conversion export (ICE) engine to import or export LDIF files and perform server-to-server migration
- A merge utility for combining eDirectory trees
- The iMonitor utility to monitor and diagnose servers in the tree from a Web browser
- An Index Manager utility to create and manage eDirectory database indexes
- A Filtered Replica Wizard for creating filtered replicas to reduce synchronization traffic between servers
- The ability to run on multiple platforms, including NetWare, Windows NT, Windows 2000, Linux, Solaris, and Tru64 Unix

To properly manage and troubleshoot eDirectory, you need to understand how eDirectory works and how it is different from previous NDS implementations.

NDS Operation

NDS versions that shipped with NetWare 4 and 5 use the RECMAN database, which consists of data and stream files in a hidden directory on the SYS volume. The RECMAN database files use fixed-length record data-storage methods and are used for the following purposes:

- The Partitio.nds file lists the database partitions, which includes the schema and any external references.
- The.Entry.nds file contains records for the properties of each object.
- The Value.nds file contains the property values (attributes) for each object.
- The Block.nds file holds overflow value data from the Value.nds file.

NDS uses Novell's Transaction Tracking System (TTS) to ensure that database transactions, such as creating new objects or changing objects' property values, are completely posted to each file in the RECMAN database. If a system problem prevents all files from being correctly updated, TTS backs out the incomplete transaction from all affected files. The transaction can then be reapplied later.

The main difference between the NDS versions that shipped with NetWare 4 and NetWare 5 is the database filenames. Table 12-2 lists the database filenames for both versions of NDS.

Table 12-2 NDS Filenames in NetWare 4 and 5

NetWare 4 NDS Filenames	NetWare 5 NDS Filenames
Entry.nds	0.dsd
Value.nds	1.dsd
Block.nds	2.dsd
Partitio.nds	3.dsd

eDirectory Operation

Instead of the fixed-length record files used in previous versions of NDS, eDirectory uses FLAIM, a highly scalable indexed database. The structure and purpose of the files in this database are different from the NDS database system:

- The NDS.db file acts as the control file for the database and contains the rollback log used to abort incomplete transactions.

- The 00000001.log file in the SYS_NetWare\NDS.rfl directory tracks committed transactions as well as the current transaction. By default, the 00000001.log file is installed in No Keep mode, which means the transactions are eventually overwritten and no additional log files are created. The log file can be changed to Keep mode if additional backup is required. In Keep mode, additional log files named 0000002.log, 00000003.log, and so on are created when specified log file conditions, such as maximum size, are met.

- The NDS.xx files contain all records and indexes stored on the server. When an NDS.xx file reaches the maximum of 2 GB, files named NDS.02, NDS.03, and so forth are created for the remaining data. Limiting these files to 2 GB allows scalability but still offers high performance. The following indexes are maintained in the NDS.xx files to enhance performance:

  - Attribute substring indexes for the CN and uniqueID fields

  - Attribute indexes for the Object Class and dc fields

  - Attribute indexes that include strings beginning with CN, uniqueID, Given Name, and Surname

- The Stream files have an .nds extension and are named with hexadecimal characters (0-9, A-F). Stream files are used to hold information such as print job configurations and login scripts.

In place of the TTS system used to back out incomplete transactions in the NDS system, eDirectory's FLAIM database uses log files to back out and roll forward transactions in the event of a system failure. Completed transactions, called "committed transactions," are placed in the log file. Non-committed, or incomplete, transactions may or may not be placed in the log file. In a system failure, eDirectory can roll forward to reapply any committed transactions in the log file that might not have been fully written to the disk. Earlier versions of NetWare can be updated to use eDirectory 8.6 and take advantage of its higher performance and scalability. These enhancements, along with eDirectory's capability to run on multiple operating systems, make it the most versatile and scalable directory service available today. In this chapter, you learn how to install eDirectory on a new NetWare 6 server and how to upgrade NetWare servers running earlier versions of NDS to the new eDirectory service.

12

PREPARING FOR NETWARE INSTALLATION

As in other network activities, preparation is vital to the success of your NetWare server installation. Preparing for NetWare installation involves determining the server's hardware configuration and identifying the physical and logical network environment where the server will be installed. In the following sections, you learn how to prepare for server installation by following the process Eric Kenton used to identify the hardware configuration and network information for installing NetWare 6 on the UASHOST server.

The Server Planning Worksheet

To perform a successful NetWare 6 server installation, you need to supply information about your server's hardware devices and setup options to the installation program. To help plan for all the information needed during server installation, Eric developed the NetWare Server Planning Form, shown in Figure 12-8.

The form has fields for documenting the server's hardware environment and sections to enter the information required by the installation program. In addition, Eric designed the NetWare Server Planning Form so that it divides the information required during NetWare 6 server installation into nine sections: Server Identification, System Information, Disk Driver Information, Partition Information, Network Card Information, Protocol Information, Server Context, Installation Component Options, and Port Usage. In the following sections, you learn what information is required in each section and apply it to filling out a NetWare Server Planning Form for your NetWare server, as described in Activity 12-2 at the end of this section.

NetWare Server Planning Form

Page 1 of 2

Server Identification

File server name: _UASHOST_   **Server ID #:** _____

Domain name: _uas.com_   Random _X_ or Assigned _____

System Information

Computer make/model: _____

CPU: _Intel Pentium III_   Clock Speed: _1.5 GHz_ Bus: _PCI_

Memory capacity: _512 MB_

Disk Driver Information

Disk Controller 1

    Type: _SCSI_   Manufacturer/model : _Adaptec 2940_

    Interrupt: _5_   I/O address: _340-343_   DMA channel: _3_

    Memory address: _____ - _____

    Disk driver name: _AHA2940_

Drive Address	Type	Speed Manufacturer	Capacity
0	SCSI	Western Digital	12 ms/60GB

Disk Controller 2

    Type: _SCSI_   Manufacturer/model : _Adaptec 2940_

    Interrupt: _11_   I/O address: _350-353_   DMA channel: _3_

    Memory address: _____ - _____

    Disk driver name: _AHA2940_

Drive Address	Type	Speed Manufacturer	Capacity
0	SCSI	Western Digital	12 ms/20GB

Partition Information for Initial Installation

Partition	Type	Pool/Volume/Capacity
1	NSS	SYS_Pool/SYS/4GB

Network Card Information

Card Number	Network Type	Manuf. ID	LAN Driver	Bus	I/O Port	Memory Address	IRQ/DMA
1	100BaseT	Microdyne	NE2000	PCI	300	0D000	10/None

Figure 12-8   NetWare Server Planning Form

NetWare Server Planning Form

Page 2 of 2

Protocol Information

Network card: Microdyne, card number 1
TCP/IP frame type: Ethernet II
IP address: 192.168.1.51
Subnet mask: 255.255.255.0
Gateway: 192.168.1.1
_____ **IPX protocol**

　　　Frame type(s): _802.2_　　　 _____ _____

　　　Network address: _1EEE8022_ _____ _____

Server Context

Tree name: _UAS Tree_　　　 Organization: _UAS_　 Organizational Unit: _____

Installation Component Options: ("D" are installed by default)

　　　_D_　**Novell Certificate Server (Only one per tree)**
　　　_D_　**NDS iMonitor Services**
　　　_D_　**NetWare Remote Manager**
　　　_D_　**Storage Management Services**
　　　_D_　**ConsoleOne 1.3.2**
　　　_X_　**iPrint/NDPS**
　　　___　**NetWare Enterprise Web Server**
　　　___　**NetWare Web Manager**
　　　___　**NetWare FTP Server**
　　　___　**NetWare Web Search**
　　　___　**Novell DNS/DHCP Services**
　　　___　**WAN Traffic Manager Services**
　　　_X_　**Novell Native File Access Protocol**
　　　_X_　**Novell Advanced Audit Service**
　　　___　**NetWare Web Access**
　　　___　**Novell iFolder Storage Services**
　　　___　**eDirectory iManager Service**
　　　___　**Novell NetStorage**

Port Usage

Service	IP Address	Ports	
iFolder	_____	____	____
NetStorage	_____	____	____
iPrint	_____	____	____

Figure 12-8 NetWare Server Planning Form (continued)

Server Identification

Each NetWare server needs a unique identification to communicate with and provide services to the network. The identification information for a NetWare 6 server consists of three major components: the server's name, internal identification number, and DNS name. The server's name can be from 2 to 47 alphanumeric characters and, although it can contain underscores and dashes, no spaces or periods are allowed. The server identification number is used with the IPX protocol to create an internal network within the server for routing packets of data between modules on the software bus. The server ID number can consist of up to eight hexadecimal digits, and can be a random number assigned by the installation program or a specific number identified by the organization. If your server is using IPX to communicate on a WAN with other IPX servers you do not administer, you might want to register your internal IPX number with Novell to make sure it's unique. If you do not need a registered IPX number, the best alternative is to allow the NetWare installation program to assign a random number and then record the assigned internal network number on the NetWare Server Planning Form. Because the UAS server did not need a registered number, Eric selected the Random option to let the installation program supply an eight-digit hexadecimal value. You'll learn how to find and document your server's identification number in the "Working with the Server Console" section.

If your network uses or will be using a DNS server, as described in Appendix B, you should assign a unique DNS name to your NetWare server during installation. Because UAS has registered the domain name "uas.com" on the Internet, Eric selected the name "uashost.uas.com" for the server's DNS name. The same name can then be used to access services from the local intranet or the outside world over the Internet. Before installing NetWare 6, it's important to plan and document the server's name, IPX identification assignment, and domain name on your NetWare Server Planning Form.

System Information

As described in Chapter 1, NetWare is a network operating system (NOS) designed to perform server functions. Essentially, NetWare 6 consists of an operating system kernel (Server.exe) that provides core NetWare server services to the network and a software bus that allows other modules containing specialized services and control functions to be loaded and unloaded, as shown in Figure 12-9.

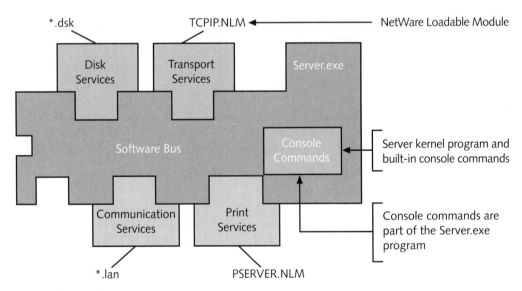

Figure 12-9   NetWare software bus

In addition to providing core NetWare services and support for loadable modules, the NetWare 6 kernel has been designed to support Java applications and provide Internet services using HTTP. These capabilities require additional system resources, such as processor speed and memory, that were not needed in earlier NetWare versions. Because of its modular design, the hardware requirements needed to run NetWare 6 vary based on the number of modules and services that will be loaded and the number of users logging in. The minimum hardware environment for a NetWare 6 server is shown in Table 12-3.

Table 12-3   NetWare 6 minimum hardware requirements

Processor	Although a Pentium II or an AMD K7 processor is required, Novell recommends that a Pentium II 700 MHz or higher be used for improved performance
Disk space	Minimum 200 MB free on DOS partition; 2 GB free space on SYS volume for standard NetWare products, with 4 GB recommended for use with Internet services
Memory	256 MB of RAM for standard NetWare products, with 512 MB recommended for additional services
Network	A NetWare 6-compatible network board
CD drive	A CD drive that can read ISO 9660-formatted CDs
Display adapter	Super VGA or higher
Mouse	Serial, USB, or PS/2 recommended

Eric used the System Information section of the NetWare Server Planning Form to identify the CPU and memory requirements he felt were necessary to meet the processing needs of the modules and services that will be running on the UAS server.

Disk Driver Information

NetWare 6 disk drivers are modular, with separate drivers called **Host Bus Adapters (HBAs)** to manage the controller cards and **Custom Device Modules (CDMs)**, which work with the HBA to control the individual storage devices attached to the controller card. Disk controllers that do not have HBAs and CDMs included with NetWare need to have their NetWare drivers loaded from a floppy disk supplied by the manufacturer before they can be used with NetWare. NetWare 6 includes HBAs and CDMs for Intelligent Drive Electronics (IDE) controllers that can handle most IDE and Enhanced IDE (EIDE) type and drives. Although servers supporting a small number of users and devices can use IDE disk controller cards, large servers that support more storage devices, such as large hard drives, CD-ROMs, and tape backup systems, often use SCSI controllers because they have higher speeds and support a wider range of devices than IDE controllers. To ensure better speed and expansion capability, UAS selected a SCSI disk controller. The company is planning to expand its storage devices in the near future, and SCSI controllers will support additional high-speed disk drives and an optical disk system for archiving engineering designs.

You should also identify the make and model on the NetWare Server Planning Form to be sure that the correct driver is selected during installation. NetWare 6 can detect the most popular IDE and SCSI disk controllers, such as the Adaptec 2940 that UAS uses. Therefore, to make installation simpler, when selecting a SCSI disk controller for a server, check to see that the disk controller you select is included with NetWare. In most cases, you can ensure this by purchasing controller cards that are NetWare 6 certified. Before installation, you should identify the disk system components and drivers to be used on your server, and then document them on your NetWare Server Planning Form.

Partition Information

The next step in preparing for server installation is defining the amount of disk storage to be allocated to DOS and the NetWare system partition. Additional partitions and volumes can be added later, as described in Chapter 3. On a NetWare server, disk storage space is divided into two or more areas called partitions— one partition for use by DOS in starting the server, and the other partitions for use by the NetWare operating system. The DOS partition is quite small; usually 200 MB is sufficient for basic server operation, with 1 GB recommended to hold memory dump files if your server crashes. The remainder of the disk space on the drive is reserved for the NetWare partitions shown on the NetWare Server Planning Form. As described in Chapter 3, all servers require a SYS partition of between 2 and 4 GB. The network administrator creates additional partitions to hold company data. During installation, Eric identified 4 GB of disk space for the SYS partition and left the rest of the hard drive open for company data, which will be placed in separate volumes.

12

Another consideration in planning NetWare partitions is disk mirroring or duplexing. As described in Chapter 3, disk mirroring is the process of duplicating data on two different NetWare partitions. Duplexing occurs when the partitions are on drives attached to different controller cards. To do mirroring or duplexing, the NetWare partitions on the drives to be mirrored must be the same size. Filling out the Partition Information section on your NetWare Server Planning Form with the size of your DOS and NetWare partitions before starting the NetWare 6 installation will help ensure that the correct values are used during the installation.

Network Card Information

To communicate with other devices on the network, a server needs at least one network interface card. Additional NICs can be installed to allow access to the server from multiple network cable systems. When multiple NICs are installed in a server, the server acts as a router, passing packets of data through network cable systems, as shown in Figure 12-10.

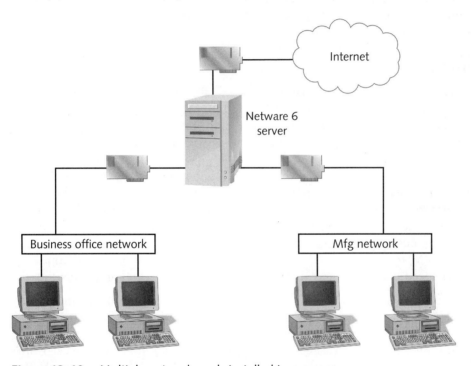

Figure 12-10   Multiple network cards installed in a server

To access NICs, NetWare requires a driver to be identified during NetWare installation. As a result, you need to identify the make, model, and configuration for each NIC in your server before installing NetWare. To make installation easier, NetWare contains drivers for many popular NICs. As with disk controllers, one of the best ways to be sure a driver for your NIC is included with NetWare is to purchase a card that has been Novell certified. During installation, you also need to supply the hardware configuration for the card, which can consist of an interrupt, a Direct Memory Access (DMA) channel, an input/output port, and a memory address. You can configure the card by using special software or by placing jumpers or setting switches on the card itself. The NetWare Server Planning Form shows the network card and configuration Eric identified for use with the UAS server.

Protocol Information

After you have identified the server's hardware environment, the other major consideration is identifying the network environment in which the server will operate. The network environment consists of network protocols along with the network address and any special frame types to be used for each NIC in the server. In addition to providing the legacy IPX (Internet Packet eXchange) protocol, Novell enables NetWare 6 to communicate directly by using TCP/IP. The IPX protocol has the advantages of being simpler to set up and providing compatibility with older NetWare servers and clients. Although more complex to implement, TCP/IP is a more universal protocol and enables you to connect the server to the Internet through an ISP or to provide services directly to a company intranet. Because of the existing clients and applications, UAS has decided to install support initially for both IPX and TCP/IP on the server. After converting all workstations and applications to TCP/IP, the corporation can remove support for IPX from the NetWare 6 servers.

The IPX Protocol

When installing the IPX protocol, each network cable system requires a unique network address and frame type. The **frame type** specifies the format of the data packets to be sent across the network cable. To communicate, all computers need to use a common frame type and network address. Because the default Ethernet frame type used with IPX packets is Ethernet 802.2, Eric has entered Ethernet 802.2 for the frame type on the NetWare Server Planning Form.

The IPX network address works much like a zip code: It allows packets to be efficiently delivered to the correct network of the recipient. As a result, if your network has the first server on the network cable, you can use any network address consisting of up to eight hexadecimal digits. Additional servers attached to the same network cable need to use the same network address of the existing server. As the NetWare Server Planning Form shows, Eric has selected a network address of 1EEE8022 for the 10BaseT network card to stand for the IEEE 802.2 standard used by this Ethernet card.

The TCP/IP Protocol

In addition to the IPX protocol, NetWare supports TCP/IP. The NetWare Server Planning Form can be used to identify TCP/IP information that will be configured during installation. To install support for TCP/IP during installation, you need to supply the server with an IP address and mask. As described in Appendix B, an IP address consists of a 32-bit (four-byte) number divided into a network address and a host (or node) address. The network part of the address must be the same for all computers on the same network cable segment. The host address must be unique for each computer on that network segment. The network mask identifies which bytes in an IP address make up the network address. The number 255 in the network mask identifies the entire byte as part of the network address. Zeros in the network mask identify bits that are part of the host address.

On your NetWare Server Planning Form, determine whether you will be using the IPX protocol. If so, fill in the IPX section with the frame types and corresponding IPX network address information. If you will be using TCP/IP, fill in the Protocol Information section with the IP address, mask, and gateway information.

Server Context

During NetWare installation, you have a choice of placing the new server in an existing tree or creating a new tree. To place the server in an existing tree, you need to be able to log in as the Admin user of the existing tree and enter the context of the container where the server will be created. To create a new tree, you need to determine its name and the context of the container where the new server object and Admin user will be placed. As a result, an important step in preparing for NetWare installation is to identify where the server will be placed in the eDirectory tree. On the NetWare Server Planning Form, Eric has identified the context for the new UASHOST server as being the UAS Organization within a new tree named UAS_Tree.

Installation Component Options

This section is used to identify which components should be installed during the initial server installation. Installing a minimum number of components is recommended, as additional components can be installed later. Selecting multiple components during server installation makes it more difficult to select the correct configuration options for each component. Table 12-4 contains a brief description of each component on the NetWare Server Planning Form.

Table 12-4   NetWare 6 component descriptions

Installation Component	Description
Novell Certificate Server	Provides secure transmission for e-mail, Web sites, and applications using public key cryptography. Required component for the first server installed in a tree. This service is described in Chapter 10.
NDS iMonitor Services	Allows administrators to monitor and manage the eDirectory tree structure from an Internet browser (see Chapter 9).
NetWare Remote Manager	Allows administrators to access and manage the server from an Internet browser (see Chapter 9).
Storage Management Services	Provides backup and restore software (see Chapter 3).
ConsoleOne 1.3.2	Installs ConsoleOne software on the server, enabling access to ConsoleOne through the NetWare X Server - Graphical Console.
iPrint/NDPS	Enables the use of NDPS and iPrint software on the server (see Chapter 8).
NetWare Enterprise Web Server	Installs the NetWare Enterprise Web Server product needed to host Web sites on the server (see Chapter 10).
NetWare Web Manager	Installs the Web Manager product used to manage the Web and FTP services.
NetWare FTP Server	Installs the NetWare FTP server used to host FTP sites on the server (see Chapter 10).
NetWare Web Search	Installs a search engine on the NetWare server that's used to build an index of information on available Web sites.
NetWare DNS/DHCP Services	Installs DNS and DHCP services (described in Appendix B) on the server. After the services are installed, they need to be configured and enabled by using Remote Manager.
WAN Traffic Manager Services	Allows control of WAN traffic through policies that can be applied to the use of WAN links by network services.
Novell Native File Access Protocol	As described in Chapter 2, NFAP allows access to NetWare files directly from workstations without having to install Novell Client.
Novell Advanced Audit Service	Enables auditing of services running on the network.
NetWare WebAccess	Provides an interface to NetWare 6 Web utilities using Novell Portal Services technology. By default, port 2200 is used to access other Web-based utilities, such as iManager and Remote Manager.
Novell iFolder Service	Installs the iFolder service (see Chapter 9).
eDirectory iManager Service	Installs the iManager service needed to manage eDirectory objects from a Web browser (see Chapter 4).
Novell NetStorage	Installs the NetStorage software used to access network files from a Web browser (see Chapter 9).

As shown on the NetWare Server Planning Form, Eric selected only the NDPS, NFAP, and Advanced Audit Service components. He later installed the iFolder, NetStorage, and Web Access components, as described previously in Chapters 9 and 10. During the installation, Eric documented the URLs and port numbers for the component services he installed on the NetWare Server Planning Form. The Port Usage section is for documenting port numbers and IP address information that is important later when you're accessing, troubleshooting, and managing these services. In the following activity, you apply what you have learned about planning for a NetWare 6 installation by filling in a NetWare Server Planning Form for your version of the UAS server.

Activity 12-2: Planning a NetWare 6 Server Installation

Time Required: 30 minutes

Objective: Plan a NetWare 6 server installation.

Description: In this activity, assume you'll be installing a new server for the AeroDyn branch of UAS. Your first step is to get a copy of the NetWare Server Planning Form from Appendix D. You'll use this form to collect and document the information needed for the installation, as described in the previous sections. If you will be installing NetWare 6 on an actual server, you should work with your instructor to determine the server hardware settings for disk partitions and NICs. If you will not be using the NetWare Server Planning Form to perform an actual server installation, you should select a computer you would like to use as the AeroDyn server and then document the hypothetical server's configuration.

1. Make a copy of the NetWare Server Planning Form from Appendix D.

2. Document the server's ID information, including server name, ID number, and domain name, in the Server Identification section.

3. In the System Information section, document system information for the server you'll be installing NetWare 6 on.

4. In the Disk Driver Information section, document your server's disk controller and drive information.

5. In the Partition Information section, identify the type, pool, capacity, and drive to be used for your SYS volume.

6. In the Network Card Information section, identify the make and model of your network card along with any special hardware settings.

7. In the Protocol Information section, identify the TCP/IP address information for your server and indicate whether the IPX protocol will be installed.

8. In the Server Context section, identify the name of the tree and context for your server.

9. Use the Installation Component Options section to select any optional installation components.

10. The Port Usage section will be filled in during the NetWare 6 installation.

INSTALLING NETWARE 6

The NetWare 6 server installation process can be divided into three major phases: preparation of the DOS partition, initial installation and file copying, and graphical user interface (GUI) installation. The GUI installation phase is subdivided into three general steps: server setup, eDirectory installation, and license/component installation. In the next sections, you follow Eric as he performs each installation step to set up the UASHOST server, as documented on the NetWare Server Planning Form.

Phase 1: Preparation of the DOS Partition

There are two paths you can take when preparing the DOS partition: You can let the NetWare installation program create and format the DOS partition for you, or you can manually create and format the partition. If you're using a computer that already has a Windows operating system you want to preserve, you should manually create the DOS partition by using FDISK or the Windows Disk Management utility. If you're installing NetWare 6 on a clean hard drive, you can configure your BIOS to start from the CD-ROM, and then use the NetWare Installation program to create and format a DOS partition. If your computer does not have CD-ROM startup enabled, you can use Windows 98 to make a startup disk and then start the computer from the startup disk and select the Start with CDROM support option. After obtaining a DOS prompt from the startup disk, you enter the drive letter assigned to your CD-ROM drive, type INSTALL, and press Enter to start the initial file copying and text-based installation. To install NetWare 6 on the server, Eric first configured the BIOS to start from the CD-ROM and then performed the following steps to create the DOS partition:

1. First, Eric inserted the CD-ROM in the server and then began the server software installation by starting from the CD-ROM.

2. When the language selection menu was displayed, he pressed Enter to accept the default English language.

3. Next, he selected the Accept License Agreement option, and then pressed Enter.

4. To create a DOS partition, he selected the Create a New Boot Partition option, and then pressed Enter.

5. He pressed Enter to accept the default partition size of 200 MB, selected Continue, and then pressed Enter to create the DOS partition.

6. After the DOS partition was created, he pressed the spacebar to restart the server.

7. After the system restarted, the DOS partition was automatically formatted and the initial file copying began.

Phase 2: Initial Installation and File Copying

The installation program first copies files to the C:\Nwserver directory on the DOS partition and then starts the NetWare server kernel and proceeds with the text-based installation. During this phase, you need to select your installation method, identify the disk and network card drivers, and create the SYS volume. Eric performed the following steps during the initial installation of the UASHOST server:

1. After reading the JReport runtime License Agreement, Eric pressed F10 to continue and display a NetWare Installation window.

2. After pressing Enter to select the Custom installation option, he then pressed the down arrow key to highlight Continue and pressed Enter to open the Server Settings window containing the server ID number, reboot, and SET options.

3. He recorded the server ID number on the NetWare Server Planning Form, and then pressed Enter to continue with the default server settings.

4. He pressed Enter to continue with the default regional settings, including country, code page, and keyboard.

5. He again pressed Enter to continue with the default mouse type and video mode settings and start the initial file copying.

6. Initial files were then copied to the server's C:\Nwserver directory, after which NetWare displayed the window listing device types and driver names, similar to the one in Figure 12-11.

7. Because NetWare 6 detected the Adaptec AHA2940 adapter, Eric simply highlighted the Continue option and pressed Enter to load the detected storage drivers. If the storage drivers had not been automatically detected, he could have used the Modify option to select the correct storage drivers from the list.

8. After the storage device drivers were loaded, a window was displayed, showing the detected network boards, as shown in Figure 12-12.

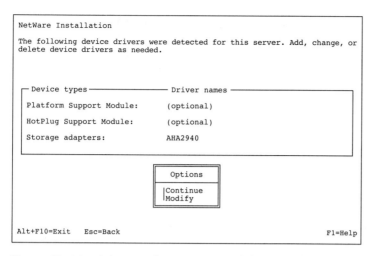

Figure 12-11 Selecting device types and drivers

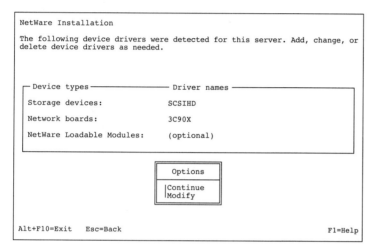

Figure 12-12 The network card information window

9. Because he purchased a Novell-certified NIC, Eric simply verified that the correct driver was detected, highlighted the Continue option, and pressed Enter to continue the installation. If your NIC is not automatically detected, you can use the Modify option and follow these steps to install a NIC driver from a floppy disk:

- Highlight the Modify option, and press Enter.

- Press the down arrow key to highlight the Network Boards field, and press Enter to display the Drivers window.

- Press Insert to display a list of known network board drivers.

- Press the down arrow key to find and highlight your network board, and then press Enter. If your network board is not included in the list, press Insert to display the Path to be Scanned window. Insert a floppy disk containing the drivers, and press Enter again to scan for the driver files. Press Enter to select your driver file.

- Press Enter to return to the Drivers window.

- Press the down arrow key to select the Return to driver summary option, and then press Enter. Your new driver should now appear in the Drivers window.

- Press the down arrow key to return to the Options menu.

- Highlight the Continue option, and press Enter to load the selected network and disk drivers. The network driver will then be loaded.

10. After the installation software detected the drive's free space, Eric saw the Create a NetWare partition and volume SYS window, similar to the one in Figure 12-13.

11. To accept the default size of 4 GB, he highlighted Continue and pressed Enter to begin the file-copying process. During file copying, the installation program creates the system directories on the SYS volume, as described in Chapter 3, and then copies files from the CD-ROM to the correct directories. After file copying is finished, the installation software starts the GUI console to complete the installation.

Phase 3: GUI Installation

Most of the server setup and configuration information is supplied by using the NetWare GUI. The GUI installation can be subdivided into three general phases. In the server setup phase, you supply the server name, create additional volumes, select protocols, supply IP address information, enter the DNS name and domain of the server, and identify your time zone. The eDirectory installation phase involves installing eDirectory and identifying the tree and context information for the server. In the license and component phase, you enter your license information and select additional components. In the following sections, you follow the steps Eric performed in these GUI phases to install NetWare 6 on the UASHOST server.

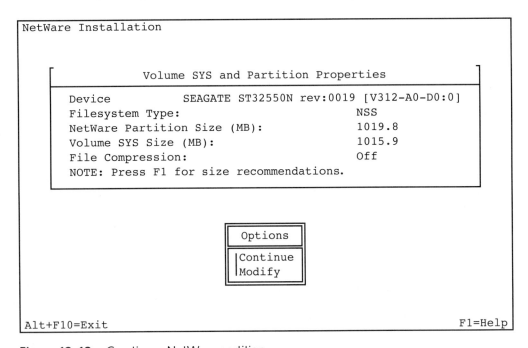

```
NetWare Installation


                      Volume SYS and Partition Properties

        Device                 SEAGATE ST32550N rev:0019 [V312-A0-D0:0]
        Filesystem Type:                       NSS
        NetWare Partition Size (MB):           1019.8
        Volume SYS Size (MB):                  1015.9
        File Compression:                      Off
        NOTE: Press F1 for size recommendations.




                           Options

                           Continue
                           Modify




Alt+F10=Exit                                                   F1=Help
```

Figure 12-13   Creating a NetWare partition

Server Setup

The server setup phase starts with asking for the server name and then proceeds to obtain the initial encryption license information. Before performing this phase, you should have access to a license that contains the Novell Cryptographic License file (extension .nkf) for your server.

1. When asked for the server name, Eric entered UASHOST, and then clicked Next to display the Encryption license window.

2. In the Encryption license window, Eric clicked the Browse button and navigated to the directory on the floppy disk containing his license files. He then clicked the NFK license file and clicked OK to place the filename and path in the Location text box.

3. He then clicked Next to accept the encryption license and display the Configure File System window, similar to the one in Figure 12-14.

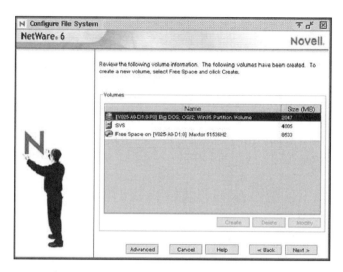

Figure 12-14   The Configure File System window

4. Because Eric was planning to create additional storage pools and volumes later, he clicked Next to accept the existing information and display the Protocols window, similar to the one in Figure 12-15.

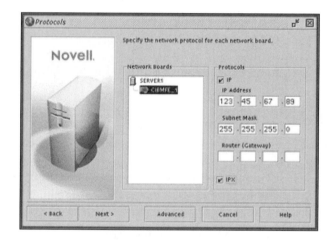

Figure 12-15   The Protocols window

5. Eric clicked the IP check box and entered the server's IP address and subnet mask, as defined on the NetWare Server Planning Form.

6. To install support for the IPX protocol, Eric clicked the IPX check box and then clicked the Advanced button to document the network address assigned to each network frame type on the NetWare Server Planning Form. Eric wanted to be sure that the network address detected for each frame type was the same for all servers using IPX.

7. After documenting the IPX address information, he clicked OK to return to the Protocols window and then clicked Next to display the Domain Name Service window.

8. Eric entered uashost in the Host name text box and entered uas.com in the Domain text box. Because Eric had no DNS server on the network, he left the Verify the DNS information check box and Name Server text boxes blank, clicked Next, and responded to the DNS warning by clicking OK.

9. After completing the DNS information, Eric selected his time zone in the Time Zone window, and then clicked Next to begin the eDirectory installation.

eDirectory (NDS) Installation

The eDirectory installation involves selecting an existing tree or creating a new tree. In either case, you will be asked to enter the context for the new server. When creating a new tree, the installation program asks for the context and password of the Admin user. By default, the Admin user account is created in the same context as the server it's installed into. Eric installed eDirectory on the UASHOST server by performing the following steps:

1. To create a new eDirectory tree, Eric clicked the New NDS tree option, and then clicked Next to display the tree information window.

2. In the tree window, he entered the following data:
   - Tree name: UAS_Tree
   - Context for server: UAS
   - Admin name: admin
   - Admin context: O=UAS
   - Password: Eric started with a password of "novell" and then changed the password later to something more secure.

3. He then clicked Next to install eDirectory and display a summary window. Eric recorded the following information for later reference:
   - eDirectory tree name
   - Server context
   - Administrator name

4. After documenting the preceding information, Eric clicked Next to close the summary window and display the Licenses window.

License and Component Installation

The final phase of the installation process is to locate and select the NetWare server and connection licenses and then select any additional components to install. As a general rule, it's best to select a minimum number of additional components at first and install additional features by using the GUI console. Eric performed the following steps to complete the installation of the UASHOST server by installing the Novell license and selecting the initial server components:

1. Only a single server license can be installed during NetWare 6 installation; user licenses are installed later with iManager. When the Licenses window was displayed, Eric noticed that multiple licenses were listed in the Licenses to be installed section.

2. At this time, only server licenses can be installed. Because more than one license was listed in the Licenses to be installed section, Eric clicked each license to see its description. He then clicked the Remove button to remove all user licenses, leaving only the NetWare 6 Server License in the window.

3. He clicked Next after verifying the license information to display the Components Selection window.

4. The NFAP component was selected by default. Eric also selected the iPrint/NDPS and Novell Advanced Audit Service components, and then clicked Next.
   - iPrint/NDPS
   - Novell Advanced Audit Service (optional)
   - Web Access

5. He clicked Next to accept the default options in the Configure IP-based Services window.

6. He clicked Next to accept the default options in the Certificate Server 2.21 Objects window.

7. He then read the Organizational CA Warning message, and clicked OK.

8. Eric then performed the following steps to configure the Native File Access Protocol installation:

   a. In the LDAP Configuration window, Eric clicked the Allow Clear Text Passwords check box, and then clicked Next.

   b. He clicked to remove the checks from the Native File Access for Macintosh and Native File Access for Unix check boxes. With only the Native File Access for Windows selected, he then clicked Next.

   c. Eric verified that UASHOST_W was displayed in the Server Name window and entered the comment "UASHOST Native File Access for Windows" in the Server Comment text box.

   d. He then clicked Next to display the NFAP Authentication window. He verified that LOCAL was selected and that "workgroup" was displayed in the Workgroup Name text box, and then clicked Next to display the IP Addresses window.

   e. He verified that the Enable CIFS on all addresses option was selected, and then clicked Next to display the Share Point Setup window.

   f. He verified that the Share all Mounted Volumes check box was selected, and then clicked Next to share all mounted volumes and display the Context Setup window.

9. Eric entered UAS in the Context text box, clicked the Add button to have the NFAP search the UAS Organization and all OUs for user names, and then clicked Next.

10. Eric then performed the following steps to configure the WebAccess component:

    a. He clicked Next to accept the default WebAccess.UAS context.

    b. He then clicked the appropriate check boxes to enable the Print and File Gadgets options.

    c. In both the Print Gadget and File Gadget Location text boxes, he replaced uashost.uas.com with the server's IP address, and then clicked Next to display the iManage Install Options window.

    d. He clicked Next to continue and display the Products to be Installed window.

11. Finally, he clicked Finish to accept the product selections and start the file-copying process. The GUI installation program then copies all necessary files to the system. This process takes 30–45 minutes, depending on CD-ROM and disk speed. After all files were copied, Eric removed the CD-ROM and restarted the server.

If you have access to a computer that can be used to install NetWare 6, you can use the NetWare Server Planning Form you completed in Activity 12-2 to perform Activity 12-3.

Activity 12-3: Installing NetWare 6

Time Required: 30–45 minutes

Objective: Install NetWare 6 on a new server.

Description: If you have access to a computer that can be used to perform a NetWare 6 installation, in this activity, you follow the steps Eric performed for the UASHOST server to install your version of the UASHOST server, using the information you documented on your NetWare Server Planning Form.

1. Start the NetWare 6 installation from your NetWare 6 CD. If you cannot start from your CD-ROM, use Windows 98 to create a start disk, and then use that disk to start your computer and begin the installation by running the Install program from the NetWare 6 CD.

2. Accept the license agreement, create a DOS partition of at least 200 MB, and restart the server.

3. Press **F10** to accept the JREPORT runtime license agreement.

4. Press the **Enter** key to select the Custom option and then continue the installation.

5. Complete the installation steps described in the "Phase 2: Initial Installation and File Copying" section.

6. Use your NetWare Server Planning Form to complete the steps described in the "Phase 3: GUI Installation" section.

7. Use your NetWare Server Planning Form to complete the steps described in the "eDirectory (NDS) Installation" section.

8. Complete your installation by performing the steps described in the "License and Component Installation" section. Record any port usage information on your NetWare Server Planning Form.

9. Restart your server, and log in as the Admin user.

WORKING WITH THE SERVER CONSOLE

As described in the "Preparing for NetWare Installation" section, a NetWare server contains at least two disk partitions: one for DOS and one for NetWare. A NetWare server starts first from the DOS partition (C: drive). As shown previously in Figure 12-9, the NetWare server consists of the Server.exe kernel software and modules that are loaded to provide services. The Server.exe kernel supplies the core NetWare services, such as file sharing, and provides a software bus for NetWare Loadable Modules and Java applications. Most network services, such as Novell Distributed Print Services (NDPS) and Novell eDirectory, and device drivers are provided by software modules called **NetWare Loadable Modules (NLMs)**, which are loaded during or after the server startup process.

To start the NetWare server, you run the Server.exe program from the DOS partition. During installation, the Server.exe program, its support files, and its disk driver modules are stored on the DOS partition in the Nwserver directory. If you choose to automatically start the server during the installation process, the commands needed to start the server are placed in the Autoexec.bat file. When the computer starts, DOS automatically performs the commands placed in the Autoexec.bat file. For example, because Eric chose to automatically start the server, the following commands were placed in the Autoexec.bat file of the UASHOST server:

```
C:\>cd nwserver
C:\nwserver>server
```

As the Server.exe program is loading, it reads commands from the Startup.ncf file, also located in the C:\Nwserver directory. This file contains the names of the disk drivers and other configuration commands, as shown in Figure 12-16.

```
                          File: STARTUP.NCF

LOAD IDEHD.CDM
LOAD IDECD.CDM
LOAD IDEATA.HAM PORT=1F0 INT=E
LOAD IDEATA.HAM PORT=170 INT=F
```

Figure 12-16   Sample Startup.ncf file

After Server.exe has loaded its disk drivers, it mounts the SYS volume and continues to read commands from the Autoexec.ncf file stored in the System directory of the SYS volume. As illustrated in Figure 12-17, the Autoexec.ncf file contains commands that identify the server's name, internal address, and any NLMs, such as the network card drivers, that must be loaded for server operation.

```
                        File: AUTOEXEC.NCF

# WARNING!!
FILE SERVER NAME UASHOST
# WARNING!!
# If you change the name of this server, you must update
# all the licenses that are assigned to this server. Using
# NWAdmin, double-click on a license object and click on
# the Assignments button. If the old name of
# this server appears, you must delete it and then add the
# new server name. Do this for all license objects.
SERVERID E0704B6
LOAD IPXRTR
LOAD NGRPCI.LAN SLOT=3 FRAME=ETHERNET_802.2  NAME=NGRPCI_1_E82
BIND IPX NGRPCI_1_E82 NET=10BA5E2
```

Figure 12-17   Reading commands from the Autoexec.ncf file

After startup, the server console screen finally displays the Novell X-Windows Graphics Console screen. You can change the background of this screen by clicking Start, pointing to Settings, and then clicking Backgrounds. In addition to the Graphics Console, NetWare 6 has a text-based console screen and console screens for several NLMs. You can flip between console screens with the Alt+Esc key combination, or you can select a console screen by pressing Ctrl+Esc to display all consoles and then entering the number of the screen you want to display (see Figure 12-18). Although some NLMs, such as the Broker or NDPS Manager, display information on the console, many NLMs, such as disk and LAN drivers, simply provide operating system extensions and need no separate console screen.

```
Current Screens

    1. System Console
    2. Logger Screen
    3. X Server -- Graphical Console
    4. NDPS Manager
    5. NDPS Broker
    6. HP NDPS Console Screen
    7. NWConfig Screen

Select screen to view:
```

Figure 12-18   The Ctrl+Esc Console Selection window

For example, to change to the System Console screen, press Ctrl+Esc to display the list of console screens, enter 1, and then press Enter to display the console prompt, as shown in Figure 12-19.

```
UASHOST:
UASHOST:load nwconfig
Loading Module NWCONFIG.NLM                          [NOT MULTIPLE]
UASHOST:
```

Figure 12-19   The NetWare system console

Console Commands

To become a CNA and effectively operate a server console, you need to know how to use the basic **console commands** built into the NetWare operating system, so you should know the purpose and use of the console commands listed in Table 12-5. The following sections describe these console commands in more depth and provide examples of using the commands to perform server operations.

Table 12-5 Essential console commands

Command Syntax	Description
BIND *protocol* TO *drive\board_name* [*drive_parameters*]	Attaches a protocol to a LAN card. Replace *protocol* with the protocol name (IPX or IP, for example). Replace *drive\board_name* with the name of the network interface card (NIC) or an optional name assigned to the network board. You can optionally replace *drive_parameters* with the hardware settings that identify the NIC (such as I/O port and interrupt).
LOAD [*path*]*module_name* [*parameters*]	Loads an NLM in the file server's RAM. Optionally replace *path* with the DOS or NetWare path leading to the directory containing the module to be loaded. Replace *module_name* with the name of the NLM you want to load. Optional *parameters* can be entered depending on the module being loaded.
CONFIG	Displays configuration information about each network card, including hardware settings, network address, protocol, and frame type.
DISPLAY SERVERS	Displays all servers in the file server's IPX router table, including the number of routers (hops) to get to each server. This command is not available unless IPX is selected during server installation.
MEMORY	Displays the total amount of memory available to the file server computer.
SET TIME	Allows you to change the file server's current system date and time.
CLS/OFF	Clears the file server console screen.
DISABLE/ENABLE LOGIN	Prevents or enables new user logins.
BROADCAST	Sends the specified message to all currently logged-in users.
DOWN	Closes all files and volumes, disconnects all users, and takes the file server offline.
MOUNT *volume_name* [ALL] DISMOUNT *volume_name*	Places a volume online or offline. Replace *volume_name* with the name of the volume you want mounted, or use ALL to mount all NetWare volumes.
MODULES	Lists all currently loaded modules starting with the last module loaded.
SECURE CONSOLE	Provides additional security to help protect the server from unauthorized access.
SEND *"message"* [TO] *user_name\connection_number*	Sends a message to a specified user. Replace *message* with the message line you want to send, and replace *user_name\connection_number* with the name of the currently logged-in user or the connection number assigned to the user. The *connection_number* can be obtained from the Connection option of the MONITOR NLM.
UNBIND *protocol* [FROM] *LAN_driver\board_name*	Removes a protocol from a LAN card. Replace *protocol* with the name of the protocol stack (such as IPX) you want to remove from the card. Replace *LAN_driver\board_name* with the name of the driver program that has been loaded for the network card or the name assigned to the network card by the LOAD command.
UNLOAD *module_name*	Removes an NLM from memory and returns the memory space to the operating system. Replace *module_name* with the name of the currently-loaded module, given in the MODULES command.
VOLUMES	Displays a list of all mounted volumes along with the volume type (NSS or Traditional) and supported namespaces.
PROTOCOLS	Displays a list of all currently loaded protocols.
HELP *command*	Displays information on the specified command. For example, to get information on the syntax and use of the BIND command, enter HELP BIND, and press Enter.

The BIND [protocol] TO [driver] Command

The BIND command attaches a protocol stack to a network card and is necessary so that workstations using that protocol can communicate with the file server. Replace the *protocol* parameter with the name of the protocol stack you want to attach to the network card. Replace *driver* with the name of the network card. For example, TCP/IP can be bound to the NE2000 card driver by entering the command BIND IP TO NE2000 and then supplying the network address, as shown in Figure 12-20.

```
UASHOST:
UASHOST:
UASHOST:BIND IP TO NGRPCI_1_EII ADDR=172.20.0.60 MASK=255.255.0.0

TCPIP-6.3-112: Wed Mar 20 08:07:37 2002
Bound to board 2 with IP address 172.20.0.60 and mask FF.FF.00.00.
IP LAN protocol bound to NETGEAR FA310TX Fast Ethernet PCI Adapter driver

 3-20-2002   8:07:39 am:    SLP-2.2-0
    SLPTCP bound to 172.20.0.60

UASHOST:
```

Figure 12-20   Sample BIND command

The CONFIG Command

The CONFIG command displays information about the server and network card configuration, as shown in Figure 12-21.

```
File server name: UASHOST
IPX internal network number: 0E0704B6
Server Up Time:  1 Hour 44 Minutes 6 Seconds

NETGEAR FA310TX Fast Ethernet PCI Adapter driver
     Version 2.25    February 12, 1999
     Hardware setting: Slot 3, I/O ports 7800h to 78BFh, Interrupt Ah
     Node address: 00A0CC543065
     Frame type: ETHERNET_802.2
     Board name: NGRPCI_1_E82
     LAN protocol: IPX network 010BA5E2

NETGEAR FA310TX Fast Ethernet PCI Adapter driver
     Version 2.25    February 12, 1999
     Hardware setting: Slot 3, I/O ports 7800h to 78BFh, Interrupt Ah
     Node address: 00A0CC543065
     Frame type: ETHERNET_II
     Board name: NGRPCI_1_EII
     LAN protocol: ARP
     LAN protocol: IP Addr:172.20.0.60 Mask:255.255.0.0

Tree Name: .UAS TREE.
```

Figure 12-21   Sample CONFIG command

Notice that in addition to displaying the file server's name and internal network address, the CONFIG command displays the following information about each network adapter in the file server:

- Name of the LAN driver
- Board name assigned when the LAN driver was loaded
- Current hardware settings, including interrupt, I/O port, memory address, and DMA channel
- Node (station) address assigned to the network adapter
- Protocol stack that was bound to the network adapter
- Network address of the cabling scheme for the network adapter
- Frame type assigned to the network adapter

You should use the CONFIG command before installing network adapters in the server so that you have a current list of all hardware settings on the existing network boards. This will help you to select unique interrupt and I/O address settings for the new cards. In addition, the CONFIG command can be used to determine the network address of a cable system before adding another server to the network. If you accidentally start another server using a different network address for the same cable system, router configuration errors between the servers will interfere with network communications.

The DISPLAY SERVERS Command

The DISPLAY SERVERS command, as shown in Figure 12-22, can be useful when using the IPX protocol to determine whether the server is correctly attached to a multiserver network. This command, included with the IPX protocol, is not available if only TCP/IP is loaded.

```
UASHOST:
UASHOST:
UASHOST:
UASHOST:DISPLAY SERVERS
    BSER4.00-7.0  0   CTS_HOST     1   CTS_HOST     2   CTS_PSERVER  2
    REMOTE        0   UASHOST      0   UASHOST      0   UASHOST      0
    UASHOST       0   UAS_BROKER   0   UAS_TREE____ 0   UAS_TREE____ 0
There are 12 known services.
UASHOST:
```

Figure 12-22   Sample DISPLAY SERVERS command

When a server using the IPX protocol is first started, it sends out broadcasts advertising its services to all machines on the network. From these broadcasts, the servers and workstations on the network build lists that include the names of all servers and eDirectory trees on the network. The DISPLAY SERVERS command also lists other services, such as print servers and NDPS Brokers. If a new server does not appear in other server lists, and the new server does not "see" the other servers on the network, your server is not communicating properly with the network. The most common problems are that IPX has not been bound to the network card or the NIC driver is using a different frame type than the other servers. Another common problem when using TCP/IP is that the server has been configured with the wrong network address or subnet mask.

If the new server shows up on other servers, but no servers are showing up on the new server, it could mean that the network card in the new server has a conflicting interrupt or memory address and cannot receive network packets from other servers. You should use the CONFIG command to check for an overlapping interrupt or memory address.

The DISABLE/ENABLE LOGIN Commands

The DISABLE LOGIN command prevents new users from accessing services on the NetWare server. Before shutting down the server, you should issue the DISABLE LOGIN message to prevent any additional users from accessing the server, and then use the BROADCAST command to send a message to all logged-in users telling them that the server will be shutting down in the specified time period and they should close all files and log out of the server. If the DISABLE LOGIN command is not issued, new users might log in to the server after the message was broadcast and not be aware the server was shutting down shortly. Another use of the DISABLE LOGIN command is to temporarily prevent users from logging in while you perform maintenance work, such as loading new drivers or backing up the system. After the work is finished and the server is ready for use, you can issue the ENABLE LOGIN command to allow users to log in again and use the server.

The DOWN Command

The DOWN command deactivates the NetWare server operating system, removes all workstation connections, and returns the server to the DOS prompt. Before issuing the DOWN command, you should disable new logins and broadcast a message to all users, as shown in Figure 12-23. If active sessions exist, the NetWare operating system will issue a warning message asking you if you want to terminate active sessions.

```
UASHOST:
UASHOST:DISABLE LOGIN

 3-20-2002   8:19:52 am:    CONNMGR-5.60-85  [nmID=90013]
    Login is now disabled

UASHOST:BROADCAST Server going down in 15 minutes. Please save work and logout.
UASHOST:
UASHOST:DOWN
Java: Cleaning up resources, Please Wait.
```

Figure 12-23   Shutting down a server

If you see this message, you should cancel the DOWN command, use the MONITOR utility (described in "Using the MONITOR Module," later in this chapter) to determine which connections have open files, and then send a message to users to log out. If no one is at any of the workstations and data files have been left open, you might need to go to individual workstations to close the files and log the users out. Therefore, be sure to remind users that their workstations should not be left unattended while data files are open.

The LOAD Command

The LOAD command loads an NLM into memory and runs it. By default, the LOAD command searches for the requested module in the SYS:System directory unless a different path is specified. Valid paths can include NetWare volume names as well as DOS local drive letters. When a module is loaded into memory, it remains there until the console operator ends the program or uses the UNLOAD command to remove the software from memory. Optional parameters can be placed after the LOAD command, depending on the needs of the module being loaded.

Beginning with NetWare 5 and continuing with NetWare 6, using the LOAD command to run an NLM is no longer necessary. If you simply type the name of the NLM, the system automatically performs the loading process.

The MODULES Command

The MODULES command lists all currently loaded modules along with their names, version numbers, and dates. The modules are listed in sequence, starting with the last module loaded and ending with the first module loaded. The MODULES command is also useful for quickly checking a module's version number and date to determine NetWare compatibility or to look for network problems known to be caused by defective versions of certain modules.

The MOUNT and DISMOUNT Commands

Mounting a volume is the process of loading information from the volume's directory entry table (DET) into the file server's RAM, thereby making the volume available for access by users and the file server's operating system. The MOUNT command is needed to mount a volume that has been taken offline with the DISMOUNT command or that did not mount correctly when the file server was started. Normally, the MOUNT ALL command is inserted into the file server's Autoexec.ncf startup file during installation and attempts to mount all volumes when the file server is started. However, in some cases, such as after a file server crash, some volumes might not mount because of errors in their file allocation tables (FATs) or DETs. When this happens to traditional volumes, you must use the VREPAIR module (see "NetWare Loadable Modules (NLMs)" later in this chapter for more information) to correct the FAT problem and then use the MOUNT command to bring the repaired volume online. When working with NSS volumes, you must dismount the volume and then use the NSS /poolrebuild command (described in the next section) rather than VREPAIR to identify and correct NSS pool and volume problems.

The NSS /poolrebuild Command

The NSS command has a number of options for viewing and repairing the state of NSS components, such as pools and volumes. For example, the NSS /poolrebuild=*poolname* command can be used to rebuild the SYS volume pool when server errors occur. You need to deactivate the pool and all volumes in the pool before the rebuild. Rebuilding the SYS volume pool copies any errors into an error file named *volume_name*.RLF at the root of the server's SYS volume. Every time you rebuild a particular NSS volume, the previous error file is overwritten. Novell recommends using the NSS /poolrebuild command only as a *last resort* to recover the file system because it could result in lost data. Therefore, you should verify that you have a good backup of the volume before using the NSS /poolrebuild command.

The SECURE CONSOLE Command

The SECURE CONSOLE command adds the following security features to help protect the server from unauthorized access:

- Prevents loading NLMs from other sources, such as floppy disks, the DOS partition, or CDs.

- Allows only the console operator to modify the date and time.

- Prevents keyboard entry into the internal debugger software. This is important because programmers could use the debugger to change operating system parameters.

The SEND Command

The SEND command on the server console is used to send a message to a specific client. The most common use of the SEND command is to request a user to log out before shutting down the file server. Messages can be sent to a user's login name or connection number. For example, to send a message to a user at connection number 9, enter the following command:

```
SEND "Server going down in 5 minutes" TO 9
```

The SET TIME Command

The SET TIME command is used to change the current server time or date. In a multiple server network tree consisting of 30 or fewer servers, a single server is designated as a reference server. All other servers on the network synchronize their time to the reference server, so in a multiple-server network, you should change the time only on the reference server. Novell recommends checking the time from DOS or CMOS and then making any corrections before starting the Server.exe program. The following commands show several ways of using SET TIME to change the file server's current date and time to 3:00 P.M., October 30, 2002:

```
SET TIME 10/30/2002 3:00p
SET TIME October 30, 2002 3:00p
SET TIME October 30, 2002
SET TIME 3:00
```

The UNBIND Command

The UNBIND command is used to unload a protocol stack from a LAN driver, causing the server to stop communicating with other machines using that protocol. The most common use of the UNBIND command is to take a defective server off the network. If, for example, you have bound the IPX protocol to a LAN driver and used the wrong network number for the cable system, almost immediately the servers on the network will complain that another router is calling the network a different name. To stop this problem, you can use the UNBIND command to remove the protocol from the network card and then reissue the BIND command using the correct network address. In the following activity, you use console commands to work with your server's console.

Activity 12-4: Using Console Commands

Time Required: 10 minutes

Objective: Use the NetWare system console commands.

Description: To perform this activity, you need to have access to your server's system console. You'll use several console commands to record information on your student answer sheet. An important task for every network administrator is developing and maintaining documentation on the network and server configurations. Use the following steps to record the requested server and network information.

1. Use the CONFIG command to record the following server data on your student answer sheet:
   - Server name
   - Internal IPX number (if your server is using IPX protocol)
   - Network card driver
   - Interrupt
   - Port
   - Network address
   - Node address
   - Frame type
   - Bindery context
   - Currently mounted volumes

 If IPX is not installed on your server, skip the following step.

2. If using the IPX protocol, enter the DISPLAY SERVERS command, and record up to two servers on your student answer sheet.

3. Use the MEMORY command, and on your student answer sheet record the amount of RAM on your server.

4. Use the VOLUMES command, and record the name of each volume on your student answer sheet.

NetWare Loadable Modules (NLMs)

One of the strengths of NetWare is its use of NetWare Loadable Modules (NLMs) to add functionality to the core operating system. Because NLMs play such an important role in tailoring the NetWare network, CNAs must be familiar with the standard NLMs included with the NetWare operating system. As shown in Table 12-6, NLMs can be classified into four general categories based on their function, with each category having its own extension.

Table 12-6 NLM categories

Category	Extension	Description
Disk drivers	.ham and .cdm	Controls access to the NetWare disk partitions. Commands to load these modules are usually placed in the Startup.ncf file.
LAN drivers	.lan	Each network card must be controlled by a compatible LAN driver. Commands to load these modules are placed in the Autoexec.ncf file.
Namespace	.nam	Contains logic to support other workstation-naming conventions, such as those used with Macintosh, OS/2, or Unix-based computers. Commands to load namespace modules are usually placed in the Startup.ncf file.
General-purpose	.nlm	Adds additional services and functions to the file server's operating system.

12

In addition to the special modules for controlling disk and network cards, NetWare comes with a number of general-purpose NLMs in the SYS:System directory with the extension .nlm. These NLMs can be used for a wide range of capabilities, as shown in Table 12-7. In the following sections, you learn about several of these modules that CNAs must be able to use to manage their network file servers.

Table 12-7   General-purpose NLMs

CDROM.NLM	Used to mount a CD when it's first inserted in the server's CD-ROM drive. After this module is loaded, it automatically detects the removal and insertion of CDs.
NWCONFIG.NLM	Used to work with NetWare partitions, volumes, and system files.
MONITOR.NLM	Used to monitor file server performance, hardware status, and memory usage.
REMOTE.NLM	Used to view and operate the NetWare server console from a remote workstation. Requires a password.
RSPX.NLM	Allows the REMOTE module to send and receive console screen commands over the local network cable.
RS232.NLM	Allows the REMOTE module to send and receive console screen commands over the Asynchronous port.
RCONAG6.NLM	Provides an IP-based remote Java console for use with ConsoleOne (described in Chapter 9).
SCRSAVER	Provides a way to lock the server console with a password. To access the server console, the operator must enter the specified password or the Admin user's password.
VREPAIR.NLM	Checks the specified traditional volume for errors and allows the operator to write corrections to the disk volume. This command works only with traditional volumes. To correct problems with NSS volumes, use the NSS /rebuild command.
DSREPAIR	Checks the eDirectory tree replicas for any problems and synchronizes all replicas with the master. See the "Upgrading the Existing Tree to eDirectory 8.6" section later in this chapter for an example of using DSREPAIR.

Using the MONITOR Module

The MONITOR utility module is useful for monitoring and configuring system performance. In this section, you learn how to use it to lock the server console and to view server performance, connection information, and disk and network statistics. After loading the MONITOR utility, the main monitor screen, shown in Figure 12-24, is displayed.

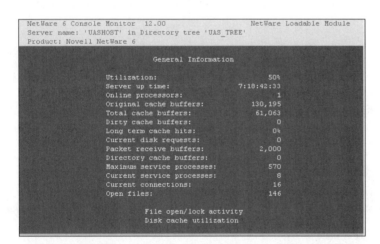

Figure 12-24   The console screen for the MONITOR utility

The screen displays the version and date of the NetWare operating system along with several important system parameters about your server's available memory and performance. The lower half of the screen displays a menu of monitor options. You can view a menu of Available Options (shown in Figure 12-25) by pressing the Tab key.

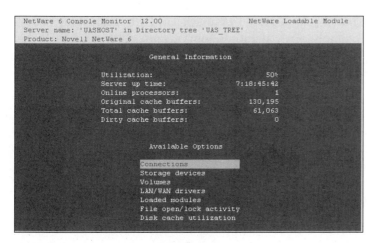

```
NetWare 6 Console Monitor  12.00            NetWare Loadable Module
Server name: 'UASHOST' in Directory tree 'UAS_TREE'
Product: Novell NetWare 6

                         General Information

            Utilization:                      50%
            Server up time:              7:18:45:42
            Online processors:                    1
            Original cache buffers:         130,195
            Total cache buffers:             61,063
            Dirty cache buffers:                  0


                          Available Options

            Connections
            Storage devices
            Volumes
            LAN/WAN drivers
            Loaded modules
            File open/lock activity
            Disk cache utilization
```

Figure 12-25   The Available Options menu

Some of the system parameters and items in the General Information menu are described in the following list:

- *Utilization*—Shows the percentage of time the processor is busy. In most cases, utilization should be less than 70%.

- *Server up time*—Measures the length of time the server has been running since it was last started.

- *Original cache buffers*—Contains the number of buffers (in 4 KB blocks) available when the server was first started.

- *Total cache buffers*—Contains the number of buffers currently available for file caching. If the number is less than 40% of the original cache buffers, your server is running low on memory and you should unload modules or add more RAM as soon as possible.

- *Dirty cache buffers*—Contains a count of the number of buffers that have had modifications but are waiting to be written to disk. A high number of dirty cache buffers indicates that the disk system is bogging down, and a faster disk or an additional disk controller card might be necessary.

- *Current disk requests*—Shows how many requests for disk access are currently waiting to be processed. Like the dirty cache buffers, this number can be used to determine whether disk performance is slowing down the network.

- *Packet receive buffers*—Indicates the number of buffers established to receive packets that the server has received and are waiting to be serviced. If this number approaches the default maximum of 10,000, your file server is falling behind in servicing incoming packets and, therefore, slowing down the network. You might need to get a faster server, increase the disk speed, or add more memory, depending on the other statistics.

- *Directory cache buffers*—Indicates the number of buffers that have been reserved for disk directory blocks. Increasing the number of available directory cache buffers when the server first starts can sometimes improve its performance.

- *Service processes*—Indicates the number of "task handlers" that have been allocated for station requests. If the number of station requests in the packet receive buffers exceeds a certain limit, the server adds extra task handlers to process the requests. Of course, this in turn reduces the amount of memory and processing time for other activities. If the number of service processes approaches the default maximum of 570, and you have a high processor utilization rate, you might need to unload NLMs or add another file server to decrease the load on the current server.

- *Connections*—Quickly shows how many stations are turned on and connected to the server. A station does not have to be logged in to appear in this statistic because any computer accessing the server from the local network or Internet uses up a connection on the file server.

- *File open/lock activity*—Helps determine whether any files are currently open before shutting down the server.

12

The server's Utilization, Total cache buffers, Packet receive buffers, and Dirty cache buffers can give you a quick picture of your server's health; simply verify that utilization is under 70%, total cache buffers are at least 50% of the original cache buffers, and dirty cache buffers are less than 30% of the total cache buffers. Table 12-8 summarizes the MONITOR statistics, including certain key values.

In addition to the General Information window, the MONITOR utility contains several menu options for viewing information about your server's performance and operation. Selecting the Connections option displays a window showing all active connections and the name of the user currently logged in. If no user is logged in to a given connection number, the message "NOTLOGGED-IN" appears next to the connection number. You can use this option to check for user activity before shutting down the server. You can also disconnect a user by highlighting the user name and pressing the Delete key. To view information about any connection, select the connection number and press Enter.

Table 12-8   MONITOR statistics

Statistic	Description	Values
Utilization	Percentage of time the processor is being used	Generally should not be higher than 80%
Server up time	Length of time the NetWare server has been running since it was last started	Used to determine when the server was last started
Online processors	Number of enabled processors	Used to verify whether all CPUs are running when using a multiprocessor system
Original cache buffers	Number of cache buffers available when the server is first started; represents the amount of memory in your server after the NetWare kernel is loaded	Used along with total cache buffers to determine the amount of memory the server is using
Total cache buffers	Number of buffers available for file caching	Decreases as modules are loaded into memory (Novell recommends that total cache buffers be at least 40% of the original cache buffers)
Dirty cache buffers	Number of buffers containing information that needs to be written to disk	If consistently 30% or more of total cache buffers, check the disk system's speed to see if installing additional disk controllers or faster drives would improve speed
Long term cache hits	Number of times the server found requested data in memory instead of having to read it from disk	For best performance, should be 80% or higher; adding more memory can increase long term cache hits
Current disk requests	Number of disk requests in a queue waiting to be serviced	A consistently high value along with a high number of dirty cache buffers could indicate a slow disk system
Packet receive buffers	Number of buffers available to receive requests from workstations	Default value of 2,000 should be more than enough; on smaller networks with fewer than 50 workstations, can be decreased to 1,000 to provide more memory for cache buffers
Directory cache buffers	Number of buffers allocated for directory caching	Normally does not need to be adjusted
Service processes	Number of task handlers allocated for user workstation requests	Normally does not need to be adjusted
Current connections	Number of licensed and unlicensed connections currently in use by the server	Should consistently be less than the number of connections in the license; if the value approaches the maximum available licensed connections, additional connections might need to be purchased
Open files	Number of files being accessed via the network server in user workstations	Tracking this value can help determine server usage

The Volumes option lists all mounted volumes along with the percentage of volume space used. The LAN/WAN drivers options displays information on all LAN drivers loaded, including driver name, frame type, port, and interrupt. The System resources option is a convenient way to view the percentage of cache buffers used. The Disk cache utilization option, used to open the Cache Utilization Statistics window, shown in Figure 12-26, is a good way to determine whether your server has enough memory.

 Novell recommends that the long term cache hits should be more than 90%. If this figure is less than 90%, adding more memory or unloading NLM will improve server performance.

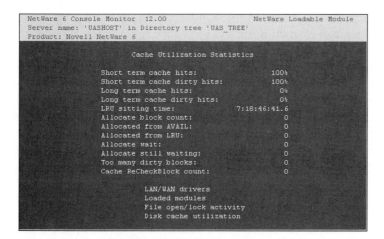

Figure 12-26   The Cache Utilization Statistics window

Select the Server parameters option to modify server configuration parameters, such as the maximum number of packet receive buffers or server time type. In the following activity, you use the MONITOR utility to document your server configuration and performance settings.

Activity 12-5: Using the MONITOR Utility to Document Performance Settings

Time Required: 10 minutes

Objective: Use the MONITOR utility to view file server performance.

Description: After the UASHOST server was installed and running, Eric used the MONITOR utility to create a baseline of server activity, which helps identify changes that can reduce network performance. In this activity, you use the MONITOR utility to create a baseline of server activity for your UASHOST server. To perform this activity, you need access to the server console so that you can use the MONITOR utility to record server performance statistics.

1. At the Netware server, press **Ctrl+Esc** to display the Current Screen list.

2. Press **1** on your keyboard to display the System Console command-prompt screen.

3. Enter **MONITOR**, and press **Enter** to start the MONITOR utility.

4. Press the **Tab** key to display all server statistics.

5. Record the following baseline statistics on your student answer sheet:

   - Server up time
   - Original cache buffers
   - Total cache buffers
   - Dirty cache buffers

12

- Long term cache hits
- Current disk requests
- Directory cache buffers
- Current connections
- Open files

6. Press **Esc** twice, and then select **Yes** to exit the MONITOR utility.

Using Java on the Server

In NetWare 6, the server can be a highly efficient environment for running Java applications. The Java language, developed by Sun Microsystems, can be used to develop Internet applications that run on multiple platforms, including Web browsers such as Netscape. Having the capability to run Java applications opens up many possibilities for running client-server applications on the NetWare server in the future. In a client-server application, at least part of the application runs on the server, and the user interface component runs on the client workstation. The major reason many organizations, such as the UAS AeroDyn division, install servers is their ability to run server-based software. Windows NT/2000-based applications are typically limited to the Microsoft platform, but one of the strengths of Java applications is being able to run on multiple platforms. As a result, many Internet and client-server applications are being developed in Java to take advantage of operating system platform independence. As one of the most powerful and fastest Java machines, NetWare 6 is in a good position to be a preferred choice for running Java applications over the Internet or on company intranets.

Running Java applications on the server console requires extra hardware resources. Novell recommends at least 256 MB of RAM, a PS/2 or serial mouse, and a PCI video card that conforms to the VESA 1.2 or higher specification. If your video card does not meet VESA 1.2 standards, NetWare loads a default driver that supports only 640 by 480 resolution with 16 colors. The JAVA.NLM is automatically loaded along with the X Window System GUI console when your server starts. If you're not using any Java-based applications, you can exit the GUI console after your server starts and unload the Java language by entering the UNLOAD JAVA command at the server console screen.

Using the NetWare GUI Console

Novell has included a Java GUI console interface with NetWare 6. The GUI platform is provided by an implementation of the X Window System, allowing Java programs that conform to the Abstract Windowing Toolkit (AWT) to be displayed with the X Window interface. To load GUI support, you can type the command STARTX at the server console. Although the NetWare GUI is not intended to be a full-featured desktop workstation, it does offer a graphical way to interact with the NetWare console. For example, Eric used the GUI console to install the Web Access product by following these steps:

1. Eric inserted the NetWare 6 operating system CD into the NetWare server's CD-ROM drive, and then pressed Ctrl+Esc to select the system console. In the system console, Eric entered the command "CDROM" to mount the CD as a volume. He then pressed Ctrl+Esc to select the X Windows - Graphical Console.

2. In the GUI console, Eric clicked the Novell button to display a menu containing options for ConsoleOne, Install, Programs, Utilities, Settings, and Run.

3. He clicked the Install option to see a list of already installed products.

4. To install additional products, he clicked the Add button and supplied the path to the installation CD.

5. Next, he selected the product he wanted to install, and clicked Next to display a product summary window. (You can customize any of the selected products by highlighting the product and clicking the Customize button.)

6. After finishing the customization, Eric clicked the Finish button to install the selected product. After the product was installed, Eric was prompted to restart the server. Before doing so, he issued the DISABLE LOGIN command and broadcast a network message about the impending server shutdown.

The GUI console can also be used to configure video resolution, background, and keyboard configurations as well as run the ConsoleOne utility. The ConsoleOne GUI utility gives network administrators a way to work with eDirectory objects and the file system from the server console. In past versions of NetWare, all file and user maintenance had to be done from a workstation running NetWare Administrator. With the ConsoleOne addition to NetWare 6, Novell has provided network administrators with a way to manage user and file system objects from the server console so that they don't have to return to client workstations to create a user or copy a file.

Modifying the Server Startup Files

As described earlier, when the server first starts, it runs commands from the Startup.ncf and Autoexec.ncf files to load drivers, set configuration parameters, and load NLMs. Sometimes network administrators need to modify the commands in the startup files to perform such functions as modifying the server's IPX network address, preventing the GUI console from automatically loading when the server starts, or adding modules such as NDPS Broker and Manager to the startup process. The startup files can be viewed and modified from the server console by using the NWCONFIG module. For example, Eric added commands to automatically load the Broker and NDPS Manager modules whenever the server starts by using the NWCONFIG module to modify the Autoexec.ncf file:

1. From the server console, Eric pressed Ctrl+Esc to display the Current Screens menu.

2. From the Current Screens list, Eric selected the System Console option, and pressed Enter to display the system text console.

3. Next, he entered the command NWCONFIG to display the Configuration Options menu, shown in Figure 12-27.

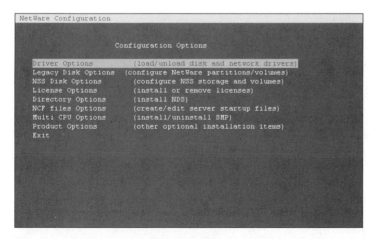

Figure 12-27   The NWCONFIG main menu

4. Eric pressed the down arrow key to highlight NCF files Options, and then pressed Enter to display the Available NCF Files Options list, shown in Figure 12-28.

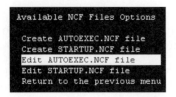

Figure 12-28   The Available NCF Files Options list

5. Eric selected the Edit AUTOEXEC.NCF file option, and then pressed Enter to display the contents of the Autoexec.ncf file.

6. He then scrolled down to the end of the file and entered the following commands after the last command (see Figure 12-29):

```
LOAD NDPSM .UAS_NDPSM.UAS
LOAD BROKER .UAS_BROKER.UAS
```

Figure 12-29   Adding new commands to the Autoexec.ncf file

7. After entering the commands, Eric pressed the F10 key, and then pressed Enter to confirm saving the new Autoexec.ncf file and return to the Available NCF Files Options list.

8. Eric pressed Esc to return to the Configuration Options menu.

9. Eric pressed Esc and then Enter to exit the NWCONFIG program.

Upgrading an Existing Network to NetWare 6

As shown in Table 12-9, there are many advantages to implementing a NetWare 6 server in an existing NetWare network.

Table 12-9   NetWare 6 features

NetWare 6 Feature	Description
Novell iPrint	Enables users to access printers from a variety of remote locations using a Web browser.
NetWare Web Access	Allows the network administrator to set up a Web-based portal that enables users to access network resources from a Web browser.
Novell Native File Access Protocol	With NFAP, Macintosh, Windows, and Unix workstations can access and store files on NetWare servers without having to install additional software (such as Novell Client).
Novell iManage	A Web-based utility that lets you easily configure and manage a variety of services, including DNS, DHCP, iPrint, NetWare Licensing, and eDirectory administration.

Table 12-9   NetWare 6 features (continued)

NetWare 6 Feature	Description
Novell iFolder	Has storage and management solutions for the problems associated with storing and retrieving data. With iFolder, users can access their data from multiple computers in different locations.
Novell NetStorage	Enables users to access NetWare files from a Web browser.
Novell NetDrive	Allows you to map a drive to your NetWare server using a Web browser, thus eliminating the need for Novell Client.
Novell Storage Services	A file storage and management system that meets the requirements of large file systems; you can quickly mount up to 255 volumes with capacities up to 8 terabytes.
NetWare Remote Manager	Enables you to use a Web browser to securely access network servers from any workstation and perform specific server-management tasks.
Novell Cluster Services	A server-clustering system that ensures high availability and manageability for critical network applications and resources.
eDirectory 8.6	A full-service, platform-independent, LDAP-compatible directory service that can store and manage millions of objects, including user applications, network devices, and data.

Many networks containing NetWare 4 and NetWare 5 servers can benefit from installing a NetWare 6 server. However, before installing a NetWare 6 server into an existing Novell Directory Services (NDS) tree, you must perform the following steps:

1. Back up the existing network data.

2. View and update servers to the latest NDS version.

3. Prepare the existing network for eDirectory 8.6 installation.

4. Update the Certificate Authority (CA) object to version 2.0 or higher.

NetWare 6 includes a new utility called Deployment Manager (Nwdeploy.exe) that runs from a client computer; it's used primarily to help prepare your existing network for a NetWare 6 eDirectory upgrade. In addition to performing network preparation tasks, such as updating servers to the latest NDS version and preparing for eDirectory 8.6 installation, Deployment Manager also supplies help information on installation and upgrading options as well as post-installation tasks. Because UAS will be installing the new NetWare 6 server into an existing NetWare environment, Eric used the Storage Management System, described in Chapter 3, to back up the existing servers. He then used Deployment Manager to update the NDS tree for the new NetWare 6 eDirectory system, updated the CA object, and installed the NetWare 6 server as described in the following sections.

Upgrading the Existing Tree to eDirectory 8.6

Although UAS installed NetWare 6 into a new tree, the AeroDyn division currently has a NetWare 5 server that management would like to continue using. To install the new NetWare 6 server into the existing NetWare 5 NDS tree, Eric needed to upgrade the existing tree to NDS version 8.6 before installing NetWare 6 on the new server. To prepare the existing NDS tree, Eric used the Novell Deployment Manager software to perform the following tasks during a time when no users were logged in to the network:

1. First, Eric made sure that the existing server was backed up by running the SBACKUP software, as described in Chapter 3.

2. After the backup was complete, Eric made sure the existing server's volumes were problem free by dismounting the volumes and running the VREPAIR utility.

3. Next, he used the DSREPAIR utility to check the existing NDS tree structure and correct any problems, if needed.

4. After checking the volumes and NDS tree, Eric downloaded the latest support pack for existing servers at *http://support.novell.com* and installed it.

5. To use Deployment Manager to update the existing UAS_tree to eDirectory version 8.6, Eric went to a client workstation and logged in to the NetWare network as Admin. He then inserted the NetWare 6 CD and started Deployment Manager by clicking NWDeploy.exe, which automatically started Deployment Manager, as shown in Figure 12-30.

6. After accepting the license agreement, Eric clicked Step 2: View and Update NDS Version, and then followed the prompts to update the existing NetWare servers to the latest NDS version.

7. Next, Eric clicked Step 3: Prepare for Novell eDirectory 8.6, and followed the prompts to update the existing NetWare tree to the new NetWare 6 eDirectory.

8. After all the upgrades were completed, Eric exited Deployment Manager, logged off, and then restarted the existing NetWare server.

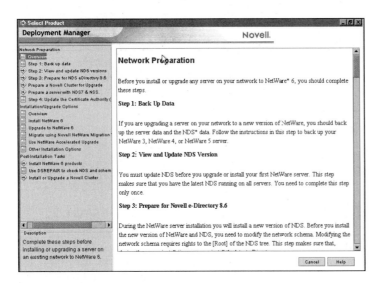

Figure 12-30 The Deployment Manager main interface

Upgrading the Certificate Authority Object

As described in Chapter 10, the Certificate Authority (CA) object plays an important role in network security by providing users and applications with private and public keys for encrypting data packets for secure transmission. Each eDirectory tree must have one, and only one, CA service running on a NetWare server. Because earlier versions of the CA are not compatible with the services that ship with NetWare 6, you must identify the server running the CA service and, if necessary, upgrade to version 2.0 or higher. Eric performed the following steps on the AeroDyn network to identify and upgrade the existing CA service to the latest version:

1. First, Eric logged in to the existing network with the Admin user name and password.

2. Next, he started ConsoleOne and expanded the Security container to display the Certificate Authority object.

3. He double-clicked the Certificate Authority object, and then clicked the General tab to display the name of the server hosting the CA service.

4. He then loaded the NWCONFIG module on the identified server, and selected Product Options to determine the version of the CA service.

5. To update the CA service to the latest version, Eric downloaded the latest CA software from *http://www.novell.com/download/#NDS*.

6. After downloading the CA software, he loaded the NWCONFIG module, and then selected the Install a product not listed option from the Product Options menu to install the latest CA service on the existing server.

7. Finally, he restarted the server with the RESTART SERVER command. Eric was then ready to install the new NetWare 6 server into the existing AeroDyn tree.

Installing a NetWare 6 Server into an Existing Tree

The process of installing NetWare 6 into an existing tree is similar to installing NetWare 6 into a new tree, except for the need to identify the tree and context where the NetWare 6 server will be installed and the user name and password for an Administrator account with Supervisor rights to the container where the server will be installed. Before Eric installed the NetWare 6 server into the existing AeroDyn tree, he filled out the NetWare Server Planning Form and then followed all the steps shown in the previous installation process, with the exception of the eDirectory installation step. Following is a summary of the steps Eric performed to install the NetWare 6 server into the existing AeroDyn tree:

1. To prepare the DOS partition and start the installation, Eric used the same steps he performed in Phase 1 when installing the UASHOST server.

2. After restarting the server, Eric performed the initial installation and file-copying phase by accepting the defaults for the server and regional settings. He then selected the disk controller and network card drivers for the new AeroDyn server. After loading the drivers, the installation program detected his disk drive's free space, and Eric created a SYS volume of 4 GB. The installation program then copied the server files to the SYS volume and started the GUI installation phase.

3. During the GUI installation phase, Eric entered the name of the server, supplied the encryption license, and selected both the IP and IPX protocols. Because he's going to create additional volumes later, he clicked Next when the Configure File System window opened. He then entered a unique IP address for the new server along with its DNS name and time zone information.

4. During the eDirectory installation phase, Eric chose to install the new server into an existing tree. He entered the name of the AeroDyn tree along with the Admin user name and password, and then supplied the context for the new server by entering "OU=Engineering.O=AeroDyn" to place the new server in the AeroDyn Engineering department's OU. After recording the eDirectory summary information, Eric clicked Next to perform the license and component installation.

5. During the license and component installation, Eric inserted the license disk containing the server connection license files. He then chose to install the Web Access, iPrint/NDPS, and NFAP components. After configuring the NDAP and Web Access components, he took a break while all the files were copied to the server.

6. After completing the final file-copying phase, Eric restarted the new server and logged in as the Administrator.

Now that the NetWare 6 server installations are finished, and the network system is up and running, Eric's job has just begun. The initial network setup requires a lot of work and time, but it's only the beginning of the ongoing process of network administration, which includes adding new software, changing configurations, training users, troubleshooting problems, securing resources, adding and managing user accounts, and upgrading software and skills. Eric found that after the new servers were up and running, his workload has increased to the point that UAS is looking to hire yet another network administrator. He wants to know if you would be interested in applying for the new position?

12

CHAPTER SUMMARY

❏ Directory services play an essential role in administering and managing networks consisting of diverse operating systems and locations. Most directory services today are based on the X.500 standard, which defines protocols for the Directory Information Base, Directory Information Tree, Directory User Agent, and Directory Service Agent.

❏ Preparing for NetWare server installation involves defining the server name and hardware information along with additional products and services. Server naming requirements include the following:
  - The server's name can be from 2 to 47 alphanumeric characters, including underscores and hyphens.
  - No spaces or periods are allowed.
  - When using IPX, each server must be assigned a unique internal network number consisting of up to eight hexadecimal digits.

❏ NetWare server installation involves three major phases: creation of the DOS boot partition, initial text-based setup, and GUI installation. The GUI installation phase is further divided into phases for server identification, eDirectory installation, and license and component selection.

❏ Console commands are built into the NetWare 6 kernel and enable the console operator to perform a variety of functions. Commonly used console commands include CONFIG, LOAD and UNLOAD, BROADCAST, DISABLE LOGIN, DISPLAY SERVERS, BIND, and TIME.

❏ NetWare enables the console operator to add services and features to the NetWare kernel by loading programs called NetWare Loadable Modules (NLMs). The MONITOR and NWCONFIG NLMs can be used to view and change server configuration parameters. The NSS and VREPAIR NLMs are used to check and correct disk volume problems. The DSREPAIR NLM can be used to view and correct problems with eDirectory, and the RCONAG6 and REMOTE NLMs provide access to the server console from a workstation.

❏ When adding a new NetWare 6 server to an existing network, it's important to perform the following steps:
  - Back up the existing server data.
  - View and update the NDS version.
  - Upgrade the existing network to eDirectory 8.6.
  - Upgrade the server running Novell Certificate Server to version 2.0 or higher.

❏ The Deployment Manager software included on the NetWare 6 operating system CD has options for viewing and updating NDS versions, updating NDS to eDirectory 8.6, and installing NetWare 6 products.

KEY TERMS

console command — A command function built into the NetWare kernel Server.exe program and, therefore, is always in memory.

Custom Device Module (CDM) — Manages disk drives through the HBA software.

Directory Access Protocol (DAP) — A protocol that handles formatting and transmitting data between the DUA and DSA.

directory database — A database used to store information about network objects.

Directory Information Base (DIB) — The name of the X.500 directory database.

Directory Information Shadowing Protocol (DISP) — A special form of the DSP that's responsible for keeping multiple copies of the DIB synchronized.

Directory Information Tree (DIT) — A tree structure for the DIB containers that represents the hierarchical relationship between entries.

Directory Schema — A set of rules for ensuring that the information in the DIB is not damaged or lost.

directory service — Software that provides discovery, security, relational management, storage, and retrieval of directory database information.

Directory Service Protocol (DSP) — A protocol that handles communication between DSAs.

Directory System Agent (DSA) — Software running on a server that consists of a collection of services and protocols that manage specific portions of the DIB.

Directory User Agent (DUA) — Runs on the user workstation and acts as a client to send requests from the user to the directory service.

entry — A record in the directory database that stores information on a particular network object.

frame type — Specifies the format of the data packet to be sent across the network cable.

Host Bus Adapter (HBA) — A modular disk driver that manages the controller card.

NetWare Loadable Module (NLM) — An external program that can be loaded into the file server's RAM to add additional functionality or control hardware devices, such as disk drives and network cards.

shadowing — The process of distributing and synchronizing the DIB among multiple locations.

X.500 — Recommendations created by the International Telecommunications Union that define directory services.

REVIEW QUESTIONS

1. In the X.500 model, which of the following components is responsible for initiating a request for directory services information?

    a. DIB

    b. DSP

    c. DUA

    d. DUP

2. Which of the following is the X.500 protocol used to communicate between different directory servers?

    a. DIB

    b. DSP

    c. DUA

    d. DUP

3. Which of the following is made up of objects called entries?

    a. DIB

    b. DSP

    c. DUA

    d. DUP

4. Which of the following is a set of rules that ensures that the directory remains well formed as modifications are made?

    a. protocols

    b. DUP

    c. Directory Schema

    d. DSP

12

5. Which of the following is the process of distributing the DIB between servers?

   a. synchronizing

   b. replicating

   c. shadowing

   d. stabilizing

6. Which of the following is not an optional NetWare 6 installation component?

   a. iPrint

   b. eDirectory

   c. NFAP

   d. iFolder

7. Which of the following commands/modules can be used to correct problems with NSS volumes?

   a. VREPAIR

   b. NSS /rebuild

   c. REBUILD

   d. DSREPAIR

8. Which of the following commands assigns a protocol to a LAN driver?

   a. BIND

   b. CONFIG

   c. LOAD

   d. NETBIND

9. Which of the following commands would be used to assign a frame type and I/O port to a LAN driver?

   a. CONFIG

   b. BIND

   c. LOAD

   d. NETBIND

10. Which of the following commands would show the total file memory available on the file server?

   a. MEMORY

   b. SYSTEM

   c. MONITOR

   d. CONFIG

11. Which of the following console commands would display the network addresses assigned to each LAN in the file server?

   a. MEMORY

   b. DISPLAY SYSTEM

   c. MONITOR

   d. CONFIG

12. Which of the following console commands would let you know if your newly installed file server could "see" other servers on the network?

   a. DISPLAY SYSTEM

   b. DISPLAY NETWORKS

   c. DISPLAY SERVERS

   d. DISPLAY ALL

13. Write a console command that would change the server's clock to 11:59 P.M., December 31, 2003:

_____

14. Write the sequence of commands a network administrator should enter before turning off the server computer in the middle of the day:

_____

_____

_____

15. After booting the file server, you notice that a traditional volume named TEXT did not mount because of errors in the FAT. Identify which NLM could be used to fix the volume and the command needed to bring the TEXT volume back online: _____

16. Suppose that after loading the NE2000 Ethernet card driver and binding the IPX protocol with the network address 1EEE8023, your server begins reporting router configuration errors that indicate other servers on the network are using the network address "10Base2" for the Ethernet LAN. Write the commands you should use to correct the problem: _____

17. Which of the following console commands prevents NetWare from loading NLMs from the SYS:Public\NLM directory?

a. SCRSAVER

b. LOCK CONSOLE

c. SECURE CONSOLE

d. CONFIG

18. Which of the following upgrade processes can be performed by using Deployment Manager? (Choose all that apply.)

a. back up data

b. prepare for NDS eDirectory 8.6

c. install NetWare 6 products

d. repair eDirectory problems

e. repair NSS volume problems

19. Which of the following NLMs must be loaded to access the server console from a workstation using ConsoleOne?

a. REMOTE

b. RCONSOLE

c. RCONAG6

d. RCONSOLEJ

20. If the number of total cache buffers displayed in the MONITOR utility is less than _____ of the original cache buffers, you need to add more memory to your file server.

a. 80%

b. 90%

c. 40%

d. 25%

12

UNIVERSAL AEROSPACE CASE PROJECTS

Case Project 12-1: Build a Server Baseline

Although the UAS network is performing fine, increased demands and equipment failures could cause future performance problems. To help identify performance problems that might occur, you should determine the server's nominal performance by using the MONITOR utility to build a baseline showing server performance during typical work periods. In this project, you use the MONITOR utility over a period of a few days to determine server baseline statistics. To do this project, you need access to the MONITOR utility from the server console or through the remote console facility. Your instructor will provide instructions on accessing the MONITOR utility.

APPENDIX

A

CNA OBJECTIVES

Table A-1 maps the Certified Novell Administrator (CNA) objectives to the corresponding chapter and section title where the objectives are covered in this book. Because the CNA exam undergoes frequent updating and revising, you should check the Novell Education Web site for the latest developments at *http://www.novell.com/education*.

 Titles of subsections are enclosed in parentheses. Bold formatting for section titles indicates where to find the primary objective coverage.

Table A-1: NetWare 6 CNA Objective Mapping

Objective	Chapter: Section
Section 1: Identify NetWare 6 Features and Services	
1.1: Identify the Features of NetWare 6	Chapter 1: **Introduction to Network Components and Services** (all subsections); Network Entities **(Server-centric Systems)**; Chapter 12: Upgrading an Existing Network to NetWare 6
1.2: Identify the Operating System Components of NetWare 6	Chapter 1: **Introduction to Network Components and Services** (all subsections); Chapter 12: Preparing for NetWare Installation **(System Information)**
1.3: Describe How NetWare Relates to Other Operating Systems	Chapter 1: Network Entities **(Servers)**
Section 2: Install NetWare 6	
2.1: Identify Prerequisite Requirements	Chapter 12: Preparing for NetWare Installation **(System Information)**
2.2: Prepare the Existing Network	Chapter 12: **Upgrading an Existing Network to NetWare 6**
2.3: Prepare the Designated Computer	Chapter 12: **Preparing for NetWare Installation** (all subsections)
2.4: Install NetWare 6	Chapter 12: **Installing NetWare 6** (all subsections)
Section 3: Manage NetWare 6	
3.1: Use Server Console Commands to Manage NetWare 6	Chapter 12: Working with the Server Console **(Console Commands)**
3.2: Use Configuration Files	Chapter 12: Working with the Server Console **(Modifying the Server Startup Files)**
3.3: Identify the Utilities to Remotely Manage NetWare 6	Chapter 2: Implementing the eDirectory Tree **(Creating Organizational Units with iManager)**; Chapter 3: Establishing the Universal AeroSpace Directory Structure **(Implementing the Directory Structure)**; Chapter 4: Creating and Managing Users and Groups **(Using iManager to Create Users and Groups)**; Chapter 9: **Using NetWare 6 Remote Management Utilities**
Section 4: Install and Manage the Novell Client	
4.1: Describe the Novell Client	Chapter 1: Introduction to Network Components and Services **(Login Security Services)**; Chapter 2: Implementing the Client **(The Novell Client)**
4.2: Install the Novell Client	Chapter 2: Implementing the Client **(The Novell Client)**
4.3: Log in to eDirectory and the Workstation	Chapter 1: Introduction to Network Components and Services **(Login Security Services)**

Table A-1:   NetWare 6 CNA Objective Mapping (continued)

Objective	Chapter: Section
4.4: Set Client Properties	Chapter 2: Implementing the Client **(The Novell Client)**
Section 5: Identify Directory Service Basics	
5.1: Identify Basic Directory Service Tasks	Chapter 1: Introduction to Network Components and Services **(Directory Services)**; Chapter 12: **Directory Services**
5.2: Identify Common Directory Service Uses	Chapter 1: Introduction to Network Components and Services **(Directory Services)**; Chapter 12: **Directory Services**
5.3: Describe How a Directory is Structured	Chapter 12: **Directory Services**
Section 6: Describe Novell eDirectory	
6.1: Identify the Role and Benefits of eDirectory	Chapter 1: Introduction to Network Components and Services **(Directory Services)**; Chapter 12: **Directory Services**
6.2: Identify How eDirectory 8.6 works	Chapter 12: Directory Services **(eDirectory Architecture)**
6.3: Identify and Describe the Composition of eDirectory	Chapter 12: Directory Services **(eDirectory Architecture)**
6.4: Identify and Describe eDirectory Object Classes	Chapter 2: Novell eDirectory Services **(eDirectory Components)**
6.5: Identify the Flow and Design of the eDirectory Tree	Chapter 2: **Designing an eDirectory Tree Structure**
6.6: Identify eDirectory Tools and When to Use Them	Chapter 2: Designing an eDirectory Tree Structure **(Introduction to eDirectory Management Utilities)**
Section 7: Manage User Objects	
7.1: Describe the Admin Object	Chapter 2: Novell eDirectory Services **(eDirectory Components)**
7.2: Create User Objects	Chapter 4: **Creating and Managing Users and Groups** (all subsections)
7.3: Modify User Objects	Chapter 4: Creating and Managing Users and Groups **(Updating Multiple User Accounts)**
7.4: Move Objects	Chapter 4: **Moving Users and Containers**
7.5: Delete User Objects	Chapter 4: **Moving Users and Containers**
Section 8: Manage eDirectory Rights	
8.1: Describe eDirectory Security	Chapter 6: **Introduction to eDirectory Security**
8.2: Determine How Rights Flow	Chapter 5: Access Right Security **(Inherited Rights)**; Chapter 6: Introduction to eDirectory Security **(Inherited Rights)**
8.3: Block Inherited Rights	Chapter 5: Access Right Security **(The Inherited Rights Filter)**; Chapter 6: Introduction to eDirectory Security **(Using the Inheritable Right)**
8.4: Determine eDirectory Effective Rights	Chapter 6: Introduction to eDirectory Security **(Assigning eDirectory Rights)**
8.5: Troubleshoot eDirectory Security	Chapter 6: Introduction to eDirectory Security **(Troubleshooting eDirectory Security)**
Section 9: Configure the User Environment	
9.1: Use Login Scripts to Configure the User Environment	Chapter 7: **Login Script Processing** (all subsections)
9.2: Plan the Login Scripts for Containers, Groups, and Users	Chapter 7: **Implementing Login Scripts for Universal AeroSpace** (all subsections)
9.3: Use Z.E.N.works for Desktops 3 to Configure the Environment	Chapter 7: **Managing User Environments with Z.E.N.works for Desktops** (all subsections)
9.4: Identify Common Configurations Created Through User Policies	Chapter 7: Managing User Environments with Z.E.N.works for Desktops **(Managing Workstations)**

Table A-1: NetWare 6 CNA Objective Mapping (continued)

A

Objective	Chapter: Section
Section 10: Implement Queue-Based Printing	
10.1: Set Up a Queue-Based Printing System	Chapter 8: Network Printing Overview **(Queue-Based Printing System Components)**
10.2: Set Up Queue-Based Printing in an IP-Only Environment	Chapter 8: Network Printing Overview **(Setting Up Queue-Based Printing)**
10.3: Configure Queue-Based Printing on the Workstation	Chapter 8: Network Printing Overview **(Setting Up Queue-Based Printing)**
10.4: Manage Queue-Based Printing	Chapter 8: Network Printing Overview **(Setting Up Queue-Based Printing)**
10.5: Troubleshoot Queue-Based Printing Problems	Chapter 8: Network Printing Overview **(Troubleshooting Queue-Based Printing)**
Section 11: Implement NDPS Printing	
11.1: Identify the Features of NDPS	Chapter 8: **Implementing Novell Distributed Print Services**
11.2: Describe NDPS Components	Chapter 8: Implementing Novell Distributed Print Services **(Setting Up NDPS Components)**
11.3: Set Up NDPS	Chapter 8: Implementing Novell Distributed Print Services **(Setting Up NDPS Components)**
11.4: Manage NDPS	Chapter 8: **Setting Up the Printing Environment** (all subsections)
Section 12: Implement Novell iPrint Printing	
12.1: Identify the Benefits and Features of Novell iPrint	Chapter 8: **iPrint and the Internet Printing Protocol (IPP)**
12.2: Describe Novell iPrint Components	Chapter 8: **iPrint and the Internet Printing Protocol (IPP)**
12.3: Install and Configure Novell iPrint	Chapter 8: iPrint and the Internet Printing Protocol (IPP) **(Enabling Printers for iPrint, Installing the iPrint Client and IPP Printers)**
Section 13: Resolve Network Printing Problems	
13.1: Apply Quick-Fix Techniques	Chapter 8: Implementing Novell Distributed Print Services **(Troubleshooting NDPS Printing)**
13.2: Troubleshoot the Most Common Problems with Printing	Chapter 8: Implementing Novell Distributed Print Services **(Troubleshooting NDPS Printing)**
13.3: Troubleshoot Problems Arising from Incompatible Printer Drivers	Chapter 8: Implementing Novell Distributed Print Services **(Troubleshooting NDPS Printing)**
13.4: Troubleshoot Printing Problems Arising from Incompatible Document Formats	Chapter 8: Implementing Novell Distributed Print Services **(Troubleshooting NDPS Printing)**
13.5: Identify the Printing Environment	Chapter 8: **Defining a Printing Environment** (all subsections)
13.6: Troubleshoot NDPS-Based Printing	Chapter 8: Implementing Novell Distributed Print Services **(Troubleshooting NDPS Printing)**
13.7: Troubleshoot Printing Problems in a Mixed Environment	Chapter 8: Implementing Novell Distributed Print Services **(Troubleshooting NDPS Printing)**
13.8: Troubleshoot Problems with iPrint	Chapter 8: Setting Up the Printing Environment **(Using the iPrint Map Utility)**
Section 14: Evaluate NetWare File Services	
14.1: Identify Network File Service Components	Chapter 3: **NetWare File System Components** (all subsections)
14.2: Identify Types of NetWare Volume Storage	Chapter 3: NetWare File System Components **(Volumes)**

Table A-1: NetWare 6 CNA Objective Mapping (continued)

Objective	Chapter: Section
Section 15: Create and Access NetWare Volumes	
15.1: Create Traditional and NSS Volumes	Chapter 3: NetWare File System Components (**Volumes**); Establishing the Universal AeroSpace Directory Structure (**Implementing the Directory Structure**)
15.2: Access Volumes through Mapped Network Drives	Chapter 3: Planning Drive Pointer Usage (**Establishing Drive Pointers**)
Section 16: Implement Directory and File Rights to Provide NetWare File System Security	
16.1: Identify the Types of Network Security Provided by NetWare	Chapter 1: **Introduction to Network Components and Services**; Chapter 4: **Establishing Login Security**
16.2: Identify How NetWare File System Security Works	Chapter 5: **Access Right Security** (all subsections); **Attribute Security** (all subsections)
16.3: Plan File System Rights	Chapter 5: **Planning File System Security** (all subsections)
16.4: Identify Directory and File Attributes	Chapter 5: Attribute Security (**File and Directory Attributes**)
Section 17: Design a Network File System	
17.1: Identify Guidelines for Planning Network Volumes	Chapter 3: Establishing the Universal AeroSpace Directory Structure (**Designing the Structure**)
17.2: Identify the Content and Purpose of NetWare SYS Directories	Chapter 3: NetWare File System Components (**Directories and Subdirectories**)
17.3: Identify the Types of Directories Used for Organizing a File System	Chapter 3: NetWare File System Components (**Directories and Subdirectories**)
17.4: Evaluate Directory Structure Types	Chapter 3: Establishing the Universal AeroSpace Directory Structure (**Designing the Structure**)
Section 18: Identify How to Back Up and Restore NetWare Systems	
18.1: Identify the SMS Backup Process	Chapter 3: Backing Up Network Data (**The Storage Management System**)
18.2: Develop a Network Backup Strategy	Chapter 3: Backing Up Network Data (**Establishing a Backup System**)
18.3: Evaluate Common Backup and Restore Software Used with NetWare	Chapter 3: Backing Up Network Data (**Establishing a Backup System**)
18.4: Identify Protection Guidelines for Backup Data	Chapter 3: Backing Up Network Data (**Establishing a Backup System**)
Section 19: Implement Novell iFolder	
19.1: Identify the Purpose and Benefits of iFolder	Chapter 9: **Working with iFolder**
19.2: Identify How the iFolder Components Help You Access and Manage Your Files	Chapter 9: **Working with iFolder**
19.3: Install and Configure iFolder	Chapter 9: Working with iFolder (**iFolder Components and Installation**)
19.4: Manage and Optimize iFolder	Chapter 9: Working with iFolder (**Managing iFolder**)
Section 20: Identify Features and Functions of Email	
20.1: Describe the Structure of Common Client/Server Email Programs	Chapter 11: **Implementing an E-mail System**
20.2: Identify the Protocols Used for Sending and Receiving Email	Chapter 11: Implementing an E-mail System (**E-mail Protocols**)
20.3: Identify Common Email Front-End (Client) Programs	Chapter 11: Implementing an E-mail System (**Common E-mail Clients**)
20.4: Identify Common Email Back-End (Server) Programs	Chapter 11: Implementing an E-mail System (**Common E-mail Back-End Servers**)

A

Table A-1: NetWare 6 CNA Objective Mapping (continued)

Objective	Chapter: Section
Section 21: Identify the Components of a GroupWise 6 System	
21.1: Understand How Messages are Routed in a GroupWise System	Chapter 11: Implementing an E-mail System **(E-mail Components)**
21.2: Identify the GroupWise Domain Directory Structure	Chapter 11: Implementing an E-mail System **(Installing GroupWise)**
21.3: Identify the GroupWise Post Office Directory Structure and Files	Chapter 11: Implementing an E-mail System **(Installing GroupWise)**
21.4: View the GroupWise System in ConsoleOne	Chapter 11: **Configuring and Managing the GroupWise System; Monitoring and Troubleshooting a GroupWise System**
Section 22: Maintain a Basic GroupWise System	
22.1: Create GroupWise Post Office Users	Chapter 11: Configuring and Managing the GroupWise System **(Creating GroupWise Post Office Users)**
22.2: Create Additional GroupWise Post Office Objects	Chapter 11: Configuring and Managing the GroupWise System **(Creating Additional GroupWise Post Office Objects)**
22.3: Delete Post Office Objects	Chapter 11: Configuring and Managing the GroupWise System **(Deleting and Renaming Post Office Objects)**
22.4: Rename a GroupWise User	Chapter 11: Configuring and Managing the GroupWise System **(Deleting and Renaming Post Office Objects)**
22.5: Establish Mailbox Security	Chapter 11: Configuring and Managing the GroupWise System **(Establishing Mailbox Security)**
Section 23: Secure Your Network	
23.1: List the Steps for Developing an Effective Security Policy	Chapter 10: **Securing Net Services** (all subsections)
23.2: Identify the Basic Methods for Internally Securing a Network	Chapter 10: Securing Net Services **(Internal Security)**
23.3: Restrict Administrative Access to the Network	Chapter 6: eDirectory Security for Universal AeroSpace **(Setting Up an Independent Container Administrator)**
23.4: Identify How to Troubleshoot Common Internal Security Problems	Chapter 10: Securing Net Services **(Internal Security)**
23.5: Identify How a Firewall Provides External Network Security	Chapter 10: Securing Net Services **(Firewall Security)**
Section 24: Protect Your Network Against Viruses	
24.1: Identify Types of Viruses	Chapter 10: Securing Net Services **(Protection Against Virus Attacks)**
24.2: List the Symptoms of an Infected Computer	Chapter 10: Securing Net Services **(Protection Against Virus Attacks)**
24.3: Describe What You Can Do to Prevent a Virus Attack	Chapter 10: Securing Net Services **(Protection Against Virus Attacks)**
24.4: List the Steps in the Virus Removal Process	Chapter 10: Securing Net Services **(Protection Against Virus Attacks)**
Section 25: Identify How Novell Products Deliver Internet Services	
25.1: Identify How Data and Services Are Delivered Over the Internet	Chapter 10: **NetWare 6 Internet Service Components**
25.2: Evaluate the Internet Delivery Components	Chapter 10: **NetWare 6 Internet Service Components** (all subsections)
25.3: Identify the Novell Products that Deliver Internet Services	Chapter 10: **NetWare 6 Internet Service Components** (all subsections)

Table A-1:   NetWare 6 CNA Objective Mapping (continued)

Objective	Chapter: Section
Section 26: Identify How to Implement a Web Server	
26.1: Identify How a Web Server Works	Chapter 10: Installing and Configuring Web Services **(Working with NetWare Enterprise Web Server)**
26.2: Evaluate Commonly Used Web Servers	Chapter 10: **Installing and Configuring Web Services**
26.3: Identify the Process of Installing and Configuring NetWare Enterprise Web Server	Chapter 10: Installing and Configuring Web Services **(Working with NetWare Enterprise Web Server)**
Section 27: Describe How to Install and Configure an FTP Server	
27.1: Describe the Role of an FTP Server	Chapter 10: Installing and Configuring Web Services **(Working with NetWare FTP Server)**
27.2: Evaluate FTP Servers	Chapter 10: Installing and Configuring Web Services **(Working with NetWare FTP Server)**
27.3: Evaluate FTP Clients	Chapter 10: Installing and Configuring Web Services **(Working with NetWare FTP Server)**
27.4: Install and Configure NetWare FTP Server	Chapter 10: Installing and Configuring Web Services **(Installing NetWare FTP Server)**
Section 28: Identify How Viruses Affect Web Services	
28.1: List the Factors That Encourage Attacks on Web Servers	Chapter 10: **Securing Net Services**
28.2: Identify What a Virus Is	Chapter 10: Securing Net Services **(Protection Against Virus Attacks)**
28.3: Identify Common Methods Used to Attack Web Services	Chapter 10: **Securing Net Services** (all subsections)
28.4: List the Measures You Can Take to Prevent Virus Attacks	Chapter 10: Securing Net Services **(Protection Against Virus Attacks)**
Section 29: Identify the Purpose and Function of a Web Portal	
29.1: Describe How Portals are Used in the Industry	Chapter 10: NetWare 6 Internet Service Components **(Novell Portal Services)**
29.2: Describe the Purpose of Novell Portal Services	Chapter 10: NetWare 6 Internet Service Components **(Novell Portal Services)**
29.3: Identify Novell Portal Services Features and Benefits	Chapter 10: NetWare 6 Internet Service Components **(Novell Portal Services)**

B

FORMS AND WORKSHEETS

Administering a network requires a great deal of planning. Network administrators must not only plan, design, and implement networks, but also keep network information in some sort of easily accessible order. Many networking professionals find a standardized set of forms and worksheets to be beneficial in keeping network data organized. To help you plan and organize your network, the following forms and worksheets are included in this appendix:

- Storage Requirements Form
- Volume Design Form
- Directory Design Form
- Group Planning Form
- User Template Planning Form
- User Planning Form
- Organizational Role Planning Form
- Directory Trustee Worksheet
- Directory Attribute Form
- eDirectory Security Worksheet
- eDirectory IRF Worksheet
- Login Script Requirements Worksheet
- Container Login Script Worksheet
- Profile Login Script Worksheet
- User Policy Planning Form
- NDPS Definition Form
- GroupWise Documentation Worksheet
- NetWare Server Planning Form

One of your first steps as a network administrator, however, should be creating an organizational chart for your company, which will help when planning your eDirectory design. An example of the Universal AeroSpace organizational chart follows:

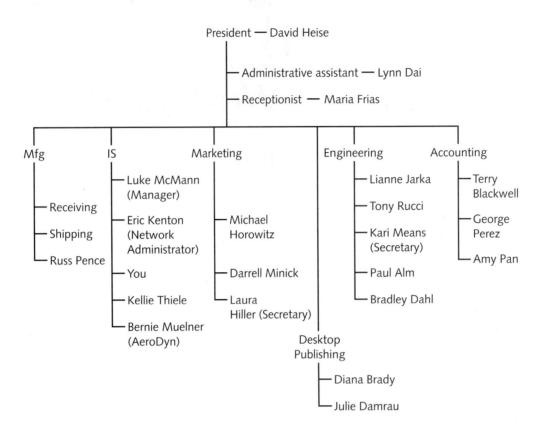

President — David Heise

— Administrative assistant — Lynn Dai

— Receptionist — Maria Frias

Mfg   IS   Marketing   Engineering   Accounting

— Receiving

— Shipping

— Russ Pence

— Luke McMann (Manager)

— Eric Kenton (Network Administrator)

— You

— Kellie Thiele

— Bernie Muelner (AeroDyn)

— Michael Horowitz

— Darrell Minick

— Laura Hiller (Secretary)

— Lianne Jarka

— Tony Rucci

— Kari Means (Secretary)

— Paul Alm

— Bradley Dahl

— Terry Blackwell

— George Perez

— Amy Pan

Desktop Publishing

— Diana Brady

— Julie Damrau

B

Storage Requirements Form

Created by:

Date:

Organization:

Workgroups:

Workgroup Name	Members

Directories:

Directory Description	Type	Users	Capacity

Volume Design Form

Designed by: _____   **Date:** _____

Volume Name: _____   Maximum Capacity: _____

Storage Pool: _____

_____ Backup   _____ Compression   _____ Data Shredding   _____ Directory Quotas
_____ Flush Files   _____ Migration   _____ Modified File list   _____ Salvage Files
_____ Snapshot – File Level   _____ User Space Restrictions

B

Directory Design Form

Designed by: _____   **Date:** _____

Volume Name: _____

Directory Name: _____   Estimated Size: _____

Directory Name

Group Planning Form			
Organization:		Page	of
Developed by:		Date:	

Group Name	Members	Context	Description

User Template Planning Form

Organization:	Page	of
Developed by:	Date:	

Template name	
Context	
Home directory path	
Minimum password length	
Require unique passwords	
Days between password changes	
Grace logins	
Valid login times	
Concurrent connections	
Groups	
Users	
Rights to Login Script	
Rights to home directory	

Template name	
Context	
Home directory path	
Minimum password length	
Require unique passwords	
Days between password changes	
Grace logins	
Valid login times	
Concurrent connections	
Groups	
Users	
Rights to Login Scripts	
Rights to home directory	

User Planning Form

Organization: _____ Page _____ of _____

Developed by: _____ Date: _____

User Name	Login Name	Initial eDirectory and Simple Password	Context	Template Name	Home Directory	Groups	Additional Properties

B

Organizational Role Planning Form

Created By:

Date:

Role Name	Context	Purpose	Primary Occupant(s)

Directory Trustee Worksheet

DIRECTORY TRUSTEE WORKSHEET for:

Page   of

Directory Path	IRF	Trustee										

B

Directory Attribute Form	
Created by:	
Date:	

Directory	Attributes

eDirectory Security Worksheet

Developed by: _____

Tree Name: _____

Object		Trustee			Property		
Name	Type	Name/Type	Entry (Object) Rights	Inheritable Right	Name	Attribute (Property) Rights	Inheritable Right

B

eDirectory IRF Worksheet

Object Name	Type	Entry (Object) Rights IRF	All Attributes IRF	Property Name	Property IRF

Login Script Requirements Worksheet

| Organization: | | Page | of | |
| Developed by: | | Date: | | |

Drive Mappings

Users	Drive	Path	Script

Messages

Users	Description	Login Script

Container Login Script Worksheet

Organization:		**Page**	**of**
Developed by:		**Date:**	
Container Context:			

REM General Commands

```
REM Created by:
REM Last modified:
```

REM Commands for_____Workgroup

REM Commands for_____Workgroup

REM Commands for_____Workgroup

REM End of Login Script Commands

Profile Login Script Worksheet

Organization:	Page	of
Developed by:	Date:	
Profile Script Name:	Container Context:	

Login script for:_____ profile object

Users: _____   _____

          _____   _____

```
REM Created by:
REM Last modified:
```

Login script for:_____ profile object

Users: _____   _____

          _____   _____

```
REM Created by:
REM Last modified:
```

B

User Policy Planning Form

Company/Department:

Date:

Created by:

Profile Name	Context	Associations	Wallpaper	Screen Saver	Desktop Scheme

NDPS Definition Form

Created by:

Date:

NDPS Manager:

eDirectory Context:

Server:

Database Volume:

Managers:

Printer Name	Make/Model	NDPS Printer Classification	Port and Interrupt	Attachment Method	Users	Associated Print Queue	eDirectory Context	Operators

Notes:

B

GroupWise Documentation Worksheet

Organization:	Page	of
Developed by:	Date:	

GroupWise Directory Structure	
GroupWise Domain Name	
GroupWise Domain Directory Path	
GroupWise Post Office Name	
GroupWise Post Office Directory Path	
Post Office Context	
POA Network Address and Port	IP address: Client-server port: Message transfer port: HTTP port:
MTA Network Address and Port	IP address: Message transfer port: HTTP port:
Web Console Information	User name: Password:

NetWare Server Planning Form

Server Identification

File server name: _____   **Server ID #:** _____

Domain name: _____   Random _____ or Assigned _____

System Information

Computer make/model: _____

CPU: _____   Clock Speed: _____   Bus: _____

Memory capacity: _____

Disk Driver Information

Disk Controller 1

       Type: _____   Manufacturer/model: _____

       Interrupt: _____   I/O address: _____   DMA channel: _____

       Memory address: _____ – _____

       Disk driver name: _____

Drive	Speed	Address	Type	Manufacturer	Capacity

Disk Controller 2

       Type: _____   Manufacturer/model: _____

       Interrupt: _____   I/O address: _____   DMA channel: _____

       Memory address: _____ – _____

       Disk driver name: _____

Drive	Speed	Address	Type	Manufacturer	Capacity

Partition Information for Initial Installation

Partition	Type	Pool/Volume/Capacity

Network Card Information

Card Number	Network Type	Manuf. ID	LAN Driver	Bus	Port	I/O Memory Address	IRQ/DMA

B

NetWare Server Planning Form

Protocol Information

Network card:

TCP/IP frame type:

IP address:

Subnet mask:

Gateway:

_____   IPX protocol

        Frame type(s): _____   _____   _____

        Network address: _____   _____   _____

Server Content

Tree name: _____   Organization: _____   Organizational Unit: _____

Installation Component Options: ("D" are installed by default)

__D__	Novell Certificate Server (only one per tree)
__D__	NDS iMonitor Services
__D__	NetWare Remote Manager
__D__	Storage Management Services
__D__	ConsoleOne 1.3.2
_____	iPrint/NDPS
_____	NetWare Enterprise Web Server
_____	NetWare Web Manager
_____	NetWare FTP Server
_____	NetWare Web Search
_____	Novell DNS/DHCP Services
_____	WAN Traffic Manager Services
_____	Novell NFAP
_____	Novell Advanced Audit Service
_____	NetWare WebAccess
_____	Novell iFolder Storage Services
_____	Novell iManager Services
_____	Novell NetStorage

Port Usage

Service	IP Address	Ports	
iFolder	_____	_____	_____
NetStorage	_____	_____	_____
iPrint	_____	_____	_____
Apache	_____	_____	_____

C

NETWORK PATHWAYS AND PROTOCOLS

As described in Chapter 1, a network pathway, along with protocols for its use, is necessary for clients to access network services and resources. LAN pathways typically consist of a cable system that connects devices to the network, but wireless networks that use infrared or radio signals are gaining popularity, providing more mobility for networked notebook and computers. Protocols are the rules for formatting and transmitting data across the network pathway. In Chapter 1, you learned about the NetBEUI, SPX/IPX, and TCP/IP protocols. Although NetBEUI and SPX/IPX are still used, TCP/IP use is rapidly growing. Because of its widespread use and added complexity, you learn more about planning and configuring TCP/IP in this appendix. Chapter 1 covers the basic network pathway and protocol objectives you need to know to pass the CNA test, but as a network administrator, you might also be required to set up and maintain your organization's network infrastructure. This appendix supplies the additional information about network pathways and TCP/IP you'll need to help plan and implement a LAN system for your organization.

DESIGNING A NETWORK PATHWAY

The infrastructure of a LAN pathway is based on the methods for connecting network entities. Wireless networks are becoming popular with notebook computer users, but higher costs and differing standards from product to product make them less feasible than cable-based systems. A network cable system consists of the cable media, the topology (or cable layout), and the network interface cards (NICs). In the following sections, you learn about different types of cables, topologies, and data transmission methods that make up network pathways and see how these pathway components are implemented in the Universal AeroSpace network.

Network Cables

The **cable media** is the physical wire used to transfer data between network components. Data is carried through a cable system using analog or digital signals. Analog signals, used in radio and television, consist of energy waves traveling through the cable at a predefined frequency, measured in number of waves per second. Analog signals have the advantage of being able to carry multiple signals, using separate frequencies, over long distances without needing to regenerate the signals. Although analog signals work well for carrying voice and video, computers are digital devices that communicate by using discrete voltage levels representing ones and zeros. To use an analog system, computer signals must be modulated into analog frequencies with a modem. This modulation and demodulation process reduces the speed of the computer transmission. High-speed modems that can operate at speeds over one million bits per second are very expensive.

Digital signals are more compatible with computers than analog signals because they consist of sending a discrete voltage over the cable to represent a "1" or "0." For example, one digital coding system uses a positive voltage to represent "1" and a negative voltage to represent "0." The disadvantages of digital signals include the relatively short distance (150–600 feet) that discrete electrical voltages can travel without being repeated and the limitation of being able to transmit only one signal on the cable at a time. Despite these limitations, LANs use digital signals for economical, high-speed transmissions of over 100 Mbps between network entities in a confined area.

The capacity or speed of the cable media is determined by its bandwidth. In digital networks, **bandwidth** is measured in megabits per second (Mbps). Depending on the type of cable, bandwidths can vary from only 2 Mbps to over 100 Mbps. Table C-1 shows the bandwidths of several common types of cables, along with their common bandwidth capacity.

Table C-1   Cable media

Medium	Cost	Installation	Capacity	Immunity from EMI and Tapping
Unshielded twisted-pair cable	Low	Simple	1–100 Mbps	Low
Shielded twisted-pair cable	Moderate	Simple to moderate	1–100 Mbps	Moderate
Coaxial cable	Moderate	Simple	10–1000 Mbps	Moderate
Fiber-optic cable	Moderate to high	Difficult	100–2000 Mbps	Very high
Infrared	Moderate	Simple	10–100 Mbps	Subject to interference from strong light sources

In the following sections, you learn about the cable media listed in Table C-1, along with the advantages and disadvantages of using each media in the UAS network.

Coaxial Cable

Although coaxial cable is seldom used in today's computer networks, it can still be found in older network systems. As illustrated in Figure C-1, **coaxial** cable consists of a central conductor surrounded by a wire mesh shield.

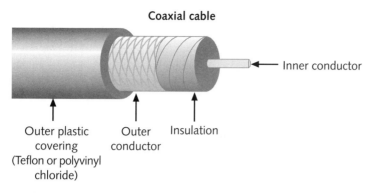

Figure C-1   Coaxial cable

The wire mesh shield is used as a ground and helps protect against the central conductor carrying electrical signals from outside interference. Because of its resistance to outside interference, UAS originally used coaxial cable in the Manufacturing department. Coaxial cable comes in several types, based on the cable size and resistance in ohms, as shown in Table C-2. To prevent network errors, you must use the correct cable type and terminating resisters with the network system you're installing. Because the connectors used on types RG-58 and RG-62 are the same, it's especially important to make sure you're using the correct cable type and terminators.

Table C-2   Coaxial cable types

Cable Type	Resistance (Ohms)	Typical Usage
RG-8	50	Thick Ethernet networks
RG-58	50	Thin Ethernet networks
RG-59	75	Cable TV and IBM broadband networks
RG-62	93	ARCnet networks

The advantages of coaxial cable include medium transmission speed and good immunity from electronic interference. However, because of the relatively high cost and bulk (compared to twisted-pair cable), Eric Kenton decided to replace the older coaxial cable network in the Manufacturing department with a combination of fiber-optic and twisted-pair cabling.

Twisted-Pair Cable

Unshielded twisted-pair cables are most commonly used with telephone and LAN systems. As shown in Figure C-2, **unshielded twisted-pair (UTP)** cables consist of pairs of two insulated wires twisted together.

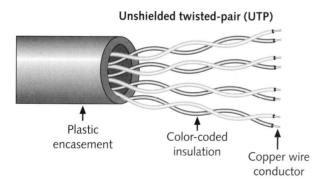

Figure C-2   Unshielded twisted-pair cable

The number of twists in the wire is important because more twists help prevent the magnetic field generated by an electrical signal in one wire from causing stray voltage in the other wire. The RJ-45 connectors on the end of the unshielded twisted-pair cable segments, similar to those used on telephone cables, are needed to connect the network cable to the hub and computer. As shown in Table C-3, UTP cable comes in several types based on its speed rating.

Table C-3   Twisted-pair cable types

Cable Type	Speed Range (Mbps)	Typical Usage
1 and 2	Under 4	Voice and low-speed data
3	Under 16	Data
4	Under 20	Data
5	Up to 100	High-speed data
Shielded twisted-pair	Up to 20	Areas where external interference is a problem

When the UAS building was wired in 1998, Eric recommended using Category 5 UTP cable for the Business office because it was relatively inexpensive, easy to install, and provided fairly high-speed transmission rates of up to 100 Mbps. The disadvantage of UTP cable is its susceptibility to electrical interference from outside sources, such as motors and fluorescent lights. Because the equipment in the Manufacturing department could cause electrical interference problems, Eric wanted to keep the use of unshielded cable to a minimum in this area.

When networks need to operate in environments with sources of external interference, such as power lines and radio broadcasts, you should consider using shielded twisted-pair or fiber-optic cables. **Shielded twisted-pair (STP)** cable increases resistance to outside noise by encasing the twisted-pair cables in a wire mesh shield. Although shielded twisted-pair cable reduces the effects of outside interference, the increased capacitance caused by surrounding the wire with a mesh shield makes it slower and bulkier to work with than UTP cable.

Fiber-optic Cable

As shown in Figure C-3, **fiber-optic** cable consists of special light-conducting glass or plastic fibers at the center of a tube of protective cladding surrounded by a tough outer sheath.

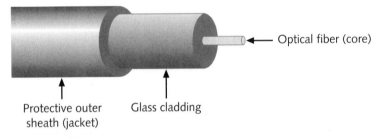

Protective outer sheath (jacket)   Glass cladding   ← Optical fiber (core)

Figure C-3   Fiber-optic cable

Lasers or light-emitting diodes transmit pulses of light through the cable that are picked up by photo detectors at the receiving end. Although more expensive, fiber-optic cable provides extremely high transmission rates over long distances with little interference. In spite of the added expense, Eric recommended using fiber-optic cable to connect the Manufacturing department to the central wiring closet.

Network Topology

The topology of the network defines the physical layout of the cables that connect network devices. The two major network cable topologies commonly used to link computers in a LAN are the star topology and the linear bus topology. Although the star topology is the most popular, each topology has its own advantages and disadvantages. In the following sections, you learn about the advantages and disadvantages of several topologies as well as how to apply them to the UAS network.

Star Topology

As shown in Figure C-4, the **star topology** consists of a central hub from which cable segments radiate to each computer on the network.

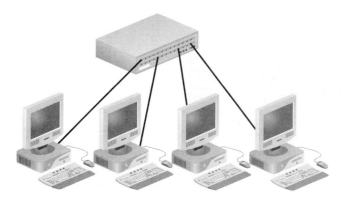

Figure C-4 Star topology

The hub in a star topology is responsible for distributing signals from one computer to other cable segments. In addition, in some network systems, the hubs act as a repeater that regenerates the signal, thus allowing it to travel longer distances. As shown in Figure C-5, star topologies often use some sort of central wiring panel, called a **patch panel**, that gives you the flexibility to easily expand the network by connecting additional computers to the hub. Patch panels are usually placed in wiring closets located near the majority of attached computers so that cable lengths can be reduced.

By using a patch panel wiring system, you can wire the entire network with a jack in each office or room leading to the patch panel. To connect a new computer to the network, you can then simply connect it to the wall jack and connect the corresponding patch panel port to the central hub. In addition to ease of network expansion, star networks are very fault-tolerant because a broken cable or bad connector normally affects only one computer. The star topology also makes troubleshooting the network easier because you can quickly isolate a faulty component to one section of the network. The UAS network uses a star topology with the main wiring closet and patch panel in the server room. Small wiring closets are located near the computers in the Receiving and Shipping departments, with fiber-optic cables running from a hub in each closet to the file server room. The fiber-optic cable's resistance to electronic interference and reliable high-speed capability over long distances make it an ideal cable system for attaching the computers in Receiving and Shipping to the central network.

Linear Bus Topology

In the past, many organizations used a linear bus topology, similar to the one in Figure C-6, to economically connect computers in a relatively small area. Originally, UAS used the linear bus topology to connect the computers in the Manufacturing department to the file server room.

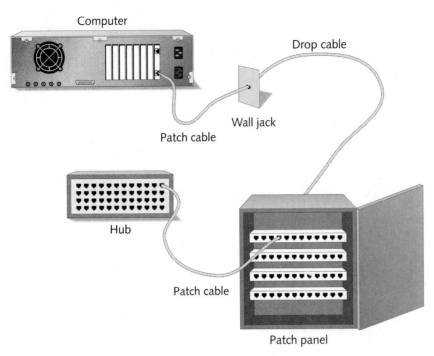

Figure C-5 Patch panel wiring

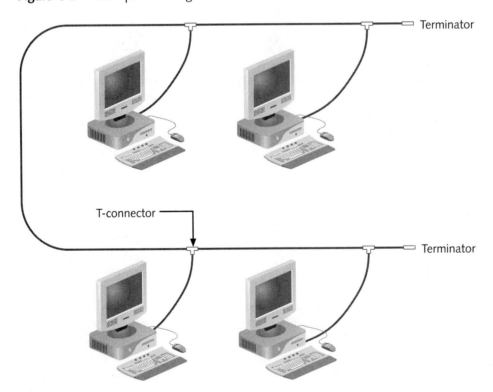

Figure C-6 Linear bus topology

As illustrated in Figure C-6, the **linear bus topology** in the Manufacturing department consisted of a coaxial cable segment that ran from each computer in the Receiving and Shipping departments with a terminator at each end and T-connectors attached to each of the computers. The terminators are important because they eliminate electrical signals when they reach the ends of the cable, preventing "echoes" on the cable that would interfere with communications. The terminator in the file server room was attached to the building ground to prevent electrical interference from other devices, such as fluorescent lights and equipment, from causing transmission errors on the network. Although the linear bus topology worked well when connecting several computers in a restricted area, Eric found it difficult to add new computers. Adding a new computer required bringing down the entire network segment to splice in a new T-connector. In addition, as the number of user workstations in the Manufacturing department increased, Eric found that the source of broken cables or bad T-connectors was difficult to locate because the problem affected all computers on the cable segment. As a result, UAS recently replaced the coaxial-based bus topology with a fiber-based star topology.

Ring Topology

A **ring topology** is similar to a bus topology, except that the ends of the cable are connected, so it has no termination points. As a result, signals on the ring topology travel around the network in one direction until they return to the sending device. When using a ring topology, each computer in the ring receives the signals and then retransmits them to the next computer in the ring. Because the signals are regenerated at each device, they can traverse longer distances, as long as another computer is located within the distance limit of each network card's transmitter.

The disadvantage of a ring topology is that extra cable might be needed to connect the ring when computers are spread out in a serial fashion. In addition, the ring topology has the same difficulties as a linear bus network in terms of taking the network down to add or remove computers. However, the ring topology is often easier to troubleshoot than a linear bus network because each computer on the ring receives and then retransmits a signal; therefore, the troubleshooter can use special software, such as network sniffers, to determine which computer is not receiving the signal. The damaged cable component can be isolated to the cable segment between the computer that isn't receiving the signal and its "upstream" neighbor. Table C-4 summarizes the advantages and disadvantages of the star, linear bus, and ring topologies.

Table C-4   Topology comparison

Topology	Wiring	Expansion	Fault Tolerance	Troubleshooting
Star	Requires the most wire because a cable must connect each computer to a central hub.	Easy to expand by using a patch panel to plug new computers into the hub.	Highly fault-tolerant because a bad cable or connector will affect only one computer.	Easiest to troubleshoot by removing suspect computers from the network.
Linear bus	Usually requires the least amount of wire because the cable is connected from one computer to the next.	Difficult to expand unless a connector exists at the new computer's location.	Poor fault tolerance because a bad connector or cable will disrupt the entire network segment.	The most difficult to troubleshoot because all computers can be affected by one problem.
Ring	Wiring requirements are more than those of a linear bus because of the need to connect the cable ends, but are less than those of a star.	Difficult to expand because of the need to break the ring to insert a new computer.	Poor fault tolerance because a bad connector or cable will disrupt the entire network segment.	With proper software, rings can be fairly easy to troubleshoot because software can identify which computer cannot receive the signal.

Mesh Topology

As shown in Figure C-7, a **mesh topology** provides multiple paths for signals. Because an entire network based on a pure mesh topology could be a real mess, the mesh topology is normally used between major computers to provide alternative paths if one line is down or overloaded. The mesh topology connects major sites on the Internet, providing multiple paths to any location. If one path is busy or down, TCP/IP provides the means to route packets by using another path. In the future, Eric would like to implement Novell's cluster technology so that several computers can share data from one shared storage device. Although NetWare clustering can be implemented using any network topology, Eric proposed creating a storage area network (SAN) by using the mesh topology, as shown in Figure C-8, to ensure fast and reliable access to the shared storage device from both NetWare 6 servers.

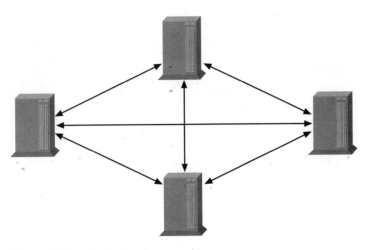

Figure C-7   Mesh topology

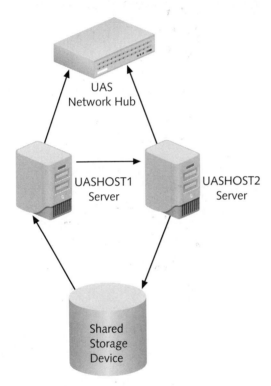

Figure C-8   The Universal AeroSpace mesh topology

Network Interface Cards

After establishing a plan for the cabling infrastructure, the next component Eric selected for the UAS network was the type of **network interface cards (NICs)** to connect each computer to the cable system. NICs are responsible for transmitting data in packets consisting of 500 to 4000 bytes. Each packet contains the address of the receiving computer's network card, much as a letter is addressed to a delivery box number. Although there are many NIC manufacturers, two major standards are commonly used today: token ring and Ethernet. The Ethernet standard can be further broken down into coaxial, 10BaseT, and 100BaseT. Each network card standard has its own method of transmitting data, thus preventing the use of more than one type of card on a network cable. Table C-5 compares the token ring, 10BaseT, coaxial, and 100BaseT network systems in terms of topology, speed, access method, and distance. In the following sections, you learn about the network card standards in Table C-5, along with their advantages and disadvantages for an organization such as Universal AeroSpace.

Table C-5 Network card comparison

Network System	Cable Types	Topology	Maximum Nodes	IEEE Standard	Speed	Access Methods	Distance
Token Ring	UTP, STP Fiber	Star	96	802.5	4–16 Mbps	Token	150 ft per cable run
10BaseT	UTP Fiber	Star	512	802.3	10 Mbps	CSMA/CD	328 ft per cable run
Coaxial (10Base2)	Coaxial	Linear bus	30 per segment with maximum of 3 populated segments	802.3	10 Mbps	CSMA/CD	607 ft per segment
100BaseT	UTP Fiber	Star	512	802.3	100 Mbps	CSMA/CD	328 ft per cable run

Token Ring

IBM originally designed the **token ring** system for industrial environments that need reliable high-speed communications. Originally, the standard token ring cards transmitted at 4 Mbps; today, most token ring cards use 16 Mbps transmission speeds. (Note that you cannot mix cards running at 4 Mbps with cards running at 16 Mbps on the same token ring network.) As shown in Figure C-9, a token ring system consists of a star topology, with each station connected by a twisted-pair cable to a central hub called a **multiple station access unit (MSAU)**.

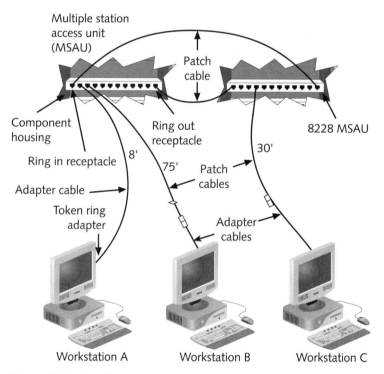

Figure C-9 A token ring network system

Although each station on the token ring is connected to the central MSAU, forming a star topology, the signals actually travel in a ring. In Figure C-9, the signal from Workstation A is transmitted to the MSAU, which relays the signal to the cable running to Workstation B. Workstation B retransmits the signal and sends it back to the MSAU. The MSAU relays the signal to the cable running to Workstation C, which transmits the signal back to the MSAU, where it's relayed to the originating Workstation A. If the cable running from the MSAU to Workstation B is broken, or if Workstation B is shut down, a relay in the MSAU passes the signal to the connection leading to Workstation C. In this manner, the token ring system is very fault-tolerant and resistant to breakdowns.

The advantages of token ring systems are consistent speed, expandability, and fault-tolerance. The transmission speeds of token rings are usually lower than high-speed Ethernet systems, but under heavy loads, token ring networks offer more consistent performance by eliminating collisions. Collisions occur on Ethernet networks when two computers sense an open cable and try to transmit simultaneously. Because each entity on a token ring network must wait for a free token before transmitting data, collisions are eliminated, resulting in better throughput. In addition, token ring systems are usually easier to troubleshoot because bad connections or cable runs can be automatically isolated.

Ethernet and 10/100BaseT

UAS originally used an **Ethernet** network in the Manufacturing department that was based on a linear bus with RG-58 coaxial cable, as shown in Figure C-10. Computers were attached to the cable by using T-connectors with a terminator on each end of the cable, and a repeater was used to connect cable segments. Repeaters work by receiving digital signals on one port and retransmitting them on the other. A single Ethernet network can support up to five cable segments connected by four repeaters. However, only three of these segments can have computers attached; the other two cable segments are used only to transmit across longer distances.

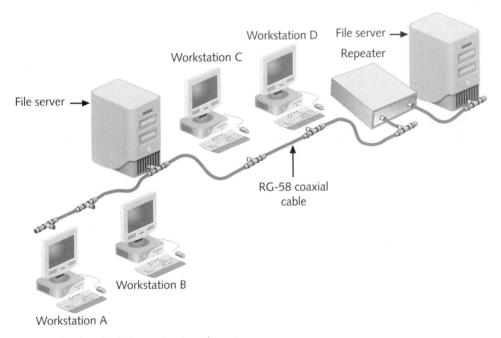

Figure C-10   An Ethernet network system

Modern Ethernets use a star network topology with twisted-pair cable and are referred to as 10BaseT or 100BaseT networks, depending on their speed. The 10/100BaseT system in Figure C-11 uses a device called a concentrator as a hub to connect all machines to the star topology network with twisted-pair cable and RG-45 connectors on each end of the cable. The term **10BaseT** or **100BaseT** comes from the Ethernet network having a transmission speed of *10* or *100* Mbps using digital *base*band signals over *t*wisted-pair cable segments. The term **baseband** is used to describe a computer network that carries digital signals representing ones and zeros, compared to a **broadband** system that carries analog signals, such as those in television and radio communications.

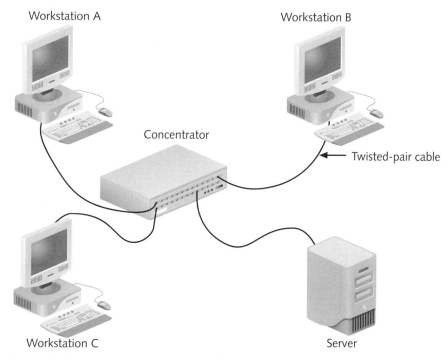

Figure C-11   A 10/100BaseT network system

To control access to the cable and prevent multiple computers from transmitting at the same time, Ethernet networks use the **Carrier Sense Multiple Access with Collision Detection (CSMA/CD)** system that was standardized by the Institute of Electrical and Electronic Engineers (IEEE) 802.3 committee. The CSMA/CD system allows a computer to transmit a message whenever it detects that the cable is not in use. You can think of this process in terms of using a CB radio. When no one is talking, you can go ahead and transmit your message. If someone else is talking, you wait for him or her to finish his or her message before you start your transmission. The problem with CSMA/CD-based access comes when two or more computers sense an open channel and start transmitting at the same time. This is called a collision, and the computers must wait for a few microseconds before retransmitting their messages.

Although the star topology is the same as that used for token ring systems, the 10/100BaseT signals are not sent from one station to the next, as in token rings, but are broadcast throughout the cable system to all stations by using the same CSMA/CD system used with Ethernet cards. Often, a UTP cable system designed for a token ring can easily be converted to support 10/100BaseT by simply replacing the MSAUs hubs with concentrators. The concentrators act as repeaters, receiving signals on one cable port and then retransmitting those signals on all other ports. Most concentrators have an uplink port that enables hubs to be linked to form larger networks (see Figure C-12).

The Ethernet rule of limiting the network to four repeaters also applies to hubs. As shown in Figure C-12, when linking hubs, it's important to ensure that a signal will not pass through more than four hubs. When two or more stations try to transmit at the same instant, a collision occurs and the stations must retransmit after waiting a specified time period. To reduce collisions, larger networks often use intelligent concentrators called switches. Switches reduce collisions, so they often increase network throughput by storing packets of data in memory and then sending them on to their correct destinations when the network cable is not being used. The network in Figure C-12 could be improved by replacing the topmost hub with a switch to help isolate packets to each of the departments and reduce collisions.

The advantages of 10/100BaseT over a token ring include high performance under light to medium loads and lower costs because the CSMA/CD system is simpler than the token ring system. Under light to medium loads, the 10/100BaseT performance can be faster than the token ring, but without using the more expensive switching hubs, the 10/100BaseT system could be bogged down with collisions when there are many stations with lots of activity. In the following activity, you have the opportunity to apply what you have learned about network pathways to designing a network infrastructure for the AeroDyn facility.

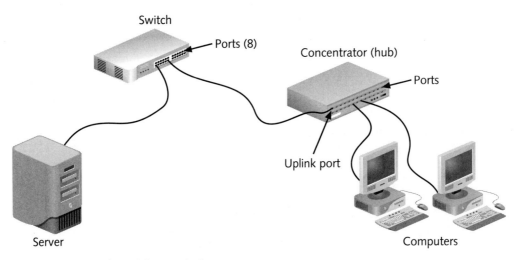

Figure C-12 Linking Ethernet hubs

Activity C-1: Designing a Network Pathway

Time Required: 10 minutes

Objective: Design a network pathway.

Description: The AeroDyn subsidiary of UAS is relocating to a new facility. Bernie Muelner, the network administrator for AeroDyn, would like you to design a network infrastructure for the new facility, which will have a centralized server to provide file, print, and application services for all clients. Three wiring centers have been identified for the network, along with the computer room (see Figure C-13).

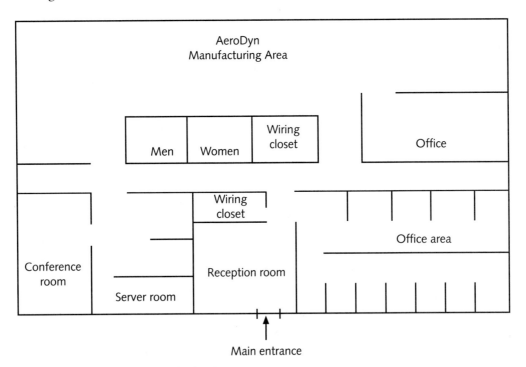

Figure C-13 The AeroDyn facility layout

Each wiring closet will have hubs that need to be attached to the computer room. Bernie would like to create two separate network cable systems: one for the Manufacturing area and the other for the Business offices. Using the diagram in Figure C-13, draw a simple sketch on your student answer sheet that identifies the following:

- Show the placement of hubs and switches, using an *H* for hubs and an *S* for switches. Identify the number of eight-port hubs needed in each wire closet.

- Indicate wire runs from the hubs to the computers. Don't show all the computers, just one or two in each of these areas: Office, Conference, and Manufacturing.

- Label the wire connections on your diagram with one of the following codes: T = twisted-pair, C = coaxial, F = fiber-optic.

- Draw a separate diagram showing how the hubs will be connected.

- Indicate the network card speed (using *10* for 10BaseT or *100* for 100BaseT) for each computer and the server.

IMPLEMENTING THE TCP/IP PROTOCOL

As described in Chapter 1, the TCP/IP protocol stack consists of four layers: Network, Internet, Transport, and Application. The Network layer represents the network pathway for delivering data packets between network entities on the same network. The Internet layer uses network addresses to deliver data packets between physical networks. The Transport layer maintains a connection between network entities and uses port numbers to deliver data packets to the correct application. The Application layer includes programs that provide network services, such as a Web server or an FTP server. Other common network application services that you'll learn about in this section include Dynamic Host Configuration Protocol (DHCP) and Domain Name Service (DNS).

IP Addressing

Because planning an IP address system is a critical part of implementing TCP/IP, in this section you learn more about IP address usage. As you learned in Chapter 1, an IP address consists of four bytes divided into two components: a network address and a host address. Based on the number of bytes in the network address component, IP addresses are classified as Class A, Class B, or Class C, as shown in Table C-6.

Table C-6   TCP/IP address classes

Address Class	Range	Address Bytes	Number of Networks	Host Bytes	Number of Hosts
Class A	1–127	1	127	3	16,777,215
Class B	128–191	2	16,128	2	65,535
Class C	192–223	3	2,097,152	1	254

A Class A address has the first byte reserved for the network address, making the last three bytes available to assign to host computers. Because a Class A address has a three-octet host address, Class A networks can support over 16 million host computers. The number of Class A Internet addresses is limited, so they are reserved for very large organizations, such as the federal government, IBM, or AT&T. Class B addresses are evenly divided between a two-octet network and two-octet host address, allowing more than 65,000 host computers per Class B network address. Large organizations and Internet service providers are often assigned Class B Internet addresses. Class C addresses have a three-digit network address and a one-digit host address, resulting in more than 16 million Class C Internet addresses, each supporting up to 254 host computers; these addresses are usually available for small-business and home use.

In addition to a unique network address, each network must also be assigned a subnet mask, used to identify the network address bits from the host address bits. A network address component is identified by placing a "1" in each bit that's part of the network address. For example, a Class A address, by default, has a subnet mask of 11111111 00000000 00000000 00000000 in binary, or 255.0.0.0 in decimal. The number 255 in the subnet mask identifies the entire first byte as part of the network address. Zeros in the last three bytes identify them as part of the host computer address. The Class B address has a default subnet mask of 255.255.0.0, indicating that the first two bytes represent the network portion of the address and the last two bytes represent the host or node. A Class C address has a default subnet mask of 255.255.255.0, indicating that the first three bytes are the network address, and only the last byte can be used to represent the node. Because 0 and 255 are not valid node values, a Class C address enables up to 254 devices to access the network at the same time.

Planning IP Address Assignments

When assigning IP addresses, you need to assign a unique network address to each network segment that is separated by a router. For example, the UASHOST server shown in Figure C-14 acts as a router separating the network into two segments: Business and Manufacturing. Using Class C addresses, Eric assigned the network address range 192.168.1.1 through 192.168.1.254 to the Business network segment and the address range 192.168.2.1 through 192.168.2.254 to the Manufacturing network segment.

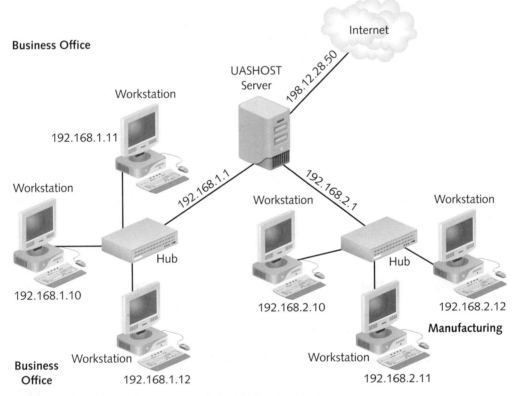

Figure C-14   The two segments of the UAS network

IP addresses can be divided into public and private address ranges. Public IP addresses are used to connect to the Internet. If your organization's network will be attached to the Internet through a dial-up, DSN, cable, or T1 connection, you'll need to obtain one or more registered IP addresses from your ISP. To obtain a range of IP addresses for connecting computers to the Internet, an organization needs to submit a request to its ISP. For a monthly fee, the ISP provides the organization with one or more IP addresses that are registered on the Internet. With a registered IP address, an organization can offer services that users can access over the Internet.

Until recently, InterNIC controlled and assigned all public IP address numbers used on the Internet. However, because the Internet's stability relies on careful management of IP address space, in 1997 the nonprofit American Registry for Internet Numbers (ARIN) was formed to administer and register IP addresses. (InterNIC continues to administer U.S. domain names.) ARIN supplies a range of IP addresses to ISPs that they can allocate to their users.

Internal or private networks that are not directly connected to the Internet could potentially use any IP address range, but ARIN has set aside the address ranges shown in Table C-7. If you're currently connecting your private network to the Internet through a router or plan to connect in the future, you should plan to use these reserved addresses for the computers on your private network.

Table C-7   Reserved private network addresses

Class	Reserved network addresses
Class A	One reserved network address: 10.0.0.0
Class B	16 reserved network addresses: 172.16.0.0 through 172.31.0.0
Class C	254 reserved network addresses: 192.168.1.0 through 192.168.254.0

To access entities and services on other networks, each computer must also have the IP address of its gateway. Before sending a packet to another computer, TCP/IP's Internet layer uses your computer's subnet mask to determine the destination computer's network address. If the destination network address is different from the sending computer's network address, the sending computer relays the packet to the IP address specified in the gateway parameter. The gateway computer then forwards the packet to its next destination. In this way, the packet eventually reaches the destination computer.

In the sample UAS network shown in Figure C-14, the UASHOST server is the gateway that enables computers on the private network to access the Internet. Each computer on the UAS private network needs to be configured with the IP address of the UASHOST server (192.168.1.1) as its gateway to access the Internet. For example, Kellie is working on the computer in Figure C-14 that has an IP address of 192.168.1.11 (its subnet mask is 255.255.255.0, and its gateway is 192.168.1.1). She starts her Web browser to send a request to a Web server with a URL of *http://198.12.28.10*. Before sending the packet, her computer applies its subnet mask of 255.255.255.0 to the IP address 198.12.28.10 and gets a resulting network address of 198.12.28. Because this network address is not equal to Kellie's network address of 192.168.1, Kellie's computer would send the packet to the IP address of the UASHOST server specified in the gateway configuration. The UASHOST computer uses Network Address Translation to transmit the request to the Internet, and the Web server on the Internet sends its Web page to the UASHOST computer, which forwards the results to Kellie's computer. In the following activity, you apply what you have learned about IP addresses to establishing an IP address scheme for AeroDyn.

Activity C-2: Planning IP Address Assignments

Time Required: 10 minutes

Objective: Plan IP address usage for a sample network.

Description: Bernie has asked you to come up with a private IP address scheme for the Manufacturing and Business office networks. On your student answer sheet, your IP address scheme should identify the following:

- Network address for the Manufacturing division
- Network address for the Business office
- Range of IP addresses to be assigned to computers in the Manufacturing division
- Range of IP addresses to be assigned to computers in the Business office
- IP addresses to be assigned to the existing server and to future servers (up to 10)

Network Address Translation

If you have a private network in your organization, you can select one of the following methods of connecting computers on your internal network to the Internet:

- Have the ISP provide each computer with a live Internet address.
- Use a proxy server to share a single Internet address.
- Use Network Address Translation to route your internal network address through a single live IP address.

The number of registered IP addresses is limited, so assigning each computer its own live Internet IP address can be expensive and difficult to implement. In addition, having computers "live" on the Internet increases your security risk of hackers accessing the computer. Although sharing a single Internet address through a proxy service can be a good solution for small or home-based networks, proxies can be difficult to configure for large networks with one or more servers that need to be accessed from the outside. NetWare 6 offers a solution to connecting large internal networks to the Internet: Network Address Translation (NAT). NAT configures your NetWare 6 server as a router between the company's internal network and the Internet. Only one registered IP address needs to be assigned to the NetWare 6 server's Internet connection. When a client needs to access a service on the Internet, its default gateway setting directs the packet to the NetWare 6 server. NAT running on the NetWare server then replaces the client's IP address with its registered "live" IP address and sends the packet to the Internet host. NAT assigns a port number to the connection with the outside host to save connection information. When the Internet host responds, NAT uses the port number assigned to that connection to retrieve the client's information and send the Internet host's response back to the requesting client.

For example, UAS will connect to the Internet through an ISP named Unlimited Horizons. To attach the UASHOST server to the Internet, Unlimited Horizons has supplied a Class C address of 198.12.28.50 for the UAS server. Rather than have Unlimited Horizons assign a live Internet address to each computer that needs Internet access, UAS decided to use the NetWare 6 NAT feature to route packets from the internal network to the Internet. By using NAT, UAS can establish its own internal IP address scheme instead of obtaining a unique Internet address for each workstation and server attached to the network. Although UAS could assign computers on its network any IP address it wanted for internal use, certain address ranges (shown previously in Table C-7) have been reserved for this purpose. Because these address ranges are considered nonroutable by Internet routers, using NAT along with one of the private address schemes on the UAS internal network increases security by preventing Internet computers from sending packets directly to a computer on the UAS internal networks. The only way for packets to be transferred between the UAS computers and the Internet is through the NetWare 6 server's NAT feature. Using the NAT feature saves UAS the cost of renting or purchasing a dedicated router to perform this function. In the following activity, you document the IP addresses assigned to computers on your classroom network.

Activity C-3: Documenting IP Address Assignments

Time Required: 10 minutes

Objective: Document the IP configuration of a network.

Description: In this activity, you use your student answer sheet to document the IP addresses assigned to the devices on your classroom network.

1. Record the IP address assigned to your classroom server.

2. Identify which of the following TCP/IP application services are running on your network:
   - DHCP
   - DNS
   - Web Server
   - NAT

3. Record the IP address of your classroom DNS server, if available.

4. Record the IP address range assigned to the student workstations.

5. Record an IP address, a subnet mask, and a default gateway that can be manually assigned to your computer.

6. If you have an Internet connection, record the IP address assigned to your network. Identify whether the address is registered to your network or assigned temporarily.

Assigning Network Addresses

To communicate on the network, each computer needs to be assigned an IP address and a subnet mask. IP addresses and masks can be assigned to network entities manually or automatically. In manual address assignment, the network administrator must enter an IP address, a mask, and a gateway when configuring each network entity, as shown in Figure C-15.

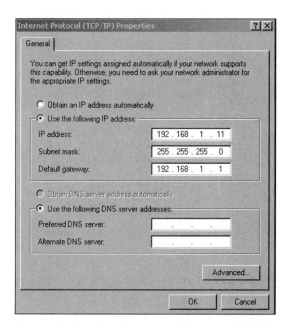

Figure C-15   Configuring a Windows 2000 IP address and gateway

The manual method works fine for assigning addresses to servers or small networks, but is too labor intensive for large networks with hundreds of network entities. When using automatic address assignment, an IP address range can be established on a server running the **Dynamic Host Configuration Protocol (DHCP)**. Network entities then "lease" IP addresses from the DHCP service when they first start up and renew their IP addresses every several days, depending on the configuration of the DHCP service. The range of IP addresses that the DHCP service is configured to distribute is referred to as the "scope." For example, UAS currently uses a DHCP service running on the NetWare 6 server to automatically assign IP addresses in the range of 192.168.1.10 to 192.168.1.200. Figure C-16 shows the range of IP addresses Eric assigned to the DHCP service running on the UASHOST server.

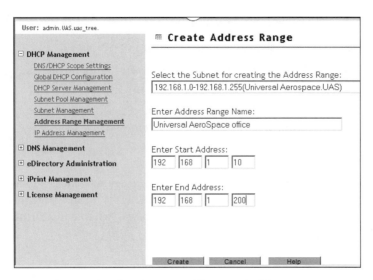

Figure C-16   Configuring a DHCP scope in iManager

In addition to providing a client with an IP address and a mask, the DHCP address scope can be configured to assign other TCP/IP settings to client computers, such as the address of the default gateway or router (see Figure C-17).

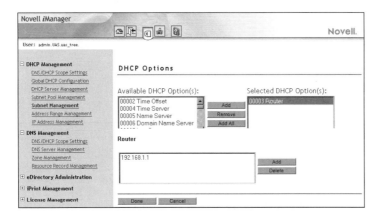

Figure C-17   Configuring an IP gateway in iManager

To configure a computer to obtain the IP address configuration from the DHCP server, perform the following steps:

1. Right-click My Network Places, and then click Properties to open the Network and Dial-up Connections dialog box.

2. Right-click the Local Area Connection icon, and then click Properties to open the Local Area Connection Properties dialog box.

3. Click Internet Protocol (TCP/IP), and then click Properties to open the Internet Protocol (TCP/IP) Properties dialog box, shown in Figure C-18.

4. Click the Obtain an IP address automatically radio button, and then click OK to save the settings and return to the Local Area Connection Properties dialog box.

5. Click OK again to save your changes, and then close the Network and Dial-up Connections dialog box. The system then obtains an IP address from the DHCP server or assigns itself an unused host address in the 169.254.0.0 network address range if no DHCP server is available.

C

Internet Protocol (TCP/IP) Properties   ? X

General

You can get IP settings assigned automatically if your network supports this capability. Otherwise, you need to ask your network administrator for the appropriate IP settings.

○ Obtain an IP address automatically
● Use the following IP address:

IP address: 172 . 20 . 0 . 112
Subnet mask: 255 . 255 . 0 . 0
Default gateway: .   .   .

○ Obtain DNS server address automatically
● Use the following DNS server addresses:

Preferred DNS server: .   .   .
Alternate DNS server: .   .   .

                                    Advanced...

                        OK   Cancel

Figure C-18   The Internet Protocol (TCP/IP) Properties dialog box

When a client is set to obtain an IP address automatically, when it starts up, it sends out a request for a DHCP server, as shown in Figure C-19.

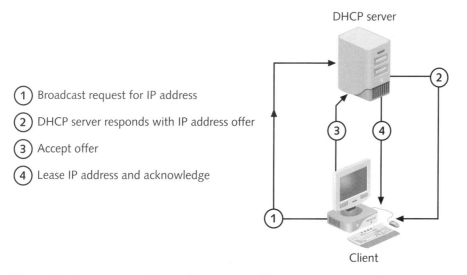

① Broadcast request for IP address

② DHCP server responds with IP address offer

③ Accept offer

④ Lease IP address and acknowledge

Figure C-19   Using DHCP to obtain an IP address

Any DHCP servers on the same network cable respond with an available IP address that the client can lease. The client takes the first response it receives and sends a packet back to the DHCP server requesting the IP address. The DHCP server then acknowledges the request and leases the IP address information to the client. If the client receives no DHCP responses, it assigns itself an available IP address in the range 169.254.*x*.*y* (*x* and *y* represent variable addresses).

To view the IP address information assigned to a client configured to obtain its address automatically, you need to enter the IPCONFIG /ALL command in the command-prompt window (see Figure C-20). If you change the DHCP scope configuration, such as changing the IP address of the gateway or DNS server, you can force the client to obtain the new information without restarting by entering the following commands in a command-prompt window:

```
IPCONFIG  /RELEASE
IPCONFIG  /RENEW
```

```
(C) Copyright 1985-1999 Microsoft Corp.

C:\>ipconfig /all

Windows 2000 IP Configuration

        Host Name . . . . . . . . . . . . : IS
        Primary DNS Suffix  . . . . . . . :
        Node Type . . . . . . . . . . . . : Broadcast
        IP Routing Enabled. . . . . . . . : No
        WINS Proxy Enabled. . . . . . . . : No

Ethernet adapter Local Area Connection:

        Connection-specific DNS Suffix  . :
        Description . . . . . . . . . . . : AMD PCNET Family PCI Ethernet Adapte
r
        Physical Address. . . . . . . . . : 00-50-56-72-32-22
        DHCP Enabled. . . . . . . . . . . : No
        IP Address. . . . . . . . . . . . : 172.20.1.200
        Subnet Mask . . . . . . . . . . . : 255.255.0.0
        Default Gateway . . . . . . . . . : 172.20.0.60
        DNS Servers . . . . . . . . . . . : 172.20.0.60
```

Figure C-20   Using the IPCONFIG command

Another useful command when testing TCP/IP communications is PING *ip_address*. The PING command allows you to send packets to another computer specified by its IP address or name and then wait for replies. By default, the PING command sends four 32-byte packets. If there's no reply in the default time period, a "Request timed out" error message is displayed. This message usually means that one of the following conditions exists:

- The target computer is not on.

- The target computer does not have the IP protocol configured.

- The target computer has a different IP address than the one used in the PING command.

- Either the target computer or the sending computer has an incorrect mask or gateway configuration.

 If a client that is configured to obtain its IP address from a DHCP server is not able to communicate on the network, use the IPCONFIG /ALL command to check its IP address. If it's assigned an IP address in the 169.254.*x.y* range, the client was unable to communicate with the DHCP server. Check to see that the DHCP server is up and running on the network.

In the following activity, you use the IPCONFIG command to document your IP configuration and then use PING to test communications with yourself and other hosts.

Activity C-4: Assigning and Testing IP Addresses

Time Required: 10 minutes

Objectives: Assign and troubleshoot IP addresses.

Description: In this activity, you document your computer's IP configuration and then modify the IP address assignment to obtain an IP address manually and automatically. You'll work with the IPCONFIG and PING commands to test your IP configuration.

1. If necessary, start your computer, and log on to the local workstation by clicking the **Workstation only** check box and entering the administrator user name and password for your Windows 2000 computer.

2. Right-click **My Network Places**, and then click **Properties** to open the Network and Dial-up Connections dialog box.

3. Right-click **Local Area Connection**, and then click **Properties** to open the Local Area Connection Properties dialog box.

4. Click the **Internet Protocol (TCP/IP)** component, and then click the **Properties** button to open the Internet Protocol (TCP/IP) Properties dialog box.

5. Record your existing IP configuration on your student answer sheet.

6. Perform the following steps if your workstation is configured to obtain an IP address manually (if not, skip to Step 7):

   a. Click the **Use the following IP address** radio button.

   b. Enter the IP address, mask, and gateway you identified for your workstation in Activity C-3.

   c. Click **OK** twice to save your changes and return to the Network and Dial-up Connections dialog box.

   d. Open a command-prompt window by clicking **Start**, **Run**, entering **cmd**, and clicking **OK**.

   e. Use the appropriate command to display your IP configuration. On your student answer sheet, record the command you use and your IP address information.

   f. Skip to Step 8.

7. Perform the following steps if your workstation is configured for an automatic IP address:

   a. Click the **Obtain an IP address automatically** radio button.

   b. Click **OK** twice to save your changes and return to the Network and Dial-up Connections dialog box.

   c. Open a command-prompt window by clicking **Start**, **Run**, entering **cmd**, and clicking **OK**.

   d. Use the appropriate command to display your IP configuration. On your student answer sheet, record the command you use and your IP address information.

8. Use the PING command to send packets to the IP address you identified for your classroom server in Activity C-3. On your student answer sheet, record the results of the PING command.

9. Enter **Exit** to return to the Windows desktop.

10. Repeat Steps 2 through 4 to return your workstation to the original IP address configuration you identified in Step 5.

11. Close any open windows, and log out.

Domain Name Service (DNS)

Another important part of implementing TCP/IP is identifying and configuring the **Domain Name Service (DNS)** for the network. No one wants to have to remember the IP addresses of other computers and Web servers that they need to access; it's much easier to use names. An additional advantage of using names is that the same name can be used to access a server even if the server's IP address changes. The DNS resolves TCP/IP names into IP addresses by having the client computer send a request to its assigned DNS server. The DNS server then looks up the name and returns the IP address to the client computer. TCP/IP names are often referred to as "domain names" because they include the server's name along with the name of the domain where the server is located. The Universal Resource Locator (URL) you use to access a Web site from your browser is an example of a domain name. For example, to access Novell's support site, you could enter the URL *http://support.novell.com*; "support" is the name of the server, and "novell.com" is the name of the domain the server resides in.

Domain names can be private or public. Private domain names are maintained on a local DNS server and are not available to computers outside the organization. To work on the Internet, public domain names need to be registered through an ISP. When a domain name is registered on the Internet, the computer's name and IP address are placed in a DNS server and made accessible to all computers attached to the Internet. As shown in Figure C-21, domain names on the Internet are organized by the Internet Corporation for Assigned Names and Numbers (ICANN) into a hierarchical structure based on the organization's type, location, and name.

The .com domain is reserved for commercial businesses, the .org domain is generally used only by non-profit organizations, the .gov domain is used for governmental agencies, and the .net domain contains names of Internet service providers. Top-level domains are also divided by country. There are more than 200 country top-level domains, such as .us, .uk, .ca, and .fr. The list of top-level domains keeps growing as new types are defined; some new types include .tv, .biz, .info, and .aero. For example, to allow outside users to access by name the UAS Web site stored on the UASHOST server, Luke McMann registered the domain name "uashost.uas.com" with the IP address 198.12.28.50.

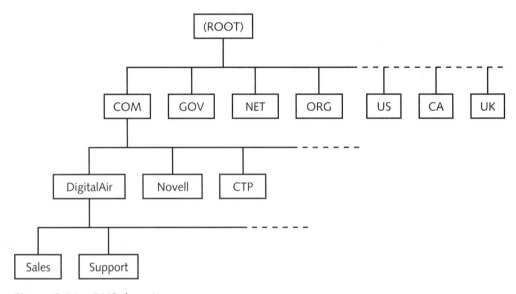

Figure C-21 DNS domains

 You can find more information on domain names and the registration process at *http://www.interNIC.net.*

There are thousands of computer domain names on the Internet, and keeping all these names on a single master DNS server would be impossible to manage. As a result, DNS servers typically contain only the names of computers in a single domain. The names for a domain are stored in a zone file, which contains all computer names for a specific domain. For example, the Novell DNS server would store the domain names of only the servers in the novell.com domain in its novell.com zone, and the Microsoft DNS server would keep track of the microsoft.com server names in its microsoft.com zone.

The top-level Internet domains are stored on 13 DNS servers referred to as the Internet (Root) servers. When a user makes a request for a server such as support.novell.com, the request is first sent to the DNS server specified in the client computer's TCP/IP configuration. The local DNS server then checks its cache to see whether the name has been used recently. If the support.novell.com name is not in the cache, the local DNS server performs a lookup process (see Figure C-22). In Step 1, the local DNS server sends a request to the (Root) server for the IP address of a DNS server responsible for the .com domain. After receiving the IP address of the .com domain server, in Step 2 the local DNS server sends a request to the .com domain server for the IP address of the server responsible for the novell.com zone. In Step 3, the local DNS server sends a request to the novell.com server asking for the IP address of the support.novell.com computer. Step 4 involves the local DNS server returning the IP address of the support.novell.com computer to the local client, which then sends a packet directly to the support.novell.com computer using the IP address it was given.

Because they are available only to computers on your network, private domain names are much simpler to set up and manage. To implement private domain names in the UAS network, Eric installed DNS on the NetWare 6 server, and then used iManager to create a zone file for the uas.com domain and add a record for the UASHOST server, as shown in Figure C-23.

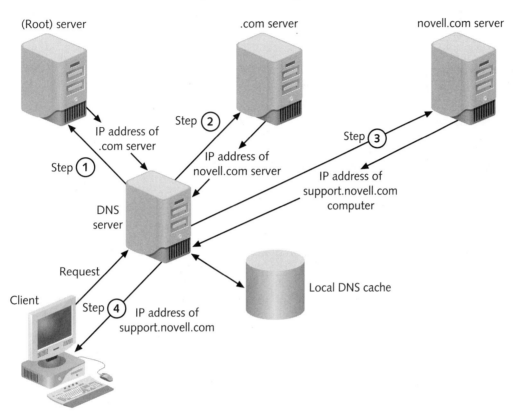

Figure C-22   The DNS lookup process

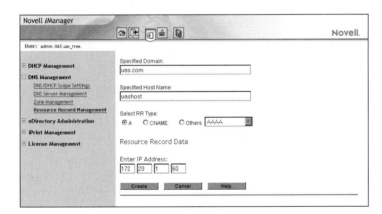

Figure C-23   Using iManager to implement private domain names

After setting up the NetWare 6 DNS sever, Eric needed to configure the computers on the UAS network to use the IP address of the UASHOST server as the primary DNS server and the address of the DNS server maintained by the ISP as the secondary name server. To configure DNS server information manually for each computer, you use the Preferred DNS server text box in the Internet Protocol (TCP/IP) Properties dialog box, as shown in Figure C-24. The information in the Alternate DNS server text box specifies the IP address of a second DNS server that the client can use if the primary DNS server does not respond and times out.

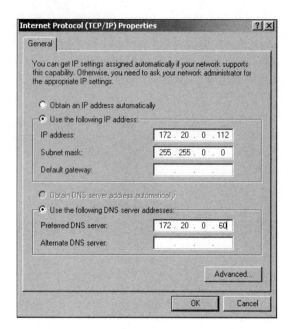

Figure C-24   Configuring DNS server information manually

Rather than manually setting primary and alternate DNS server IP addresses for each client computer, Eric configured the DHCP server scope (see Figure C-25) to automatically assign the DNS server addresses each time a computer starts.

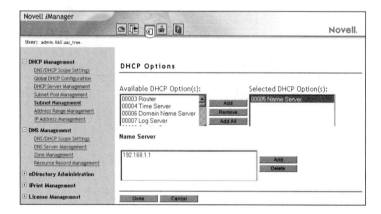

Figure C-25   Configuring the DHCP server scope

When a request is made for a domain name, the client computer consults its IP configuration to determine the IP address of its primary and alternate DNS servers. If the primary DNS server does not respond within a set time period, the client computer sends the request to the alternate DNS server. Eric selected the DNS server maintained by the ISP as the alternate name server so that users can still access the Internet domain names if the UASHOST server is down. If the alternate DNS server does not respond, an error message is displayed, telling the user that a DNS server is not available. When a DNS server receives a request from a client, it first checks to see whether it has the requested server's name and IP address in its memory cache. DNS servers keep a temporary list, or cache, of recently accessed names in memory to respond faster. If the name is not in the cache, the DNS server checks to see whether it has a copy of the zone file that contains the name and IP address information for all computers in the requested domain. When the DNS server has a zone file for the requested domain, it looks up the requested name and returns the IP address. If the name is not found in the zone file, an invalid name message is returned to the user. If the DNS server does not contain a copy of the zone file, it forwards the request to the Internet Domain Name Resolver, which returns the IP address of the server that contains the zone file for the requested domain. For example, if Eric enters the URL *http://support.novell.com* in his Web browser, the request is sent to the UASHOST server. Because the UASHOST server does not contain a copy of the novell.com domain, it forwards the request to the (Root) DNS server and obtains the address of the DNS server that has the zone file for the Novell domain. The UASHOST server then queries the Novell DNS server to obtain the IP address of the support.novell.com server. Finally, the UASHOST server returns the IP address for the support.novell.com server to Eric's Web browser, which uses the IP address to access the Novell support home page.

The NSLOOKUP command can be useful when checking your DNS server configuration. The syntax of the NSLOOKUP command is "NSLOOKUP name.domain"; "name" and "domain" represent the server name and domain stored in the DNS server. In the following activity, you configure your workstation to use your classroom server as the DNS server and then use the NSLOOKUP and PING commands to test your DNS server configuration.

Activity C-5: Using Domain Name Services

Time Required: 10 minutes

Objective: Configure a client computer to use DNS.

Description: In this activity, you configure your client to use the classroom DNS server and then test the configuration with the NSLOOKUP and PING commands. To perform this activity, you need to have a DNS server installed on your classroom network.

1. If necessary, start your computer, and log on to the local workstation by clicking the **Workstation only** check box and entering the administrator user name and password for your Windows 2000 computer.

2. Right-click **My Network Places**, and then click **Properties** to open the Network and Dial-up Connections dialog box.

3. Right-click **Local Area Connection**, and then click **Properties** to open the Local Area Connection Properties dialog box.

4. Click the **Internet Protocol (TCP/IP)** component, and then click the **Properties** button to open the Internet Protocol (TCP/IP) Properties dialog box.

5. If no DNS server is specified, click the **Use the following DNS server address** radio button, and enter the IP address (defined in Activity C-3) of your classroom DNS server.

6. Click **OK** twice to save your changes and return to the Network and Dial-up Connections dialog box.

7. Close the Network and Dial-up Connections dialog box.

8. Open a command-prompt window by clicking **Start**, **Run**, entering **cmd**, and then clicking **OK**.

9. Test your DNS server by entering the **NSLOOKUP uashost.uas.com** command and pressing **Enter**.

10. Record the results on your student answer sheet.

11. Test your DNS server by entering the **PING uashost.uas.com** command and pressing **Enter**.

12. Record the results on your student answer sheet.

13. Type **Exit**, and then press **Enter** to close the command-prompt window.

14. Log out.

Key Terms

10BaseT — A network system that uses CSMA/CD along with a star topology consisting of twisted-pair cables running from a central hub to each network device. 10BaseT networks transmit data at 10 Mbps.

100BaseT — A 100 Mbps version of the 10BaseT network system.

bandwidth — A measurement used to determine the capacity and speed of a cable system.

baseband — A network that carries digital signals consisting of ones and zeros.

broadband — A network that carries analog signals, such as those used by radio and cable television.

cable media — A wire used to transfer data between network components.

Carrier Sense Multiple Access with Collision Detection (CSMA/CD) — A method used to control access to Ethernet and 10BaseT networks by having a computer wait for an open carrier before transmitting a message. A collision occurs when two or more computers attempt to transmit at the same time, causing the computer to wait before attempting to retransmit the messages.

coaxial — A type of cable commonly used for television networks that consists of a single copper wire surrounded by a wire mesh shield.

Domain Name Service (DNS) — A service that resolves TCP/IP domain names into IP addresses by looking up the name based on the domain or zone the name belongs to.

Dynamic Host Configuration Protocol (DHCP) — A network service that automatically leases IP addresses to other computers when they're started.

Ethernet — A network system that uses CSMA/CD along with a linear bus consisting of computers attached to a coaxial cable segment by T-connectors.

fiber-optic — A cable that consists of glass fibers designed to carry light generated by pulsing lasers or light-emitting diodes. Fiber-optic cable is resistant to electronic interference and can be used for very high-speed computer networks that cover long distances.

linear bus topology — A network topology in which a single cable segment runs from one computer to the next.

mesh topology — A network topology in which each computer is attached to the others by using separate cables.

multiple station access unit (MSAU) — A central hub used to connect cables in a token ring network.

network interface card (NIC) — A hardware component used to connect each computer to the cable system.

patch panel — A centralized wiring panel used to connect individual wires coming from computers to a network hub.

ring topology — A network topology in which the signals are passed in one direction from one computer to another until they return to the original sending computer.

shielded twisted-pair (STP) — A type of cable consisting of pairs of insulated wires twisted together and encased in a wire mesh shield. The use of the grounded wire mesh shield in STP cable reduces the effect of outside interference from other electrical sources.

star topology — A network topology in which a cable runs from each network device to a central hub.

token ring — A network system that uses a star topology with twisted-pair cable running from the central MSAU hub to each computer. A token passing scheme is used to control access to the network by causing computers to wait for the token before transmitting their message, thereby eliminating collisions on CSMA/CD networks, such as Ethernet and 10BaseT.

unshielded twisted-pair (UTP) — A type of cable that consists of pairs of insulated wires twisted together to reduce electrical crosstalk.

zone file — The location in which a DNS servers keeps all computer name information for a specific domain.

D

UPGRADING TO NETWARE 6.5

In the high-tech world, change is usually depicted as a new version number, a code name, or a buzzword blasted over the Internet, such as OneNet, .NET, Sun One, and so forth. With each change, CNAs and CNEs alike wonder whether the skills they have mastered will become outdated or obsolete. Although many changes and enhancements have been made to Novell's reliable network operating system, the skills you have learned in NetWare 6 will help with what's available in NetWare 6.5. As illustrated in Figure D-1, NetWare 6.5 includes enhancements for IT administrators, end users, and software developers. In addition to the familiar ConsoleOne and NetWare Administrator utilities you learned to use in this textbook, IT administrators will benefit from version 2.0 of iManager, which now has all the capabilities of both ConsoleOne and NetWare Administrator in one Web-based administration utility. Network administrators will also appreciate the new installation and configuration capabilities of NetWare 6.5, which simplify the task of installing specialized servers and consolidating data from multiple servers into a single data center. End users will benefit from NetWare 6.5 Virtual Office, which provides a collaborative computing environment that enables users to organize and manage teams to communicate and share resources. NetWare 6.5 also furthers Novell's commitment to the open source concept by replacing the Enterprise Web Server in NetWare 6 with a second copy of the Apache Web Server as well as including open source software and Web development tools, such as PHP, MySQL, and Perl, at no additional cost. In this appendix, you update your NetWare skills by learning about many of the new administrative, end user, and software development features of NetWare 6.5.

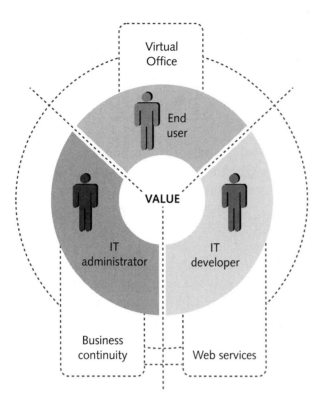

Figure D-1   Strategic areas of focus in NetWare 6.5

NetWare 6.5 Installation and Upgrading Enhancements

As networks grow, installing new servers and upgrading existing servers are ongoing processes in most multiserver organizations. One way in which NetWare 6.5 provides scalability for network growth is by adding specialized servers to the eDirectory tree. These servers, which are specialized for tasks such as running an Apache Web server or iFolder and iPrint services, can often improve network performance and management in a multiserver network.

As you learned in this book, a complete customized server installation of NetWare 6 can be rather complex and time consuming if all you want to do is set up a dedicated iFolder or Domain Name System/Dynamic Host Configuration Protocol (DNS/DHCP) server. Although the basics steps in a customized NetWare 6.5 server installation are similar to those in NetWare 6, Novell offers new server installation options called "Choose a pattern" to help simplify and speed up the installation of specialized servers, as shown in Figure D-2.

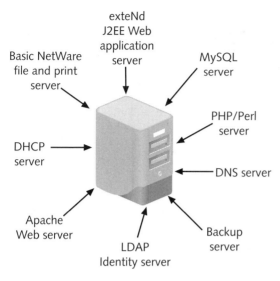

Figure D-2   NetWare 6.5 patterned server installation options

These pattern options, shown in Figure D-3, enable administrators to select what type of server they want to install.

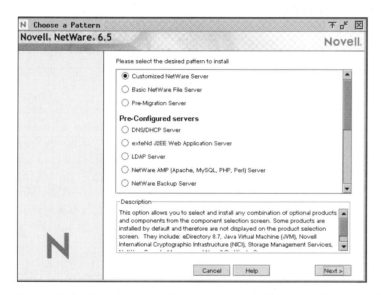

Figure D-3   Selecting a patterned server option in the Choose a Pattern dialog box

- The Customized NetWare Server pattern takes you through all the server installation and configuration options, allowing you to select and configure each option manually.

- The Basic NetWare File Server pattern simplifies the process of installing a server that will be used specifically as a NetWare file server by automatically selecting and configuring the options necessary to provide file services.

- Although some organizations are installing a NetWare 6.5 server as their first NetWare server, often it's more common to install a NetWare 6.5 server in an existing eDirectory tree or to upgrade a server running an older NetWare version. Because the hardware requirements for NetWare 6.5 are more demanding than earlier NetWare versions (see Table D-1), many administrators find it more feasible to install NetWare 6.5 on a new computer and then use the Novell Migration Wizard to migrate users and data from the earlier NetWare server to the new NetWare 6.5 server. Novell includes the Pre-Migration Server pattern to make it easier for administrators to install a server that's configured to be the target server for the migration process.

Table D-1   NetWare 6.5 Hardware Requirements

Component	Minimum Requirement
Processor	Pentium II or AMD K7 (Pentium IV recommended)
Memory	512 MB (1 GB recommended)
Disk	200 MB DOS partition (1.2 GB recommended if you have 1 GB RAM—200 MB for DOS plus 1 GB to hold memory dumps equals a 1.2 GB partition) 2 GB free for SYS volume (4 GB recommended for SYS volume)
Monitor	Super VGA

- The patterns under the Pre-Configured servers section are used to automate the installation of special-purpose servers. For example, if you indicate a DNS/DHCP installation, the pattern installation process asks for the information needed to install DNS/DHCP. After you supply the information, the pattern installation process quickly and automatically installs the necessary software and customizes the server to maximize DNS/DHCP performance. An important Novell strategy is to fully support open-source application development in NetWare 6.5. Because NetWare 6.5 offers so many open-source development tools, Novell has included the NetWare AMP (which stands for Apache, MySQL, PHP/Perl) server pattern to simplify installing and configuring a server specialized for open-source application development.

Performing a NetWare 6.5 Server Installation

A new NetWare 6.5 server installation uses many of the same steps described in the textbook for a NetWare 6 installation, but the NetWare 6.5 process follows a slightly different sequence and includes some new options, such as pattern deployment, a main menu, and several enhanced login security options (described in Appendix E).

The best way to learn about the new installation process and options is to go through an installation of a NetWare 6.5 server. Assume that you work for a network consulting company, and one of your co-workers, Kathleen Stanton, has just completed a NetWare 6.5 training class. A small startup company, Rocky Ridge Enterprises, is planning to install a NetWare 6.5 server to handle its business needs. Rocky Ridge selected NetWare 6.5 because it offers a secure and open-source environment for in-house development of Web applications. The Rocky Ridge manager has purchased new server hardware that exceeds the NetWare 6.5 minimum requirements and would like your consulting company to install the NetWare 6.5 operating system and configure the server. The following sections describe the steps Kathleen uses to install a customized NetWare 6.5 server for the Rocky Ridge organization.

If you have a computer with a blank hard disk or have VMWare installed on your workstation, you can follow these steps to practice a NetWare 6.5 installation. You can use your server to perform the activities in this appendix.

Initial Installation Phase

As in the NetWare 6 installation process, the initial installation phase uses text-based menus and screens to select language and keyboard settings, to choose disk and LAN drivers, and to create the SYS volume. The NetWare 6.5 installation process includes a new screen, the NSS Main Menu, for creating additional partitions, pools, and volumes during this installation phase. The Main Menu can be accessed after installation by entering the command NSSMU at the server console. The following steps illustrate Kathleen's progress through the initial installation phase:

1. Kathleen inserted the NetWare 6.5 (Operating System) CD 1 into the CD-ROM drive of the server and restarted it. She chose the default options: "I" to install a new server and "A" to search for a CD-ROM driver. Next, she selected "A" for Auto terminate and then "A" for Auto Execution.

2. When the installation program started, she pressed Enter to select the option to install in English.

3. She pressed Enter again to accept the default regional settings for Country, Code page, and Keyboard.

4. Next, she read the NetWare 6.5 license agreement and then pressed the F10 key to accept and continue.

5. She pressed the F10 key again to accept the JReport runtime license agreement and display the Welcome to the NetWare 6.5 server installation window shown in Figure D-4.

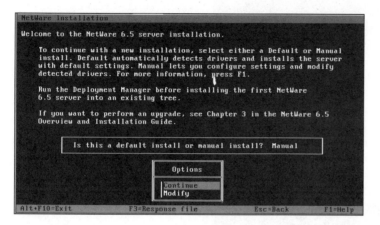

Figure D-4   The Welcome to the NetWare 6.5 server installation window

6. To customize the installation, Kathleen pressed Enter to change the default installation type to Manual. Next, she pressed the Tab key to select the Continue option and pressed Enter to display the Prepare boot partition window.

7. The Prepare boot partition window allows the installer to create a DOS boot partition within the first 8 GB of the server's hard drive. The minimum DOS partition boot size is 200 MB, but Novell recommends adding space to hold a memory dump in case the server undergoes a hardware fault. Because this server has 1 GB of RAM, Kathleen selected the Modify option, pressed Enter, highlighted Free Space, and then pressed Enter; she typed in a size of 1200 MB for the DOS partition. She pressed Enter again, and the installation program formatted the DOS boot partition and returned to the Prepare boot partition window. Kathleen pressed Tab, selected the Continue option, and then pressed Enter to display the Server Settings window.

8. Kathleen recorded the server ID number on her installation worksheet and then pressed Enter to start the file copy process. During this process, files are copied from the Operating System CD to the DOS partition. These files include the server startup software, configuration files, and drivers.

9. After the files are copied, the installation program displays the detected platform support driver. Kathleen pressed Enter to accept and load the detected driver and display the detected HotPlug and Storage adapters.

10. Kathleen verified the detected driver and adapters and pressed Enter to display the detected storage devices. Again, Kathleen verified these devices and then pressed Enter to continue and load them.

11. Next, the installation program displays the drivers that support the detected LAN adapter. Kathleen selected the driver identified by her computer hardware configuration and pressed Enter to display the Device types and Driver names window. She pressed Enter again to accept the devices and continue loading the drivers.

12. After the drivers loaded, the installation program displayed the Create SYS Volume window shown in Figure D-5.

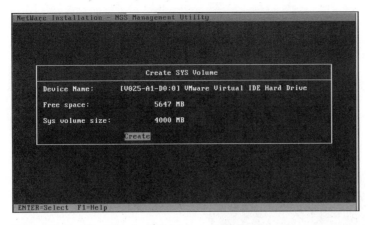

Figure D-5   The Create SYS Volume window

13. Kathleen pressed Enter to accept the default 4 GB SYS volume size and display the NSS Main Menu window shown in Figure D-6. This installation menu is a new addition to NetWare 6.5 and allows the installer to customize or change the configuration of devices, storage pools, and volumes without restarting the installation program.

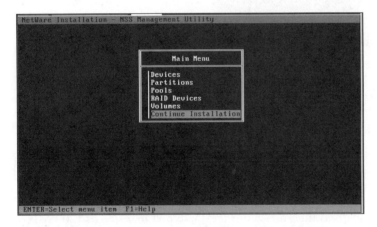

Figure D-6   The NetWare 6.5 main menu for installation

14. Kathleen performed the following steps to create an NSS pool named CORP for user data:

   a. From the NSS Main Menu, she selected the Partitions option and pressed Enter to display the Partitions window.

   b. She pressed the Insert key, selected the Free Space option, and pressed Enter to display the Select Partition Type window.

   c. Next, she verified that NSS was selected and pressed Enter to display the Create Partition window.

   d. She then used the arrow keys to select the Create option and pressed Enter to create a new partition and return to the Partitions window.

   e. She pressed Esc to return to the NSS Main Menu.

   f. Next, she selected the Pools option and pressed Enter to display the Pools window.

   g. To create a new pool, she pressed the Insert key and then typed the name CORP in the Enter new pool name text box. She pressed Enter to display the Available Partitions window.

   h. She pressed Enter to select the previously created partition and display the Pool Information window.

   i. After creating the CORP pool, Kathleen pressed Esc to return to the NSS Main Menu.

15. Kathleen used the following steps to create a new volume named USERDATA for user data:

   a. From the NSS Main Menu, she selected the Volumes option and pressed Enter to display the Logical Volumes window.

   b. She typed USERDATA in the Enter new volume name text box and pressed Enter to display the Pools window.

   c. She selected the USERDATA pool and pressed Enter to display the Change Volume Properties window.

   d. Next, she set the Directory Quotas attribute to yes, as shown in Figure D-7.

   e. She highlighted the Create option and pressed Enter to create the new volume and return to the Logical Volumes window.

   f. After creating the USERDATA volume, she used the Esc key to return to the NSS Main Menu.

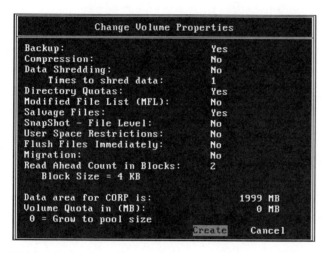

Figure D-7   The Change Volume Properties window

16. After creating the USERDATA volume, Kathleen used the Esc key to return to the main menu. She selected the Continue Installation option and pressed Enter to start another file copy process. This process copies all the system files to the SYS volume and then loads the server program. She took a short break while waiting a few minutes for the files to be copied.

Pattern Selection Phase

The pattern selection phase allows installers to select the type of server installation they want to perform and then enter the configuration information required for that type of installation. At the end of this phase, the installation process copies the necessary files into the SYS volume. The following steps show how Kathleen performed this part of the installation:

1. After the server program loaded, the Choose a Pattern dialog box shown previously in Figure D-3 was displayed. Because this server will be a general-purpose one, Kathleen left the default Customized NetWare Server radio button selected and clicked Next to display the Components dialog box shown in Figure D-8.

2. Kathleen selected the following installation options (she plans to install additional features, such as the FTP server, later):

- Apache2 Web Server and Tomcat 4 Servlet Container (required for iPrint)
- iPrint
- MySQL
- OpenSSH
- eGuide

- Novell iManager 2.0
- Novell Virtual Office Framework

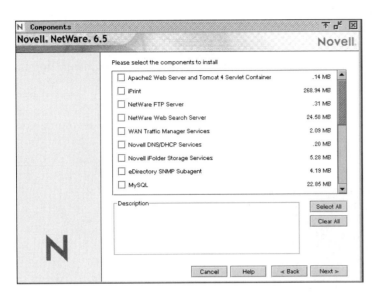

Figure D-8   The Components dialog box

3. After selecting these options, Kathleen clicked Next to display the installation summary window.

4. Kathleen verified that all the products she wanted to install at this time were included. Next, she clicked the Copy Files button and inserted the NetWare 6.5 (Products) CD 2 and clicked OK when prompted. Because this file copy takes almost 30 minutes, Kathleen decided to take a well-deserved break.

During the file copy process, windows with information about the selected products are displayed.

Server Configuration Phase

During this final phase of the server installation, installers need to enter the server name, supply the license information, select and configure any network protocols to be used, identify the time zone, install eDirectory, and select any additional login methods to be used by network clients. Kathleen used the following steps to complete this final phase of the installation:

1. After finishing the file copy, the installation process displays the Enter the server name dialog box. Kathleen entered Rocky65 in the Server Name text box and then clicked Next to display the Encryption dialog box. NetWare services encrypt data by using cryptographic files (with the extension .nfk) located on the server license diskette.

You can use the Browse button to locate cryptographic files on other media. The NetWare 6.5 Products CD contains a License folder with cryptographic and license files that can be used to install an evaluation or demonstration server.

2. Kathleen inserted her license diskette and clicked Next to configure cryptography and then display the Protocols dialog box.

3. She clicked the IP check box and entered the IP address and mask for the NetWare 6.5 server. She then clicked Next to display the Domain Name Service dialog box shown in Figure D-9.

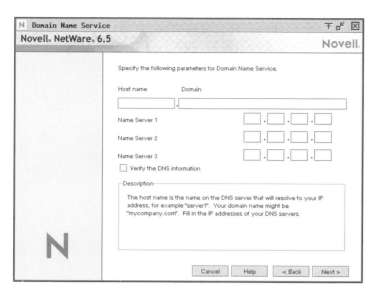

Figure D-9 The Domain Name Service dialog box

4. Because there's no DNS server on the local network, Kathleen left all fields blank and clicked Next. When she received a warning message informing her that some services will have limited functionality without the DNS service, she clicked OK to continue.

5. Next, she selected her time zone and clicked Next to initialize the eDirectory service and display the eDirectory Installation dialog box.

6. She clicked the Create a new eDirectory tree radio button, and then clicked Next to display the eDirectory Installation dialog box shown in Figure D-10.

7. Kathleen entered RR_TREE in the Tree Name text box and RockyRidge in the Context for Server Object text box. She then entered the password for the Admin user in the Password and Retype Password text boxes, and clicked Next to install eDirectory and display the eDirectory Summary window. She recorded the information from this window on her server installation worksheet and clicked Next to display the Licenses dialog box.

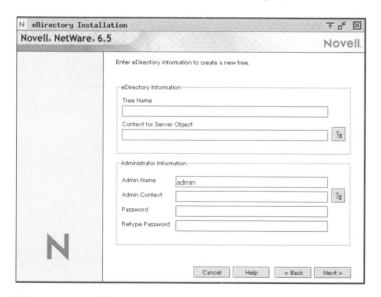

Figure D-10 The eDirectory Installation dialog box

8. The Licenses dialog box can be used to install licenses for the NetWare 6.5 server and users during server installation. License files have an .nlf extension and can also be installed after server installation by using iManager as described in the textbook. Because the Rocky Ridge company has an MLA server license, no user licenses are required. Kathleen used the Browse button to locate the MLA license certificate on her floppy diskette and then added it to the License(s) to be installed list box (see Figure D-11).

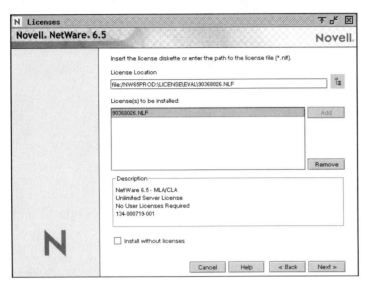

Figure D-11   The Licenses dialog box

 A sample MLA license certificate for evaluation purposes is included on the NetWare 6.5 Products CD in the License\eval folder.

9. Kathleen clicked Next to display the MLA License Certificate Context dialog box. The Select the NDS context text box allows the installer to specify the context where licenses are installed. The licenses are then valid for all users in the selected context and below. Kathleen verified that the context was set to the RockyRidge Organization, and then clicked Next to install the licenses and display the LDAP Configuration dialog box.

10. She recorded the default clear text and SSL/TLS port numbers on her server worksheet, and then clicked Next to accept the default port settings and display the Novell Modular Authentication Service dialog box shown in Figure D-12.

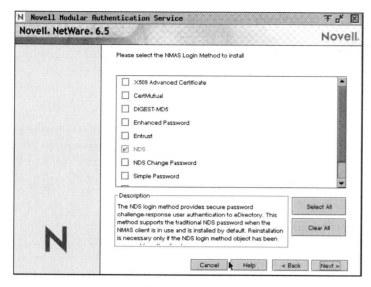

Figure D-12   Selecting a login method in the Novell Modular Authentication Service
dialog box

11. The Novell Modular Authentication Service dialog box allows the installer to select from a variety
of standard security options, described in Appendix E. In addition to the default NDS login method,
Kathleen selected the Simple Password login method so that Windows client computers in the
Marketing Department could log in without using the Novell client software. She then clicked Next
to display the MySQL Options dialog box shown in Figure D-13.

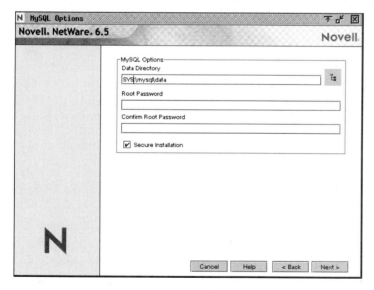

Figure D-13   The MySQL Options dialog box

12. She recorded the default path to the MySQL data directory on her server worksheet and then
entered a password in the Root Password and Confirm Root Password text boxes.

13. After she clicked Next, the installation program finished configuring each selected service.
Kathleen removed all CDs and floppy disks, and then restarted the server.

Installing NetWare 6.5 on Blade Computers

Another enhancement in the NetWare 6.5 installation process is being able to quickly and easily install
multiple NetWare servers on blade computers, which consist of one to several computers housed in a single cabinet (see Figure D-14).

In a blade system, each computer consists of a single board containing CPU, memory, disk storage, and network controller. Each server blade slides into a socket that connects it to a backplane, which supplies it with common infrastructure components, such as power supply, shared video and keyboard, CD-ROM, network switches, and system ports. Blade servers save space, improve access convenience, and reduce equipment costs and are a convenient way of clustering NetWare servers to share a common network storage device (as described earlier in the textbook).

Novell has optimized the NetWare 6.5 installation process to support simple, automated installation on multiple blade servers through the use of ZENworks images. In this textbook, you learned how to use ZENworks for Desktops to create user policies that help manage the desktop environment. With NetWare 6.5, you can also use ZENworks policies to create a server image that supplies the information for automatically installing NetWare 6.5 on a blade server.

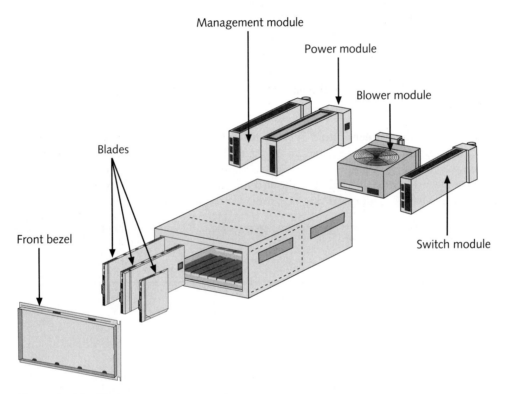

Figure D-14   Blade server components

Managing Branch Offices

For large organizations, providing network services and business continuity to branch offices distributed across a wide geographical area has traditionally been an expensive undertaking. In addition, branch offices might not have the equipment or technical support staff to perform regular backups and recover from problems, resulting in possible data loss and increased support time. For example, Novell has more than 100 branch offices located around the world. In this environment, managing and maintaining servers at remote locations can involve considerable travel and administrative expense. Although consolidating servers into a corporate data center can reduce travel and administration time, it often results in unacceptable response times for users at branch offices. Novell has helped solve these problems through the Novell Nterprise Branch Office Appliance included with NetWare 6.5. As shown in Figure D-15, Nterprise Branch Office is a multifunction software appliance that enables network administrators to centralize control and reduce costs by caching eDirectory and file system information kept at the data center on one or more servers at each branch office.

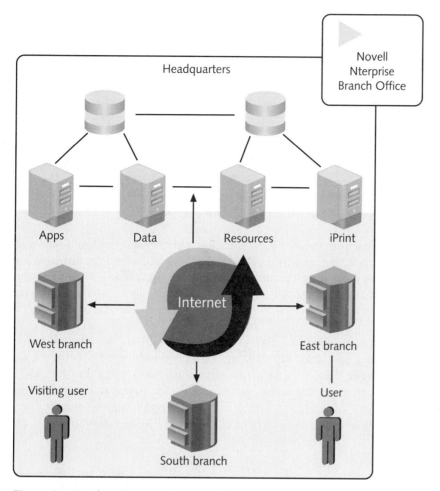

Figure D-15   The Nterprise Branch Office Appliance

Novell refers to the Nterprise Branch Office system as an "appliance" because it requires no complex installation process; you simply insert the preconfigured Nterprise CD into the computer you want to be the branch office cached server and start it up. The Nterprise Branch Office Appliance is then copied to the hard disk, and the system is up and running. The branch office will have a local cached copy of eDirectory and frequently accessed data, thus providing high performance yet still allowing centralized system management from the data center.

As shown in Figure D-15, Nterprise Branch Office servers use standardized Internet connections to communicate with the corporate office. Using the multiple network paths available on the Internet eliminates the extra expense of dedicated WAN links and helps reduce network downtime. When a user logs in at a branch office, the Nterprise Branch Office Appliance first checks its eDirectory cache for the user name and password; if the user does not exist on the local eDirectory cache, the Nterprise appliance uses LDAP to check the corporate server's eDirectory. When the user is found, a copy of the user's eDirectory data is cached on the local Nterprise appliance, a user home directory is created, and access to shared printers and folders is granted.

Server Consolidation

As organizations and their networks grow, network administrators often need to consolidate data from branch office servers into the corporate data center and merge older servers into new directory trees. NetWare 6.5's new Consolidation utility has options for automating the process of moving a server into another tree and consolidating data from multiple servers into a corporate data center. The NetWare 6.5 Consolidation utility can save network administrators many nerve-wracking hours of attempting these processes manually. For example, implementing Nterprise Branch Office Appliances at distributed offices requires moving the data currently at the branch office server to the corporate data center and then using Nterprise Branch Manager to set up a cache appliance at the branch office. Before implementing the Nterprise Branch Office Appliance, network administrators can use the Consolidation utility to move data from existing servers to servers in the corporate data center. After the data has been successfully consolidated in the data center, the Nterprise Branch Manager Appliance replaces the existing local servers.

Network administrators can also use the Consolidation utility to move data to a new location when implementing cluster volumes. To implement a cluster volume using NetWare 6.5, the network administrator would first create a clustered volume on a network storage device shared by two NetWare 6.5 servers and then copy the files and trustee assignments from the original data volumes. In NetWare 6, an administrator would need to manually copy all the files from the existing volume to the new clustered volume, reassign network rights to users and groups, and eventually delete the old data.

 As described in the textbook, a clustered volume is located on a network storage device that's shared among multiple servers. The advantages of having a clustered volume are improved performance (because two or more servers share the access load) and increased fault tolerance (because access to the volume is still possible if hardware failure or planned maintenance activities have caused a server to be down).

However, with the NetWare 6.5 Consolidation utility, this process is more automated and reliable; the administrator can now simply drag and drop the existing volume onto the new clustered volume. The Consolidation utility then moves the data, along with file attributes and trustee assignments, to the new location. The process is nondestructive, in that if the operation fails, the original data is still intact and the process can be restarted easily. The Consolidation utility can save network administrators much time and frustration and reduce expenses caused by administrative overhead and server downtime.

Remote Upgrades

In today's rapidly growing network environments, upgrading servers to newer versions and installing support packs are frequent tasks for network administrators to keep organizations' information systems current. NetWare 6.5 offers the powerful Remote Upgrade utility that enables a network administrator at one location to upgrade a server at a different site simply by identifying the server to be upgraded (the target server) and the server containing the new software (called the source server). It's even possible for the source server and target servers to be in two separate sites with the network administrator at a third location. For example, a network administrator in Utah could use the Remote Upgrade utility to instruct a source server in Sydney, Australia containing a new support pack to automatically upgrade another server in Perth. This upgrade capability promises to save large organizations the time and money currently required to keep their servers upgraded with the latest software versions.

NETWORK ADMINISTRATION AND BUSINESS CONTINUITY

In addition to installing and upgrading servers, a network administrator must perform a wide variety of tasks, including implementing and maintaining eDirectory trees, setting up and managing network users and printing, backing up data, and securing network resources. Novell refers to the network administration tasks that ensure an organization's continuous operation as the network's "business continuity needs." As networks have become more integrated and wide ranging, business continuity has become more complex to manage. The resulting increase in administrative time has resulted in extra costs for many organizations attempting to implement and maintain large networks of servers in multiple locations. After considerable research into the business continuity needs of today's integrated networks, Novell has enhanced NetWare 6.5 with several important features to reduce network administration time and costs and provide additional services, as described in the following sections.

iManager 2.0 Enhancements

Introduced in NetWare 6, iManager 2.0 is expanded and enhanced in NetWare 6.5 to include the capabilities of both ConsoleOne and NetWare Administrator, providing enhanced administrative tasks and remote server management features, such as:

- Creating and managing eDirectory objects
- Working with eDirectory partitions
- Managing storage resources
- Running server diagnostics
- Performing intrusion detection
- Creating branch office connections
- Handling outages

In the following sections, you learn how to use iManager 2.0 to perform a variety of administrative procedures, including creating objects, working with universal passwords, viewing eDirectory partition information, and creating tasks.

Starting iManager

iManager 2.0 has many new options and features not available with iManager 1.0. One of the first differences you'll notice is the startup process. As in iManager 1.0, to start iManager 2.0, you open your Web browser and enter the URL (*https://ip_address* or *Server_name*:2200) for your NetWare 6.5 server to display the login window shown in Figure D-16. Notice that by default the secure port 636 is used along with a Secure Sockets Layer (SSL) connection. More information about using SSL to create a secure connection is provided in Appendix E.

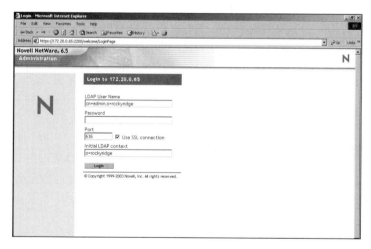

Figure D-16   The Administration login dialog box in NetWare 6.5

To start iManager 2.0, perform the following step after starting your browser and entering the URL stated previously:

1. If necessary, enter the user name and context of your Admin user.

2. Next, enter the password for the Admin user and then click the Login button to display the Welcome to NetWare 6.5 window, similar to the one in Figure D-17.

3. Click the + sign to expand the Network Management option and then click the iManager 2.0 option to display the Novell iManager 2.0 startup window shown in Figure D-18.

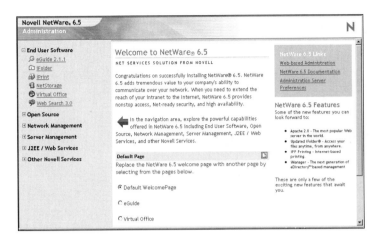

Figure D-17 The Welcome to NetWare 6.5 window

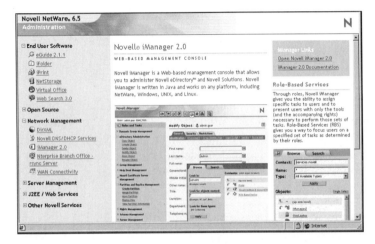

Figure D-18 The Novell iManager 2.0 startup window

4. Click the Open Novell iManager 2.0 link under the iManager Links heading at the upper-right to start the iManager 2.0 utility and display the Novell iManager window (similar to the window shown in Figure D-19).

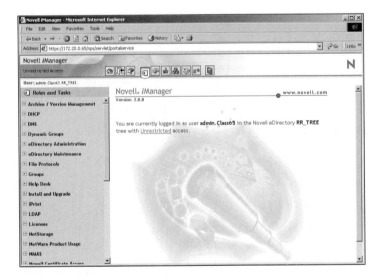

Figure D-19 The Novell iManager 2.0 main window

Notice all the options available in the Roles and Tasks frame on the left. These options are based on the tasks assigned to your login user name. Novell has enhanced iManager 2.0 so that administrators can now be assigned roles to perform all the administrative functions that previously required ConsoleOne or NetWare Administrator. For example, Kathleen performed the following steps in iManager to create a new DATA volume on the Rocky Ridge server. If you have supervisor rights to your NetWare 6.5 server, you can follow these steps to create a DATA volume on your server.

1. After opening her Web browser and logging in, Kathleen started iManager by following the steps described previously.

2. Next, she expanded the Storage option in the Roles and Tasks frame and clicked the Volumes option to open the Volume Management window.

3. She clicked the magnifying glass icon next to the Server text box and selected the Rocky65 server object to display the existing volumes (see Figure D-20).

4. To create a new volume named USERDATA, Kathleen clicked the New button to display the New Volume text box.

5. She entered the name USERDATA and clicked Next to open the New Volume window (similar to the one shown in Figure D-21).

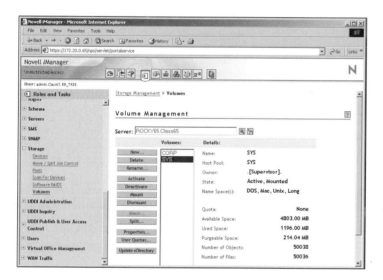

Figure D-20   The Volume Management window

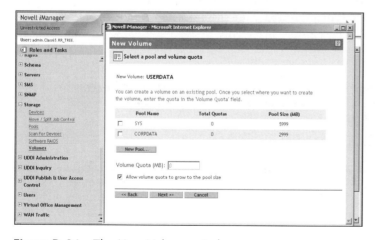

Figure D-21   The New Volume window

6. To assign the new USERDATA volume to the CORP storage pool and allow the volume to grow to CORP's maximum size, Kathleen clicked the check box next to CORP.

 To restrict the amount of space available to the USERDATA volume, you can click to clear the Allow volume quota to grow to the pool size check box and then enter a limit in the Volume Quota (MB) text box.

7. Kathleen then clicked Next to display the Attribute information window shown in Figure D-22.

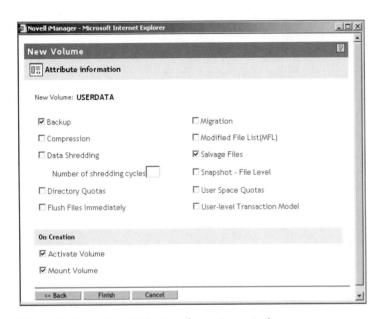

Figure D-22   The Attribute information window

8. She clicked the Directory Quotas and User Space Quotas check boxes and then clicked Finish to create the new USERDATA volume and return to the Volume Management window.

9. Kathleen clicked the Update eDirectory button to create the associated eDirectory object for the new volume, and then clicked the Home button to return to the main iManager window.

After creating the USERDATA volume, Kathleen used iManager to create user accounts with home directories on the new volume. To keep user accounts separate from other operating system objects, Kathleen decided to create an RRUSERS Organizational Unit (OU) within the RockyRidge Organization and a HOMEDIR folder on the USERDATA volume. She then created a template object to add the user accounts shown in Table D-2. To see how this is done, follow the steps in Activity D-1.

Table D-2   Marketing Users

Login Name	Full Name	Comments
##RWiggerts	Rosemarie Wiggerts	General Manager
##CDunn	Clara Dunn	Administrative Assistant
##WLocke	William Locke	Production Manager
##MHeise	Mary Heise	Marketing Manager

Activity D-1: Creating eDirectory Objects

Time Required: 20 minutes

Objective: Use iManager to create eDirectory objects

Description: As the network administrator for Rocky Ridge, you have already created a USERDATA volume and now need to create the user accounts shown in Table D-2 in the RRUSERS OU. In this activity, you use iManager 2.0 to create an RRUSERS OU within your assigned container and then create the users in Table D-2 by using a template.

1. Open your Web browser and enter the URL *https://ip_address:2200* (*ip_address* represents the IP address of your NetWare 6.5 server).

2. Follow the procedure described previously to open the iManager main window.

3. Create a HOMEDIR folder in your assigned storage area by following these steps:

   a. Click the **+** symbol next to the Servers option to expand it.

   b. Click the **Launch NetWare Remote Manager** option to open the Launch NetWare Remote Manager window.

   c. Click the **Browse** button to the right of the NCP Server name text box, and use the ObjectSelector window to select your NetWare 6.5 server.

   d. Click **OK** to open the Volume Management window.

   e. Click the volume assigned to your student account to display the NetWare File Listing window, similar to the one in Figure D-23. In this figure, 10Sample represents a storage folder assigned to a student.

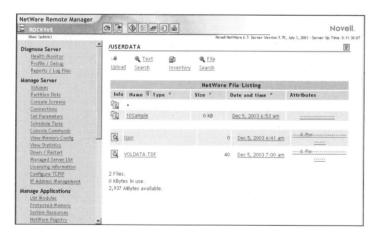

Figure D-23   The NetWare File Listing window in Remote Manager

   f. If necessary, navigate to your assigned folder by clicking on the folder name. (For example, to open the 10Sample folder, click on the name 10Sample.)

   g. Click the **Info** icon to the left of the single "." to display the Create Subdirectory button shown in Figure D-24.

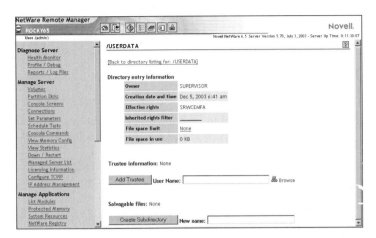

Figure D-24   Viewing file information

    h. Enter **RRHOME** in the New name text box, and click the **Create Subdirectory** button to create the new directory and return to the Volume Management window.

    i. Click the **Exit** button on the toolbar to return to the iManager window.

4. Create the RRUSERS OU in your assigned container:

    a. In the Roles and Tasks frame, click the **+** sign to expand the eDirectory Administration option.

    b. Click the **Create Object** link to open the Create Object window.

    c. Click **Organizational Unit** in the Available object classes list box, and then click **OK** to open the Create Organizational Unit window.

    d. Enter **RRUSERS** in the Organizational Unit name text box.

    e. Click the **Browse** button (magnifying glass icon) next to the Context text box to open the ObjectSelector window.

    f. If necessary, navigate down the tree until your assigned container is displayed in the Contents frame.

    g. Click your assigned container to place its name in the Context text box.

    h. Click **OK** to create the RRUSERS OU, and then click **OK** when the "Create Organizational Unit request succeeded" message is displayed.

5. Create the T_RRUSER user template in your RRUSERS OU:

    a. Click the **Create Object** link to open the Create Object window.

    b. Scroll down the Available object classes list box, click the **Template** object class, and then click **OK** to open the Create Template window.

    c. Enter **T_RRUSER** in the Template name text box.

    d. Click the **Browse** button next to the Context text box to open the ObjectSelector window.

    e. If necessary, navigate down the tree until your RRUSERS OU is displayed in the Contents frame.

    f. Click your **RRUSERS** container to place its context in the Context text box, and then click **OK** to create the object and display the "Create Template request succeeded" message. Click **OK** to return to the Novell iManager main window.

6. Configure the T_RRUSER template by performing the following steps:

    a. Click the **Modify Object** link under the eDirectory Administration heading to open the Modify Object window.

    b. Click the **Browse** button next to the Object name text box to open the ObjectSelector window.

    c. Click the **down arrow** next to the RRUSERS OU to display the T_RRUSER template object.

d. Click the **T_RRUSER** template object to place its context in the Context text box, and then click **OK** to open the Modify Object window shown in Figure D-25.

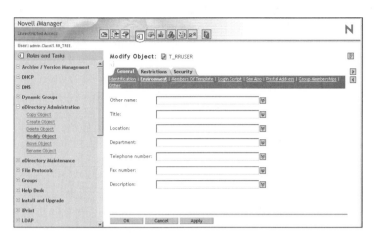

Figure D-25   The Modify Object window

    e. Explore the tabs in the Modify Object window and notice that you can set the same parameters described in the textbook when using ConsoleOne to work with templates.

    f. In the Environment tab, select the **RRHOME** folder in your assigned volume for the user home directory path.

    g. Click **OK** to save your changes, and then click **OK** again to return to the iManager main window.

7. Follow these steps to create a user account for Rosemarie Wiggerts:

    a. Click the **+** symbol to expand the Users options.

    b. Click the **Create User** link to open the Create window.

    c. Enter the user's login name, **##RWiggerts** (## represents your assigned student number), in the Username text box and **Wiggerts** in the Last name text box.

    d. Click the **Browse** button next to the Context text box, and in the Object Selector window, click your **RRUSERS** OU to place it in the Context text box.

    e. Click the **Copy from template or user object** check box, use the **Browse** button to navigate to your RRUSERS OU, and click your **T_RRUSER** template object.

    f. If necessary, click the **Create home directory** check box to enable it. Click the **Browse** button next to the Volume text box, and then navigate to your assigned volume.

    g. Click in the **Path** text box and enter the path (preceded by a backslash) to the RRHOME folder you created in Step 3.

    h. Enter a password in the Password and Retype Password text boxes, and then click the **Set simple password** check box.

    i. Scroll down and click the **OK** button to create the new user account and display the "Create User request succeeded" message box. Continue to the next step.

8. Create the remaining users shown in Table D-2:

    a. Click the **Repeat Task** button to return to the Create User window.

    b. Repeat Step 7 to create the remaining users in Table D-2. (Remember to include your assigned student number at the beginning of each user's login name.)

    c. After creating the last user, click **OK** in the "Create User request succeeded" message box to return to the main iManager window.

9. Click the **Exit** button on the toolbar to exit iManager, and then close your Web browser.

Working with Universal Passwords

In the textbook, you learned that NetWare 6 and 6.5 include the Native File Access Protocol (NFAP) feature, which makes it possible for Windows, Macintosh, and Unix workstations to access the NetWare server without installing the Novell client software. NFAP is an important feature, because many organizations want to minimize software complexity on user workstations. The downside of using the workstation's native client protocol is that certain NetWare features aren't available, such as the additional security built into Novell Client's eDirectory password encryption. When accessing the NetWare 6 or NetWare 6.5 server from a workstation that doesn't have Novell Client installed, the client computer uses its own password encryption algorithm to secure the password. This requires eDirectory to maintain two passwords, one for Novell Client encryption and another, called a "simple password," to differentiate it from the more secure eDirectory password, for native client protocols. If users need to log in from multiple workstations (some with Novell Client and some without) when using NetWare 6, they have to maintain two passwords, one for Novell Client workstations and the other for native client workstations. With NetWare 6.5, Novell simplifies the management of simple passwords by implementing a universal password option. After the universal password option is enabled in an OU, the "simple password" is automatically synchronized with the eDirectory password whenever a user in that OU logs in from a Novell client. From then on, the NetWare operating system synchronizes the two passwords, allowing the user to maintain only one password for both Novell and native client workstations. In the following activity, you enable universal passwords for your RRUSERS OU and then verify that the eDirectory password works when logging in from a Novell or Microsoft client.

Activity D-2: Enabling Universal Passwords

Time Required: 10 minutes

Objective: Use iManager to create eDirectory objects

Description: To simplify installation and maintenance, most computers in the organization access the NetWare 6.5 server using only the Microsoft client. As a result, Novell Client has been installed on only two computers. To allow users to log in to the network from these computers with only one password, Kathleen decided to implement the NetWare 6.5 Universal Password feature. In this activity, you implement universal passwords in your RRUSERS OU so that users can use the same password for the Microsoft or Novell client.

1. Open your Web browser and enter the URL *https://ip_address:2200* (*ip_address* represents the IP address of your NetWare 6.5 server).

2. Follow the procedure described previously to open the iManager main window.

3. Click the **+** sign to expand the NMAS options.

4. Click the **Universal Password Configuration** link to open the Universal Password Configuration window.

5. View the current status of your RRUSERS container by following these steps:

   a. Click the **Browse** button next to the Container text box to open the ObjectSelector window.

   b. Click the **down arrow** to navigate through the tree until the RRUSERS OU appears in the Contents frame.

   c. Click your **RRUSERS** OU to insert its context into the Container text box.

   d. Click the **View** button to display the universal password's current setting, similar to the context shown in Figure D-26.

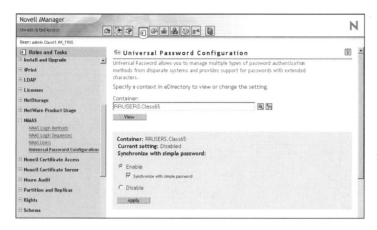

Figure D-26   The Universal Password Configuration dialog box

6. Enable the Synchronize with simple password option:

a. Verify that the Enable radio button and the Synchronize with simple password check box are selected.

b. Click the **Apply** button to enable the Universal Password option for your RRUSERS container.

c. Click the **OK** button when the "Universal Password has been enabled" message is diplayed.

7. Click the **Exit** button to end your iManager session. Users should now be able to log in from the Microsoft or Novell client with the same password.

File System Enhancements

Because information is the life blood of most organizations, network data must be secure, reliable, and protected against disaster. NetWare 6.5 has several enhanced features that increase an organization's ability to protect network data yet still provide high-speed, continuous access. The following sections describe how NetWare 6.5 file system enhancements can help protect an organization's most valuable asset.

Cluster SAN Architecture

In the textbook, you learned that storage area networks (SANs) consist of one or more storage devices directly attached to a high-speed network so that multiple servers can access and share the storage devices. NetWare 6 introduced the capability of creating a volume on a SAN that was shared by a cluster of two or more servers. As shown in Figure D-27, Novell has continued to improve server cluster technology in NetWare 6.5 with enhancements.

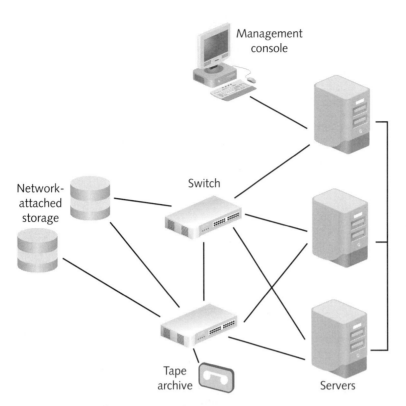

Figure D-27   Cluster SAN architecture

- Read-only shared volumes allow multiple servers to share the same content, which improves response time for user requests. This feature is especially useful in Web sites where downloading graphical data can bog down a single server. Changes can be made on only the master volume and automatically synchronized to the read-only volumes.

- The XML-based management console provides a way to monitor and manage the cluster environment from any computer. The XML-based interface also allows Novell to quickly adapt the management console to meet emerging industry standards for storage management.

- The quarantine of failing service function allows the cluster to remove a volume or service experiencing repeated failures.

- Maintenance Mode operation keeps a cluster together when one server is taken offline for normal maintenance. In NetWare 6 clusters, when a computer is shut down, the other computers in the cluster assume that the computer has failed and remove it from the cluster. When you bring the machine back online, it must be reinserted into the cluster. In NetWare 6.5, you can put a server into Maintenance Mode to inform the other cluster members that the machine has not failed. After maintenance is completed, you simply bring the machine back online to continue its role in the cluster. Using Maintenance Mode saves administrative time when performing normal maintenance.

iSCSI Support

Small Computer System Interface (SCSI) technology is a major way in which network file systems are attached to servers. A new standard called Internet SCSI (iSCSI) enables SCSI protocols to be run across a high-speed TCP/IP network. Novell has implemented the iSCSI standard in NetWare 6.5 so that servers can use LAN networks to share access to SCSI disk systems. This technology allows smaller organizations to implement a SAN at reduced costs by using a NetWare 6.5 server attached to an array of SCSI disks as a network storage device. With iSCSI, NetWare 6.5 can deliver full-featured SANs for many small and medium-sized businesses by providing server clustering at reduced costs.

Snap Shot Backups

As network storage needs have grown, tape-based backup systems (discussed in Chapter 8) have not kept up with the need for regular backups. For example, before NetWare 6.5, a server backup might have required several hours; during that time, the files being backed up must be offline to ensure that the data is correct. In a traditional backup system, open files are skipped or incorrectly copied to the backup device.

In NetWare 6.5, Novell has taken advantage of today's low-cost storage devices to make a copy of each data file to be backed up. The copy, called a "snap shot," is a picture of the actual data file at a specific time. Snap shot files can be updated frequently with little or no impact on user access to the primary data file. The snap shot file is then available to be backed up with conventional backup technology without bringing the primary file offline. Novell's snap shot technology allows data to be available around the clock, which is an important feature for NetWare 6.5 administrators.

A critical part of backing up database files is ensuring that the database is consistent before performing the backup or snap shot. To be consistent, the database must have finished its last update before the backup. To ensure database file consistency, NetWare 6.5 snap shot technology implements a set of function calls known as "freeze and thaw." By calling the freeze function, the snap shot process instructs the database application to complete its current transaction and get the database consistent for the snap shot. After the snap shot is complete, the thaw function is called to inform the database software that it can resume operation.

Another important application of the NetWare 6.5 snap shot technology is providing geographic mirroring (see Figure D-28), which combines snap shot technology and an iSCSI SAN to provide a fault-tolerant solution to data access.

Figure D-28 shows a cluster setup that includes London as the primary Logical Unit Number (LUN), with a mirrored copy of the London Snap Shot volume located in New York as the secondary LUN. If the London server or site fails, the New York cluster would promote the New York secondary volume as the primary volume. This system would keep data available despite the loss of service at any location. This type of disaster recovery or business continuance is especially important as a result of 9/11. The federal government is planning a policy that would require financial organizations seeking FDIC insurance to demonstrate that a geographic mirror is in place. In addition, business insurance rates could substantially increase (by more than 10%) for organizations that do not have a geographic disaster recovery plan or system in place.

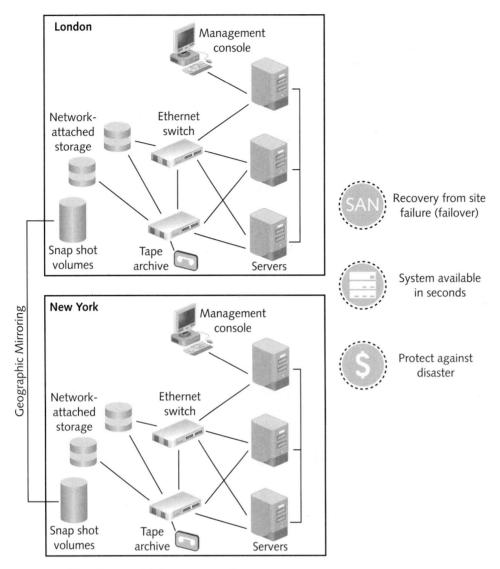

Figure D-28   Geographic business continuance

END USER ENHANCEMENTS

NetWare 6.5 continues to build on Novell's OneNet strategy of making network services available at anytime from anywhere. Throughout this book, you have learned about some key OneNet utilities, including iManager, iPrint, iFolder, and NetStorage. In NetWare 6.5, Novell has continued to enhance these utilities and added some new capabilities called Virtual Office and Virtual Teams, described in the following sections.

Virtual Office

Users are making more use of the Internet for real-time collaborative tasks, such as sharing data in development and design teams, analytical research, product design, and mergers or acquisitions. Needs for these collaborative tasks include messaging, data sharing, printing, and access to common task-specific applications, such as word processing and data management software. Users can become more productive when these tasks are independent of location and time, thus allowing the work experience to follow the user. As illustrated in Figure D-29, Virtual Office is an environment providing access to Novell's OneNet applications, including iFolder, iPrint, and the new Novell Virtual Teams and Novell eGuide.

Novell
Virtual Teams

Novell
iFolder 2.0

Novell
eGuide

Novell
iPrint

Figure D-29 The Novell Virtual Office environment

From the Virtual Office window, users can easily access their iFolder data, install and send output to their printers, interact with other users in their teams, organize and manage their contacts, and look up and access eDirectory information by using eGuide.

Virtual Teams

As shown in Figure D-29, NetWare 6.5 Virtual Teams is a place where users can exchange and share information. You can think of Virtual Teams as a group of workers who have shared purposes, accountabilities, and work activities.

As globalization and network connectivity continue to increase, so does the need for organizations to be able to conduct work across time, space, and cultural boundaries. Virtual Teams using technology such as mediated communication systems and applications to collaborate can increase productivity for organizations that can harness these technologies. In Activities D-3 and D-4, you see how to create Virtual Teams and use them to share information.

Activity D-3: Creating Virtual Office Teams

Time Required: 20 minutes

Objective: Use Novell Virtual Office to create teams

Description: The Rocky Ridge organization is working on a Web-based marketing project that involves three employees. To help communicate and share data, Rosemarie Wiggerts wants to implement a Virtual Team. In this activity, you use Virtual Office to create a Web marketing team and add the three employees.

1. On your workstation, open your Web browser and enter the URL for your NetWare 6.5 server (*https://ip_address*) to display the Welcome to NetWare 6.5 window.

2. Click the **Virtual Office** option in the left pane.

3. To log in, click the **User Login** option at the upper-right to open the Login window.

4. Enter the user name and password for your Rosemarie Wiggerts user and click the **Login** button.

5. Create a Virtual Team named RRWEBDEV:

   a. Under the Virtual Team Tasks heading on the left, click **Create Virtual Team**.

   b. In the Name text box, enter **RRWEBDEV** and click **Create**. Click **OK** to respond to the success message.

6. Members can be added to your new Virtual Team by selection or by invitation. Follow these steps to send an invitation to your William Locke and Rosemarie Wiggerts users:

   a. Under My Virtual Teams on the left, click **RRWEBDEV** to display the Virtual Team window, similar to the one in Figure D-30.

Figure D-30 The Virtual Team window

   b. Under the Team Membership heading on the left, click the **Invite a user** option.

   c. Click the **Add** button to display a search window.

   d. Enter **Locke** in the Last name text box and click **Search**.

   e. Click your **William Locke** user, and click **Add** to place William in the Virtual Team Invitations window.

7. Click the **Logout** link at the upper-right of the Virtual Office window.

8. Follow these steps to log in as William Locke and join the RRWEBDEV team:

   a. Log in with your William Locke user name and password.

   b. Click RRWEBDEV from the Virtual Team Inbox, and then click the Join button to add the RRWEBDEV team to William's My Virtual Teams list. Notice that the RRWEBDEV team is now listed under the My Virtual Teams heading located in the left column.

   c. In the left options column, click the RRWEBDEV team located under the My Virtual Teams heading and explore available team information.

   d. Click the **Logout** link to log out.

9. Log out.

Activity D-4: Working with Virtual Teams

Time Required: 20 minutes

Objective: Use Virtual Teams to share information

Description: In this activity, you upload a file to the RRWEBDEV virtual team and then log in as another team member and download the file.

1. Log in to Virtual Office as Rosemarie Wiggerts.

2. Create a team calendar by following these steps:

   a. Click the **RRWEBDEV** team.

   b. Click the **Show team calendar** option to display a calendar window, similar to the one in Figure D-31.

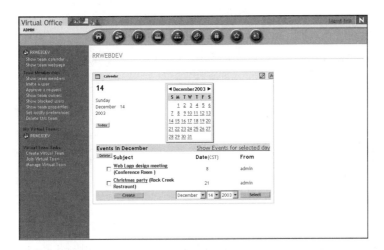

Figure D-31   The Virtual Team Calendar window

   c. Click the **Create** button to add an event for today's date.

   d. Click **Save** to save the entry, and then click **Close** to return to the RRWEBDEV Calendar window.

3. Publish a favorite URL for all team members by following these steps:

   a. Click the **Show team webpage** option to display a Team Page window, similar to the one in Figure D-32, and then click the **Edit** button.

Figure D-32   The Virtual Team Page window

   b. Click the **Published Favorites** check box, and then click the **Edit** button to open the Current Bookmarks window.

   c. Click **Add** to open the Add Bookmark dialog box.

   d. Enter **Novell** in the Name text box, and enter **www.novell.com** in the URL text box.

   e. Click **OK** to place the bookmark in the Current Bookmarks window.

   f. Click **Save** to save the new bookmark and open a Links window. Close the Links window to return to the Virtual Team Page window.

4. To upload a file, follow these steps:

   a. Click the **Published Files** check box and then click **Edit** to open the Files window.

b. Click the **Upload** button, and use the **Browse** button to navigate to your C:\WINNT\System32 (or C:\WINDOWS\System32) folder.

c. Select the **Ping.exe** program and click **Open** to insert it in the File name text box.

d. Click the **Upload** button to upload the file and notify all subscribers.

e. After the file is uploaded, click **Close** and then close the Files window.

5. Log out.

6. Log in to Virtual Office as William Locke and verify that the calendar, URL, and Ping.exe file are available.

7. Log out and close your Web browser.

NetWare 6.5 eGuide

Rapid changes in business structures and policies can make it difficult for users to find and access corporate information or know who to contact for support and problems. To improve access to an organization's internal information, NetWare 6.5 ships with Novell's new eGuide Web application. As shown in Figure D-33, the eGuide application enables users to search for names, addresses, fax numbers, and e-mail addresses stored in Novell eDirectory or on other LDAP-compatible directory services, such as Microsoft Active Directory, across the Internet.

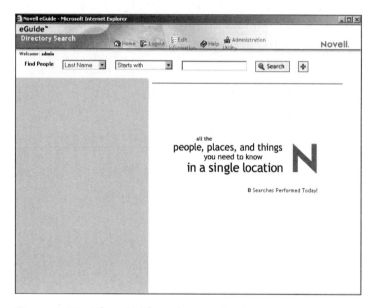

Figure D-33 The eGuide welcome window

In addition, Novell eGuide makes use of eDirectory's self-help capabilities by enabling users to manage their personal directory information and get answers to common problems, thereby reducing administrative time and costs.

iPrint Enhancements

As you learned in Chapter 11, using iPrint to easily find and access network printers through a Web browser is a powerful part of the OneNet strategy. In NetWare 6.5, Novell has expanded iPrint's capabilities by adding the following features:

- Support for Citrix and terminal server environments enables users to print to printers both inside and outside the terminal server environment.

- The iPrint client allows users to add printers to their workstations without needing to log in with administrator rights to the local workstation.

- Although Novell Distributed Print Services (NDPS) still plays an important role in supporting iPrint printers, new gateways are making it easier to set up printing through iManager without using NetWare Administrator.

- Print auditing allows organizations to track access to printers.

- With the new printer pooling feature, multiple print devices can be accessed as one logical iPrint printer.

- Because many organizations still need support for applications that print to the LPT port, the NetWare 6.5 iPrint services allow DOS-based printers to print directly through iPrint instead of sending output to a print queue.

WEB SERVICES

As you learned in the textbook, Novell has included Apache Web Server, Tomcat Servlet Engine, and NetWare Enterprise Web Server with NetWare 6.5. Novell has implemented many of its management tools as Web interfaces rather than the traditional GUI or text-mode interfaces. NetWare Remote Manager, iManager, and the like are Web-based applications or Net services that administrators use to manage their networks. The Internet has created a new breed of user, one who is sophisticated and knowledgeable. Novell understands that the learning curve to use a browser-type interface is much lower, because most administrators have experience using Internet tools, such as search engines and browsers. Web-based tools also make it possible for administrators and end users to work from anywhere in the world, with any operating system. As long as a Web browser is available, NetWare servers are available.

Developer Tools

Previous versions of NetWare had few tools for Web or application developers. Apache Web Server is included with NetWare 6, but having a Web server without the necessary Web development tools can increase costs for businesses. NetWare 6.5 comes to the rescue with some new tools and products, described in the following sections.

MySQL Database

MySQL is an open-source database application that thousands of Web developers currently use as the back-end database for e-commerce solutions. With NetWare 6.5, you get a commercial license for MySQL, enabling you to create a back-end database to your company's Web pages.

Not sure what a database is? To find some great books on the subject, visit *www.course.com* and search on the keyword "database."

Rhode Island became one of the first states to implement open-source technology for state government use, and many businesses are using open-source applications instead of proprietary vendor software as a cost-saving alternative. Other examples of open-source applications are Apache (Novell's default Web server), FreeBSD, Linux, and Perl.

In a MySQL database, information is stored electronically. When a customer places an order over the Web, for example, code written by a developer updates the database with information the customer enters or displays information from the MySQL database in a Web page for the customer to view. If you want to create a table to store contact information for employees working in an OU called InfoSystems, you could use the following code to create a table called tblinfosys with four columns—emp_id, emp_name, emp_email, and emp_phone—for the employee data:

```
CREATE TABLE tblinfosys (
  emp_id    int(4) NOT NULL,
  emp_name    varchar(50),
  emp_email    varchar(50),
  emp_phone    varchar (10),
  PRIMARY KEY (emp_id)
);
```

Even without any database experience, you can see that creating a table is not that complicated. In fact, your experience in writing login scripts will help you in this area.

PHP

NetWare 6.5 includes PHP version 4.0, an open-source scripting language for creating dynamic Web pages, which can change depending on information the user enters or on code written in the script. For example, you can display a clock with the current time of day on your Web page and have it updated every second. There are literally thousands of sites you can visit with sample code, free tutorials, support groups, and newsgroups, making it a great choice for a new Web developer wondering what scripting language to learn.

PHP is a server-side scripting language, similar to Microsoft Active Server Pages (ASP), that can be used on Web servers. One of its advantages is that you can use it to connect directly to MySQL, Oracle, and DB2 databases. PHP code is usually inserted into HTML Web pages. The following example mixes HTML code with PHP code. PHP code begins with the characters <? and ends with the characters ?>, so it's easy to determine where the two codes are being used. Note the /* and */ characters in the PHP segment. These characters separate comments from the actual PHP code. As you learned when creating login scripts, comments are essential in any scripts you write.

```
<HTML>
<HEAD>
<TITLE>CBE Labs</TITLE>
</HEAD>

<BODY BGCOLOR="white">

<H1>InfoSystems Employees</H1>
<?
/*
PHP InfoSystems Personnel
Written by William Locke
The following code counts how many records are in the
tblinfosys table. (For simplicity, the code for connecting
to the database is omitted.) */

  $query = "SELECT COUNT(*) FROM tblinfosys";
?>
```

Novell exteNd

Formerly called SilverStream exteNd, an application developed by IBM, Novell exteNd includes four software packages: exteNd Application Server, exteNd Composer, exteNd Workbench, and exteNd Director. As a Web developer, one of your tasks is formatting data for your online customers to view from their browsers. Before you can format this data, however, you need to access it. In other words, you must find out where the data is located. Is it on the company's legacy system, located in the computer room of an old dilapidated building? Or is the data on a NetWare 6.5 server running MySQL? In either case, Novell exteNd Composer can be used to access that database. You would use exteNd Director to deliver that data to your online customers. Both tools work together as a wizard and are displayed to the developer as an exteNd Workbench GUI.

 As a CNA, you probably won't be required to use many of these Web development tools. However, having a better understanding of what your NetWare server is capable of makes you a better administrator and a more valuable employee to your company.

Novell's exteNd Application Server was one of the first application servers to be Java 2 Enterprise Edition (J2EE) 1.3 certified, which requires passing more than 15,000 tests. For developers who want to deploy Java applications, this server includes all the tools needed to create anything from robust applications to interactive applets for your company's Web pages. (If needed, you can refer to Chapter 14 for an explanation of applets.) The big advantage of Java is its platform independence. As long as the computer system on which the application is running has a Java Virtual Machine (JVM), the developer has to create only one version of the program for it to run on multiple platforms. This platform independence makes Java the language of choice for the World Wide Web and the recommended programming language to study if you want to expand your computer skills. As of this writing, NetWare 6.5 includes JVM version 1.4.1.

With NetWare 6.5, administrators can create both simple Web-based applications and Web interfaces similar to iManager or Remote Manager. This gives administrators the flexibility to create their own management tools, if necessary, and to customize NetWare's management consoles by creating their own gadgets. The only limitations are the administrator's programming skills. Gone are the days of NLMs being the only method of creating applications for Novell.

NetWare 6.5 has also integrated eDirectory with Web Services, enabling you to take advantage of the security features already implemented in your network. Certificates and Secure Sockets Layer (SSL) security can be implemented with minimum coding, so your e-commerce applications can be released to your customers with reduced security risks.

NetWare 6.5 includes many new features and security enhancements that promise to make NetWare and Novell services, such as eDirectory, more prevalent in IT environments. In Appendix E, you'll learn more about the NetWare 6.5 security enhancements and how they can be used to securely access Novell services across the Internet, using a wide variety of security standards. As NetWare and Novell services continue to grow, the skills you have gained in studying to become a CNA will become even more valuable. In addition, Appendix F outlines how Novell's Nterprise for Linux can make your skills with eDirectory and iManager even more valuable in the rapidly growing Linux community.

NetWare 6.5 Security Enhancements

Security can be defined as a measure of how data and resources are protected from unauthorized access. The higher the security for a resource, the more difficult it is for an intruder to gain access to that resource. Most security systems consist of a three part model: authentication, authorization, and auditing (AAA). The AAA model begins with authentication, which is the process used to positively identify an entity as being the person or system they claim to be. Authorization is the process of giving authenticated users a set of predetermined rights to the resource they are attempting to access and ensuring that the service request actually originated from the authenticated user. Authorization security in NetWare 6/6.5 is implemented through trustee assignments and Role Based Services (RBS). As described in the textbook, trustee assignments are used to grant authenticated users rights to the NetWare file system and eDirectory objects; RBS is used to give users rights to perform administrative tasks in iManager. Appendix F explains how to set up RBS in NetWare and Linux environments. Finally, auditing is the process of logging the use of each resource. Since NetWare version 2, Novell has included auditing features in NetWare for keeping track of all changes and access attempts made to network resources. For example, you can track which users access a file or printer and record the user name, date and time of access, operation performed, and success or failure of the operation. This information can be important when tracking changes or looking for an intruder. NetWare 6.5 still uses the same basic authorization and auditing security features from previous NetWare versions, but in this appendix, you learn about new features that have been incorporated into NetWare 6.5 authentication security services.

In the past, a large part of security relied on physically isolating resources and networks. Although security has always been important to implementing computerized business applications, even on isolated or internal networks, the Internet has placed new demands on security systems by removing the physical security of isolation and placing resources and applications where they are potentially accessible to nearly anyone with a computer.

Novell has a history of implementing strong security systems in the NetWare operating system products. NetWare 6.5 continues to build on the security systems Novell has included since NetWare version 2 in the mid-1980s. As described in the textbook, NetWare security systems can be divided into login security, file system security, eDirectory security, printer security, and server console security. Using the AAA model, login security provides authentication, and the other security systems provide authorization security. In addition, since NetWare version 2, Novell has always included an auditing security system for tracking access to network resources and data. An important aspect of any type of security is preventing data from being captured and read while it's being transmitted between network entities. Secure data transmission is accomplished by scrambling or encrypting the message in a way that only the receiver can decipher. In this appendix, you learn how Novell has continued to enhance network security by implementing industry open-source standards into the NetWare 6.5 operating system.

INTRODUCTION TO ENCRYPTION SECURITY

In addition to the security options described in the textbook, security systems need to protect information from being captured and read as it's transmitted across the network. Keeping passwords and data secret is especially important when using the Internet, because intruders might have access to login and data packets as they travel across network routers and cables. Keeping passwords and data unintelligible to anyone except the intended receiver is accomplished through some type of encryption. Basically, encryption is the process of converting plain text into a secret message, which can only be read after it is decrypted by reversing the encryption process. The process used to encrypt and decrypt the message is called a cipher. The science of encrypting data, called cryptography, involves using algorithms with a special value called a key (often the user's password) to hide information from all but intended recipients by "scrambling" data packets as shown in Figure E-1. The only way to read the scrambled data packet is to decrypt the data packet by reversing the process and using the corresponding key value.

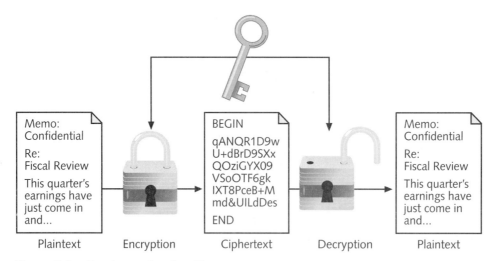

Figure E-1   Cryptography algorithm process

Cryptography Techniques

The two major types of cryptography techniques, or ciphers, are symmetric ciphers and asymmetric ciphers (also called public key cryptography). When using a symmetric key cryptography technique, the same key, usually the user's password, is used to encrypt and decrypt the message or request. The advantage of symmetric cryptography is that it's simple and efficient. The problem with symmetric cryptography is that both the sender and receiver must have the same key. Securely exchanging the same key between the server and client can be a problem when communicating over public networks such as the Internet. Asymmetric ciphers or public cryptography gets around the problem of exchanging the same key by using a set of two keys: a public key and a private key. An entity's public key is exchanged with other systems and used to encrypt data being sent to that entity. The entity's private key is then used to decrypt the data that was encrypted with its public key, as illustrated in Figure E-2.

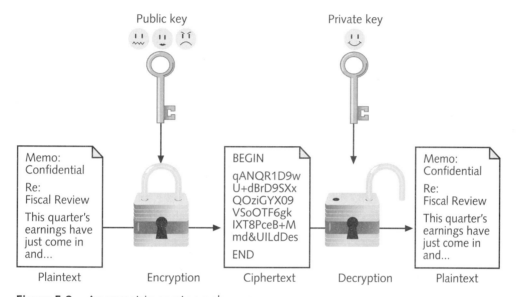

Figure E-2   Asymmetric cryptography process

In addition to encrypting data packets, public and private keys can be used to create and verify digital signatures. A digital signature is important because it shows that a message or request is from the actual entity, since only that entity could create a signature readable by its public key.

Private and public keys are provided to network entities or users through a certificate issued by a Certificate Authority (CA). Public Key Cryptography Standards (PKCS) provides a set of standards maintained by the RSA Data Security organization for the purpose of implementing public key cryptography on the Internet. PKCS-compatible CAs use the X.509 standard to format certificates that can be used to encrypt and decrypt data by any PKCS-compatible system. There are PKCS standards for different encryption needs. For example, PKCS#7 is an extensible message format that represents the results of cryptographic operations on data. The PKCS#12 standard is often used for encrypting login requests and is included as a NetWare 6.5 login option.

CAs can be defined as private or public. Most network operating systems, including NetWare, Windows 2000/2003, and Linux, include private CA software that allows the server to issue X.509 certificates to clients. Although a private X.509 certificate issued by the local network operating system works fine for users who have accounts on that organization's network, to operate on the Internet an organization needs an X.509 certificate that's digitally signed by a recognized CA, such as VeriSign. This digital signature is analogous to having a passport, a driver's license, or other certified picture ID rather than a company or student ID card. Although a student ID card can get you into campus activities, it isn't recognized as a valid form of ID at the airport. A digitally signed certificate is considered more valid than a locally issued certificate because a CA verifies the identity of the user or organization requesting the certificate. Just as a passport is recognized as a valid form of ID at the airport, a digitally signed certificate is accepted as valid identification by most Web browsers and servers, including Netscape, Windows Internet Explorer, and Novell NetWare 6.5.

Encryption Protocols

A number of encryption protocols can be used to secure data and passwords transmitted across networks. Most protocols can be configured to use symmetric or asymmetric cryptographic techniques, depending on security and performance needs. When exchanging keys isn't necessary, symmetric protocols require less processing overhead, so they are often used to encrypt data transmitted on private networks, and keys for each user can be stored in a directory service on the server. Public systems that allow access by users who are unknown to the server often use asymmetric cryptography in the encryption protocol to exchange keys securely. Some protocols use a combination of symmetric and asymmetric cryptography, thus taking advantage of the security of asymmetric cryptography to exchange a key that a symmetric protocol then uses to encrypt and decrypt data packets. The following sections introduce some common protocols for securing network transmissions and securing access to your NetWare 6.5 console.

IP Security Protocol (IPSec)

Data transmitted across the network can also be secured by performing the data encryption process at Layer 3 (the Network layer) of the Open Systems Interconnect (OSI) model, which eliminates the need to encrypt passwords. The IP Security (IPSec) protocol, developed by the Internet Engineering Task Force (IETF), secures the Network layer by using Encapsulating Security Payload (ESP) to perform encryption and decryption at the IP packet level. Either symmetrical or asymmetrical encryption can be used. Because IPSec packets have a standard TCP/IP header, they can be routed through the network using standard devices that might not be IPSec aware. The main disadvantage of IPSec is the additional processing time needed to encrypt and decrypt all IP packets. Security systems that work at a higher level can selectively encrypt sensitive data packets, thereby improving network performance.

SSL and TLS Protocols

Secure Sockets Layer (SSL) and Transport Layer Security (TLS) are some of the most widely used protocols for securing message transmission across the Internet. Originally developed by Netscape, SSL and TLS are also supported by Microsoft and Novell as well as many other Internet application developers. Although TLS is essentially the latest version of SSL, it's not as widely available in Web browsers. Both SSL and TLS use a hybrid of the symmetric and asymmetric encryption ciphers to encrypt data packets. First, the sending computer uses the receiver's X.509 certificate to verify the receiver's identity. Next, the sender's computer randomly picks a symmetric key and then encrypts it using the public key from the receiving computer's digital certificate. The sending computer then sends the encrypted key to the receiving computer, which decrypts the data packet using its private key. After the sender and receiver identify the secret symmetric key, the computers can use this shared key to perform standard symmetric encryption of data packets more efficiently than using the asymmetric technique to encrypt and decrypt each data packet. The length of the symmetric key also plays a role in secure transactions. Web browsers that use 40- and 56-bit keys are considered to have weak encryption because these key sizes can be cracked in a short time (approximately one week on average) by using commonly available processing power along with specialized software. The 40- and 56-bit browsers are common because of U.S. government regulations on exporting strong (128-bit) cipher keys.

 Key lengths are not the sole characteristic that makes the security of a key weak or strong; the security of a key also depends on the encryption algorithm. Keys based on certain encryption algorithms can be 10 to 20 times stronger for a given length than keys based on a weaker algorithm.

The HTTPS Protocol

Secure Hypertext Transfer Protocol (HTTPS) is a secure communications protocol designed to transfer encrypted information between computers over the Web. HTTPS is essentially an implementation of the widely used HTTP protocol that uses SSL/TLS for secure data transmission. The major difference between HTTPS and SSL/TLS is that SSL/TLS is used to encrypt a persistent connection whereas HTTPS uses SSL to encrypt a single page. After a digital certificate is installed on a Web server, an SSL-enabled Web browser, such as Netscape or Internet Explorer, can connect to the Web server using HTTPS and securely exchange information. HTTP combines with SSL/TLS to enable secure communications by following these steps:

1. By accessing a URL with HTTPS, the client requests a secure transaction and negotiates an encryption algorithm.

2. The server sends the client the server's digital certificate containing the public key and a list of supported ciphers and key sizes in priority sequence.

3. The client compares the CA that issued the certificate to a list of trusted CAs and verifies that the certificate has not expired.

4. The client generates a secret symmetric key based on the list of ciphers and then encrypts the key using the server's public key and sends it to the server.

5. The server then decrypts the new symmetric session key using its own asymmetric private key.

6. After the symmetric key has been identified, both the server and client use that key along with the negotiated algorithm to secure all further communication between the two entities.

Message Digest Security

Another important aspect of securing data transmitted across the Internet is ensuring that data has not been tampered with or changed since it left the sender. Data transmissions can be secured against tampering by using a hashing algorithm to create a fixed-length message called a message digest, as shown in Figure E-3.

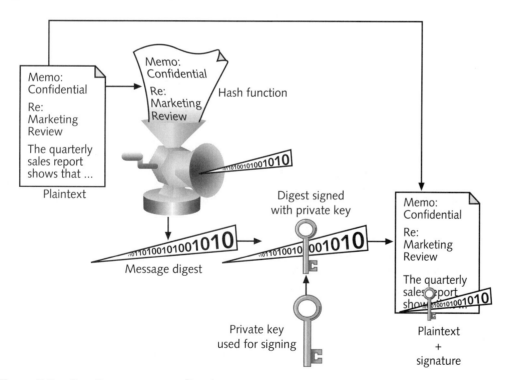

Figure E-3   Creating a message digest

The message digest is signed with the user's private key and appended to the message transmission. The receiver then opens the transmission and uses the sender's public key along with the hash algorithm to compute a message digest from the original message. If the message digests match, the receiver knows that no bits in the message have changed since it was signed by the sender. In some ways, a message digest is similar to the Cyclic Redundancy Check (CRC) code attached to each data packet by TCP/IP. The CRC is also calculated by applying a mathematical algorithm to the data packet's contents to create a relatively simple code consisting of 8 to 16 bits. When the packet is received, the receiver applies the same algorithm to the data packet's contents and then checks its results against the sender's CRC. If the results are different, the receiver assumes the bits in the packet were changed or damaged by the transmission process.

The difference between using a message digest and the normal CRC that TCP/IP attaches to data packets is that the CRC notifies the receiver of transmission errors, but doesn't allow the receiver to detect falsified data packets in which the hacker has modified the CRC to match the new data content. Two major hashing algorithms are in use today. Secure Hash Algorithm 1 (SHA-1), developed by the National Security Agency (NSA), produces 160-bit message digests and is considered the most secure. Message Digest 5 (MD5), developed by RSA Data Security, produces 128-bit digests and has been placed in the public domain. Because it requires no licensing, as of this writing MD5 is the most commonly used hashing algorithm, but cryptography experts fear it has flaws that could cause it to be broken in the future.

The Secure Shell Protocol: OpenSSH

The Secure Shell (SSH) protocol is used with remote login and file transfer programs, such as Telnet and File Transfer Protocol (FTP), to provide an encrypted link between the client and server. SSH uses asymmetric public key cryptography techniques to establish an encrypted, secure connection between the user and the remote machine. After the secure connection is established, user names, passwords, and all other data can be securely transmitted over the secure connection. Because of its popularity, many network applications and operating systems, including NetWare 6.5, now support SSH ports, and free clients are available for logging on to an SSH-compatible server. Novell supports the open-source version of SSH called OpenSSH and includes it as an installation option (see the NetWare 6.5 installation section in Appendix D).

Originally, the FTP file transfer program did not ensure secure encrypted data transmission between client and server. As a result, several attempts have been made to fix FTP's security shortcomings, but they have not been widely adapted. The most commonly used file transfer program that provides encrypted security is called Secure File Transfer Protocol (S/FTP). S/FTP is not a rework of the traditional FTP, but is a new component of SSH that has the same command syntax as FTP but performs all operations over an encrypted transport. S/FTP can also use SSH features, such as public key authentication and compression. Novell has included S/FTP with OpenSSH in NetWare 6.5 to provide the following advantages over the traditional FTP service:

- Because S/FTP uses the underlying OpenSSH protocol, it offers strong authentication using a variety of methods, including X.509 digital certificates.

- By using OpenSSH, all authentication information, commands, and data transferred between the S/FTP client and the Novell server are encrypted and secured.

- S/FTP uses a single TCP connection port, making it relatively easy to configure on a firewall. On the other hand, the older FTP service uses two connection ports: the initial connection that uses port number 21 and a second reverse connection that opens a random high port number. Assigning a random port number for the second connection makes firewall configuration more difficult.

- As described in the textbook, many networks use Network Address Translation (NAT) to route packets between a secured private network and the Internet. S/FTP makes NAT configuration easier because it doesn't need to negotiate a separate IP address for the data connection, as with traditional FTP clients and servers.

Because Novell includes OpenSSH with NetWare 6.5, you can use one of several client programs to securely access the NetWare 6.5 server console. One popular choice is PuTTy. You can download the PuTTy utility from several sources, including *www.chiark.greenend.org.uk/~sgtatham/putty/download.html*. In the following activity, you use PuTTy to securely access your NetWare 6.5 server's console.

Activity E-1: Using the OpenSSH Protocol

Time Required: 15 minutes

Objective: Use OpenSSH and PuTTy to securely access the NetWare 6.5 console

Description: As a consultant for the Rocky Ridge organization, you need to access the server console periodically to perform server maintenance. To do this, you have downloaded the OpenSSH PuTTy utility and plan to use it to securely access the Rocky Ridge server console. Follow these steps to access your NetWare 6.5 server console with PuTTy:

1. At the server console, type **SSHD** and press **Enter** to start the OpenSSH service, which replaces the less secure rlogin and Telnet services.

2. At the server console, type the command **SCP** and press **Enter** to start the SCP (remote console) service. Then type **SFTP** and press **Enter** to start the S/FTP service.

3. If necessary, download the PuTTy client from *www.chiark.greenend.org.uk/ ~sgtatham/putty/ download.html*.

4. From your workstation desktop, open the SSH-compliant client by running the PuTTy application.

5. In the Host Name text box, enter the IP address of your NetWare 6.5 server, and then click the **SSH** radio button to change the port to 22.

6. To begin the session, click **Open**.

7. If necessary, click **Yes** twice to trust the host and continue with the connection.

8. Enter your assigned Admin user name and password at the "login as:" prompt. The server console screen should then be displayed on your desktop.

9. Explore the functionality of the SSH session by using the following keyboard commands:

   - **Ctrl+Z** to open the screen list (GUI not supported)
   - **Ctrl+Z** to toggle between server screens
   - **Ctrl+Q** to display the SSH keyboard commands help screen

10. Press **Ctrl+X** and enter **y** to exit the SSH session and close the PuTTy application.

NETWARE 6.5 AUTHENTICATION SECURITY ENHANCEMENTS

As described earlier, authentication security provides a way to ensure that the entity attempting to access the system is a valid user and is actually the user it claims to be. For example, you might know that Rosemarie Wiggerts is an employee of the Rocky Ridge company, but how do you determine that the entity attempting to gain access is actually Rosemarie? In the real world, we often identify people by checking authorized picture IDs, by verifying signatures, or by knowing the person personally. Most network authentication security relies heavily on user names and passwords to identify a valid user. For example, if an entity supplies the user name RWiggerts along with the proper password, that entity is assumed to be Rosemarie Wiggerts and is granted Rosemarie's access to the system resources. As you learned in this textbook, NetWare includes the following optional features to help strengthen authentication security:

- Minimum password lengths
- Password expiration
- Unique password
- Intruder detection
- Time restrictions
- Station restrictions

Although Novell's eDirectory uses a highly secure system of password encryption and storage, it's a proprietary system that requires the Novell client to provide the encryption services needed to access eDirectory passwords. Because NetWare 6.5 is designed to allow access from other clients, including Web browsers, Novell offers additional authentication options in the installation process (as described in Appendix D) to secure the transmission of passwords and ensure that the login attempt is from an authorized entity. In the following sections, you learn more about these login methods and how they enhance the NetWare security environment.

NDS Passwords

The NDS password option is the default authentication method the NetWare 6.5 server uses. NDS passwords are stored in eDirectory using Novell's proprietary encryption method. An NDS password requires the Novell client to be installed on user workstations to provide the necessary encryption algorithm. As described in the textbook, when you create a user account in ConsoleOne or iManager, you have the option of entering an NDS password for the user. In NetWare 6.5, an NDS password is required for the user to log in from the Novell client. If you don't enter an initial NDS password, a message (see Figure E-4) is displayed warning you that a password is required for the user to log in.

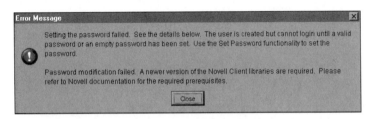

Error Message

Setting the password failed. See the details below. The user is created but cannot login until a valid password or an empty password has been set. Use the Set Password functionality to set the password.

Password modification failed. A newer version of the Novell Client libraries are required. Please refer to Novell documentation for the required prerequisites.

Close

Figure E-4   The NDS password warning message

Simple Passwords

In the textbook, you learned that NetWare 6 and 6.5 include Native File Access Protocol (NFAP), which allows Windows, Macintosh, and Unix workstations to access the NetWare server without having Novell Client installed. NFAP is an important feature because many organizations want to minimize software complexity on user workstations. The downside to using a workstation's native client protocol is that certain NetWare features aren't available, such as the additional security built into the Novell client's NDS password encryption. When a client workstation without Novell Client accesses the NetWare 6.0 or 6.5 server, it uses its own password encryption algorithm to secure the password. This requires eDirectory to maintain two passwords: one for Novell Client encryption and another for native client protocols, called a "simple password," to differentiate it from the more secure NDS password. NetWare stores the simple password separately from the NDS password, using a different encryption system that's compatible with the workstation's native client.

Universal Passwords

One of the inconveniences of simple passwords is that users might need two different passwords, one for Novell Client workstations and the other for native Windows workstations. With NetWare 6.5, Novell has simplified this process by adding universal passwords. Administrators enable this option in a container of the eDirectory tree, and then eDirectory stores one password that all workstations use. When the Universal Password option is enabled in an Organizational Unit (OU), the simple password is automatically synchronized with the eDirectory password whenever a user in that OU logs in from a Novell client. The NetWare operating system keeps the two passwords synchronized so that users need to use and maintain only one password for Novell and native client workstations. Universal passwords decrease the security of NDS passwords, but because they can be enabled on a container-by-container basis, administrators can pick and choose which users need this flexibility. Because of the reduced security of native client passwords, however, the Universal Password option should not be enabled on highly sensitive user accounts that require stronger security, such as the Admin user. In the following activity, you enable universal passwords for your RRUSERS OU so that the same password will work when logging in from the Novell or Microsoft client.

Activity E-2: Enabling Universal Passwords

Time Required: 10 minutes

Objective: Enable universal passwords

Description: To simplify installation and maintenance, most computers in the Rocky Ridge organization access the NetWare 6.5 server using only the Microsoft client, so the Novell client has been installed on only two computers. Kathleen has decided to implement universal passwords so that users can log in to the network using only one password. In this activity, you implement universal passwords in your RRUSERS OU:

1. Open your Web browser and enter the URL *https://ip_address:2200* (*ip_address* represents the IP address of your NetWare 6.5 server).

2. Follow the procedure described in Appendix D to open the iManager main window.

3. Click the **+** sign to expand the NMAS options.

4. Click the **Universal Password Configuration** option to open the Universal Password Configuration window.

5. View the current status of your RRUSERS container by following these steps:

   a. Click the **Browse** button next to the Container text box to open the ObjectSelector window.

   b. Click the **down arrow** to navigate down the tree until the RRUSERS OU appears in the Contents frame.

   c. Click your **RRUSERS** OU to insert its context into the Container text box.

   d. Click the **View** button to display the current setting for universal passwords, similar to the window shown in Figure E-5.

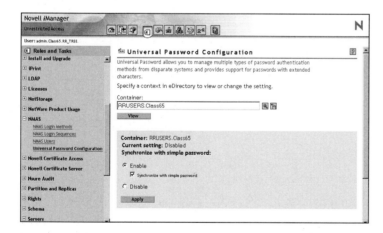

Figure E-5   The current setting for universal passwords

6. Enable the Synchronize with simple password option:

   a. Verify that the Enable radio button and the Synchronize with simple password check box are selected.

   b. Click the **Apply** button to enable universal passwords for your RRUSERS container.

   c. Click **OK** to complete the update.

7. Click the **Exit** button to end your iManager session. Users should now be able to log in from the Microsoft or Novell client with the same password.

Message Digest 5 (MD5)

Message Digest 5 performs a hashing encryption method that uses a one-way function to mix the contents of a password and make it an unintelligible entry in a password table. Microsoft uses MD5 encryption in Microsoft Challenge Handshake Authentication Protocol (MS-CHAP) when logging on to Active Directory. By incorporating an MD5 login method in NetWare 6.5, Novell makes it easier for NetWare servers to co-exist in a Windows 2000 or 2003 network.

CertMutual

As described in the textbook, Lightweight Directory Access Protocol (LDAP) is an industry-standard protocol designed to govern access to directory services over a TCP/IP network. In addition to defining a hierarchical naming system and directory information tree, LDAP provides authentication security by using a standards-based interface called Simple Authentication and Security Layer (SASL). LDAP provides three levels of authentication:

- *No authentication*—Use this option if the directory is published publicly and there is no need to restrict access to certain individuals.

- *Simple authentication*—This LDAP security option passes login information across the network in clear text, which creates a security risk because intruders could use packet-capturing software to capture and read passwords. The clear text security risk can be lessened if lower-level protocols, such as IPSec, are used for password encryption.

- *SASL*—This option uses one of several security methods, such as TLS and IPSec, to encrypt data over a connection-oriented protocol. When LDAP authentication is used, TLS/SSL is the most common method used with the LDAP version 3 included in NetWare 6.5.

Universal Smart Card

Security tokens are authentication devices that are assigned to users to eliminate the need to type a password. They help increase security by preventing passwords from being captured at the keyboard and by providing a way to authenticate from non-keyboard devices, such as entry locks. A universal smart card is an active security token that creates an encrypted base key each time the owner tries to authenticate. A smart card is a plastic card, about the size of a credit card, that has an embedded chip with an integrated circuit containing memory and a programmable microprocessor. Universal smart cards can be plugged directly into a computer or other device and act as an employee badge, credit card, electronic building key, or access-granting certificate. In addition to storing user name and password information, smart cards can securely store personal information, such as biometric information that confirms the owner's identity, health records, digital certificates, and private/public keys. Because of the growing use of universal smart cards in IT environments, Novell has included a smart card authentication option in the NetWare 6.5 installation process.

X.509 Certificate

As described earlier, public key cryptography uses X.509 certificates to exchange keys and verify the identity of the sender and receiver. Since NetWare version 5, Novell has included a private CA that allows network administrators to issue and use private X.509 certificates for use within an organization. In the following activity, you use iManager to create an X.509 certificate from the NetWare 6.5 CA software.

Activity E-3: Creating an X.509 Certificate

Time Required: 10 minutes

Objective: Use iManager to create an X.509 certificate from the NetWare 6.5 CA

Description: Rocky Ridge wants to install an X.509 certificate on its e-mail server to enable secure message transmissions. Follow these steps to create an X.509 certificate for your NetWare 6.5 server:

1. Open your Web browser and enter the URL *https://ip_address:2200* (*ip_address* represents the IP address of your NetWare 6.5 server).

2. Follow the procedure described in Appendix D to open the iManager main window.

3. Log in with your assigned Admin user name and password.

4. Expand the **Novell Certificate Server** option and view the available certificate options.

5. Click the **Create Server Certificate** option to display the Create Server Certificate Wizard shown in Figure E-6.

Figure E-6   The Create Server Certificate Wizard

6. In the Server text box, enter **ROCKY65.Class65**. (Note that the context might vary, depending on your classroom setup.)

7. In the Certificate nickname text box, enter **RRCert**.

8. Leave the Standard radio button selected as the creation method, and then click **Next**.

9. Review the summary information, and then click **Finish**.

10. When you see the message informing you that the certificate was successfully created, click **Close**.

11. Click the **Exit** button to end your iManager session, and then close your Web browser.

NOVELL SERVICES FOR LINUX

Linux is proving to be a viable enterprise-wide network operating system that can help organizations reduce costs yet still provide robust and secure network services. As a result of this track record, there's a growing demand for Linux in almost every area of the IT industry, including Web servers, e-mail servers, application servers, and user desktops. To meet the growing demand for Linux services and support, Novell and other leading vendors are bringing many new services and support to the Linux environment. In this appendix, you learn about the growing demand for Linux and how Novell is helping meet this demand through services, support, and certification.

GROWTH OF LINUX

Most IT professionals agree that Linux and the open-source movement have changed the landscape of the IT industry. According to the market research firm IDC (*www.idc.com*), between 2002 and 2007 Linux is projected to grow at a compounded annual rate of 14%. Forrester Research (*www.forrester.com*) surveyed companies earning more than $1 billion dollars and also confirmed the growth of Linux. Of the 50 companies responding to the survey, 72% plan to increase their Linux use over the next two years, and more than half plan to use Linux in place of their existing operating systems.

An important part of the growth of Linux is open-source licensing, which enables developers to build systems with open-source software without paying royalties or other fees, as long as they release the source code with their product. According to CIO research (*www.cio.com*), 64% of 375 companies surveyed use open-source products and cite the lower total cost of ownership (TCO) as a key advantage. An article in the December 2002 issue of *CIO* magazine states that company CIOs (chief information officers) mentioned the following benefits of using open-source products: lower TCO (total cost of ownership), reduced capital investment, and increased reliability and uptime compared to existing systems. In this same article, IT executives said that open-source products offer more flexibility and faster, cheaper application development.

Linux Benefits

Although the open-source concept has been part of academic and scientific computing for many years, only recently have many business organizations started to take it seriously. Part of the reason for this increased interest in open source has been the cutback in IT budgets and the increased costs and headaches of maintaining proprietary software licenses. In addition, many organizations are examining new open-source business applications and services in an effort to stay competitive. Some benefits organizations can reap from open-source solutions include the following:

- Support for a wide variety of hardware environments
- Reduction in software costs
- Availability, reliability, and scalability
- Reduced operating costs
- Experienced development resources
- Rapidly growing number of applications and tools

The following sections explain these benefits and how they can affect organizations.

Hardware Choices

One of Linux's greatest strengths is its capability to run on many types of computer hardware, ranging from mainframe computers to laptops and PDAs. Many hardware vendors, such as IBM, Dell, Hewlett-Packard, and Sun Microsystems, have options to include and support Linux with their computer systems. In addition, because of Linux's efficient use of hardware resources, such as processors and memory, many organizations find they can support more users and applications with less hardware investment. Although some versions of UNIX require an expensive reduced instruction set computer (RISC) processor, Linux runs fine on Intel processors, so organizations can realize significant cost savings.

Reduced Software Costs

Open-source Linux is free, but bundled distributions from companies such as Red Hat and SuSE can range from $50 to $1500, depending on additional features and support. However, because most commercial Linux distributions don't require user licensing, a company can save substantially by buying a single copy and installing it on several machines in the network.

Availability, Scalability, and Reliability

Many organizations have selected Linux to run their Web applications because of its reputation for stability. Linux system uptime is often measured in years rather than days or weeks. Windows-based systems often need to be entirely shut down and restarted to install a patch or upgrade, but Linux systems generally require stopping and restarting only a single service or process. Performance and reliability are improved with Linux systems because multiprocessors are supported and because Linux servers can be linked to form computing clusters. As with NetWare 6 clusters, when any Linux computer in the cluster fails or needs to be shut down for maintenance, users of the cluster don't experience interruptions because another computer in the cluster continues to provide the downed computer's resources and services. With estimates of revenue losses running as high as $1 million per hour for some enterprises, clustering is becoming an important part of the IT environment.

Reduced Operating Costs

In a cost-of-ownership study, the Robert Frances Group found that salaries for operators of Linux Web servers are lower than salaries for operators of proprietary operating systems (Sun Solaris, Microsoft Windows, and Novell NetWare) and that operators of Linux servers can support more machines per operator. One reason for this finding is that the same software image can run on a variety of hardware platforms, reducing the cost of training system operators and support staff when different operating systems are needed for each distinct hardware platform. For example, in an environment where servers such as the IBM AS400 are used with Sun and Intel-based workstations, multiple proprietary operating systems can require a lot of system operator time and training. In this case, running Linux on all hardware platforms can reduce administrative costs.

Software Development Resources

Organizations using Linux benefit from the combined efforts of thousands of experienced open-source developers who collaborate on many different projects. Compared to proprietary operating systems, the open-source community of developers and experts continually improves on Linux at little or no cost to end user organizations. Because of open-source agreements, companies can modify the Linux operating system and other open-source software to enhance their capabilities, as long as the source code modifications are made available to the open-source community. This process creates constant growth in the product based on needs rather than marketing strategies.

Applications and Tools

Linux seems to have reached a threshold at which developers are starting to see a viable market for applications and software tools. As a result, many applications from independent developers and the open-source community are readily available. Open-source applications, such as StarOffice and OpenOffice, have been designed and written to be compatible with and comparable with major proprietary products, such as Microsoft Office. Graphical desktop environments, such as Ximian Desktop, create a Windows-like look and feel and support several applications and tools, including Novell services. Other leading companies, such as Computer Associates, IBM, Oracle, PeopleSoft, Sybase, and SAP, have converted or are planning to convert their applications, tools, and databases to the Linux environment. As the number of Linux users increases, you can look for the number of software choices to continue growing rapidly.

LINUX CONCERNS

As shown in Figure F-1, a study conducted by Forrester Research (*www.forrester.com*) showed that some of the biggest concerns organizations express when considering open-source solutions such as Linux are support, number of applications, product maturity, security, and lack of in-house skills. The following sections briefly examine these concerns.

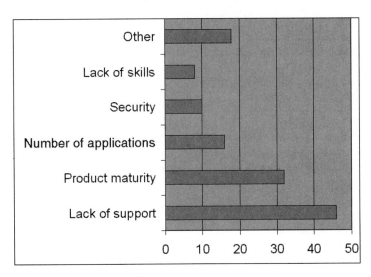

Figure F-1   Factors affecting adoption of open-source solutions

Support

Concern about 24-hour support is probably one of the key factors preventing many organizations from adopting Linux and other open-source solutions. Corporate-level support must go beyond a hotline that customers can call when a problem comes up. When implementing a large-scale system, IT departments need to consider many issues, such as network infrastructure, training (technical and end user), availability, support, and data integration. Organizations tend to feel more confident having support from a large vendor with extensive experience in operating systems, networks, and IT infrastructure, such as Microsoft, Novell, or IBM.

Number of Applications and Product Maturity

Although versions of Linux have been available for more than 10 years, only in the past few years has Linux been recognized as a viable operating system for business applications in corporate environments. The list of Linux-based business applications is growing rapidly, but the software is relatively new compared to proprietary operating systems, such as UNIX, Macintosh, or Windows. Today, most application development is based on Microsoft .NET and Java. Because it's unlikely that Microsoft .NET development software will ever be available on Linux, most Linux software developers currently use a Java or Java 2 Enterprise Edition (J2EE) environment. This could change in the future if an open-source implementation of .NET called the Mono Project becomes an alternative to Java-based development tools.

Another concern is network, system, and application management software. Linux has many excellent utilities for software distribution, metering, account management, and backup, but there's concern in the IT industry that these utilities haven't been adequately stress-tested or integrated into enterprise-wide IT environments. In addition, most existing Linux utilities operate only on Linux, making it difficult to integrate them into an enterprise-wide system consisting of Windows, NetWare, and UNIX systems. The good news is that large vendors, including Novell, are developing and converting proven software management tools to the Linux platform. Several of these solutions are discussed in the "Novell Services for Linux" section later in this appendix.

Security

In this textbook and in Appendix E, you learned about several ways to secure a network from internal and external intruders. Organizations that deploy Linux must be assured that it can effectively meet their enterprise-wide security requirements for single login, firewalls, encryption, and virus protection. As an operating system, Linux plays a critical but limited role in authenticating user identity and ensuring that users have access only to the system resources they are authorized for. Novell eDirectory can solve many of these Linux security issues by providing a secure directory service that can be shared among many servers of different operating system types.

Lack of Skilled Staff

Many NetWare and Windows-based IT organizations are concerned about not having the specialized skills required to effectively set up, use, and maintain the Linux operating system. Organizations currently running UNIX-based systems find that they can leverage their UNIX expertise to manage Linux systems. By implementing Novell Linux services, most NetWare-based IT organizations can make use of the skills they have developed with eDirectory and Novell utilities, such as iManager, in the Linux environment. In addition, Novell has developed the Certified Linux Engineer (CLE) program to help bring IT staff up to speed on maintaining a system that integrates Linux and NetWare servers. This certification program is discussed in more depth in the "Training and Certification" section later in this appendix.

NOVELL SERVICES FOR LINUX

Novell announced a major Linux strategy at BrainShare 2003: making a commitment to deliver a complete range of Linux-related products and services to the market. A key component is the availability of Novell services to customers running Linux instead of NetWare. Novell's commitment is to make all services associated with the NetWare operating system available on Linux in an effort to become a provider of services that run on both NetWare and Linux servers. The Novell Linux strategy has the following major components:

- A comprehensive set of support services

- Products and solutions

- A commitment to the open-source community

- Training and certification

The following sections introduce these components and explain how Novell is implementing them in the Linux strategy.

Support Services

In addition to a phone hotline, support services include finding and obtaining the latest patches and drivers and offering technical support information on problems and fixes. As described in the previous section, IT organizations are concerned about open-source software not having the level of support normally offered by proprietary software vendors, such as Microsoft and Sun. Novell has provided a high level of support services for NetWare operating systems since the early 1980s and is now committed to bringing that same level of professionalism and support services to the Linux platform. Novell has many experienced consultants around the world who are prepared to deliver a comprehensive portfolio of services that help clients make the transition to Linux and open-source systems. Table F-1 lists some of the key support services Novell has made available to the Linux and open-source community.

Table F-1 Key Support Services for Linux

Service	Description
Discovery	Consulting services designed to help business leaders understand the ramifications of implementing Linux. These services include a summary of business and tactical goals, a high-level technical and business justification, and recommended steps for implementing Linux in the organization's IT environment.
Strategy	A more in-depth assessment of the business justification for implementing Linux and its effect on the organization's IT infrastructure.
Implementation	Implementation options, such as training, software design and development, techniques for migrating from existing systems to Linux, integration with existing systems, testing, and deployment.
Application	Enables clients to work with Novell consultants to effectively implement a wide variety of applications on the Linux platform.

Products and Solutions

Although the Linux operating system provides a solid open-source environment that offers many advantages, it doesn't have some of the higher level services and utilities that network administrators have come to expect from an enterprise operating system. Novell has made the commitment to enable Linux environments to run many of the same Novell services that are available on the NetWare kernel. Novell Nterprise Linux Services 1.0 is a comprehensive set of products and utilities that give the Linux operating system many of NetWare 6.5's enterprise service capabilities. The Nterprise Linux Services product not only enhances the Linux platform; it also leverages a large support base of IT professionals with experience in managing NetWare networks using these same services and tools. As shown in Table F-2, Nterprise Linux Services is a bundle of Novell network services and utilities running on enterprise-class Linux distributions.

Table F-2 Nterprise Linux Services

Service	Description	Comparable NetWare Product
Identity services	Novell eDirectory service that includes connectors to NT domains, Active Directory, and Web address books	eDirectory for Linux
File services	Personal file management services with automatic built-in file encryption, anywhere/anytime Internet access, and automatic synchronization between server and client	iFolder and NetStorage
Print services	Internet Printing Protocol (IPP)-based printing for Windows, Macintosh, and Linux clients	iPrint
Messaging services	A message and calendaring system that supports up to 50,000 users per server	GroupWise and NetMail
Web services	A Web access system based on the open-source Apache Web Server and Tomcat Java Virtual Machine (JVM) to access Nterprise Linux Services	Apache and Tomcat
Management services	Patch and application distribution to Linux servers in Remote Patch Management (RPM) format	Remote Manager

Table F-2   Nterprise Linux Services (continued)

Service	Description	Comparable NetWare Product
Install services	Server-based install services that support express (single server) or custom (distributed) deployments	ZENworks for Desktops
Administration services	Browser-based single point of administration for all Nterprise Linux Services	iManager 2.0, eGuide, Novell Modular Authentication Service (NMAS)

F

As you can see in Table F-2, Nterprise Linux Services enables you to apply much of what you have learned about NetWare 6 and 6.5 to managing Linux-based network environments. A key to Novell's success in getting Linux-based IT organizations to adopt Nterprise Linux Services will be reaching the necessary threshold of market share through Linux distribution channels. Red Hat and SuSE are the major distributors of enterprise-level Linux operating systems. Red Hat is a leading distributor of Linux in the United States, and SuSE is the main European distributor. With Novell's acquisition of SuSE in the fall of 2003, Nterprise Linux Services can be packaged with SuSE Linux distributions, making it available to many European Linux-based organizations. In addition, Novell has partnered with IBM, Hewlett-Packard, and Dell, who will also be shipping Nterprise Linux Services to their customers. These combined distribution channels should help jumpstart the Linux community by providing a set of standard and well-known network services. As a Certified Novell Administrator for NetWare 6, you'll be well on your way to having the skills and knowledge needed to manage a Linux-based network environment. In the following section, you learn how to install Novell's iManager utility on the Linux operating system.

Installing iManager 2.0 on Linux

You have learned how to use iManager to perform many administrative tasks on NetWare 6 and 6.5 servers. In addition to serving as a browser-based administrative tool for NetWare, iManager 2.0 has been enhanced to provide a single point of administration for Novell eDirectory and other network resources on operating systems such as Linux, Windows, and Solaris. In this section, you learn how to install iManager 2.0 on a Linux server, but first you need to meet the prerequisites listed in Table F-3.

Table F-3   iManager 2.0 for Linux Prerequisites

Requirement	Prerequisite Value
Operating system	SuSE Linux Enterprise Server 8.x, Red Hat Linux 8
Java Virtual Machine	Sun JVM 1.4.1 or later
Processor	Pentium III 800 MHz or higher
RAM	360 MB
Rights	Root (Supervisor) rights to the Web server
eDirectory	eDirectory version 8.7.1 or later must be installed on Linux
Ports	Apache, Tomcat, and JVM are installed with iManager 2.0 and by default need to use the following ports: 80 and 443 for Apache and 8080, 8005, and 8009 for Tomcat; to avoid port conflicts that interfere with iManager operations, be sure existing applications on the Linux host are not using these ports
Gettext software	Use the Gettext -v command to verify that your Linux server has the latest version of the Gettext software (obtained from your Linux distributor)

If you're installing iManager with Nterprise Linux Services, follow the prerequisites and instructions in the accompanying installation guide.

After verifying that your Linux environment meets the prerequisites in Table F-3, you can use these steps to install iManager 2.0 on your Linux server:

1. Mount the CD containing Novell iManager on your Linux file system.

2. Use the following command to extract iManager from the compressed file:

   ```
   tar -zxvf iMan_202_linux.tgz
   ```

3. Open a shell and change to the iManager_linux directory (a subdirectory of the directory where you copied or extracted the iManager files in Step 2).

4. Enter the following command to start the installation process:

   ```
   ./install.sh
   ```

5. Follow the onscreen prompts and instructions. Press Enter to accept the default text shown in brackets.

6. When prompted to enter the iManager server addresses or DNS host name, the IP address is automatically detected. Press Enter to accept it.

7. Use dot notation when entering the Admin user name (for example, cn=admin.o=RockyRidge).

8. If you're installing iManager 2.0.1, use these steps to set a password for the the Portal Configuration Object (PCO):

   a. In an eDirectory tree with an existing PCO, you need to use the existing password, which is stored in the PortalServlet properties files in the TOMCAT_HOME\webapps\nps\WEB-INF directory. Search for the System Password=[password] field.

   b. When setting a new password, don't use the password for your Admin users. The default password of "novell" should be changed for increased security.

9. The default LDAP server IP address is the local machine. Be sure to use the IP address of the eDirectory LDAP server for the eDirectory tree in which you're installing iManager.

10. After finishing the installation, start a supported browser (Netscape or Internet Explorer) and enter the URL https://*ip_address*:port/nps/iManager.html (replacing *ip_address* with the IP address of the server running iManager). The port number can be left blank if you're using the default port of 443 for secure connections. Be careful when entering the URL, as it's case sensitive.

Setting Up Role Based Services

As described in Appendix E, authorization is the security system component that assigns a set of rights or permissions to authenticated users for the purpose of accessing and managing network resources. Because both Linux and NetWare have separate systems for granting users permission to access and maintain data in the file system, NetWare administrators need to learn about Linux file system security to manage Linux environments. With Role Based Services (RBS), Novell has created a standardized system of delegating authority to users to use iManager on both Linux and NetWare servers. RBS consists of administrative tasks grouped into roles that can be assigned to users within a specific eDirectory context. RBS consists of a number of objects, described in Table F-4.

Table F-4   RBS eDirectory Objects

RBS Icon	Name	Description
	rbsCollection	A container object that holds all RBS Role and Module objects. A tree can have multiple rbsCollection objects located in any of the following containers: Country Domain Locality Organization Organizational Unit The main rbsCollection is normally located in the same container as the server holding the master copy of the eDirectory partition.
	rbsRole	Specifies the tasks that users who are members of the role are allowed to perform. rbsRole is a container object that holds rbsTasks and can be located only within a rbsCollection container. Role members can be users, groups, or Organizational Units and are associated with a specific context in the tree called a scope. rbsRole objects are automatically created and deleted as necesssary by Role Based Services.
	rbsTask	Represents a leaf object that holds a specific function, such as creating printers or resetting passwords.
	rbsBook	Represents a leaf object located in an rbsModule that consists of pages containing roles and tasks for members.
	rbsScope	Represents a leaf object used for access control list (ACL) assignments instead of assigning rights for each user object. rbsScope objects define the context in the tree where a role will be performed and are associated with rbsRole objects.

RBS objects are placed in the eDirectory tree as shown in Figure F-2.

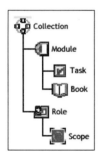

Figure F-2   RBS tree objects

By default, RBS is not installed with iManager, so only the eDirectory administrator can use iManager to manage network objects. To give other users rights to administer eDirectory objects in a Linux or NetWare environment, first you need to use these steps to install RBS:

1. Open your Web browser and use the steps in Appendix D to start iManager. Log in as the Admin user.

2. Click the Configure button to display the RBS configuration options, expand the RBS Configuration item, and click the Configure iManager link to display the Available Options window (see Figure F-3).

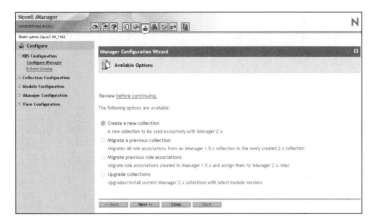

Figure F-3   RBS installation options

3. Select the Create a new collection radio button and click Next to display the Collection Information window (similar to the one in Figure F-4). In this window, you enter the name and context where the new rbsCollection object will be located. Enter a name for the rbsCollection object in the Name text box and the context of the container where the collection will be stored in the Container text box. Click Next to display the setup window shown in Figure F-5.

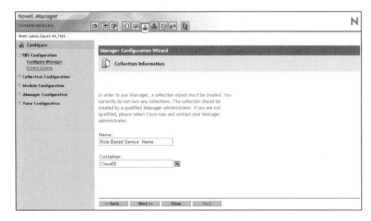

Figure F-4   The Collection Information window

Figure F-5   Selecting RBS modules

4. Select the modules to be installed (all are selected by default), and enter a scope for your administrative user name in the Scope text box.

Several tasks in iManager require users to have Supervisor rights in the container to perform updates. When assigning roles to users or groups, the administrator is prompted for a scope that defines the area of the tree in which the user or group's role will be effective. To automatically assign the eDirectory rights necessary for the selected user or group to perform the tasks in the assigned role, click the Assigned Rights check box, as shown previously in Figure F-5.

5. Leave the Assign Rights and Inheritable check boxes selected to automatically assign the eDirectory rights users need to perform the tasks listed in each role. With these check boxes selected, you can simply add a user to an administrative role, and RBS will assign that user eDirectory Entry and Attribute rights.

6. Click the Start button to install RBS and set up the roles and tasks for the modules you selected in Step 4.

7. After completing the setup, exit iManager and close your Web browser. You can now assign users to administrative roles as described in the textbook.

Commitment to Open Source

NetWare 6.5 has continued to enhance the commitment to open source that Novell started with NetWare 6. As described in Appendix D, NetWare 6.5 comes with a number of open-source features, such as a second copy of Apache Web Server for hosting corporate Web sites, the Tomcat Servlet engine, and several developer tools, including MySQL, PHP and Perl scripting languages, and Novell exteNd. Although these open-source tools and utilities are available to the public, Novell has made them more usable by integrating them with NetWare 6.5 and providing support services. NetWare 6 includes a copy of Apache Web Server, but it was intended only to support Novell Web services, such as iPrint, iFolder, and NetStorage. NetWare 6 also includes NetWare Enterprise Web Server so that organizations can host their own Web sites on the NetWare 6 server. A major change in NetWare 6.5 is replacing NetWare Enterprise Web Server with a second copy of Apache. Apache Web Server is the most popular Web server on the Internet. As of this writing, 62% of all Web sites are hosted by Apache Web servers. Along with the enterprise version of Apache Web Server, NetWare 6.5 includes the Apache Web Server utility for managing and maintaining Apache Web sites hosted on Linux and NetWare 6.5 servers.

Apache Web Server is configured by using directives stored in the httpd.conf file. Figure F-6 shows these directions displayed in Apache Manager. Apache Web Server reads the httpd.conf file at startup and periodically during operation to maintain the Web server's configuration. The httpd.conf file is a simple text file containing all the directives needed to configure the Web server and any other modules that might be loaded. These directives and modules are well documented on the Apache Web site, making it relatively easy to configure and manage your server.

However, changing the configuration requires knowledge of the httpd.conf file's directives and their syntax. When manually editing the httpd.conf file, it's easy to introduce errors by incorrectly typing a directive name or omitting necessary components of the syntax, which can cause interruptions in the organization's Web services that require extra troubleshooting and configuration time. In addition, if you're managing several installations of Apache, keeping all their httpd.conf files synchronized can waste time and cause additional problems.

Configuration view: sys:/apache2/conf/http

ServerRoot	"SYS:/APACHE2"
Timeout	300
KeepAlive	On
MaxKeepAliveRequests	100
KeepAliveTimeout	15
ThreadStackSize	65536
StartThreads	25
MinSpareThreads	10
MaxSpareThreads	50
MaxThreads	1024
MaxRequestsPerChild	0
Listen	80
SecureListen	443 "SSL CertificateDNS"
ServerAdmin	you@your.address
ServerName	172.20.0.65
UseCanonicalName	Off
DocumentRoot	"SYS:/APACHE2/htdocs"
DirectoryIndex	index.html index.html.var
AccessFileName	.htaccess
TypesConfig	conf/mime.types
DefaultType	text/plain
HostnameLookups	Off

Figure F-6 Viewing the default Apache configuration file in Apache Manager

NetWare 6.5 solves many of the problems of administering Apache Web Server running on Linux or NetWare servers with a new Web-based administration tool: Apache Manager. Apache Manager is more than a simple GUI interface for editing the httpd.conf file. With the multiple-server administration mode, you can manage several installations of Apache running on multiple servers from eDirectory (sometimes referred to as a "server farm"). Because Apache Manager is a Java application, it runs on both Linux and NetWare 6.5. This tool offers the following advantages over manually configuring the httpd.conf configuration file:

- Changes to directives are made electronically, reducing the risk of errors.

- You don't have to know all the Apache directives or modules to configure Apache.

- You can manage multiple installations of Apache Web Server from a single interface.

- You don't need to edit and maintain several configuration files, in which many of the same directives are used on each Apache Web server.

In the chapter on installing and configuring Web services, you learned how to use NetWare Enterprise Web Server to start and stop the Novell Enterprise Web server, change the path of the default Web content, and create a virtual document directory. In the following sections, you learn how to use Apache Manager to perform some of the same functions on the Apache Web server. If you have access to an administrative user name and password, you can perform these configuration changes on your Apache Web server.

Starting and Stopping Apache Web Server

The Rocky Ridge company is using the copy of Apache Web Server that came with NetWare 6.5 to host its own Web site. After installing the server, Kathleen used the following steps to check the Apache Web server's status:

1. She started her workstation, clicked Start, Run, and entered the URL https://*ip_address*:2200 (replacing *ip_address* with the address of the NetWare 6.5 server) to open the Login window.

2. She entered her Admin user name and password and clicked the Login button to display the Welcome to NetWare 6.5 window.

3. In the navigation frame on the left, she clicked the Open Source heading and then the Apache 2.0 link (see Figure F-7).

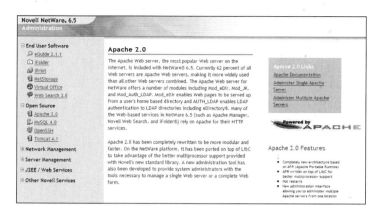

Figure F-7   Starting Apache Manager

4. Kathleen clicked the Administer Single Apache Server link under the "Apache 2.0 Links" heading on the right to open the Apache Manager Server Status window shown in Figure F-8.

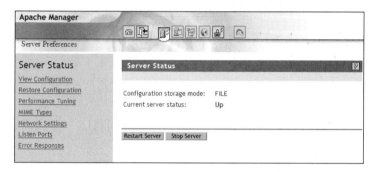

Figure F-8   The Server Status window

From the information in this window, Kathleen knows that the server configuration is coming from the httpd.conf file and the server is up and running. She can use the toolbar buttons to view server logs, modify Web site content locations, view loaded modules, and change administration mode. Two buttons at the bottom of the Server Status window are available for restarting or stopping the Apache Web server. If Web server configuration changes don't seem to be working, restarting the Apache Web server to reload the httpd.conf directives is a good idea.

Changing Administration Mode

Novell Apache 2.0 Web Server can be configured via directives in the httpd.conf file or eDirectory. When you're administering only a single Apache Web server, using the default httpd.conf file to store configuration directives is often simpler. However, if you're administering a server farm consisting of several Apache Web servers running on different server platforms, working with multiple httpd.conf configuration files can be time-consuming and increase the chance of inconsistencies. Changing the administration mode to eDirectory simplifies managing multiple Apache Web servers by storing configuration directives as an eDirectory object, where they can be accessed by all Apache Web servers. To change the administration mode of the Rocky Ridge Apache Web server to eDirectory, Kathleen performed the following steps:

1. She clicked the Administration Mode button on the Apache Manager toolbar to display the Administration Mode window shown in Figure F-9.

2. She clicked the eDirectory Import Wizard radio button, and then clicked the Save button to start the Administration Mode Wizard.

3. She clicked Next to display the Change from File to Directory Mode window, clicked the Create a new server object radio button, and then clicked Next again.

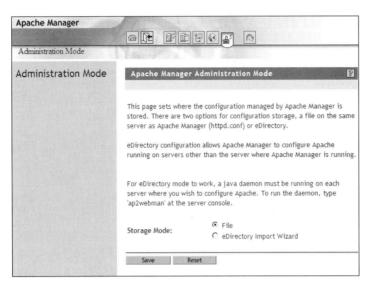

Figure F-9 Selecting an administration mode for Apache Manager

4. She selected a server group and entered the NetWare 6.5 server's name and IP address (see Figure F-10).

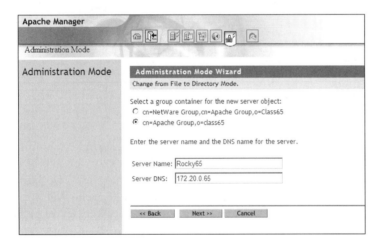

Figure F-10 The Administration Mode Wizard

5. She clicked Next to display a window asking whether to use the httpd.conf file or the inherited eDirectory configuration. She verified that the Import configuration from httpd.conf radio button was selected, and then clicked Next to display a summary window.

6. She clicked Finish to complete the conversion from File to eDirectory administration mode.

7. She clicked the Logout button to return to the Login window, and then closed her browser.

Changing the Path of the Default Web Content

To prevent the SYS volume from filling up, Kathleen wants to move the Rocky Ridge Web site content to the USERDATA volume. Before starting Apache Manager, Kathleen created an Apache2 directory on the USERDATA volume and a RockyRidge subdirectory under the Apache2 directory. To configure Apache Web Server to use the new directory, Kathleen clicked the Content Management button to display the Primary Document Directory window shown in Figure F-11.

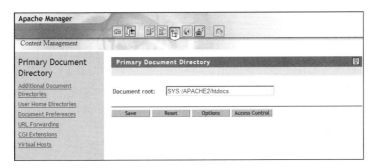

Figure F-11   The Primary Document Directory window in Apache Manager

F

She entered the path USERDATA:Apache2\RockyRidge in the Document root text box, and then clicked the Save button. Next, she clicked the Logout button on the toolbar to close the Apache Manager utility and return to the Login window. Apache Web Server will now look to the new directory for all incoming Web server requests.

Creating a Virtual Document Site

As you learned in the chapter on installing and configuring Web services, in organizations with several departments, giving each department a separate content directory can simplify management. In the following activity, you learn how to use Apache Manager to create a virtual document directory for your Web content.

Activity F-1: Creating a Virtual Document Site

Time Required: 15 minutes

Objective: Use Apache Manager to configure your own virtual document site

Description: In this activity, you use Apache Manager to set up an additional document site that points to a subdirectory in your assigned directory. To perform this activity, you need access to a user name and password that has rights to administer Apache Web Server.

1. Follow these steps to start Apache Manager:

   a. Click **Start, Run** and enter **https://*ip_address*:2200** (replacing *ip_address* with the ip address of your server). Press **Enter** or click **OK**. If necessary, click **Yes** to close the security alert message box and open the Login dialog box.

   b. Enter the password for the Admin user and click **Login** to display the Welcome to NetWare 6.5 window.

   c. Click the **Open Source** heading, and then click the **Apache 2.0** link.

   d. Click **Administer Single Apache Server** under the "Apache 2.0 Links" heading on the right to display the Server Status window.

2. Follow these steps in Content Management to create an additional document directory:

   a. Click the **Content Management** button on the toolbar.

   b. Click the **Additional Document Directories** link in the navigation frame on the left (see Figure F-12).

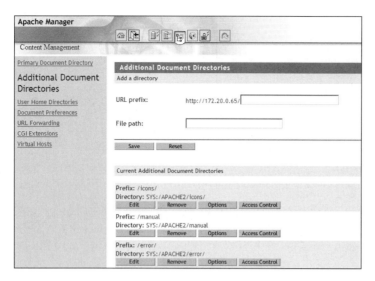

Figure F-12   The Additional Document Directories window

    c. In the Additional Document Directories window, enter **##RRHome** in the URL prefix text box (replacing ## with your assigned student number).

    d. Enter the path to your assigned student directory (for example, Rocky65\USERDATA\ ##UserData) in the File path text box.

    e. Click **Save** to open the Save and Apply Changes dialog box.

    f. Click **Save and Apply** to apply your changes to the httpd.conf file and display the Success! message box.

    g. Click **OK** to close the message box and return to Apache Manager.

3. Click the **Logout** button to close Apache Manager and return to the Login window.

4. Close the Login window, and exit your Web browser. Your Web site should now be ready for testing.

Training and Certification

There's a growing demand for Linux in the IT industry, and Novell is fueling this growth by offering support and a host of mature network services and utilities with the Nterprise Linux Services product. IT staff need a combination of Linux and Novell skills to implement Nterprise Linux Services on enterprise networks. To help train and certify network administrators for this new Linux enterprise environment, Novell has worked with other Linux-based companies, such as Red Hat and SuSE, to create the Certified Linux Engineer (CLE) program. As a CNA, you'll already have much of the knowledge and skills you need to complete this certification. With a CLE certification, you can capitalize on the growing demand for Linux and open-source solutions. As you learned earlier in this appendix, Novell currently offers several products for Linux, and others are on their way. The CLE exam tests your abilities with the Linux operating system and with Novell services. Figure F-13 illustrates the process of getting your CLE certification.

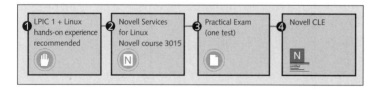

Figure F-13   The Novell Certified Linux Engineer certification process

Before taking the CLE exam, you should pursue the Linux Professional Institute's (LPI's) LPIC 1 certification. This certification isn't a requirement for the CLE exam, but the skills you gain in preparing for the LPIC 1 certification are important in knowing how to set up and maintain the Linux operating system kernel. With the LPI knowledge as a base, next you should become familiar with Nterprise Linux Services by taking the Novell 3015 course or comparable training or by studying self-paced material available from Novell. After becoming familiar with how to implement Nterprise Linux Services, you should be ready to take the CLE certification, which consists of one practical exam. Following is a list of objectives for the CLE exam:

- Objective 1: Be able to install the Linux operating system
- Objective 2: Be able to install Ximian Desktop 2
- Objective 3: Demonstrate basic Linux skills necessary for using Novell Nterprise Linux Services (NNLS)
- Objective 4: Describe NNLS
- Objective 5: Perform an NNLS installation
- Objective 6: Update NNLS with Red Carpet
- Objective 7: Describe the purpose of a directory
- Objective 8: Describe how eDirectory works
- Objective 9: Perform eDirectory maintenance tasks
- Objective 10: View user information with eGuide
- Objective 11: Manage user accounts with Linux User Management (LUM)
- Objective 12: Manage user objects with iManager
- Objective 13: Describe the purpose of DirXML
- Objective 14: Identify how DirXML works
- Objective 15: Install and implement the DirXML drive for eDirectory
- Objective 16: Describe what iFolder is and how it works
- Objective 17: Synchronize files between PCs
- Objective 18: Describe Samba
- Objective 19: Secure and back up files using iFolder
- Objective 20: Describe what iPrint is and how it works
- Objective 21: Identify iPrint features
- Objective 22: Identify clients supported by iPrint
- Objective 23: Install a printer using iPrint
- Objective 24: Describe NetMail and how it works
- Objective 25: Identify standards that NetMail conforms to
- Objective 26: Identify calendaring features of NetMail
- Objective 27: Describe Virtual Office and how it works
- Objective 28: Identify security features of Virtual Office
- Objective 29: Identify benefits of Web experience unification

F

G

COMMAND-LINE UTILITIES

Numerous workstation utilities and commands make it easier to adminster a NetWare network. Some of these utilities come packaged with NetWare 6. Some are legacy utilities from NetWare 3.12, NetWare 4.11, and NetWare 5.x. Most can be run on a Windows 2000 Professional client from Start, Run or from a command prompt (click Start, Run, enter "command" or "cmd," and click OK). Certain commands, such as MAP, work best when using "command" to open the command-prompt window because "command" starts a 16-bit DOS-based environment; "cmd" opens a Windows 2000 32-bit command-line interface. Many of the earlier NetWare commands were designed to work in a 16-bit DOS environment and could perform differently when run from a Windows 2000 command prompt. To discover all the possible options for these commands, use the following syntax:

```
command /?
```

NetWare 6 Workstation Utilities

Many administrative utilities that are part of the NetWare 6 operating system are Java based, such as ConsoleOne, or GUI based (NetWare Administrator, for example). Additionally, there are other utilities, native to NetWare 6, that are not Java or GUI based. The workstation utilities in Table G-1 are shipped with NetWare 6 and can help you administer a NetWare 6 network.

Table G-1   NetWare 6 Workstation Utilities

Command	Description	Path
CAPTURE	Used to redirect a workstation's printer port to a network print queue; provides backward-compatibility for non-NDPS printing environments. It can be run from a command prompt or within a login script to establish a user's printing environment.	SYS:\Public
CONSOLEONE	Used to manage eDirectory and the file system on a NetWare 6 network; the main Java-based utility for network administrative tasks in NetWare 6. Generally, it's run from the Start, Run option, not from a command prompt.	SYS:\Public\Mgmt\ConsoleOne\1.2\bin
CX	Used to change a client's current context; most often used with the /R /A /T switches. For example, CX /R /A /T displays all objects (/A) in all containers (/T), up to and including the [Root] object (/R).	SYS:\Login SYS:\Public
FILER	Enables an administrator to manage files, folders, and volumes on a server. The Filer utility should be protected from user access because of the options it offers, such as deleting all files and directories in the file system. For that option alone, many administrators move Filer from SYS:\Public to SYS:\System to prevent user access. It's a great tool to facilitate administrative tasks in the file system, but can cause problems when used by uninformed users.	SYS:\Public

Table G-1   NetWare 6 Workstation Utilities (continued)

Command	Description	Path
FLAG	Used to assign attributes to files and folders. When copying numerous read-only (Ro) files from one folder to another, for example, you can use FLAG to disable the Ro attribute on all the files at the same time. After you've finished copying the files, use FLAG again to enable the Ro attribute on the files.	SYS:\Public
LOGIN	Used to authenticate a user to the network from a workstation. There are several versions of LOGIN, including one that runs from a command prompt and one that can be run in a graphical interface.	SYS:\Login SYS:\Public
LOGOUT	Used to log out (leave the network).	SYS:\Public
MAP	Used to map logical drive letters to network file system resources. It can be run from a command prompt or within a login script to establish a user's drive mappings.	SYS:\Login SYS:\Public
NCOPY	Used to copy files and folders from a source directory to a destination directory. The advantage of using NCOPY instead of DOS COPY or XCOPY is that NCOPY maintains all NetWare trustee assignments and attributes. For example, to copy all files and subdirectories from the Utility directory located on the SYS volume to the Utility directory in your ##CORP volume, enter NCOPY SYS:Software.cti\Utility*.* ##CORP:Apps\Utility /S/E/V.	SYS:\Public
NDIR	Used to list a directory's files, subdirectories, and pertinent NetWare information, including owner, effective rights, IRFs, and attributes. To explore this command's many options, use the following syntax from the command prompt: NDIR /?. Some of NDIR's options include the following: • /DO to display only directories • /FO to display only files • /S to display not only files in the path, but also subdirectories and any files in those subdirectories • /SORT to sort files and directories based on the SORT criteria, such as GR for greater than, SI for file size, and AC for last accessed date To list all files in the SYS:Public directory that are more than 500,000 bytes, for example, enter NDIR SYS:Public*.* /SI GR 500000. To list all files that have not been accessed this month, enter NDIR SYS:Public*.* /AC BEF month/01/year.	SYS:\Public
NLIST	Used to list information about eDirectory objects and resources, including containers, users, and servers. Be sure to explore all the available options with the syntax NLIST /? ALL. For example, to list all users in the organization who have the job title "Manager," enter the following commands: CX /R (change to the [Root] of the eDirectory tree) NLIST USER WHERE "Title" EQ Manager /S	SYS:\Public
NPRINTER	Used to route printing jobs to the correct printer. This queue-based printing utility requires IPX/SPX for DOS and Windows 3.1 workstations.	SYS:\Public
NPTWIN95	Used on Windows 9x computers to load a port driver for queue-based printing.	SYS:\Public\Win95

Table G-1   NetWare 6 Workstation Utilities (continued)

Command	Description	Path
NWADMN32	Used to manage NDS and the file system in pre–NetWare 5 versions. It is still a vital tool for managing some key administrative processes, including the management of NDPS resources.	SYS:\Public\Win32
NWBACK32	Used to back up and restore files, folders, and resources from Target Service Agents, servers, and workstations. This utility is the workstation equivalent of SBACKUP, which is the main server-based utility for backing up NetWare 6 files, directories, and eDirectory across a NetWare network.	SYS:\Public
RIGHTS	Used to display or change effective rights to a directory. This workstation utility can be run from a command prompt or within a login script. To display the trustee assignments for all users in the current directory structure, for example, enter RIGHTS *.* /S /T.	SYS:\Public

G

LEGACY WORKSTATION UTILITIES COMPATIBLE WITH NETWARE 6

Those who have grown familiar with utilities from earlier versions of NetWare will be pleased that many of those utilities can still be used in the NetWare 6 environment. The utilities listed in Table G-2 do not ship with NetWare 6, but can be copied from your existing SYS:\Public folder to the SYS:\Public folder in NetWare 6.

Many of the utilities in Table G-2 require associated message files (.msg and .hep files), found in the SYS:\Public\Nls\English folder in your existing SYS:\Public directory. When copying the files to a NetWare 6 server, be sure to copy the executable and any associated files. All the utilities in Table G-2 can be run from a command prompt.

Table G-2   Compatible Workstation Utilities from Earlier NetWare Versions

Command	Description	Path
FLAGDIR	Used to modify the attributes on a directory.	SYS:\Public
GRANT	Used to make a trustee assignment for a user; often used in a batch file to create numerous users with trustee assignments to the file system.	SYS:\Public
MAKEUSER	Used to create users and objects, primarily when creating many users and objects simultaneously.	SYS:\Public
NETADMIN	Used to provide an administrative interface for managing NDS and eDirectory objects in NetWare 4x through NetWare 6; has the look and feel of the NetWare 3.x SYSCON utility.	SYS:\Public
NVER	Used to display information on the server name, IPX/SPX version, NDS/eDirectory version, and LAN driver version.	SYS:\Public
PURGE	Used by administrators to permanently erase files and folders from a NetWare server.	SYS:\Public
RCONSOLE	Used to allow a directly connected workstation using IPX/SPX to start a server session from the workstation. The workstation keyboard and monitor emulate the server keyboard and monitor. In NetWare 6, with the trend toward TCP/IP, RCONAG6 is the utility of choice.	SYS:\Public
REMOVE	Used by administrators to remove a user or group from a file or directory's access control list.	SYS:\Public

Table G-2   Compatible Workstation Utilities from Earlier NetWare Versions (continued)

Command	Description	Path
RENDIR	Used to rename directories; not used as much now because this feature is available with Windows Explorer.	SYS:\Public
REVOKE	Used by administrators to revoke a user's rights to a file or directory but keep the user in the file or directory's access control list.	SYS:\Public
SALVAGE	Used to recover a file or directory that was previously deleted. This utility is available from a command prompt, in NetWare Administrator, and in Filer.	SYS:\Public
SEND	Used to send a message to another workstation.	SYS:\Public
SETPASS	Used by administrators and users to change a password.	SYS:\Public
WHOAMI	Used to display your user name, connection ID, and the server you are logged in to.	SYS:\Public

Glossary

10BaseT — A network system that uses CSMA/CD along with a star topology consisting of twisted-pair cables running from a central hub to each network device. 10BaseT networks transmit data at 10 Mbps.

100BaseT — A 100 Mbps version of the 10BaseT network system.

Access Control [A] right — An access right that allows the user to grant access rights for a directory to other users.

access right — A file system permission that can be granted to users, groups, or containers. Access rights include Supervisor, Read, Write, Create, Erase, Modify, File Scan, and Access Control.

Add Self Attribute right — A special case of the Write Attribute right that allows trustees to add or remove their membership in a group.

Admin — An important user object with supervisor rights to the entire eDirectory tree.

administrative role — A group of administrative tasks that can be assigned to Admin users so that they can perform administrative functions, such as managing eDirectory, printing, licensing, and DHCP/DNS services.

alias object — An object used as a pointer to another object located in a different container of the eDirectory tree.

application service — A service that assists client computers in running certain software functions.

Archive Needed (A) — A file attribute that indicates the file has been changed since it was last backed up.

attribute — A flag or code associated with files and directories to control what type of processing can be performed on them.

Attribute rights — A group of eDirectory security rights used to define the rights granted to read and modify data in the properties of an object. Attribute rights include Read, Compare, Write, Add Self, Inheritable, and Supervisor.

authentication — The part of NetWare security that helps protect against hackers by validating each network packet to guarantee that it was sent from the authorized user.

AutoComplete addressing — An e-mail client feature used to search the address book for matching names when a user enters an e-mail address.

automatic load printer — A printer that is attached directly to the server's printer port or to a port on the workstation.

back-end process — Software such as an e-mail server that processes the data or messages received from the front-end process running on a client.

balanced tree (B-tree) — An indexing system used with the NSS file system that enables NSS volumes to be mounted more quickly and with less RAM than traditional volumes.

bandwidth — A measurement used to determine the capacity and speed of a cable system.

baseband — A network that carries digital signals consisting of ones and zeros.

block — The smallest unit of disk storage on a NetWare volume. NSS volumes use a block size of 4 KB, but the block size in traditional volumes can be set from 4 KB to 64 KB.

broadband — A network that carries analog signals, such as those used by radio and cable television.

Broker — An NDPS component responsible for sending printer messages and notifications, using the Event Notification System (ENS), Resource Management Service (RMS), and Service Registry Services (SRS).

Browse Entry right — An eDirectory security right that grants the right to view an object.

caching mode — An e-mail client feature that automatically stores all messages and attachments on the local hard disk of the user workstation.

Can't Compress (Cc) — A file attribute indicating that the operating system was unable to compress the file.

Carrier Sense Multiple Access with Collision Detection (CSMA/CD) — A method used to control access to Ethernet and 10BaseT networks by having a computer wait for an open carrier before transmitting a message. A collision occurs when two or more computers attempt to transmit at the same time, causing the computer to wait before attempting to retransmit the messages.

centralized application service — A system in which all processing is done on a centralized server. The workstations act as terminals to send and receive data from the server computer.

Certified Novell Administrator (CNA) — An administrator who has passed the Novell Certified Administrator certification test; the objectives for this test are covered in this book.

circuit-level gateway — A firewall gateway that inspects packet heading information, including type of service, port number, user name, and DNS name.

client — A computer that accesses network services such as shared files, printers, applications, or communication systems.

coaxial — A type of cable commonly used for television networks that consists of a single copper wire surrounded by a wire mesh shield.

Compare Attribute right — A special case of the Read right that allows trustees to find an object without viewing property information.

console command — A command function built into the NetWare kernel Server.exe program and, therefore, is always in memory.

container login script — A login script that is a property of a container object and is run by all users in that container when they log in to the network.

container object — An eDirectory object used to contain other objects.

context — The location of an object in the eDirectory tree.

controlled access printer — An NDPS printer that exists as an object in the eDirectory tree. By default, only users in the same container as the controlled access printer can send output to it.

Copy Inhibit (Ci) — A file attribute that prevents Macintosh computers from copying the file.

Country container object — A special type of container object used to group Organization container objects by country. Country containers must be assigned a valid two-digit country code and can exist only at the root of an eDirectory tree.

Create [C] right — An access right that allows users to create files and subdirectories.

Create Entry right — An eDirectory security right that grants the right to create objects in a container.

current context — The default location of the client computer in the eDirectory tree.

Custom Device Module (CDM) — Manages disk drives through the HBA software.

date variable — A login script variable that contains date information, such as day of week, month, and year.

default login script — Commands stored in Novell Client that run when a user does not have a personal user login script.

Delete Entry right — An eDirectory security right that grants the right to delete an object in a container.

Delete Inhibit (Di) — An attribute that protects a file or directory from being deleted.

denial-of-service — A form of network attack that loads the server with packets to shut down network services.

differential backup — A backup strategy in which only files that have changed since the last full backup are copied to the backup tape. When performing a differential backup, the SBACKUP program backs up all files that have the Archive attribute enabled but does not reset the Archive attribute, thus making it easier to restore all data after a disaster.

Directory Access Protocol (DAP) — A protocol that handles formatting and transmitting data between the DUA and DSA.

directory database — A database used to store information about network objects.

directory entry table (DET) — A storage location at the beginning of each volume for storing information on files and directories, including name, size, location, owner, and access dates.

Directory Information Base (DIB) — The name of the X.500 directory database.

Directory Information Shadowing Protocol (DISP) — A special form of the DSP that's responsible for keeping multiple copies of the DIB synchronized.

Directory Information Tree (DIT) — A tree structure for the DIB containers that represents the hierarchical relationship between entries.

Directory Map object — An object in the eDirectory tree that contains the path to a volume and directory in the network file system.

directory partition — A division of the eDirectory structure that starts with a single container and includes any subcontainers.

Directory Schema — A set of rules for ensuring that the information in the DIB is not damaged or lost.

directory service — A network service that provides discovery, security, relational management, storage, and retrieval of information on network objects, such as users, printers, groups, and containers, in a global database that's accessible to all network servers.

Directory Service Protocol (DSP) — A protocol that handles communication between DSAs.

Directory System Agent (DSA) — Software running on a server that consists of a collection of services and protocols that manage specific portions of the DIB.

directory trustee — A user, group, or container object that has been granted access rights to a directory.

Directory User Agent (DUA) — Runs on the user workstation and acts as a client to send requests from the user to the directory service.

disk partition — An area of hard disk storage formatted for a specific operating system. NetWare 6 uses NSS-formatted disk partitions to form storage pools.

distinguished name — A name that uniquely identifies an object in the eDirectory database.

distributed application service — A system that supports each user's computer running its own software.

distribution list — A GroupWise object consisting of a set of users who can be addressed as a group by using a unique name.

document management — An e-mail client feature that enables you to share documents with a group of users.

Domain Name Service (DNS) — A service that resolves TCP/IP domain names into IP addresses by looking up the name based on the domain or zone the name belongs to.

Don't Compress (Dc) — A file attribute that tells the operating system not to compress the file. When applied to a directory, none of the files in the directory will be compressed.

Don't Migrate (Dm) — An attribute that prevents files or directories from being migrated to a high-capacity storage device.

Don't Suballocate (Ds) — A file attribute that tells the operating system not to use block suballocation on the file.

drive pointer — A letter used to reference storage areas in the file system.

duplexing — A technique to increase file service reliability by keeping two disks attached to separate controller cards synchronized on the server.

Dynamic Host Configuration Protocol (DHCP) — A network service that automatically leases IP addresses to other computers when they're started.

eDirectory — A Novell global directory service containing information on all network objects, including users, groups, printers, and volumes, that is available to all servers.

effective rights — A subset of access rights that controls which functions a user can perform in a directory or file.

entry — A record in the directory database that stores information on a particular network object.

Entry rights — A group of eDirectory security rights used to control what a user can do with an object. Consists of Browse, Create, Delete, Inheritable, Rename, and Supervisor rights.

Erase [E] right — An access right that allows the user to delete files and remove subdirectories.

Ethernet — A network system that uses CSMA/CD along with a linear bus consisting of computers attached to a coaxial cable segment by T-connectors.

Execute Only (X) — A file attribute that can be applied to .com and .exe files to prevent them from being copied. Once applied, the Execute Only attribute cannot be removed.

external entity — An object type created to give users outside the organization an account in a GroupWise post office.

extranet — A network system that uses the Internet to connect different organizations for business transactions.

failover — The process of switching from a failed server to an operational server.

fiber-optic — A cable that consists of glass fibers designed to carry light generated by pulsing lasers or light-emitting diodes. Fiber-optic cable is resistant to electronic interference and can be used for very high-speed computer networks that cover long distances.

file compression — A NetWare technique to save disk space by automatically compressing files that have not been accessed for a specified time period.

File Scan [F] right — An access right that allows the user to view a directory of file and subdirectory names.

file service — A service that enables client computers to access and save data on its disk storage system.

file trustee — A user, group, or container object that has been granted access rights to a file.

firewall — A point of access between an organization's internal private network and the Internet, used to filter packets and reduce the risk of unauthorized access to or malicious attacks on the organization's private network system and services.

frame type — Specifies the format of the data packet to be sent across the network cable.

front-end process — Software such as an e-mail client that runs on a user's workstation and provides an interface that allows users to communicate with services running on a server.

full backup — A backup strategy in which all data is copied to the backup tape daily, regardless of when it changed.

gateway — The NDPS component that works with the printer agent to send output from the printer agent to the network print device.

Hidden (H) — A file or directory attribute that prevents standard DOS and Windows applications from seeing the associated file or directory.

home directory — A directory created for each user for storing his or her own files and documents.

Host Bus Adapter (HBA) — A modular disk driver that manages the controller card.

host server — The NetWare server that runs the backup program and has the attached tape or other backup media.

hub — A central connecting point for computers attached to a star topology network.

identifier variable — A login script variable used in login script commands to represent such information as the user login name, date, time, and DOS version.

iFolder — A NetWare service that enables files to be kept on a local computer (or one that's not attached to the network) and synchronized with the network.

Immediate Compress (Ic) — A file or directory attribute that tells the system to compress a large file immediately after it has been used.

incremental backup — A backup strategy that backs up only the files that have changed (the Archive attribute is on) that day, and then resets the Archive attribute on all files that are backed up.

information theft — A form of network attack that uses wire taps and sniffer software to illegally intercept data.

Inheritable Attribute right — An eDirectory security right that enables leaf objects and subcontainers to inherit Attribute rights in a container trustee assignment.

Inheritable Entry right — An eDirectory security right that allows leaf objects and other subcontainers to inherit the trustee's assignments.

inherited rights — A group of Entry or Attribute rights that flow down to other containers or leaf objects.

Inherited Rights Filter (IRF) — A method of reducing inherited rights in a subdirectory or file by allowing only the access rights specified in the filter to be inherited.

Internet Message Access Protocol (IMAP) — A standardized protocol used to access and store messages from the post office server.

intruder detection — A part of login security that works at the container level by setting a limit on the number of incorrect login attempts that can be made on a user account in that container during a specified time period.

intrusion — A form of network attack that involves gaining unauthorized and illegal access to an organization's information, usually through obtaining a user's account and password.

Java servlet — An application written in the Java programming language to run on a Web server.

leaf object — An eDirectory object used to represent network entities, such as users, groups, printers, and servers. Leaf objects must exist within Organization or Organizational Unit containers.

Lightweight Directory Access Protocol (LDAP) — A simplified version of X.500 that makes it easier for compatible systems to exchange directory information.

Lightweight Directory Interchange Format (LDIF) — An ASCII text file format that uses a standardized syntax to add, change, or delete objects in LDAP-compatible directory systems.

linear bus topology — A network topology in which a single cable segment runs from one computer to the next.

local area network (LAN) — A high-speed communication system consisting of cables and cards (hardware) along with software that enables different types of computers to communicate and share resources over short distances, such as within a single building or room.

local drive pointer — Drive letters that point to physical devices on the local computer, such as the floppy drive, hard drive, or CD-ROM drive.

logging in — The process of authenticating yourself to a Novell network by supplying a user name and password.

logging on — The process of authenticating yourself to a Windows network by supplying a user name and password.

Login directory — A required NetWare operating system directory that contains files and programs needed by DOS clients to log in to the network.

login script — A list of commands performed when you first log in to the network. An important use of the login script is establishing the initial drive pointer mappings.

login script variable — A reserved word in the login script language with a variable value that's unique to the user logging in. For example, the HOME_DIRECTORY variable contains the path to the user's home directory.

manual load printer — A remote printer attached to a port on a networked workstation and controlled by the print server.

mesh topology — A network topology in which each computer is attached to the others by using separate cables.

message service — A network service responsible for sending and receiving network messages and notifications.

Message Transfer Agent (MTA) — A software component that assists the core post office software in transferring messages between mailboxes.

metropolitan area network (MAN) — A network that uses fiber-optic or microwave towers to connect computers in the same geographical area.

Migrated (M) — A file attribute set by the system indicating that a file has been moved to an archive data medium.

mirroring — The process of automatically synchronizing the information on two partitions located on different disk drives attached to the same controller.

mode switching — An e-mail client feature that allows users to change their mailbox modes between online, caching, and remote.

Modify [M] right — An access right that allows the user to change file and directory names—without changing the file contents—and use the FLAG command to change attribute settings on files or subdirectories.

multiple station access unit (MSAU) — A central hub used to connect cables in a token ring network.

NDPS Manager — The NDPS component that manages the printer agent for printers that do not have an embedded printer agent.

NetBEUI — A Microsoft nonrouting protocol stack commonly used on Windows.

Net Services — A set of hardware and software components that work together to provide access to information services across the Internet or company intranet.

NetWare Core Protocol (NCP) — A protocol used by NetWare to access services on a NetWare server.

NetWare Loadable Module (NLM) — An external program that can be loaded into the file server's RAM to add additional functionality or control hardware devices, such as disk drives and network cards.

NetWare 6 Server certificate — A license certificate installed during the NetWare 6 server installation; this certificate is necessary for the server to run.

NetWare 6 User certificate — A UAL license certificate that supports user connections to the network. This certificate is not installed during the NetWare 6 server installation; it's installed later by using iManager.

network drive pointer — A letter, usually F: through Z:, used to represent directory paths and volumes in the network file system.

network interface card (NIC) — A hardware component used to connect each computer to the cable system.

network operating system (NOS) — The software that runs on server computers to provide services to the network.

nickname — A GroupWise object that assigns an account name to a role or position in the company.

Normal (N) — A directory attribute that removes all other directory attributes.

Novell Distributed Print Services (NDPS) — A new printing system developed by Hewlett-Packard and Novell to make network printer configuration and access more convenient.

Novell Directory Services (NDS) — Used in versions before NetWare 6, a global database containing information on all network objects, including users, groups, printers, and volumes, that are available to all servers.

Novell NetStorage — A NetWare service that gives users secure access to files on the NetWare server from any Internet location.

Novell Portal Services (NPS) — A Net Services component running on a NetWare server that provides customized pages or portals for users based on users' rights and personal style specifications.

Novell Storage Services (NSS) — The file system used primarily by NetWare 6. In NSS, logical volumes are created from storage pools that consist of one or more disk partitions.

object — A network component of the eDirectory database.

OneNet — Novell's strategy of making multiple networks, consisting of diverse clients and services, work together as one network.

Organization container object — An eDirectory object used to group objects that belong to an organization. Organization objects can exist at the root of an eDirectory tree or within a Country container.

Organizational Role object — An object type that enables you to assign rights to an object rather than a specific user.

Organizational Unit (OU) container object — An eDirectory object used to group leaf objects that belong to a subdivision of an Organization container. Organizational Unit containers can exist within an Organization container or within another Organizational Unit.

packet filtering — A process performed by a screening router to determine whether a packet is from a trusted, untrusted, or unknown network.

parallel port (LPTn) — A common printer port used on personal computers. Parallel ports require thicker cables to transmit several bits of information at one time.

patch panel — A centralized wiring panel used to connect individual wires coming from computers to a network hub.

path — The location of a file or directory in the network file system.

peer-to-peer — A network operating system in which a computer can be both client and server.

Policy Package object — An eDirectory object used to manage the way users access their workstations and connect to the network.

Post Office Agent (POA) — A e-mail software component that is responsible for transferring messages from the client to the correct mailbox on the E-mail server.

Post Office Protocol (POP) — A standardized client/server protocol used for sending and receiving e-mail messages between the client and the e-mail server.

print queue — A network object representing a holding area where print jobs are kept until the printer is available. In NetWare, a print queue is a subdirectory of the Queues directory, located in the volume specified during print queue creation.

print server — A component of queue-based printing that manages network printers by taking jobs from print queues and sending them to the appropriate network printer.

print service — A network service that makes printers attached to the network available to user workstations.

printer agent — The software component of NDPS that transfers output from the client and controls the physical printer.

private key — The digital key code used in public key cryptography that is kept solely by the owner and used to decode data and create digital signatures.

profile login script — An eDirectory object that contains login commands common to multiple users.

property — A field containing information about an object. Not all object types have the same properties.

protocol stack — The collection of protocols responsible for formatting and routing packets of data between network devices.

proxy service — A high-level firewall service that works at the application level to give clients on an organization's network both incoming and outgoing access to Internet services.

public access printer — An NDPS printer that is attached to the network but does not have an eDirectory object in the tree. Any user attached to the network can send output to a public access printer without having to log in to the network.

Public directory — A required NetWare operating system directory that contains NetWare utility programs and commands available to all users.

public key — The digital key code used in public key cryptography for clients to encrypt data being sent to a host and to verify a host's digital signature.

public key cryptography — An Internet security system that uses public and private keys to encrypt and decrypt data and create digital signatures for authenticating users.

[Public] trustee object — A special trustee object created during the NetWare installation that consists of all client computers attached to the network.

Purge (P) — A file or directory attribute that prevents a file or all files in a directory from being salvaged after deletion.

queue — A space in the e-mail database where the server temporarily stores outgoing messages while waiting to contact the destination server at a predefined interval.

queue-based printing — A printing system implemented in NetWare 3 that's designed to support simple printers and DOS-based applications.

Read Attribute right — An eDirectory security right that includes the Compare right and allows the trustee to view values stored in an object's property fields.

Read [R] right — An access right that allows the user to read files or run programs in a directory.

Read Only (Ro) — A file attribute that prevents the contents of a file from being modified.

Read Write (Rw) — A default file attribute that allows the contents of a file to be changed.

regular drive pointer — A drive pointer that is assigned to a data directory on each volume.

relative name — Starts with the current context of the client, but omits the leading period.

remote printer — A printer attached to the port of a networked workstation and controlled by the print server.

Rename Entry right — An eDirectory security right that grants the right to change the name of an object.

Rename Inhibit (Ri) — A file or directory attribute that prevents the name of a file or directory from being changed.

replica — A copy of the eDirectory database stored on a NetWare server.

resource — A GroupWise object representing a physical asset that can be checked out or scheduled, such as a conference room or a company vehicle.

ring topology — A network topology in which the signals are passed in one direction from one computer to another until they return to the original sending computer.

root drive pointer — A regular drive pointer that acts as though it were the root of the volume.

[Root] object — An eDirectory object representing the beginning of the network directory service tree.

[Root] partition — The initial division of the eDirectory tree that starts at the root of the tree.

[Root] trustee object — A special trustee object that represents all users defined in the eDirectory tree. All users who have logged in to the eDirectory tree are part of the [Root] trustee object.

rule — A GroupWise object containing actions that are applied to incoming messages that meet certain conditions.

search drive pointer — A drive pointer that is used to reference executable files and application directories by using a DOS path.

security service — A network service that authenticates users to the network and determines which network rights they have.

serial port (COMn) — A port often used to connect communication devices, such as modems and printers, to send signals over long cables. Serial ports send only one bit of data at a time, so serial cables can consist of only a few wires.

server — A computer that provides one or more network services.

server-centric — A network operating system, such as NetWare 6, in which server functions run on a designated computer.

server clustering — A setup in which two or more servers can share a common disk system, making the data available in case one of the servers has a hardware failure.

Server Connection Licensing (SCL) — The license model used by pre–NetWare 6 servers that requires each server to have a license for each connection, including connections made by printers and other non-user resources.

Server Management console — The iFolder component that enables network administrators to perform administrative tasks, such as managing iFolder user accounts.

shadowing — The process of distributing and synchronizing the DIB among multiple locations.

Sharable (Sh) — A file attribute that allows multiple users to use a file at the same time.

shielded twisted-pair (STP) — A type of cable consisting of pairs of insulated wires twisted together and encased in a wire mesh shield. The use of the grounded wire mesh shield in STP cable reduces the effect of outside interference from other electrical sources.

Simple Mail Transfer Protocol (SMTP) — A TCP/IP-based e-mail protocol used to transfer messages between e-mail servers.

spoofing — A method of illegally accessing network resources or attacking a network service by creating falsified packets that appear to come from an authorized entity.

spooling — The process of sending output from a user's computer to a print job storage area.

star topology — A network topology in which a cable runs from each network device to a central hub.

Storage Management System (SMS) — The NetWare backup service that includes several NetWare Loadable Modules, along with workstation software that enables the host server to back up data from one or more target devices by using the SBACKUP NLM.

storage pool — An NSS file system component used to group one or more partitions into a storage area that can be divided into one or more volumes.

suballocation — A feature of traditional volumes that divides blocks into smaller 512-byte increments so that multiple files can share the same block, thus saving disk space.

Supervisor Attribute right — An eDirectory security right that grants all rights to a property unless blocked by an object's IRF.

Supervisor Entry right — An eDirectory security right that grants all access privileges, including the Supervisor right to all the object's attributes or properties.

Supervisor [S] right — An access right that grants all rights to a directory and its subdirectories; this right cannot be blocked or reassigned at a lower subdirectory or file level.

syntax — Rules to be followed when writing login script commands.

System (Sy) — A file or directory attribute that flags a file or directory for operating system use.

System directory — A required NetWare-created operating system directory that contains system software and commands available only to the server and Admin user, not to other users.

target server — A server whose data is backed up by a host server.

thread — A process that's currently being worked on by the CPU.

thin client — The workstation component of a centralized application service that acts as an input/output terminal to an application running on the server.

time variable — A login script variable that contains system time information, such as hour, minute, and a.m. or p.m.

token ring — A network system that uses a star topology with twisted-pair cable running from the central MSAU hub to each computer. A token passing scheme is used to control access to the network by causing computers to wait for the token before transmitting their message, thereby eliminating collisions on CSMA/CD networks, such as Ethernet and 10BaseT.

topology — The physical layout of the cable system.

Transaction Tracking System (TTS) — A system that protects the Transactional attribute, ensuring that all transactions are completed or left in the original state.

Transactional (T) — A file attribute used on database files to enable the system to restore the file to its previous state if a transaction is not completed.

Transmission Control Protocol/Internet Protocol (TCP/IP) — The protocol commonly used to format and route packets between Unix computers; also used on the Internet.

trusted network — A network with an IP address range that's known to be safe or can be controlled and monitored by your organization.

trustee assignment — An entry in the ACL for a file or directory that makes the user a trustee of a directory or file.

typeful name — A distinguished name that includes object type abbreviations (O, OU, and CN).

typeless name — A distinguished name that assumes object type based on position instead of including the object type abbreviations.

uninterruptible power supply (UPS) — A backup power system that uses batteries to supply continuous power to a computer during a power outage.

unknown network — A network that is not specified as a trusted or untrusted network in a firewall. Firewalls treat unknown networks as untrusted networks.

unshielded twisted-pair (UTP) — A type of cable that consists of pairs of insulated wires twisted together to reduce electrical crosstalk.

untrusted network — An IP address range that might contain hackers or other malicious entities. Packets from networks listed as untrusted are inspected by the network firewall.

User Access Licensing (UAL) — The NetWare 6 licensing system, in which each user account is provided with a fixed license to access any server in the tree the first time the user logs in.

user-defined variable — A login script variable that allows users to enter parameters for their personal user login scripts.

user login script — Personalized login script commands for a single user that are stored in the Login Script property of a user's eDirectory account. A user's personal login script runs after any container or profile script commands are finished.

user template — A property that defines standard settings and configures restrictions for each user in a particular container.

virtual private network — A trusted network that sends packets over an untrusted network, such as the Internet.

virus — A self-replicating program that can be embedded in software to propagate between computers and eventually can be triggered to affect computer performance or destroy data.

volume — The major division of NetWare storage. All files are stored in volumes associated with a specific NetWare server.

volume object — A pointer to physical data volumes on the server, used to access data and store volume configuration and status information.

Web Services — A set of hardware and software components that provide WWW and FTP information services to clients located on the Internet or company intranet.

wide area network (WAN) — A network that uses carriers such as the phone system to connect computers over long distances.

workgroup — A group of two or more peer-to-peer networked computers.

workstation variable — A login script variable that contains information about the workstation's environment, such as machine type, operating system, operating system version, and station node address.

Write Attribute right — An eDirectory security right that includes the Add Self right and allows the trustee to change information in property fields.

Write [W] right — An access right that allows the user to change or add data to files in a directory.

X.500 — Recommendations created by the International Telecommunications Union that define standard directory service functions and formats.

Zero Effort Networking (Z.E.N.works) for Desktops (ZfD) — A Novell product that enables network administrators to centrally manage users' desktop environments.

zone file — The location in which a DNS server keeps all computer name information for a specific domain.

Index

* (asterisk), 294, 301
\ (backslash), 37
. (period), 26, 168
+ (plus sign), 63, 164
; (semicolon), 294, 301

A

Access Control Lists. *See* ACLs (Access Control Lists)
Access Control right, 153, 186–189
access right(s). *See also* effective rights; inherited rights
   administrative roles and, 268–273
   assigning, 189–190, 194–204, 208–211, 239–240, 243–244, 248–249
   basic description of, 186–204
   blocking, 265–266
   default, 253–255
   delegating, 260–262
   eDirectory services and, 236–240, 249–255, 260–263, 268–273
   Enterprise Web Server and, 443–444
   guidelines, 205–208
   login scripts and, 262–263
   needed for each user, identifying, 205–208
   planning, 205–208, 232
   required for common functions, list of, 187
   troubleshooting, 249–251
account(s). *See also* login; user names
   creating, 32, 158–161
   disabled, 149, 171
   establishing login security for, 142–148
   iFolder, 395–396
   intruder detection limits for, 145–148
   locking, 147–148
   managing, 141–183
   restrictions, setting, 142–145
   securing, 149–150
   using multiple, 165
Account Locked check box, 148
ACL property, 236, 250–251
ACLs (Access Control Lists), 186, 188, 236, 250–251
Active Directory, 12
ACU (Automatic Client Upgrade), 42
adapter settings, viewing, 24, 414
Add button, 40, 152
Add Filter button, 247
Add Printer icon, 341
Add Printer Wizard, 334
Add Property dialog box, 247, 251, 252
Add Replica button, 71
Add Replica dialog box, 71
Add Self right, 239, 273
Address Restrictions option, 144
Admin object, 48

Admin user accounts, 9–11, 106
   backup, 149–150, 171
   disabled, 149, 171
   eDirectory services and, 13, 54, 58, 59, 62, 63
   file salvage operations and 115
   increasing security for, 149–150
   locking out, 149
   NetWare Administrator and, 54
   open policy packages for, 317–320
   passwords, changing, 10–11
   renaming, 149
   restrictions for, 143–145
   Role Based security and, 163
   viewing TCP/IP settings with, 28
administrative roles
   assigning rights through, 268–273
   creating groups and, 164
   defined, 163
   viewing, 162–163
Administrator rights, 28
Advanced Audit Service (Novell), 457
Advanced button, 8, 9, 10
Advanced Login tab, 44
Advanced Menu Settings tab, 44
Advanced Settings tab, 45, 88
AFP (AppleTalk Filing Protocol), 35
alias objects
   defined, 47, 60
   creating, 60–62
All Attributes Read check box, 260
Allow forward references check box, 170
American Standard Code for Information Interchange. *See* ASCII (American Standard Code for Information Interchange)
AM_PM variable, 289
Apache directory, 93
Apache Web Server, 93, 433–435, 437–438
   administration mode and, 669–670
   content paths and, 670–671
   starting/stopping, 668–669
   virtual document sites and, 671–672
AppleTalk Filing Protocol. *See* AFP (AppleTalk Filing Protocol)
applets, 393–394, 396, 400, 402. *See also* Java
application(s)
   -oriented directory structure, 99–100
   services, basic description of, 7, 16–18
Application Launcher, 315
Application layer, 26
Apply Changes button, 440
Apps directory, 117
Archive Needed attribute, 217, 218
ARCserve for NetWare, 128–129

ASCII (American Standard Code for Information Interchange)
   files, displaying, 298–302
   LIDF and, 168
Assign Simple Password check box, 158, 160
Associations dialog box, 320
asterisk (*), 294, 301
attribute(s). *See also specific attributes*
   basic description of, 186, 217–227
   defining, 232–233
   directory, 217, 219–227
   documenting, 225–227
   file, 217–219, 222–227
   implementing, 222–224
   rights, 236–237
Audit directory, 93
authentication, 6–8, 67, 68. *See also* login
   certificate services and, 451–453
   defined, 142
   NetWare 6.5 enhancements to, 651–655
AutoComplete addressing, 477
Automatic Client Upgrade. *See* ACU (Automatic Client Upgrade)
automatic load printers, 335. *See also* printers
Available Classes dialog box, 164

B

back-end processes, 474, 477–479
backslash (\), 37
backup(s)
   of Admin user accounts, 149–150, 171
   basic description of, 127–133
   centralized, 78
   determining storage needs for, 130
   differential, 85, 130–131
   disaster recovery procedures and, 132–133
   full, 130–131
   importance of, 21
   incremental, 130–131
   policy-based, 129
   rotation system, 132–133
   SMS, 127–133
   snap shot, 635–636
   software, running, 131–132
   strategies, 130–131
   systems, 130–133
   tape, 21–22, 132–133
   testing, 131, 132
   third-party software packages for, 128–129
   users, assigning, 131
   weekly, 133
   bandwidth, 57
baseband systems, 594

batch files, 125
battery power, 21
BEGIN command, 300
Bestart.ncf, 129
Bestop.ncf, 129
Bid.frm, 113, 114, 116
BIND command, 536–537
BindView Solutions for Novell, 457
blade computers, 621–622
block(s)
    defined, 86, 135
    size, 86, 98
    suballocation of, 86–87, 98
boot diskettes, 463
boot sector viruses, 462. *See also* viruses
Border Manager (Novell), 466
branch offices, managing, 622–623
Brightstor ARCserve Backup for NetWare,
    128–129
broadband systems, 594
Broker component, 346–348, 350–351, 361, 408
Browse button, 15, 56
Browse rights, 237–238
browser(s), 14, 16, 437
    certificates and, 161
    creating user and group accounts from,
        163–165
    eDirectory services and, 35, 36, 53
    entering server addresses in, 161
    iFolder and, 390–396, 402–403
    iManager and, 62–64, 161
    NPS and, 435
B-trees (balanced trees), 82–83
bugs, recovering files corrupted by, 132. *See also*
    debugging; errors
BURGLER.NLM, 457
business continuity, 624–641

C

cable(s)
    choosing, 23–24
    described, 586–588
    fiber-optic, 588
    network pathway component and, 6, 23–24
    printers and, 22
    twisted-pair, 587–588
    unshielded twisted-pair (UTP), 587–588
caches, 14, 477
    disabling, 88
    Novell Client and, 45
    power supplies and, 21
Can't Compress attribute, 217, 218
CAPTURE command, 300, 334, 675
Carrier Sense Multiple Access with Collision
    Detection. *See* CSMA/CD (Carrier Sense
    Multiple Access with Collision Detection)
CAs (Certificate Authorities), 391, 451–453,
    549–550. *See also* certificates
Cascade Windows button, 55
catalog views, 129
CD command, 121
CDMs (Custom Device Modules), 523, 552

CD-ROM drives, 21, 32, 43–44, 78
certificate(s). *See also* CAs (Certificate
    Authorities)
    creating directories and, 109
    defined, 161
    information, viewing, 109
    services, 450–453
    viewing, 161
Certificate Server (Novell), 453–454
Change Context button, 55
Change Password button, 10, 11
check boxes (listed by name). *See also* options
    (listed by name)
    Account Locked check box, 148
    All Attributes Read check box, 260
    Allow forward references check box, 170
    Assign Simple Password check box, 158, 160
    Create another Directory check box, 108
    Create another User check box, 159, 160
    Create Home Directory check box, 65
    Define Additional Properties check box, 318
    Detect intruders check box, 147
    Force Password Change check box, 159, 160
    Force periodic password changes check
        box, 155
    Limit Concurrent Connections check
        box, 155
    Limit grace logins check box, 144, 155
    Lock account after detection check box, 147
    Reconnect at logon check box, 39, 43
    Require a password check box, 155
    Require unique passwords check box,
        144, 155
    Run Login Script check box, 41
    Set Password check box, 159
    User Extensible Policies check box, 318,
        320, 321
    Workstation only check box, 10, 28, 62
CIFS (Common Interface File System), 34–35
circuit-level gateways, 461. *See also* gateways
Citrix, 16
CLEAR STATION command, 411
client(s). *See also* Novell Client
    defined, 6, 29
    eDirectory services and, 34–45
    iFolder, 393–395, 400, 402
    implementing, 34–45
    network printing and, 332, 366, 377–379
    options, 36
    protocols, 34–35
    removing, 37–38
    -server application services, 16–17
Client tab, 44
Clients directory, 43
Clipboard, 113, 303
Close automatically option, 281
Close command, 165
CLS command, 294, 411
clustering, 14, 82–84, 633–634
CNA (Certified Novell Administrator), 1, 3,
    29, 557–562

collision detection. *See* CSMA/CD (Carrier
    Sense Multiple Access with Collision
    Detection)
command(s). *See also* commands (listed
    by name)
    character restrictions for, 294
    DOS, 92
    external program execution, 299–300
Command Antivirus, 463
commands (listed by name). *See also* commands
    BEGIN command, 300
    BIND command, 536–537
    CAPTURE command, 300, 334, 675
    CD command, 121
    CLEAR STATION command, 411
    CLS command, 294, 411
    CONSOLEONE command, 675
    CONTEXT command, 296
    Copy command, 117
    CX command, 50, 92, 675
    DISABLE/ENABLE LOGIN command, 538
    DISMOUNT command, 539
    DISPLAY command, 298
    DISPLAY SERVERS command, 538
    Exit command, 14, 23, 124, 125, 282, 301
    FDISPLAY command, 298
    FILER command, 119, 675
    FIRE PHASERS command, 301
    FLAG command, 186, 225–227, 233, 676
    FLAGDIR command, 677
    GRANT command, 677
    IPCONFIG command, 28, 143
    LOAD command, 539
    LOAD SMDR command, 131
    LOGIN command, 676
    LOGOUT command, 676
    MAKEUSER command, 677
    MAP command, 122–125, 281, 291, 294–295,
        299, 676
    Merge Partition command, 176
    MODULES command, 539
    MOUNT command, 539
    Move command, 173
    NCOPY command, 676
    NDIR command, 676
    NETADMIN command, 677
    NLIST command, 676
    NO_DEFAULT command, 295
    NPRINTER command, 676
    NPTWIN95 command, 676
    NVER command, 677
    NWADMN32 command, 677
    NWBACK32 command, 677
    Open command, 311
    PAUSE command, 296, 299
    Print command, 23, 303, 311
    PURGE command, 677
    RCONSOLE command, 677
    REM command, 301–303, 308
    REMOVE command, 677
    RENDIR command, 678
    REVOKE command, 678

RIGHTS command, 677
SALVAGE command, 678
Save As command, 23
SCRSAVER command, 456, 457
SECURE CONSOLE command, 456, 457, 540
Select All command, 117
SEND command, 540, 678
SET TIME command, 540
SETPASS command, 678
UNBIND command, 540
UNLOAD JAVA command, 316
WHOAMI command, 678
WRITE command, 297
Command Software Systems, 463
command-line utilities, 675–678.
    See also commands
Compaq, 21
Compare Attribute right, 238
Compare right, 238
components. *See also* objects
    defined, 6
    eDirectory services and, 46–48
    file sharing and, 19–20
    identifying, 22–24
    installing, 40–42
    introduction to, 6–18
    major, diagram displaying, 7
    network printing and, 332–336, 345–359
    removing, 38
    sample, 18
compression
    defined, 135
    NetWare file systems and, 82, 85
    volumes and, 82
Computer Management console, 10–11
Computer object, 47
conditional statements, 300–301
CONFIG command, 411, 537
Configure button, 24
Configure Toolbar button, 55
Confirm New Password text box, 10
Confirm Password text box, 11
console(s)
    command, 535–541
    NetWare installation and, 534–548
    screen savers, 456, 457
    server, 417–419, 534–548
CONSOLEONE command, 675
ConsoleOne (Novell)
    advantages of, 53
    assigning attributes with, 222
    assigning rights with, 194–204, 208–211, 243–244, 248–249
    basic description of, 59–60
    completing tree structures with, 64–66
    copying files with, 113–114
    creating directories with, 106–109
    creating groups with, 151–152
    creating objects with, 65–66, 105–106, 126, 172–173
    creating partitions with, 79, 102

creating storage pools with, 102–104
creating user templates with, 154–156
creating volumes with, 100–101, 103–105
creating user accounts with, 158–161
deleting objects with, 173–174
establishing login restrictions with, 145
exploring tree structure with, 13–14
handling login scripts with, 282, 283–284, 310–313
handling trustee assignments with, 189–191, 194–195, 210–211, 213–216, 457
importing users with, 169–171
installing, 57–59
modifying user accounts with, 165
moving directories with, 113
moving objects with, 173–177
renaming objects with, 173–174
securing Admin user accounts with, 149–151
setting directory size restrictions with, 111
setting IRFs with, 197–198
setting password restrictions with, 143–145
snap-ins, adding, 490–495
testing intruder detection and, 148
troubleshooting effective rights with, 458–459
updating users with, 166–168
viewing directory information with, 94–95
viewing effective rights with, 190–192, 200
viewing inherited rights with, 200
viewing NSS information with, 87, 88–91
viewing volume information with, 92
container(s). *See also* container login scripts; container objects
    administrators, independent, 266–268
    assigning access rights to, 189–191, 207–216
    blocking rights to, 265–266
    creating user objects in, 156–158
    drive mappings and, 15–16
    intruder detection and, 145–148
    tree structure design and, 51–60
    trustee assignments and, 189–191, 194–195, 244–246
    updating users in, 166–168
container login script(s). *See also* login scripts
    business, 327–328
    defined, 281–282, 286
    entering, 283–284, 328
    printing, 310–311
    testing, 328, 329
    worksheets, 305–308
    writing, 327–328
Container Login Script Worksheet, 577
container objects. *See also* containers
    country, 46
    defined, 46–47
    eDirectory services and, 46–49
    moving, 174–175
    naming, 48–49
content directory, 437
Content Management button, 440
context
    concept of, 8
    current, 49–50

defined, 48–49, 72
    network printing and, 372–373
    selecting, 9–10
    setting, 57
Context button, 9
CONTEXT command, 296
Context text box, 8
Contextless Login tab, 45
Control Panel policy, 319
controlled access printers, 353, 375.
    See also printers
controller card(s)
    failures, 80
    NetWare file systems and, 80–81
Copy command, 117
Copy Inhibit attribute, 217, 218
Copy Trustees dialog box, 114
copying
    files, during installation, 528–530
    files, with ConsoleOne, 113–114
    login scripts, 303
CORP volume, 79, 86, 98–100
    defined, 21
    drive pointers and, 121, 122
    eDirectory services and, 37, 39
    objects, 105–106
    partitions, 80–81, 102
    storage pool, 103–104
country container objects, 46. *See also* container objects
CPUs (central processing units)
    iFolder and, 400
    monitoring, 413–414
    requirements, 57, 78, 315
Create a New Logical Volume Wizard, 104
Create a new NSS partition dialog box, 102
Create a New Pool Wizard, 101, 103
Create a New Traditional Volume Wizard, 101
Create another Directory check box, 108
Create another User check box, 159, 160
Create Directory Map dialog box, 126
Create Entry right, 238
Create Group button, 55
Create Group dialog box, 164
Create Home Directory check box, 65
Create Network Address dialog box, 144
Create Object button, 55, 61
Create Organizational Unit window, 64
Create Partition button, 71
Create Print Queue button, 55
Create Print Queue dialog box, 337
Create Printer Agent dialog box, 354–355
Create rights, 186–189, 237
Create Subdirectory button, 111
Create User button, 55
Create User dialog box, 165
Create Volume dialog box, 61–62
cryptography, 450–451, 647–648.
    See also encryption
CSMA/CD (Carrier Sense Multiple Access with Collision Detection), 595
Ctrl+Alt+Del keystroke combination, 9, 10, 11

current context. *See also* context
  defined, 49
  viewing, 50
Current Memory Usage graph, 408
CX command, 50, 92, 675

D

DAP (Directory Access Protocol), 515–517, 552
data shredding, 82, 85, 112
Data Shredding attribute, 85, 112
dates
  creation/modification, 92
  file access, 113
Dates and Time tab, 92
DAY variable, 288–289
DAY_OF_WEEK variable, 288–289
Deactivate button, 91
debugging, 313–314. *See also* errors
default login scripts, 281, 283
Default Tree and Context option, 41
Define Additional Properties check box, 318
DEL parameter, 294
Delete Entry right, 238
Delete File button, 115
Delete Inhibit attribute, 217, 218, 220
Delete right, 237, 264
Deleted.sav directory, 112
Demilitarized Zone. *See* DMZ
  (Demilitarized Zone)
denial-of-service attacks, 454, 464–466
Design folder, 320
Design group, 151
Designs directory, 20
desktop
  accessing iFolder from, 401–402
  creating, with Z.E.N.works, 320–322
  policies, 321, 329
  shortcuts, creating, 53–54
  standard user, 320–322
  wallpaper, 321
Desktop directory, 107
DET (directory entry table), 111–112, 135, 186
  IRFs and, 196
  trustee assignments and, 188
Details on Multiple Users button, 55
Details tab, 109
Detect intruders check box, 147
device(s)
  drivers, 24, 25, 34, 356, 359
  information, viewing, 89–90
DHCP (Dynamic Host Configuration
  Protocol), 163, 601–602
DHCP Management administrative role, 163
dial-up connections, 16–17
DIB (Directory Information Base), 513–514,
  517, 552
digital signatures, 451
directories. *See also* directory services
  accessing, 20, 23
  attributes of, 217–227, 232
  creating, 65, 106–111
  defined, 92–94
  designing, 98–99

displaying hidden, 224
entries in, 512
generated during installation, 94
installing Novell Client from, 43–44
modifying, 208–211
moving, 112–113
partitions and, 68
shared, 20, 94–99
size restrictions for, 105, 111
structure of, establishing, 95–117
sub-, 107–113, 119
suggested, 94
system-created, 92–93
virtual document, 441–442, 444–445
Directory Attribute Form, 232, 573
Directory Design Form, 98–99, 567
Directory Map objects
  assigning rights to, 259–260
  basic description of, 125
  creating, 126
directory services. *See also* directories;
  eDirectory services
  architecture of, 518–520
  basic description of, 7, 12–13
  components of, identifying, 517–518
  NetWare installation and, 511–519
  Novell (NDS), 12, 45, 170–171, 518, 532
Directory Trustee Worksheet, 209–214, 572
DirXML (Novell), 436
DISABLE/ENABLE LOGIN command, 538
disaster recovery procedures, 132–133.
  See also backups
Disconnect button, 16
disk duplexing
  defined, 80
  enabling, 80–81
  file services and, 14
Disk Operating System. *See* DOS (Disk
  Operating System)
DISMOUNT command, 539
DISP (Directory Information Shadowing
  Protocol), 516–517, 552
DISPLAY command, 298
DISPLAY SERVERS command, 538
distinguished names
  defined, 48
  LDAP, 168
  typeful, 48–49, 73
  typeless, 49–50, 73, 115
  using, 49–50
distribution lists, 494, 510
DIT (Directory Information Tree), 515, 553
DMZ (Demilitarized Zone), 455
DNS (Domain Name System), 391, 605–609
  Management administrative role, 163
  NetStorage and, 404
  NetWare installation and, 521–522
document(s). *See also* forms; worksheets
  opening, 23
  preferences, configuring, 442–443
Document directory, 48
Domain Name System. *See* DNS (Domain
  Name System)

Don't Compress attribute, 217, 218, 220
Don't Migrate attribute, 219
Don't Suballocate attribute, 217, 218
DOS (Disk Operating System)
  backups and, 127, 128, 129
  clients, 92
  commands, 92
  drive mappings and, 120, 121, 122, 123
  drive pointers and, 118, 119, 124, 125
  login scripts and, 299–300
  NetWare installation and, 527–528, 534
  network printing and, 334, 362, 377
  Novell Client and, 42
  partitions, 78–79
  paths, 119
  prompt, creating directories from, 106
  SMS and, 127, 128
downloading components, 395
DPA (Distributed Printing Application)
  standard, 344
drive(s). *See also* drive mappings
  removing, 40
  requirements, 315
  space restrictions, 85–86
drive mapping(s)
  defined, 15
  eDirectory services and, 38–40, 43–44
  login scripts and, 280–286, 288
  moving directory structures and, 112–113
  Novell Client installation and, 43–44
  planning, 120–122
  purging deleted files and, 116–117
  of search drives, 124–125
  working with, 15–16
drive pointer(s)
  application, 121
  creating, 123–124
  defined, 118
  establishing, 122–123
  implementing, 124–125
  local, 118
  network, 118
  planning, 120–125
  regular, 118, 119
  root, 118, 119, 121, 123–124
  search, 119–122, 124–125
  usage, planning, 118–120
Driver Installation dialog box, 34
Driver tab, 24
drivers, device, 24, 25, 34, 356, 359, 523
DSA (Directory System Agent), 515, 553
DSP (Directory Service Protocol),
  516–517, 553
DSREPAIR, 417
DSTRACE, 415
DUA (Directory User Agent), 515
duplexing, disk
  defined, 80
  enabling, 80–81
  file services and, 14
Dynamic Host Configuration Protocol. *See*
  DHCP (Dynamic Host Configuration
  Protocol)

E

eDirectory service(s)
  Administration administrative role, 163, 164, 268–273
  architecture, 518–520
  backups and, 128, 129, 131
  browsers and, 35, 36, 53, 62–64
  components, 46–48
  defined, 12
  development of, 45
  directory context and, 48–49
  Directory Map objects and, 125–126
  drive mappings and, 38–40, 43–44
  hierarchical structure of, 12
  iManager and, 53, 62–64
  iMonitor and, 414–417
  implementing, 33–76
  information, viewing, 13–14
  IRF Worksheet, 258–259, 265–266, 575
  managing user accounts and, 142, 153, 156–158, 163, 164
  moving container objects in, 174–175
  NetWare file systems and, 87, 125–126, 128, 129, 131
  network printing and, 336, 372–373
  Novell's OneNet strategy and, 2
  object types, 46–48
  partitioning, 66, 68–72
  Remote Manager and, 412–413
  replication, 66–68
  security, 6, 8, 186, 235–278
  Security Worksheet, 258, 574
  templates and, 153, 156–158
  tree structure, 13, 46–66, 76
  troubleshooting, 249–251
  upgrades and, 549–550
Edit menu
  Copy command, 117
  Merge Partition command, 176
  Paste command, 117
  Select All command, 117
effective rights
  calculating, 200
  defined, 188
  troubleshooting, 458–459
  viewing, 190–191
Effective Rights dialog box, 194, 198, 199, 203, 246, 249, 458
Effective Rights option, 250
e-mail. *See also* GroupWise (Novell); messaging services
  clients, 475–479, 485–490
  components, 474–475
  protocols, 475
  security for, 498–499
  sending/receiving, 488–489
  servers, 477–479
emergency boot diskettes, 463
encryption, 37, 456
  described, 646–651
  iFolder and, 390, 391

protocols, 648–651
  security certificates and, 109
EngData object, 125, 126, 259–260
ENGHOST server, 67, 68
EngScript.txt, 310–311
ENS (Event Notification Service), 346
Enter Network Passwords dialog box, 37, 39, 109–110, 115
Enterprise Web Server (Novell)
  basic description of, 436–444
  changing the path of Web content with, 441, 444
  configuring, 439–443
  configuring document preferences with, 442–443
  creating virtual directories with, 441–442, 444–445
  installing, 438–439
  restricting access with, 443–444
  starting/stopping services with, 441
entire contents option, 39
entities, defined, 6, 18–23
entry rights, defined, 236–237
Environment option, 154, 166
EpsonNet, 353
Erase rights, 186–189
error(s). *See also* bugs; debugging correction, 82
  recovering files corrupted by, 132
Ethernet
  cards, 24
  described, 594–595
Eudora, 476
Event Notification Service. *See* ENS (Event Notification Service)
Execute Only attribute, 217, 218, 222
Exit button, 55
Exit command, 14, 23, 124, 125, 282, 301
Exit ConsoleOne button, 66
Expense.rtf, 401, 403
Expense.txt, 401
Explorer
  creating directories with, 106
  making trustee assignments with, 210–211
eXtensible Stylesheet Language. *See* XSL (eXtensible Stylesheet Language)
exteNd (Novell), 642–643
external program execution commands, 299–300
extranets, defined, 437

F

facility printer maps, 379–381
Facts tab, 95, 113, 114
failover, 83
FAT (File Allocation Table)
  viruses and, 462
  volumes and, 82
fault tolerance
  clustering and, 83
  file services and, 14
  NetWare file systems and, 78, 80–81, 83
  replicas and, 67

FDISPLAY command, 298
fiber-optic cable
  advantages of, 23
  cost of, 23
  described, 23, 588
  network pathway component and, 23–24
file(s)
  access dates, 113
  attributes, 217–219, 221–227
  compression, 82, 85, 135
  copying, 113–114
  deleted, salvaging, 85, 93, 112, 115–116
  deleting, 115
  downloading, 395
  information, viewing, 113
  interleaving, 128
  -name extensions, 113
  planning the location of, in file systems, 111–112
  purging, 112
  saving, immediately, 84–85
  sharing, 19–20
  snapshots, 85
  trustees, defined, 188
  uploading, 114–115
File Caching option, 45
File Caching parameter, 88
File Download dialog box, 367, 395
File menu
  Close command, 165
  Exit command, 14, 23
  Move command, 173
  Open command, 311
  Print command, 23, 303, 311
  Save As command, 23
  File Scan rights, 131, 186–189, 195–196
file servers. *See also* servers
  accessing, 14–16, 38–40
  NetBEUI and, 27
file services. *See also* specific services
  defined, 7, 14–15
  drive mappings and, 15–16
  eDirectory services and, 35
file system(s). *See also* specific systems
  backups and, 127–133
  components, 78–95
  defining processing needs for, 95–97
  designing, 75–140, 205
  NetWare upgrades and, 633–636
  planning the location of files in, 111–112
FILE_SERVER variable, 290
FILER command, 119, 675
Filtered replica, 67
Find Object button, 55
Finish button, 39
FIRE PHASERS command, 301
firewalls, 455, 459–461, 466
FLAG command, 186, 225–227, 233, 676
FLAGDIR command, 677
Flush Files Immediately attribute, 84–85

folder(s). *See also* directory services
accessing, 20, 23
attributes of, 217–227, 232
creating, 65, 106–111
defined, 92–94
designing, 98–99
displaying hidden, 224
entries in, 512
generated during installation, 94
installing Novell Client from, 43–44
modifying, 208–211
moving, 112–113
partitions and, 68
shared, 20, 94–99
size restrictions for, 105, 111
structure of, establishing, 95–117
sub-, 107–113, 119
suggested, 94
system-created, 92–93
virtual document, 441–442, 444–445
Folder Options dialog box, 224
Force Password Change check box, 159, 160
Force periodic password changes check box, 155
forms. *See also* worksheets
described, 563–583
Directory Attribute Form, 232, 573
Directory Design Form, 98–99, 567
Group Planning Form, 150–151, 568
NDPS Definition Form, 370–371, 372, 373, 386, 580
NetWare Server Planning Form, 582–583
Organizational Role Planning Form, 172, 571
Storage Requirements Form, 96–97, 565
User Planning Form, 157, 159, 166, 570
User Policy Planning Form, 579
User Template Planning Form, 153–155, 569
Volume Design Form, 566
Forms directory, 23, 114, 115, 116
frame type, 525, 553
Friday.txt, 298
.frm file extension, 113
front-end processes, 474
FTP (File Transfer Protocol), 432–433, 437.
See also FTP Server (NetWare)
folders/files, accessing, 449
TCP/IP and, 26
FTP Server (NetWare). *See also* FTP (File
Transfer Protocol)
configuring, 446–449
described, 445–449
installing, 446
working with, 449–450
Full Control permissions, 20
FULL_NAME variable, 289–290

G

gateways
circuit-level, 461
network printing and, 353–354
General tab, 14
Get Pass Phrase dialog box, 396
GRANT command, 677
GREETING_TIME variable, 289

group(s)
assigning rights to, 189–193, 208–216
creating, 149, 150–154
defining, 150–151
managing, 149–171
objects, 47
planning, 150–151
trustee assignments and, 243–244
viewing members of, 57
Group Planning Form, 150–151, 568
GroupWise (Novell)
agents, 499–500
basic description of, 473–510
clients, 477, 485–490
configuring, 489–499
distribution lists, 494, 510
Documentation Worksheet, 581
external entities, 494–495
installing, 479–495
mail servers, 478–479
managing, 489–499
monitoring, 499–503
nicknames, 494
Post Office objects, 495–498
resources, 494
snap-ins, adding, 490–495
troubleshooting, 499–504
GUIs (graphical user interfaces), 16, 530–533

H

hard drives. *See also* drive mappings; hardware
removing, 40
requirements, 315
space restrictions, 85–86
hardware. *See also specific devices*
compatibility lists, 34
failures, 14, 84
requirements, 78, 315
server, viewing, 413–414
Have Disk button, 34
HBAs (Host Bus Adapters), 523, 553
Help button, 55
Hewlett-Packard, 344, 353–354, 358–359
Hidden attribute, 217, 218, 220
Hide Toolbar button, 55
home directories. *See also* directories
creating, 65, 154
defined, 135
drive pointers and, 121
eDirectory services and, 65
moving, 112–113
templates and, 153, 154
updating users and, 166
HOME_DIRECTORY variable, 289–291
host(s)
defined, 26
servers, 127
hot fixes
file services and, 14
partitions and, 80
volumes and, 82
Hot Fix option, 80
HOUR variable, 289

HOUR24 variable, 289
HTML (HyperText Markup Language), 403, 435
HTTP (HyperText Transfer Protocol), 403, 436
eDirectory services and, 35, 36
iMonitor and, 415
Secure (HTTPS), 648–649
hubs
defined, 23, 29
network pathway component and, 23

I

IAB (Internet Access Board), 25
IBM (International Business Machines), 24
Identification dialog box, 57
identifier variables, 300
iFolder (Novell), 2, 14
accessing, 401–403
Apache Web Server and, 433
basic description of, 390–403
client, 393–395, 400, 402
components, 391–394
configuration settings, 397–399
defined, 390
installing, 391–396
Java applets and, 393–394, 400, 402
managing, 396–400
server, optimizing, 399–400
user accounts, 395–396
Web site, customizing, 396
Welcome window, 394–395
iFolderClient.exe, 395
IF...THEN...ELSE statements, 300–302
iManager (Novell)
administrative roles and, 268–273
advantages of, 53
Apache Web Server and, 433
creating Broker objects with, 346–348
creating NDPS Managers with, 348–354
creating OUs with, 62–64
creating printer agents with, 375–377
creating users and groups with, 161–165
defined, 53
enhancements, 625–528
installing, 663–664
Linux and, 663–664
Login window, 162
main window, 269
Novell Licensing Services and, 419, 420–422
starting, 625–628
testing printers with, 368–370
Z.E.N.works and, 315
IMAP (Internet Message Access Protocol), 475
Immediate Compress attribute, 217, 218, 220
iMonitor (Novell)
described, 414
Trace Configuration window, 415–416
using, 415–417
importing objects, 168–171
Increase Size button, 91
independent container administrators, 266–268
information theft, 454
Inheritable Attribute right, 238, 251–253

Inheritable Entry right, 238
  inherited rights, 195–198. *See also* IRFs
    (Inherited Rights Filters)
  eDirectory services and, 238, 239,
    246–249, 273
  reassigning, 200–202
  trustee assignments and, combining, 198–200
  using, 248–249
Inherited Rights and Filters dialog box, 201
INS option, 124
INS parameter, 294
Install button, 40, 44
installation
  of components, 40–42
  ConsoleOne, 57–59
  directories created during, 94
  Enterprise Web Server, 438–439
  FTP Server, 446
  GroupWise, 479–495
  iFolder, 391–396
  Microsoft Client Service for NetWare, 40–42
  NetWare Administrator, 53–54
  Novell Client, 42–44
  Novell NetWare, 21, 94, 511–556
  preparing for, 519–527
  printer, 359–361, 367–368, 378–380
  SYS volumes created during, 21
  Z.E.N.works, 316
Internet Access Board. *See* IAB (Internet
  Access Board)
Internet Explorer browser. *See also* browsers
  certificates and, 161
  eDirectory services and, 35, 36, 53, 62–64
  file services and, 14
  iManager and, 62–64
Internet layer, 26
Internet Packet Exchange/Sequenced Packet
  Exchange. *See* IPX/SPX (Internet Packet
  Exchange/Sequenced Packet Exchange)
Internet Printing Protocol. *See* IPP (Internet
  Printing Protocol)
Internet Protocol. *See* IP (Internet Protocol)
  addresses
Internet service components. *See also specific*
  components
  configuring, 437–450
  installing, 437–450
  overview of, 431–471
  security for, 454–466
interrupts, viewing available, 414
intruder detection
  defined, 146, 454, 456
  enabling, 146–148
  limits, setting, 145–146
  testing, 148
Intruder Detection button, 147
Intruder Detection dialog box, 147
Inventory directory, 39–40
IP (Internet Protocol) addresses
  assignment of, 27, 598–605
  configuration information, viewing, 28
  described, 26–27, 597–600

iFolder and, 392, 394
managing user accounts and, 143–144,
  161, 170
NAT and, 460–461
NetStorage and, 404–405
network printing and, 367
TCP/IP model and, 26–27
testing, 604–605
in URLs, 161
IPCONFIG command, 28, 143
iPlanet Web server, 438
IPP (Internet Printing Protocol), 16, 344, 365,
  366, 368
IPPSRVR, 365–366
IPPSRVR.NLM, 366
iPrint (Novell)
  client, 366
  described, 365
  enabling printers for, 365–370
  enhancements, 640–641
  installing printers with, 367–368, 379–380
  Management administrative role, 163
  Map utility, 379–381
  NDPS support for, 344
  Novell's OneNet strategy and, 2
  Web site, 366
IPSec (IP Security), 648
IPX/SPX (Internet Packet
  Exchange/Sequenced Packet Exchange)
  basic description of, 25
  eDirectory services and, 34, 36, 42
  elimination of, 26
  gateways, 461
  NetWare installation and, 521–522, 525
  RConsoleJ and, 417
IRFs (Inherited Rights Filters), 131, 195,
  196–198, 202. *See also* inherited rights
  blocking rights and, 265–266
  changing, 210–211
  eDirectory services and, 238, 246–248,
    265–267, 277
  implementing, 266–267, 277
  minimizing the use of, 204, 205–208
IS container, 46–47, 57, 286–288, 292–296,
  297–302
iSCSI support, 634
ISMgrs group, 57, 151, 152, 155
ISO DPA standard, 344
ISS directory, 109–111

J

Java
  applets, 393–394, 396, 400, 402
  backup software and, 129
  GUI console interface, 546–547
  iFolder and, 393–394, 396, 400, 402
  servlets, 434–436
  using, on servers, 546–547
Java directory, 93
JPEG (Joint Photographic Experts Group)
  files, 379–380

L

land attack, 465. *See also* denial-of-service
  attacks
LANs (local area networks)
  basic description of, 2
  network entities and, 18–23
  network pathway component and, 23–24
  network services and, 6
  Novell's OneNet strategy and, 2–3
  security proposals for, 455
  TCP/IP model and, 26, 27
laptop computers, 16–17
laser_5.gif, 380
LDAP (Lightweight Directory Access
  Protocol), 12, 438
  defined, 168
  iFolder and, 392–393, 397, 398
  importing objects with, 168–171
  NetStorage and, 404
LDAP Settings tab, 392
LDIF (Lightweight Directory Interchange
  Format)
  command syntax, 168
  importing objects and, 168–171
leaf objects
  defined, 47
  moving, 173
  naming, 48
Lexmark, 353
License Agreements, 58, 316, 532–533
license certificates. *See also* certificates
  defined, 420
  installing, 420–421
  viewing, 421–423
License Management administrative role, 163,
  420, 422
License Management option, 420, 422
Licensing Services (Novell), 419–423
Lightweight Directory Access Protocol.
  See LDAP (Lightweight Directory Access
  Protocol)
Lightweight Directory Interchange Format.
  See LDIF (Lightweight Directory
  Interchange Format)
Limit Concurrent Connections check box, 155
Limit grace logins check box, 144, 155
linear bus topology, 589–591. *See also* topology
Linux
  benefits, 658–659
  commitment to open sources and, 667–672
  concerns, 659–661
  eDirectory services and, 45
  growth of, 658–659
  hardware choices and, 658
  iMonitor and, 415
  Internet service components and, 433
  Novell's OneNet strategy and, 2–3
  products/solutions, 662–664
  protocols and, 25
  role-based services and, 664–667
  service, 657–673
  software costs and, 658

support, 660, 661–662
training/certification, 672–673
LOAD command, 539
LOAD SMDR command, 131
Local Area Connection Properties dialog box,
    38, 40–42, 44–45, 88
Local Users and Groups icon, 10
Lock account after detection check box, 147
Log Off Windows dialog box, 15
logging off
    after changing passwords, 10
    described, 29, 15
login. *See also* authentication; login scripts;
    passwords
    advanced options for, 44
    before browsing UAS tree structures, 13–14
    defined, 7, 29
    failed, 10
    file sharing and, 20
    iFolder and, 395–396, 397, 402–403
    importance of, 9
    managing user accounts and, 142–148
    names, 156–158
    NetStorage and, 404
    Novell Client and, 44, 45
    printing and, 22–23
    procedure, detailed description of, 9–10
    protocol configuration and, 27–28
    security, establishing, 142–148
    security services, 7–8
    Z.E.N.works and, 17
LOGIN command, 676
Login directory, 92, 93, 95
Login Restrictions dialog box, 155
login script(s). *See also* login
    commands, 280
    copying, 303
    creating, 286–303
    debugging, 313–314
    default, 281, 283
    defined, 135
    designing, 304–305
    Directory Map objects and, 125
    documenting, 303
    drive mappings and, 122, 123
    e-mail and, 486
    entering, 310–311, 283–284
    execution, preventing, 295–296
    external program execution commands and,
        299–300
    IF statements in, 300–302
    implementing, 304–314
    pasting, 303
    printing, 303, 310–311
    processing, 280–286
    programming, 286–303
    relationship between, 280–281
    REM statements in, 303–301, 308
    requirements, identifying, 304–305
    rights, checking, 262–263
    testing, 281, 313–314, 328, 329
    types of, 281–283
    user templates and, 153, 156

variables and, 288–293
worksheets, 304–309
writing, 293–295, 305–309
writing messages with, 297–298
Login Script property, 263, 281, 282
Login Script Requirements Worksheet,
    304–305, 576
Login Script tab, 283, 287, 292
Login.exe, 92
LOGIN_ID variable, 289–290
LOGOUT command, 676
Lotus Notes, 477

M

MACHINE variable, 290
Macintosh
    eDirectory services and, 35
    NetWare file systems and, 78, 98
    protocols and, 25
macro viruses, 462. *See also* viruses
Mail directory, 93
mainframes, 24
MAKEUSER command, 677
Manage Object Rights button, 55
management utilities. *See* ConsoleOne
    (Novell); iManager (Novell); Novell NetWare
    Administrator
MANs (metropolitan area networks), 2–3
MAP command, 122–125, 281, 291, 294–295,
    299, 676
Map Drive dialog box, 169
Map Network Drive dialog box, 43–44
Master replicas, 67, 70
Mbps (megabits per second), 24
MD5 (Message Digest 5) protocol, 654
media pooling, 128
Media tab, 89, 90, 102
Members button, 57
Members dialog box, 57
Members tab, 60, 152
Memberships dialog box, 167
Memberships tab, 155, 160, 167
Memo.frm, 115, 405–406
memory. *See also* RAM
    (random-access memory)
    file services and, 14
    monitoring, 408, 410–411
    requirements, 57, 78, 315
    servers and, 19
    volumes and, 82
Merge Partition command, 176
Merge Partition dialog box, 176
mesh topology, 591–592. *See also* topology
message digest security, 649–650
messaging services. *See also* e-mail
    clients, 475–479, 485–490
    components, 474–475
    defined, 7, 11–12
    protocols, 475
    security for, 498–499
    sending/receiving messages with, 11–12,
        488–489
    servers, 477–479

MfgData directory, 108
MfgData object, 125
MfgScrpt.txt, 311
Mgmt folder, 108, 166
MgmtData object, 125
microprocessors
    iFolder and, 400
    monitoring, 413–414
    requirements, 57, 78, 315
Microsoft Client Service for NetWare
    accessing NetWare services with, 38–40
    defined, 36, 40
    eDirectory services and, 36–42
    installing, 40–42
    removing, 41–42
Microsoft Exchange 2000 Server, 478
Migrated attribute, 218
MINUTE variable, 289
Mirror button, 89
mirroring
    defined, 135
    duplexing and, comparison of, 80–81
    use of the term, 80
mode switching, 477
Modified File List attribute, 85
Modified File List feature, 82, 85
Modify Members button, 270
Modify Members window, 271
Modify rights, 131, 186–189
Modify Tasks button, 270
MODULES command, 539
Monday.txt, 298–299
MONITOR utility, 542–546
MONTH variable, 289
MONTH_NAME variable, 289
MOUNT command, 539
Move command, 173
Move dialog box, 173, 175
MSAU (multiple station access unit), 593–594
Mspaint.exe, 115
MTA (Message Transfer Agent), 475, 483–485,
    499–502
My Computer
    accessing directories with, 23
    accessing workgroup information with, 38
    assigning rights with, 190
    creating directories with, 106
    disconnecting network drives with, 40
    identifying drive letters with, 15
    making trustee assignments with, 210–211
    purging files with, 112, 117
    salvaging files with, 112
    viewing/verifying drive mappings with, 39, 43
My Network Places
    mapping drives from, 122
    purging files with, 112, 116
    salvaging deleted files with, 112, 116
    viewing components with, 38
    viewing network adapter settings with, 24
    viewing TCP/IP settings with, 28
    viewing volumes with, 37
MySQL, 641–642

N

NAT (Network Address Translation), 460–461, 600
Native File Access Protocol. *See* NFAP (Native File Access Protocol)
Navigation frame, 13, 59–60, 102–104, 114, 145
NCP (NetWare Core Protocol)
   basic description of, 25
   eDirectory services and, 35
NCOPY command, 676
NDAY_OF_WEEK variable, 288–289
NDIR command, 676
NDPS (Novell Distributed Print Services)
   basic description of, 344–364
   Broker component, 346–348, 350–351, 361, 408
   Definition Form, 370–371, 372, 373, 386, 580
   Manager, 347–354, 361–363, 370–371, 373
   printers, installing, 359–360, 378–380
   troubleshooting, 361–364
NDS (Novell Directory Services), 12, 45, 170–171, 518, 532
NDS Import/Export Wizard, 170–171
NDS Import/Export Wizard dialog box, 170–171
NDS passwords, 652
Net Services (Novell), 433
NETADMIN command, 677
NetBasic directory, 93
NetBEUI, 27, 29, 34
NetBIOS, 27, 34
NetList.doc, 23
Netscape Communicator, 14. *See also* browsers; Netscape Navigator browser
Netscape Navigator browser. *See also* browsers
   eDirectory services and, 36, 62–64
   iManager and, 62–64
NetShield (Network Associates), 463
NetStorage (Novell)
   accessing files with, 405–406
   described, 403–404
   installing, 404–405
NetStorage directory, 93
NetWare 6.5 (Novell)
   blade computers and, 621–622
   branch offices and, 622–623
   business continuity and, 624–641
   developer tools, 641–643
   eGuide, 640
   end user enhancements, 636–641
   installation, 612–624
   legacy workstation utilities compatible with, 677–678
   network administration and, 624–641
   objects, creating, 628–631
   security enhancements, 645–655
   upgrades, 611–643
   Web services, 641–643
NetWare 6.5 Server (Novell)
   configuration phase, 618–621
   consolidation, 623–624
   installation, 614–617

NetWare Administrator (Novell), 40, 87, 315
   assigning rights with, 192–193
   browsing with, 54–59
   creating objects with, 60–62
   described, 53
   desktop shortcut for, 53–54
   enabling intruder detection with, 146–148
   installing, 53–54
   making trustee assignments with, 211, 212–213
   modifying multiple user accounts with, 165
   network printing and, 334, 337–338, 340–341, 343–344, 354–359, 373–382
   renaming objects with, 173
   starting, 55
   toolbar, 55
   viewing effective rights with, 190–192
NetWare Core Protocol. *See* NCP (NetWare Core Protocol)
NetWare Resource Browser dialog box, 15
NetWare Remote Manager dialog box, 110
NetWare Security dialog box, 10, 11
NetWare Send Message dialog box, 11, 12
NetWare Server Planning Form, 582–583
NetWare Utilities option, 11
NetWare Web Manager dialog box, 109, 114–115
network(s). *See also specific types*
   adapter information, viewing, 24, 414
   topology, 589–592
   types of, 2–3
   unknown, 460
   untrusted, 460
   upgrading, to NetWare 6, 548–551
Network Address Translation. *See* NAT (Network Address Translation)
Network Identification tab, 38
network interface cards. *See* NICs (network interface cards)
Network layer, 26, 27
Network Neighborhood, 210–211
NETWORK_ADDRESS variable, 290
New button, 101
New Directory dialog box, 108
New Group button, 152
New Group dialog box, 151–152
New Object button, 107, 108, 126
New Object dialog box, 61, 107, 172
New Organizational Unit dialog box, 65
New Password text box, 10, 11
New Template dialog box, 154
New User button, 160
New User dialog box, 11, 66, 159, 160, 158
New Volume dialog box, 105
NFAP (Native File Access Protocol), 25, 78
   drive mappings and, 38–40
   eDirectory services and, 35–40
NFS (Network File System), 35
NICI (Novell International Cryptography Infrastructure), 454
NICs (network interface cards)
   compatible, list of, 34

described, 592–596
   device drivers for, 24–25, 34
   identification of, as components, 6
   installing, 34, 524
   network pathway component and, 6, 24
   properties of, 24
   protocols and, 25
   selecting, 24
   speed of, 24
   troubleshooting, 24
Nipp.exe, 367
NLIST utility, 92, 303, 310, 311, 676
NLMs (NetWare Loadable Modules), 457, 534–535, 541–545
NO_DEFAULT command, 295
noise, during transmissions, 23
Normal attribute, 220
Norton Antivirus Corporate Edition (Symantec), 463
Norton Disk Doctor (Symantec), 85
NOSs (network operating systems)
   clients and, 34–35
   dedicated, 21
   defined, 19, 29
   eDirectory services and, 34–35
   network services and, 19
Notepad, 169, 303, 310–311
Novell Advanced Audit Service, 457
Novell Application Launcher, 317
Novell Border Manager, 466
Novell Certificate Server, 453–454
Novell Client
   customizing, 44–45
   described, 36, 42–43
   eDirectory services and, 34–38, 42–45, 66
   installing, 42–44
   login with, 7, 10, 280, 281, 283
   mapping drives with, 15
   NetStorage and, 405
   network printing and, 366, 379
   protocols and, 25
   removing, 37–38
   salvaging deleted files with, 115–116
   variables and, 290, 291
   versions of, 42
Novell ConsoleOne
   advantages of, 53
   assigning attributes with, 222
   assigning rights with, 194–204, 208–211, 243–244, 248–249
   basic description of, 59–60
   completing tree structures with, 64–66
   copying files with, 113–114
   creating directories with, 106–109
   creating groups with, 151–152
   creating objects with, 65–66, 105–106, 126, 172–173
   creating partitions with, 79, 102
   creating storage pools with, 102–104
   creating user templates with, 154–156
   creating volumes with, 100–101, 103–105
   creating user accounts with, 158–161

deleting objects with, 173–174
establishing login restrictions with, 145
exploring tree structure with, 13–14
handling login scripts with, 282, 283–284, 310–313
handling trustee assignments with, 189–191, 194–195, 210–211, 213–216, 457
importing users with, 169–171
installing, 57–59
modifying user accounts with, 165
moving directories with, 113
moving objects with, 173–177
renaming objects with, 173–174
securing Admin user accounts with, 149–151
setting directory size restrictions with, 111
setting IRFs with, 197–198
setting password restrictions with, 143–145
snap-ins, adding, 490–495
testing intruder detection and, 148
troubleshooting effective rights with, 458–459
updating users with, 166–168
viewing directory information with, 94–95
viewing effective rights with, 190–192, 200
viewing inherited rights with, 200
viewing NSS information with, 87, 88–91
viewing volume information with, 92
Novell Directory Services (NDS), 12, 45, 170–171, 518, 532
Novell DirXML, 436
Novell Distributed Print Services (NDPS)
  basic description of, 344–364
  Broker component, 346–348, 350–351, 361, 408
  Definition Form, 370–371, 372, 373, 386
  Manager, 347–354, 361–363, 370–371, 373
  printers, installing, 359–360, 378–380
  troubleshooting, 361–364
Novell Enterprise Web Server
  basic description of, 436–444
  changing the path of Web content with, 441, 444
  configuring, 439–443
  configuring document preferences with, 442–443
  creating virtual directories with, 441–442, 444–445
  installing, 438–439
  restricting access with, 443–444
  starting/stopping services with, 441
Novell GroupWise
  agents, 499–500
  basic description of, 473–510
  clients, 477, 485–490
  configuring, 489–499
  distribution lists, 494, 510
  external entities, 494–495
  installing, 479–495
  mail servers, 478–479
  managing, 489–499
  monitoring, 499–503
  nicknames, 494

Post Office objects, 495–498
resources, 494
snap-ins, adding, 490–495
troubleshooting, 499–504
Novell iFolder, 2, 14
  accessing, 401–403
  Apache Web Server and, 433
  basic description of, 390–403
  client, 393–395, 400, 402
  components, 391–394
  configuration settings, 397–399
  defined, 390
  installing, 391–396
  Java applets and, 393–394, 400, 402
  managing, 396–400
  server, optimizing, 399–400
  user accounts, 395–396
  Web site, customizing, 396
  Welcome window, 394–395
Novell iManager
  administrative roles and, 268–273
  advantages of, 53
  Apache Web Server and, 433
  creating Broker objects with, 346–348
  creating NDPS Managers with, 348–354
  creating OUs with, 62–64
  creating printer agents with, 375–377
  creating users and groups with, 161–165
  defined, 53
  enhancements, 625–528
  installing, 663–664
  Linux and, 663–664
  Login window, 162
  main window, 269
  Novell Licensing Services and, 419, 420–422
  starting, 625–628
  testing printers with, 368–370
  Z.E.N.works and, 315
Novell iMonitor
  described, 414
  Trace Configuration window, 415–416
  using, 415–417
Novell International Cryptography Infrastructure (NICI), 454
Novell iPrint
  client, 366
  described, 365
  enabling printers for, 365–370
  enhancements, 640–641
  installing printers with, 367–368, 379–380
  Management administrative role, 163
  Map utility, 379–381
  NDPS support for, 344
  Novell's OneNet strategy and, 2
  Web site, 366
Novell Licensing Services, 419–423
Novell Login window. See also login
  changing passwords and, 10–11
  opening, 9
Novell Net Services, 433
Novell NetStorage
  accessing files with, 405–406

described, 403–404
installing, 404–405
Novell NetWare 6.5 (Novell)
  blade computers and, 621–622
  branch offices and, 622–623
  business continuity and, 624–641
  developer tools, 641–643
  eGuide, 640
  end user enhancements, 636–641
  installation, 612–624
  legacy workstation utilities compatible with, 677–678
  network administration and, 624–641
  objects, creating, 628–631
  security enhancements, 645–655
  upgrades, 611–643
  Web services, 641–643
Novell NetWare 6.5 Server (Novell)
  configuration phase, 618–621
  consolidation, 623–624
  installation, 614–617
Novell NetWare Administrator, 40, 87, 315
  assigning rights with, 192–193
  browsing with, 54–59
  creating objects with, 60–62
  described, 53
  desktop shortcut for, 53–54
  enabling intruder detection with, 146–148
  installing, 53–54
  making trustee assignments with, 211, 212–213
  modifying multiple user accounts with, 165
  network printing and, 334, 337–338, 340–341, 343–344, 354–359, 373–382
  renaming objects with, 173
  starting, 55
  toolbar, 55
  viewing effective rights with, 190–192
Novell OneNet strategy, 2–3, 5, 78
  eDirectory and, 12, 35, 36, 62
  Internet service components and, 431
  managing user accounts and, 163
  protocols and, 25
  utilities and, 389–390
Novell Portal Services (NPS), 434–436
Novell RConsoleJ, 417–419
Novell Remote Manager, 79, 406–414, 435
  defined, 406–409
  creating directories with, 106, 109–111
  managing servers with, 410–411
  managing volumes with, 411–412
  monitoring server health and performance with, 407–410
  uploading files with, 114–115
  viewing license information with, 422–423
  viewing partitions with, 413–414
  viewing volume information with, 87
Novell Storage Services (NSS)
  backups and, 128
  defined, 78–79, 135
  file snapshots and, 85
  information, viewing, 87–91

partitions, 79–81
salvage file operations and, 86
storage pools and, 81, 83
volumes, 81–87, 98, 100, 104–105
NPRINTER command, 676
NPTWIN95, 335, 336, 362, 676
NSS (Novell Storage Services)
backups and, 128
defined, 78–79, 135
file snapshots and, 85
information, viewing, 87–91
partitions, 79–81
salvage file operations and, 86
storage pools and, 81, 83
volumes, 81–87, 98, 100, 104–105
NVER command, 677
NWadmin32, 54, 55, 146, 677
NWBACKUP32, 128, 677
NWCONFIG, 87, 102, 547–548

O

object(s). *See also specific objects*
accessing, 49–50
alias, 47, 60–62
creating, 60–66, 76, 105–106, 126
defined, 46, 73
deleting, 173–174
directory context and, 48–50
eDirectory services and, 46–48, 51–60, 73
importing, 168–171
leaf, 47, 48, 173
moving, 173–175
names, 48–49, 173–174
properties of, 48, 73, 156, 157–158
selecting, 56
tree structure design and, 51–60
viewing, 56–57
Object frame, 13, 14, 59–60
Odbc directory, 93
Office directory, 107
Old Password text box, 10, 11
OneNet strategy (Novell), 2–3, 5, 78
eDirectory and, 12, 35, 36, 62
Internet service components and, 431
managing user accounts and, 163
protocols and, 25
utilities and, 389–390
Open command, 311
Open New Browser Window button, 55
OpenSSH, 650–651
optical disks, 21
options (listed by name)
Account Locked option, 148
Address Restrictions option, 144
All Attributes Read option, 260
Allow forward references option, 170
Assign Simple Password option, 158, 160
Close automatically option, 281
Create another Directory option, 108
Create another User option, 159, 160
Create Home Directory option, 65
Default Tree and Context option, 41

Define Additional Properties option, 318
Detect intruders option, 147
Effective Rights option, 250
entire contents option, 39
Environment option, 154, 166
File Caching option, 45
Force Password Change option, 159, 160
Force periodic password changes option, 155
Hot Fix option, 80
INS option, 124
License Management option, 420, 422
Limit Concurrent Connections option, 155
Limit grace logins option, 144, 155
Lock account after detection option, 147
NetWare Utilities option, 11
Novell ConsoleOne option, 58
Partitions option, 102
Printer Status option, 342
Reconnect at logon option, 39, 43
Rename option, 173
Require a password option, 155
Require unique passwords option, 144, 155
Restore option, 132
Rights to Other Objects option, 156
Run Login Script option, 41
Run scripts option, 280–281
Send Message option, 11
Set Password option, 159
Share as option, 20
Share this folder option, 20
Show Connected Servers option, 11
Target Service option, 132
To Users option, 11
Traditional Volumes option, 101
User Extensible Policies option, 318, 320, 321
View Certificate option, 161
Workstation only option, 10, 28, 62
Oracle, 436
Order.frm, 115
organization container objects, 46–51
Organizational Role objects, 171–172,
206–207, 209, 458
Organizational Role Planning Form, 172, 571
OS/2, 127, 128, 129
OS_VERSION variable, 290
OU (Organizational Unit) objects
creating, 62–64, 75–76
defined, 46–47
eDirectory services and, 263–264, 286–288
intruder detection and, 145–148
login scripts and, 286–288
managing, 263–264
moving, 175–177
naming, 49
tree structure design and, 51–52
Outlook (Microsoft), 476. *See also* e-mail
Outlook Express (Microsoft), 476.
See also e-mail
overbooking volumes, 84–85
oversized UDP packets attack, 465.
See also denial-of-service attacks

P

packages
creating, 317–320
defined, 317
open policy, 317–320
packet(s)
capturing, 142
filtering, 460
Paint (Microsoft), 20, 115
Parallel Communication dialog box, 339–340
parallel ports, 335. *See also* ports
partition(s)
creating, 71–72, 102, 175
duplexing, 80–81
eDirectory services and, 66, 68–72
fault tolerance and, 80–81
NetWare file systems and, 78–81
NetWare installation and, 523–524, 527–528
NSS volumes and, 83
viewing, 70–71, 89–90, 101, 103, 412–413
Partition Mirror Group dialog box, 89–90
Partitions option, 102
Partitions tab, 89
password(s). *See also* authentication; login
accessing objects and, 49–51
assigning, 9–12, 44, 66, 142, 150, 158–159
-breaking programs, 456
case sensitivity of, 10
changing, 9–12, 44, 142, 159
eDirectory services and, 36–44, 49–51, 55, 66
entering, 8, 9, 10
expiration of, 144
guessing, preventing, 145–148, 456
insuring the security of, 142–143, 145–148
intruder detection and, 145–148
length restrictions, 144
login script processing and, 280
NetStorage and, 404
NetWare file systems and, 109–110, 115
peer-to-peer networks and, 19
restrictions on, 10, 143–145, 155, 456
simple, 37, 158–159
templates and, 153, 155
testing, 10
universal, 632–633, 652–653
Password Restrictions dialog box, 144, 157
Passwords text box, 8
patch panel, 589
path, defined, 135
Path property, 245, 260
pathways
described, 6, 7, 23–24, 585–610
designing, 586–597
protocols and, 25–28
pattern selection phase, 617–618
PAUSE command, 296, 299
PDS (Print Device Subsystem), 354, 356
peer-to-peer operating systems
defined, 19
eDirectory services and, 37
file sharing and, 19–20
superiority of server-centric systems over, 21

PeopleSoft, 436

period (.), 26, 168

peripheral devices, identification of, as components, 6

Perl directory, 93

permissions, 14, 20. *See also* access rights

Permissions button, 20

PH (Port Handler), 354

PHP (Personal Home Page), 642

ping of death attack, 465. *See also* denial-of-service attacks

platforms. *See also specific platforms*
  backup software and, 127, 128
  eDirectory and, 12, 35, 45
  NetWare file systems and, 78, 127, 128
  protocols and, 25

plus sign (+), 63, 164

POA (Post Office Agent), 475, 484–485, 499–503

policies
  iFolder and, 399
  workstation, 317–320

Policy Package objects, 317

Policy Package Wizard, 318

polymorphic viruses, 462. *See also* viruses

POP3 (Post Office Protocol), 433

port(s)
  parallel, 335
  printer, 335, 339–340, 354
  numbers, 161, 433
  serial, 335

Portal Services (Novell), 433

Post Office Protocol. *See* POP3 (Post Office Protocol)

Postal Address property, 252

power supplies
  backup, 21
  uninterruptible (UPS), 21

Print command, 23, 303, 311

Print Device Subsystem. *See* PDS (Print Device Subsystem)

print queue(s)
  creating, 336, 337–338, 377–378
  defined, 332–336
  for non-NDPS clients, 377–378
  objects, 48, 337–338
  gateways and, 354
  setting up, 336–343
  troubleshooting, 343–344

Print Queue dialog box, 338, 342, 343

print server(s)
  creating, 340–341
  defined, 332, 336–337
  gateways and, 353
  loading, 342–343
  object, defined, 47
  testing, 342–343

print services, defined, 7, 16. *See also* NDPS (Novell Distributed Print Services)

printer(s). *See also* printing
  agents, 352–359, 362, 373, 375–377
  attachment methods, 22–23, 334–336, 339–340, 371–372

automatic load, 335

basic description of, 334–336

configuring, on client computers, 378–379

controlled access, 353, 375

default, setting, 23

defining, 346, 337

drivers, 356, 359

eDirectory services and, 47, 48, 52, 55

enabling, 365–370

gateways, 353–358

installing, 359–361, 367–368, 378–380

location, determining, 371–372

maps, 379–381

names, defining, 372

objects, 48, 336, 338–340

ports, 335, 339–340, 354

public access, 353, 373–375

requirements, defining, 370–371

setting up, 341–342, 345–346

testing, 368–370, 381–382, 387

troubleshooting, 343–344, 361–364, 381–382, 387

Printer dialog box, 341

Printer Status option, 342

printing. *See also* print servers; printers
  environments, defining, 370–373
  floor plans, 22–23
  implementing, 331–388
  login scripts, 303, 310–311
  overview of, 332–334
  queue-based, 332–344
  setting up, 336–343, 386
  troubleshooting, 343–344, 361–364, 381–382, 387

private keys, defined, 451

processing needs, defining, 95–97

processors
  iFolder and, 400
  monitoring, 413–414
  requirements, 57, 78, 315

profile login script(s). *See also* login scripts
  defined, 284
  entering, 284–286, 311–313, 328–329
  worksheets, 308–309
  writing, 328

Profile Login Script Worksheet, 578

Programs button, 440

properties
  adding, 251–252
  changing, 165
  defined, 47, 73, 156
  Inheritable Attribute right and, 251–253
  of objects, 48, 73, 156, 157–158

protocol(s). *See also* protocols (listed by name)
  basic description of, 24–28, 585–610
  identifying, 27–28
  NetWare installation and, 524–525
  network pathway component and, 6
  nonproprietary, 25
  proprietary, 25
  stack, defined, 25–27

protocols (listed by name). *See also* IP (Internet Protocol) addresses
  AFP (AppleTalk Filing Protocol), 35
  DAP (Directory Access Protocol), 515–517, 552
  DISP (Directory Information Shadowing Protocol), 516–517, 552
  DSP (Directory Service Protocol), 516–517, 553
  FTP (File Transfer Protocol), 26, 432–433, 437, 445–450
  HTTP (HyperText Transfer Protocol), 35–36, 415, 403, 436
  IMAP (Internet Message Access Protocol), 475
  IPP (Internet Printing Protocol), 16, 344, 365, 366, 368
  LDAP (Lightweight Directory Access Protocol), 12, 168–171, 392–393, 397, 398, 404, 438
  NCP (NetWare Core Protocol), 25, 35
  NFAP (Native File Access Protocol), 25, 35–40, 78
  POP3 (Post Office Protocol), 433
  SMTP (Simple Mail Transfer Protocol), 475
  TCP/IP (Transmission Control Protocol/Internet Protocol), 25–28, 30, 34, 93, 432, 433, 525, 597–609
  UDP (User Datagram Protocol), 26

proxy services, 461

PUBHOST server, 68–70

public access printers, 353, 373–375. *See also* printers

Public directory, 92, 93, 95, 135

public key(s)
  cryptography, 450–453
  defined, 451

Purge All button, 117

Purge attribute, 218, 220

PURGE command, 677

Purge Network Files dialog box, 117

purging deleted files, 116–117

Pvsw directory, 93

Q

queue(s)
  creating, 336, 337–338, 377–378
  defined, 332–336, 504
  e-mail, 504
  for non-NDPS clients, 377–378
  objects, 48, 337–338
  gateways and, 354
  setting up, 336–343
  troubleshooting, 343–344

Queues directory, 93

R

RAID (redundant array of independent disks)
  defined, 22
  fault tolerance and, 84
  volumes and, 82

RAM (random-access memory). *See also* memory
  drive pointers and, 119

iFolder and, 399
requirements, 57
volumes and, 82
RCONAG6.NLM, 417, 418
RCONSOLE command, 677
RConsoleJ (Novell), 417–419
Read Only attribute, 20, 219, 222, 226
Read rights, 131, 186–189, 195–196, 238
Read Write attribute, 219
Read-Only replica, 67
Reboot button, 44
Reconnect at logon check box, 39, 43
recovery procedures, 132–133. *See also* backups
redundant array of independent disks.
      See RAID (redundant array of
      independent disks)
Registry, 317
relative names, using, 50–51
REM command, 301–303, 308
Remote Manager (Novell), 79, 406–414, 435
defined, 406–409
creating directories with, 106, 109–111
managing servers with, 410–411
managing volumes with, 411–412
monitoring server health and performance
      with, 407–410
uploading files with, 114–115
viewing license information with, 422–423
viewing partitions with, 413–414
viewing volume information with, 87
remote printers. *See also* printers
attaching, 372
defined, 335
gateways and, 354
REMOVE command, 677
Rename Inhibit attribute, 219, 220
Rename option, 173
Rename rights, 238
RENDIR command, 678
replicas
adding, 71
described, 66–68
eDirectory services and, 67–68
partitions and, 68–72
viewing, 70–71
Require a password check box, 155
Require unique passwords check box, 144, 155
Resource Management Service. *See* RMS
      (Resource Management Service)
Resources tab, 24
Restore option, 132
restoring data
disaster recovery procedures and, 132–133
SMS and, 131
testing backups by, 132
Restrictions tab, 143, 145, 167
REVOKE command, 678
Rich Text Format. *See* RTF (Rich Text Format)
rights
administrative roles and, 268–273
assigning, 189–190, 194–204, 208–211,
      239–240, 243–244, 248–249

basic description of, 186–204
blocking, 265–266
default, 253–255
delegating, 260–262
eDirectory services and, 236–240, 249–255,
      260–263, 268–273
Enterprise Web Server and, 443–444
guidelines, 205–208
login scripts and, 262–263
needed for each user, identifying, 205–208
planning, 205–208, 232
required for common functions, list of, 187
troubleshooting, 249–251
Rights to Other Objects option, 156
RIGHTS utility, 211, 216–217, 677
ring topology, 591. *See also* topology
RMS (Resource Management Service), 346
role-based security, 162–163, 268–273
root
certificates, 391
drive pointers, 118, 119, 121, 123–124
objects, 47, 236, 253–254
partitions, 68, 70, 175–177
Rover directory, 109–111
RPS directory, 108
RTF (Rich Text Format), 401
Run Config Report, 408–409
Run Login Script check box, 41
Run scripts option, 280–281
R/W (Read/Write) replicas, 67, 68

S

SALVAGE command, 678
Salvage All button, 116
Salvage Network Files dialog box, 116
salvaging deleted files, 85, 93, 112, 115–116
SANs (storage area networks), 22, 83, 633–636
SAPs (Service Advertising Packets), 346
Save As command, 23
Save button, 23
Save Settings button, 55
SBACKUP, 127, 128, 131, 132
SBCON menu, 132
scalability, 659
SCL (Server Connection Licensing), 419
SCSI (Small Computer Systems Interface), 634
screen savers, console, 456, 457
Script tab, 287, 290, 293
SCRSAVER command, 456, 457
SECOND variable, 289
SECURE CONSOLE command, 456, 457, 540
security. *See also* access rights; authentication;
      login; passwords
alert message boxes, 109–110, 115
attributes and, 217–227
eDirectory, 235–278
encryption and, 37, 109, 390, 391, 456
firewalls and, 455, 459–461, 466
guidelines, 205–208, 256–259
internal, 455–458
Internet service components and, 454–466
Linux and, 660
NetWare 6.5 enhancements to, 645–655

NetWare file systems and, 78, 109–110,
      235–278
planning, 204–217
role-based, 162–163, 268–273
services, 6, 7–8
troubleshooting, 249–251
violations, common, 456–457
viruses and, 132, 454, 461–464
worksheets, 258
Select All command, 117
Select button, 11
Select Network Component Type dialog
      box, 40
Select NetWare Logon dialog box, 41
Select Network Client dialog box, 40–41
Select Object dialog box, 56–57, 61–62, 152,
      155, 167, 172
Select Printer Drivers dialog box, 356
semicolon (;), 294, 301
Send button, 11
SEND command, 540, 678
Send Message option, 11
Send Message Results dialog box, 11
serial ports, 335
server(s). *See also* file servers; print servers
accessories, 21–22
application services and, 16–18
association of volumes with, 21
-centric operating systems, 19, 21
classification of, as entities, 6, 19
clustering, 14, 82–84
component, defined, 6
consoles, 417–419, 534–548
described, 30
eDirectory services and, 35, 37, 67–70
e-mail, 477–479
file sharing and, 19–20
hardware environments, 413–414
identification of, 521–522
installing, 35
managing, 410–411
monitoring, 407–410, 413–414
NetWare installation and, 519–522, 525–526,
      530–531, 534–548, 551
object, default rights assigned to, 254–255
organization of, into workgroups, 37
partitions and, 68–70
planning forms (NetWare Server Planning
      Form), 519–521, 525–526, 533
print, 22, 47, 332, 336–337, 340–343
startup files, 547–548
target, 127
Server Management console, 391, 396–399
Server Preferences button, 440
Server Protect (Trend Micro), 463
Server Status button, 440
Service Advertising Packets. *See* SAPs (Service
      Advertising Packets)
Service Message Blocks. *See* SMBs (Service
      Message Blocks)
Service Registry Services. *See* SRS (Service
      Registry Services)

services. *See also specific services*
  common, 6–7
  network, introduction to, 6–18
servlets, 434–436. *See also* Java
Set Context dialog box, 146
Set Password button, 11, 159, 160
Set Password check box, 159
Set Password dialog box, 11, 66, 150
SET TIME command, 540
SETPASS command, 678
shadowing, 517, 553
Sharable attribute, 219
Share as option, 20
Share Properties dialog box, 20
Share this folder option, 20
shared directories
  defined, 94
  defining processing needs for, 95–97
  designated, 20
  designing, 98–99
  permissions and, 20
shared storage devices
  configuring, 32
  defined, 22
Shell policy, 319
SHELL_TYPE variable, 290
SHORT_YEAR variable, 289
Show Connected Servers option, 11
Show Device button, 90
SLDAP (Standalone LDAP), 438
SMACHINE variable, 290
smart cards, universal, 654
SMBs (Service Message Blocks)
  defined, 27
  NetBEUI and, 27
SMS (Storage Management System)
  defined, 127–130, 136
  testing, 131–132
SMTP (Simple Mail Transfer Protocol), 475
smurf attack, 465. *See also* denial-of-service
  attacks
sniffer software, 456
Software.cti directory, 39, 113, 117, 320
SOFTWARE.CTI Properties dialog box, 39
Solaris, 415
Sort button, 55
SOURCE volume, 98, 100–102
spoofing, 332, 454
SRS (Service Registry Services), 346
SSH (Secure Shell) protocol, 650
SSL (Secure Socket Layer), 648
StaffDev.frm, 401
Standalone LDAP. *See* SLDAP
  (Standalone LDAP)
star topology, 23, 589, 591. *See also* topology
startup files, 547–548
STATION variable, 290
Stations.ldif, 169–170
Statistics tab, 92
stealth viruses, 462. *See also* viruses
storage area networks. *See* SANs (storage area
  networks)

storage pool(s), 79, 81
  block size and, 86
  creating, 103–104
  defined, 136
  information, viewing, 89
  logical division of, into volumes, 83
  names, 98
  overbooking and, 84
  size specifications, 84–85
  viewing, 104
Storage Management System. *See* SMS
  (Storage Management System)
Storage Requirements Form, 96–97, 565
STP (shielded twisted-pair cable), 588
Styles button, 440
suballocation, of blocks, 86–87, 98
subdirectories
  creating, 107–111
  drive pointers and, 119
  moving, 112–113
Subordinate replica, 67
Supervisor rights
  changing, 203–204
  defined, 186–189, 202
  eDirectory services and, 13, 237, 238, 264–267
  granting, 203
  IRF and, 202, 266–267
  NetWare file systems and, 111, 113
  reassigning, 264–266
  templates and, 153
  working with, 202
SYN packet flooding attack, 465.
  See also denial-of-service attacks
syntax
  defined, 293–294
  for login scripts, 293–294
SYS volume, 57, 58
  defined, 21
  directories, 94–95
  drive pointers and, 121, 122
  objects, 60–62, 105–106
  partitions, 80–81
  reservation of, for operating system files, 98
  salvage operations and, 86
  size requirements, 78
  storage pools and, 81
SysOp Organizational Role object, 260
System attribute, 219, 221
System directory, 92, 93, 95, 129
System policy, 319
System Properties dialog box, 38

T

tape backups, 21–22, 132–133. *See also* backups
target server(s)
  defined, 127
  SMS and, 127
Target Server Agents. *See* TSAs (Target
  Server Agents)
Target Service option, 132
TCP/IP (Transmission Control
  Protocol/Internet Protocol)
  basic description of, 25–27, 30

development of, 25
directories and, 34, 93
implementing, 597–609
Internet service components and, 432, 433
model, 25–27
NetWare installation and, 525
port numbers and, 433
settings, viewing, 28
teardrop attack, 465. *See also* denial-of-service
  attacks
Telnet, 433
templates, 152–158
Terminal Server (Microsoft), 16
testing
  backups, 131, 132
  e-mail systems, 509
  login scripts, 313–314, 328, 329
  passwords, 10
  print servers, 342–343
  printers, 368–370, 381–382, 387
thin clients, defined, 16, 30
threads, defined, 400
Tile Windows button, 55
time
  restrictions, on passwords, 143–145, 155, 167
  variables, 289
TLS (Transport Layer Security), 648
Tmp directory, 93
To Users option, 11
Token Ring networks, 24, 593
Tomcat Servlet Engine (Apache), 434–435
topology
  described, 23, 30, 589–592
  network pathway component and, 23
Traditional Volume Attribute dialog box,
  101–102
Traditional Volumes dialog box, 101
Traditional Volumes option, 101
Transaction Tracking System. *See* TTS
  (Transaction Tracking System)
Transactional attribute, 219
Transmission Control Protocol/Internet
  Protocol. *See* TCP/IP (Transmission Control
  Protocol/Internet Protocol)
Transport layer, 26
tree structure
  browsing, 59–60
  completing, with ConsoleOne, 64–66
  designing, 51–60
  implementing, 60–66
  information, selecting, 8
  modifying, 76
  server-centric operating systems and, 21
Trojan horses, 462. *See also* viruses
trusted
  certificates, 109
  networks, 460
trustee assignments
  in ACLs, 186
  basic description of, 188–189
  containers and, 189–191, 194–195, 244
  creating, 190, 240–243

default, 254–255
defining, 256–259, 271
documenting/listing, 216–217, 232
eDirectory services and, 240–244,
    254–259, 271
grouping, 192–193
implementing, 210–216, 232, 271
inherited rights and, combining, 198–200
listing of, in security worksheets, 259
minimizing the use of, 204, 206–207
modifying, 189–190
user, 188–191
Trustees tab, 95
TSAs (Target Server Agents), 127–128
TTS (Transaction Tracking System), 219
twisted-pair cable, 587–588
typeful distinguished names, 48–49, 73
typeless distinguished names, 49–50, 73, 115

U

UAL (User Access Licensing), 419
UasAdmin user accounts, 150, 151, 163–164,
    412, 417
UASFloor.jpg, 381
UASHOST server, 11, 13, 15, 17
    eDirectory services and, 37, 42, 61, 67, 70–71
    file sharing and, 19–20
    iFolder and, 391–392
    NetStorage and, 404, 405
    NetWare file systems and, 80, 87, 89, 90, 111
    protocols and, 25
    RConsoleJ and, 418
    Remote Manager and, 410–411
    virus protection techniques and, 462
    volumes and, 21
UASHOST_CORP volume, 15, 154
UASHOST_SYS volume, 62, 65, 87, 92
UDP (User Datagram Protocol), 26
UNBIND command, 540
UNC (universal naming convention), 37, 116
Uniform Resource Locators. See URLs
    (Uniform Resource Locators)
Uninstall button, 38, 42
Unix, 12, 35, 78, 98, 433
unknown networks, 460
UNLOAD JAVA command, 316
untrusted networks, 460
Up one Context Level button, 71
updating users, 166–168
upgrades, 548–551
uploading files, 114–115
UPS (uninterruptible power supply), 21
Upzip button, 58
URLs (Uniform Resource Locators), 161
user(s). See also user accounts
    assigning access rights to, 189–191, 205–211,
        213–216
    creating, 11, 149–171
    -defined variables, 290–292
    displaying all, 10–11
    login scripts, 281, 282
    managing, 149–171
    naming conventions, 156

templates, 152–158
updating, 166–168
variables, 289–290
user account(s). See also login; user names
    creating, 32, 158–161
    disabled, 149, 171
    establishing login security for, 142–148
    iFolder, 395–396
    intruder detection limits for, 145–148
    locking, 147–148
    managing, 141–183
    restrictions, setting, 142–145
    securing, 149–150
    using multiple, 165
User Datagram Protocol. See UDP (User
    Datagram Protocol)
User Extensible Policies check box, 318,
    320, 321
User Extensible Policies dialog box, 318–319
user names. See also users; user accounts;
    passwords
    entering, 9, 10
    finding, 9
    login security services and, 7–8
    selecting, 10
User object, defined, 48
User Planning Form, 157, 159, 166, 570
User Template Planning Form, 153–155, 569
USER_ID variable, 289–290
Users and Space Restrictions tab, 92
Users and Groups button, 440
Utility directory, 107, 116, 117, 169
UTP (unshielded twisted-pair) cable, 587–588

V

variables
    creating, 292–293
    using, 291–292
Variables button, 290
vehicle.bmp, 20
VERITAS Backup Exec for NetWare, 129
View Certificate button, 109
View Certificate option, 161
virtual
    document directories, 441–442, 444–445
    document sites, 671–672
Virtual Office (Novell), 636–641
virtual private networks. See VPNs (virtual
    private networks)
Virtual Teams (Novell), 637–640
viruses, 132, 454, 461–464, 504
volume(s)
    accessing, 37
    compression and, 85
    creating, 83, 92, 98, 100–101, 104–105
    defined, 21
    designing, 98–100
    division of, into directories, 92–94
    drive pointers and, 121
    information, viewing, 92
    managing, with Remote Manager, 411–412
    maximum number of, 82
    objects, 48, 60–62, 73, 87, 105–106

overbooking, 84–85
quota settings, 104–105
suballocation feature, 86–87
traditional, 86–87
Volume Design Form, 566
VPNs (virtual private networks), 460

W

Wallpaper policy, 321
WANs (wide area networks)
    defined, 2, 30
    network printing and, 348
    Novell's OneNet strategy and, 2–3
    replicas and, 68
    TCP/IP and, 25, 26
Web Access (Novell), 433
Web browser(s), 14, 16, 437
    certificates and, 161
    creating user and group accounts from,
        163–165
    eDirectory services and, 35, 36, 53
    entering server addresses in, 161
    iFolder and, 390–396, 402–403
    iManager and, 62–64, 161
    NPS and, 435
Web Client (Novell), 36
Web Console (Novell), 501
Web Manager (Novell), 161–162, 433, 437
    administrative roles and, 268–273
    NPS and, 435
Web Search Server (Novell), 433, 434, 436
Web Services (Novell), 432
Webapps directory, 93
WebDAV (Web Distributed Authoring and
    Versioning), 35, 36, 403, 440
Welcome to NetWare Administrator window, 55
WHOAMI command, 678
Win32 dialog box, 54
Win32 folder, 54
windows
    opening new, 56, 57
    tiling, 57
Windows (Microsoft). See also specific versions
    assigning rights with, 192–193
    eDirectory services and, 12, 36, 40
    iFolder and, 391
    iMonitor and, 415
    network printing and, 335
    protocols and, 25, 27
    setting attributes from, 222–224
    trustee assignment and, 190, 211–212
Windows 9x (Microsoft). See also Windows
    (Microsoft)
    eDirectory services and, 36, 40
    network printing and, 335
Windows Explorer
    creating directories with, 106
    making trustee assignments with, 210–211
Windows NT (Microsoft). See also Windows
    (Microsoft)
    eDirectory and, 12
    iFolder and, 391
    iMonitor and, 415

login security services and, 8
Novell's OneNet strategy and, 2–3
policies and, 320
Z.E.N.works and, 315
Windows 2000 (Microsoft). *See also* Windows (Microsoft)
backup software and, 129
drive mapping and, 122
eDirectory services and, 12, 36, 40, 45
file sharing and, 19–20
iFolder and, 391
iMonitor and, 415
Internet service components and, 433
login, 7–8, 10
network printing and, 335
Novell's OneNet strategy and, 2–3
passwords, changing, 10-11
policies and, 320, 321
Professional, 19–20, 66
workgroup size restrictions, 19
Z.E.N.works and, 315
WINNT folder, 115
Winsetup, 43
WinZip Self-Extractor dialog box, 58
Wizards
Add Printer Wizard, 334
Create a New Logical Volume Wizard, 104
Create a New Pool Wizard, 101, 103
Create a New Traditional Volume Wizard, 101
iPrint Installation Wizard, 367–368
NDS Import/Export Wizard, 170–171
Policy Package Wizard, 318
WordPad (Microsoft), 23, 303, 403, 406
printing documents with, 342, 369
saving files with, 401

workgroups
defined, 19, 30
eDirectory services and, 37, 52
organization of servers into, 37
peer-to-peer operating systems and, 19
size restrictions, 19
tree structure design and, 52
worksheets. *See also* forms
described, 563–583
Directory Trustee Worksheet, 209–214, 572
eDirectory IRF Worksheet, 258–259, 265–266, 575
eDirectory Security, 258, 574
Login Script Worksheets, 304–309, 577, 579
workstation(s)
classification of, as entities, 19
desktop, creating, 320–322
environments, configuring, 279–230
file sharing and, 19–20
identification of, as components,
installing ConsoleOne on, 57–59
login and, 7, 8, 280–286
policies, 317–320
printers and, 22, 23, 341–342, 359–361, 367–368, 378–380
protocols, identifying, 27–28
uploading files from, 114–115
variables, 290
Workstation Manager, 315
Workstation only check box, 10, 28, 62
worms attacks, 462. *See also* viruses
WP directory, 113, 124, 125
WRITE command, 297
Write rights, 186–189, 238, 239, 282

X

X.500 standards, 45, 48, 168, 512–517, 654–655
Xerox, 344, 353–354
XML (eXtensible Markup Language), 403
XSL (eXtensible Stylesheet Language), 435
XTier directory, 93

Y

YEAR variable, 289

Z

Z.E.N.works
application management with, 315, 316
basic description of, 17–18, 315
directories and, 93, 94
distributing virus signature updates with, 463
eDirectory services and, 40, 42
hardware requirements, 315
installing, 316
managing user environments with, 314–316
Microsoft NetWare client and, 40
Novell Licensing Services and, 419
Novell's OneNet strategy and, 2
protocols and, 25
remote control with, 315
software requirements, 315
workstation management with, 315, 316, 317–322
zip files, extracting, 58
zone files, 583, 606